THE KIERKEGAARDIAN MIND

Søren Kierkegaard (1813–1855) remains one of the most enigmatic, captivating, and elusive thinkers in the history of European thought.

The Kierkegaardian Mind provides a comprehensive survey of his work, not only placing it in its historical context but also exploring its contemporary significance. Comprising thirty-eight chapters by a team of international contributors, this handbook is divided into eight parts covering the following themes:

- Methodology
- Ethics
- Aesthetics
- Philosophy of Religion and Theology
- Philosophy of Mind
- Anthropology
- Epistemology
- Politics.

Essential reading for students and researchers in philosophy, Kierkegaard's work is central to the study of political philosophy, literature, existentialist thought, and theology.

Adam Buben is Universitair Docent 1 in Philosophy at Leiden University in the Netherlands.

Eleanor Helms is Associate Professor of Philosophy at California Polytechnic State University in San Luis Obispo, USA.

Patrick Stokes is Associate Professor of Philosophy at Deakin University, Melbourne, Australia.

THE ROUTLEDGE PHILOSOPHICAL MINDS

In philosophy past and present there are some philosophers who tower over the intellectual landscape and have shaped it in indelible ways. So significant is their impact that it is difficult to capture it in one place. The Routledge Philosophical Minds series presents a comprehensive survey of all aspects of a major philosopher's work, from analysis and criticism of their major texts and arguments to the way their ideas are taken up in contemporary philosophy and beyond. Edited by leading figures in their fields and with an outstanding international roster of contributors the series offers a magisterial and unrivalled picture of a great philosophical mind.

THE NIETZSCHEAN MIND
Edited by Paul Katsafanas

THE HUMEAN MIND
Edited by Angela Coventry and Alexander Sager

THE ROUSSEAUIAN MIND
Edited by Eve Grace and Christopher Kelly

For more information on this series, please visit: https://www.routledge.com/Routledge-Philosophical-Minds/book-series/RPM

THE KIERKEGAARDIAN MIND

*Edited by Adam Buben, Eleanor Helms,
and Patrick Stokes*

LONDON AND NEW YORK

First published 2019
by Routledge
4 Park Square, Milton Park, Abingdon, Oxon OX14 4RN
605 Third Avenue, New York, NY 10017

First issued in paperback 2023

Routledge is an imprint of the Taylor & Francis Group, an informa business

© 2019 selection and editorial matter, Adam Buben, Eleanor Helms, and Patrick Stokes; individual chapters, the contributors

The right of Adam Buben, Eleanor Helms, and Patrick Stokes to be identified as the authors of the editorial material, and of the authors for their individual chapters, has been asserted in accordance with sections 77 and 78 of the Copyright, Designs and Patents Act 1988.

All rights reserved. No part of this book may be reprinted or reproduced or utilised in any form or by any electronic, mechanical, or other means, now known or hereafter invented, including photocopying and recording, or in any information storage or retrieval system, without permission in writing from the publishers.

Trademark notice: Product or corporate names may be trademarks or registered trademarks, and are used only for identification and explanation without intent to infringe.

British Library Cataloguing-in-Publication Data
A catalogue record for this book is available from the British Library

Library of Congress Cataloging-in-Publication Data
Names: Buben, Adam, 1977- editor.
Title: The Kierkegaardian mind / edited by Adam Buben, Eleanor Helms, and Patrick Stokes.
Description: 1 [edition]. | New York : Routledge, 2019. | Series: The Routledge philosophical minds | Includes bibliographical references and index.
Identifiers: LCCN 2018061160| ISBN 9781138092716 (hardback : alk. paper) | ISBN 9780429198571 (e-book)
Subjects: LCSH: Kierkegaard, Søren, 1813-1855.
Classification: LCC B4377 .K4995 2019 | DDC 198/.9—dc23
LC record available at https://lccn.loc.gov/2018061160

ISBN: 978-1-03-257013-6 (pbk)
ISBN: 978-1-138-09271-6 (hbk)
ISBN: 978-0-429-19857-1 (ebk)

DOI: 10.4324/9780429198571

Typeset in Bembo
by Apex CoVantage, LLC

Publisher's Note
The publisher has gone to great lengths to ensure the quality of this reprint but points out that some imperfections in the original copies may be apparent.

CONTENTS

Acknowledgements ix
List of abbreviations for Kierkegaard's Works x
List of contributors xiv

    Introduction: Kierkegaard's life, context, and legacy 1
    Adam Buben, Eleanor Helms, and Patrick Stokes

PART 1
Methodology 15

  1 The passion of Kierkegaard's existential method 17
    Lee C. Barrett

  2 Johannes Climacus and the dialectical method: from dialectics back to existence 28
    Claudine Davidshofer

  3 Kierkegaard's experimenting psychology 39
    William McDonald

  4 Methodology and the Kierkegaardian mind 52
    Jamie Turnbull

PART 2
Ethics 65

  5 Ethical reflection as evasion 67
    Rob Compaijen and Pieter Vos

6	Kierkegaard on moral particularism and exemplarism *Karl Aho*	78
7	Beyond worry? On learning humility from the lilies and the birds *John Lippitt*	89
8	Did Napoleon teleologically suspend the ethical? A dilemma for some 'Hegelian' readings of *Fear and Trembling* *Ryan S. Kemp*	100
9	An ethics of home and hope: Kierkegaard's exile and Heidegger's emigrant *Megan Altman*	110
10	Love for humans: morality as the heart of Kierkegaard's religious philosophy *Sharon Krishek*	122

PART 3
Aesthetics   133

11	The ethical life of aesthetes *Ulrika Carlsson*	135
12	Kierkegaard on nature and natural beauty *Anthony Rudd*	145
13	Kierkegaard's transfigurations of the sublime *Samuel Cuff Snow*	156
14	Kierkegaard on the value of art: an indirect method of communication *Antony Aumann*	166
15	Deleuze on Kierkegaard *Andrew Jampol-Petzinger*	177

PART 4
Philosophy of religion and theology   189

16	Kierkegaard's existential mimesis *Wojciech Kaftanski*	191
17	Becoming a subject: Kierkegaard's theological art of existence *Peder Jothen*	203

18	Engendering atonement: Kierkegaard on the cross Deidre Nicole Green	215
19	On faith and reason(s): Kierkegaard's logic of conviction K. Brian Söderquist	227
20	Coming to an understanding with the paradox Mark A. Wrathall	239
21	Kierkegaard's defense of nature and theology against natural theology Will Williams	254

PART 5
Philosophy of mind — 267

22	Consciousness, self, and reflection Patrick Stokes	269
23	Conscience, self-deception, and the question of authenticity in Kierkegaard Claudia Welz	281
24	Imagination and belief Eleanor Helms	293
25	Agency, identity, and alienation in *The Sickness unto Death* Justin F. White	305

PART 6
Anthropology — 317

26	Kierkegaard's post-Kantian approach to anthropology and selfhood Roe Fremstedal	319
27	Images of the closed self in *The Sickness unto Death* Anna Louise Strelis Söderquist	331
28	The Kierkegaardian self: convergences and divergences Jack Mulder, Jr.	341
29	Kierkegaard and the desirability of immortality Adam Buben	351

PART 7
Epistemology — 363

30 Christian epistemology and the anthropology of sin: Kierkegaard on natural theology and the concept of 'offense' — 365
Karen L. Carr

31 Varieties of existential uncertainty — 376
Rick Anthony Furtak

32 Irony and the conversion experience — 386
Walter Wietzke

33 Logic, language, and existential knowledge — 397
Mélissa Fox-Muraton

34 The incognito of a thief: Johannes Climacus and the poetics of self-incrimination — 409
Martijn Boven

PART 8
Politics — 421

35 Lukács, Kierkegaard, Marx, and the political — 423
Alison Assiter

36 Kierkegaard: the dialectical self and the political — 435
Shoni Rancher

37 Kierkegaard, Hegel, and Augustine on love — 446
Thomas J. Millay

38 The covetous canary: Kierkegaard on the problem of social comparison and the cultivation of social courage — 457
Paul Carron

Index — 468

ACKNOWLEDGEMENTS

Putting together a volume of this size is not for the faint of heart. Fortunately, with an editorial team evenly spread across the globe, it can honestly be said that the sun never set on this project. But it wasn't just our hard work that brought it to fruition, and we'd like to take this opportunity to express our gratitude to those who helped make this book a reality.

To begin with, this project has been supported by our respective home institutions: Leiden University in the Netherlands, California Polytechnic State University in the United States, and Deakin University in Australia. For a number of reasons, which include hosting conferences and other events that helped forge the ideas presented in this volume, we are also grateful to the Hong Kierkegaard Library at St. Olaf College in Northfield, Minnesota, and the Søren Kierkegaard Research Centre at the University of Copenhagen.

We are especially grateful to the late Robert L. Perkins, series editor of the *International Kierkegaard Commentary* (Mercer University Press), whose list of abbreviations is used throughout the volume. We'd also like to offer our thanks to the following people who have provided help and encouragement at various stages of the project: Andrew Burgess and Janice Schuetz, Jon Stewart, John Davenport, Gordon Marino, Joakim Garff, and Rebecca Shillabeer and Gabrielle Coakeley at Routledge.

Finally, we thank our respective friends and families for their support and encouragement, and especially Megan Altman for her assistance with various last-minute editorial tasks.

ABBREVIATIONS FOR KIERKEGAARD'S WORKS

Standard English translations

BA	*The Book on Adler*, H.V. Hong and E. H. Hong (trans), Princeton, NJ: Princeton University Press, 1995.
CA	*The Concept of Anxiety*, R. Thomte in collaboration with A. B. Anderson (trans), Princeton, NJ: Princeton University Press, 1980.
CD	*Christian Discourses* and *The Crisis and a Crisis in the Life of an Actress*, H.V. Hong and E. H. Hong (trans), Princeton, NJ: Princeton University Press, 1997.
CI	*The Concept of Irony*, together with 'Notes of Schelling's Berlin Lectures,' H.V. Hong and E. H. Hong (trans), Princeton, NJ: Princeton University Press, 1989.
CUP 1	*Concluding Unscientific Postscript to 'Philosophical Fragments,'* vol. 1, H.V. Hong and E. H. Hong (trans), Princeton, NJ: Princeton University Press, 1992.
CUP 2	*Concluding Unscientific Postscript to 'Philosophical Fragments,'* vol. 2, H.V. Hong and E. H. Hong (trans), Princeton, NJ: Princeton University Press, 1992.
COR	*The 'Corsair' Affair*, H. V. Hong and E. H. Hong (trans), Princeton, NJ: Princeton University Press, 1982.
EO 1	*Either/Or*, vol. 1, H. V. Hong and E. H. Hong (trans), Princeton, NJ: Princeton University Press, 1987.
EO 2	*Either/Or*, vol. 2, H.V. Hong and E. H. Hong (trans), Princeton, NJ: Princeton University Press, 1987.
EPW	*Early Polemical Writings*, J. Watkin (trans), Princeton, NJ: Princeton University Press, 1990.
EUD	*Eighteen Upbuilding Discourses*, H. V. Hong and E. H. Hong (trans), Princeton, NJ: Princeton University Press, 1990.
FSE	*For Self-Examination* and *Judge for Yourself!* H.V. Hong and E. H. Hong (trans), Princeton, NJ: Princeton University Press, 1990.
FT	*Fear and Trembling* and *Repetition*, H.V. Hong and E. H. Hong (trans), Princeton, NJ: Princeton University Press, 1983.
JC	*Johannes Climacus*. See *Philosophical Fragments*.
JFY	*Judge for Yourself!* See *For Self-Examination*.

JP	*Søren Kierkegaard's Journals and Papers*, seven vols., H. V. Hong and E. H. Hong, assisted by G. Malantschuk (eds and trans), Bloomington, IN: Indiana University Press, 1967 (vol. 1); 1970 (vol. 2); 1975 (vols. 3 and 4); 1978 (vols. 5–7).
KJN 1	*Kierkegaard's Journals and Notebooks: Volume 1, Journals AA-DD*, N. J. Cappelørn, A. Hannay, D. Kangas, B. H. Kirmmse, G. Pattison, V. Rumble, and K. B. Söderquist (eds), Princeton, NJ: Princeton University Press, 2007.
KJN 2	*Kierkegaard's Journals and Notebooks: Volume 2, Journals EE-KK*, N. J. Cappelørn, A. Hannay, D. Kangas, B. H. Kirmmse, G. Pattison, V. Rumble, and K. B. Söderquist (eds), Princeton, NJ: Princeton University Press, 2008.
KJN 3	*Kierkegaard's Journals and Notebooks: Volume 3, Notebooks 1–15*, N. J. Cappelørn, A. Hannay, D. Kangas, B. H. Kirmmse, G. Pattison, V. Rumble, and K. B. Söderquist (eds), Princeton, NJ: Princeton University Press, 2010.
KJN 4	*Kierkegaard's Journals and Notebooks: Volume 4, Notebooks NB-NB5*, N. J. Cappelørn, A. Hannay, D. Kangas, B. H. Kirmmse, G. Pattison, J. D. S. Rasmussen, V. Rumble, and K. B. Söderquist (eds), Princeton, NJ: Princeton University Press, 2011.
KJN 5	*Kierkegaard's Journals and Notebooks: Volume 5, Journals NB6-NB10*, N. J. Cappelørn, A. Hannay, D. Kangas, B. H. Kirmmse, G. Pattison, J. D. S. Rasmussen, V. Rumble, and K. B. Söderquist (eds), Princeton, NJ: Princeton University Press, 2012.
KJN 6	*Kierkegaard's Journals and Notebooks: Volume 6, Journals NB11-NB14*, N. J. Cappelørn, A. Hannay, B. H. Kirmmse, G. Pattison, J. D. S. Rasmussen, V. Rumble, and K. B. Söderquist (eds), Princeton, NJ: Princeton University Press, 2013.
KJN 7	*Kierkegaard's Journals and Notebooks: Volume 7, Journals NB15-NB20*, N. J. Cappelørn, A. Hannay, D. Kangas, B. H. Kirmmse, D. D. Possen, J. D. S. Rasmussen, V. Rumble, and K. B. Söderquist (eds), Princeton, NJ: Princeton University Press, 2014.
KJN 8	*Kierkegaard's Journals and Notebooks: Volume 8, Journals NB21-NB25*, N. J. Cappelørn, A. Hannay, D. Kangas, B. H. Kirmmse, D. D. Possen, J. D. S. Rasmussen, and V. Rumble (eds), Princeton, NJ: Princeton University Press, 2015.
KJN 9	*Kierkegaard's Journals and Notebooks: Volume 9, Journals NB26-NB30*, N. J. Cappelørn, A. Hannay, D. Kangas, B. H. Kirmmse, D. D. Possen, J. D. S. Rasmussen, and V. Rumble (eds), Princeton, NJ: Princeton University Press, 2017.
PC	*Practice in Christianity*, H. V. Hong and E. H. Hong (trans), Princeton, NJ: Princeton University Press, 1991.
P	*Prefaces* and *Writing Sampler*, T. W. Nichol (trans), Princeton, NJ: Princeton University Press, 1997.
PF	*Philosophical Fragments* and *Johannes Climacus*, H. V. Hong and E. H. Hong (trans), Princeton, NJ: Princeton University Press, 1985.
PV	*The Point of View*, including *On My Work as an Author*, *The Point of View for My Work as an Author*, and *Armed Neutrality*, H. V. Hong and E. H. Hong (trans), Princeton, NJ: Princeton University Press, 1998.
R	*Repetition*. See *Fear and Trembling*.
SLW	*Stages on Life's Way*, H. V. Hong and E. H. Hong (trans), Princeton, NJ: Princeton University Press, 1988.
SUD	*The Sickness unto Death*, H. V. Hong and E. H. Hong (trans), Princeton, NJ: Princeton University Press, 1980.
TDIO	*Three Discourses on Imagined Occasions*, H. V. Hong and E. H. Hong (trans), Princeton, NJ: Princeton University Press, 1993.

TA	*Two Ages*, H.V. Hong and E. H. Hong (trans), Princeton, NJ: Princeton University Press, 1978.
TM	*The 'Moment' and Late Writings*, H.V. Hong and E. H. Hong (trans), Princeton, NJ: Princeton University Press, 1998.
UDVS	*Upbuilding Discourses in Various Spirits*, H.V. Hong and E. H. Hong (trans), Princeton, NJ: Princeton University Press, 1993.
WA	*Without Authority*, H.V. Hong and E. H. Hong (trans), Princeton, NJ: Princeton University Press, 1997.
WL	*Works of Love*, H.V. Hong and E. H. Hong (trans), Princeton, NJ: Princeton University Press, 1995.

Danish texts (Søren Kierkegaards Skrifter)

SKS 1	*Af en endnu Levendes Papirer; Om Begrebet Ironi*, N. J. Cappelørn, J. Garff, J. Kondrup, and F. H. Mortensen (eds), Copenhagen: Gads, 1997.
SKS 2	*Enten–Eller. Første del*, N. J. Cappelørn, J. Garff, J. Kondrup, and F. H. Mortensen (eds), Copenhagen: Gads, 1997.
SKS 3	*Enten–Eller. Anden del*, N. J. Cappelørn, J. Garff, J. Kondrup, and F. H. Mortensen (eds), Copenhagen: Gads, 1997.
SKS 4	*Gjentagelsen; Frygt og Bæven; Philosophiske Smuler; Begrebet Angest; Forord*, N. J. Cappelørn, J. Garff, J. Kondrup, and F. H. Mortensen (eds), Copenhagen: Gads, 1997.
SKS 5	*Opbyggelige taler, 1843–44; Tre Taler ved tænkte Leiligheder*, N. J. Cappelørn, J. Garff, J. Knudsen, J. Kondrup, and F. H. Mortensen (eds), Copenhagen: Gads, 1998.
SKS 6	*Stadier paa Livets Vei*, N. J. Cappelørn, J. Garff, J. Knudsen, J. Kondrup, and F. H. Mortensen (eds), Copenhagen: Gads, 1999.
SKS 7	*Afsluttende uvidenskabelig Efterskrift*, N. J. Cappelørn, J. Garff, J. Knudsen, and J. Kondrup (eds), Copenhagen: Gads, 2002.
SKS 8	*En literair Anmeldelse; Opbyggelige Taler i forskjellig Aand*, N. J. Cappelørn, J. Garff, and J. Kondrup (eds), Copenhagen: Gads, 2004.
SKS 9	*Kjerlighedens Gjerninger*, N. J. Cappelørn, J. Garff, and J. Kondrup (eds), Copenhagen: Gads, 2004.
SKS 10	*Christelige Taler*, N. J. Cappelørn, J. Garff, and J. Kondrup (eds), Copenhagen: Gads, 2004.
SKS 11	*Lilien paa Marken og Fuglen under Himlen; Tvende ethisk-religieuse Smaa-Afhandlinger; Sygdommen til Døden; »Ypperstepræsten«–»Tolderen«–»Synderinden«*, N. J. Cappelørn, J. Garff, A. M. Hansen, and J. Kondrup (eds), Copenhagen: Gads, 2006.
SKS 12	*Indøvelse i Christendom; En opbyggelig Tale; To Taler ved Altergangen om Fredagen*, N. J. Cappelørn, J. Garff, A. M. Hansen, and J. Kondrup (eds), Copenhagen: Gads, 2008.
SKS 13	*Dagbladsartikler 1834–48; Om min Forfatter-Virksomhed; Til Selvprøvelse*, N. J. Cappelørn, J. Garff, A. M. Hansen, J. Kondrup, T. A. Olesen, and S. Tullberg (eds), Copenhagen: Gads, 2009.
SKS 14	*Bladartikler*, N. J. Cappelørn, J. Garff, A. M. Hansen, J. Kondrup, T. A. Olesen, and S. Tullberg (eds), Copenhagen: Gads, 2010.

SKS 15	*Et Øieblik, Hr. Andersen!; Johannes Climacus eller De omnibus dubitandum est; Polemik mod Heiberg; Bogen om Adler*, N. J. Cappelørn, J. Garff, J. Kondrup, T. A. Olesen, and S. Tullberg (eds), Copenhagen: Gads, 2012.
SKS 16	*Synspunktet for min Forfatter-Virksomhed; Hr. Phister som Captain Scipio; Den bevæbnede Neutralitet; Dømmer Selv!*, N. J. Cappelørn, J. Garff, J. Kondrup, T. A. Olesen, and S. Tullberg (eds), Copenhagen: Gads, 2012.
SKS 17	*Journalerne AA-DD*, N. J. Cappelørn, J. Garff, J. Knudsen, and J. Kondrup (eds), Copenhagen: Gads, 2000.
SKS 18	*Journalerne EE-KK*, N. J. Cappelørn, J. Garff, J. Knudsen, and J. Kondrup (eds), Copenhagen: Gads, 2001.
SKS 19	*Notesbøgerne 1–15*, N. J. Cappelørn, J. Garff, J. Knudsen, and J. Kondrup (eds), Copenhagen: Gads, 2001.
SKS 20	*Journalerne NB-NB5*, N. J. Cappelørn, J. Garff, J. Knudsen, and J. Kondrup (eds), Copenhagen: Gads, 2003.
SKS 21	*Journalerne NB6-NB10*, N. J. Cappelørn, J. Garff, J. Knudsen, and J. Kondrup (eds), Copenhagen: Gads, 2003.
SKS 22	*Journalerne NB11-NB14*, N. J. Cappelørn, J. Garff, A. M. Hansen, and J. Kondrup (eds), Copenhagen: Gads, 2005.
SKS 23	*Journalerne NB15-NB20*, N. J. Cappelørn, J. Garff, A. M. Hansen, and J. Kondrup (eds), Copenhagen: Gads, 2007.
SKS 24	*Journalerne NB21-NB25*, N. J. Cappelørn, J. Garff, A. M. Hansen, and J. Kondrup (eds), Copenhagen: Gads, 2007.
SKS 25	*Journalerne NB26-NB30*, N. J. Cappelørn, J. Garff, A. M. Hansen, and J. Kondrup (eds), Copenhagen: Gads, 2008.
SKS 26	*Journalerne NB31-NB36*, N. J. Cappelørn, J. Garff, A. M. Hansen, and J. Kondrup (eds), Copenhagen: Gads, 2009.
SKS 27	*Løse papirer*, N. J. Cappelørn, J. Garff, A. M. Hansen, and J. Kondrup (eds), Copenhagen: Gads, 2013.
SKS 28	*Breve og dedikationer*, N. J. Cappelørn, J. Garff, A. M. Hansen, and J. Kondrup (eds), Copenhagen: Gads, 2013.

Each volume in the *Søren Kierkegaards Skrifter* series is accompanied by a commentary volume. Where the commentary is cited, a 'K' is added before the volume number (e.g., SKS K12).

CONTRIBUTORS

Karl Aho is Assistant Professor of Philosophy at Tarleton State University (Stephenville, TX), a member of the Texas A&M University System. In addition to Kierkegaard, his recent publications engage Augustine of Hippo and William James.

Megan Altman is Assistant Professor of Philosophy at Cornell College in Iowa. She is a co-editor (with Hans Pedersen) of *Horizons of Authenticity in Phenomenology, Existentialism, and Moral Psychology* (Springer, 2014). Her work has appeared in *Frontiers of Philosophy in China* and *Concrescence: The Australasian Journal of Process Thought*.

Alison Assiter is Professor of Feminist Theory at the University of the West of England, Bristol, UK. Her latest book is *Kierkegaard, Eve and Metaphors of Birth* (Rowman and Littlefield, 2015). She has published a number of books and articles in feminist philosophy and political philosophy, and most recently on Kant, Kierkegaard, and realism.

Antony Aumann is Associate Professor of Philosophy at Northern Michigan University. He's held positions at the Ohio State University and St. Olaf College. He publishes on Kierkegaard, Nietzsche, and issues in contemporary aesthetics, and he is the author of *Art and Selfhood: A Kierkegaardian Account* (Lexington, 2019).

Lee C. Barrett is the Henry and Mary Stager Professor of Theology at Lancaster Theological Seminary in Pennsylvania. He has published numerous essays on Kierkegaard in the *International Kierkegaard Commentary* series and in the *Kierkegaard Research: Sources, Reception and Resources* series. His books include *Eros and Self-Emptying: The Intersections of Kierkegaard and Augustine* (Eerdmans, 2013).

Martijn Boven has lectured at Leiden University and Radboud University Nijmegen (both in the Netherlands) since completing his dissertation, *Metaphor and Metamorphosis: Paul Ricoeur and Gilles Deleuze on the Emergence of Novelty*. His work has appeared in *Kierkegaard Research: Sources, Reception and Resources* and *International Journal of Philosophy and Theology*.

Adam Buben is Universitair Docent 1 in Philosophy at Leiden University in the Netherlands. He is the author of *Meaning and Mortality in Kierkegaard and Heidegger: Origins of the Existential*

Philosophy of Death (Northwestern University Press, 2016), a co-editor (with Patrick Stokes) of *Kierkegaard and Death* (Indiana University Press, 2011), and a contributor to several edited volumes and book series addressing the thought of Kierkegaard.

Ulrika Carlsson received her PhD in Philosophy from Yale University. Her work on Kierkegaard has focused on *The Concept of Irony* and *Either/Or*. She also engages with contemporary ethics on love and value incommensurability. She is an Assistant Professor of Philosophy at Moscow's National Research University Higher School of Economics.

Karen L. Carr is the McNaughton Rosebush Professor of Liberal Studies and Professor of Religious Studies at Lawrence University. She earned a BA from Oberlin College in Philosophy and Religion, and then her AM and PhD in Religious Studies from Stanford University. She has published on Kierkegaard, Nietzsche, and nihilism in the nineteenth and twentieth centuries.

Paul Carron is Assistant Professor of Philosophy in the Baylor Interdisciplinary Core Program at Baylor University, Waco, Texas. His work has appeared in a range of journals, including *International Journal for Philosophy of Religion, Biology and Philosophy, Epoché: A Journal for the History of Philosophy, Journal of Cognition and Neuroethics, Teaching Ethics,* and *Southwest Philosophy Review*.

Rob Compaijen is a post-doctoral researcher at Radboud University Nijmegen in the Netherlands. He specializes in ethics, philosophy of religion, and nineteenth-century thought. He is the author of *Kierkegaard, MacIntyre, Williams, and the Internal Point of View* (Palgrave Macmillan, 2018).

Samuel Cuff Snow is a joint PhD candidate in Philosophy at Monash University and Freie Universität Berlin. His doctoral thesis investigates the existential and transformative significance of aesthetic experience in Kant and Kierkegaard. He has published in edited collections and journals, including *Continental Philosophy Review* and *Critical Horizons*.

Claudine Davidshofer is Assistant Professor of Philosophy at High Point University in North Carolina. She completed her PhD at Emory University. Her research focuses on the relationship between Kierkegaard and Hegel, and especially on the themes of movement, modality, and dialectics.

Mélissa Fox-Muraton is Professor of Philosophy at the École Supérieure de Commerce de Clermont (France) and affiliated with the Research Centre Philosophies et Rationalités (Université Clermont Auvergne). She is the author of *Ontologie de la chair: Phantasmes philosophiques et médicaux de la conceptualisation narrative* (Lambert Lucas, 2013).

Roe Fremstedal is Professor of Practical Philosophy at UiT, the Arctic University of Norway. His publications include *Kierkegaard and Kant on Radical Evil and the Highest Good* (Palgrave Macmillan, 2014) and articles in *Kantian Review, Kierkegaard Studies Yearbook, Journal of Religious Ethics, Journal of Value Inquiry,* and *Religious Studies*.

Rick Anthony Furtak is Associate Professor of Philosophy at Colorado College. He is the author of *Wisdom in Love: Kierkegaard and the Ancient Quest for Emotional Integrity* (University of Notre Dame Press, 2005) and *Knowing Emotions: Truthfulness in Affective Experience* (Oxford University Press, 2018). He has edited volumes of essays on Kierkegaard and Thoreau, and published a translation of Rilke's *Sonnets to Orpheus*.

Deidre Nicole Green is a post-doctoral fellow at the Neal A. Maxwell Institute for Religious Scholarship. She has previously held fellowships at the Søren Kierkegaard Research Centre in Copenhagen and the Hong Kierkegaard Library at St. Olaf College. She is the author of *Works of Love in a World of Violence: Feminism, Kierkegaard, and the Limits of Self-Sacrifice* (Mohr Siebeck, 2016).

Eleanor Helms is Associate Professor of Philosophy at California Polytechnic State University in San Luis Obispo, California. Her work has appeared in a range of journals including *Res Philosophica*, *International Philosophical Quarterly*, *Philosophy and Literature*, *Environmental Philosophy*, *Business and Professional Ethics*, and *Philosophy and Management*.

Andrew Jampol-Petzinger is a post-doctoral teaching fellow in Philosophy at Fordham University. He defended his dissertation on the topics of ethics and selfhood in Kierkegaard and Deleuze in 2018.

Peder Jothen teaches in the Religion Department at St. Olaf College, Northfield, Minnesota. His book, *Kierkegaard, Aesthetics, and Selfhood: The Art of Subjectivity* was published by Ashgate in 2014. His PhD in Religious Ethics is from the University of Chicago.

Wojciech Kaftanski is a post-doctoral research fellow in the Institute of Philosophy at KU Leuven in Belgium. He is a former House Foundation Fellow at the Hong Kierkegaard Library at St. Olaf College and a Visiting Fellow at the Søren Kierkegaard Research Centre in Copenhagen. His work has appeared in *Kierkegaard Studies Yearbook*, *Kierkegaard Research: Sources, Reception and Resources*, and *Heythrop Journal*.

Ryan S. Kemp is Assistant Professor of Philosophy at Wheaton College, where he focuses on Kant, German Idealism, and Kierkegaard. He completed his PhD at the University of Notre Dame, and he is the author of the forthcoming *Routledge Philosophy Guidebook to Kierkegaard and Either/Or*.

Sharon Krishek is a lecturer in the Philosophy Department at the Hebrew University of Jerusalem. She is the author of *Kierkegaard on Faith and Love* (Cambridge University Press, 2009), *Kierkegaard's Philosophy of Love* (in Hebrew, 2011), and various articles in journals such as *Faith and Philosophy*, *International Journal for Philosophy of Religion*, and *European Journal of Philosophy*.

John Lippitt is Professor of Ethics and Philosophy of Religion at the University of Hertfordshire and Honorary Professor of Philosophy at Deakin University. His publications include *Humour and Irony in Kierkegaard's Thought* (Palgrave Macmillan, 2000), *Kierkegaard and the Problem of Self-Love* (Cambridge University Press, 2013), and the *Routledge Guidebook to Kierkegaard's Fear and Trembling* (second edition, 2015). He is co-editor of *The Oxford Handbook of Kierkegaard* (with George Pattison, 2013) and *Narrative, Identity and the Kierkegaardian Self* (with Patrick Stokes, Edinburgh University Press, 2015).

William McDonald is Chair of Philosophy at the United Arab Emirates University and an Adjunct Associate Professor of Humanities at the University of New England. He is co-editor, with Jon Stewart and Steven Emmanuel, of the six-volume *Kierkegaard's Concepts* (Routledge, 2013–2015), translator of Kierkegaard's *Prefaces* (Florida State University Press, 1989), and author of many articles on Kierkegaard, including the entry in the *Stanford Encyclopedia of Philosophy*.

Thomas J. Millay is a PhD student in Theology and Ethics at Baylor University and a contributing editor for the *Los Angeles Review of Books*. He has published on Kierkegaard in *Modern Theology* and the *International Journal of Systematic Theology*, and he has contributed to the *Kierkegaard Research: Sources, Reception and Resources* book series. His book *You Must Change Your Life: Kierkegaard and the End of Reading* is forthcoming from Cascade Press.

Jack Mulder, Jr. is Professor of Philosophy at Hope College. He is the author (with Bertha Alvarez Manninen) of *Civil Dialogue on Abortion* (Routledge, 2018), *What Does It Mean to Be Catholic?* (Eerdmans, 2015), *Kierkegaard and the Catholic Tradition: Conflict and Dialogue* (Indiana University Press, 2010), and *Mystical and Buddhist Elements in Kierkegaard's Religious Thought* (Edwin Mellen Press, 2005).

Shoni Rancher earned his PhD from SUNY Binghamton's Social, Political, Ethical, and Legal Philosophy program, and has held teaching positions at Misericordia University, the University of West Georgia, and Georgia State University. His work has appeared in the *Kierkegaard Research: Sources, Reception and Resources* series, the *Acta Kierkegaardiana* series, and the *APA Newsletter on Hispanic/Latino Issues in Philosophy*.

Anthony Rudd is Associate Professor of Philosophy at St. Olaf College, Minnesota. He is the author of *Kierkegaard and the Limits of the Ethical* (Oxford University Press, 1993), *Expressing the World: Skepticism, Wittgenstein and Heidegger* (Open Court, 2003), and *Self, Value and Narrative: A Kierkegaardian Approach* (Oxford University Press, 2012). His articles have appeared in journals such as *Inquiry*, *The European Journal of Philosophy*, *Faith and Philosophy*, and *Philosophy East and West*.

Anna Louise Strelis Söderquist is Lecturer in Philosophy at DIS (Study Abroad in Scandinavia) and an Affiliated Researcher with the Søren Kierkegaard Research Centre at the University of Copenhagen Faculty of Theology in Denmark. She is the author of *Kierkegaard on Dialogical Education: Vulnerable Freedom* (Lexington, 2016) and has articles appearing in *Acta Kierkegaardiana*, *Res Philosophica*, and *Philosophical Forum*.

K. Brian Söderquist is Lecturer in Philosophy at DIS (Study Abroad in Scandinavia) and an Affiliated Researcher with the Søren Kierkegaard Research Centre at the University of Copenhagen Faculty of Theology in Denmark. He is the author of *The Isolated Self: Truth and Untruth in Kierkegaard's 'On the Concept of Irony'* (C. A. Reitzel, 2007), as well as numerous articles. He has also served as co-editor of *Kierkegaard Studies Yearbook* and *Kierkegaard's Journals and Notebooks*.

Patrick Stokes is Associate Professor of Philosophy at Deakin University, Melbourne, Australia, and an honorary fellow at the University of Hertfordshire, UK. He is the author of *The Naked Self* (Oxford University Press, 2015) and *Kierkegaard's Mirrors* (Palgrave Macmillan, 2010), and co-editor with John Lippitt of *Narrative, Identity, and the Kierkegaardian Self* (Edinburgh University Press, 2015) and with Adam Buben of *Kierkegaard and Death* (Indiana University Press, 2011).

Jamie Turnbull is an independent scholar. He has been a House Foundation Fellow at the Hong Kierkegaard Library, St. Olaf College, and is a former editor of *Acta Kierkegaardiana*. He is interested in the relation between the historical Kierkegaard and contemporary depictions of him.

Pieter Vos is Lecturer in Ethics at the Protestant Theological University (Amsterdam) and director of the International Reformed Theological Institute (IRTI). He has published on moral formation, virtue ethics, Reformed theology, and Kierkegaard. His publications on Kierkegaard include *The Solace of the Moment: Kierkegaard on God and Suffering* (in Dutch; Ten Have, 2002) and *Reading Søren Kierkegaard* (in Dutch; Kok, 2010).

Claudia Welz is Professor of Systematic Theology at the University of Copenhagen, with special responsibilities in Ethics and Philosophy of Religion, and Founding Director of the Center for the Study of Jewish Thought in Modern Culture. She is the author of *Love's Transcendence and the Problem of Theodicy* (Mohr Siebeck, 2008), *Vertrauen und Versuchung* (Mohr Siebeck, 2010), and *Humanity in God's Image: An Interdisciplinary Exploration* (Oxford University Press, 2016).

Justin F. White is Assistant Professor of Philosophy at Brigham Young University in Provo, Utah. He focuses on nineteenth- and twentieth-century European philosophy (especially phenomenology) and the philosophy of agency. His work has appeared in *Midwest Studies in Philosophy* and *The Southern Journal of Philosophy*.

Walter Wietzke is Visiting Assistant Professor of Philosophy at University of Wisconsin–River Falls. His work has appeared in a range of journals and publications including *Res Philosophica*, *The European Legacy*, *Kierkegaard Studies Yearbook*, and *Lutheran Quarterly*.

Will Williams teaches Religion and Philosophy at LeTourneau University in Longview, Texas. He was previously a Kierkegaard House Foundation Fellow at St. Olaf College in Northfield, Minnesota, and he is the author of *Kierkegaard and the Legitimacy of the Comic* (Lexington, 2018).

Mark A. Wrathall is Professor of Philosophy at the University of Oxford, where he is also a fellow and tutor at Corpus Christi College. He is the author and editor of numerous books focusing on the thought of Martin Heidegger, and he was featured in the 2010 documentary *Being in the World*.

INTRODUCTION: KIERKEGAARD'S LIFE, CONTEXT, AND LEGACY

Adam Buben, Eleanor Helms, and Patrick Stokes

A short, strange life

Kierkegaard's life and authorial career are deeply unusual, even eccentric, by the standards of both his age and our own. Yet Kierkegaard is also very much a product of a quite particular place and moment in European history. His life fits snugly within the period known to us now as the Danish Golden Age, an era of dramatic cultural, intellectual, scientific, political, and artistic flourishing bookended by twin national humiliations: the bombardment of Copenhagen by the British in 1807, and the loss of the southern provinces to Prussia after the Second Schleswig War in 1865. It was a period that produced its share of problematic geniuses, from the brilliant but insufferable Hans Christian Andersen to the restless political and religious energy of N. F. S. Grundtvig and the cultural dominance of Johann Ludvig Heiberg. Thanks in large part to the last figure, Kierkegaard was also both the product and chief critic of a philosophical and theological milieu in which the philosophy of G. F. W. Hegel was exerting an increasing, though never total, hegemony on Danish intellectual life.

Søren Aabye Kierkegaard was born on May 5, 1813, in Copenhagen, the city where he would spend almost all of his life.[1] His father, Michael Pedersen Kierkegaard, was born into poverty, but in his early teens he became an apprentice to a merchant and went on to a prosperous business career, retiring at just forty. In 1794 he married the sister of a business connection, Kirstine Nielsdatter Røyen. At Kirstine's death on March 23, 1796, they were childless. Michael's next marriage, to Ane Sørensdatter Lund, drew attention for two reasons: she was the family's maid, and she was pregnant with their first child at the time of their marriage on April 26, 1797. (This also meant that their romance occurred within the expected year of mourning following the death of a spouse.) Søren was the last of their seven children.

While his childhood seems largely unremarkable, Kierkegaard did experience a great deal of familial loss throughout his adolescence. Only he and his brother, Peter Christian, would make it past 1838, and Michael apparently believed that his own youthful indiscretions had brought on a curse that was to blame for the premature demise of most of his children. Whatever Kierkegaard may have thought about his father's odd dark legacy, it is clear that his father also left him with sufficient financial security to sustain his education at the University of Copenhagen and, ultimately, his career as an independent author. He defended his Magister thesis (equivalent to a modern PhD), *The Concept of Irony*, in 1841, the same year he infamously broke off his engagement to Regine Olsen.

Kierkegaard had met Olsen at the house of a mutual friend when she was just fifteen. Over the next two years, until she was old enough to court officially, Kierkegaard endeared himself to her and her family. Despite what appears to be a deep and sincere affection for her, Kierkegaard decided that he could not accomplish his goals as an author while maintaining a life as a dedicated husband. The break was painful, not least because of Olsen's distress and the humiliation of her father. (Kierkegaard actually tried to present himself to the gossipy Copenhagen society as a cad, being seen apparently enjoying himself in public, in order to rescue his former fiancée's reputation.) This scandalous decision, and his continued concern for Olsen, had a profound effect on much of his early work. Many of his books and discourses are addressed to 'that single individual, whom I in joy and gratitude call my reader' – a reference both to every individual reader and to one very specific reader in particular. To the end of his life he remained clear that he was, in a sense, spiritually married to Olsen. When he died, he left his estate to Regine, by now married to Kierkegaard's old rival Fritz Schlegel and living in tropical dissatisfaction as First Lady of the Danish Virgin Islands. She declined all but his old letters to her.[2]

Having concluded both his thesis and his engagement, Kierkegaard soon left for Berlin, where he attended the lectures of Friedrich Wilhelm Joseph Schelling alongside several other soon-to-be notable intellectuals from this era (including Friedrich Engels). While in Berlin, he composed significant portions of what would become his first major work, *Either/Or* (1843). This marked the beginning of his 'first authorship,' and over the next few, very productive, years, Kierkegaard published the majority of his most famous philosophical works from a variety of pseudonymous perspectives, while simultaneously producing a series of lesser known 'upbuilding' discourses under his own name. Among others, this period saw the emergence of *Fear and Trembling* (1843), *The Concept of Anxiety* (1844), *Philosophical Fragments* (1844), and *Stages on Life's Way* (1845). With the completion of *Concluding Unscientific Postscript to 'Philosophical Fragments'* (1846), Kierkegaard believed that his work as an author had come to an end. This belief seems to have been based in part on worries that the old family curse would not allow him to exceed the age at which Jesus Christ was crucified, but it was also due to his plan to become a rural pastor. As it turned out, neither the curse nor his plan would be realized, and his 'second authorship' commenced instead.

Kierkegaard's writings after *Concluding Unscientific Postscript* were marked by expanding interest in, and commentary on, the social-political climate in Denmark, including the role of the church in secular society. The first work from this period was a literary review of a novel by Thomasine Gyllembourg titled *A Story of Everyday Life*. Kierkegaard took the literary review as an opportunity to express, under his own name, the ways in which he thought Danish society had become weak-willed and empty, not in spite of, but as a result of, its intellectual growth. It had, he charged, become an 'age of reflection' rather than an 'age of revolution.' This critique was published around the time of his quarrel with *The Corsair*, a satirical periodical that had taken to mocking notable figures in Copenhagen. When Kierkegaard publicly called out this irresponsible behaviour and demanded that he be targeted as well, thinking that his fellow citizens would come to his defence, *The Corsair* cruelly obliged. Instead of defending him, however, the public seemed to enjoy and even participate in the mockery. This experience with the mob, and the form of mass communication that incited it, led Kierkegaard to avoid the streets of Copenhagen (on which he had formerly enjoyed frequent strolls and conversations), to recommit himself to writing, and to rethink what could be expected of his audience.

In most of the major works of the 'second authorship,' including *Upbuilding Discourses in Various Spirits* (1847), *Works of Love* (1847), *Christian Discourses* (1848), and *For Self-Examination* (1851), no pseudonyms are used, and his critique of the way Christianity is understood and practiced in contemporary Danish society becomes increasingly straightforward and biting. In the rare cases when he does employ a pseudonym – such as in *The Sickness unto Death* (1849) and *Practice in Christianity* (1850) – the point is to provide a thoroughly Christian perspective that brings all its terrible rigours to the fore with the kind of religious authority that Kierkegaard does not possess himself. His hope was that this new forthright, and sometimes brutally harsh, approach to presenting what is involved in genuine Christianity would disturb the 'Christians' of Copenhagen and awaken them from their complacent adherence to the tranquilized distortion of Christianity then making its way from pulpits to pews. Unfortunately, his hope would not be fulfilled.

Frustrated by what he saw as a continued failure to address the many shortcomings of the Danish state church (despite his numerous attempts to bring them to the attention of the church leadership), and outraged by the views of his former teacher (and new bishop) Hans Lassen Martensen, Kierkegaard spent the last two years of his life engaged in a direct attack on the church. He argued in essays published in *The Fatherland*, for example, that clergy should either take their prestige from their religious calling (and live in poverty) or claim a respectable salary and comfortable secular life – but not both. Kierkegaard's frustrations were part of a wider egalitarian shift in Denmark at the time, affecting the government as well as the church, with a concrete turning point at the end of A. S. Ørsted's (the brother of physicist H. C. Ørsted) government in 1854. During the time of Kierkegaard's publications in *The Fatherland* (1854–1855) and *The Moment* (1855), it seems that Bishop Grundtvig was replying to Kierkegaard's most recent essays on a weekly basis. The prevailing opinion was that Kierkegaard was a troublemaker and perhaps even a traitor to the cultural elite he ought to have defended during a time of political and social upheaval. Instead, Kierkegaard turned the changing political climate to his advantage: following the end of Ørsted's government and the implementation of new laws supporting freedom of speech, it was more difficult for Martensen and others to challenge Kierkegaard's criticisms in court. He took full advantage.[3]

Despite new political protections, this series of attacks still left Kierkegaard in a difficult position: his inheritance from his father was about to run out, yet he had virulently and very publicly attacked the sole employer for the only job for which he was qualified. As it turned out, fate had other plans. Following some disturbing health incidents, Kierkegaard collapsed in the street in October 1855. There is no settled fact of the matter about what ultimately led to his demise. The doctors evidently suspected spinal tuberculosis (Pott's Disease), and this does make a good deal of diagnostic sense, though other conditions have been suggested as well.[4] Regardless of what the doctors thought, when Kierkegaard checked himself in to Frederiks Hospital, he was himself convinced he would not be coming out alive. Indeed, he seems to have told the admitting physician that his imminent death would be a sort of denouement of his religious mission. He came not to be healed, but to be martyred.

Over the next month he refused to see and reconcile with his older brother, Peter Christian, refused final communion, and ultimately died around 9 pm on November 11. At his funeral a week later, his nephew Henrik Lund made a loud protest that the church was appropriating in death someone who had been its implacable enemy in life. (For his trouble, Lund was fined and very nearly imprisoned.) Kierkegaard lies in the family plot in Assistens Cemetery, in the city's inner north – just a few yards away from the grave of 'that single individual,' Regine Schlegel *nee* Olsen. Not long before her own death in 1904, Regine, now a sprightly widow in her eighties, had berated a young Danish theology graduate for the unforgivable sin of not knowing the work of Søren Kierkegaard.

Kierkegaard's third century

More than a century and a half after his death, Kierkegaard remains one of the most enigmatic, captivating, and elusive thinkers in the history of European thought. As much orthogonal to his own age as ours, his influence has been at once both pervasive and cryptic, shaping key philosophical and theological currents from Existentialism to Post-structuralism and beyond in ways that may not always be apparent, even to those who have been the conduits of Kierkegaardian themes. His legacy of unconventional, genre-busting, frequently pseudonymous, often unpublished and unfinished texts, dripping with irony and as playful as they are melancholy, remains a rich and still largely untapped resource for contemporary thought. As Kierkegaard enters his third century, his full relevance, far from diminishing, is only beginning to come into view.

Yet the very expansiveness and variety of Kierkegaard's thought makes it hard for the reader to find a foothold when grappling with this protean and often evasive thinker. With themes often being developed by different voices, in different terminology, over the course of several works, it can be difficult to know where to begin with Kierkegaard. *The Kierkegaardian Mind* seeks to give a synoptic view of the many currents in Kierkegaard's thought and advance new arguments showing their ongoing relevance for contemporary philosophy, theology, literature, and politics. A recurring theme in Kierkegaard's work is a distrust of systematization and mediation, and a corresponding insistence on leaving tensions in place. In keeping with this Kierkegaardian tradition, *The Kierkegaardian Mind* allows the reader to see the full spectrum of tensions, contradictions, and divergent possibilities in Kierkegaard's work and in his ongoing reception.

A wide range of Kierkegaard scholars from around the world and from various disciplinary backgrounds have been assembled to cover the full sweep of Kierkegaard's thought. Some of the leading Kierkegaard commentators of the last three decades, along with exciting emerging voices in the field, guide the reader through key concepts, themes, and debates within and around Kierkegaard's thought. Chapters have been grouped into sections on Kierkegaard's Methodology, Ethics, Aesthetics, Philosophy of Religion/Theology, Philosophy of Mind, Anthropology, Epistemology, and Politics.

Methodology

Kierkegaard's methodology is at once captivating and elusive. The use of different names, or pseudonyms, in many writings makes it difficult to know Kierkegaard's own position. Pseudonymous works, as well as those written in his own name, often rely on metaphor, extended parables, satire, and other literary devices. In addition to making sense of Kierkegaard's writing on various topics through the stylistic challenges, what can we learn about Kierkegaard from these unusual methods themselves?

Acknowledging that Kierkegaard's writing does not fit neatly with expected patterns of philosophical argument, Lee C. Barrett argues in 'The Passion of Kierkegaard's Existential Method' that there are nevertheless 'metastrategies' in Kierkegaard's writing that amount to a method, including his use of specific philosophical tropes and even his use of literary forms. His strategies fit with his goal of clarifying different options for living, including the role of pathos in each, rather than persuading readers of the superiority of one view. His work influenced a turn of attention in later nineteenth-century thinkers and beyond toward the way a reader encounters and 'uses' a text for self-reflection and to facilitate imagining different points of view.

Claudine Davidshofer's 'Johannes Climacus and the Dialectical Method: From Dialectics Back to Existence' provides a helpful orientation in the way this method has been employed throughout the history of philosophy, before situating Kierkegaard's peculiar appropriation of dialectics relative to the approaches of Socrates and Hegel. Focusing on the works attributed to the pseudonym Johannes Climacus, primarily *Philosophical Fragments*, Davidshofer gives a detailed account of his dialectical analysis of, first, the Socratic/pagan relationship with eternal truth, and then the Christian. Unlike Hegel, Climacus can see no way of resolving the tensions inherent in both the pagan and the Christian notions of reaching such truth. Thus, he concludes that the highest achievement of the dialectical method is to make individuals (whether pagan or Christian) take seriously the task of living with these tensions.

Examining one significant implication of the focus on self-consciousness, in 'Kierkegaard's Experimenting Psychology' William McDonald shows how Kierkegaard, along with Swiss psychiatrist Ludwig Binswanger (1881–1966), avoids a problem in post-Kantian psychology that Foucault (1994: 318–22) calls the 'empirico-transcendental doublet.' The problem pointed out by Foucault is that the transcendental conditions for the possibility of empirical knowledge can only be discovered by relying on empirical – rather than purely transcendental – inquiry. Kierkegaard avoids this problem by treating the self as a mode of being rather than an object to be reflected on and by making exemplary cases (rather than abstract reflection) the means of disclosing the self. McDonald then further traces Kierkegaard's influence on nineteenth-century psychology in Denmark, including the importance of Kierkegaard's emphasis on mood and Kierkegaard's understanding of the self as self-relating and self-interpreting.

Such non-theological uses of Kierkegaard are not universally welcomed, however. Jamie Turnbull's chapter, 'Methodology and the Kierkegaardian Mind,' considers a range of interpretations of Kierkegaard's method of indirect communication (as exemplified in the use of pseudonyms and poetic writing style) and finds the literary, psychological, and philosophical interpretations wanting. Only a theological interpretation, grounded in the notion of Christ qua incarnation as absolute paradox and sensitive to the intellectual horizons and concerns of Golden Age Denmark, can fully make sense of indirect communication. If that is so, claims Turnbull, then psychological, biographical, or philosophical understandings of Kierkegaard's methodology are deficient, and indeed any reading of Kierkegaard not grounded in supernaturalism will hopelessly distort what Kierkegaard is trying to do.

Ethics

While not an ethicist in the sense of someone who tries to determine what sort of actions are morally permissible or impermissible, a great deal of Kierkegaard's writing is clearly ethical in character, even when he is critical of the limits of 'the ethical' itself as a category. Indeed, it is part of Kierkegaard's genius as a moral psychologist that he sees how talk of ethics can actually be used in the service of *un*ethical approaches to existence. As Rob Compaijen and Pieter Vos argue in their chapter 'Ethical Reflection as Evasion,' although Kierkegaard sees that thinking about the ethical is a necessary component of living well, he is also very much alive to the ways in which *thinking* about ethics can be a way of avoiding having to *act* ethically. In particular, Kierkegaard is suspicious of the claim that ethical reflection is a knowledge-generating exercise like the sciences, and that like the sciences it requires a certain dispassionate detachment on the part of the contemplator – a stance that, as Kierkegaard claims, is wholly incompatible with living ethically in an existential situation.

Even though Kierkegaard's approach to ethics clearly runs counter to much of contemporary ethical theory, there are nonetheless fascinating points of intersection. One distinctive feature of Kierkegaard's ethics is that he rejects the idea of a system based on moral rules or abstract principles, instead concentrating on concrete exemplars and illustrations. Karl Aho's 'Kierkegaard and Moral Particularism and Exemplarism' brings Kierkegaard into dialogue with two recent ethicists who are likewise suspicious of rules-based ethical systems: the moral particularist Jonathan Dancy and the moral exemplarist Linda Zagzebski. Both thinkers emphasize the role of narratives in moral judgment, as does Kierkegaard. But, argues Aho, Kierkegaard goes further by bringing the narrators themselves into the situation being considered. Moreover, his claims that such successful moral self-narration is rare, and that admiration is problematic in the present age, offer important complications and challenges for both Dancy and Zagzebski.

Despite not being particularly concerned with the ethical permissibility of particular actions, nor with establishing normative, action-guiding principles, Kierkegaard nonetheless has been seen as contributing to various metaethical positions, such as divine command ethics and virtue ethics. John Lippitt, in his chapter 'Beyond Worry? On Learning Humility from the Lilies and the Birds,' shows one way in which Kierkegaard's account of the virtues is useful both philosophically and existentially. Lippitt focusses on Kierkegaard's discussion of humility, a virtue illustrated in his discourse on the teaching of the lilies of the field and the birds of the air (Matt. 6: 25–32). What these natural exemplars can show us, according to Lippitt, is a particular variety of humility that is other-directed rather than self-absorbed, one that is nonetheless compatible with a concern for self-improvement.

Kierkegaard's pursuit of lived virtues, and his critique of more dispassionate and contemplative approaches to the ethical, largely arise in response to the Hegelianism then dominating the Copenhagen intellectual scene. In 'Did Napoleon Teleologically Suspend the Ethical? A Dilemma for Some 'Hegelian' Readings of *Fear and Trembling*,' Ryan S. Kemp takes on a prominent interpretation of Kierkegaard's famous text, which suggests that the apparently unethical actions of Abraham, while contrary to prevailing cultural norms, can find justification in some kind of higher rationality. The problem with such an interpretation is that it seems to remain compatible with Hegel's description of the movers and shakers of world history, while the account of the teleological suspension of the ethical provided by Kierkegaard's pseudonym Johannes de silentio is explicitly intended to *conflict* with Hegel's views. Kemp argues that a proper understanding of this important concept in *Fear and Trembling* involves a more radical break with rational justification than Hegel would be willing to condone.

Moving from Kierkegaard's reception of earlier thinkers to his influence on later ones, one topic that has been heavily discussed in the literature is Kierkegaard's connections to and influence upon Martin Heidegger (given how Kierkegaardian so many of Heidegger's concerns in *Being and Time* appear to be). However, less has been said specifically about what Heidegger's *ethical* thought, a contentious issue in itself, owes to Kierkegaard. One obvious answer is 'not much': while both Kierkegaard and Heidegger present the individual self as thrown into the world, Kierkegaard offers a religious hope for a 'return' that seems to be absent in Heidegger. In 'An Ethics of Home and Hope: Kierkegaard's Exile and Heidegger's Emigrant,' Megan Altman shows that, in fact, Heidegger's work contains an existential hope in place of Kierkegaard's eschatological hope, one grounded in the etymological origins of 'ethics' in meanings of 'home' and 'dwelling.' Such hope allows us, as Altman claims, to find holy things in the most humble of places.

While hope receives a lot of attention in Kierkegaard's writings, especially in his more explicitly religious and edifying work, love is an even more ubiquitous theme throughout the corpus. Sharon Krishek's 'Love for Humans: Morality as the Heart of Kierkegaard's Religious Philosophy' considers the discussions of love in *Fear and Trembling* and *Works of Love*, arguing that a life well lived involves putting one's natural potential for loving others into practice. With the help of an example from contemporary literature, Krishek connects this actual love for others with the account of selfhood in *The Sickness unto Death*. On her view, failure to love amounts to a form of despair in which one does not achieve an appropriate balance between the eternal/

universal and temporal/particular elements of what one is. Because achieving this balance is necessary for genuine selfhood, and such selfhood (according to *Sickness*) entails being in a genuine relationship with the divine, actual love for one's fellow humans is an integral component of faith in God.

Aesthetics

A standard reading of Kierkegaard has existence falling into discrete spheres or 'stages': the aesthetic, the ethical, and the religious, with the aesthetic sphere being our default, immediate mode of being from which we are ethically enjoined to emerge. Kierkegaard also has views on aesthetics in the academic sense of questions about art, beauty, sensory experience, and enjoyment of nature. The chapters in this section examine all these different aspects of the 'aesthetic' in Kierkegaard.

As a description of someone in a particular stage of existence, 'aesthete' is thus not a compliment in Kierkegaard's nomenclature. *Either/Or* exemplifies this schema, with the first volume's aesthetic musings by a jaded young man known only as 'A' being countered by the ethical exhortations of the older, married Judge William in the second part. Yet this standard picture may be a little too neat and simplistic. In 'The Ethical Life of Aesthetes,' Ulrika Carlsson takes on the standard view of *Either/Or* that sees the ethical critiques in the second part of the book as successfully diagnosing what is wrong with the aesthetic way of life presented in the first part. In addition to addressing complicated questions about which pseudonym, or perhaps pseudonyms, might be responsible for the different components of the first part, Carlsson also makes compelling arguments that the aesthete 'A' is far more sophisticated when it comes to matters of love, faith, and meaning than the ethicist Judge (as well as many a Kierkegaard commentator) would have the reader believe. Ultimately, Carlsson thinks that, for someone incapable of the sort of unquestioned, foundational religiosity of the Judge, the aesthetic way of life offers hope for another (more ancient) sense of significance.

Kierkegaard also addresses aesthetic value in terms of what is pleasing to the senses (that is, as addressing questions of beauty and enjoyment of the physical world). Anthony Rudd argues in his chapter, 'Kierkegaard on Nature and Natural Beauty,' that Kierkegaard's view of the value of nature is more compatible with Romanticism's view of the natural world than often thought. Rudd shows that Kierkegaard conceives of nature as a *theophany* – a revelation of God – and that virtues of silence and obedience are a stance of 'active receptivity' needed to learn from nature so understood. Allegories like the lilies of the field and the birds of the air, far from being mere teaching aids we are meant to learn from and dispense with, turn out to be instances of an ongoing appreciation of the natural world that forms part of our ongoing relationship to God.

Along with Romanticism, Immanuel Kant's views on beauty and sensory experience are a foundation for much of Kierkegaard's thinking about art and nature. Kant found certain natural phenomena of overwhelming scale and force to be sources of the experience of the sublime, which was a strong feeling of fear or discomfort nevertheless accompanied by a higher kind of pleasure in one's autonomy, experienced as nature's inability to dominate our rational powers. In 'Kierkegaard's Transfigurations of the Sublime,' Samuel Cuff Snow argues that in *Either/Or*, Kierkegaard takes the conflict in the Kantian sublime between the need for representation and that which is unrepresentable, and transfigures it into figures like Antigone and the 'silhouettes.' Caught between irreconcilable demands, condemned thereby to anxiety and grief, these figures both embody a form of the sublime that echoes Kant's account and yet point beyond it, towards new possibilities for living, governed ethico-religiously by love.

Not only sublime experiences, but also works of art in general, can offer new ways of understanding one's self and fresh sources of meaning. In 'Kierkegaard on the Value of Art: an Indirect Method of Communication,' Antony Aumann explains Kierkegaard's 'cognitivist' approach to artwork. Unlike many thinkers of his day, Kierkegaard believed that not only can artwork teach us important truths about ourselves, but it can also be a better occasion for such instruction than works of philosophy and science. Relying on examples from the world of painting and literature, Aumann connects Kierkegaard's views on art with his famous affinity for indirect communication. Good artwork serves as a kind of mirror that allows one to see oneself in the image or character depicted and reflects one's own shortcomings in a more personal and compelling way than is possible when they are directly pointed out.

Kierkegaard's emphases on the aesthetic aspects of self-development need not be thought of as separate from their religious character. In 'Deleuze on Kierkegaard,' Andrew Jampol-Petzinger gives new consideration to Giles Deleuze's proposal that Kierkegaard's work is ambiguously religious and aesthetic, such that efforts to distinguish those dimensions reveal a mere difference in tone. Like a work of art, Kierkegaard's writing presents itself as a concrete object of encounter that provokes a reaction to the underlying reality it expresses. The Deleuzian interpretation brings out the creativity of both the religious person and the artist when faced with the task of making oneself at home in a situation that has become impossible and uninhabitable, such as that of Abraham in *Fear and Trembling* as well as the desolation of Europe after WWII. As with the other treatments of art, beauty, and sublimity above, creativity offers a way of becoming oneself even in a strange or hostile environment.

Philosophy of religion/theology

Kierkegaard almost never refers to himself as a philosopher, and while his magisterial thesis was largely focused on philosophy (Socrates, Fichte, and Hegel, among others), it was actually written for a theology degree. His influence within both theology and philosophy of religion (in addition to the other areas examined here) has been immense and his contribution unique. This section of *The Kierkegaardian Mind* explores some of the key themes within this aspect of his work: imitation, atonement, reason, paradox, and, above all, faith.

In 'Kierkegaard's Existential Mimesis,' Wojciech Kaftanski surveys different accounts of 'imitation' in Kierkegaard scholarship, arguing that it is helpful to relate it along with representation and emulation in a broader concept of mimesis. He uncovers a tension in the demand to imitate things that have a consciousness very unlike ours, including Christ as prototype (since Christ has a divine nature) and the 'lilies of the field' and 'birds of the air' (who lack the capacity for disobedience). Kaftanski suggests we can imitate them indirectly, by taking on the same goals but pursuing different means.

In 'Becoming a Subject: Kierkegaard's Theological Art of Existence,' Peder Jothen argues that imitation of Christ must be understood existentially as an ongoing task. Through a close reading of the youth who is shown a picture of Christ suffering in *Practice in Christianity*, Jothen argues that art can be part of the task of becoming a Christian. Most importantly, art engages the passions and aids the development of a subject who is both theological (an infinite creature made in God's image) and aesthetic (a finite body). Despite some suggestions (by Kierkegaard himself, as well as interpreters) that Kierkegaard has a negative view of art, Jothen shows that art can be a means to higher self-reflection. In the task of selfhood, we learn to see the ideal, the suffering Christ, as something we must become in existence, in this way becoming works of art ourselves.

In 'Engendering Atonement: Kierkegaard on the Cross,' Deidre Nicole Green suggests possible Kierkegaardian contributions to a debate amongst feminist theologians about the ostensibly violent nature of atonement in Christianity. She does this by providing detailed analyses of two prominent discussions of women from scripture in Kierkegaard's work – Sarah from the apocryphal Book of Tobit, and the sinful woman who anoints Christ's feet in the Book of Luke. Because Kierkegaard holds the actions of these women up as important and informative parallels for Christ's act of atonement via crucifixion, Green argues that Kierkegaard is emphasizing more traditionally feminine aspects of the atonement that often go unnoticed. Specifically, she highlights gentleness, humility, and openness to the help of others.

Whether and to what extent Kierkegaard should be read as a fideist who denies the capacity of human reason to determine matters of ultimate truth has been a heavily contested issue. K. Brian Söderquist's 'On Faith and Reason(s): Kierkegaard's Logic of Conviction' revisits this highly contentious topic in Kierkegaard studies, and argues that, because his notion of faith is necessarily opposed to human understanding, trying to provide reasons in its defence misses the point. Through a helpful comparison with William James's views on religious conviction, Söderquist makes a case that, for Kierkegaard, genuine faith requires the passive experience of something inherently private, yet remarkably convincing on a personal level (in addition to an active willingness to remain open to such an experience). Although one can never eliminate the impulse to try to make oneself and one's set of beliefs comprehensible, at least to oneself, a life of faith means embracing one's seemingly indefensible conviction without ever satisfying this impulse.

Mark A. Wrathall, in 'Coming to an Understanding with the Paradox,' takes on the challenge of the incomprehensibility of Christianity, which is a characteristic of God as both human and divine that Kierkegaard treats as a strength and essential feature of Christianity rather than a criticism. Wrathall distinguishes between 'believing nonsense' and 'having faith that is contrary to the understanding' and proposes that Kierkegaard is an 'adoxalist': faith is a practical stance of ready attention to relevant information together with characteristic reactions. In this way, the cognitive question of what one believes becomes a practical question of how one lives. The inability to describe the Christian relation to the God-man, or what Wrathall calls 'Climacus's Puzzle,' turns out to be no more mysterious than our inability to discursively describe other areas of skilled activity.

Despite the positive view of nature found in many of Kierkegaard's works (as discussed for instance in the chapters by Rudd and Lippitt), Will Williams finds a note of theological concern in the way Kierkegaard's era conceived of the natural world. In his chapter, 'Kierkegaard's Defense of Nature and Theology Against Natural Theology,' Williams traces Kierkegaard's disdain both for a form of romanticism that thinks we can simply read ethical lessons directly from nature and, more significantly, with natural sciences that step outside their proper bounds and reduce fundamental ethical and religious phenomena to questions of taxonomy and mechanical explanation. Such sciences, for Kierkegaard, always claim to be on the verge of solving fundamental mysteries which are not in fact their proper domain to begin with. Kierkegaard ultimately concludes that whatever the microscope may reveal about the structure of the natural world, only the eyes of faith can see the ultimate truth of Christianity.

Philosophy of mind

From Plato's account of the soul onward, philosophers have examined what it means to have a mind or consciousness and how thought relates to the finite, material body. While not typically thought of as a philosopher of mind (he never asks, for example, how the mind relates to the brain), Kierkegaard does in fact have interesting and important things to say about the nature of consciousness, experience, and the relationship between thought and existence. In 'Consciousness, Self, and Reflection,' Patrick Stokes outlines the structure of consciousness, the account of the nature of reflection, and the place of 'higher immediacy' beyond reflection, in Kierkegaard's account of mind. While Kierkegaard's remarks on the nature of consciousness are brief, schematic, and unfinished, the tripartite structure and account of reflection he develops has ramifications both throughout his moral-religious psychology and, more surprisingly, throughout the history of twentieth-century phenomenology.

Other themes from Kierkegaardian psychology were no less influential on European thought in the last century – and no less important today. Claudia Welz explores three such themes in her chapter, 'Conscience, Self-Deception, and the Question of Authenticity in Kierkegaard.' How can self-deception be possible? What is it to live authentically, and how can this be achieved? What is the call of conscience? All such questions are familiar to students of figures like Sartre and Heidegger, yet their wellsprings, as well as important answers to them, lie within Kierkegaard.

In 'Imagination and Belief,' Eleanor Helms examines the role of imagination and possibility in forming beliefs about the real world, comparing Kierkegaard's view to that of phenomenologist Maurice Merleau-Ponty. In ordinary perception for both philosophers, she argues, experiences have a teleological character, which motivates belief in the reality of what is perceived. Judge William's critiques of the aesthete in *Either/Or*, as well as A's review of the novel *A First Love*, reveal the important work of the imagination (usually faulted as the source of illusion) in enabling us to recognize what is real.

In 'Agency, Identity, and Alienation in *The Sickness unto Death*,' Justin F. White clarifies the role of practical identity in achieving selfhood. He considers experiences of not being oneself, such as when actions do not seem to be our own, as for example when we are overcome with emotion, when we are in different types of despair, or when suffering from self-deception or ignorance. While acknowledging the influence of concrete roles and externalities (e.g., son, parent), White shows how we are always more than our practical identities. Selfhood, he argues, is aspirational: it includes the attitude we take toward the inheritances and necessities that make up an indispensable aspect of our identities. Rather than being alienated from the aspects of our lives we do not choose, viewing them as merely external, we can understand them as opportunities to increase our agency as we make choices in light of the parts of our lives that are not up to us.

Anthropology

Kierkegaard's views on the difficult task of achieving selfhood are intimately bound up with his understanding of human nature. Given his core theological commitments, Kierkegaard primarily understands the human in relation to the divine and the cultivation of genuine selfhood as a properly religious endeavour. This is not to say that his work is free of secular analogues, but providing these will never be the ultimate goal of his treatment of such topics. While he has a great deal to say about selfhood and human nature throughout his writings, the book that makes a theme of them is (pseudonym) Anti-Climacus's *The Sickness unto Death*, and unsurprisingly, this is where most of the chapters in this section direct their gaze.

In 'Kierkegaard's Post-Kantian Approach to Anthropology and Selfhood,' Roe Fremstedal discusses the relation between philosophical and theological anthropology in Kierkegaard's thought, and explains his negative approach to anthropology that prioritizes the issue of despair. Whereas the first part of *Sickness* provides a philosophical anthropology that distinguishes between inauthentic (non-conscious) and authentic (conscious) despair, the second part develops a theological anthropology that involves the despair before God known as sin. Because human nature turns out to be a synthesis of opposites, avoiding despair and cultivating a genuine self means fostering the proper relationship between these opposites through wholeheartedness and religious faith.

In 'Images of the Closed Self in *The Sickness unto Death*,' Anna Louise Strelis Söderquist offers further analysis of 'climbing the ladder of despair.' Describing faith and genuine selfhood as a kind of openness to dependency and vulnerability, Strelis Söderquist spends much of her chapter explaining the many ways a person can instead remain closed off by being unreflective, independent, or even defiant. The most unique element of her approach to the much-discussed issue of these different types of despair is her exploration of the metaphorical imagery Anti-Climacus employs to make his account more relatable. In the first part of *Sickness*, he relies on different door-themed images (e.g., the false door), and in the second part, metaphors of war take over (e.g., the defensive fortification).

In 'The Kierkegaardian Self: Convergences and Divergences,' Jack Mulder, Jr., identifies three important elements of the famously challenging definition of the self in *Sickness* and then places them in conversation with significant philosophical and theological forebears. In the case of the basic metaphysical foundation on which the project of becoming a self can be pursued, Mulder sees potential for fruitful comparison with Aristotelian and Thomistic hylomorphism. When it comes to self-awareness and self-relation, Mulder argues that Kierkegaard offers an important historical and communal corrective to the Lockean sense of self that is largely based on personal memory continuity. Finally, Mulder calls attention to some interesting points of connection between Kierkegaard and St. John of the Cross on the issue of relating to God.

Moving on to some of Kierkegaard's other discussions of the task of cultivating selfhood, Adam Buben's 'Kierkegaard and the Desirability of Immortality' addresses the increasing amount of attention paid to Kierkegaard within the recent philosophical debate about the desirability of immortality. His views on boredom and what makes life worth living seem like they would be especially helpful in responding to Bernard Williams's famous argument that immortality would become tedious. Nonetheless, there has been some disagreement about the extent to which Kierkegaard would be opposed to Williams's position and about the former's relevance in what is a largely secular debate. Ultimately, Buben concludes, even if Kierkegaard would not be entirely in favour of precisely the sort of immortality under consideration here, his notion that becoming a proper self lasts 'as long as life lasts' (CUP 1, 163/SKS 7, 152) provides some reason to think it could be worthwhile.

Epistemology

Any living person deals with uncertainty, weighs the cost of commitment to actions and ideals, and gains and loses a variety of beliefs over time. The stakes are particularly high when the beliefs and commitments in question relate to eternity and one's soul, and when there is a possibility our powers of reasoning and willing are damaged or deceived from the outset. As a thinker deeply concerned with the limits of human reason and the inability (as both he and Lutheran orthodoxy see it) of fallen humanity to work our way out of our predicament using our own cognitive resources, it should come as no surprise that epistemology is an important, if not always overt, issue in Kierkegaard's thought.

In 'Christian Epistemology and the Anthropology of Sin: Kierkegaard on Natural Theology and the Concept of "Offense,"' Karen L. Carr charts a course a through a few of the pseudonymous works of Climacus and Anti-Climacus as she attempts to explain the relationship between faith, sin, reason, and offense in Kierkegaard's thought. Because the human self is inherently dependent upon God, it can never be its own master. Among the implications of such an understanding of selfhood is the one that says an individual's own rational capacity will never be sufficient for grasping eternal truths and having a genuine relationship with the divine. Accepting this kind of limitation is not easy for the individual with delusions of autonomy, and so a common reaction involves rejecting this view of the self and other related teachings. Carr maintains that the possibility of such rejection is the constant companion of Christian faith.

Rick Anthony Furtak's 'Varieties of Existential Uncertainty' explores some of the ways in which uncertainty shows up as a constitutive feature of human experience in Kierkegaard's work. Beginning with the uncertainty surrounding religious experience, exemplified by Abraham's reaction, in *Fear and Trembling*, to the (allegedly) divine command to sacrifice Isaac, Furtak goes on to consider the inherent uncertainty associated with the tasks involved in becoming subjective, tasks that *Postscript* claims could occupy an individual indefinitely. Finally, turning to literary examples drawn from *Stages on Life's Way* and the work of Marcel Proust, Furtak considers the various uncertainties of relating to other people. The upshot of all these discussions is that uncertainty is not something to be avoided and overcome, but rather, something we must find a way to live with.

Uncertainty also plays a significant role in the experience of conversion, argues Walter Wietzke in 'Irony and the Conversion Experience.' Wietzke identifies a significant tension in Kierkegaard's concept of conversion. On the one hand, the conversion from one existential 'sphere' to another is grounded in the subjective features of human agency, such as irony and the will, rather than being causally dependent on God or divine grace. Yet on the other hand, these concepts don't seem to be able to explain all the personally transformative aspects of conversion. On Wietzke's account, this does not mean there must be further 'external' conditions for conversion to occur, but simply that risk and uncertainty are a key element of the conversion experience.

Yet risk and uncertainty should not lead us to stop pursuing knowledge. In 'Logic, Language, and Existential Knowledge,' Mélissa Fox-Muraton re-examines the role of logic in Kierkegaard and offers reasons for optimism. Far from being an irrationalist, she argues, Kierkegaard is a realist about language (in the sense that language has roots in the empirical world). He thinks moreover that language can refer meaningfully to non-physical realities once we understand they cannot be talked about in the same way as physical things (that is, objectively). While Kierkegaard insists there are limits to knowledge, he at the same time urges us to use all the theoretical tools available to answer all the questions we can, including moral and existential ones.

Even when the situation looks bad for acquiring knowledge, there may be unexpected ways forward. In 'The Incognito of a Thief: Johannes Climacus and the Poetics of Self-Incrimination,' Martijn Boven reveals ambiguities in *Philosophical Crumbs* (or *Philosophical Fragments*) as Climacus, the pseudonymous author, plays the role of a plagiarizer by pretending to invent Christianity while also drawing attention to his deception. Boven shows the text indirectly implicates the reader, as any truth beyond Socrates must be stolen from somewhere. One paradoxical result is that, to the extent Climacus is a plagiarist, the appearance he takes on in order to deceive turns out to be his true identity. In this way, it is possible to begin with a deception and end with the truth.

Politics

Kierkegaard lived in what proved to be a period of decisive political significance for Denmark, the only place in Europe where the democratic gains of 1848 were both permanent and achieved without bloodshed. Being something of an instinctive conservative and distrustful of mass movements, his direct comments on the politics of his time are largely negative if not dismissive. Yet we can trace deeper elements of political critique in Kierkegaard and can also recover important resources for political theorizing.

Despite being near-contemporaries and formed by many of the same intellectual currents in German Idealism, Marx and Kierkegaard would seem to have radically different preoccupations. While Kierkegaard offers a notoriously individualistic view of salvation, Marx's soteriology is worldly, political, and collective. The Marxist György Lukács argued that there are in fact important points of commonality between Marx and Kierkegaard, but insisted that Marx's systematic thinking is opposed to Kierkegaard's deep opposition to all system-building. Yet as Alison Assiter argues in 'Lukács, Kierkegaard, Marx, and the Political,' things are not so clear as Lukács claims; there is indeed a role for systems in Kierkegaard, and more commonality between Marx and Kierkegaard than might appear.

In 'Kierkegaard: the Dialectical Self and the Political,' Shoni Rancher develops an account of Kierkegaard's political commitments that gives priority to the individual, concluding that Kierkegaard's politics is strongly egalitarian. Authoritarian commitments are ruled out by Kierkegaard's emphasis on dialectic and incompleteness, which means that no single figure, community, or ideal can become a final authority. Instead, an ongoing, dialectical tension is created by the dual insistence that (1) each individual must relate to an ideal and that (2) individuals must relate to the *same* ideal. The possibility of a shared ideal reserves a space for political community in Kierkegaard's thought, while the emphasis that each individual must have the ideal rules out any kind of authoritarianism or coercion in pursuit of the ideal.

In 'Kierkegaard, Hegel, and Augustine on Love,' Thomas J. Millay argues for a more specific view of the individual, namely the importance of love as upbuilding the individual in her relationship with God. One implication is that suffering is not always to be avoided. Millay relates Kierkegaard's work to Augustine's earlier insistence that material things become good or bad depending on their role in enabling one to love God. Millay challenges the limited focus of Augustinian liberalism on improving material situations in a political community; he argues instead, following other interpretations of Augustine, that spiritual growth (i.e., upbuilding) may mean voluntarily taking on *more* suffering by sacrificing the comforts of a bourgeois society. Augustine and Kierkegaard together issue a call to be careful of being overly comfortable or aiming to avoid suffering as a community's (or individual's) highest goal.

In 'The Covetous Canary: Kierkegaard on the Problem of Social Comparison and the Cultivation of Social Courage,' Paul Carron re-examines Kierkegaard's notion of 'the crowd' in light of social comparison theory in contemporary psychology. He examines ways in which humans make sense of our surroundings by comparing ourselves to others, as illustrated by the bystander effect and other experiments showing how the presence of others alters both our behaviour and our attention. Carron then goes on to show that Kierkegaard was aware of the same social influences and considered them an obstacle for true selfhood and a kind of dehumanization. Kierkegaard also offers a solution, he proposes, in the goal of standing alone before God, which enables one to develop the inwardness required to actualize one's humanity even when surrounded by more passive others. Resisting the default of finding identity by comparing oneself to others means accepting one's position as 'lowly,' which requires social courage.

Conclusion

The diversity of themes assembled in this volume gives a sense of, though by no means exhausts, the richness and fecundity of Kierkegaard's thought. In its third century, the Kierkegaardian mind continues to seduce, perplex, challenge, and enlighten those who engage it. The contributions to this volume demonstrate that Kierkegaard's thought can still challenge, critique, and offer surprising ways forward, even in established fields of academic inquiry. Kierkegaard had a gift for turning attention back to questions that must be faced in new ways in every time period: What counts as good and valuable? What can we know, and how? What are the standards for success as a human being? Kierkegaard used his startling talent and considerable literary abilities to keep people from avoiding the difficult questions. His way of doing so turns out to be uniquely embedded in his Copenhagen and yet strangely universal. The ability to find deep meaning in all of life, in any place and time period, is at the heart of Kierkegaard's own struggle as a thinker and writer to find 'an unshakable certainty in oneself won from all experience' (EPW, 76/SKS 1, 32).

Notes

1 The following section draws on the several impressive biographies of Kierkegaard available, including Lowrie (2013), Hannay (2003), Garff (2005), and the collection of contemporary accounts in Kirmmse (1990).
2 On Regine's life during this period and beyond, see Garff (2017).
3 On Kierkegaard's social and political engagement with his contemporaries, as well as how the cultural climate influenced his writing, see Kirmmse (1990).
4 Schioldann and Søgaard (2013) survey some of the health problems that have variously been attributed to Kierkegaard and the theories advanced as to what killed him, the latter including syphilis, Guillain-Barré syndrome, and porphyria. On the case for Potts Disease (spinal tuberculosis) with paraplegia as the cause of death, see Brown (2005) and Weismann and Staubrand (2014); against this, see Schioldann and Søgaard (2014).

References

Brown, J. (2005) 'The health matter briefly revisited epilepsy, "hunchback," and that tiny word (tubercl?),' *Søren Kierkegaard Newsletter*, 49: 16–20.
Foucault, M. (1994) *The order of things: An archaeology of the human sciences*, New York: Vintage Books.
Garff, J. (2017) *Kierkegaard's muse: The mystery of Regine Olsen*, A. Hannay (trans), Princeton, NJ: Princeton University Press.
Garff, J. (2005) *Søren Kierkegaard: A biography*, B. Kirmmse (trans), Princeton, NJ: Princeton University Press.
Hannay, A. (2003) *Kierkegaard: A biography*, Cambridge: Cambridge University Press.
Kirmmse, B. (1990) *Kierkegaard in golden age Denmark*, Bloomington, IN: Indiana University Press.
Lowrie, W. (2013) *A short life of Kierkegaard*, new edition with 'How Kierkegaard got into English' and introduction by A. Hannay, Princeton, NJ: Princeton University Press.
Schioldann, J. and Søgaard, I. (2014) 'Soren Kierkegaard's primary cause of death was not tuberculous spondylitis,' *History of Psychiatry*, 25, no. 1: 134.
Schioldann, J. and Søgaard, I. (2013) 'Søren Kierkegaard (1813–55): A bicentennial pathographical review,' *History of Psychiatry*, 24, no. 4: 387–98.
Weismann, K. and Staubrand, J. (2014) 'Søren Kierkegaard's disease,' *History of Psychiatry*, 25, no. 1: 133.

PART 1
Methodology

1
THE PASSION OF KIERKEGAARD'S EXISTENTIAL METHOD

Lee C. Barrett

Introduction

Kierkegaard's 'method' of engaging philosophical and theological issues has often been regarded as an anomaly in the history of Western thought. 'Method' has usually suggested a rigorously standardized procedure for addressing puzzlements about general features of life in the world, typically with supporting arguments to demonstrate that the particular method in question is superior to its rivals. However, Kierkegaard's authorship does not fit neatly into the methodological frameworks of such high-profile nineteenth-century traditions as Kantianism, Idealism, Empiricism, etc. Consequently, a discussion of his work often has been relegated to an appendix to histories of nineteenth-century theology and philosophy. This is understandable, for his peculiar writings do not resemble anything remotely like the standard philosophical or theological texts of his era. They are filled with multiple voices, pseudonymous authors, books-within-books, thick irony, and abrupt shifts in topic. Although some of his pages look like logical argumentation, even these arguments are often disrupted by unexpected digressions. In many passages Kierkegaard seems to deliberately eschew any disciplined development of a theme, something which would be anathema to any methodologically driven thinker.

Given such a peculiar authorship, it is inevitable that interpretive questions would abound concerning the nature and purpose of his work, and the method, if any, that informed them. Was the basic thrust of his writings an advocacy of subjective relativism? Were his texts designed to be antidotes to all totalizing ideologies and complacent closures? Or were his works an odd sort of apologia for a specific doctrinal position? Philosophically, was his method a proto-phenomenology of religious experience, the application of a Hegel-like dialectic to the development of the individual, a harbinger of Heidegger-style existentialism, a Wittgenstein-like clarification of the uses of specific bits of religious language, or an anticipation of post-structuralism? Theologically, was his *oeuvre* a presentiment of Barth's Christocentrism (only with more subjective fervour), a foreshadowing of Tillich's method of correlation, or an ancestor of Bultmann's call to authenticity? Was he an orthodox Lutheran, an odd sort of Pietist, or a crypto-Catholic? The difficulty of classifying Kierkegaard's literature in terms of some curricular niche in the academy is so severe that many do not regard him as a *bona fide* philosopher or theologian at all. Perhaps his work should be approached as open-ended imaginative literature. Maybe he was a literary provocateur, with no message to communicate, no specific meaning to promote, and no particular method to pursue (Poole 1993).

Nevertheless, the fact that Kierkegaard's writings have inspired the development of a host of divergent theological and philosophical methods suggests that something of methodological significance may have been implicit in his texts. In spite of the elusive and idiosyncratic nature of his work, he may still count as a theologian and philosopher who thought in a disciplined way. Kierkegaard himself was not averse to this characterization of his work, for he once observed that his task 'was to situate Christianity in reflection' (KJN 6, 300/SKS 22, 298), with 'reflection' being one of his principle characterizations of the critical abstraction associated with philosophy and theology. Accordingly, Kierkegaard frequently borrowed such tools from philosophy as conceptual clarification, the ferreting out of hidden assumptions, and the exposure of fallacious arguments. However, he employed these standard conceptual strategies for a particular purpose. In his authorship Kierkegaard was trying to provoke a profound transformation in the reader, enabling the reader to become more self-reflective and responsible. In order to catalyze this self-reflection, he borrowed strategies from the histories of philosophy and theology in a rather promiscuous and ad hoc way. But there was a method to his seeming madness. An overarching vision of what theological and philosophical writing should be like governed his use of more specific traditional philosophical tropes and even his employment of fables, biblical stories, and jokes. This pervasive metastrategy could be considered his 'method.'

Kierkegaard's methodological context

No matter how much their methods might differ in other regards, most of Kierkegaard's contemporaries assumed that philosophy and theology involved the straightforward description of highly general and foundational features of the nature of the cosmos, human experience, divine revelation, or alleged transcendent realities. It was further assumed that these descriptions would take the form of propositions employing fairly univocal, stable concepts, aiming at clarity. Furthermore, these propositions were to be logically arranged, exhibiting an orderly progression from one topic to another, a progression often determined by almost geometric patterns of entailments. The desired result was a comprehensive explanatory system in which all the propositions would fit neatly together. Ideally, arguments should be advanced to defend the truth of the individual propositions and of the system as a whole. The arguments should be persuasive enough to compel cognitive assent, or at least present a plausible case.

This understanding of philosophy and theology was common to the plethora of schools that flourished in the early nineteenth century, in spite of their evident differences in method. Doctrinally inclined theologians regarded their propositions as referring to objective supernatural states of affairs, authorized by the Bible and the confessional tradition. The scriptural propositions only needed to be organized in a more logical order, so that their implications for the understanding of God, Christ, and humanity would be more transparent. Kierkegaard was well familiar with this heritage through the work of the 'Old Orthodox' party of Andreas Rudelbach in Denmark (KJN 5, 36–7/SKS 21, 39). The neo-Kantians saw their foundational propositions as referring to the necessary a priori structures of human cognitive, moral, and aesthetic experience. Although in Kierkegaard's day the legacy of Kant was going out of fashion, it lived on in a muted form in the textbooks Kierkegaard used by Karl Bretschneider (1828). The Hegelians regarded their assertions as objective descriptions of the dialectical movement of Spirit, manifested both in logic and in the history of consciousness. Kierkegaard was well aware of this tradition through the influence of Johan Ludvig Heiberg and Hans Lassen Martensen on Danish culture (Stewart 2007a; 2007b). Even thinkers influenced by Pietism, who might have been expected to write in a more emotive or expressive manner, treated their assertions as second-order descriptions of the contents of religious experience or of the dynamics of subjectivity. This was evident in the lectures of H. N. Clausen (KJN 3, 3–82/SKS 19, 7–85) and in the work of Friedrich Schleiermacher, whom Kierkegaard studied under the direction of Martensen. Even philosophers affected by Romanticism, who assumed that the ephemeral and eternal aspects of experience could be synthesized in an intuition of harmony and wholeness, regarded philosophy as the systematic exposition of the underlying unity of the cosmos (Pattison 2002). All of these traditions assumed that theology and philosophy should offer a unified, cohesive, clear, and rationally defensible system.

Kierkegaard's fluid, fractured, and shifting authorship was an implicit rejection of all this. His resistance to theology and philosophy as 'science' was rooted in his different understanding of the purpose of philosophical and theological thinking and writing. For Kierkegaard, theological and philosophical reflection should first and foremost enable an individual to assume responsibility for the shape of her own life and to feel the ultimate importance of doing this. Kierkegaard was consistent about this throughout his authorship, insisting that the genuine purpose of philosophical and theological writing is to encourage a deep and sincere engagement with the question of how one should live one's life. The closure that most philosophies promised militated against the risk and passion that existential engagement requires. Kierkegaard objected that the closed, didactic systems that traditional philosophy and theology have generated are only abstract ideals, which lack the power to transform individuals. Thinking by itself can only heal life's fissures in the imagination, not in reality.

The plurality of life-view options

A major part of this task of coaching self-reflection and self-responsibility required that an individual realize that there are multiple options for her life and appreciate what those options are. One of Kierkegaard's most persistent fears was that individuals would simply conform to the dominant cultural ethos, without questioning it and without considering alternatives. For this reason, he appreciated Socrates, whose use of irony (although it was largely negative) tried to liberate Athenians from automatic adherence to the mores of their *polis* (CI, 204–9/SKS 1, 249–53). More particularly, Kierkegaard was worried that the distinctiveness of the Christian way of life would be obscured through its conflation with vague notions of bourgeois propriety and dutiful citizenship, or even with the pursuit of a pleasurable existence. Consequently, the clarification of the differences among various ways of life became a primary goal of Kierkegaard's project.

In this regard Kierkegaard was helped by the concept of a 'life-view' elaborated by the poet and philosopher Poul Møller (1839–1843). Although Kierkegaard sometimes uses the phrase to designate any manner of living that encompasses a broad range of behaviour, he more typically restricts it to intentional and comprehensive ways of giving coherence and direction to an individual's existence, integrating its affective, volitional, and ideational dimensions. Life-views are efforts to give unity to an individual's life by actualizing an enduring ideal that can withstand fluctuations of mood, the vagaries of temperament, and the contingencies of fortune. A life-view enables an individual to see her existence as something more than a random congeries of reactions to external circumstances (TA, 14–6/SKS 8, 16–9). Each life-view is implicitly an informal network of concepts, attitudes, values, hopes, and fears that structures the way life is experienced.

Kierkegaard uses 'life-view' in a more expansive and protean way than his more familiar term 'stages of life.' The concept of 'stages,' particularly as articulated by the pseudonym Climacus, seems to refer to only four existential options (the aesthetic, the ethical, the generically religious, and the Christian) with some boundary territories (such as irony and humour). However, Kierkegaard's other voices instantiate or describe ways of life that cannot be reduced to one of the classic four stages or their boundaries. For example, Stoicism's resignation is described as a life-view, even though it is neither purely ethical nor fully religious (EPW, 76/SKS 1, 32). Similarly, in *Two Ages* Kierkegaard depicts a stance of hopeful and trusting resignation as a distinctive life-view (TA, 12–3/SKS 8, 15–6).

Because life-views are crucial for human flourishing but are also multiple, Kierkegaard's main concern became the clarification of the differences among them, with an eye to highlighting the distinctiveness of Christianity. Kierkegaard feared that the modern age had obscured the differences among life-views; consequently, his practice of philosophy and theology concentrated on communicating the essential differences among them. Kierkegaard sought to make the uniqueness of these ways of living come alive for a culture that had blurred their boundaries. This project of clarification was fraught with philosophical and theological significance, for each life-view suggested a unique way of construing the issues dear to philosophers and theologians, including the nature of time, the self, intersubjectivity, the virtues, etc.

According to Kierkegaard, the contours of a life-view, even ones that the individual has not embraced or experimented with, can be communicated because the imagination can present an ideal way of life to the self (Gouwens 1989). The imagination can foster a partial grasp not only of the concepts and values, but also of the passions and modes of action that constitute that way of life. The imagination can mediate between the ideal and the real by helping individuals to project themselves into alternative ways of living. Of course, in order for this to happen the individual's imaginative powers must be activated.

Communicating life-views

Kierkegaard's novel way of engaging in theological and philosophical reflection is most evident in his scattered remarks about communicating life-views and in his general practice of communicating matters of existential significance. Because the imagination had to be stimulated, attention to the literary dimensions of his work became crucial to the way he engaged in the philosophical and theological tasks. Kierkegaard's reliance upon images, parables, rhetorical disjunctions, and other literary devices sharply differentiated his method of communication from those of his contemporaries. He was convinced that matters related to the meaning and purpose of human life cannot be communicated without the use of the appropriate evocative rhetorical strategies. In *Concluding Unscientific Postscript* Kierkegaard's pseudonym Johannes Climacus encapsulated this theme in his celebrated dictum that in subjective communication the 'how' is more important than the 'what' (CUP 1, 202/SKS 7, 185). In his journals Kierkegaard put this even more forcefully, writing that 'the difference in life is not what is said, but how' (KJN 7, 90/SKS 23, 91). Therefore, attempting to paraphrase an existential communication into something didactic would be a gross distortion; in fact, it would evacuate the statement of meaning. Accordingly, Kierkegaard remarked, 'What I have to say must not be lectured. As a lecture it would become something completely different' (KJN 4, 322/SKS 20, 321). If promoting a deeper engagement with life was the goal of Kierkegaard's authorship, then an engaged literary style had to provide the indispensable form for his authorship. It was this conviction that made Kierkegaard's theory and practice of communication so distinctive.

Kierkegaard's conviction about the link between literary strategies and the communication of life-views was evident in his proposal that a literary work has enduring value only in so far as it communicates a coherent life-view. Otherwise, the emotional responses that a text elicits would be fleeting, disconnected, and fluctuating, producing no deeper engagement with life. In fact, ideally, the entire literary production of an author should exhibit a particular life-view. Kierkegaard praised the novelist Madame Gyllembourg for having been consistent throughout her career as an author (TA, 12–4/SKS 8, 15–6). Each new work exhibited continuity with her past productions, showing that she had been faithful to her life-view and to her project of communicating it to her readers. Most importantly, she consistently communicated the pathos that underlay her unique life-view. Kierkegaard found the works of Hans Christian Andersen to be sadly wanting in this regard, for they lacked a unifying life-view and simply expressed the vagaries of his personality (EPW, 74/SKS 1, 30). If the communication of the pathos of a life-view was essential for literary works, it was even more essential for philosophical and theological texts.

Kierkegaard's authorship signalled a revolution in the understanding of the significance of literary devices for the doing of theology and philosophy, for in the composition of his own texts he was experimenting with the ways in which texts could communicate life-views. Most strikingly, by wrestling with the issue of communicating a Christian life-view, Kierkegaard problematized the boundary between theological literature and the types of devotional and upbuilding literature that could be put to Christian purposes. Kierkegaard's unconventional way of writing about religious matters, so often noted by commentators, was inspired by his convictions concerning the unique nature of authentic religious communication. It is this sensitivity to the requisites of Christian communication that led him to forge a new method of reflection different from the legacies of Protestant scholasticism, the Enlightenment, Kantianism, Hegelianism, or Romanticism.

In 1847 Kierkegaard sketched the contours of his novel theory of communication in a set of outlines for a series of lectures concerning the unique challenges of communicating matters pertaining to ethical and religious ways of life (JP 1, 267–308/SKS 27, 389–434). He had already wrestled with these issues in his massive pseudonymous work, *Concluding Unscientific Postscript* (CUP 1, 72, 251/SKS 7, 72, 228), and had been ruminating about them for years in his journals. The issue of existential communication was so crucial for him that he was never fully content with his various lecture drafts and never delivered them or made them public.

Kierkegaard's fundamental conviction about communication was that the meaning of any existentially significant text, or even a single existentially significant statement, is not an intrinsic, stable property of the formal definitions of the written words themselves or of their seeming ability to refer to some objective state of affairs. The words only acquire meaning and reference when they are put to an appropriate use in such activities as exhorting, repenting, praising, and rejoicing, and that use is understood by the hearer/reader. More generally, the ability to grasp the discursive import of any assertion requires the ability to understand its typical performative function in a nexus of human concerns and purposes. For example, to say 'my sister has a dangerous infection' in most instances is to do much more than convey a bit of biological data. It is typically an expression of deep anxiety, presupposing a context of familial attachment and concern. To not appreciate this expressive use is to have a deficient grasp of the concept 'sister,' for the word is used to do much more than refer to a genetic relationship. To illustrate the importance of the performative use of a statement, Climacus offers the example of a madman who escaped from an asylum and tried to prove his sanity by proclaiming an indubitable objective truth. To accomplish this he placed a ball in the tail of his coat so that it would bump his rear when he moved, and with every impact he would announce: 'Boom, the earth is round' (CUP 1, 194–5/SKS 7, 178–9). The absence of any context of intelligible motivations and purposes made it unclear what the lunatic was trying to say, or even what he was referring to. Before questions of the truth and reference of a bit of language can even be raised, the question of its meaning must first be considered, and that can only be grasped by situating it in a performative context.

Most importantly, concepts pertaining to 'the meaning of life' cannot be communicated as if they were neutral bits of data to be transmitted from one mind to another. For example, Kierkegaard complained that the 'zeal of the orthodox' for the 'divine word' is really an attempt to substitute subscription to ecclesially endorsed objective propositions for the transformation of lives (CUP 1, 194–5/SKS 27, 163). But religious convictions and philosophical proposals cannot be treated as predigested morsels of truth. For example, part of the meaning of the assertion 'God is good' is the imperative to cultivate gratitude for whatever happens in life. To not know that writings about God's providence are trying to encourage a disposition of thankfulness is to not know the full meaning of 'providence' (EUD, 297–326/SKS 5, 291–316). In fact, to discourse about God as if God were some sort supernatural object divorced from contexts of passionate response is to rob the concept of any meaning. Summarizing this point about the importance of a context of pathos in his lecture notes, Kierkegaard excoriated the tendency of modernity to reduce religious communication to the transfer of objective knowledge (JP 1, 267–308/SKS 27, 389–434). The effort to discourse about life from a neutral standpoint ignores the ways that existentially significant bits of language are intended to have an impact on the reader/hearer's self-understanding. The root problem is that information by itself does not possess the power to show how the data should be used to affect the reader's life. Kierkegaard concludes that understanding any ethical or religious communication requires a grasp of the intelligible network of passions, purposes, and concerns in which it is embedded. By doing so, Kierkegaard was implicitly shifting the focus from the formal properties of ethical and religious assertions to their uses.

The dimension of pathos

In regard to the appropriate uses of bits of religious and ethical language, Kierkegaard paid particular attention to the desires, hopes, and fears (often referred to in terms of 'pathos,' 'subjectivity,' or 'inwardness') that should attend their employment, for it was this aspect of their use that had been most obscured in contemporary Denmark. The crucial dimension of pathos is a constitutive part of the meaning of any existentially significant statement or text; the passions are not merely affective addenda to meanings that could be grasped purely cognitively. For example, in the unpublished *Johannes Climacus, or De omnibus dubitandum est*, the pseudonymous author shows how talk about 'doubt' as an epistemological problem, which was common in much of modern philosophy, does not make sense apart from particular worries about the direction of a person's life (JC, 113–70/SKS 15, 13–59). Similarly, in *The Concept of Irony* the young Kierkegaard contended that talk about irony, which is the exposure of the contradiction between actuality and ideality, should not be allowed to evaporate into a universal and indiscriminate negation of actuality in general (as happened with late Romanticism's infinite absolute negativity), but should lead to an impassioned disquietude with specific forms of cultural smugness and mindless conformity (as was the case with Socratic irony) (CI, 239–331/SKS 1, 279–357). In much the same way, the statement that 'Jesus is the atonement for sin' cannot be fully understood apart from the capacity to imagine debilitating dissatisfaction with the state of one's moral and spiritual life, and to appreciate the joyful relief of forgiveness (WA, 44/SKS 11, 48). Even if a person is not presently feeling profound contrition, she must at least be capable of imagining what it would be like to experience the fear and trembling of moral despair as well as the joy of reconciliation. Without that pathos, talk about the 'atonement' makes no sense.

This conviction that understanding existentially significant texts requires the ability to grasp a specific type of pathos had enormous consequences for the doing of philosophy and theology. As we have seen, Kierkegaard feared that most academic philosophical and theological discourse erroneously assumed that religious meanings can be communicated merely through the precise definition of concepts and the exhibition of the logical relations that obtain among them. Against this commonly held opinion, Kierkegaard argued that religious and ethical concepts are not amenable to direct communication through simple declarative sentences and certainly not through the construction and defence of a formal system of such propositions. Rather, the communication of ethical and religious meaning involves the evocation of the passion-laden dimensions of the given concepts and a clarification of the ways those concepts could shape emotions and passions. An existential communication must somehow trigger fear and trembling over the direction of a person's life and encourage an intense and all-encompassing sense of responsibility for it. Consequently, Kierkegaard sought to elucidate basic life-encompassing beliefs and dispositions by encouraging the proper pathos through the manner of writing itself (Strawser 1997). For Kierkegaard, only the use of a wide range of evocative rhetorical strategies could vivify the passions that are ingredients of the meanings of ethical, religious, and specifically Christian concepts.

The importance of eliciting the appropriate pathos was therefore intrinsic to Kierkegaard's efforts to communicate life-views. Kierkegaard assumed that religious and ethical communication should enable individuals to imagine a life-view defined by a particular set of passions that the individual had not previously been aware of or had not adequately appreciated (TA, 12–23/SKS 8, 15–24). Theological and philosophical writing should capacitate the individual by expanding her imaginative grasp of the passional dimensions of life-view options and helping her to feel their attractive and repellent power. For example, for Kierkegaard, faith is most essentially a matter of heartfelt repentance, reckless commitment, extravagant love, and resilient expectation; consequently, any piece of theological writing must display those passions in its literary form. Kierkegaard became almost obsessed with finding the most apt literary form for his particular texts so that they would be most suited for eliciting the passions that are constitutive of particular life-views. His dizzying combinations of unexpected rhetorical devices, including shifts in voice, abrupt changes of mood, elusive parables, and anomalous metaphors, are not mere literary embellishments of themes that could have been communicated more expeditiously through a discursive essay. By developing a more rhetorical style of theological writing, Kierkegaard was appropriating the theme of the congruence of form and content, of idea and medium, which had been characteristic of nineteenth-century aesthetic theory from the Classicists, through the Romantics, to the Hegelians (Soderquist 2007). What was unusual was Kierkegaard's extension of this dictum to theological and philosophical works.

Given the fact that different life-views involve different passions, Kierkegaard concluded that their communication requires different corresponding moods, different styles, different genres, and even different authorial voices. Each concept essential to a life-view needed to be matched with the literary form uniquely appropriate to it. For example, 'God's love' requires a mood of joy and delight, while 'sin' requires a mood of candid and sober self-critique. Because of these differences in pathos, the communication of different existentially significant concepts must be distributed to very different types of texts, with different evocative potentialities.

According to Kierkegaard, the selection of literary genre is absolutely crucial for the communication of existentially significant concepts. For example, a work exposing the disjointed nature of the aesthetic life should be a chaotic anthology of essays, diaries, and aphorisms, exhibiting sudden oscillations and disorienting changes of topic. By contrast, an exploration of the ethical life, which should embody what it is to be ethical, is more aptly presented through an extended epistle, in which the author expresses and enacts ethical solicitude for the recipient. Similarly, because an analysis of Christian love should itself be an example of love for the neighbour, it should assume the form of a discourse solicitously and tenderly addressing the reader in order to help the reader grow in love. To do justice to the wide spectrum of types of pathos, Kierkegaard employed first-person novellas, sermons, literary reviews, disjointed aphorisms, and philosophical treatises.

Kierkegaard's penchant for inventing pseudonymous authors, many of whom exhibited elaborate and complex personal characteristics, was rooted in the fact that the authorial voice must instantiate the passions associated with the concept to be communicated. In matters of religious seriousness, there must be congruence between the implied author's life and the author's speech, for without the testimony of the author's life, the meaning of the author's words will not be clear. Kierkegaard contended that the meaning of a communication depends on the particularities of who said it, on what occasion, and in what situation (KJN 7, 90–1/SKS 23, 91). He remarked, 'In one person's mouth the same words can be so full of substance, so trustworthy, and in another person's mouth they can be like the vague whispering of leaves' (WL, 11–2/SKS 9, 19–20). Of course, the reader encounters the implied author through the author's self-presentation in the text; therefore Kierkegaard carefully constructed his authorial personae to exhibit the emotional dynamics of a particular way of life. For example, the pseudonymous author of Part Two of *Either/Or*, Judge William, not only writes about the resolution and steadfastness that a life of duty requires, but instantiates these qualities in his life as a devoted husband, civil servant, and dutiful citizen. On the other hand, Johannes Climacus, to whom *Philosophical Fragments* and *Concluding Unscientific Postscript* were ascribed, self-identifies as a 'humourist,' someone who has an empathic but amused sense of the incongruities that characterize human life (CUP 1, 502/SKS 7, 455). Nevertheless, he has not made a decision to commit himself to any alternative way of life, although he is clearly fascinated by religious options and confesses a desire to acquire an 'eternal happiness' (CUP 1, 17/SKS 7, 26). His persona manifests the ambivalence and instability of this existential option. Vigilius Haufniensis, who describes himself as an objective psychologist, exhibits a different kind of ambivalence. In spite of his protestations that he is a disinterested observer of human foibles, he manifests a very passionate fascination with the story of Adam and Eve, thereby instantiating the anxious attraction/repulsion that precedes the fall into sin (CA, 25–51/SKS 4, 332–56).

Kierkegaard's careful attention to the author's voice was not restricted to his pseudonymous works. Even when writing his signed texts, Kierkegaard would modulate his voice and style in order to suit the passional requirements of the particular theological concept at hand. For example, when writing about the daunting loftiness of the ideal of following Christ, Kierkegaard would adopt the voice of a repentant spiritual mediocrity. This is evident in his self-presentation in *For Self-Examination*, in which he confesses, 'I have become convinced that I am not an honest soul but a cunning fellow' (FSE, 24/SKS 13, 52). To instantiate the contrition he hoped to elicit from the bourgeois Danish church, Kierkegaard included himself among the vast array of those average people who fail to follow after the example of Christ's life in its full rigour, and addressed the reader as one penitent to another. But when writing about the attractive sublimity of the ideal of a life of love, as he does in *Works of Love*, he would adopt the voice of an enrapt enthusiast for love, lauding its spiritual satisfactions.

The pedagogy of freedom

Besides encouraging the communication of pathos, Kierkegaard's work is animated by another concern: the desire to enable the reader to read existentially relevant texts in the right way. Sometimes Kierkegaard does this through direct exhortation. For example, in *For Self-Examination* Kierkegaard highlighted the role of the reader in gleaning personal edification from the Bible (FSE, 15–51/SKS 13, 43–76). His observations about the reading of Scripture can be more broadly construed as instructions concerning how to read all existentially relevant texts, including his own. Throughout the book Kierkegaard draws a sharp distinction between reading from a perspective of academic neutrality and reading from a stance of earnest concern for the quality of one's own life. The Bible (and, by extension any significant ethical or religious text) should be engaged with the intensity and urgency with which one would read a letter from one's beloved. To read from a perspective of interpretive distance is to fail to comprehend it. Rather than being treated as an artefact to be deciphered, the Bible should function as a mirror in which we see ourselves (FSE, 25–35/SKS 13, 53–62). The reader should engage the text with caution, saying, 'It is about me that it is speaking' (FSE, 35–44/SKS 13, 62–70). The cultivation of this earnest self-referentiality is ultimately the reader's own responsibility.

Kierkegaard wanted to write in such a way that the act of reading in itself would be a pedagogy in assuming responsibility for one's own life. To read his texts, or any potentially life-shaping text, facilely or complacently would militate against the growth of this earnestness. To prevent a superficial reading, Kierkegaard teases the reader with multiple interpretive possibilities, interrupts the development of his arguments, introduces tangents, points the reader in multiple directions, shatters standard genre expectations, and generally makes hermeneutic closure impossible. Reading his texts is often exhausting work, for the reader is frequently left wondering if a passage is making a serious point or is simply jesting. The author may have been playing with a poetic fancy or may have been wrestling with a profundity, or both, or neither. The evident tension between earnestness and playfulness in many of Kierkegaard's texts forces the reader to decide whether to be amused, offended, or inspired.

Kierkegaard did not design his texts to be so enigmatic because the conceptual content was esoteric or because he took a sadistic delight in confounding his readers. Rather, ambiguity and multivocity were crucial to his project. He not only wanted the reader to become familiar with the differences among life-views and their various forms of pathos, but he also wanted the reader to be confronted with the task of choosing from among multiple interpretive possibilities. This task, like the task of living earnestly, requires passion, and passion requires risk. Kierkegaard's pseudonym Climacus writes, 'For without risk, no faith; the more risk, the more faith; the more objective reliability, the less inwardness (since inwardness is subjectivity); the less objective reliability, the deeper is the possible inwardness' (CUP 1, 209/SKS 7, 192). Kierkegaard sought to write in such a way that the reader would have to accept responsibility for her own reading and risk an interpretation of his pages. Forcing the reader to self-consciously make interpretive decisions was part of his broader strategy of provoking the reader to assume responsibility for the shape of the reader's own life. For Kierkegaard, that assumption of responsibility was essential for the development of any sort of earnest pathos. (For him, this is particularly true of commitment to the Christian life, which requires an extreme degree of risk and accountability.) The communication itself must be a pedagogy in freedom; the author cannot naively assume that the reader is already free and responsible. The very act of choosing a construal of the text is an exercise in self-responsibility; the act of reading becomes a school for passionate inwardness.

Obviously, this way of doing theology and philosophy rules out the effort to provide apodictic proofs for various convictions. Any quest for certainty is really a covert epistemological justification for the abdication of personal responsibility. An indubitable revelation, or an absolutely compelling argument, would sabotage the possibility of engaging life with passion. The longing for metaphysical reassurance is always an evasion of the daunting task of accepting the risk that a passionate engagement with life requires. Consequently, Kierkegaard rejected all efforts to show that the doctrines of Christianity can be rationally demonstrated, or that the veracity of Christian revelation is historically probable, or even that Christianity is culturally relevant.

Given his antipathy to objective certainty, Kierkegaard not only condemned arguments for the existence of God and other metaphysical propositions, but also refused to attempt to prove that Christianity can satisfy the deepest longings of the human heart. Some expositors have construed his 'theory of the stages' as a kind of apologia for Christianity, suggesting that it functions as a foundational anthropology showing that human subjectivity is structured in such a way that only Christian faith can truly satisfy it (Pojman 1984). According to this view, reflection on the dynamics of selfhood should lead an individual to realize that the tensions in the aesthetic, ethical, and generically religious stages can only be resolved by embracing Christian faith. But this sort of justification of Christianity would subvert Kierkegaard's primary goal of intensifying passion. Certainly, he does urge the individual to nurture certain passions and dispositions (particularly Christian ones) by displaying their possible attractiveness, but he does not develop an argument to show that only these passions and dispositions can lead to a fulfilling life. In fact, he goes out of his way to make sure that the individual is also aware of how offensive the pathos of Christianity can be (PC, 69–144/SKS 12, 81–147). All that he sought to do was to help the individual become aware of the crucial differences among various life-views, present the Christian life-view in such a way that the attractiveness (and the offensiveness) of its pathos could be imaginatively felt, and hope that the reader might choose that way of life. But he could not guarantee that the individual would be transformed through the act of reading.

Conclusion

Kierkegaard's way of engaging theological and philosophical issues had several startling features. First, the purpose of philosophy and theology is not to develop an indubitable 'system' or to prove that a particular view of life is superior to others, but rather to clarify the differences among various existential options, particularly the forms of pathos ingredient to them. Second, in order to vivify the passions of a life-view, Kierkegaard gave new prominence to the rhetorical dimensions of theological and philosophical texts. The reader must always be attentive to the particularities of voice, context, and purpose of any of Kierkegaard's volumes in order to be able to imagine what it would be like to live in a unique way, pursuing distinctive goals, and cultivating distinctive passions. Because some forms of pathos, and particularly Christian pathos, are so difficult to imagine, communication about matters of existential importance must employ dramatic literary strategies to clarify them. Kierkegaard sought to show through the form of his writing what a life-view involves, rather than simply saying it. His rhetorical performance is not an optional embellishment; it contributes to the meaning of his texts. Third, Kierkegaard was convinced that writing about matters of existential importance had to preserve the precious elements of risk and choice, for without them passion would be impossible.

Kierkegaard's philosophical and theological practice has had significant implications for these disciplines. Rather than focusing on the intrinsic propositional qualities of theological and philosophical texts, Kierkegaard shifted attention to their uses in the pursuit of religious and moral purposes. That crucial issue of 'use' applies to both the author and the reader, both to the production of a text and to its reception. In order for a text to have existential meaning, the author must be attempting to do something to the reader, such as comfort her, accuse her, destabilize her, challenge her, or inspire her. Conversely, the reader must be willing to use the texts for the purposes of self-examination and edification, or at least be willing to imagine what it would be like to do so. Kierkegaard's new attention to engaged, passionate 'use' was a harbinger of the intense interest in the functions of philosophical and theological works that would finally come to fruition in the twentieth-century.

Related topics

'Methodology and the Kierkegaardian mind,' Jamie Turnbull; 'Johannes Climacus and the dialectical method: from dialectics back to existence,' Claudine Davidshofer.

References

Bretschneider, K. G. (1828) *Handbuch der Dogmatik der evangelisch-lutherischen Kirche*, vols. 1–2, 3rd ed., Leipzig: Johann Ambrosius Barth.
Gouwens, D. (1989) *Kierkegaard's dialectic of imagination*, New York: Peter Lang Publishing.
Møller, P. (1839–1843) *Efterladte Skrifter*, vols. 1–3, Copenhagen: C. A. Reitzel.
Pattison, G. (2002) *Kierkegaard, religion and the nineteenth century crisis of culture*, Cambridge: Cambridge University Press.
Pojman, L. (1984) *The logic of subjectivity: Kierkegaard's philosophy of religion*, Tuscaloosa, AL: University of Alabama Press.
Poole, R. (1993) *Kierkegaard: The indirect communication*, Charlottesville, VA: University Press of Virginia.
Soderquist, K. B. (2007) *The isolated self*, Copenhagen: C. A. Reitzel.
Stewart, J. (2007a) *A history of Hegelianism in golden age Denmark*, tome 1 (*The Heiberg Period: 1824–1836*), Copenhagen: C. A. Reitzel.
Stewart, J. (2007b) *A history of Hegelianism in golden age Denmark*, tome 2 (*The Martensen Period: 1837–1842*), Copenhagen: C. A. Reitzel.
Strawser, M. (1997) *Both/and: Reading Kierkegaard from irony to edification*, New York: Fordham University Press.

Further reading

Caputo, J. D. (2008) *How to read Kierkegaard*, New York: W. W. Norton.
   Caputo reads Kierkegaard in the light of post-structuralist thought in such a way that his religious and ethical concerns are not minimized.

Hanson, J. (ed) (2010) *Kierkegaard as phenomenologist: An experiment*, Evanston, IL: Northwestern University Press.
   This anthology of articles proposes that Kierkegaard not only inspired the philosophical method known as phenomenology, but actually exhibited its main characteristics in his own texts.

Rae, M. (2010) *Kierkegaard and theology*, London: T. & T. Clark.
   Rae presents Kierkegaard as a Christian thinker who deals with standard doctrinal topics, but avoids casting him as a traditional systematic theologian.

Stewart, J. (2015) *Søren Kierkegaard: Subjectivity, irony, and the crisis of modernity*, Oxford: Oxford University Press.
   Stewart situates Kierkegaard in his historical context of Denmark and the cultural movements of Romanticism and Hegelianism, showing how these issues affected his way of doing philosophy.

2

JOHANNES CLIMACUS AND THE DIALECTICAL METHOD: FROM DIALECTICS BACK TO EXISTENCE

Claudine Davidshofer

Introduction

In Kierkegaard's day, there was much chatter in Danish intellectual society about 'dialectics' and the 'dialectical method.' Hegel's dialectical philosophy had taken hold in academic circles, and Kierkegaard's contemporaries were busily applying Hegelian dialectical thinking to everything in sight – from logic, to existence, to religion.[1] Kierkegaard and his pseudonyms often worry that, because modern speculative thought (i.e., Hegelian dialectical thinking) requires the individual to abstract himself from concrete existence in order to assume an abstract viewpoint of pure thought, it distracts the individual from his own everyday existence. The modern speculative thinker is so absorbed in dialectical thought that he forgets that his existence continues on each day, whether or not he is invested in living it.

Even though Kierkegaard harshly criticizes dialectical thinking for distracting the individual from existence, Kierkegaard and his pseudonyms often use the dialectical method to analyze human existence. In *The Point of View for My Work as an Author*, Kierkegaard claims that the dialectical method is particularly effective for leading the individual 'away from speculative thought, away from the system' and back to everyday existence (PV, 78/SKS 16, 58). This is somewhat curious, for it suggests that Kierkegaard uses dialectics to critique dialectics, and uses dialectical thinking to lead the individual away from dialectical thinking.

While many of Kierkegaard's pseudonyms use aspects of the dialectical method to analyze human existence, I will focus here specifically on how Johannes Climacus uses the dialectical method in *Philosophical Fragments*.[2] In *Fragments*, Climacus constructs an impressive dialectical thought experiment to analyze human existence, as it is defined by paganism and Christianity, respectively. In this chapter, I will explore the following questions: Why does Climacus use the dialectical method to analyze human existence?, and How does the dialectical method lead the individual back to everyday existence?

General pattern of the dialectical method

Before we consider how Johannes Climacus uses the dialectical method in *Philosophical Fragments*, we need to clarify what is meant by 'dialectics' and 'dialectical method.' Throughout the history of philosophy, many philosophers use the dialectical method – most notably, Socrates,

Plato, Aristotle, Kant, and Hegel. While each philosopher may use the dialectical method slightly differently, there is still a main purpose and main argument pattern that these philosophers tend to follow. Dialectics is one specific method that we use to think our way to the truth. In particular, we use the dialectical method in order to discover definitions, that is, to discover the stable essences, concepts, and principles that underlie all change and variability in reality. We use dialectics to answer the question 'What is X?' – where 'X' stands for any conceptual essence abstracted from its instantiation in concrete particularity. For example: What is Being? What is Nothing? What is The Good? What is Knowledge? The dialectical method helps us to understand what these definitions really mean in and of themselves.

In general, the dialectical method tends to follow the same pattern, which we can breakdown into three major steps. Step One: We posit a definition as our initial starting point. We posit that 'X is Y.' We are not asserting that this initial definition is necessarily true, but rather, we are merely positing that this definition is hypothetically true. We are saying: 'Let us hypothetically assume that X is Y.' Step Two: We test this hypothetical definition. We carry out a thought experiment to rationally scrutinize this definition to determine what it really means and what conclusions would follow from it if it were indeed true. We think through the definition according to an 'If – Then,' or conditional, thought structure. We ask, '*If* X is Y, *then* what does this assertion really mean and what conclusions follow from it?'

Step Three: We assess the results of our thought experiment. We are primarily checking for the absence or presence of contradiction within our definition, checking to see if it is internally self-consistent or self-contradictory. If the definition proves to be self-consistent, then we can conclude that it is a pretty good definition and is worth hanging onto. If, however, the definition proves to be self-contradictory, then we should conclude that it is not a good definition and should be discarded. If the definition 'X is Y' leads us to the opposite definition, that 'X is ~Y,' then the definition is self-contradictory, because it means both that 'X is Y' and also that 'X is ~Y.' Accepting this definition would mean accepting that 'X is Y' and also that 'X is ~Y,' that the definition is both itself and the opposite of itself. Since we generally assume that something cannot be self-contradictory, we should conclude that our initial definition is somehow erroneous and should be discarded. But we can then revise our definition based on what we have learned from the dialectical process and repeat the dialectical process with this revised definition as our new hypothetical starting point. If necessary, we can repeat the process again and again, using ever-better definitions each time, until we eventually discover a definition that is self-consistent.[3]

I will now briefly explain how Socrates and Hegel each execute the main steps of the dialectical pattern.[4] As we will see, Johannes Climacus situates his own dialectical method alongside Socratic dialectics and Hegelian dialectics.[5] For Socrates, the dialectical method is performed through dialogue, through questions and answers between Socrates and his interlocutor(s). Step One: Socrates invites his interlocutor to posit the initial hypothetical definition. Step Two: To test the definition, Socrates asks questions to help his interlocutor draw out the meaning and implications of his definition. Step Three: If the definition withstands rational scrutiny, then Socrates is willing to accept the definition, though he says that he is always willing to re-test and even discard the seemingly good definition later on. If, however, as is most often the case, the definition is self-contradictory, then Socrates concludes that the definition is erroneous and must be discarded. Socrates is usually eager to repeat the dialectical method with a revised definition, but his interlocutor often becomes impatient and gives up before a good definition is found. While Socratic dialectics is very effective at exposing poor definitions, rarely, if ever, does it allow Socrates to discover a good definition.

For Hegel, the dialectical method is performed not in dialogue between interlocutors, but within speculative thought itself. Step One: Thought posits a definition. Step Two: Thought questions and answers itself and draws out the meaning and implications of its definition. Step Three: According to Hegel, thought always discovers that its initial definition is self-contradictory – that it is both itself and its opposite. But thought also always generates a new definition from out of this self-contradictory definition. Thought necessarily mediates the two contradictory moments into a new definition that both cancels and preserves the contradictory moments within itself. Thought can repeat the dialectical process again and again – each time discovering the definition is self-contradictory and moving beyond it to a new definition – forming ever-more sophisticated and comprehensive definitions each time. To give a brief example, in the opening of Hegel's *Science of Logic* (Hegel 1969: 82–3; cf. Hegel 1975: §84–8), when thought tests the definition of Being, it quickly discovers that this definition really means the opposite of Being – that is, the definition of Being is really the definition of Nothing. Realizing that the definition is self-contradictory, thought then mediates the two contradictory moments, Being and Nothing, into a new definition – that is, Becoming. Being and Nothing are preserved within the definition of Becoming, because Becoming means the movement from Being to Nothing or from Nothing to Being. But the active contradiction between Being and Nothing is also cancelled, because it is subsumed into the higher definition of Becoming. Thought can then repeat the dialectical process again by testing the definition of Becoming.

Hegel claims that Socrates fails to find good definitions, because when he hits a contradiction, he repeats the dialectical process with an arbitrarily chosen new definition. Had Socrates realized that speculative thought generates the new definition from out of the self-contradictory definition itself, then he could have moved from a merely negative dialectics (exposing poor definitions) to a positive dialectics (finding good definitions) (Hegel 1969: 26–9, 53–9; 1975: §79–82; 1977: §32–7, §58–9).

The consensus among scholars is that Kierkegaard's dialectics is opposed to, and even a direct response to, Hegel's dialectics. Kierkegaard does agree with Hegel that definitions are 'dialectical' – that is, they are internally self-contradictory and therefore are a tense relation between self and opposite. But unlike Hegel, Kierkegaard does not believe that thought can mediate the two opposing moments into a new definition that resolves this tension. For Kierkegaard, definitions simply are self-contradictory, a tense relationship between self and opposite (Burns 2015: 61–6; Diem 1959: 46–50; Dunning 1981: 383–6; Dunning 1985: 6–12; Piper 2004; Walsh 2005: 5–7). While Hegel advances a dialectic of mediation, Kierkegaard advances a strict 'dialectic of paradox' (Dunning 1985: 8) – that is, an 'inverse dialectic' (Walsh 2005: 7), a 'non-dialectical dialectic' (Piper 2004: 498), or a 'fractured dialectic' (Burns 2015: 61–6).

Furthermore, scholars emphasize that Kierkegaard constantly defines human existence according to a dialectic of paradox. Dunning (1981; 1985) argues that the paradoxes of inner/outer and self/others define aesthetic, ethical, and religious existence. These are paradoxes, Dunning explains, because the opposites constantly exist together as unresolved, self-contradictory unities within the individual. The individual can never resolve this tension, because human existence simply *is* this tension between opposites. The individual must continually live as this unresolved push-and-pull between contraries. Piper (2004) and Taylor (2000) argue that the paradox of god/human defines religious existence. Walsh (2005) defines Christian existence according to four main paradoxes: consciousness of sin/faith and forgiveness, possibility of offense/faith, dying to the world/new life in the spirit, and suffering/joy. I certainly agree with this consensus that Kierkegaard advances a dialectic of paradox over a dialectic of mediation and that he defines human existence as paradox. But I will focus here more specifically on how Kierkegaard (as Johannes Climacus) uses the *dialectical method*, as described above, to analyze human existence and lead the individual back to existence, and not simply on how Kierkegaard defines the human according to dialectical opposites.

Dialectics applied to paganism

In *Philosophical Fragments*, Johannes Climacus tries to answer the following question: How can the human learn the eternal truth? How can the human – this temporal, finite creature – relate to the eternal truth in his everyday existence? Climacus believes that there are two ways to answer this question: according to paganism and according to Christianity. For paganism, the human is able to learn the eternal truth because he already possesses the eternal truth and the ability to learn the eternal truth. For Christianity, the human is able to learn the eternal truth, even though he does not already possess the eternal truth or the ability to learn the eternal truth (PF, 9–15/SKS 4, 218–25). In *Fragments*, Climacus uses the dialectical method to test the definition of paganism and the definition of Christianity in order to discover what each really means. He uses the dialectical method to answer the following questions: What is paganism? How does the human relate to the truth in paganism? What is Christianity? How does the human relate to the truth in Christianity?

Since Socrates devoted his entire life to trying to 'know himself' (PF, 37/SKS 4, 242) – to understanding human existence – Climacus chooses Socrates as his exemplary representative for all versions of paganism in general. But what Climacus says about Socratic paganism can also be applied to any other version of paganism – that is, to any other 'pagan' philosopher (such as Plato, Spinoza, Hegel, or the 'modern speculative thinker' of Danish society) who assumes that the human is able to learn the truth by his own effort alone.

The dialectical structure is evident throughout *Philosophical Fragments*. Climacus describes his work as a 'thought-project' (PF, 9/SKS 4, 218), a 'metaphysical caprice' (PF, 37/SKS 4, 242), and a 'whimsical idea' (PF, 109/SKS 4, 305). He says it is all a 'hypothesis' (PF, 109/SKS 4, 305), and he constructs the work according to a conditional thought structure. He continually uses the 'If – Then' language of the dialectical method and continually reminds us that he is not asserting that either paganism or Christianity is definitely true, but is merely hypothetically positing each as true to discover what each really means. Climacus is asking, If Socratic paganism were true, then what does this really mean and what follows from it? If Christianity were true, then what does this mean and what follows from it? Does one definition withstand rational scrutiny better than the other definition?

We will follow Climacus as he uses the dialectical method to test each definition. I will have to simplify and condense much of his complex, sprawling argument, and I admit that I am presenting the argument in a perhaps more straightforward and step-by-step manner than Climacus himself does. But I think that this re-structured approach will allow us to draw out most clearly the argument's 'dialectical rhythm' and 'dialectical clarity,' of which Climacus himself seems so proud (CUP 1, 10/SKS 7, 20).

Climacus first uses the dialectical method to rationally scrutinize the definition of Socratic paganism (see Dunning 1985: 166–81; Howland 2006: 28–56). Step One of the dialectical method: Climacus posits Socratic paganism as hypothetically true – that is, paganism asserts that the human is able to learn the eternal truth because the human already possesses the eternal truth (PF, 9–13/SKS 4, 218–21). Step Two of the dialectical method: Climacus tests this hypothetical definition. In order to test this definition, Climacus draws out a few important implications of this definition.

First Implication: If the human already possesses the eternal truth, then how does the human learn the eternal truth? Climacus confronts Meno's Paradox (cf. Plato 1997: 80c–82). It seems impossible for the human to learn the truth. If the human already has the truth, then he cannot learn the truth, because he already has it and does not need to learn it. If the human does not already have the truth, then he cannot learn the truth, because he would not know how to search for it or what to search for. According to Socrates, Climacus explains, the human has the eternal truth, but he has it in the mode of temporarily not-having it, of having temporarily forgotten it. The human simply needs a teacher to be the 'occasion' (PF, 11/SKS 4, 220) that reminds him that he has the truth and the ability to find the truth, and then he can re-acquire the truth by his own effort alone (PF, 9–13/SKS 4, 218–22). So, the human is able to learn the truth, because he is 'recollecting' (PF, 9/SKS 4, 218) the truth that he already has but has temporarily lost.

Second Implication: If the human recollects the truth, then how does he initially acquire the truth? According to Socrates, Climacus says, the human soul is immortal, and the god himself directly places the truth into the human soul 'from eternity' (PF, 13/SKS 4, 221). The god gives the human everything that he needs to relate to eternal truth while he lives in temporal existence. (PF, 9–13/SKS 4, 218–22). So, the god himself gives the human the truth from eternity.

Third Implication: If the god gives the human the truth, then how does the human lose the truth? Socrates did not directly address this question, so Climacus tries to puzzle it out on his own. Climacus maintains that it would not make sense for the god to give the human the truth from eternity, but then to take the truth away from him while he is in temporal existence. Since it 'cannot have been due to an act of god,' then it must have been 'due to himself' (PF, 15/SKS 4, 223). The human must somehow lose the truth through his own fault, through his own error. So, the human himself is responsible for losing the truth given to him by the god.

Fourth Implication: If the human loses the truth by his own fault, then how can he recollect the truth by his own effort? Climacus confronts Meno's Paradox all over again. The human no longer has the truth (he lost it somehow), and so it seems impossible that the human can recollect the truth by himself, because he does not know how to search for the truth or what to search for. The teacher cannot simply remind him that he has the truth and the ability to recollect the truth, because the human precisely does not have the truth or the ability to search for the truth anymore. To regain the truth, Climacus wonders, wouldn't the god have to directly give the human the truth once more, as he had originally done 'from eternity'? Since the human loses the truth by his own error, it seems impossible that he could regain the truth by his own effort (PF, 14–5/SKS 4, 222–4). So, the human is unable to learn the eternal truth, because he does not possess the eternal truth or the ability to learn the eternal truth on his own.

Step Three of the dialectical method: Climacus assesses the results of his dialectical thought-project. In thinking through the definition of Socratic paganism, Climacus has hit a contradiction, or, as he says, 'a paradox' (PF, 37/SKS 4, 242). He originally posited that Socratic paganism asserts that the human can learn the eternal truth because he already possesses the eternal truth. But this definition has led to the opposite definition, namely, that paganism claims that the human cannot learn the eternal truth because he does not possess the eternal truth. The dialectical method reveals that paganism is internally self-contradictory; it is paradoxical. Paganism means that the human is truth and is able to learn the truth, and also that the human is untruth and is unable to learn the truth. Accepting the definition of paganism would mean accepting a paradoxical view of the human: the human has the truth and the human has lost the truth; the human is able to learn the truth and the human is unable to learn the truth.

Climacus claims that Socrates himself was likely aware of this 'Socratic Paradox' at the centre of his definition of the human. As Climacus notes, Socrates admits in the *Phaedrus* that he is 'still not quite clear about himself, whether he (a connoisseur of human nature) was a more curious monster than Typhon or a friendlier and simpler being, by nature sharing something divine,' and this 'seems to be a paradox' that Socrates reaches (PF, 37/SKS 4, 242; cf. Plato 1997: 230a). While Socrates generally assumes that the human 'shares something divine,' he also wonders whether the human is like Typhon: a complex, prideful beast-god with 100 hissing, howling snake heads, who battles Zeus for control of the cosmos, only to be thrown into Tartarus and buried under a mountain. Perhaps, like Typhon, the human is given the ability to relate to the divine by the god himself, but, like Typhon, his own prideful error causes him to squander this privilege and lose his ability to relate to the divine. According to Climacus, Socrates is on the verge of discovering 'consciousness of sin' (PF, 51/SKS 2, 255), but he can only describe it indirectly through the Typhon metaphor, because the human intellect cannot discover the concept of sin by itself. Sin has to be directly revealed to the human by God himself.[6]

Climacus's dialectical method shows us that the definition of paganism is self-contradictory. Why is this important? What has Climacus really accomplished? Climacus's dialectical thought-project yields two major results: a negative and a positive result. First, the negative: Climacus's dialectical method is a 'disintegrating' dialectic (Diem 1959: 46). It disintegrates the definition of Socratic paganism by showing that it is paradoxical for thought. Since Socratic paganism is the stand-in for all versions of paganism (Plato, Spinoza, Hegel, modern speculative thought), Climacus disintegrates the definition of paganism in general, by showing that all versions of paganism will end in some version of the Socratic Paradox – the human can and cannot learn the truth. Climacus uses the dialectical method to force the pagan philosopher to confront the paradox at the very centre of his definition of the human. Climacus shakes paganism's certainty in itself.

Second, the positive result: By disintegrating the rational certainty of paganism, Climacus leads the pagan philosopher up to the point where he hopefully chooses to become a subjective thinker – to appropriate the truth into his daily life. According to Climacus, Socrates is indeed a subjective thinker. When thought dissolves his definition of the human, Socrates is forced out of abstract thought and is thrown back upon his own everyday existence, back upon himself as this single existing individual. Socrates must ask himself what role searching for the eternal truth plays in his everyday existence and if it is important enough to his daily life that he is willing to cling to this paradoxical definition and continue searching for the eternal truth, even though thought shows him his endeavour is uncertain. Socrates chooses to 'risk the belief' (Plato 1997: 114d; cf. CUP 1, 201–2/SKS 7, 184–5),[7] and he 'stakes his whole life' (CUP 1, 201/SKS 7, 185) on something he cannot know.

According to Climacus, this '"fragment" of uncertainty helped Socrates' (CUP 1, 202/SKS 7, 185) to become a subjective thinker. Socrates realizes that he thinks not just to think, but he thinks in order to exist, because searching for the truth helps him to live well in daily life. Socrates is passionately invested in the search for the truth; he integrates and expresses the truth in his everyday existence (CUP 1, 201–5/SKS 7, 184–7). As Howland (2006: 198) writes, Socrates 'shuttles ceaselessly between being and becoming, truth and life – an up-and-down process . . . which always begins with, and returns to, questions that arise within the sphere of daily existence.' Socrates wishes to know the divine, eternal truth for the sake of his concrete, temporal existence.[8]

At the end of the day, Climacus's dialectical thought-project is really aimed at the paganism of modern speculative thought. Socrates thinks in order to exist, but the modern speculative philosopher thinks in order to think, and his existence is a mostly forgotten afterthought (CUP 1, 368, 375–84/SKS 7, 335, 341–50). He is so absorbed in abstract thought – busily trying to finish 'the system' – that his thinking is detached from his existing (CUP 1, 106–25/SKS 7, 103–20). Because speculative thinking is so commonplace in Danish intellectual society, Climacus believes that he cannot directly communicate to the speculative thinker that he has forgotten how to exist in the truth. So, he uses the dialectical method to indirectly communicate with the speculative thinker. By using the same dialectical style that speculative thought uses, and by focusing on Socrates rather than targeting speculative thought directly, Climacus keeps the speculative thinker reading up until the end, gradually leading him up to the point where he realizes that the Socratic Paradox is also his paradox and that the entire thought-project was likely aimed at him.

By disintegrating the rational certainty of paganism, Climacus forces the speculative thinker out of abstract thought and forces him to confront the role that thinking plays in his everyday existence. When faced with the paradox of paganism, would the speculative thinker still decide that speculative thinking is important enough to his daily life that he is willing to continue speculating, even though he knows that he may not reach the truth? Would he still spend so much time absorbed in abstract thought, trying to finish the grand system? Would he perhaps speculate only on questions that are important to his everyday existence? Climacus's dialectical method encourages the 'interior assimilation of thought in the whole process of existence' (Diem 1959: 193). Climacus leads the speculative thinker up to the point where he hopefully chooses to become a subjective thinker, like Socrates.

Dialectics applied to Christianity

Having found this paradox, this 'decisive heterogeneity' (CUP 1, 368/SKS 7, 335), at the centre of paganism, Climacus now uses the dialectical method to test the Christian definition of human existence. Step One of the dialectical method: Climacus posits the Christian definition of human existence as hypothetically true. According to Christianity, the human is able to learn the eternal truth, even though he does not possess the eternal truth or the ability to learn the eternal truth by his own effort alone. Put another way, the human 'is untruth'; the human 'is sin.' According to Christianity, the human 'himself has forfeited and is forfeiting' the truth and the condition 'through [his] own fault' (PF, 15/SKS 4, 224), and so he cannot learn the truth on his own, because he does not know how to search for the truth or what to search for. Step Two: Climacus tests the definition of Christianity.

First Implication: If the human cannot learn the truth by himself, then how is he able to learn the truth? Climacus explains that the god himself must directly intervene and radically transform the human by giving him both the truth and the condition to understand the truth. The human must undergo a decisive change, a change of *'rebirth'* (PF, 19/SKS 4, 227), wherein he becomes 'a *new* person' (PF, 18/SKS 4, 227). He goes from being untruth – not having the truth or the condition – to being truth – having both the truth and the condition. The human must undergo a *'conversion'* (PF, 18/SKS 4, 227) and *'repentance'* (PF, 19/SKS 4, 227), wherein he rejects his old self (sin, self-imposed untruth) and accepts his new self (truth, given to him by the god) (PF, 15–21/SKS 4, 223–9). So, the god himself must deliver the human from self-imposed untruth and restore him to truth.

Second Implication: If the god intervenes, then does the god bring the human the truth and the condition by an ascent? Perhaps, Climacus ventures, the god directly reveals himself and reveals the eternal truth as he himself understands it, thereby lifting the human out of untruth and exalting the human to the level of eternal truth, to the level of the god himself. But, Climacus explains, in this union 'the love does not become happy' (PF, 29/SKS 4, 236). It forgets that the human is indeed a human and not the god, and what the god wants most of all, Climacus explains, is for the human to relate to him in his uniquely human way, by using his human intellect and his capacity to freely decide to unite with him (PF, 29–30/SKS 4, 235–7). So, the god does not bring the human the truth and the condition by an ascent.

Third Implication: If the god does not bring the human the truth and the condition by an ascent, then does it happen by a descent? It must be, Climacus concludes, that the god descends to the level of the human. The god must appear not as the god, but as a human, and he must reveal the truth not as he himself understands it, but as the human can understand it. In order to be understood by all humans, the god must appear as the 'lowliest of persons' (PF, 31/SKS 4, 238), in the 'form of a *servant*' (PF, 31/SKS 4, 238). And in order to fully take on the form of the human, the god must suffer the worst of human sufferings, even being 'forsaken in death' (PF, 32/SKS 4, 239). So, an absolute paradox must occur: the god must become human, the eternal must enter time; the omnipotent god must walk upon the earth as a human servant (PF, 31–5/SKS 4, 238–40).

Fourth Implication: If this absolute paradox must occur, then what is the truth and the condition that the god-man brings to the human? The truth is the absolute paradox itself, which is the god-man himself. The condition is faith, which is a new ability or 'new organ' (PF, 111/SKS 4, 306) that allows the human to receive the absolute paradox as the truth. According to Climacus, 'faith is not a knowledge' (PF, 62/SKS 4, 263) of the paradox. Rather, faith allows the human to understand that the paradox is indeed a paradox – that it unites the most contradictory contradictories – and yet to still freely choose to 'constantly cling firmly' (PF, 62/SKS 4, 264) to the absolute paradox of the god-man as the absolute truth (PF, 59–66/SKS 4, 261–4).[9]

Step Three of the dialectical method: Climacus assesses the results of his dialectical thought-project. When subjected to dialectical scrutiny, the Christian definition of human existence fares even worse than the pagan definition of human existence. Climacus ends up with a double paradox; the Christian definition is even more absurd and even more paradoxical to thought. Climacus begins where Socrates ends, by defining the human as the Socratic Paradox (now as Christian sin-consciousness): the human is unable to learn the truth because he lost the truth and the condition by his own fault. To solve this paradox, Climacus ends with the absolute, Christian paradox: the god must become human to deliver the human from his self-imposed untruth (sin) and restore him to truth.

So, what has Climacus's dialectical method accomplished? As was the case with paganism, Climacus achieves both a negative and a positive result. First the negative: Here again, Climacus's dialectical method is a 'disintegrating' dialectic (Diem 1959: 46). Climacus completely disintegrates the definition of Christianity by showing it to be doubly paradoxical – beginning in the Socratic Paradox (sin) and ending in the absolute Christian paradox (the god-man) – and therefore to be utterly absurd to thought. Climacus uses the dialectical method to force the Christian to confront the double paradox at the very centre of his definition of human existence. He shakes the Christian's certainty in himself – that he knows what Christianity is and that he himself is a Christian – by showing that Christianity requires the human to perform the absurdly difficult task of constantly clinging to the absolute paradox in his daily life.

Second, the positive result: Here again, by disintegrating the definition of Christianity, Climacus throws the Christian back upon himself and forces him to confront whether being a Christian is important enough to his daily life that he will continue being a Christian, even though Christianity is utterly paradoxical and being a Christian is an utterly difficult task. Faced with the absolute paradox of Christianity, the Christian realizes that he is not a Christian because Christianity is rationally certain, but rather, he is a Christian because Christianity is important enough to his daily life that he is willing to stake his life on something so uncertain (CUP 1, 380–95, 429–32/SKS 7, 346–60). Here again, Climacus's 'negatively emancipating dialectic' (Diem 1959: 46) leads the Christian up to the point where he hopefully chooses to become a subjective thinker – to become passionately invested in Christianity for the sake of his everyday existence. As Climacus writes, 'the dialectical is like oil on the fire and extends the range of inwardness and intensively inflames the passion' (CUP 1, 385/SKS 7, 352).

Climacus's dialectical thought-project is aimed at both the casual Christian of Christendom and the modern speculative thinker, for both have forgotten what it means to be a Christian (CUP 1, 50–7, 373–81/SKS 7, 54–61, 340–7). The casual Christian believes that he already knows what Christianity is and that he himself is a Christian – after all, he is baptized in infancy, goes to church on Sundays, and rattles off scriptural passages with ease. He has a complacent, detached attitude toward Christianity. When confronted with the paradox of Christianity, would the casual Christian still decide that Christianity is important enough to his everyday existence that he is willing to continue being a Christian, even though it is an utterly difficult task? Would he become more passionately invested in Christianity and appropriate it differently into his everyday life?

The modern speculative thinker believes that he can subsume and go beyond Christianity in speculative thought – after all, he subsumes everything else into his grand philosophical system. He has an abstract, detached attitude toward Christianity. When confronted with the paradox of Christianity, would the speculative thinker still believe he can subsume and go beyond the paradox of Christianity in philosophical thought? Would he decide to leave Christianity out of speculative thought and only speculate about those matters that admit of speculation? Climacus uses the dialectical method to 'impinge on the hearer's existence,' and to 'both make him aware of the wrongness of the way in which he is engaged and recall him from it' (Diem 1959: 82, 193).

Because Christianity is so commonplace in Danish society, Climacus believes that he cannot directly communicate to the members of this society that they do not know what it means to be a Christian. Climacus writes, 'But while everyone is busy with learnedly defining and speculatively understanding Christianity, one never sees the question "What is Christianity?" presented in such a way that one discovers that the person asking about it is asking in terms of existing and in the interest of existing. And why does no one do that? Ah, naturally because we are all Christians as a matter of course' (CUP 1, 373/SKS 7, 340). Climacus instead uses the dialectical method to indirectly communicate with them, to gradually lead them up to the point where they must confront the paradoxicality of Christianity and what it means to be a Christian in everyday life. As Diem (1959: 53) writes, Climacus's purpose is to 'free from all materialistic self-deception those who are already convinced of Christian truth and think they have made the decision for faith, and this he does by instilling into them a passionate concern about existence itself as the unavoidable preliminary condition for Christian living.'[10]

Conclusion

In the end, Climacus's dialectical thought-project shows us that both the pagan and the Christian definitions of human existence are self-contradictory. According to the dialectical method, then, Climacus should discard both definitions and repeat the dialectical process until he discovers a definition of human existence that withstands rational scrutiny. But Climacus explicitly states that he will go no further. He will not search for a better definition, and he will not endorse either Socratic paganism or Christianity as the better definition. Since paganism and Christianity are absolute opposites – they are the only two ways that we can define the human – any other definition that pretends to 'go beyond' these opposites will still end in paradox (PF, 108–11/SKS 4, 304–6). As Mackey (1971: 165) writes, 'Climacus forces his reader into a corner where he must admit . . . that there is no honest way of understanding human existence that can avoid contradiction.' Climacus merely presents the issue – by working through both definitions – and then leaves the reader to fend for himself.

Climacus claims that the 'good dialectician' (PF, 108/SKS 4, 304) should stop the dialectic here: at the stalemate between the two paradoxical definitions. Climacus is speaking to the dialecticians of modern speculative thought – who, presumably, are 'poor' dialecticians – because they cannot tolerate contradiction and they insist on mediating opposing definitions into a new definition. The good dialectician, by contrast, can accept contradiction, because he knows that dialectics is less about proving the rational certainty of the truth and more about inspiring the individual's existential certainty of the truth. Climacus, good dialectician that he seems to be, encourages the individual, whether he is pagan or Christian, to accept contradiction and to confront the rational uncertainty of searching for the truth, all so that he may become existentially certain of the importance of searching for the truth for the sake of his everyday life.

Related topics

'The passion of Kierkegaard's existential method,' Lee C. Barrett; 'Logic, language, and existential knowledge,' Mélissa Fox-Muraton; 'Varieties of existential uncertainty,' Rick Anthony Furtak; 'Coming to an understanding with the paradox,' Mark A. Wrathall.

Notes

1 For a discussion of Hegelian philosophy in nineteenth-century Denmark – of the Danish Hegelians and their critics – see Stewart (2003: especially 45–89) and Thulstrup (1980: 14–58).
2 Climacus is arguably Kierkegaard's pseudonym with the most genuine love for and well-trained skill in dialectical thinking. In *De Omnibus Dubitandum Est*, Climacus explains that he has always been 'ardently in love' (JC, 118/SKS 15, 17) with dialectical thinking. Even as a child, he would spend hours practicing the movements of dialectical thinking and listening to his father engage his friends in Socratic-style dialectical conversation, always marvelling at how his father could trap his friends in contradiction (JC, 118–9, 121–5/SKS 15, 20–4).
3 A notable exception is Kant, who argues, in the 'Antimonies of pure reason,' that dialectical reason can 'prove' both the 'thesis' and the 'antithesis,' but it cannot resolve these two contradictory views (Kant 1998: 459–550).
4 For a discussion of how Socrates, Hegel, and Kant each use the dialectical method, see Maybee (2009: 10–6; 2016); for a discussion of Socrates and Hegel, see Diem (1959: 11–30).
5 Malantschuk (1974: 103–78) thoroughly discusses how Kierkegaard employs the principle of 'consistency' throughout his works. He writes that the 'central and determining concept for Kierkegaard in the structuring of this method becomes the concept of *consistency*' (Malantschuk 1974: 105).
6 In *The Sickness unto Death*, Anti-Climacus also constructs his work according to a dialectical structure, claiming that it is best suited to thinking through despair, that is, the concept of sin (SUD, 5–6/SKS 11, 117–8). Anti-Climacus specifically uses the same dialectical method as Johannes Climacus in the section titled 'The Socratic definition of sin.' Anti-Climacus uses the same hypothetical 'If – Then' thought structure to test the Socratic (i.e., pagan) and Christian definitions of sin. When subjected to dialectical scrutiny, the Socratic definition of sin (i.e., sin is ignorance) proves to be self-contradictory, and the Christian definition of sin (i.e., sin is wilful ignorance of sin) proves to be doubly paradoxical and doubly absurd (SUD, 87–104/SKS 11, 201–8).
7 In the *Phaedo*, Socrates says, 'No sensible man would insist that these things are as I have described them, but I think it is fitting for a man to risk the belief – for the risk is a noble one – that this, or something like this, is true about our souls and their dwelling places' (Plato 1997: 114d).
8 For an in-depth discussion of the Socratic Paradox and Socrates' view of his own self-knowledge, see Howland (2006: 102–28) and Diem (1959: 37–50); for Kierkegaard's view of Socrates as a subjective thinker, see Howland (2006: 188–208).
9 In *Fear and Trembling*, in the 'Problemata' section, Johannes de silentio uses the same 'If –Then' dialectical method to test the pagan and Christian definitions of faith. De silentio also discovers that, when subjected to dialectical scrutiny, the pagan definition of faith proves to be self-contradictory and the Christian definition of faith proves to be doubly paradoxical (FT, 54–120/SKS 4, 121–207).
10 For an explanation of the relationship between Kierkegaard's dialectical method and Christian revelation and Church doctrine, see Diem (1959: 81–102, 157–85).

References

Burns, M. O. (2015) *Kierkegaard and the matter of philosophy: A fractured dialectic*, New York: Roman & Littlefield.
Diem, H. (1959) *Kierkegaard's dialectic of existence*, H. Knight (trans), London: Oliver & Boyd.
Dunning, S. N. (1985) *Kierkegaard's dialectic of inwardness: A structural analysis of the theory of stages*, Princeton, NJ: Princeton University Press.
Dunning, S. N. (1981) 'The dialectic of contradiction in Kierkegaard's aesthetic stage,' *Journal of the American Academy of Religion*, 49, no. 3: 383–08.
Hegel, G. W. F. (1977) *Hegel's phenomenology of spirit*, A. V. Miller (trans), Oxford: Oxford University Press.
Hegel, G. W. F. (1975) *Hegel's logic: Part one of the encyclopaedia of the philosophical sciences*, W. Wallace (trans), Oxford: Oxford University Press.
Hegel, G. W. F. (1969) *Hegel's science of logic*, A. V. Miller (trans), New York: Humanity Books.
Howland, J. (2006) *Kierkegaard and Socrates: A study in faith and philosophy*, Cambridge: Cambridge University Press.
Kant, I. (1998) *Critique of pure reason*, P. Guyer and A. Wood (trans), Cambridge: Cambridge University Press.
Mackey, L. (1971) *Kierkegaard: A kind of poet*, Philadelphia, PA: University of Pennsylvania Press.
Malantschuk, G. (1974) *Kierkegaard's thought*, E. Hong and H. Hong (trans), Princeton, NJ: Princeton University Press.
Maybee, J. (2016) 'Hegel's dialectics,' *Stanford Encyclopedia of Philosophy*. Retrieved from <https://plato.stanford.edu/entries/hegel-dialectics/> [accessed September 10, 2017].
Maybee, J. (2009) *Picturing Hegel: An illustrated guide to Hegel's encyclopaedia logic*, Lanham, MD: Lexington Books.
Piper, H. B. (2004) 'Kierkegaard's non-dialectical dialectic or that Kierkegaard is not Hegelian,' *International Philosophical Quarterly*, 44, no. 4: 497–17.
Plato (1997) *Plato: Complete works*, J. M. Cooper (trans), Indianapolis, IN: Hackett Publishing Company.
Stewart, J. (2003) *Kierkegaard's relations to Hegel reconsidered*, Cambridge: Cambridge University Press.
Taylor, M. C. (2000) *Journeys to selfhood: Hegel and Kierkegaard*, New York: Fordham University Press.
Thulstrup, N. (1980) *Kierkegaard's relation to Hegel*, G. L. Stengren (trans), Princeton, NJ: Princeton University Press.
Walsh, S. (2005) *Living Christianly: Kierkegaard's dialectic of Christian existence*, University Park, PA: Pennsylvania University Press.

Further reading

Diem, H. (1959) *Kierkegaard's dialectic of existence*, H. Knight (trans), London: Oliver & Boyd.
   Diem examines Kierkegaard's dialectical method, especially in relation to Socrates' and Hegel's dialectical methods. Diem argues that Kierkegaard employs a 'disintegrating' dialectical that leads the individual back to existence.

Dunning, S. N. (1985) *Kierkegaard's dialectic of inwardness: A structural analysis of the theory of stages*, Princeton, NJ: Princeton University Press.
   Dunning focuses on Kierkegaard's pseudonymous texts, arguing that the 'dialectic of paradox' (i.e., inner/outer, self/others) characterizes the aesthetic, ethical, and religious stages of existence.

Walsh, S. (2005) *Living Christianly: Kierkegaard's dialectic of Christian existence*, University Park, PA: Pennsylvania University Press.
   Walsh focuses on Kierkegaard's religious texts, arguing that Christian existence is characterized by four main paradoxes: sin/faith and forgiveness, possibility of offense/faith, dying to the world/new life in the spirit, and suffering/joy.

3
KIERKEGAARD'S EXPERIMENTING PSYCHOLOGY

William McDonald

Introduction

With his experimenting (*experimenterende*) psychology, Kierkegaard develops an alternative to eighteenth-century rational, empirical and transcendental psychologies, which aims to preserve the subjective nature of first-person experience while adhering to the scientific requirements of objectivity and universal validity. It is an idealist psychology whose method includes identifying instantiations of psychological forms in order to exemplify the psychological experience of particular existential types. These instantiations and exemplars – experiments – may be found in actual life, history, myth, and literature or might be constructed by Kierkegaard or his pseudonyms. Kierkegaard uses the term 'experimenting' to qualify 'psychology' in the subtitle of *Repetition*, and part of the subtitle of 'Guilty? Not Guilty?' in *Stages on Life's Way* is 'A Psychological Experiment.' He refers to experiments and experimentation in association with psychological concepts throughout his authorship from *On the Concept of Irony* to *The Sickness unto Death*. To understand Kierkegaard's notion of experimenting psychology, and to appreciate its originality and power, we need to see how it fits into the history of the development of psychology as a science. This requires us to identify the relevant features of eighteenth-century German psychology and the trajectory psychology takes in nineteenth-century Denmark. We will then trace a parallel between Kierkegaard's approach to psychology and Ludwig Binswanger's existential psychotherapy in order to solve a problem that otherwise vitiates post-Kantian psychology. But first we will sketch some of the features of Kierkegaard's experimenting psychology and existential anthropology.

Experimenting psychology and existential anthropology

Kierkegaard does not develop a systematic psychology – indeed he resists dispassionate, objective, systematized reflection on the psyche in favour of a personalized approach. His experimenting psychology is far removed from the empirical method of what came to be known as experimental psychology and is equally removed from eighteenth-century German empirical and rational psychology. It owes more to the use of observation, self-reflection, and literary characterization found in the work of Friedrich Schlegel and F. C. Sibbern and might better be called an *art* – though Kierkegaard refers to it as a science (*Videnskab*) (CA, 51/SKS 4, 356). It also engages with themes in Kant and post-Kantian German Idealism, especially the notions of subjectivity, freedom, and self-consciousness.

Kierkegaard requires of the psychological observer that he has 'a poetic originality in his soul so as to be able at once to create both the totality and the invariable from what in the individual is always partially and variably present' (CA, 55/SKS 4, 359–60). He draws on the principle *unum noris omnes* (if you know one, you know all), where the one you know is yourself (CA, 79n/SKS 4, 382n). However, the one you know must be an 'existing subjective individual' and 'a real [*virkeligt*] human being' (CUP 1, 571–2/SKS 7, 519; translation modified). This is to rule out purely abstract self-knowledge or extrapolation from dispassionate, systematic thought as bases for psychological insight. Kierkegaard's art of experimenting psychology uses self-observation, recollection, and imagination to identify exemplars, which instantiate general features of the fundamental ontology of 'the existing individual.' His approach is not to identify universal laws, nor to infer regularities, of human behaviour. Nor is it primarily focused on psychopathologies – although he has been referred to as a 'physician of the soul' (Podmore 2009) and his analysis of despair was thought by Ludwig Binswanger (1958: 297) to define schizophrenia 'with the keen insight of genius.' More accurate is Alastair Hannay's (1998: 110) description of the project in *The Sickness unto Death* as a 'pathology of selfhood.' Kierkegaard's experimenting psychology illustrates features of existential anthropology, whether pathological or not, which apply in principle to all human beings.

Kierkegaard's psychology seeks an objective understanding grounded in self-understanding (Nordentoft 1978: 2–3). Self-understanding comes not primarily from introspection, which had already been thoroughly criticized by Kant as a reliable method (Kitcher 1990: 11), but from broader self-observation and recollection (Evans 1990: locations 526–33). Its objectivity does not consist in impartial observation or double-blind testing against a control group. Rather, its objectivity consists in its accurate analysis of the fundamental ontology that conditions all existing human beings. It starts with observation, which is followed up by the 'original thinking through of that which has been observed' (Nordentoft 1978: 1). The perspicacity of the observation is proportional to the degree of engagement of the observer:

> An inquisitively interested observer sees a great deal, a scientifically interested observer is worthy of respect, a concerned interested observer sees what others do not see, but a mad [*sindssvag*] observer perhaps sees the most of all; his observations are sharper and more persevering, just as certain animals have sharper senses than do human beings. But, of course, his observations must be verified.
>
> *(SLW, 281/SKS 6, 262; translation modified)*

Verification is by means of confirming those observations in oneself. They can be verified by either recollecting their truth from one's own experience or repeating their truth in one's own experience, through inward appropriation. Observations can be falsified by finding a contradiction between what the observer says and how the observer exists '*qua* human being' (CUP 1, 304/SKS 7, 276). Observations can also be falsified by finding a contradiction in the mood, between what is appropriate to the object and what is presented, as for example 'when sin is brought into aesthetics, the mood becomes either light-minded or melancholy,' whereas its proper mood is 'earnestness' (CA, 14–5/SKS 4, 322).

Kierkegaard's psychology is dialectical and must be conducted in a proper mood and be subject to the category of appropriation (CA, 14n/SKS 4, 322n), where to appropriate is to make something truly one's own, in heartfelt inwardness (cf. CUP 1, 21, 203, 242/SKS 7, 29, 186, 220;

CI, 328/SKS 1, 356). Because of the dynamic nature of mental phenomena, the psychological observer needs to have 'a life-view' and 'a life-development' (EPW, 64–5/SKS 1, 20–1) as stable bases for viewing mental phenomena dialectically and seeing how they fit into a totality. These are also requisites for the poet or novelist. Psychology, poetry, and religion are contiguous domains, as is suggested in the subsection of 'Guilty? Not Guilty?' called 'the Last Frontier between the Esthetic and the Religious Lies in the Psychological' (SLW, 446/SKS 6, 412).

Kierkegaard's art of experimenting psychology often involves the imaginary construction of existential types, such as the aesthete, the ethicist, the Christian, the ironist, and the humourist.[1] At other times the exemplar is found in actual life, as in the case of Adolf Adler, in whom Kierkegaard finds an exemplar of the contemporary confusion of religious and secular categories (BA, 91–2/SKS 15, 248–9). Actual existing figures always contain something accidental, so are not as open to 'the pure ideality of possibility' as poetically created exemplars (BA, 91/SKS 15, 248), yet even his imaginary constructions are ultimately grounded in Kierkegaard knowing himself as a real existing individual. Each of the imaginary constructions constitutes the instantiation of an existential type and can be used as an exemplar towards which we can comport ourselves in our own life projects. Kierkegaard typically removes himself from authoritative authorship of these exemplary characters by presenting them in texts by pseudonyms. He also shows us pseudonyms who create their own exemplary characters in order to observe their dialectical developments, as, for example, Constantine Constantius does with the Young Man in *Repetition* or Frater Taciturnus does with Quidam in 'Guilty? Not guilty?' This indirect communication is to facilitate the activity of the reader in relating herself to herself, guided by the exemplars, as part of the process of becoming a self. The creation of exemplary existential types resembles Friedrich Schlegel's series of biographical sketches of great men, including Voltaire, Herder, Goethe, and Lessing, which Schlegel called 'characteristics,' in which he sought a unifying pattern that both individuates the men and makes their lives exemplary (Crowe 2010: 70). Schlegel, however, presented these biographical sketches directly, unlike Kierkegaard, who presents his existential exemplars indirectly in order to hold up a mirror to the reader as an existing individual.[2]

Kierkegaard's works also show us instantiations of particular moods, to demonstrate how these have the potential to disclose something fundamental about coming-into-existence as a self or spirit. He shows how existential irony discloses that consciousness is not stuck in immediate perception, sensation, and cognition, but can become self-reflexive, as a step on the path to becoming a self. He shows how boredom discloses that the individual is a temporal being, who can take time that seems bereft of meaning either as an occasion to seek distraction or as a spiritual trial. Anxiety opens up the possibility of self-consciousness, firstly in the sense of awkward self-awareness, by disclosing that one exists *for another* and that one has the freedom (and responsibility) to choose to act on the basis of being oneself or on the basis of the expectations of others. Kierkegaard also shows how despair discloses that one is ultimately dependent, in becoming self/spirit, on the power that established one's self – that is, we are not self-sufficient self-creators, as some German Idealists and Romantics believed. In the case of all these ambiguous moods, no particular determinate outcome is guaranteed; they are all potential moments in which to exercise freedom, and so, various outcomes are possible depending on the choices made. Dialectical skill is therefore required of the psychologist to follow the possible developments on the basis of different existential choices.

Kierkegaard's experimenting psychology fits with other sciences and in particular with his anthropology. He takes the proper object of psychology to be the *coming-into-existence of the self*, so that the fundamental ontology of the existing human being must be taken into account in order to understand the nature and limits of psychology. Unlike Kant and the rational psychologists, Kierkegaard does not think human beings are *essentially* thinking beings. Kierkegaard, perhaps following Schelling, takes human beings to be part of nature and always in the process of coming into being (Assiter 2015: 66–7). The human self or spirit, according to Kierkegaard, emerges in a process of dynamic self-relation, in which it strives to become 'a synthesis of the finite and the infinite, of the temporal and the eternal, of freedom and necessity' (SUD, 13/SKS 11, 129). Furthermore, the human being is 'a synthesis of psyche and body sustained by spirit' (CA, 48/SKS 4, 354). Ultimately, Kierkegaard's anthropology includes the idea that this dynamic synthesis must relate itself not only to itself, but also 'to that which established the entire relation' (SUD, 13/SKS 11, 129) – God. This theological component built into Kierkegaard's anthropology also includes the idea that human beings are sinners and that sin is a form of error. Because of this, human beings live in 'untruth' and are prone to self-deception. The psychologist, then, needs to be aware of this propensity – both in the subject and object of observation.

Kierkegaard makes some explicit remarks about the relations among various academic disciplines, which are related to his views on the faculty-based conception of mind derived from eighteenth-century philosophical psychology, especially in the work of Christian Wolff, Johannes Nikolaus Tetens, and Immanuel Kant. For example, Kierkegaard regards the faculty of imagination as 'the capacity *instar omnium* [for all capacities],' because it is 'the medium for the process of infinitizing' and 'the possibility of any and all reflection, and the intensity of this medium is the possibility of the intensity of the self' (SUD, 31/SKS 11, 147).

Kierkegaard thinks that a science of psychology must operate within certain limits. But, contra Kant, he thinks psychology is not limited to transcendental deductions about the conditions of possibility of cognition, sensation, and perception. Its limits are determined by: (1) its specific objects; (2) the discourses, sciences, or spheres of existence that seek to take those as their objects; (3) the relations between psychology and the other sciences that seek to understand the same object; (4) the relationship between observer and observed; (5) the nature of the psychologist as an existing human being; and (6) the fundamental ontology of the self or spirit.

As an example of the limits set by the object of observation and other sciences with the same object, let us take psychology when its object is anxiety about sin. It is bounded on one side by the science of dogmatics (which deals by authority with what is true about sin) and on another side by the science of ethics (which deals, in an ideal way, with how it is right and wrong to act). Ultimately, all three sciences fail to take sin itself as their proper object, because sin exists as a possibility for a free individual and only comes into being in the moment of choice, whereas sciences typically deal with persistent states of being (CA, 21/SKS 4, 329). Sin is the proper object of a sermon rather than any science (CA, 15/SKS 4, 323). On the other hand, psychology can properly deal with the *effects* of the idea of sin on the human psyche. The primary effect is to make people anxious, so anxiety is the proper object of the science of psychology when it attempts to deal (indirectly) with sin (CA, 14/SKS 4, 321). Anxiety is a category of reflection (EO 1, 155/SKS 2, 154), and an ambiguous mood, which, at least initially, lacks a determinate intentional object (CA, 42/SKS 4, 348). This lack of a determinate intentional object distinguishes it from fear (SKS K4, 348).[3]

However, psychology in other contexts, when it pays attention to different objects, is bounded by other sciences or spheres of existence. When it takes guilt as its object, psychology operates in the space between aesthetics and religion (SLW, 446/SKS 6, 412). When it takes despair as its object, it operates on the margins of Christian faith for the purpose of 'upbuilding' and 'awakening' (SUD, iii/SKS 11, 115). In every context it is a science that, 'just as much as poetry and art, presupposes a mood in the creator as well as in the observer' (CA, 14n/SKS 4, 322n). Just what is the appropriate mood for the observer in the science of psychology? It is a mood that preserves inviolate the phenomenon it observes, by allowing the phenomenon to disclose itself rather than mastering the phenomenon by fitting it to a preconceived concept (CI, 9/SKS 1, 71). This point is made in the negative, when the pseudonym Vigilius Haufniensis observes that if 'sin is dealt with in psychology, the mood becomes that of persistent observation,' but thereby the 'concept becomes a different concept, for sin becomes a state. However, sin is not a state. Its idea is that its concept is continually annulled' (CA, 15/SKS 4, 323). In this requirement of psychology, Kierkegaard distinguishes his approach from both Hegelian speculative philosophy, which seeks ultimate mastery of the phenomenon in an absolute science, and Kant, for whom all phenomena are squeezed into predetermined categories of experience.

Because mental phenomena are rarely states, but more often transitory events, and because they cannot be analyzed into perfectly discrete objects to be laid out in taxonomic tables for scientific inspection, their rigorous observation requires that the observer enter into the appropriate mood, so that the observer can follow empathetically the psychological motions of the observed.[4] In the case of the psychologist who is observing the effect of sin on the psyche, the appropriate mood is 'a discovering anxiety' (CA, 15/SKS 4, 323). This enables the psychologist to understand the phenomenon under investigation by means of empathy, but it is also appropriate to the (indirect) study of sin because it reflects the proper degree of earnestness. Moreover, the psychologist who investigates sin in a mood of anxiety 'is in anxiety over the portrayal that [he himself] brings forth' (CA, 15/SKS 4, 323). Vigilius Haufniensis defines anxiety as '*a sympathetic antipathy* and *an antipathetic sympathy*' (CA, 42/SKS 4, 348). The psychologist who examines the psychological effects of sin with a discovering anxiety, then, simultaneously maintains empathetic awareness and critical distance, while also being anxious about her own potential freedom to sin or err.

The nature of consciousness is of course a primary concern for any science of psychology, including Kierkegaard's. For Kant (see 1998: 246–8), consciousness conceived as 'the unity of apperception' is a necessary condition of all experience. Moreover, it is a necessary precondition of Kant's (1998: 246–7) transcendental deduction – by means of which he deduces the conditions of possibility of all experience – and it must take the form of self-consciousness. Self-consciousness plays an equally indispensable role for Descartes, Leibniz, and Fichte, and is also of the highest importance to the post-Kantian Idealists and Romantics, even as they reject the foundational role it was given by Kant and Fichte (Frank 2004: 53).

For Kierkegaard, consciousness and self-consciousness are not given or presupposed but are to be achieved. He conceives of consciousness as 'an inherently first-personal, agent-bound, reflexive subjective state' (Stokes 2014: 55) and distinguishes it from 'immediacy' – or what we might think of as mere sentience or sensory awareness. Nor is consciousness simply the folding back upon itself of immediacy in 'reflection.' In his unpublished work *Johannes Climacus, or De omnibus dubitandum est*, Kierkegaard introduces the idea of consciousness as the medium in which sensory input from *reality* (*Virkelighed*) meets the *ideality* of language – but these are contradictory elements: 'the moment I make a statement about reality, contradiction is present, for what I say is ideality' (JC, 168/SKS 15, 55). Consciousness actively relates reality to ideality and becomes a third element in the relation without solving the contradiction (JC, 169/SKS 15, 57). Here Kierkegaard uses a pun on the Danish word for interest (*interesse*) and its Latin meaning 'being-between.' 'Reflection is *disinterested*. Consciousness, however, is the relation and thereby is interest, a duality that is perfectly and with pregnant double meaning expressed in the word interest (*interesse* [being between])' (JC, 170/SKS 15, 57). If we take the interestedness of consciousness to be 'the subjective, affective correlate' of self-awareness, then consciousness can be a matter of degree (Stokes 2014: 59) – the more interest, the more consciousness. Similarly, the 'more consciousness, the more self; the more consciousness, the more will; the more will the more self. A person who has no will at all is also not a self; but the more will he has, the more self-consciousness he has also' (SUD, 29/SKS 11, 145). Self-consciousness is achieved when we take our consciousness as an object for our consciousness. But each individual's consciousness, hence self-consciousness, is utterly unique. 'The most concrete content that consciousness can have is consciousness of itself, of the individual himself' (CA, 143/SKS 4, 443). Kierkegaard's account of self-consciousness, then, constitutes a rejection of what Manfred Frank (2004: 68) refers to as 'the reflection-model of self-consciousness,' which runs from Descartes through Kant to Fichte, and with which the post-Kantian Idealists and Romantics grapple.[5]

Kierkegaard's psychology addresses the themes of consciousness, subjectivity, and freedom, which are at the centre of his German predecessors' philosophical psychology. But we need to look a bit more broadly at that context in order to understand where he is coming from when he develops his experimenting psychology.

Transcendental psychology and reflection philosophy

German psychology in the eighteenth century was dominated by the work of Gottfried Wilhelm Leibniz, Christian Wolff, and the critical philosophy of Immanuel Kant. Wolff divided the discipline into rational and empirical psychology (Teo 2005: 53). Rational psychology was taken to be an a priori science, which 'deduces the essential properties of the soul that contain the sufficient reason for whatever actually occurs in the soul or can occur in it' (Kitcher 1990: 12). Both parts of Wolff's division were then subject to critique by Kant, who criticized the notion of rational psychology in his *Critique of Pure Reason* and the notion of empirical psychology in his *Metaphysical Foundations of Natural Science*. Kant concluded on the basis of these critiques that a science of psychology, as conceived by his predecessors, is impossible. He sought to avoid the problems of rational and empirical psychology by using pure reason to deduce the conditions of the possibility of experience – in his *transcendental psychology*. The transcendental deduction is a legitimate use of reason, unlike the rational psychologists' 'paralogisms' (Kant 1998: 411). Once the transcendental deduction has identified all and only those features of the mind required for experience, empirical psychology can resume within well-defined limits, as a phenomenology of experiences.

Kant's transcendental deduction identifies features of the mind that are required for cognition, sensation, and perception. In order to understand, sense, or perceive something, the mind has to organize sensory inputs under concepts, then synthesize the information in a unifying consciousness. This unifying function Kant (1998: 232) calls 'the transcendental unity of apperception.' The unity of apperception is the single, identical subject of all experience and thereby constitutes one of the main pillars of the mind. Another concern, for Kant, is how the mind represents objects, using the categories of experience.

Kant (1998: 225) identifies three capacities or faculties of mind, 'which contain the conditions of possibility of all experience and cannot themselves be derived from any other faculty of the mind.' These are sense, imagination, and apperception. These three capacities for all possible experience are 'subjective sources of cognition,' each of which 'can be considered empirically ... or [as] foundations a priori that make this empirical use itself possible' (Kant 1998: 236). In empirical consciousness they ground our perception, association and reproduction, and recognition, respectively (Kant 1998: 236).

Kant's transcendental psychology is embedded within his larger project to reconcile the causally deterministic realm explored by empirical science and the realm of reason, where he thinks freedom dwells. His solution is to confine science to a description of the world of appearances, or representations – that is, to phenomena as they are manifest to our consciousness – without drawing any conclusions about the way the world actually is.

This solution, according to at least some of the post-Kantian German Idealists, is flawed. Hegel, for example, in his early work *Faith and Knowledge*, accuses Kant of *subjectivism*, that is 'the position that the truth about objects is just the truth of our conceptual scheme, without our categories being actually exemplified by the real things in themselves' (Schulting 2017: 344). Moreover, Hegel criticizes Kant for adhering to 'reflection philosophy,' which 'remains stuck in its reflective oppositions (mind/world, form/content, a priori/a posteriori, subject/object, unity/manifold, reality/ideality, finitude/infinitude, etc.), while failing to *reflect on* these reflective oppositions' (Schulting 2017: 347). Kierkegaard, as we have seen, takes actively relating to reflective oppositions like these to be constitutive of selfhood.

The problem of 'reflection philosophy,' especially as it bears on the understanding of consciousness, is central to post-Kantian Idealist and Romantic psychology. Johann Gottlieb Fichte is 'the first to have shown conclusively that from Descartes, via German Rationalism and British Empiricism, up to Kant, self-consciousness was misconceived of as the result of an act of reflection by which a second-order act bent back upon a first-order act that is identical to itself' (Frank 2004: 53). In other words, if self-consciousness is attained by reflecting upon ourselves, how can the observing self (subject) be identical to the observed self (object)? The subject/object split creates a difference between these two 'selves.' Fichte's solution is to posit a pre-reflective unitary self, which is spontaneously free (unlimited, infinite). He then seeks to use this self-conscious 'I' as the starting point from which to derive all valid propositions about 'objective necessity and limitation (finitude),' which in turn is taken to be a transcendental condition for the possibility of the 'I' (Breazale 2018). Fichte thereby oscillates between ungrounded positing of the 'I' and transcendental deduction of its conditions of possibility. The German Romantics also confront the problem of self-consciousness conceived of as self-reflection. However, unlike Fichte they do not take self-consciousness to be a foundational principle of philosophy, and instead found self-consciousness on either transcendent Being or a non-conceptual form of consciousness such as feeling or intuition (Frank 2004: 53).

As we have seen, Kierkegaard avoids these abstract speculations on the nature and origin of self-consciousness. Instead he grounds self-consciousness in the concrete existence of the individual and gives a development account both of coming-into-existence as a self and of becoming self-conscious through moods, emotions, recollections, and actively relating the real and the ideal – including by reduplicating exemplars. In addition, Kierkegaard provides an anthropological framework through which to understand what it is to be, or become, an existing individual.

Eighteenth-century Danish psychology

J. N. Tetens, the Danish mathematician and philosopher, introduced a tripartite division of the psyche into understanding (*Verstand*), feeling (*Gefühl*), and willing (*Willen*), which became orthodoxy for eighteenth- and nineteenth-century German faculty psychology and the systematic basis for Kant's critical philosophy (Teo 2005: 43). Tetens also emphasized the importance of empirical, controlled experiments in establishing psychology as a natural science (SKS K7, 2). He thought that psychology should be based on observation, starting with introspective self-observation and ending with metaphysical synthesis (Teo 2005: 43).

F. C. Sibbern developed Tetens' tripartite division by means of his notion of 'collaterals.' This is the idea that thinking, feeling, and willing don't happen in isolation, but occur together (see Malantschuk 1980: 162–76). He also developed Tetens' philosophy of personality (SKS K7, 2), in which thinking, feeling, and willing are of equal value as expressions of life and which 'constitute the psychological basis of his principle of subjectivity' (Koch 2016: 236). This adumbrates Kierkegaard's notion that the self is performative, an act of relating oneself to one's multiple constitutive relata.

Sibbern, like Kierkegaard, thought that philosophy should be focused on existence rather than abstract thought (Kirmmse 1996: 217). He thought that human life is subject to a dialectical development, where the 'final goal is the full and complete development of the human being as a moral and spiritual being, that is, as a person' (Koch 2016: 234). Sibbern also emphasized the necessity of personal appropriation of truth and the individual's inner emotional connection with the universal life source (Koch 2016: 239–41).

Sibbern had introduced psychology as the core subject in the philosophy curriculum at the University of Copenhagen, where his textbook on psychology was used in the *examen philosophicum* (Pind 2014: 18). Kierkegaard probably had Sibbern as a teacher in the foundations of psychology course and there are traces of many of Sibbern's most distinctive ideas in Kierkegaard's psychology. Nevertheless, Kierkegaard's psychology is more dynamic than Sibbern's, which attempts to treat emotions merely collaterally rather than dialectically and existentially (Nordentoft 1978: 4).

Both Kierkegaard and Sibbern were very influential for the next generation of Denmark's philosophical psychologists, Harald Høffding and Kristian Kroman. Both Høffding and Kroman turned to philosophy after reading Kierkegaard at university, though both reacted against his theology and idealism and took a positivistic turn (Pind 2009: 34–7). However, when Høffding turned his attention to psychology in 1874, he returned to Kierkegaard for his critique of the British associationists (Pind 2009: 35–6). In Kierkegaard he 'came to see the importance of a thought which had lain behind Kierkegaard's philosophizing and had much earlier been deliberately emphasized by Kant, namely the idea of the assembling and unifying character of human consciousness' (Høffding 1928: 69).

Høffding distinguishes between 'active' and 'inactive' psychology. The latter he takes to be characteristic of British associationist psychology, in which mental associations are supposed to follow mechanically from one another. While Høffding thinks this outlook helped liberate psychology from metaphysics, it is also limited because it views mental elements in isolation. To be understood properly, mental events need to be seen in context. The idea of a 'relational law' among mental events was so important to Høffding that he claimed it was 'the guiding idea of his psychology' (Pind 2009: 36). In this we find echoes of Sibbern's collateral thinking and Kierkegaard's self as dialectically active self-relating.

Høffding (1891: 1) views psychology as 'a pure science of experience,' though he is aware of the problems of introspection as a means of accessing experience – for the reasons Kant had already given, viz. that thoughts and feelings are not steady, abiding, or discrete (Høffding 1891: 16–7). Høffding maintains a strict distinction between inner and outer experience and, like Kierkegaard, gives methodological preference in psychology to observation of inner experience. He thinks that physiological approaches to psychology cannot take us very far in understanding mental phenomena, as physiology really only deals with 'reflex actions' (Høffding 1891: 10). The feeling of pain, on the other hand, is a phenomenon that belongs to inner experience and is directly accessible only to consciousness (Høffding 1891: 11). Psychology deals with thoughts, feelings, and sensations, which belong to inner experience; all psychological approaches, therefore, have to take inner experience as their starting point, even physiological psychology insofar as it deals with mental phenomena. However, despite the fact that inner and outer experience are quite distinct as experiences, that fact alone is insufficient to conclude that they have as their objects different substances or principles (Høffding 1891: 12–3).

For Høffding (1891: 14) psychology should be a science 'without a soul,' since it should make no presuppositions about the metaphysical status of that upon which inner experience is founded. He therefore excludes from psychology both materialism and spiritualism, opting instead for a phenomenological method (Høffding 1891: 15).

Høffding (1891: 16) follows Descartes and Kant in regarding time as 'the form of mental phenomena' – just as space is the form of material phenomena. This is a source of the problem for introspection as a method since inner experience won't stand still to be observed. So, again like Kierkegaard, Høffding (1891: 17–8) prefers recollection as a method for accessing inner phenomena, since it enables different currents of observation to be unified in retrospect.

Individual observation of inner experience, however, is subjective. Yet psychology aspires to be an objective science. Observations not only between different individuals, but within and by the same individual, can vary. This can be offset to some extent by comparing observations across time and trying to take account of subjective bias, but this is an imperfect method to arrive at what is universal (Høffding 1891: 18–9). We can do a certain amount by means of classification and analysis, but we should not leap from identifying a species of mental life to attributing causal powers to it, since classification is often done on the basis of observing a prominent characteristic, rather than rigorously analysing 'the individual elements and the laws of their connection and interaction,' especially in the context of classifying faculties of mind (Høffding 1891: 19). In any case, we should not confuse these observations with explanations or theories: 'The mere observation and description of [mental products], therefore, are of value as a basis only' (Høffding 1891: 20). The subjectivity of psychological observation needs to be 'supplemented by physiological and historical (sociological) inquiries, or, as we may say... *subjective* psychology must be supplemented by *objective*' (Høffding 1891: 24). However, objective psychology 'always rests on an inference by analogy,' when as objective psychologists 'what we think we discover of mental life outside our own consciousness, we reproduce in ourselves by means of a sympathy closely connected with analogy. But these analogies may afford indispensable correctives to our subjective observation' (Høffding 1891: 24).[6]

A more rigorous way to ensure objectivity, according to Høffding (1891: 21), is experimentation.[7] Høffding and Kroman had been instrumental in opening the way for Alfred Lehmann to establish a laboratory for experimental psychology at the University of Copenhagen. Høffding had written a letter to Wilhelm Wundt, asking that he accept Lehmann into his experimental psychology laboratory in Leipzig and later kept up a correspondence with Lehmann in Leipzig. He and Kroman supported Lehmann's application for a position at the University of Copenhagen and for funding to establish a laboratory on his return from Leipzig. Despite a personal falling out over a scientific disagreement, in which Lehmann purported to disprove experimentally Høffding's theory of 'unmediated recognition,' Høffding continued to support Lehmann professionally. This ultimately resulted in the establishment of a master's degree in applied and theoretical psychology at the University of Copenhagen in 1918, and in the recognition of the University of Copenhagen as a pioneering centre of experimental psychology (Pind 2009).

Existential psychotherapy and fundamental ontology

The combination of Høffding's positivism and Lehmann's experimental psychology proved fatal for Kierkegaard's experimenting psychology, at least in Copenhagen. However, his work remained inspirational for others. Elements of his work were taken up directly by existential psychotherapists such as Ludwig Binswanger, Rollo May, Carl Rogers and Irvin Yalom (Stewart 2011a), and indirectly thanks to Kierkegaard's influence on philosophers such as Karl Jaspers, Martin Heidegger, Maurice Merleau-Ponty, and Jean-Paul Sartre (Stewart 2011b).

We will restrict ourselves here to a consideration of some parallels between Kierkegaard's experimenting psychology and Binswanger's method of psychotherapy, which potentially avoid what Foucault (1994: 318–22) calls 'the empirico-transcendental doublet.' This is a methodological flaw in the human sciences, analogous to the 'paralogisms' Kant found in rational psychology. Foucault traces the problem to Kant's 'contamination' of transcendental deduction – on the basis of pure reason – with his anthropology, which outlines the empirical limits of human knowledge. Our self-knowledge entails viciously circular reasoning when we seek its conditions of possibility in the limits 'discovered' by the very empirical investigations those limits make possible. That is, the same conditions or limits that are discovered by the empirical human sciences are also those that condition the discoveries. It is a fatal methodological flaw in much of the post-Kantian psychology, whose history we have traced above.

Binswanger's method, like Kierkegaard's, avoids vicious circularity because it starts with the idea of human *existence* as an open process of coming-into-being through free, self-relating activity rather than as limited by fixed, transcendental conditions of possibility. It steers a middle way between the transcendental and the empirical by making human being 'neither a transcendental structure nor a concrete particular, but the instantiation of the first in the second' (Han-Pile 2016: 7). In order for this approach to avoid the pitfalls of the empirico-transcendental doublet, 'the particular cases of [human-being] examined in existential analysis have to be regarded as exemplary' (Han-Pile 2016: 7).[8] It does this by taking existential instances (case studies) to be exemplary in disclosing ways of being-in-the-world, towards which the observer or reader are free to comport themselves. Kierkegaard takes this potential comportment to be the dialectical element in both observation and coming-to-be a self. Binswanger starts with existence, which 'is not human life empirically understood, let alone an empirical fact about an entity . . . but the self-interpreting activity that is both presupposed by and expressed in all forms of Dasein's comportment' (Han-Pile 2016: 7).[9] This is very similar to Kierkegaard's notion of understanding the self as a self-relating activity.

In his case studies, Binswanger begins with observations of the patient's history, behaviour, and communication. He then applies an existential analysis, before concluding with a psychopathological-clinical analysis. The existential analysis consists in identifying the patient as an *instantiation* of a mode of being-in-the-world. This includes an account of how the patient comports herself towards the elements that make up that mode of being-in-the world. The analysis also shows how the patient *exemplifies*, in her comportment, the conditions of possibility of her being-in-the-world. The psychopathological-clinical analysis consists in applying the categories of psychoanalysis and clinical psychiatry to the existential analysis, with a view to therapeutic treatment.

In his case studies of Ellen West and Lola Voss, Binswanger finds that they have narrowed their possible modes of being-in-the-world by taking one aspect (anxiety) *in* the world and intensifying it until it becomes a fixed dimension (dread) *of* their world. This process Binswanger (1963b: 284) calls 'mundanization [*Verweltlichung*].' This is the 'process in which the Dasein is abandoning itself in its actual, free potentiality of being itself, and is giving itself over to a specific world-design' (Binswanger 1963b: 284). From the point of view of the psychological observer, the patient as an exemplar discloses not only the limits of her specific world-design but also other possible ways of being-in-the-world, both the possibility she instantiates and the possibilities she abrogates.

Binswanger's existential anthropology, then, resembles Kierkegaard's insofar as it regards being-in-the-world as a process of self-interpreting activity, in which one of the poles is freedom/necessity. Moreover, both agree that being human is a dialectical process and that, in undertaking a scientific, psychological investigation, we ought not to forget ourselves in the process (Binswanger 1963b: 169–71).

There are many detailed parallels between Kierkegaard's experimenting psychology and Binswanger's *Daseinsanalyse* (cf. Basso 2011: 29–54). For example, in his study of Lola Voss, Binswanger discusses the relationship between anxiety, 'the sudden,' and discontinuity in communication, just as Kierkegaard discusses their relationship, mediated by the notions of 'the demonic' and 'inclosing reserve,' in *The Concept of Anxiety* (CA, 129–32/SKS 4, 430–3). Binswanger (1963b: 300) also discusses, in terms very similar to Kierkegaard's, how the process of 'mundanization' as 'displacement of ... responsibility and guilt onto an outside "fate" ... has to be paid for with the loss of freedom and compulsive entanglement in the net of external circumstances' (cf. CA, 97/SKS 4, 400). Both place great emphasis on the role of freedom in coming-to-be as a self (Binswanger 1963a: 167). Both also emphasize the salvific role of love in connecting us to others in a way that opens us radically to existential possibilities, in contrast to the way demonic forces foreclose such possibilities. Love has the capacity to grant insight on the basis of non-judgmental acceptance of, and care for, others, and so plays an important role in the art of understanding others.

However, we can't pursue these detailed parallels further. The main task was to show how Kierkegaard's experimenting psychology and Binswanger's *Daseinsanalyse* potentially solve the problem of the empirico-transcendental doublet, which has remained a problem in post-Kantian psychology, thereby demonstrating the continuing relevance of Kierkegaard's experimenting psychology.

Related topics

'Imagination and belief,' Eleanor Helms; 'Consciousness, self, and reflection,' Patrick Stokes.

Notes

1 In *Kierkegaard's Writings*, Howard and Edna Hong often translate 'Experimenter' as 'imaginary constructions.' Cf. the translation of 'psychologiske Experimenter og uvirkelige Constructioner' as 'imaginary psychological constructions and unreal fabrications' instead of 'psychological experiments and unreal constructions' (SLW, 191/SKS 6, 178–9).
2 Cf. '*Solche Werke sind Spiegel: wenn ein Affe hinein guckt, kann kein Apostel heraus sehen* [Such works are mirrors: when an ape looks in, no apostle can look out]. LICHTENBERG' (SLW, 8/SKS 6, 16).
3 This means of distinguishing anxiety and fear is also offered by Kant (cf. 2007: 357). Note, however, that for Kant anxiety is also distinguished from fear by intensity, that is more by quantitative than qualitative means.
4 Observation for Kierkegaard can include self-observation, but the latter is distinct from what Kant and the eighteenth-century empirical psychologists called 'introspection.' Introspection was taken to be a reliable source of real-time data by means of looking inside oneself as mental events occur. Kierkegaard is as sceptical as Kant about the reliability of this type of introspection. Instead, his method requires critical recollection (cf. Evans 1990: locations 526–33).
5 Contra Frank (2004: 53), we should note that Kierkegaard does not found self-consciousness 'on transcendent Being, a prior non-conceptual consciousness (feeling).'
6 Høffding (1891: 25) takes 'sociological psychology' to deal 'with mental life as it reveals itself in movement and action, in literature and art.'
7 Høffding (1891: 22–3) thinks that there is one important thing that can be measured quantitatively in psychology and that is the intensity of sensation.
8 According to Philip Pettit the difference between instantiation and exemplification is as follows: 'Instantiation is a two place relationship between a set of examples and a rule and it certainly has the feature of being a one-many relationship: one finite set of examples instantiates many rules ...

Exemplification is a three place relationship, not a two place one. It involves not just a set of examples and a rule but also a person for whom the examples are supposed to exemplify the rule' (quoted in Han-Pile 2016: 15–6).

9 'Dasein' – literally 'being there' – is used as a technical term by Heidegger to displace the subject/object opposition found in metaphysical conceptions of the human/world relationship. Dasein is not a subject over against an objective world. Rather, subject and object are mutually constitutive as being-in-the-world. The concept of Dasein is instrumental in enabling Binswanger's alternative to the empirico-transcendental doublet, and arguably has its roots in Kierkegaard's views on the self as a self-relating activity.

References

Assiter, A. (2015) *Kierkegaard, Eve and metaphors of birth*, London/New York: Rowman & Littlefield International.

Basso, E. (2011) 'Ludwig Binswanger: Kierkegaard's influence on Binswanger's work,' in J. Stewart (ed), *Kierkegaard Research: Sources, Reception and Resources*, vol. 13 (*Kierkegaard's Influence on the Social Sciences*), London: Routledge.

Binswanger, L. (1963a) 'Freud's conception of man in the light of anthropology,' in J. Needleman (trans), *Selected Papers of Ludwig Binswanger*, New York: Harper Torchbooks.

Binswanger, L. (1963b) 'The case of Lola Voss,' in J. Needleman (trans), *Selected Papers of Ludwig Binswanger*, New York: Harper Torchbooks.

Binswanger, L. (1958) 'The case of Ellen West,' in R. May, E. Angel, and H. F. Ellenberger (eds), *Existence– A New Dimension in Psychiatry and Psychology*, New York: Simon & Schuster.

Breazale, D. (2018) 'Johann Gottlieb Fichte,' *The Stanford Encyclopedia of Philosophy*. Retrieved from <https://plato.stanford.edu/archives/sum2018/entries/johann-fichte/> [accessed May 22, 2018].

Crowe, B. D. (2010) 'Friedrich Schlegel and the character of Romantic ethics,' *Journal of Ethics*, 14: 53–79.

Evans, C. S. (1990) *Kierkegaard's Christian psychology: Insight for counseling and pastoral care*, Kindle edition, Regent College Publishing.

Foucault, M. (1994) *The order of things: An archaeology of the human sciences*, New York: Vintage Books.

Frank, M. (2004) 'Fragments of a history of the theory of self-consciousness from Kant to Kierkegaard,' *Critical Horizons*, 5, no. 1: 53–136.

Han-Pile, B. (2016) 'Phenomenology and anthropology in Foucault's "Introduction to Binswanger's dream and existence": A mirror image of "The order of things,"' *History and Theory*, Theme Issue, 54: 7–22.

Hannay, A. (1998) 'Kierkegaard: The pathologist,' *Enrahonar*, 29: 109–14.

Høffding, H. (1928) *Erindringer*, Copenhagen: Gyldendal.

Høffding, H. (1891) *Outlines of psychology*, Suffolk: Richard Clay & Sons.

Kant, I. (2007) 'Anthropology from a pragmatic point of view,' in G. Zöller and R. Louden (eds), *Anthropology, History, and Education*, Cambridge: Cambridge University Press.

Kant, I. (1998) *Critique of pure reason*, P. Guyer and A. W. Wood (trans), Cambridge: Cambridge University Press.

Kirmmse, B. H. (1996) *Encounters with Kierkegaard: A life as seen by his contemporaries*, Princeton, NJ: Princeton University Press.

Kitcher, P. (1990) *Kant's transcendental psychology*, Oxford: Oxford University Press.

Koch, C. H. (2016) 'Frederik Christian Sibbern: "The lovable, remarkable thinker, Councilor Sibbern" and "the political simple-Peter Sibbern,"' in J. Stewart (ed), *Kierkegaard Research: Sources, Reception and Resources*, vol. 7 (*Kierkegaard and His Danish Contemporaries*), tome 1, ebook, London: Routledge.

Malantschuk, G. (1980) *Frihed og ekistens: Studier i Søren Kierkegaards tænkning*, Copenhagen: C. A. Reitzel.

Nordentoft, K. (1978) *Kierkegaard's psychology*, B. H. Kirmmse (trans), Pittsburgh, PA: Duquesne University Press.

Pind, J. L. (2014) *Edgar Rubin and psychology in Denmark*, Basel: Springer International.

Pind, J. L. (2009) 'A tale of two psychologies,' *Journal of the History of Behavioral Sciences*, 45, no. 1: 34–7.

Podmore, S. (2009) 'Kierkegaard as physician of the soul: On self-forgiveness and despair,' *Journal of Psychology and Theology*, 37, no. 3: 174–85.

Schulting, D. (2017) *Kant's radical subjectivism: Perspectives on the transcendental deduction*, London: Palgrave Macmillan.

Stewart, J. (ed) (2011a) *Kierkegaard research: Sources, reception and resources*, vol. 13 (*Kierkegaard's Influence on the Social Sciences*), London: Routledge.

Stewart, J. (ed) (2011b) *Kierkegaard research: Sources, reception and resources*, vol. 9 (*Kierkegaard and Existentialism*), London: Routledge.

Stokes, P. (2014) 'Consciousness,' in S. Emmanuel, W. McDonald, and J. Stewart (eds), *Kierkegaard Research: Sources, Reception and Resources*, vol. 15 (*Kierkegaard's Concepts*), tome 2, London: Routledge.

Teo, T. (2005) *The critique of psychology: From Kant to postcolonial theory*, Dordrecht: Springer.

Further reading

Kosch, M. (2006) *Freedom and reason in Kant, Schelling, and Kierkegaard*, Oxford: Clarendon Press.
   This book's analysis of moral agency in Kant, Schelling, and Kierkegaard discloses important aspects of their moral psychology as well as the importance of Schelling for Kierkegaard's theory of agency.

McCarthy, V. A. (2015) *Kierkegaard as psychologist*, Evanston, IL: Northwestern University Press.
   This book gives an accessible overview of Kierkegaard as a psychologist, paying attention to his analysis of sex and sexuality, moods, narcissism, repetition compulsion, melancholia, anxiety, and despair, as well as relating his philosophical psychology to that of Schelling and Heidegger.

4
METHODOLOGY AND THE KIERKEGAARDIAN MIND

Jamie Turnbull

Introduction

The question of how we understand Kierkegaard's methodology, and the issue of our own methodological approach to Kierkegaard's thought and work, are inextricably linked. For *how* we approach Kierkegaard (or, in the parlance of this volume, how we approach the Kierkegaardian mind) will dictate *what* we take his thought to be, and, in turn, what we take his methodology to consist in. Put otherwise the question of Kierkegaard's methodology – just what he took himself to be doing, and the account that we can give of it – is necessarily connected to the approach that we adopt in reading him.

This chapter falls into four parts. In the first I articulate why the question of Kierkegaard's methodology, the matter of indirect communication, is important to understanding him, and give a general overview of interpretative approaches. Part two argues that to understand the Kierkegaardian mind, and its thinking about indirect communication, we need to locate it within its cultural and intellectual context. Situating Kierkegaard's work and thought in this context reveals his project to be formulated against what he takes to be the theological naturalism of his contemporaries, and grounded in a logic of relations that finds its home in his Christology.

In the third part of the chapter I attempt to anticipate and answer objections to the account developed in part two. The fourth part of the chapter argues that, if the account that I have developed is correct, then certain approaches to Kierkegaard's methodology of indirect communication cannot be veridical, on the basis of their methodological presuppositions alone. Indeed, if I am correct, then philosophical, secular, and theologically naturalistic attempts to understand the methodology of indirect communication must necessarily fail, on the grounds that they a priori rule out of account the very concepts necessary to making sense of the Kierkegaardian mind on this issue.

Why indirect communication?

Kierkegaard has been, and continues to be, subject to a huge diversity of interpretation. For instance, he has been read as a poet, post-modernist, existentialist, phenomenologist, pragmatist, proto-Wittgensteinian, moral-perfectionist, Aristotelian moral perceptualist, virtue ethicist, moral epistemologist, anthropologist, sociologist, and moral-religious psychologist. Each of these interpretations comes with *some* conception of Kierkegaard's method: of what he is trying to achieve, and how he goes about it. If we are going to be able to adjudicate between different readings and appropriations of Kierkegaard, then it is important to pay attention to his own conception of what he takes himself to be doing.

Kierkegaard stresses the importance of indirect communication to his work. For instance, in the midst of a series of lectures he prepared on the subject, he states that distinguishing between reflecting upon the *object* and reflecting upon the communication 'is *decisive for my whole project*' (JP 1, 306/SKS 27, 433; emphasis added). Similarly, when he comes to offer an autobiographical overview of his life as an author, in *The Point of View*, it is the topic of indirect communication which occupies him; Kierkegaard is concerned with outlining just why, and how, he has structured his authorship on such a method (PV, 41–56/SKS 16, 23–38). There is, thus, evidence that Kierkegaard held the subject of indirect communication to be important to understanding his thought and work.

Kierkegaard scholars themselves commonly recognize the importance of understanding indirect communication. For instance, as far back as 1956, Ralph McInerny maintained that the notion of indirect communication was 'the key to what he [Kierkegaard] had to say' and was, as such, 'central to an understanding of Kierkegaard' (1956: 219–21). More recently, and in a similar vein, C. Stephen Evans claims that an 'understanding of this concept is *essential* to understanding the Kierkegaard corpus as a whole' (1983: 9; emphasis added). The claim that indirect communication is important to understanding Kierkegaard's thought and work will, I should think, be regarded as uncontentious by the majority of Kierkegaard scholars. That scholars hold indirect communication to be important to understanding Kierkegaard is attested to by the frequency with which it is mentioned in both introductory and advanced studies on his thought and writing.

Despite this attention, I think that the impact of *how* we go about attempting to understand indirect communication on *what* we take Kierkegaard to be saying is underappreciated. For our own, often tacit, methodological commitments and presuppositions can have a profound influence on what we take indirect communication to be and on the applications it is held to have outside of Kierkegaard's work. Indeed, the question of our own methodology in reading Kierkegaard has consequences for the very question of how we understand his place in the history of Western philosophy, and for how we classify his thought and work. One of the aims of this chapter is to show just how the assumptions of certain methodological trends delimit the understanding of indirect communication that can result.

Methodological approaches

I will now give the reader a flavour of some of the various ways in which indirect communication has been approached and understood by commentators. Kierkegaard's methodology has been held to concern, amongst other things, the literary style of his works, his own psychology, the cultural situation in which he was writing, and his use of biblical passages. Although not mutually exclusive, for the sake of convenience the different accounts found in the literature might be grouped under the following headings: literary, psychological, biographical, philosophical, and theological. I will briefly treat each of these in turn.

There are those that claim that indirect communication is to be identified with, or understood in terms of, certain features of natural language and its use: features such as irony, satire, metaphor and humour. Both Evans (1983: 105) and John Lippitt (2000: 5) claim that irony and humour are 'forms' of indirect communication. Similarly, Steven Emmanuel (1996: 141) holds irony and humour to be the means by which Kierkegaard's works are to be understood as indirect; and Edward Mooney (1997: 9; emphasis added) labels these same literary devices 'prominent *tokens of* indirect communication.' Kierkegaard's texts undoubtedly employ such devices. The claim these commentators make is that the method of indirect communication is to be understood in terms of, or identified with, these literary features of Kierkegaard's works.

In contrast, Joakim Garff interprets indirect communication psychologically. As is well known, at the age of twenty-four, Kierkegaard met a young girl named Regine Olson, and fell in love. Three years later, when Regine was eighteen, Kierkegaard proposed, only to break the engagement off less than a year later. Kierkegaard's relations with Regine undoubtedly had a profound effect on both his life and work. According to Garff, indirect communication can be understood as concerning messages between Kierkegaard and particular individuals, such as Regine. For instance, of Kierkegaard's love letters to Regine, Garff claims that:

> [B]y virtue of their indisputably aesthetic qualities, the letters make it clear that their author was to become not a husband but a writer. So they were actually farewell letters, *grandiose exercises in the art of indirect communication*: With enormous discretion and employing the entire panoply of the most nuanced shades of language, they try to make Regine realize that the person who sings her praises in letter after letter has long since disappeared from her life because he has lost himself in recollection of her and is thus utterly unsuited to married life.
>
> *(Garff 2005: 179; emphasis added)*

Garff (2005: 246) makes a similar case in respect to Kierkegaard's work *Repetition* (interestingly Garff thinks that this is why Kierkegaard rewrote the end of that book, once he learned of Regine's engagement to Friedrich Schlegel). Similarly, we are told that the monumental *Concluding Unscientific Postscript* contains indirect messages to Bishop Jakob Peter Mynster, as well as Kierkegaard's university tutor and adversary Hans Lassen Martensen (Garff 2005: 404, 426). For Garff, then, indirect communication can be understood in terms of Kierkegaard's psychology, and private messages to particular significant others in his life.

Jon Stewart has proposed a similar biographical, and historical, conception of indirect communication. Stewart suggests that indirect communication consists in Kierkegaard's use of anonyms to refer to his contemporaries. For

> [W]hen he wanted to criticize one of his contemporaries, he often did so *indirectly*; instead of using the names of his opponents, he made use of anonyms . . . Just as Kierkegaard used pseudonyms in an attempt to remain anonymous as an author, so also he used anonyms for his intellectual enemies in order to give them at least a semblance of anonymity.
>
> *(Stewart 2003: 43; emphasis added)*

Stewart suggests that indirect communication consists in Kierkegaard's use of code words and stock phrases to refer to his contemporaries. Indeed the use of such code words, we are to understand, 'is typical of Kierkegaard's strategy of criticizing his opponents indirectly' (Stewart 2003: 278). Kierkegaard employed such devices, according to Stewart (2003: 454), because they gave him a way of criticizing others in the close knit social world of 1840s Copenhagen, and avoided the scandal a more direct attack would provoke.

There are those that hold that there is more going on in Kierkegaard's methodology than can be accounted for in terms of the literary, psychological, or biographical detail. For these commentators, indirect communication is also a notion with substantive philosophical or theological merit in its own right. For instance, it has been claimed that indirect communication allows for the communication of non-conceptual content, or a certain kind of subjective cognition (Ramsland 1987: 330; Gurray 1990: 200; Evans 1983: 96). Kierkegaard's ideas, it has also been argued, bear substantial connection to those of the philosophers of language Paul Grice, J.L. Austin and Ludwig Wittgenstein. In the case of Grice, this has consisted in connecting indirect communication with the notion of 'conversational implicature' (Ramsland 1987: 330; Fredsted 1998: 527). Robert Solomon (1987: 79) has argued that Austin's notion of a 'performative utterance' can help illuminate the Kierkegaardian notions of subjective truth and communication. Similarly, James Conant (1989: 254–5; 1993: 209; 1995: 266–7) and Genia Schönbamsfeld (2007: 13) have argued that Kierkegaard's project of indirect communication can be understood in terms of a Wittgensteinian project of conceptual clarification.

Finally, there are those that suggest indirect communication is more pertinent to theology than philosophy. For instance, Jolita Pons has argued that indirect communication is to be accounted for in terms of Kierkegaard's use of biblical passages. Indeed Pons (2004: 146) claims that Kierkegaard's use of such passages 'instantiate[s] indirect communication,' and is 'perhaps the only tangible proof of such communication.' Similarly, George Pattison holds that Kierkegaard's form of communication is affected by 'the specific content of Christian communication.' According to Pattison we are to understand that, for Kierkegaard, 'the dialectics of communication go all the way back to *the nature of* the [absolute] paradox itself' (Pattison 1992: 86; emphasis added). The 'absolute paradox' is Kierkegaard's term for what he takes to be the correct conception of Christ's nature, and the subject of Christian faith.

As is evident from the above, Kierkegaard scholarship contains many different notions of indirect communication: of what it is, how it proceeds, and how it is to be understood. While Garff and Stewart may be right that Kierkegaard employed certain strategies in his work to communicate with, or about, particular individuals, I hope to show that the concept of indirect communication is more substantive than this. A purely psychological, biographical, or sociocultural account will, I think, necessarily fail to do justice to Kierkegaard's thinking about indirect communication.

Many scholars adopt a common methodology with respect to indirect communication (and, indeed, Kierkegaard more generally), by approaching the topic in the wake of a subsequent philosopher or 'ism,' and attempting to interpret and understand Kierkegaard's thought within those terms of reference. This trend stands in contrast to a method that begins by attempting to situate Kierkegaard in his immediate historical and intellectual context, and trying to understand him within *his own* terms. The latter is an approach that pays attention to the intellectual culture in which Kierkegaard's views developed, and to the particular problems, issues, and debates constitutive of the intellectual environment in which his thinking evolved. As shall become evident, to understand the thoughts of the Kierkegaardian mind with respect to indirect communication we need to approach that mind within the historical and cultural context formative of it; it is to that end that we shall now turn.

Indirect communication in context

The context in which Kierkegaard's thinking about indirect communication developed is provided by the debates sparked by the reception of Hegel's thought in Denmark in the late 1830s and 1840s, and specifically the issues that arose for the nature and communication of Christianity. I will briefly outline the Hegelian position that Kierkegaard takes issue with, as well as what he envisages to follow from that position for the communication of Christianity. I will then outline how Kierkegaard responds to the Hegelian position, and make the case that the claims that he makes about indirect communication form an ineliminable part of that response. If this is correct, Kierkegaard's conception of indirect communication will prove to be central to his rejection of what he takes to be the Hegelian-inspired theologically naturalistic views espoused by his contemporaries, and a logical consequence of his own Christology.

Hegelianism became a force in Danish Golden Age intellectual culture through figures such as Johan Ludvig Heiberg and Martensen. Yet, rather than simply being accepted as the *status quo*, Hegel's views were highly contentious (Stewart 2003: 109; 2007b: 378–9). Kierkegaard often casts himself as a lone force combatting a Hegelian orthodoxy yet, as Jon Stewart (2007a: 57) has argued, he is more accurately thought of as one of a number of figures who were both positively and negatively influenced by Hegelian views. Hegel's thought, and particularly the application of his views on logic to Christian doctrine, sparked a number of debates amongst Kierkegaard's contemporaries. These debates were primarily theological in nature, and included the so-called rationalism/supernaturalism debate, as well as debate on the doctrine of immortality, and on the relationship of Christianity to philosophy, and faith to knowledge (Heiberg 2005: 51).

At issue, primarily, was Hegel's criticism of the laws of traditional Aristotelian logic (the law of identity, the law of contradiction, and the law of the excluded middle), Hegel's own subsequent conception of mediation, and how those applied to Christian doctrine (Mynster 2009: 6). Hegel criticizes the law of identity as a meaningless tautology (Mynster 2009: 9; Stewart 2015: 238). Similarly he views the law of contradiction as abstract and uninformative, taking the absolute difference asserted by it as merely an abstract relation of something to itself, attained simply by negating the quality in question (i.e., P and ¬P) (Mynster 2009: 12; Stewart 2015: 242). Likewise Hegel claims that the law of the excluded middle is based on a fallacious view of the nature of concepts, and one that overlooks the essential unity that exists between pairs of categories. For in stating that a subject either possesses a particular property or attribute or it does not, the law of the excluded middle rules out the possibility of a third intermediate term between contradictory statements. According to Hegel, contraries are always united in virtue of a third term. P and ¬P are united by P, which remains despite it being posited or negated. The third, or middle term, is the underlying concept that unites the other two (Mynster 2009: 15–7; Stewart 2015: 245). The job of philosophy, for Hegel, is to grasp the underlying conceptual unity, or mediation, that exists between such concepts.

As opposed to thinking of God and human as absolutely different, Hegel's criticisms of traditional logic, and his conception of mediation, suggested that divinity and humanity are in fact, on some level, metaphysically identical. While Christ's incarnation was traditionally regarded as a divine mystery and wonder, Hegel's criticism of the law of the excluded middle suggested that human beings can come to make sense of how contradictory predicates can attach to the same subject. In this way Hegel's views appeared to entail that it was possible for human beings to come to understand the nature of God through human reason, and that the relationship between mankind and God might be better understood through philosophy.

One nexus of debate about the attempted application of Hegelian logic to Christian theology, the so-called rationalism/supernaturalism debate, concerned whether Christianity could be wholly understood in terms of human reason, and thereby rationalized or naturalized, or whether it rather rested upon a divine supernatural basis (Mynster 2009: 97, 101, 105). The attempted application of Hegelian mediation to Christian doctrine had consequences for: the nature of God and his relationship to human beings; the theological nature of human beings; the relationship between reason and divinity; the relationship between faith and knowledge; and the very identities of Christianity, Philosophy, and Theology. These were some of the issues forming the immediate intellectual environment in which Kierkegaard's own views evolved and took shape. Specifically, if there is one overriding issue or question animating Kierkegaard's thinking in the wake of these issues, it might be expressed as: how can God and humans be both absolutely different and come into relation with each other, and in such a way that these terms are not relativized to each other, or mediated, in the process? (We might formulate this question, in philosophical parlance: how can subject and object be both absolutely separate and yet necessarily related to each other?) Kierkegaard's thinking about indirect communication, as we shall see, is his answer to this question.

Kierkegaard characterizes the Hegelian position in many ways, as: objective, abstract, and speculative. One claim that he makes about the Hegelian view is that it asserts that a *direct relation* between God and human beings is possible (PC, 126, 128/SKS 12, 131, 133). In accord with the reception of Hegelian logic, and its application to Christian doctrine, Kierkegaard's claim appears to be that the Hegelian holds that the relationship between humanity and divinity can be conceived of as a logical relation. Divinity is not held to be something that is absolutely different, and so which must lie beyond mankind's capacity of conceptualization and reason, but as something that can be conceived of and incorporated into a holistic system of philosophy. When Kierkegaard asserts that the Hegelian holds that a direct relation between God and humankind is possible, the claim is that there can be a *direct cognitive relation* between human and God, such that divinity becomes knowable and understandable in terms of human reason and philosophy – specifically, of course, Hegelian philosophy (CUP 1, 220–3/SKS 7, 201–4).

For Kierkegaard the attempt to apply a logic of mediation to Christian doctrine is intellectually dishonest, and ethically and religiously perilous. With respect to humanity's relationship to God, in dissolving the law of the excluded middle, Kierkegaard holds the Hegelian to make that relation tautological, and so meaningless. For rather than mankind's relation to God being one which obtains between an individual human being and an absolutely different and transcendent God, given the metaphysical implications of mediation (that humans and God are, at bottom, identical) a relation of faith becomes a relation of a human being to themselves (or to mankind in general). The consequences of this, as Kierkegaard envisages them, are the naturalization of the supernatural (PF, 95–6/SKS 4, 292–4; CUP 1, 367–8/SKS 7, 333–5), a corrupt conception of divinity (PC, 126–8/SKS 12, 131, 133), and the deification of mankind and society in God's place (PC, 87/SKS 12, 95–6).

The severity of the threat facing Christianity, in the wake of this changing conception of the relation between God and humankind, is increased by Hegelianism's claiming to be a *Christian* theology and philosophy. This threat to Christianity comes not from outside, but from within Christian theology itself; and this fact, for Kierkegaard, makes Hegelianism all the more dangerous (CUP 1, 396/SKS 7, 361). For, whilst claiming to be a Christian philosophy, Kierkegaard thinks that Hegelianism is actually peddling a fallacious conception of both God and mankind's relationship to Him. In Kierkegaard's eyes the Hegelians masquerade as Christian theologians but, should their views become commonly accepted, it would herald the advent of secular rationalism. Mediation will, Kierkegaard fears, give rise to nominal Christianity: communities and cultures which identify themselves as Christian, but are in reality simply pagan by another name (CUP 1, 50–1, 361, 368/SKS 7, 55–6, 329, 335; PC, 43–4/SKS 12, 56–7).

Kierkegaard also thinks that the Hegelian position has further consequences for how Christianity can be talked about, or communicated, between human beings. For just as the Hegelian view is said to espouse the possibility of a direct relation between humanity and divinity, so too it is said to hold to a *direct communication* between God and human being (PC, 123, 128/SKS 12, 128–9, 132–3). Just as the Hegelian position holds that divinity can be conceptualized, so too it holds that God's message to human beings can be expressed and conveyed in terms of human language. The idea is not just that it is possible for God to communicate with mankind in human language, but for human beings to directly communicate with each other *about* God and their relationship to him (PC, 141/SKS 12, 144).

For Kierkegaard, there are numerous problems with this conception of Christian communication. For him, the media of thought and language cannot express the absolute difference between humankind and God; claiming that God can be thought and spoken about (in a manner similar to any other human being) automatically misrepresents the true nature of the God-relationship. Moreover, if an individual's relationship with God can be conceptualized and expressed within the generalities of human thought and language, then in principle what it is to be a Christian can be incorporated into human history and culture (and, with them, into the Hegelian system of philosophy) (CUP 1, 214–6/SKS 7, 196–8).

Hegelianism views the movement of reason as embodied in modern rational society. The unfortunate consequence of this, for Kierkegaard, is that coming into the right relationship with other human beings, or becoming acculturated to modern Danish society, is thought to be sufficient for (or even equivalent to) becoming a Christian (CUP 1, 50–1, 244/SKS 7, 55–6, 222). Yet, as Kierkegaard points out, such a conception of Christianity, and what it is to become a Christian, leaves *no* role for a supernatural God to play. Kierkegaard's charge is that when Christians are defined objectively, in terms of how they stand to other human beings and society, then they can be called such despite having *no* subjective relation of faith and grace to a transcendent God. Indeed, if the Hegelian conception of what it is to communicate Christianity is veridical, then the idea that a transcendent God, who brings faith and grace, has a role to play in one becoming a Christian drops out as irrelevant. In this situation Kierkegaard envisages 'Christian' becoming a tautological and meaningless accompaniment of 'human' (CUP 1, 345–6, 366–7/ SKS 7, 316–7, 333–4).

Kierkegaard's response to the attempted application of Hegelian mediation to Christology is well understood. The Hegelian position holds Christ's nature as both man and God to constitute a paradox, but a paradox than can be resolved by human reason; through the dissolution of the law of the excluded middle, and the subsequent operations of mediation, 'God' and 'man' are understood to attach to the same subject. Kierkegaard's rejoinder to this is that Christ does not constitute a *relative* paradox that can be better understood by reason and philosophy, but an *absolute paradox* that resists reason and understanding *per se* (PF, 45–6/SKS 4, 249–50; CUP 1, 217–8, 379/SKS 7, 198–9, 344–5).

In this rebuttal Kierkegaard is clear that Christ was a man, and as such shared ratiocinatory and linguistic capacities with his fellow human beings. *Qua* man, it is possible for human beings to understand Christ in the same way as they can understand other men. In terms of his existence as a man, Christ is a possible object of human judgement and so one can stand in *direct* cognitive relations to him in the same way that one can to other human beings (PC, 124–5/ SKS 12, 129–30). However, Kierkegaard is also clear that, *qua* God, Christ is *absolutely different* from other human beings. Christ is both human and divine, and divinity is not a possible object of human judgement. In terms of his existence *qua* divinity, Christ exists beyond the limits of human reason and language; thus, cognitive relations between mankind and Christ *qua* God are *impossible* (CUP 1, 217–8/SKS 7, 198–9; PC, 134/SKS 12, 138).

The last point *does not*, of course, entail that it is impossible for human beings to come into relation with God, for Kierkegaard. Yet the relation with God that human beings can come into is not one that obtains through human reason or understanding, but through Christian faith and grace. To be related to Christ *qua* God, for Kierkegaard, it is not sufficient to stand in relation to him *qua* man, but it is necessary to have faith in him and his paradoxical claim to be God. Thus, while direct relations between human beings and divinity are impossible for Kierkegaard, *indirect relations* to divinity *via* Christ's humanity are possible (indeed, not only *possible* but *necessary* if human beings are to come to stand in the right relation to God) (PC, 126–7, 134–5/SKS 12, 131–2, 138–9).

The above outlines the logic of relations between human beings and God contained in Kierkegaard's conception of the incarnation as absolute paradox. What has been little appreciated by Kierkegaard scholars is that the concept of indirect communication is a consequence of this logic of relations. To appreciate this, let us outline three claims that Kierkegaard makes about indirect communication:

(1) Indirect communication has a determinate content (PC, 125–6/SKS 12, 130–1; PF, 102/SKS 4, 299).
(2) What indirect communication relates is essentially private (CUP 1, 78–80/SKS 7, 78–80).
(3) Indirect communication is a matter of necessity (CUP 1, 73–4, 325/SKS 7, 74–5, 296–7; PC, 126–7, 134–5/SKS 12, 131–2, 138–9).

Taken together, these three claims comprise a logic of indirect communication. In conjunction these claims might be thought to be problematic (after all, how can a communication both have a determinate content and be essentially private?). Yet, when placed within the context of Kierkegaard's Christological views they can be said to be both intelligible and consistent.

Firstly, *qua* man, Christ's words can be said to have a *determinate content*. We can, in principle, agree on *what* he says, even if the meaning of those words appears ambiguous or paradoxical (claim 1). Secondly, what those words attempt to convey, or what Christ aims to achieve by them, is to bring the believer into an essentially first-personal relation of faith and grace to God. Such a relation cannot be conceptualized in terms of human reason, or expressed in the generality of human language, and so it is *essentially private* to the individual believer (claim 2). Thirdly, only *via* his human words and paradoxical claim to be God can Christ bring human beings to faith or offence at the absolute paradox, and so into the right relation to God (claim 3). For Kierkegaard, indirect communication *follows from* Christ's nature as the absolute paradox. Pattison is right, the logic of indirect communication leads all the way back to the nature of the absolute paradox. Indeed, the Christology of the absolute paradox makes Kierkegaard's apparently problematic claims about indirect communication both intelligible and consistent.

Kierkegaard's Christology, and his conception of indirect communication, gives us an alternative to the Hegelian view of how Christianity is communicated between human beings. For Kierkegaard, while it is true that Christ's human words can be incorporated into human history and culture, and passed to subsequent generations, the mere fact that these words survive in the culture is not sufficient to make the members of that culture Christian. Christ's words, rather, are said to provide the occasion for human beings to be able to come into relation with a transcendent God (PF, 100, 104/SKS 4, 297, 300–1; PC, 140–1/SKS 12, 143–4). To come into such a relation, it is necessary for a human being to respond to Christ in faith, and receive the gift of grace; the believer then comes to stand in an essentially first-personal relation of faith and grace to a supernatural God. In the face of the Hegelian view, which is said to naturalize the communication of Christianity to the mechanisms of human language, history, and culture (PF, 95–6/SKS 4, 292–4; CUP 1, 345–6, 383/SKS 7, 316–7, 349), Kierkegaard reintroduces the divine intervention of a transcendent God. One does not become Christian through culture, or the operations of reason, Kierkegaard maintains, but by responding to a supernatural God, and coming into a personal relation of faith and grace to him.

What about Socrates?

The reader is likely to have objections to the above account, which I shall now attempt to anticipate. First, the reader might object that Kierkegaard's writings contain clear examples of indirect communication that cannot be accommodated by the above account. Take, for example, the epigraph to *Fear and Trembling*: the quotation from Johan Georg Hamann, 'What Tarquinius Superbus said in the garden by means of the poppies, the son understood but the messenger did not' (FT, 3/SKS 4, 100). This epigraph, so the objection goes, is a clear example of indirect communication not grounded in Kierkegaard's Christology.

The problem with this objection is that it presupposes that the distinction between direct and indirect communication is just obvious: as if cases can simply be intuited. Yet the distinction between direct and indirect communication is not one commonly encountered outside of Kierkegaard scholarship. The concept of indirect communication is, rather, a technical one within Kierkegaard's thought; and one which he himself can be seen to be in the process of exploring and refining throughout his treatments of it. The proponents of this objection must answer how, in terms of any chosen example, direct communication is held to be *impossible* and indirect communication *necessary*. Specifically what, in such cases, plays the role of the middle term that allows indirect communication to obtain whilst simultaneously denying the possibility of direct communication? (In the case of Tarquinius' communication to his son, for example, what is communicated can, in principle, be directly stated. Yet if, to account of such cases, we move to weaken the conditions that need to be met for something to count as an instance of indirect communication, this raises the question of what sense or use there is in appealing to the term at all?) Giving a coherent answer to the above questions will, I think, prove too strong a burden of proof for its proponents to bare.

A second objection: Kierkegaard holds Socrates to be an indirect communicator. The indirect communication practised by Socrates cannot be premised on Christology, because Socrates existed pre-incarnation. In the figure of Socrates, then, we have a model by means of which we can give an account of indirect communication in a secular, or theologically naturalistic, way. To this objection the same burden of proof applies. Whence the source of necessity in such alleged indirect communication? Kierkegaard certainly takes there to be affinities between Socrates methods of communication and his own methodology, yet Socrates is a complicated and ambivalent figure in Kierkegaard's writings whom is made to play different roles. The main problem with the above objection is that what purports to be a reason why we should appeal to Socrates as a model of indirect communication is, in fact, the very reason why he cannot be so regarded. Whatever similarities Kierkegaard takes to exist between Socrates' methodology and his own, he is also clear that what is true for Socrates (in relation to truth and divinity) and what is true for he himself (and us) post-incarnation are absolutely different (CUP 1: 206/SKS 7, 188). In the *Postscript* we read:

> [T]he subject cannot be untruth eternally or be presupposed to have been untruth eternally; he must have become that in time ... *a change so essential has taken place in him that he in no way can take himself back into eternity by Socratically recollecting*. To do this is to speculate, to be able to do this but, by grasping the inward deepening in existence, *to annul the possibility of doing it is the Socratic*. But now the difficulty is that *what accompanied Socrates as an annulled possibility has become an impossibility* ...
> Let us now call the individual's untruth *sin*.
> (CUP 1: 208/SKS 7, 190–1; emphasis added)

While Socrates can, in principle, recollect the truth of his own nature, Kierkegaard is clear that for us (post-incarnation) such recollection is *impossible*. In the wake of the incarnation, and the consciousness of sin that Christ makes possible, human beings are foreclosed from divining the truth about their own natures, but must rely on a truth brought to them by God which can be arrived at only through faith and grace.

Put otherwise, for Socrates there is no break in human nature, for that break only comes with Christ's incarnation, and the consciousness of sin (CUP 1: 573, 583/SKS 7, 520, 530–31). Yet it is precisely this break which conditions the impossibility of direct communication, and demands the necessity of indirect communication. That Socrates exists pre-incarnation is, therefore, the very reason why he cannot serve as a basis on which to give an account of indirect communication for Kierkegaard (or, indeed, for us), as post-incarnation human beings.

God, history, and the Kierkegaardian mind

If the above account is correct then there is more going on in indirect communication than can be accounted for in terms of psychological or biographical detail alone. For the concept of indirect communication appears as an integral part of Kierkegaard's Christology, and of his response to what he takes to be the Hegelian-inspired theological naturalism of his contemporaries. Furthermore, it also follows that literary interpretations must fall short of being able to give an account of indirect communication, for it cannot simply be identified with or understood in terms of satire, metaphor, irony or humour.

What indirect communication demands, as we have seen, is *both* an absolute distinction *and* a necessary connection between subject and object, between words and what they mean (or the function that they are aiming to perform). No feature of natural language can both *necessarily foreclose* an interpreter from being able to understand its meaning, and yet be the *only* way in which communication can take place (which is just to say that there is no feature of natural language equivalent to the logical role that Christ plays within Kierkegaard's thought). If the literary features of language, or the literary features of Kierkegaard's works, have a role to play in our understanding indirect communication, then that can only happen when they are placed *within* the larger, more substantive theological context in which indirect communication makes sense.

Moreover, if the above reading is correct, it follows that God has an essential role to play in understanding the Kierkegaardian mind's thinking about indirect communication. For Christ serves to *both* absolutely separate *and* necessarily connect divinity and humanity, or subject and object, but not in such a way that they are mediated as a result. As such, the nature of Christ conditions the possibility of indirect relations obtaining between human beings and God, and so conditions the possibility of indirect communication. Indeed, as we have seen, the success of indirect communication is thought to depend upon the divine intervention of a transcendent and supernatural God bringing faith and grace to the Christian believer. For this reason, it is not as if we can simply subtract the figure of Christ, or Christian theology, from Kierkegaard's thinking about indirect communication and have that thinking continue to make sense to us.

If this is correct then those commentators that seek to understand Kierkegaard's methodology of indirect communication independently of his Christian theology, on an *a*historical, *a*cultural, and secular philosophical basis alone, are automatically depriving themselves of the very conceptual resources necessary to understand the logic of indirect communication. Such scholars are destined to misunderstand Kierkegaard's notion of indirect communication in virtue of their methodological presuppositions. For if we only ever approach Kierkegaard and indirect communication on the basis of assumptions that can be licenced from secular metaphysics or epistemology, then we will never arrive at the concepts necessary to understand indirect communication: the absolute paradox, a supernatural God, and the essentially first-personal nature of faith. To approaches such as these the Kierkegaardian mind must remain forever closed.

Related topics

'Johannes Climacus and the dialectical method: from dialectics back to existence,' Claudine Davidshofer; 'On faith and reason(s): Kierkegaard's logic of conviction,' K. Brian Söderquist.

References

Conant, J. (1995) 'Putting two and two together: Kierkegaard, Wittgenstein, and the point of view for their work as authors,' in T. Tessin and M. von der Ruhr (eds), *Philosophy and the Grammar of Religious Belief*, London: Palgrave Macmillan.
Conant, J. (1993) 'Kierkegaard, Wittgenstein, and nonsense,' in T. Cohen, P. Guyer and H. Putnam (eds), *Pursuits of Reason*, Lubbock, TX: Texas Tech University Press.
Conant, J. (1989) 'Must we show what we cannot say?' in R. Fleming and M. Payne (eds), *The Senses of Stanley Cavell*, Lewisburg, PA: Bucknell University Press.
Emmanuel, S. M. (1996) *Kierkegaard and the concept of revelation*, New York: State University of New York Press.
Evans, C. S. (1983) *Kierkegaard's 'Fragments' and 'Postscript': The religious philosophy of Johannes Climacus*, Atlantic Highlands, NJ: Humanities Press International.
Fredsted, E. (1998) 'On semantic and pragmatic ambiguity,' *Journal of Pragmatics*, 30, no. 5: 527–41.
Garff, J. (2005) *Søren Kierkegaard: A biography*, Princeton, NJ: Princeton University Press.
Gurray, C. (1990) 'Faith and the possibility of private meaning,' *Religious Studies*, 26: 199–05.
Heiberg, J. L. (2005) *Heiberg's on the significance of philosophy for the present age and other texts*, S. Stewart (trans), Copenhagen: C. A. Reitzel.
Lippitt, J. (2000) *Humour and irony in Kierkegaard's thought*, London: Palgrave Macmillan.
McInerny, R. (1956) 'Ethics and persuasion: Kierkegaard's existential dialectic,' *The Modern Schoolman*, 33: 219–39.
Mooney, E. F. (1997) 'Exemplars, inwardness, and belief: Kierkegaard on indirect communication,' in R. L. Perkins (ed), *International Kierkegaard Commentary*, vol. 12 (*Concluding Unscientific Postscript to 'Philosophical Fragments'*), Macon, GA: Mercer University Press.
Mynster, J. P. (2009) *Mynster's 'Rationalism, supernaturalism' and the debate about mediation*, J. Stewart (trans), Copenhagen: Museum Tusculanum Press.
Pattison, G. (1992) *Kierkegaard: The aesthetic and the religious*, London: Palgrave Macmillan.
Pons, J. (2004) *Stealing a gift: Kierkegaard's pseudonyms and the Bible*, New York: Fordham University Press.
Ramsland, K. M. (1987) 'Grice and Kierkegaard: Implication and communication,' *Philosophy and Phenomenological Research*, 48: 327–34.
Schönbamsfeld, G. (2007) *A confusion of the spheres: Kierkegaard and Wittgenstein on philosophy and religion*, Oxford: Oxford University Press.
Solomon, R. C. (1987) *From Hegel to existentialism*, Oxford: Oxford University Press.
Stewart, J. (2015) *The cultural crisis of the Danish golden age: Heiberg, Martensen and Kierkegaard*, Copenhagen: Museum Tusculanum Press.
Stewart, J. (2007a) *A history of Hegelianism in golden age Denmark*, tome I (*The Heiberg Period: 1824–1836*), Copenhagen: C. A. Reitzel.
Stewart, J. (2007b) *A history of Hegelianism in golden age Denmark*, tome II (*The Martensen Period: 1837–1842*), Copenhagen: C. A. Reitzel.
Stewart, J. (2003) *Kierkegaard's relations to Hegel reconsidered*, Cambridge: Cambridge University Press.

Further reading

Mynster, J. P. (2009) *Mynster's 'rationalism, supernaturalism' and the debate about mediation*, J. Stewart (trans), Copenhagen: Museum Tusculanum Press.

This is a translation into English of some of the sources comprising the rationalism/supernaturalism debate, and the debate about mediation, in the Danish literature of the 1830s and 1840s. It is an important historical resource in understanding the context of Kierkegaard's thinking about indirect communication.

Turnbull, J. (2014) 'Communication/indirect communication,' in S. M. Emmanuel, W. McDonald and J. Stewart (eds), *Kierkegaard Research: Sources, Reception and Resources*, vol. 15 (*Kierkegaard's Concepts*), tome 2, Farnham: Ashgate.

This is an overview of Kierkegaard's different treatments of indirect communication, and the connections and differences between them, as they appear in *Concluding Unscientific Postscript, Practice in Christianity* and *The Point of View*.

Turnbull, J. (2013) 'Is Socrates Kierkegaard's 'natural man'?' in R. Králik, A. Khan, P. Šajda, J. Turnbull and A. Burgess (eds), *Acta Kierkegaardiana*, vol. 6 (*Kierkegaard and Human Nature*), Slovakia: Kierkegaard Society in Slovakia & Kierkegaard Circle.

This paper examines the attempt to use Socrates as a guide to interpreting Kierkegaard's view of human nature. It argues that, for Kierkegaard, Socrates (as a *pre*–Christian pagan) cannot be used as a model to understand what is natural for *post*–incarnation human beings.

Turnbull, J. (2009) 'Kierkegaard's religious, and our methodological, crisis,' in R. Králik, A. Khan, P. Šajda, J. Turnbull and A. Burgess (eds), *Acta Kierkegaardiana*, vol. 4 (*Kierkegaard and the Religious Crisis in Europe*), Slovakia: Kierkegaard Society in Slovakia & Kierkegaard Circle.

This paper draws out some of the consequences of Kierkegaard's notion of subjectivity as essentially private for the attempt to read him in philosophical, or naturalistic, terms alone.

PART 2
Ethics

5
ETHICAL REFLECTION AS EVASION

Rob Compaijen and Pieter Vos

Introduction

Human beings are reflective creatures. Our capacity for reflection enables us to turn our attention towards our beliefs, feelings, intuitions, expectations, circumstances, and so forth, and allows us to (temporarily) detach ourselves from them. Not only is this capacity a structural feature of our existence, we also deem it important. While Socrates' remark that the unexamined life is not worth living (Plato 1997: 38a5–6) might be too radical,[1] most of us feel that a life well-lived typically includes significant reflective activity. Ethics, as the systematic reflection on morality, is one area in human existence which clearly demonstrates our reflective capacities. Ethical reflection is generally considered to be of crucial importance. Through reflection we are able to examine the legitimacy of our moral beliefs: reflection might show us that our moral beliefs are (or are informed by) harmful prejudices. Reflection, that is, enables us to revise or improve our moral beliefs. Moreover, ethical reflection enables us to ease or perhaps even solve moral uncertainty. During our lives, most of us will (at least sometimes) feel uncertain about ethically salient choices. We ask questions such as 'how should I live?' or 'what should I, here and now, do?' Ethical reflection, it seems, can help us to come up with plausible answers to such questions.

In light of these observations, it is fascinating that Kierkegaard is suspicious of ethical reflection as we have described it so far.[2] While he values our reflective capacities, he is, at the same time, wary of its tendency towards disengagement and procrastination. On Kierkegaard's view, ethical reflection can be – and, as a matter of fact, frequently *is* – a clever way of evading ethical action and life. This is a topic that is sometimes noted in the literature on Kierkegaard's thought, but has not been explored very systematically. The present contribution will attempt to make sense of Kierkegaard's idea that ethical reflection tends to involve evasion, and we do so by drawing primarily (though not exclusively) on his unpublished 1847 lectures 'The Dialectic of Ethical and Ethical-Religious Communication.' Although unfinished and generally lacking structure, these notes and lectures provide us with several important ideas that help us make sense of Kierkegaard's views on this issue. They also shed light on what Kierkegaard believes ethics should be concerned with, as well as on the kinds of reflection in ethics that he does regard as valuable.

The outline of this chapter is as follows. First, we will clarify in which respects Kierkegaard believes ethical reflection is an evasion. Subsequently, we will explore how Kierkegaard characterizes the task that is central to ethics, and the kinds of reflection that he argues are appropriate to that task. In the conclusion we will make clear in which respects Kierkegaard's thoughts on these matters are important for contemporary moral philosophy, but we will also point out that they themselves can involve an evasion.

Misunderstanding ethics: knowledge and disengagement

Despite the value we generally acknowledge ethical reflection to have, there is something peculiar about it. As *ethical* reflection, it is essentially directed towards the domain of practice, dealing with action, choice, and existence. As ethical *reflection*, however, it moves in the opposite direction, away from practical life. We take it that this 'ambivalent' nature of ethical reflection forms the background of Kierkegaard's suspicion of it. Elaborating this line of thought, David Gouwens (1996: 32) argues that the problem with ethical reflection for Kierkegaard is more specifically the application of the kind of reflection that is appropriate in the sciences to ethical questions: 'The difficulty with Western philosophical thought, for Kierkegaard, is that the model of objective reflection, which is ... quite within its rights in certain realms such as science, is inappropriately applied to the realm of subjectivity (particularly ethics and religion).'

In 'The Dialectic of Ethical and Ethical-Religious Communication,' Kierkegaard confirms this analysis with the following bold claim: 'The whole modern science of ethics is, ethically understood, an evasion' (JP 1, 269/SKS 27, 393). Kierkegaard's critique of ethical reflection as being evasive seems to be strongly related to the idea that ethics, in modernity, is typically regarded as a science. We find further confirmation of this idea in other notes, where he refers to the modern tendency of 'physics supplanting ethics' and the distinctly 'modern statistical approach to morality' (JP 1, 408/SKS 18, 281). In 'The Dialectic of Ethical and Ethical-Religious Communication,' Kierkegaard does not explain how he understands the notion of 'science.' (He uses '*videnskab*,' a term that is cognate with the German '*Wissenschaft*' and has a broader application than the English 'science,' which usually refers to the natural, and sometimes the social, sciences.) It seems plausible that he is thinking of specifically two features. First, science can be understood as a sophisticated and systematic attempt to acquire knowledge. Second, to be able to do that adequately, it should detach itself to a greater or lesser degree from the particular standpoint and the lived experience of the scientist(s). It is important to see that the degree of detachment that is deemed fitting differs among the various sciences: most people will agree that, for example, the radical objectivity of the standpoint of theoretical physics is inappropriate for social psychology. Nevertheless, each of the sciences aspires to adopt a standpoint that is as objective as seems adequate to acquire knowledge in its respective field of study.

Kierkegaard's claim that ethical reflection can be a clever way of evading ethical action and life thus seems to involve two important ideas. First, ethical reflection can be an evasion when it is taken to be a process in which the reflective agent radically *detaches* herself from (what we could call) her 'existential situation.' Second, it can be an evasion when it is directed towards *acquiring knowledge* that will enable the agent to answer the questions of what one should do or how one should live. But what exactly does Kierkegaard mean when he suggests that, in modernity, ethics is concerned with aspiring towards a disengaged standpoint as well as with acquiring knowledge?

Kierkegaard writes that modernity deeply misunderstands the ethical (JP 1, 269/SKS 27, 392), and the misunderstanding seems intimately related to both of the features that we have mentioned. There is, first, the misunderstanding that the ethical should be approached in a spirit of disengagement. Johannes Climacus makes this clear in *Concluding Unscientific Postscript*. Ethical questions, he writes, are 'concerned questions' (CUP 1, 193/SKS 7, 177). Attempting to answer questions like 'what should I do?' or 'how should I live?' should therefore not involve adopting a detached viewpoint in which that concern has vaporized. Or, put another way, the answers that will appear adequate and satisfying from a detached standpoint cannot be meaningfully related to the existential situation of the agent who asks such questions. Expressing this insight, Climacus writes: 'All decision, all essential decision, is rooted in subjectivity. At no point does an observer ... have an infinite need for a decision, and at no point does he see it' (CUP 1, 33/SKS 7, 39).

Second, for Kierkegaard, modernity's misunderstanding of the ethical is even more obvious in light of its idea that ethics should be concerned with acquiring knowledge. He argues that, while science is concerned with the transition from ignorance to knowledge, ethical thought (when understood correctly) is concerned with the transition from knowledge to realization (JP 1, 271/SKS 27, 394). What that means is something we will explore in the next section. Modern thought – in arguing, according to Kierkegaard, that the primary task of ethics is to acquire knowledge – presupposes that human beings *lack* the knowledge they need to be able to live ethically. Kierkegaard challenges this presupposition and argues that human beings already possess the ethical (CUP 1, 144/SKS 7, 134; JP 1, 271/SKS 27, 394). The idea that we already possess the ethical can be unpacked in different ways, but one crucial element is the idea that we already possess all ethical *knowledge*: in some sense (to be explored further), we already know what to do and how to live.

Does Kierkegaard provide us with some kind of background theory for the idea that we already possess the ethical in this sense? The idea itself should remind us of Plato's Socrates, who famously claimed that we already possess all knowledge, although we have forgotten most of it. He invoked the idea that the soul, before being united with the body, gathered all knowledge in the world of Ideas. Kierkegaard does not endorse this 'theory,' but in 'The Dialectic of Ethical and Ethical-Religious Communication' we do find two indications that might help us understand what he means. The first is his claim that, with regard to ethics, God is our only teacher (JP 1, 272–3/SKS 27, 395–6). Kierkegaard observes that, just as Prometheus provided human beings with knowledge of good and evil, God provided us with the ethical. The second is that we can only make sense of our experience of ethical obligation when we believe that we already possess the ethical. 'The ethical presupposes that every person knows what the ethical is, and why? Because the ethical demands that every man shall realize it at every moment, but then he surely has to know it' (JP 1, 271/SKS 27, 394).[3] Kierkegaard's reasoning, which seems to boil down to 'ought implies knowing,' can therefore be interpreted as an allusion to the Kantian phrase '*Du kannst, denn du sollst*' ('ought implies can'). Just like Kant argued that our experience of being bound to the moral law teaches us that we are capable of acting in accordance with the moral law, Kierkegaard seems to argue that this experience teaches us that we already possess all the knowledge that is required for living ethically.

What does Kierkegaard mean when he says that we already possess all ethical knowledge? We can unpack this idea as follows: either we actually know everything there is to know with regard to what to do and how to live, or we possess it but somehow do not have immediate access to all of it. Kierkegaard does not make clear which of these views he ascribes to, but it seems plausible to suppose that he believes the latter. After all, the idea that we *actually* know all ethical knowledge seems very unlikely in light of the fact that we can be genuinely uncertain about what we should do or choose. Moreover, that Kierkegaard holds the latter view is also suggested by his indebtedness to Socrates – an indebtedness which, of course, is particularly clear with regard to the ethical. On a Socratic view, human beings already possess all knowledge, but since they have forgotten most of it, they need to be brought to remembrance about it. In like manner, Kierkegaard seems to hold that, although we already possess the ethical, we need to come to know ourselves in order to actually come to know what to do and how to live (JP 1, 269/SKS 27, 393). (We will explore the role of self-knowledge in these matters below.)

One might argue, however, that moral pluralism – which we understand here as the diversity of moral beliefs among individuals and groups – undermines the idea that we already possess all ethical knowledge. This is a route sometimes taken by Kierkegaard scholars. Objecting that Kierkegaard's critique of ethical reflection betrays 'a stunning blindness to the possibilities of genuine disagreement,' Patrick Stokes (2013: 379) makes clear that he assumes Kierkegaard to believe that we all possess the exact same ethical knowledge. This is also suggested by Mark Tietjen (2013: 54) who argues that, for Kierkegaard, the idea that we already possess the ethical implies that each of us possesses 'innate, universal ethical knowledge.' Yet, Kierkegaard nowhere suggests that this is what he has in mind. Rather, he seems to argue that each of us in a sense already knows what to do and how to live, whether this knowledge matches the knowledge of others or not.

However, moral pluralism in the sense explicated above can give rise to fundamental doubt: how could we ever reach certainty about what to do and how to live when these questions are answered in so many different ways? Kierkegaard is aware of this line of thought and phrases it as follows: 'If someone were to say: There are quite different concepts of the ethical in different countries and in different ages. How is this doubt halted?' (JP 1, 271/SKS 27, 394). Kierkegaard responds to this worry by acknowledging that, from a scientific or scholarly point of view, the doubt cannot be halted because we will never be able to complete our survey of all the different moral beliefs in the world. He writes that this issue 'can result in scholarly folios and still not stop' (JP 1, 271/SKS 27, 394). The uncertainty whether my answers to ethical questions are the *right* answers therefore cannot be dismissed from a scientific or scholarly point of view. However, Kierkegaard makes it very clear that, from the point of view of the ethical, the uncertainty can be taken away: 'the ethical seizes the doubter with ethical consistency and says, what concern is it of yours? You shall do the ethical at every moment, and you are ethically responsible for every moment you waste' (JP 1, 271/SKS 27, 394). According to this remarkable line of thought, the diversity of moral beliefs in the world is completely irrelevant from an ethical point of view, since we already possess the ethical within ourselves: we already know what to do and how to live.

We are now in the position to understand what Kierkegaard means when he writes that '[t]he whole modern science of ethics is, ethically understood, an evasion' (JP 1, 269/SKS 27, 393). This becomes most clear in light of his conception of what the task of ethics should be. For Kierkegaard, since we already possess all the ethical knowledge we require, ethics should be concerned only with 'realization' – that is, with choosing, acting, becoming, and existing. When ethics, on the other hand, is conceived as a scientific endeavour, ethical reflection is an evasion because – by seeking to acquire ethical knowledge and (in so doing) aspiring to adopt a standpoint that is disconnected from the existential situation of the agent – it makes us inattentive to the task of actually *living* ethically. Ethical reflection, understood along these lines, makes us neglect the concrete ethical tasks, responsibilities, and choices that we face and that we in a sense already know how to respond to.

Numerous texts in Kierkegaard's authorship give witness to these evasive movements. For example, a substantial part of *Concluding Unscientific Postscript* is devoted to Climacus' argument that subjectivity and (thereby) the ethical are lost when viewed from a detached standpoint, '*sub specie aeterni*' as he describes it (e.g. CUP 1, 305/SKS 7, 277–8). Arguing that the movement of detachment is essentially different from what the ethical demands, he writes: 'The demand of abstraction upon him is that he become disinterested in order to obtain something to know; the requirement of the ethical upon him is to be infinitely interested in existing' (CUP 1, 316/SKS 7, 288). Note also how Climacus relates the issue of detachment to the issue of acquiring knowledge. With regard to the latter, consider for example the following, paradigmatic passage:

> How many an individual has not asked, 'What is truth?' and at bottom hoped that it would be a long time before truth would come so close to him that in the same instant it would determine what it was his duty to do at that moment. When the Pharisee, 'in order to justify himself' asked, 'Who is my neighbor?' he presumably thought that this might develop into a very protracted inquiry, so that it would perhaps take a long time and then perhaps end with the admission that it was impossible to define the concept 'neighbor' with absolute accuracy – for this very reason he asked the question, to find an escape, to waste time, and to justify himself.
>
> (WL, 96–7/SKS 9, 101)[4]

Another clear example is in *For Self-Examination*, where Kierkegaard regards the academic study of Scripture as an evasion (FSE, 32/SKS 13, 59–60). Scripture, Kierkegaard argues, summons us to read it as a mirror: one has to read it so as to understand what it means for one's life and to discern the things that one is commanded to do. A clever way to refrain from doing that is to focus on the parts of Scripture that one does not (yet) understand, and to demand more time and books: only when one has understood Scripture completely, one is willing to act in accordance with it.

At this point, the reader might feel irritated. 'Surely, doing the right thing requires us to ask such questions as, for example, "who is my neighbour?" and "what is Scripture demanding exactly?" If Kierkegaard dismisses such questions as evasive, he is oversimplifying!' Although the topic of this article has not received much systematic attention in the literature about Kierkegaard, the authors who display sensitivity to this aspect of his thought tend to express this sentiment. Consider the following two examples. Referring to doubts about the right course of action in applying the ideal of neighbour-love, John Lippitt (2013: 5) writes, 'Such considerations suggest that not every reflection on what my duty implies in a particular case (or every request for more information) can be dismissed with the haste Kierkegaard sometimes betrays in the face of such questions.' A particularly clear example is Patrick Stokes' (2013: 378–9) critique of Kierkegaard, which, in a similar vein, objects that reflective questions are legitimate and inevitable:

> In *Christian Discourses* he insists that there should never be a question about what my duty *is* but simply about whether I have done my duty [CD, 205/SKS 10, 214], and that asking such questions about the content of duty is therefore simply an evasion of the demand to *do* my duty. In *For Self-Examination* we are told that it is an evasion to continue to try to understand the content of Scripture completely, rather than seeking to carry out those of its demands one *has* understood, however imperfectly [FSE, 32/SKS 13, 59–60]. Yet 'what is my duty here?' and 'what precisely does Scripture require of those who believe in its moral authority?' seem to be perfectly philosophically (and theologically and philologically) respectable questions – even ones that might be essential to practical reason. Kierkegaard seems to betray both an over-confidence in the clarity of scripture and a stunning blindness to the possibilities of genuine moral disagreement.

Lippitt's and Stokes' critiques seem to suggest that Kierkegaard is completely dismissive of reflection in ethics. And perhaps our analysis so far has suggested the same. However, we do not think that Kierkegaard is critical of every kind of reflection with regard to the ethical. Rather, we follow Gouwens in his illuminating analysis of Kierkegaard's views on (and critique of) reflection. Gouwens (1996: 31) argues that the reason Kierkegaard dismisses certain kinds of ethical (and religious) reflection is related to their 'direction.' Kierkegaard distinguishes between 'subjective' and 'objective reflection,' and the latter implies 'a direction of thought away from the self' (Gouwens 1996: 33). This is clear with regard to the two aspects of Kierkegaard's critique of ethical reflection that we have highlighted: both the tendency towards disengagement, and the attempt to acquire additional knowledge direct ethical reflection away from the agent and his or her existential situation. If Kierkegaard acknowledges the importance of another kind of ethical reflection, it will have to have a direction towards the agent's self.

Existential ethics: education, double-reflection, and self-knowledge

The analysis in the previous section raises two important questions. First, what *is* the proper task of ethics? As we have seen, ethics should not be understood as having the task of acquiring ('external') knowledge in a disengaged way, but instead, ethics is concerned with 'realization' – with enabling people to live ethically. But what does that mean? Second, does Kierkegaard dismiss every kind of ethical reflection, or is there a kind of ethical reflection that he does allow for?

Ethics as learning to use one's potential competence

In his notes on communication, Kierkegaard importantly argues that the ethical should not be communicated as science or scholarship (which is the confusion of the modern age) but as an art. How is the idea of ethics as an art to be understood? The basic elements of such 'art' can be clarified with reference to an example that Kierkegaard himself uses: the educational process of a country boy becoming a soldier. The corporal who has the task of turning the country lad into a soldier 'does not explain to the soldier what it is to drill, etc.; he communicates it to him as an art, he *teaches* him to use militarily the abilities and the *potential competence* he already has' (JP 1, 269/SKS 27, 392; emphasis added). This example indicates that the proper ethical task is to teach and to learn to use one's potential competence. This includes at least three basic elements.

First, it means that the ethical has the character of *competence* or capability (*Dygtighed*), and more specifically, 'oughtness-capability' (*Skullen-Kunne*) (JP 1, 307/SKS 27, 434), in the sense that one becomes able to do what one ought to do. The ethical is an unconditional 'to be obliged,' and therefore it is not dependent on particular conditions and differences between people. Since the ethical is related to the universally human, every human being is already 'in possession of the capacity to be able to do it if only he wanted to,' as Kierkegaard states elsewhere in his notebooks (KJN 6, 74/SKS 22, 78). The ethical is a competence or capability in the sense of *knowing how to use* what one already possesses. The proper ethical task is to develop this capability, not to acquire ethical knowledge.

Second, the ethical competence one already possesses is *potential*; that is, it is not something which is already completely given in the sense that no further efforts are needed. Rather, it is possible that it will remain only potential. Just as the country lad is not yet a soldier, the human being by nature is not yet an 'ethical' being. This is why Kierkegaard states that the ethical consists in *realizing* what one already knows. The ethical task is to actualize what is potentially available.

Third, this is to be accomplished by a particular kind of education, which can be qualified as *training* and *formation*. Continuing the metaphor of the army, Kierkegaard explains what this means: 'Science probably can be pounded into a person, but the ethical has to be pounded out of him – just as the corporal, precisely because he sees the soldier in the farm boy, might say: I certainly will have to pound the soldier out of him; on the other hand, with respect to the manual of field tactics (what an army is, what sentry duty is, etc.) the corporal might say: Well, that will have to be pounded into him' (JP 1, 269–70/SKS 27, 392). The ethical potential of the human being is in need of formation in order to become 'truly human' (JP 1, 269/SKS 27, 393). Elsewhere in 'The Dialectic of Ethical and Ethical-Religious Communication,' Kierkegaard speaks of upbringing (*Opdragelse*), by which one becomes what one essentially is regarded to be (JP 1, 279/SKS 27, 402). Understood in this way, ethics is basically concerned with the moral formation of what is potentially given. The aim is 'luring the ethical out of the individual, because it is *in* the individual. The corporal begins essentially by regarding the farm boy as a soldier, because he is this κατα δυναμιν [*kata dynamin*, "in potential"]' (JP 1, 269/SKS 27, 392).

Self-knowledge and double-reflection

The second question is whether the ideas that we already know the ethical and that ethical reflection is an evasion imply the complete exclusion of any kind of reflection. We will defend the claim that Kierkegaard does not object to ethical reflection as such, only to a particular kind of ethical reflection, which he labels as 'scientific,' as we have seen. Since according to Kierkegaard ethics is not a science but an art, the kind of reflection that is adequate to such an understanding of ethics may be warranted. We will call this 'existential ethical reflection.'

In his notes and lectures on communication an alternative reflection is indeed suggested, for instance when Kierkegaard states: 'relatively little knowledge is needed to be truly human – but all the more self-knowledge' (JP 1, 279/SKS 27, 402). These phrases indicate that not all knowledge and reflection is excluded from the ethical. Not only is a little ethical knowledge needed, just as the soldier must know something of the army and its sentry duty from the manual of field tactics, but also and decisively a different kind of reflection is needed: self-knowledge. Since self-knowledge should be distinguished from the kind of knowledge that is important in the scientific understanding of ethics, Kierkegaard comes to the paradoxical statement that '[i]nsofar as the ethical could be said to have a knowledge in itself, it is 'self-knowledge,' but this is improperly regarded as a knowledge' (JP 1, 289/SKS 27, 417). The ethical is knowledge in the sense of 'self-knowledge,' but is not knowledge in the sense of 'information.' What is decisive is not information about ethical concepts and theories, but becoming aware of what I must do in my existential situation. Kierkegaard qualifies this as 'primitivity,' knowing 'what it means to be a human being' (JP 1, 268/SKS 27, 391). When a boy gathers information about the army and studies the manual of field tactics this does not yet make him a soldier. What is needed is to *exist* as a soldier. Only then – as 'self-knowledge' – does his knowledge about the army make sense.

Similarly, from the perspective of the *ethicist* ethical knowledge is not wholly abandoned, but still a further reflection is needed to cure what Gouwens (1996: 27–54) calls 'the disease of reflection' in ethics. In this disease of reflection, 'seeking to live ethically' becomes reduced to the study of 'ethics.' In this way it is no longer understood as a quest for the good, a striving, but an objective enterprise, as we have seen. Rather than being engaged in the question 'how then shall I live?' one becomes absorbed in an ethical 'ideal' or 'issue.' This can be described as the failure to live in the concepts one reflects on (Gouwens 1996: 33–4). The remedy is to bring 'reflection back from inhuman abstraction and forgetfulness to the concrete concerns of existence'

(Gouwens 1996: 43). The concern is not only with the ethical object of thought, but also with how the ethicist relates to the object of thought. Kierkegaard calls such ethicist an 'existing ethicist' (*Existerende Ethiker*). The existing ethicist is still an ethicist, but an ethicist working in the way of the corporal, a maieutic who 'pounds' the ethical 'out' not only of the other but also of himself. This requires a particular reflection. The existing ethicist 'remains conscious of himself and in reflection returns into himself to be that which he teaches, and he presupposes – that every human being is the same κατα δυναμιν [*kata dynamin*, "in potential"]' (JP 1, 269/SKS 27, 392). Here reflection is not in a disengaged way directed to an object (ethics as a science), but one's own life is reflected into ethics. The task is to live within the concepts one reflects on. Following this line of thought, we could say that the ethical questions 'what is duty?' or 'what is the good life?' become transformed into 'what should *I* do?' and 'how should *I* live?'

It is not without meaning that Kierkegaard calls 'living within what one thinks' 'double-reflection.' In this sense the ethical seems to require even *more* reflection than the modern ethics he attacks. In his notes on communication Kierkegaard describes double-reflection in the following cryptic way: 'the first is the reflection in which the communication is made, and the second is that in which it is recaptured' (JP 1, 274/SKS 27, 397). Elsewhere in his works we find more extensive descriptions, for instance: 'When a thought has gained its proper expression in the world, which is attained through the first reflection, there comes the second reflection, which bears upon the intrinsic relation of the communication to the communicator and renders the existing communicator's own relation to the idea' (CUP 1, 76/SKS 7, 77). Taking these two descriptions together the first reflection is the sphere in which an idea is communicated. This presupposes that the communicator links himself to both the communicated thought and its form. In the second reflection the communicator reflects on the first reflection, which makes it possible to attain an attitude towards the communicated truth (Kaftanski 2014). This kind of reflection prevents the ethicist from evasion because in the second reflection the question becomes how he or she is related to what is communicated.

That reflection is intensified rather than diminished also becomes clear in how thinking functions in Kierkegaard's understanding of the subjective existing thinker. Characteristic of such a subjective thinker is that he is 'an existing person, and yet he is a thinking person. He does not abstract from existence and from the contradiction, but is in them, and yet he is supposed to think. In all his thinking, then, he has to include the thought that he himself is an existing person' (CUP 1, 351/SKS 7, 321). This makes ethical reflection more demanding. As Climacus remarks, whereas 'one is soon finished' with humanity in general and 'with faith viewed abstractly,' one 'will find it inexhaustible when his faith is to be declined in the manifold *casibus* [cases] of life' (CUP 1, 351/SKS 7, 321). Applied to the question to what extent ethical reflection is part of ethics understood as an art, we could say that such reflection becomes more difficult. 'Instead of having the task of understanding the concrete abstractly, as abstract thinking has, the subjective thinker has the opposite task of understanding the abstract concretely' (CUP 1, 352/SKS 7, 322). This suggests that abstract and systematic ethical thinking – e.g. thinking about the good, ethical principles, duty etc. – is not abandoned, but that something decisive is added: what the abstract means in one's own concrete existence, that is, in the manifold cases of life.

Conclusion

The kind of ethical reflection Kierkegaard positively aims for is reflection which is essentially related to one's own 'existential situation.' Ethics does not consist in leaving the subjective behind in order to seek objective ethical truths. There is always something at stake in ethical reflection. In the Kierkegaardian sense the question is: 'what concern is it of yours?' (JP 1, 271/ SKS 27, 394). How am I involved in asking the ethical question at stake?

We can probably extend this analysis to ethical reflection as it nowadays takes place in all kinds of contexts. Although ethics can be practised as an abstract, theoretical endeavour, this is not its ultimate goal. If we would understand ethics in this way it is indeed an evasion from the real questions of life. Rather, in asking questions like 'do we have an obligation to assist people who regard their life as "fulfilled" in committing suicide?' or 'is genetic engineering of stem cells allowed?' there is something at stake. The questions are asked because of a certain urgency, for instance because people actually regard their life as fulfilled and ask for such assistance, or because the option to cure a genetic disease by way of genetic engineering is medically possible and felt as morally desirable. Ethical reflection with regard to thought experiments such as the trolley problem,[5] on the other hand, typically lacks urgency because the scenario is not related to our existential situation. (We usually do not find ourselves next to a fat man on a railroad bridge, deliberating whether it would be best to throw him off so as to prevent the killing of five people working down the railroad track.) Reflecting on such issues is not genuine ethics. It has only a limited worth (which does not mean it is completely worthless). Kierkegaard reminds us time and again that devoting oneself to such issues may become an evasion if we limit ourselves to them. What matters in ethics is not asking these questions or developing (the correct) theory, but helping to understand the real questions of moral life. In genuine ethical reflection there is always something at stake. Ethical reflection is existential in nature. The task is to think the abstract in the concrete.

On the other hand, Kierkegaard's emphasis on self-knowledge and self-reflection runs the risk of becoming evasive as well. This becomes clear in, for example, the second lecture of 'The Dialectic of Ethical and Ethical-Religious Communication' where he distinguishes the reflection of the primitive person from the reflection of the person who lacks such primitivity. The primitive person is concerned about the issue of 'what it is to be a human being' (JP 1, 304/ SKS 27, 431). Yet, it seems that in focusing on this issue the ethical reflection can remain abstract. 'A man in whom there is not much primitivity will come to consider the question of which girl he should marry. He will reflect: There is a choice, and the question is – which girl? The more primitive person perhaps will so immerse himself in the question of what reality there is in marrying that he never gets married' (JP 1, 305/SKS 27, 431–2). It seems that according to Kierkegaard the question should not be about which girl I should marry but, rather, about whether I should marry or not. However, in our view the latter question may be as abstract as the former. A concrete question would be: what does it mean to marry this particular girl I already love? Similarly, according to Kierkegaard, with regard to getting a professional position the more primitive person would 'so immerse himself in the question of whether this mode of existence is essential for man that he never gets a position' (JP 1, 305/SKS 27, 432). Contrary to what one would expect given his intention to think the abstract concretely, Kierkegaard phrases this question as a general question 'for man' about 'this mode of existence.' However, is not the question about my particular calling, whether *I* should remain a religious author or become a pastor, for instance, much more concrete than asking what is 'essential'? Concrete responsibility is not just about the question whether one is existing in what one thinks, but also about what the particular situation in which I am involved requires from me. Or to phrase it in other words, thinking the abstract concretely means not only to relate one's thinking permanently to one's own existence, but also to take the particularity of the *casibus* of life into consideration as *my* concern. The examples Kierkegaard provides of how existential ethics may work tend to evade concrete responsibility that comes with real contradictions in life. In *Works of Love*, for instance, the nature of neighbour-love is spelled out. All emphasis is on the interiority of the *how*, not on the *what*. This becomes clear in the way he explains mercifulness as a deed of love. That mercifulness is a deed of love does not mean that it consists particularly of *doing* those things that relieve people from their needs. Mercifulness is rather to be understood as an inner quality of love; 'then generosity will follow of itself and come to itself accordingly as the individual is capable of it' (WL, 315/SKS 9, 312–3). The focus on neighbour-love as an inner quality can also distract us from actually doing what is needed in a concrete situation, namely helping this particular other in this particular situation. According to Kierkegaard, '*being able* to be merciful certainly is a far greater perfection than to have money and then *to be able* to give' (WL, 317/SKS 9, 314). Nevertheless, shouldn't we say that in some situations it still matters more to give *actually* than to be *able* to be merciful? Concrete ethical responsibility can be evaded by limiting oneself to reflections on the *how* of the ethical obligation. The *what* may be an equally or even more urgent part of the ethical task to think the abstract in the concrete.

Related topics

'Consciousness, self, and reflection,' Patrick Stokes; 'The passion of Kierkegaard's existential method,' Lee C. Barrett.

Notes

1. Compare Iris Murdoch's (1970: 1) famous remark that 'an unexamined life can be virtuous.'
2. It is important to note that, while Kierkegaard is attentive to the capacity and phenomenon we describe in terms of 'reflection,' he himself uses the notion of 'reflection' in different senses throughout his authorship. See, for example, Robert C. Roberts' (1984) and Patrick Stokes' (2010: 35–40) work on this topic.
3. See also Kierkegaard's remark: 'For if I am supposed to get to know something first of all, then this 'shall' is not foremost, not absolute' (JP 1, 285/SKS 27, 409).
4. Dietrich Bonhoeffer (2015: 37) discusses a similar line of thought in *The Cost of Discipleship* ('*Nachfolge*'), where he claims that '[a]ll along the line we are trying to evade the obligation of single-minded, literal obedience.' He gives the following example of our reflective tendency to evasion in Christianity: 'If a father sends his child to bed, the boy knows at once what he has to do. But suppose he has picked up a smattering of pseudo-theology. In that case he would argue more or less like this: "Father tells me to go to bed, but he really means that I am tired, and he does not want me to be tired. I can overcome my tiredness just as well if I go out and play. Therefore though father tells me to go to bed, he really means: 'Go out and play'"' (Bonhoeffer 2015: 37).
5. The trolley problem is an influential thought experiment introduced by Philippa Foot (1967) in ethical theory. In its original version, it asks us to imagine a scenario where we are standing next to a lever close to a railroad. A runaway trolley is speeding our way. We notice that a little further down the railroad tracks five people are tied up. There is a sidetrack to which we can divert the trolley by pulling the lever. However, on the sidetrack there is one person tied to the railroad tracks. The question the thought experiment wants us to reflect on is: should we pull the lever?

References

Bonhoeffer, D. (2015) *The cost of discipleship*, R. H. Fuller and I. Booth (trans), London: SCM Press.
Foot, P. (1967) 'The problem of abortion and the doctrine of the double effect,' *Oxford Review*, 5: 5–15.
Gouwens, D. (1996) *Kierkegaard as religious thinker*, Cambridge: Cambridge University Press.
Kaftanski, W. (2014) 'Double-Reflection,' in S. Emmanuel, W. McDonald and J. Stewart (eds), *Kierkegaard Research: Sources, Reception and Sources*, vol. 15 (*Kierkegaard's Concepts*), tome 2, Farnham: Ashgate.
Lippitt, J. (2013) *Kierkegaard and the problem of self-love*, Cambridge: Cambridge University Press.
Murdoch, I. (1970) *The sovereignty of good*, London: Routledge & Kegan Paul.

Plato (1997) 'Apology,' in J. M. Cooper and D. S. Hutchinson (eds), G. M. A. Grube (trans), *Complete Works*, Indianapolis, IN: Hackett Publishing Company.

Roberts, R. C. (1984) 'Passion and reflection,' in R. L. Perkins (ed), *International Kierkegaard Commentary*, vol. 14 (*Two Ages*), Macon, GA: Mercer University Press.

Stokes, P. (2013) 'Death,' in J. Lippitt and G. Pattison (eds), *The Oxford Handbook of Kierkegaard*, Oxford: Oxford University Press.

Stokes, P. (2010) *Kierkegaard's mirrors: Interest, self, and moral vision*, London: Palgrave MacMillan.

Tietjen, M. (2013) *Kierkegaard, communication, and virtue: Authorship as edification*, Bloomington, IN: Indiana University Press.

Further reading

Compaijen, R. (2018) *Kierkegaard, MacIntyre, Williams, and the internal point of view*, London: Palgrave MacMillan.

This book explores Kierkegaard's relations to contemporary moral philosophy, and in so doing elaborates questions about (among other things) practical rationality, the first-personal point of view and abstraction, and education and communication in ethics.

Cruysberghs, P., Taels, J., and Verstrynge, K. (eds) (2003) *Immediacy and reflection in Kierkegaard's thought* (Louvain Philosophical Studies 17), Leuven: Leuven University Press.

This anthology brings together a number of established Kierkegaard scholars who consider various topics concerning the relation of immediacy and reflection, such as whether reflection can be halted, reflection in the present age, and the relation between immediacy and reflection in love.

6

KIERKEGAARD ON MORAL PARTICULARISM AND EXEMPLARISM

Karl Aho

Introduction

This chapter connects Kierkegaard and contemporary Anglophone moral philosophy by putting *Two Ages* into conversation with Jonathan Dancy's moral particularism and Linda Zagzebski's moral exemplarism.[1] Moral particularism is the view that ethics does not consist in the application of moral principles to cases (Dancy 2004: 1). Advocates of principles, such as the utilitarian principle 'that the right action is the one that has the best consequences for human welfare,' seem committed to the view that the properties that feature in those principles 'play the same role on every new appearance' (Dancy 1993: 66). By contrast, Dancy (1993: 55–6) claims that 'a property F of one action may be a reason for me to do that action, even though the F-ness of another action may be morally indifferent or even count as a reason against doing it.' What results is a perceptual model of ethics that stresses the shape of the situation itself rather than the principles we might otherwise invoke to evaluate it.

Writing on the present age nearly 150 years earlier than Dancy's *Moral Reasons*, Kierkegaard also cautions against basing ethics on principles:

> One can do anything and everything on principle, participate in anything and everything, and personally be a non-human nonentity. A man can be interested in establishing a brothel on principle (as a matter of fact, there are many public health pronouncements on the subject), and the same man can on principle be interested in a new hymnbook.... Thus everything is permissible on principle, and just as the police 'in line of duty' enter many places where others are not admitted, so also we can do everything on principle and shirk all personal responsibility.
>
> *(TA, 101–2/SKS 8, 96–7)*

Like Dancy, Kierkegaard does not think ethics should be based on principles. And like Dancy, Kierkegaard emphasizes narratives, particularly narratives that implicate and impact the lives of their narrators. Despite their stylistic differences, they (along with other contemporary theorists who do not base ethics on principles, such as Zagzebski) could be fruitful interlocutors – or so I argue in this chapter. To defend this thesis, I first briefly recount some key particularist commitments, such as the distinction between epistemological and metaphysical forms of particularism. Then I show how *Two Ages* shares several of these commitments. Kierkegaard's concerns about systematizing morality anticipate some aspects of Dancy's epistemological particularism. Yet his commitment to each human sharing the same task of becoming who they are suggests that he would reject Dancy's metaphysical particularism. Finally, I introduce the work of Zagzebski, who like Dancy seeks to minimize the role of principles in ethics. She uses Kierkegaard's account of envy in *Two Ages* to support her account of the way we admire moral exemplars. However, attending to the context of Kierkegaard's discussion of envy, especially in relation to his criticisms of principles, could strengthen her account.

If successful, my account will illuminate the ways Kierkegaard often anticipates, sometimes resists, and could fruitfully inform contemporary criticisms of principles. It will also shed light on both Kierkegaard's texts and those of Dancy and Zagzebski. Finally, it will provide an additional path forward for future engagements between Kierkegaard and Anglophone moral philosophy.

Kierkegaard and moral particularism

Dancy's particularism takes two forms. Though he himself does not call them epistemological particularism and metaphysical particularism, he describes the evolution of his view using that distinction (Dancy 2004: 140). The earlier epistemological form found in *Moral Reasons* claims moral judgments are not exclusively choices between already-available options. Instead, such judgments involve choosing how to correctly describe the shape of a situation such that its salient features are emphasized (Dancy 1993: 112–3). Principles are at most reminders of important facets of that shape. Dancy compares principles to a checklist of properties that may make a difference in a given situation. For example, 'it is important to be honest' may be on our list of principles that can be important. But appeals to principles cannot tell us in advance if honesty is important or the sole important property in that situation (Dancy 1993: 67–8). The later metaphysical particularism of *Ethics Without Principles* emphasizes how actions get to be right or wrong. Here Dancy stresses the skill of discerning the salient features of a situation and that situation's shape. Moral judgments still involve the salient features of situations, but instead of choosing how to describe a situation, we must exercise our ability to determine the role that these features play (Dancy 2004: 143). Dancy emphasizes agents' moral competence to recognize the world's features ('what reasons are present in the case before us'). Rules or principles on this view 'would be at best a dispensable crutch for judgment' (Dancy 2004: 142). Having introduced both forms of Dancy's particularism, I will develop each in turn. I will first discuss the content, the role of principles, and the methods of Dancy's epistemological particularism. Next I will consider how Kierkegaard anticipates and affirms them. Then I will show how Kierkegaard anticipates and resists metaphysical particularism, especially its characterization of moral judgment as an ability that everyone naturally learns.

Epistemological particularism

Dancy (1993: 112) characterizes epistemological particularism as requiring moral agents to correctly describe situations: 'What we are doing is telling the story of the situation, and our narrative has to follow the shape that the situation has.' He compares this storytelling process to describing the aesthetic characteristics of a building. When someone describes a building, they do not start from an arbitrary location, such as moving from left to right. Rather, the way they begin their description of the building reveals its properties according to its shape, such as starting with the features vital to its architectural structure. A good description includes the relevant features of the building in the right order and omits irrelevant ones. Describing a building in this way involves persuasively appealing to one's audience to see the building as one sees it oneself (Dancy 1993: 112). On Dancy's view, moral justification is also narratival in nature. A parent who tells their child not to steal flowers does not appeal to principles (such as 'stealing is wrong'). Instead, the parent directs them to 'the most salient feature of the situation,' such as the fact that the flowers belong to someone else (Dancy 1993: 113).

After introducing particularism as affirming a narrative account of justification, Dancy notes that his method in *Moral Reasons* fits his theory. Instead of arguing in favour of his own position, he merely seeks to describe its most salient features. Dancy claims 'the best way to win [critics] over is to show them in detail what [my] view is and rely on its persuasiveness to attract them, rather than trying to browbeat them with principles of rational choice or judgment.' Accordingly, 'rationality here [. . .] is more like the ability to listen to and appreciate a story' (Dancy 1993: 114). I introduce this methodological consideration because it is one similarity between Dancy and Kierkegaard. Kierkegaard's writings frequently use narrative forms of argumentation instead of appeals to rational choice. Kierkegaard decries calculative forms of reason as distracting people by emphasizing their own shrewd cleverness (Tietjen 2007: 177–84). Both authors share a preference for narrative arguments over principle-based ones. Their preference is rooted in a shared emphasis on rightly describing the situations agents find themselves in. To see why, let us return to Kierkegaard's *Two Ages*, which I quoted at the beginning of this chapter.

Two Ages is a representative text for considering Kierkegaard's affinities with moral particularism because of its preoccupation with rationality. In contrast with the passionate age of the French revolution, Kierkegaard describes the present age as sensible and reflecting (TA, 68/SKS 8, 66). While these may seem like positive qualities, he worries that they keep people from acting at all – let alone taking moral action. Thus he writes that 'it would be extremely difficult to be a prosecuting attorney against an age such as this, because the whole generation is expert on legal matters, and its competence, its sensibleness, its technical skill consist in letting matters reach a verdict and decision without ever acting' (TA, 69/SKS 8, 66–7). Like Dancy, Kierkegaard is sceptical of forms of argumentation that rely on appeals to rational principles or sensibleness. As we will see, Kierkegaard thinks that the inaction of those in the present age is a result of their misdescribing moral situations in a way that licenses inaction.

Kierkegaard contrasts the ways a passionate age and a reflective age (such as his present age) would describe the same situation: an ice skater risking his life to secure a treasure that everyone covets (TA, 71–2/SKS 8, 69). Observers from both ages see the same situation, but they identify different features of it as central. In a passionate age, viewers would see the skater as brave and celebrate his success or grieve his death. By contrast, 'in a reflective age devoid of passion' watchers would agree that the skater's mission is foolish and view his success as insignificant. In the former age, the skater's bravery is seen as 'an inspired venture'; in the latter age, it is 'an acrobatic stunt' (TA, 72/SKS 8, 69). The same feature of the world – skating on thin ice, that is, taking a risk for the sake of a worthwhile reward – is in the former case admirable and in the latter case foolhardy. Kierkegaard will later ascribe the spectators' seeing the skater as foolish to envy: 'Characterless envy does not understand that excellence is excellence . . . but wants to degrade it, minimize it, until it actually is no longer excellence' (TA, 84/SKS 8, 80). Compare Kierkegaard's account here with Dancy's (1993: 117) account of rival narrative descriptions of a situation's shape: 'the two narratives are in conflict with each other, because though one can consider the situation as having either [shape], one cannot take it actually to have both.' Since those in the reflective age do not value the skater's bravery, they cannot celebrate his success like those in a passionate age might. Instead of authentically admiring him, they enviously minimize his efforts. Kierkegaard's point here is two-fold. First, we see that the way the observers see the skater determine their responses to him. Moral perception leads to moral action (or in the case of those merely spectating, inaction). Second, Kierkegaard sees the passionate age's account of the situation as superior to the story the reflective age tells about it. It would be better if we were to passionately participate in the skater's daring rather than enviously spectating it, as calculative reason or rational choice theories might recommend. As will become apparent later, Kierkegaard does not think those in the present age should merely reiterate the passionate age's approach by striving to admire heroes ourselves. But he does prefer admiring the skater to envying him. Like Dancy, Kierkegaard sees moral justification as narratival. How we narrate situations matters, and there are right ways and wrong ways to tell such stories.

Initially, Kierkegaard's ice skater story and his concerns about principles may seem parallel rather than related. The skater's spectators refuse to participate or act whereas the person of principles uses principles to license any kind of action. The only connection seems to be that in both cases people avoid acting morally. But for Kierkegaard the spectators' narrative and consequent inaction stems from the same source as the principled immorality he decries. 'The generality of the formlessness in a reflective age expresses itself in the very opposite: a dominant propensity and inclination to act "on principle"' (TA, 100/SKS 8, 95). Kierkegaard's term 'formlessness' names one of several features of the present age *Two Ages* discusses. Each feature involves the distinction between acting essentially and acting inessentially (TA, 96/SKS 8, 91). For example, philandering annuls the difference between essentially loving and being essentially debauched. The philanderer pursues many partners and loves them inessentially rather than pursuing many without loving (like the debauchee) or loving a single partner essentially. And 'acting on principle is also philandering, because it vitiates moral action to the point of abstraction' (TA, 103/SKS 8, 97). Acting essentially (whether to love or to debauch) requires commitment – something that both the spectators and the person of principles lack. The person of principles is formless because she annuls the difference between form and content. Both the spectators and the person of principles can utter truths about their situations. Kierkegaard claims that their formlessness can contain truths. But those truths are generalities; they 'expand all-inclusively, all-intrusively' (TA, 100/SKS 8, 95). In short, these truths are not essentially true for people of principles, and therefore do not impel them to act. For example, the ice skater's spectators describe their situation in a way that licenses their inaction. Principles substitute something external to the situation for something internal to it. They do not appeal to the situation's form, or in Dancy's terms, its shape. Consequently, principles can justify any action. They cannot compel the person of principles to act essentially. Appeals to principles are for Kierkegaard akin to the spectators mis-narrating the ice skater's bravery. Misdescribing the situation prevents it from impelling moral action in the person describing it.

We are now in a position to evaluate Kierkegaard's anticipation of Dancy's epistemological particularism. This particularism is comprised of a criticism of appeals to principles, a corresponding embrace of narratival accounts of situations that attend to their salient features, and a methodology that favours narrative arguments over appeals to rational choice. Kierkegaard affirms each of these elements to some degree. He criticizes appeals to principles much like Dancy's epistemological particularism does. And he appeals to narrative arguments throughout his authorships. However, Kierkegaard's approach to narratival accounts of situations as an alternative to principles differs from Dancy's. For Dancy (1993: 117), the right narrative of a situation is the most persuasive one. Whereas Dancy invites his readers to merely listen to and appreciate stories, Kierkegaard goes further. He constructs his stories as mirrors, so that readers see themselves in them (Stokes 2010: 111–33). This self-implicating narrative practice provides a model for how Kierkegaard would commend others to narrate situations. The right narrative to tell about a situation is the one that is true for its viewer – not in a relativistic sense, that is, true for me and not for you, but true in the sense of reflecting and prompting moral action on the part of the storyteller. For example, the ice skater's bravery calls for admiration in his observers. One cannot describe the situation without choosing whether to construe the skater as brave or foolish. While Kierkegaard does not call for a return to a passionate age where admiration of heroes is the norm, the ice skater scenario shows that we cannot interpret stories without attending to our own roles in them. Kierkegaard anticipates and affirms much of Dancy's epistemological particularism and its focus on narratives, but develops a different account of what makes for a narrative that attends rightly to a situation's salient features and shape.

Metaphysical particularism

Perhaps the best way to consider the difference between epistemological and metaphysical particularism is to survey the different accounts of moral judgment they produce. *Moral Reasons* emphasizes epistemology – correctly describing situations through narratives that attend to their salient features and shape. The latter terms are almost absent from *Ethics Without Principles*. Instead of emphasizing narratives about the salient features of situations, Dancy (2004: 143) describes moral judgment as a process of deliberation that discerns the salience of those features: 'Our competent moral judge can tell when a feature is operating normally ... when one feature's contribution is intensified or diminished by another ... and so on.' To see how this differs from epistemological particularism, recall Dancy's comparison between morally narrating a situation and describing a building. From the perspective of epistemological particularism, describing a building requires attending to its shape and central features. By contrast, a metaphysical particularist might describe the building or situation by listing each of its features and their functions. They need not emphasize its central features. This change in emphasis is prompted by a corresponding change in Dancy's argumentative method. Whereas *Moral Reasons* argues for a narrative-driven epistemology, *Ethics Without Principles* emphasizes metaphysics, such as the wrong-making features of situations themselves (Dancy 2004: 108, 140). Instead of omitting non-salient features of the situation, metaphysical particularism affirms a holism about reasons that emphasizes the way each feature of the situation contributes to the situation's shape. Holism about reasons is the view that 'a feature that is a reason in one case may be no reason at all, or an opposite reason, in another' (Dancy 2004: 43). All features matter. Dancy views 'the overall evaluative shape of the situation as the demands it makes of us, demands that are built of the various favourings to be found in it, in non-additive ways.' The competent judge can recognize these demands upon coming across them, even if the differences that make a difference in a given situation cannot be articulated in propositional terms (Dancy 2004: 143). Rules or principles would be for this judge 'at best a dispensable crutch for judgment' (Dancy 2004: 142).

Despite sharing Dancy's distaste for principles as we have previously discussed, Kierkegaard would reject Dancy's metaphysical particularism. Kierkegaard opposes the calculative approaches characteristic of a reflective age. While he would likely approve of Dancy's appeals to the situation itself rather than principles, Kierkegaard would be sceptical of metaphysical particularism's deliberation-based approach. He writes, 'Another danger in reflection is the impossibility of seeing whether it is a resolution reached by deliberation that saves a person from doing evil or whether it is fatigue brought on by deliberation that weakens one and prevents one from doing evil' (TA, 77/SKS 8, 80). In addition to emphasizing our inability to credit deliberation with preventing evil, Kierkegaard would also reject the holism about reasons that motivates metaphysical particularism. To see why, recall the difference between Dancy and Kierkegaard's approach to narrating moral situations. For Kierkegaard, the right narrative about a situation implicates the narrator in it. Kierkegaard is concerned with finding the personally decisive reasons about a situation – not about attending to the roles every reason plays. He warns his readers of the threat posed by 'inhumanely confusing [one]self with some abstract thing, with the times, our age, etc.'; he exhorts his readers to instead cultivate their 'own proper grasp of what it is to be a human' (TA, 112/SKS 8, 106). This idea of what it means to be human will require further development, but it also introduces another reason why Kierkegaard would reject metaphysical particularism.

Kierkegaard would reject metaphysical particularism because of the understanding of moral education accompanying it. Dancy describes moral judgment as a sophisticated ability that children develop through training as they grow up. We need no special form of moral education because moral reasons are just like any other sort of reason (Dancy 2004: 142–3). For Dancy, moral education is just like any other kind of education. By contrast, for Kierkegaard moral motivation does not come from reasons (whether supplied by principles or otherwise) alone. This explains why despite being in an age of reflection, people in the present age are not morally better than those in other ages. 'So the present age is basically sensible, perhaps knows more on the average than any previous generation, but it is devoid of passion. Everyone is well informed; we all know everything, every course to take and the alternative courses, but no one is willing to take it' (TA, 104/SKS 8, 99). This passage provides further evidence that Kierkegaard would reject Dancy's holism about reasons. Even if people actually knew everything, that knowledge would not be sufficient for action. Second, the passage points us towards Kierkegaard's positive alternative to both principles and particularism. We have already observed that the person of principles and the present age lack passion. Here we see that passion both motivates the Kierkegaardian moral agent to act and provides a surer source of moral guidance than principles do. So whatever Kierkegaard's positive account of moral education entails, it must involve passion. Yet the source of that passion matters – Kierkegaard is not merely advising us to follow our inclinations or our bliss.

Despite emphasizing passion over principles, Kierkegaard forestalls attempts to make the present age a passionate or heroic age again. He calls for an alternative sort of moral education – one that emphasizes human equality rather than heroic superiority (TA, 84/SKS 8, 81). The source of this equality is vitally important. The spectators in the ice skater narrative who derided the skater's efforts were equal in their attempts to bring the skater down to their level by minimizing his achievement (TA, 71–2/SKS 8, 69). Their envy united them. By contrast, Kierkegaard sees humans as equal because they are human. This equality is coopted by reflection when people see each other abstractly, through the lens of 'pure humanity' (TA, 87–8/SKS 8, 84–5). Since pure humanity is an abstraction, we cannot rely on appeals to pure humanity to prompt moral action. Kierkegaard instead exhorts his readers to each cultivate their own grasp of what it means to be human and thus to be equal to others. His understanding of equality directs us not towards an abstraction, but back towards ourselves.

Properly understood, recognizing our equality can provide an alternative to reflection. Kierkegaard writes: 'if the individual is unwilling to learn to be satisfied with himself . . . with ruling himself instead of over the world . . . if he is unwilling to learn to be inspired by this as supreme because it expresses . . . equality with all men, then he will not escape from reflection' (TA, 88–9/SKS 8, 85). We must take moral action ourselves rather than celebrating it or spectating it in others. For example, we cannot rely on others to morally narrate situations for us. Kierkegaard writes that the individual 'will be educated to make up his own mind instead of agreeing with the public . . .

to find rest within himself . . . instead of in counting and counting' (TA, 92/SKS 8, 88). Such individuals find rest because they know their equality with other humans empowers them to judge for themselves. They need not imitate or minimize the achievements of others – doing so would entail denying their human equality with those others. Moral education in the present age involves each person learning to narrate their moral situation for themselves rather than merely agreeing with others, the abstract principles they may cite, or the counting or calculation they might recommend. We must be passionate in a way that is directed by our own moral narration of situations.

With this account of Kierkegaardian moral education in mind, we can compare and contrast Kierkegaard's nascent particularism with Dancy's developed versions. Like both forms of particularism, Kierkegaard is sceptical of accounts that base moral action on principles. Like epistemological particularism, Kierkegaard emphasizes narratives. But unlike Dancy, Kierkegaard thinks individuals must be involved in these situations rather than merely their narrators. To return to Dancy's metaphor of describing a building, Kierkegaard would have us include ourselves and our relationship to that building in our description. Going into an opera house prompts us to comport ourselves differently than going into a church, no matter how many architectural features the two buildings share. A Kierkegaardian moral description includes the describer's relationship to what is described. Similarly, Kierkegaard thinks that each individual must narrate for themselves rather than viewing the world from some other perspective, such as that of the community or some other form of association. Metaphysical particularism's holism about reasons requires attending to all of the features of a situation. It does not emphasize the particular features of the situation that are significant for the agent describing that situation. For Kierkegaard, these features are typically decisive. The reasons that matter are the ones that prompt the individual to act. According to Kierkegaard, considering all of the features of a situation is at best irrelevant and at worst a condemnable evasion of action. Kierkegaard thus anticipates several of Dancy's insights while proffering an alternative account of narrating moral situations. In the remainder of this paper, I will put the foregoing account of Kierkegaard's criticism of principles into conversation with moral exemplarism, a moral theory that, like particularism, seeks to provide an alternative to principle-based approaches.

Kierkegaard and exemplarism

Linda Zagzebski (2017: 3) claims that moral concepts can be defined through direct reference to moral exemplars. Exemplars are paradigmatically good persons who anchor our moral concepts. By directly referring to exemplars, we can identify moral concepts without first describing them (Zagzebski 2017: 15–6). Appealing to Kripke's theory of direct reference, she compares the way we identify moral exemplars to the way we identify the reference of natural kind terms like 'water.' After the reference of 'water' is fixed by ostension, empirical research into water can discover water's nature (Zagzebski 2017: 13). Zagzebski thinks we can directly refer to and subsequently research moral exemplars through a similar process. We identify exemplars through the emotion of admiration. Exemplars are the most admirable persons, and therefore the persons we ought to imitate (Zagzebski 2017: 15). One advantage of exemplarist moral theory is that it does not require people to agree about substantive matters from the outset. Instead, Zagzebski (2017: 18–9) claims that we can use empirical resources such as psychological studies, as well as narratives about moral exemplars, to inquire into moral concepts. Since moral inquiry can proceed empirically, principles are secondary at best. As Zagzebski (2017: 28) says, 'many elements of moral practice are more trustworthy than any theory we devise to justify them.' Given her scepticism towards principles and emphasis on narratives about moral exemplars, we might expect both Dancy and Kierkegaard to be sympathetic to Zagzebski's project. I will discuss how they might evaluate it in turn.

Given the comparatively minimal role she assigns principles, we can view Zagzebski's proposal to make moral exemplars central to moral theory as similar to Dancy's moral particularism. For Dancy, narrating a moral situation is the key practice that provides us with an alternative to relying on principles. Zagzebski thinks we can identify moral exemplars as sources of action guidance. Dancy and Zagzebski each emphasize narratives, but narratives of different sorts – of situations themselves, on the one hand, and of exemplars we might imitate while navigating moral situations, on the other. Unlike Dancy, who defines particularism as the negation of generalism, Zagzebski characterizes her methodology as collaborative. Like a map includes landmarks of various sorts, her theory seeks to include central elements of other approaches, such as principles (Zagzebski 2017: 5–7). Thus, she 'doubt[s] that we will find many exemplars whose moral judgment is fully and consistently explained by any standard theory, but it can be revealing to find out what sort of principles wise persons use and how they apply those principles' (Zagzebski 2017: 231–2). This Aristotelian aspect of Zagzebski's approach more closely resembles epistemological particularism than metaphysical particularism. Dancy's earlier view is that principles could help remind us of the roles the salient features of situations might play. Zagzebski's account is similar – maps can help us understand where we are, even if they cannot tell us where to go. Moreover, a good map must account for the way its readers view the region the map describes. For Zagzebski (2017: 6), 'if people sometimes use the principle of utility or a principle that all persons ought to be treated with respect, a good theory should include those principles.' Her theory does not preclude principles, but like both of Dancy's forms of particularism it denies the centrality of principles.

Zagzebski introduces Kierkegaard into her exemplarist theory in order to invoke his understanding of admiration. She does so in the context of considering the 'psychological and cultural forces' that distort admiration (Zagzebski 2017: 50). Her use of Kierkegaard occurs in an important part of her overall argument for an exemplarist moral theory. It would do no good to construct a moral theory based on admiration if people reject admiration as a moral category (Zagzebski 2017: 50–1). Zagzebski identifies envy as one reason for this rejection. She sees Kierkegaard as supporting her diagnosis: 'Kierkegaard argued that envy is a constant temptation for people who feel admiration, and some ages handle it better than others' (Zagzebski 2017: 57). As evidence, she cites his claim in *Two Ages* that the Greek practice of ostracism was a form of envy that did not deny that the person being ostracized was worthy of admiration (Zagzebski 2017: 57; cf. TA, 83/SKS 8, 79–80). Importantly, forms of envy take place in the context of particular cultures and the language they use concerning admiration (Zagzebski 2017: 58). Zagzebski (perhaps unintentionally) also echoes Kierkegaard's emphasis on equality's role in envy. She sees admiration as turning to envy 'when equality is the main motivating value' (Zagzebski 2017: 59). In so doing, she echoes Kierkegaard's claim that 'The dialectic of antiquity was oriented to the eminent. . . . The dialectic of the present age is oriented to equality, and its most logical implementation, albeit abortive, is leveling' (TA, 84/SKS 8, 81). We have already seen levelling (one of the forms of envy Kierkegaard identifies) at work in the ice skater scenario, in which the spectators were unified by their disdain for the skater's bravery. Both Zagzebski's view of equality motivating envy and her account of admiration have implications for how Kierkegaard might respond to her exemplarist theory.

The sort of equality Kierkegaard recommends to individuals in the present age challenges Zagzebski's account of envy. This equality is not abstract, that is, of the sort that emphasizes a speculative idea of pure humanity. Nor is it the negative sort of equality achieved by reducing everyone to the same level (like the equality pursued by the ice skater's spectators). Instead, Kierkegaard sees equality as prompting individuals to be satisfied acting on their own behalf rather than for the sake of recognition by other people. He compares the single individual's satisfaction to that of a pastor whose only audience is himself and an author whose only reader is himself (TA, 89/SKS 8, 85). Since the single individual does not seek recognition, they will avoid the evasions that often keep people in the present age from acting. Kierkegaard's single individual acting on the basis of the equality with others they already possess provides a plausible counter-example to Zagzebski's hypothesis that equality as a motivating force is always linked with envy. Such an individual sees herself as equal to others without trying to rule over them. Perhaps attending to this element of Kierkegaard's understanding of equality might help Zagzebski construct a more egalitarian approach to admiration that does not always associate equality with envy.

Kierkegaard's account of equality also limits the role admiration might play in the present age. In his description of the ice skater, Kierkegaard describes admiration for the skater as prompting observers to imitate the skater. In this scenario, an admiring response is prompted by the recognition that the skater is exceptional in a way that the admirer is not (TA, 72/SKS 8, 70). But if the single individual is equal to others, this sort of admiration is not called for. So admiration, like envy, may also be an avenue for evading moral action. Someone might use admiring others as a way to downplay their own abilities and consequently avoid acting. Since Kierkegaard is also critical of those who admire others rather than recognizing and acting on the basis of their equality with them, Zagzebski ought not invoke his criticisms of envy without also attending to his concerns about admiration.

Kierkegaard's account of the single individual's anonymity also limits the contexts in which we might use admiration to identify moral exemplars. In a passionate age, important figures – both the admirable ones Zagzebski identifies as well as prominent people or leaders – were recognizable. In the present age, people of excellence 'will be without authority precisely because they have divinely understood the diabolical principle of the leveling process. Like plainclothes policemen, they will be *unrecognizable*, concealing their respective distinctions' (TA, 106–7/SKS 8, 101). Unlike the important figures of ages past, what makes the single individual distinctive – their recognition of equality with other people – does not appear to others as something exceptional. Since we cannot recognize exemplars in the present age, we cannot use them to inform our moral practice. This concern need not be fatal for Zagzebski's project. She might still appeal to historical exemplars, although envy might prompt us to diminish their achievements also. But if Kierkegaard's diagnosis of admiration in the present age is accurate, present-day morally admirable individuals will be unrecognizable and thereby unable to serve as moral exemplars for Zagzebski's project.

Conclusion

We have seen that Kierkegaard anticipates several aspects of Dancy's moral particularism. His writings also influence Zagzebski's account of admiration even while they challenge some of the ways she applies that account. What have we gleaned from putting Kierkegaard into conversation with these contemporary moral theorists? First, the foregoing has shown that Kierkegaard and his interlocutors in this chapter are more similar than they might appear. All three share a preference for narrative over principle. They each attend to the actual situations people find themselves in, even if their responses to those situations differ. Dancy seeks to understand how people navigate such situations. Zagzebski seeks to give them a better map for navigating them.

Kierkegaard's approach is somewhat different, in that he thinks human equality entails that people must judge for themselves. Since he cannot tell his readers how they should judge, he writes in such a way that encourages them to do so: by composing texts that are mirrors, both to the present age and to their readers. In *Two Ages* he calls this 'giving negative support and helping the individual to the same decisiveness he himself has' (TA, 108/SKS 8, 102). This project is akin to those of both Dancy and Zagzebski. Like Dancy, Kierkegaard exhorts his readers to make their own judgments without relying on principles or other external sources of authority. Like Zagzebski, he encourages them to make such decisions, although he does not seek to simplify such decisions like her account of theories as maps does. In short, Kierkegaard's project is not as foreign to these contemporary moral theories as some might suggest.

The similarities between Kierkegaard's project, particularism, and exemplarism yield a second reason for reading these projects alongside each other. Doing so allows each project to illuminate the others. Some critics describe moral particularism as lacking an account of moral education (Hooker 2000: 15). Reading Dancy in light of Kierkegaard helped us to develop a particularist account of moral formation as cultivating the ability to narrate moral situations. Similarly, reading *Two Ages* alongside Dancy enabled us to trace the thread of Kierkegaard's criticism of principles throughout that text. Despite its importance for *Two Ages*, that criticism is embedded in the book's overall structure such that it might be easy to miss without having Dancy's arguments against generalism at the ready. This may be why *Two Ages* is read in search of moral insights far less frequently than other works by Kierkegaard such as *Fear and Trembling* or *Works of Love*. Reading *Two Ages* alongside Dancy's work can help us better appreciate this text's significance. Doing so may also set the stage for future work putting Dancy into conversation with other moral theorists that emphasize principles, such as Hegel. Finally, considering the context of Kierkegaard's discussion of envy could help hone Zagzebski's account of admiration. Contemporary moral theorists and Kierkegaardians do not only share ethical and methodological commitments – their projects can fruitfully inform each other. In particular, Kierkegaard's writings can supplement those of the particularists and others (some of whom are listed in the 'Further Reading' section below) who propose alternatives to principle-based moral theories. My hope is that this chapter's staging a conversation between Kierkegaard, particularism, and exemplarism will encourage others to pursue their own similar projects in the future.

Related topics

'Ethical reflection as evasion,' Rob Compaijen and Pieter Vos; 'Did Napoleon teleologically suspend the ethical? A dilemma for some 'Hegelian' readings of *Fear and Trembling*,' Ryan S. Kemp.

Note

1 I first briefly discussed the affinities between Kierkegaard and moral particularism, along with C. Stephen Evans, in Aho and Evans (2019).

References

Aho, K. and Evans, C. S. (2019) 'The single individual is higher than the universal: Kierkegaard,' in J. Shand (ed), *A Companion to Nineteenth Century Philosophy*, Oxford: Blackwell.
Dancy, J. (2004) *Ethics without principles*, Oxford: Oxford University Press.
Dancy, J. (1993) *Moral reasons*, Oxford: Blackwell.
Hooker, B. (2000) 'Moral particularism: Wrong and bad,' in B. Hooker and M. O. Little (eds), *Moral Particularism*, Oxford: Oxford University Press, 1–23.

Stokes, P. (2010) *Kierkegaard's mirrors: Interest, self, and moral vision*, London: Palgrave Macmillan.

Tietjen, M. A. (2007) 'Aristotle, Aquinas, and Kierkegaard on prudence,' in R. L. Perkins (ed), *International Kierkegaard Commentary*, vol. 17 (*Christian Discourses and the Crisis and a Crisis in the Life of an Actress*), Macon, GA: Mercer University Press, 165–89.

Zagzebski, L. (2017) *Exemplarist moral theory*, Oxford: Oxford University Press.

Further reading

Bakhurst, D. (2005) 'Particularism and moral education,' *Philosophical Explorations*, 8, no. 3: 265–79.

Like this chapter, Bakhurst defends the possibility of particularist moral education. His version emphasizes agents as authors of their moral judgments.

Blum, L. A. (1998) 'Moral exemplars: Reflections on Schindler, the Trocmes, and others,' *Midwest Studies in Philosophy*, 13, no. 1: 196–21.

Blum proposes kinds of moral exemplars. His idea of the moral saint – someone who is moral throughout their lives rather than for a single sustained period like Oscar Schindler – resonates with Kierkegaard's, since unlike moral heroes, moral saints need not be recognizable.

Miles, T. P. (2013) *Kierkegaard and Nietzsche on the best way of life: A new method of ethics*, London: Palgrave Macmillan.

Miles identifies Kierkegaard and Nietzsche as introducing a new ethical concept, the way of life. This concept may serve as another alternative to principles, much like moral exemplars do.

Stokes, P. (2016) 'The problem of spontaneous goodness: From Kierkegaard to Løstrup (via Zhuangzi and Eckhart),' *Continental Philosophy Review*, 49, no. 2: 139–59.

Stokes sees spontaneous moral response as the moral ideal Kierkegaard prescribes. This sort of response might serve as an alternative to principles while capturing Kierkegaard's suspicion towards calculative reasoning.

7

BEYOND WORRY? ON LEARNING HUMILITY FROM THE LILIES AND THE BIRDS

John Lippitt

'Therefore do not worry about tomorrow: tomorrow will worry about itself. Each day has enough trouble of its own.'

– Matthew 6: 34

Introduction

How on earth do I stop worrying? In *Worrying: A Literary and Cultural History*, Francis O'Gorman (2015: x) suggests that worries 'are, of nature, like a strangling weed: they can't be eradicated even if they can be cut back. They keep growing. They smother. They are exceptionally good at spoiling the view.' In this chapter, I shall argue that part of the answer to the problem of worry is to be found in a certain view of humility: one that can be teased out from several Kierkegaardian discourses, and which has recently been gaining increasing support – from both philosophers and psychologists – against competing views of humility. Humility is understood not in terms of self-abasement, underestimating oneself, or being ignorant of one's good qualities, but rather in terms of being focused on others and sources of value besides oneself: thinking not *less* of oneself, but thinking less *about* oneself. In exploring the centrality of future-oriented worries to Kierkegaard's lily and bird discourses, it will be important to notice how such worries often stem from excessive self-absorption, a particular aspect of Luther's (and the wider Lutheran tradition's) general objection to self-centred desire, and how the motive of our heart is 'curved in on itself' (*incurvatus in se*).[1] As O'Gorman (2015: 54) suggests:

> Worrying can be a form of vanity. It can be a species of self-indulgence, a way of extending ego into a conversation, or of somehow confirming *selfness* in the head. To worry silently is to feel a certain kind of closeness to oneself, to the 'real' needy person that one may believe oneself to be. To *talk* to others about worries is, in some ways, always to declare: look at me; listen to *my* pains; listen to what *I* live with; *I* am important in my own worry.[2]

Humility as it will be understood here provides an alternative to this debilitating self-absorption. O'Gorman (2015: 139) also suggests that the worrier might relax by being a bit more humble, suggesting that a partial solution to the pain of worrying is 'to moderate expectation; to be kinder to myself; to accept that I fail; to be ready to apologize; to be ready to take criticism.' He seems to be suggesting a sort of pragmatic 'realism,' a recognition of one's abilities unclouded by the distortions of a problematic kind of pride: 'we worriers,' he says, should not suppose we are 'too good for failure, or too proud to deal with objections, or too grand to take responsibility for something that went wrong, or so grand that if anything goes wrong it *must* be our responsibility' (O'Gorman 2015: 140). That all sounds sensible enough, but – apart from perhaps the final suggestion – still sounds highly self-focused.[3] The kind of humility I have in mind takes us much further beyond self-focus into other-focus. Let us get there via Kierkegaard's 'unlikely teachers,' the lilies in the field and the birds of the air.

The lilies and the birds

Kierkegaard wrote fourteen discourses on Matthew 6: 24–34, a key gospel passage in which Jesus discusses the lilies and birds. Here I shall focus mostly on those from 1847 (the second part of *Upbuilding Discourses in Various Spirits*) and 1849, though with some complementary references to parts of the *Christian Discourses* of 1848.[4] Both worry [*Bekymring*[5]] and joy are recurrent themes of these discourses.

The 1847 discourses

The gospel passage 'addresses itself to those who are worried' (UDVS, 160/SKS 8, 260), and the prayer in the preface presents the lilies and birds as 'counselor[s] to the worried' (UDVS, 157/SKS 8, 258). The first discourse, 'To Be Contented with Being a Human Being,' presents the silence of the lilies and birds as part of their qualifications to be teachers: they are 'silent – out of solicitude for the worried person' (UDVS, 160/SKS 8, 260). Here we start to see the importance of the shift of attention necessary in learning from these teachers: *the worried person needs to forget himself in contemplating them* (UDVS, 161/SKS 8, 261). This is why it is *silent* ones who have been 'divinely appointed' to teach us (UDVS, 157/SKS 8, 258): silence compares favourably with the potentially destructive power of *comparison* that is inherent in speech (since injunctions to rejoice, 'be glad!' or 'be strong!' imply: 'as I am' [UDVS, 161/SKS 8, 260–1]). Amongst the lilies, the human can be contented with being a human being – because we can be taken out of ourselves, forgetting our worries in contemplation of the lilies and their beauty.

The theme of 'the worried inventiveness of comparison' (UDVS, 165/SKS 8, 265) is central to one of the most memorable parts of this discourse, Kierkegaard's parable of the 'worried lily' (UDVS, 167ff./SKS 8, 266ff.). The basic thought behind this seems to be that a huge amount of human misery is the result of unproductive comparisons of ourselves to others, and that such comparisons produce an unhealthy kind and degree of anxiety.[6]

In this parable, Kierkegaard draws a parallel between the beauty of a lily and that of a human being. The sheer wonder of being alive, and of being human, is typically forgotten through comparison's corrosive effects. In the parable, the life of a beautiful, carefree lily is complicated by the arrival of a capricious little bird who, instead of delighting in the lily's beauty, stresses its difference (being free to come and go) and induces the lily's worry by chattering about the beauty of other lilies encountered on its travels. Predictably, the lily becomes increasingly insecure. Its static life, previously unproblematic, starts to seem restrictive, and – falling prone to the spirit of comparison – it begins to feel humiliated, wishing it was a Crown Imperial, which the bird has told it is the most gorgeous lily of all. In a subtle twist, the lily convinces itself that its desire is reasonable, since it is not 'asking for the impossible, to become what I am not, a bird, for example. My wish is only to become a gorgeous lily, or even the most gorgeous' (UDVS, 168/SKS 8, 267–8).

Confessing its worries, the lily and bird together hatch a plan that will see the bird peck away the soil restricting the lily to its spot, uproot it, and fly it to where the most gorgeous lilies grow (UDVS, 168–9/SKS 8, 268). But inevitably, once uprooted, the lily withers and dies. The message seems to be that the anxious worry which led to its demise is a human, all too human trait. The lily is the human being, while the 'naughty little bird' is 'the restless mentality of comparison, which roams far and wide, fitfully and capriciously, and gleans the morbid knowledge of diversity' (UDVS, 169/SKS 8, 268). Further, the little bird is 'the poetic and the seductive in the human being' (UDVS, 169/SKS 8, 268), and the poetic is a mixture of truth and untruth. While the diversity it notes between human beings is not a falsehood, the poetic 'consists in maintaining that diversity . . . is the supreme, and this is eternally false' (UDVS, 169/SKS 8, 268). The bird's influence causes the lily to become problematically *proud* and *envious* (UDVS, 168/SKS 8, 267). But as noted, it convinces itself that it is not asking for anything unreasonable: it fails to see that wanting to become the most gorgeous lily does not become a reasonable desire simply in virtue of not being a wish to change species. Ultimately, the problem arises from stressing the diversity that results from the spirit of comparison – 'status anxiety'? – more than our *common humanity*. From this Kierkegaard advances the bold claim that 'all worldly worry' is based upon an 'unwillingness to be contented with being a human being' (UDVS, 171/SKS 8, 270).

A second parable introduces a sub-theme: worry about making a living (an obvious example of future-oriented worry). Here the worrier is not a lily but another bird. Kierkegaard contrasts a wood-dove, also previously happy with its existence, with a tame dove it meets. Initially, the wood-dove has effectively taken the gospel passage's advice: to take each day as it comes. But the tame dove's one-upmanship starts to worry the wood-dove. As the farmer loads grain into the barn, the tame dove brags that it and its mate are well provided for. Again, the worry centres on envy at the tame dove's apparent knowledge of financial security: the wood-dove is 'struck by the thought that it must be very pleasant to *know* that one's living was secured for a long time, whereas it was miserable to live continually in uncertainty so that one never dares to say that one *knows* one is provided for' (UDVS, 175/SKS 8, 274). The wood-dove becomes worried about its *possible future need* – even though, crucially, it does not suffer *actual* need now. (My investment portfolio is doing well – but suppose the markets crash tomorrow?) Through entrapping itself in 'the idea' (UDVS, 176/SKS 8, 274) of its need for security, the bird's future-oriented worry causes it to lose its joy (UDVS, 175/SKS 8, 274). Like the worried lily, the wood-dove convinces itself that this is reasonable, since it too is not wishing to change its species: it wants to be like the wealthy tame doves, not to become a human being like the farmer. The dove changes its behaviour, trying to store up food for the future, eventually hatching a scheme whereby it can join the tame doves, sneaking into the dovecote one night. Its fate is no happier than that of the worried lily: finding the strange interloper, the farmer places it in a box and kills it the next morning (UDVS, 176/SKS 8, 275).

Again, Kierkegaard explains that the wood-dove is the human being – albeit this time with a qualification. His point is not to urge against saving for the future. Rather, what he is cautioning against is *overlooking our dependence upon God in an attitude of misguided self-sufficiency*: 'It is certainly praiseworthy and pleasing to God that a person sows and reaps and gathers into barns, that he works in order to obtain food; but if he wants to forget God and thinks he supports himself by his labors, then he has worry about making a living' (UDVS, 177/SKS 8, 276). The claim is that ultimately, without God, neither rich nor poor can provide for themselves in the deepest sense. We are – in a phrase that will become important in the next section – *radically dependent*.

Kierkegaard traces this problem to the 'spirit of comparison' too, in at least two ways. First, to want to be self-sufficient is to want 'security by himself' (UDVS, 178/SKS 8, 277), which only God can have. And second, 'the actual pressing need of the day today' has been replaced by 'the idea of a future need': it is this in which the worry about making a living in its problematic sense consists (UDVS, 178–9/SKS 8, 277). For some, this takes the form of the desire to be rich; for others, merely the desire to be fairly secure – but both stem from the spirit of comparison. And all this can be traced to the unwillingness to be contented with being a human being.

The second discourse, 'How Glorious It Is to Be a Human Being,' continues the theme of escaping worry. Again, the focus is on escaping worry *by looking away from it* (down at the lily or up at the bird) (UDVS, 183–4/SKS 8, 281). The picture is that by focusing on something of value outside the self – things of value in the world – many of one's worries are quietened (see e.g., UDVS, 194/SKS 8, 291). Through a discussion of the lily, Kierkegaard claims that the 'invisible glory' of the human being is 'to be spirit' (UDVS, 193/SKS 8, 290), here associated with being a worshipper. The focus, through worship, on how glorious it is to be a human being occupies the worried person such that his attention shifts away from his worries. And what do we learn from the bird? Again, matters are here slightly more complex. The bird lives only in the moment, yet a human has consciousness [*Bevidsthed*] in which 'he is eternally far ... beyond the moment' (UDVS, 195/SKS 8, 292); he becomes aware of the future. Indeed, the human has 'a dangerous enemy that the bird does not know – time' (UDVS, 195/SKS 8, 292) (hence the worry about making a living).

The bird is the teacher of the human in the same way as the child is of the adult: in 'jesting earnestness' (UDVS, 196/SKS 8, 293). That our teachers are dumb flora and fauna like the lily and the bird is one of the reasons that Kierkegaard labels these discourses, and the parable of the worried lily in particular, 'humorous.'[7] And this adds a further complicating factor: the bird is the pattern or exemplar [*Forbillede*] for the human – insofar as it has a worry-free existence – and yet insofar as the human is 'higher' than the bird, the human always recalls the true pattern, Christ (UDVS, 197/SKS 8, 293). Here – initially seeming to radicalize the issue about saving for the future mentioned above – Kierkegaard recalls the biblical passage about the Son of Man having no place to lay his head (Matthew 8: 20). Yet he goes on to say that it is, in the human, 'a perfection' to be able to worry about making a living (UDVS, 197/SKS 8, 294); it is a perfection to be able to *work* (UDVS, 198/SKS 8, 294), which the bird cannot do (the bird does not sow, reap, or gather into barns). But what is being proposed here is a radically different view of the significance of work. Far from being a necessary evil – necessary because of worries about one's future if one *doesn't* work – work is presented as a good insofar as it enables us to avoid the sin of sloth and to become 'God's co-worker' (UDVS, 199/SKS 8, 295).[8] Part of the message seems to be: instead of worry being the motivation for work (as with the wood-dove), think how glorious it is to be a human being, a key element of which is how glorious it is to work (as God's co-worker). In this way, *work itself, far from being a curse or of merely instrumental value, can be the source of joy*. The point is that viewing work as either co-creation, vocation, or some combination of the two, offers a radically different view of its meaning from that tacitly assumed by the worried wood-dove (and us, insofar as we resemble it).

The 1849 discourses

The focus on addressing worry is continued into the 1849 lily and bird discourses. The focus of each discourse is, respectively, silence, obedience, and joy. In the first, equivalences are drawn between 'seeking first God's kingdom' (as in the gospel passage), becoming nothing before God, and learning to be silent (WA, 10–1/SKS 11, 16–7), and this is further connected with prayer

(WA, 11–2/SKS 11, 17–8). Wanting to speak can be corrupting, a claim Kierkegaard illustrates through an example of someone who wants to ensure that he communicates a matter of grave importance to God with the greatest possible clarity, accuracy, and completeness (WA, 11/SKS 11, 17). In prayer, as Kierkegaard tells it, the more fervent one becomes, the less one has to say, leading ultimately to silence: 'Then what happened to him if he did really pray with all his heart? Something amazing happened to him. Gradually, as he became more and more fervent in prayer, he had less and less to say, and finally he became completely silent' (WA, 11–2/SKS 11, 17). Instead of wanting to speak, one learns how to listen: to be receptive to divine wisdom.

Gregory Beabout (2007: 145–6) describes this silence as the typically unnamed virtue of 'active receptivity' or 'welcoming openness.' Such receptivity, which is importantly different from a passivity constituted merely by lack or deficiency, involves 'attentively opening oneself up and waiting' (Beabout 2007: 144); this is 'the practice of silence.' This connects to other spiritual qualities valorised in Kierkegaard's discourses, namely patience and hope.[9] One obvious link to humility here is our being urged not to become more important to ourselves than the lily and bird who are our teachers. At first, this might sound like a *ranking* view of humility: don't overestimate your own importance. But the wider context enables us better to understand this. The listening that is the ultimate attitude of prayer does not begin and end in isolation before God. Elsewhere, such as in *Works of Love*, Kierkegaard stresses in various passages how love of God may be expressed through love of neighbour. For instance: 'If you want to show that your life is intended to serve God, *then let it serve people*, yet continually with the thought of God' (WL, 161/SKS 9, 161; emphasis added); 'To love people is the only thing worth living for, and without this love you are not really living' (WL, 375/SKS 9, 368); 'In the Christian sense, to love people is to love God, and to love God is to love people – *what you do unto people you do unto God*' (WL, 384/SKS 11, 376; emphasis added). In combination, this seems to valorise a kind of *God-saturated loving attention to the other* (as opposed to self-focus). I suggest that other-centred humility of this sort looks like a plausible answer to the question of what it means to embody the 'listening,' receptive, or attentive attitude in the way one lives.

The second discourse focuses on the unconditional *obedience* to God that the lily and bird are also said to teach (WA, 24/SKS 11, 29). This discourse builds on the first insofar as to become silent is said to be the first condition for truly being able to obey (WA, 24/SKS 11, 29). But in a discussion of a lily assigned to a place 'as unfortunate as possible' (WA, 27/SKS 11, 31), Kierkegaard seems to get at this obedience in terms of a contrast between what he takes to be the typical attitude of the human to such a scenario and that of his imagined lily. Humility seems quite central to this contrast. The human, Kierkegaard claims, would say:

> it is too much to endure. To be a lily and as lovely as a lily, and then to be assigned a spot in such a place, to have to flower there in surroundings as unfavourable as possible, as if the intention were to destroy the impression of one's loveliness – no, it is too much to endure; indeed, it is a self-contradiction on the part of the Creator!
> *(WA, 27/SKS 11, 31–2)*

But the lily's response is one of humility: 'I myself, of course, have not been able to determine the place and the conditions; this is not in the remotest way my affair. That I stand where I stand is God's will' (WA, 27/SKS 11, 32). And the attitude behind this humility becomes easier to acquire if one's focus is not constantly on oneself.

The third discourse focuses on joy. Here exemplarity is important: joy is best taught by the joyful, who have nothing else to do but to 'be joy'; to be 'unconditionally joyful' (WA, 36–7/SKS 11, 40–1). In other words, the bird *embodies* joy. But the *content* of its 'teaching of joy' is:

'There is a today – and there is no worry . . . about tomorrow or the day after tomorrow' (WA, 38/SKS 11, 42). This is 'the joy of silence and obedience' (WA, 38/SKS 11, 42) that links the three discourses. But how does this connect with humility – and again, of what sort?

Addressing worry through humility

Before sketching in more detail the kind of humility that I suggest is at work in Kierkegaard's discourses, a caveat. It is commonplace in writing on humility to note the bad press this quality typically receives, writers typically being keen to distinguish 'virtuous' humility from various forms of excessive self-abasement, insincere duplicitous manipulation (think Dickens' Uriah Heep), or the qualities that led Hume (1975: 270) to dismiss humility as a 'monkish virtue.' The discussion above shows that we also need a conception of humility in which comparison with others is downplayed (at least as much as possible). In much recent debate about humility (or modesty), scholars disagree about whether it involves a disposition to *underestimate* accomplishments or self-worth in some respect (and if so to what degree),[10] or whether it involves, on the contrary, *accurate* self-assessment which nonetheless does not *exaggerate* one's importance.[11] Such accounts risk relying too heavily on 'the spirit of comparison.' As noted, what we need is an account in which the humble person is characterized not by thinking *less* of themselves (like the worried lily and wood-dove, comparing themselves with others and ranking themselves relatively low), but by thinking *about* themselves less. They resist the temptation towards a mindset and orientation towards the world in which the self, its needs, concerns, and accomplishments are uppermost. Different aspects of such a view of humility have recently been emphasized by Joseph Kupfer, Robert C. Roberts, and Nicolas Bommarito.[12] In what follows, I shall aim to show that the seeds of such a view can be found in some of Kierkegaard's discourses.

In a valuable article, Joseph Kupfer (2003) has argued for four dimensions of the 'moral perspective of humility.' First is acknowledgement of our *radical dependence*: the need to acknowledge how much of whatever we might have achieved depends upon people, institutions, and circumstances beyond our control, which ties humility to *gratitude* (Kupfer 2003: 252–3, 260–1). The obvious contrast here is with the 'vice of pride' that Robert C. Roberts (2016: 66) labels 'hyper-autonomy,' such as in cases where, having been rescued from, say, financial disaster by a friend's efforts, one secretly resents the friend because he is a constant reminder of one's dependency on others. The ultimate source of 'every good and every perfect gift' (EUD, 31–48/SKS 5, 39–56) for Kierkegaard is of course God, and it is this recognition of radical dependence that such an attitude primarily registers.[13] There are several examples of this in the first part of the *Christian Discourses*, 'The Worries [*Bekymringer*] of the Pagans.' For instance, Kierkegaard's discussion of the person who prays for his daily bread (CD, 14/SKS 10, 26), in his discourse on the worry of poverty. But also, and less obviously, in his discussion in the immediately following discourse on the worry of abundance, of the relatively wealthy person who manages to lose 'the *thought of possession*' (CD, 26/SKS 10, 38); the thought that the abundance that he has is really *his*. This latter is achieved in two ways. First, by realizing that to 'be secure *for* tomorrow,' one must 'be sure *of* tomorrow' – and yet the attitude of 'this very day' bears in mind the possibility that one might die 'this very night' (CD, 27/SKS 10, 38–9).[14] Second, by realizing that everything one has can be lost: indeed, being loseable is its 'essential feature' (CD, 27/SKS 10, 39). One is only a steward of what one has: it is on loan from God (CD, 29/SKS 10, 40). Radical dependence also emerges in some of the later discourses, such as in 'The Worry of Presumptuousness [*Formastelighedens*],' in which the Christian who lacks this worry is said to avoid it by recognizing that to need God is a human being's highest perfection (CD, 64/SKS 10, 73), such that he lacks all 'self-will,' craving only to be satisfied with God's grace.

The second feature of Kupfer's moral perspective of humility arises in response to a concern – prevalent in much recent writing on humility – about how those of particularly impressive achievements may nevertheless remain humble. He notes that a focus on morally exemplary people helps to keep our 'technical' (e.g., sporting, academic, or professional) achievements in perspective: someone of exceptional achievements of this kind may thereby come to realize that their 'technical' inferior is their moral superior, say in terms of the time, energy, or resources they give to others (2003: 253).[15] For Kierkegaard, the key focus on the exemplary concerns the relation to Christ as pattern, but there are other, more surprising, examples. In the fourth discourse in 'The Gospel of Sufferings,' the repentant robber crucified alongside Jesus emerges as such an exemplar. His 'depth and humility' (UDVS, 272/SKS 8, 368) inheres in grasping that to suffer as guilty (the headline topic of the discourse), to recognize oneself as a sinner, 'is an alleviation [*Lindning*] in comparison to' the pain of Christ's death (UDVS, 272/SKS 8, 368–9). Now, the focus on another person illustrated here is hardly one in which the robber joyfully forgets his own sufferings – a tall order while nailed to a cross – yet the emphasis is that, even in such circumstances, he is able to recognize Christ's goodness, such that even here he can realize that there is one final task: repentance (UDVS, 280–1/SKS 8, 376–7). And in more everyday examples, we can sometimes be taken out of our worries altogether by a focus on others. A further example of this kind of valuable self-forgetting can be found in 'The Worry of Lowliness,' in which the 'lowly' Christian's focus on God as the pattern in 'faith's joy' over divine glory enables him to forget his own lowliness. However, the most obvious parallel with Kupfer's claim occurs in Kierkegaard's fourth 'worries' discourse, 'The Worry of Loftiness [*Højhedens*],' in a discussion of how a relatively 'eminent' [*fornemme*] Christian avoids this worry. Such a person recognizes, however the world treats him, that all human beings are of equal value in the eyes of God: our common humanity is again what matters. The challenge he faces – in the light of various admirers and hangers-on – parallels that facing those of great 'technical' achievements in Kupfer's discussion. What keeps such a person's feet on the ground is his belief that all are equal in the sight of God; that he too is a sinner in need of God's forgiveness; and that nobody comes to Christ except as lowly (CD, 51–2/SKS 10, 61–2). Thus the first criterion – recognition of our radical dependence – is combined with the second.

In Kupfer's third criterion, setting high moral ideals enables even the morally exemplary to keep their ethical achievements in perspective, as the infinite nature of the ethical demand means that there is always more to be done. When they succeed, they are aware of how much more is to be done, so rather than bask in their success they just get on with doing more of what is needed. Their focus is on the pursuit of the good, rather than their own achievements in pursuing the good. (What makes this possible is, perhaps, that they are not hindered by what Roberts calls the 'vices of pride': such features as the desire for domination, hyper-autonomy, vanity, arrogance, and envy.) The fourth and final dimension of Kupfer's (2003: 253, 256) moral perspective of humility is an orientation towards objectively valuable things in the world such that we appreciate and promote the value of these goods (e.g., scientific and artistic achievements, the glories of nature) *apart from their instrumental value to ourselves*. Outstanding people of great humility, claims Kupfer (2003: 257), are typically 'committed to serve something outside themselves, such as art or science, mankind or God, because it is worthwhile in itself.' The upshot of this is that the humble person's attention is outwardly directed, as a result of which they 'are disposed not to dwell on themselves' (Kupfer 2003: 251). The 'spirit of comparison' against which Kierkegaard warns is dispelled: as their humility deepens, 'they are less inclined to compare themselves with others – on either technical or moral grounds' (Kupfer 2003: 253). But this lack of self-absorption need not – *pace* Driver – entail self-ignorance. Roberts (2009: 129), who sees humility as the absence of 'the vices of pride,' presents a similar picture of humility as 'a trait marked by the absence of a certain kind of concern or concerned attention' such that the humble person is focused on value-not-necessarily-related-to-the-self rather than herself. Nicolas Bommarito (2013: 111) also echoes such a view in his account of humility as a 'virtue of attention,' characterized by '*inattentiveness* to good qualities that reflect well on oneself, the value of such qualities, and one's own role in bringing them about.' The last seems to me crucial. It cannot be only inattention or the right kind of attention (to such qualities or their value) which makes such humility a virtue. This is why Kupfer's initial focus on our 'radical dependence' on others is important, as it highlights the significance of gratitude in developing the virtue of humility. The person who simply does not dwell on his good qualities or their value seems *ceteris paribus* less humble than the person who does not do so *because he recognizes what he owes to others*.

This focus also enables us to highlight another important point. Distinguishing *acting* immodestly (a social vice) from actually *being* immodest, Bommarito asks what is wrong with the latter when it does not manifest itself in the former. After all, plenty of people short on humility have mastered the idea that *acting* immodestly is socially vulgar, yet they remain lacking in humility even if they are not so clumsy as regularly to *display* this fact. Consistent with the view I have been sketching here, Bommarito (2013: 114–5) persuasively suggests that their problem is one of overattending to their own goodness at the expense of attending to the good qualities of others. Such immodesty is a vice of self-centeredness (which, I have argued elsewhere [Lippitt 2013: 115–6], is different from the vice of selfishness). The absence of such self-centredness might itself be described as a 'virtue of (in)attention.'

Moreover, this also enables us to see that the humble person's not dwelling on her own qualities does not rule out the possibility of self-improvement. It might be thought that only by focusing on my strengths and weaknesses – and thus comparing myself to others in the relevant respects – can I ever hope to improve. Bommarito suggests that one can still *pay attention* to something about one's qualities without *dwelling* on them. The person seeking self-improvement will have to pay more attention to her shortcomings than her good qualities: 'what is essential is attending to her present weaknesses – the very things she will try to improve. She will also attend to the good qualities of *others* that she wishes to emulate' (Bommarito 2013: 109–10). This is precisely the purpose of the focus on moral exemplars in Kupfer's account of humility. However, in that account, the first two features (radical dependence and moral comparison) 'tend to fade in importance the more humility is informed by the latter dimensions of moral ideal and objective valuation.' Kupfer (2003: 265) concludes: 'Paying less rather than more attention to ourselves is the hallmark of the deepest, most advanced humility.... The more individuals are occupied with their guiding ideals and standards, and what they find objectively worthwhile in the world, the less they will attend to themselves.'[16]

If – as I believe to be the case – this is broadly right, then this highlights the need to clarify something important about Kierkegaard's 'spirit of comparison.' As the case of the humble person striving for self-improvement illustrates, comparison can have a positive value. But much of what I take Kierkegaard to mean by the 'spirit of comparison' is something quite different from that manifested in our humble self-improver. We can see this by considering a possible objection to the account sketched here. Why don't the achievements of the morally exemplary, in comparison to my own, inspire the same anxiety that troubled the worried lily? Why should I not feel the same inadequacy in the face of their achievements as the lily felt in comparison to the Crown Imperials? The answer is that the lily's problem was its *competitive ego*. Without this ego's demands, it is possible genuinely to enjoy, to delight in, the achievements of others, including their moral achievements.[17] The virtuously humble do not feel this anxiety insofar as they have 'died' to a significant extent to their competitive egos (a central element in the talk of 'dying to the self' that runs through Kierkegaard's writings). This gives them what Roberts

(2007: 81) describes as 'a transcendent form of self-confidence' stemming from a worldview in which – despite the great differences of achievement, moral and otherwise – everyone is viewed as of ultimately equal value, rather than others being viewed as 'the competition.' The ideal here, which Roberts (2007: 90; emphasis added) discusses in the context of raising a child in a healthily loving environment, is a sense of one's own worth which, 'if carried into adulthood by becoming articulated in a definite life view, would *be the radical self-confidence that Christians call humility*: a self-confidence so deep, a personal integration so strong that all comparison with other people, both advantageous and disadvantageous, slides right off him.' He has a sufficient sense of his own worth neither to be distressed by the fact that others are in several respects ahead of him in aspects of life, nor to take a gleeful pleasure in the respects in which he is himself ahead. Thus, the humble high achiever neither basks in his success nor feels the lily's debilitating anxiety about his failures. *Kierkegaardian joy, I suggest, can be an expression of this rather unusual form of 'self-confidence.'* Such an attitude manifests a self-acceptance that enables one to keep worry in its place, and is rooted in considering our common humanity to be more important than the differences highlighted by 'comparison' as competition.[18]

It is in this light, finally, that I suggest we see Kierkegaard's focus on avoiding the worries of 'tomorrow' or 'the next day': the future-oriented worry that has been our central theme. In 'The Worry of Self-Torment,' Kierkegaard describes 'the next day' in nautical terms as the grappling-hook by which worries seize hold of one (CD, 72/SKS 10, 81), but claims that 'the next day' does not exist for the Christian who has got beyond the worry of self-torment, since he has taken to heart the gospel's claim that tomorrow will worry about its own troubles – so he need not. In a memorable image, Kierkegaard suggests that just as a rower turns his back to his direction of travel, so does the person who lives absorbed in today turn his back on future-oriented worry (CD, 73/SKS 10, 82). The problems of tomorrow do not thereby disappear in a puff of smoke. But the worries that stem from pointlessly focusing on issues beyond one's control and which render any action in pursuit of the good likely to seem pointless, can indeed be dispelled. I suggest that the conception of humility sketched here is a major way in which one transcends such debilitating worry: at the very least, one does not add to the ordinary forms of 'torment' life can throw at us this additional, avoidable self-torment that is the cost of excessive self-absorption in light of the 'spirit of comparison.' In other words, the humility we can learn from the lilies and the birds is a major part of the proposed cure.

Related topics

'Love for humans: morality as the heart of Kierkegaard's religious philosophy,' Sharon Krishek; 'Kierkegaard on nature and natural beauty,' Anthony Rudd; 'Kierkegaard's defense of nature and theology against natural theology,' Will Williams.

Notes

1 In his wide-ranging history of the concept of joy (a concept of great interest to Kierkegaard), Adam Potkay (2007: 78) suggests that Luther is the author who turned the word *angst* (and its cognates in other languages) towards its modern sense of 'pervasive gloom and oppressive, future-oriented worry.'
2 Though 'vanity' is not, in my view, quite the right term for this kind of self-absorption or self-centredness.
3 In terms of other available views of humility – more of which later – this sounds more like either the 'accurate self-assessment' or 'owning one's limitations' view.
4 The remaining discourse – in addition to the three each in *Upbuilding Discourses in Various Spirits* and *Without Authority*, and the seven in *Christian Discourses* – is found in *Judge for Yourself!*

5 This is the term translated 'care' in the Hong translation of *Christian Discourses*, in its discussion of 'the cares of the pagans.' The term 'worry' strikes me as less ambiguous, so I shall use that translation in what follows.
6 I have suggested elsewhere (Lippitt 2016) that Kierkegaard seeks to oppose such anxiety with a certain kind of self-acceptance, rooted in a sense of life as a gift and a fundamental trust in the goodness thereof. The next couple of paragraphs are adapted from this other paper.
7 For more on this, and the combination of jest and earnestness more generally, see Lippitt (2018).
8 The hardworking apostle Paul is presented as exemplary here (UDVS, 199–200/SKS 8, 296).
9 It also suggests comparisons with the notion of 'attention' in such thinkers as Iris Murdoch and Simone Weil.
10 Julia Driver has been the most prominent proponent of the underestimation view. For some key discussions in this debate, see Driver (1989; 1999; 2001) and Schueler (1997; 1999). Nicolas Bommarito (2013: 95) notes that 'The bulk of the contemporary philosophical literature on modesty is made up of various responses to Julia Driver's account.' Taking his terminology from this discussion, Bommarito (2013: 93n1) uses the term 'modesty,' while acknowledging this term and 'humility' to be interchangeable. Likewise, I reject the distinction between humility and modesty made in some of this literature, also treating them as interchangeable terms, but I shall not argue that case here.
11 See for instance Richards (1992: 8); Flanagan (1990); Whitcomb, et al. (2017) (though this latter offers a distinct view, 'owning one's limitations,' that I have no room to discuss here).
12 Aspects of this view are also prevalent in many of the accounts found in Worthington, et al. (2017). In noting these commonalities, I do not mean to imply that the accounts offered by each of these writers are identical.
13 I have argued elsewhere (Lippitt 2018) that this is a key feature of what Kierkegaard calls 'jest.'
14 In an 1847 journal entry, Kierkegaard notes: 'Augustine has said it so well: Certainly God has promised you forgiveness – but he has not promised you the next day' (KJN 4, 273/SKS 20, 56).
15 I see this as a particular twist on a more general claim made by Flanagan (1990: 425): that the world's fastest runner, say, 'might think that being the world's fastest human is not so important *sub specie aeternitatis*.'
16 Similarly, I suggest that in more advanced states of humility, the gratitude discussed earlier may be the background assumption against which a life operates rather than being the continual focus of conscious attention.
17 Both Kupfer and Bommarito make this point of the humble person, and it is at least implicit in Roberts' inclusion of envy as one of the vices of pride. The ability thus to delight, one might claim, is an aspect of love.
18 One of the editors raises an interesting question here: is there room for the humble person to be disappointed in their moral progress in comparison with others? The suggestion is that this may be morally beneficial despite having a comparative element. She asks: Would the person who has a sufficient sense of his or her own worth never feel this kind of distress? Consider Frank, someone who readily admits his faults – but who does not take any fault very seriously. Surely – goes the objection – such a person as Frank suggests that contentment with one's moral progress is not the right attitude? While debilitating anxiety about one's failures is clearly unhelpful, is there a *healthy* anxiety about those failures? I think the answer to this question is probably yes. To clarify, then: I am not claiming that Kierkegaard's lilies and birds discourses can properly be used to justify *complacency* (which is, I take it, the charge against Frank). I am not valorizing contentment as complacency. What Kierkegaard is *inter alia* offering us, in my view, is rather a kind of encouragement in the face of disappointment with ourselves, as an alternative to an attitude that allows that disappointment to become distress.

References

Beabout, G. R. (2007) 'The silent lily and bird as exemplars of the virtue of active receptivity,' in R. L. Perkins (ed), *International Kierkegaard Commentary*, vol. 18 (*Without Authority*), Macon, GA: Mercer University Press.
Bommarito, N. (2013) 'Modesty as a virtue of attention,' *Philosophical Review*, 122, no. 1: 93–117.
Driver, J. (2001) *Uneasy virtue*, Cambridge: Cambridge University Press.
Driver, J. (1999) 'Modesty and ignorance,' *Ethics*, 109: 827–34.
Driver, J. (1989) 'The virtues of ignorance,' *Journal of Philosophy*, 86: 373–84.

Flanagan, O. (1990) 'Virtue and ignorance,' *Journal of Philosophy*, 87: 420–8.
Hume, D. (1975) *Enquiries concerning human understanding and concerning the principles of morals*, Oxford: Oxford University Press.
Kupfer, J. (2003) 'The moral perspective of humility,' *Pacific Philosophical Quarterly*, 84, no. 3: 249–69.
Lippitt, J. (2018) 'Jest as humility: Kierkegaard and the limits of earnestness,' in L. Moland (ed), *All Too Human: Laughter, Humor, and Comedy in 19th-Century Philosophy*, Dordrecht: Springer.
Lippitt, J. (2016) 'What can therapists learn from Kierkegaard?' in M. Bazzano and J. Webb (eds), *Therapy and the Counter-tradition*, London: Routledge.
Lippitt, J. (2013) *Kierkegaard and the problem of self-love*, Cambridge: Cambridge University Press.
O'Gorman, F. (2015) *Worrying: A literary and cultural history*, London: Bloomsbury.
Potkay, A. (2007) *The story of joy: From the Bible to late romanticism*, Cambridge: Cambridge University Press.
Richards, N. (1992) *Humility*, Philadelphia, PA: Temple University Press.
Roberts, R. C. (2016) 'Gratitude and humility,' in D. Carr (ed), *Perspectives on Gratitude: An Interdisciplinary Approach*, London: Routledge.
Roberts, R. C. (2009) 'The vice of pride,' *Faith and Philosophy*, 26, no. 2: 119–33.
Roberts, R. C. (2007) *Spiritual emotions: A psychology of Christian virtues*, Grand Rapids, MI: Eerdmans.
Schueler, G. F. (1999) 'Why is modesty a virtue?' *Ethics*, 109: 835–41.
Schueler, G. F. (1997) 'Why modesty is a virtue,' *Ethics*, 107: 467–85.
Whitcomb, D., Battaly, H., Baehr, J., and Howard-Snyder, D. (2017) 'Intellectual humility: Owning our limitations,' *Philosophy and Phenomenological Research*, 94: 509–39.
Worthington, E. L., Jr., Davis, D. E., and Hook, J. N. (eds) (2017) *Handbook of humility: Theory, research, and applications*, London: Routledge.

Further reading

Pattison, G. and Møller Jensen, H. (2012) *Kierkegaard's pastoral dialogues*, Eugene, OR: Wipf & Stock.
This book is a representation of some key insights from Kierkegaard's upbuilding discourses – including those on the lilies and birds – in the form of dialogues between a believer and a non-believer. It includes three brief distinct responses to the dialogues.

Roberts, R. C. (2007) *Spiritual emotions: A psychology of Christian virtues*, Grand Rapids, MI: Eerdmans.
This book is an accessible account of several of the New Testament's 'fruits of the Spirit' as 'emotion-virtues,' rooted in the author's extensive work on the philosophy of the emotions, and set against the background of a discussion of 'humility as a moral project.'

Worthington, E. L., Jr., Davis, D. E., and Hook, J. N. (eds) (2017) *Handbook of humility: Theory, research, and applications*, London: Routledge.
This book is something of a contemporary 'state of the art' collection on accounts of humility, mostly from psychology and counselling studies, but also including contributions from scholars of philosophy and religion.

8

DID NAPOLEON TELEOLOGICALLY SUSPEND THE ETHICAL? A DILEMMA FOR SOME 'HEGELIAN' READINGS OF *FEAR AND TREMBLING*

Ryan S. Kemp

Introduction

Most scholars agree that you need to know a little Hegel before you can really appreciate the full aim and scope of Kierkegaard's philosophical project. This seems especially true in the case of *Fear and Trembling*, where a slew of recent and not-so-recent commentators have argued that *Fear and Trembling*'s account of ethics is uniquely 'Hegelian,' and that this has important implications for how we interpret what de silentio[1] means by 'going beyond ethics.' If ethics is understood in a 'Kantian' sense, then de silentio recommends a faith that is strongly absurd; he requires the would-be Abraham to transgress moral commands that are universally valid. Luckily, as these interpreters see it, *Fear and Trembling*'s account of ethics is 'Hegelian.' This means that ethical norms are relative to particular historical communities, which means that Abraham is not invited to transgress universal moral norms, which means he is not so extreme after all (cf. Evans 2006; Stern 2012; and Westphal 1998). Disaster averted![2]

In one respect, these interpreters (I refer to them respectfully as Local Norm Interpreters and shortly as LNI-ers) are obviously right: Hegel is uncontroversially the historical model for *Fear and Trembling*'s account of the ethical. Not only do references to the 'system' adorn the work's preface, de silentio thinks of philosophy's task in uniquely Hegelian terms: to render 'the whole content of faith into conceptual form' (FT, 7/SKS 4, 103). Additionally, when de silentio poses the question of the teleological suspension of the ethical, he writes, 'For if the ethical, i.e. the ethical life [*det Sædelige*], is the highest and nothing incommensurable remains in a human being in any way other than that incommensurability constituting evil . . . then one needs no other categories than what the Greek philosophers had. . . . Hegel should not have concealed this' (Kierkegaard 2006: 47-8/SKS 4, 149).[3] Here de silentio explicitly invokes Hegel's notion of the ethical when he modifies 'ethical' [*Ethiske*] with 'ethical life' [*det Sædelige*]. 'Det Sædelige' is the Danish equivalent of the German 'die Sittlichkeit,' the term of art Hegel uses to refer to his own account of ethics, an account that – as I explain below – emphasizes the role of concrete social and institutional norms.

Where Local Norm Interpreters appear to go wrong is in their further suggestion that being 'Hegelian' in this way means that you think ethics is relative to particular historical communities. Though it is strictly speaking correct to say that Hegel's account of ethics as *Sittlichkeit* moves away from – as Westphal (1998: 109) puts it – a 'historically unmediated ethics of pure reason,' this does not mean that just any set of historical customs and institutions qualify as fully rational. In texts like *Elements of the Philosophy of Right*, Hegel makes it clear that *Sittlichkeit* is a normative ideal that arises in a historical context in which various inadequate practical frameworks have been superseded by an ideally rational network of institutions and practices.[4] This means that every normative framework that exists prior to this idealized state fails to qualify as fully ethical precisely insofar as it fails to live up to a universal rational standard, albeit one that is grounded in communal and institutional practices.

My case against the Local Norm Interpretation depends on showing that its account of the teleological suspension of the ethical (for short, TSE) does not permit a sufficient break with Hegel. I argue that de silentio expressly presents the TSE as a move that Hegel cannot in principle endorse. I then show that on the LNI account Hegel can – at least in some cases – endorse it. This is because the LNI account is broad enough to include Hegel's 'world historical agent' – a person whose actions are rationally justified even though they conflict with local ethical norms. If I am right to think that (1) de silentio develops the teleological suspension of the ethical as a move that is not open to Hegelian analysis, and (2) the Local Norm Interpretation of the TSE is broad enough to include Hegel's world historical agent, then I will have provided a strong *prima facie* reason to think that the LNI camp is mistaken. Teleologically suspending the ethical is not merely a break with the mores of some local community: it is a break with all possible communities.

Here is the basic structure of the chapter. I begin with a brief sketch of a recent and prominent Local Norm Interpretation. Next, I offer an account of Hegel's world historical agent that reveals her actions to be fully compatible with LNI accounts of the teleological suspension of the ethical. Finally, I explain why this is significant. I argue that it suggests that LNI descriptions of the teleological suspension of the ethical fail to satisfy one of de silentio's chief criteria: the exclusion of practical justification.

The local norm interpretation

Fear and Trembling is a thought experiment. It invites the reader to imagine what faith would have to be in order to enjoy genuine independence from philosophy. Assuming that faith occupies a distinct normative space, it must – at least sometimes – require a person to break with practical reason, or ethics, as the philosopher understands it. Furthermore, de silentio makes it clear, as we said above, that it is Hegel's understanding of ethics that is at issue: each of *Fear and Trembling*'s three problems begins by inviting an account that could avoid Hegelian analysis.[5] De silentio suggests that a sufficient condition for avoiding such analysis is teleologically suspending the ethical: insofar as someone makes this move, they have also left Hegelian justification behind. My concern is that some recent and fairly significant interpreters of *Fear and Trembling* have described the TSE in such a way that Hegel *could* understand at least some agents who make this move. In this section I sketch an especially influential version of this thesis.

C. Stephen Evans has been a major force in Kierkegaard scholarship over the last four decades.[6] One of his primary goals has been to uproot a longstanding interpretation of Kierkegaard that portrays him as an advocate of a strongly irrational faith. With this in mind, Evans defends a reading of *Fear and Trembling* that presents 'faith as the telos of morality.' He claims that, 'The main point of *Fear and Trembling* . . . is not that faith is opposed to morality, but that genuine religious faith cannot be reduced to a life of moral striving, or completely understood using only the categories of a rationalistic morality' (Evans 2006: 210). In faith, Evans goes on to say, we receive not a cancelling of ethics but its ultimate fulfilment in a higher rationality. '[This] new conception differs from the old one in two fundamental ways: (1) the basis of the ethic is not collective judgments of society but the transcendent message of God; (2) the ethic does not merely prescribe ideals but concerns itself with the concrete conditions that make it possible to realize ideals' (Evans 2006: 222). It is the first feature, transcendence of societal judgments, which is supposed to distinguish de silentio's person of faith from the merely ethical person. In his later essays, Evans characterizes the account of ethics offered in *Fear and Trembling* as specifically 'Hegelian.' While this much seems right, we need to get a better handle on what Evans means by this.

Evans (2006: 216) characterizes the Hegelian account as one 'that sees the highest life as . . . devoted to the furtherance of social institutions and socially sanctioned values. . . [T]his life is conceived . . . as in some sense absolute or final.' As a description of a feature of Hegel's account there is not much to argue with here. There is no question that Hegel (unlike, say, Kant) thinks that ethical norms are embodied in a concrete social world. The problem with this sketch is that it does not highlight the sense in which, for Hegel, some ethical worlds are better than others. This is the story of Hegel's *Phenomenology of Spirit*. 'Spirit' (or 'Reason' or 'God') comes to fuller self-consciousness in subsequent epochs of history with a final culmination in a social order that is absolutely rational. The norms that are present at the end of this historical narrative have final authority precisely because 'Spirit' is fully present in community life.

This extra bit of the Hegelian story raises questions for Local Norm Interpreters, especially when we consider that Hegel thinks human agents are often the impetus for normative change. Hegel's 'world historical agent' presents a challenge to her social world's norms for the sake of Spirit: she has a 'higher reason' that transcends the local. On the Local Norm Interpretation, we would say that the world historical agent teleologically suspends the ethical. But if this is right, it follows that such a suspension is explainable from within the Hegelian system. Hegel is in a position to fully endorse at least some figures who break with local ethical norms. Given this possibility, it is in our interest as students of *Fear and Trembling* to look at this aspect of Hegel's account in closer detail. Depending on what we discover, Local Norm Interpreters may need to modify their interpretation.

Hegel's world historical figure

In his *Lectures on the Philosophy of World History*, Hegel provides an analysis of world historical individuals that helps explain their relationship to the ethical world they inhabit. 'The great individuals of world history,' he claims,

> are those who seize upon [a] higher universal and make it their own end . . . Indeed, their justification does not lie in the prevailing situation, for they draw their inspiration from another source, from that hidden spirit whose hour is near but which still lies beneath the surface and seeks to break out without yet having attained an existence in the present.
>
> (Hegel 1975: 82–3)

One question we need to answer concerns the justification of this 'higher universal.' Are the actions of the world historical person ethically justified so that even their contemporaries ought to recognize the goodness of their actions? Or, does Hegel imagine a distinct form of rational justification that transcends mere ethical evaluation? For our purposes, a lot hangs on how this gets spelled out.

The question of whether the world historical person's commitment to a higher universal amounts to a teleological suspension of the ethical is not new to Hegel scholarship. In *Hegel's Ethical Thought*, Allen Wood argues precisely this (1990). Working from LNI assumptions about what Kierkegaard means by a teleological suspension of the ethical, Wood claims that the world historical person's transgression of ethical norms is fully justified by a higher rational norm. In a recent essay, Mark Alznauer challenges Wood on this point. He looks to show that the actions of the world historical agent 'do not involve any transcendence of the situated ethical point of view' (Alznauer 2012: 585). I will briefly develop Alznauer's objection before returning to defend the idea, shared by both Alznauer and Wood, that there is some sense in which the world historical agent's actions are justified. She transcends local ethics, but not universal reason.

Alznauer's chief concern is to show that, against initial appearances, Hegel does not think that there can be justified violations of ethical norms. Alznauer's motivation is familiar to the reader of *Fear and Trembling*: it is uncomfortable (both philosophically and morally) to claim that a person, even a rather special one, can justifiably violate the moral law. Though Alznauer spends much of his essay addressing this issue as it arises in various forms in Hegel's philosophy, he identifies the passages on the world historical agent as an especially serious objection to his thesis.

Alznauer notes two ways in which Hegel appears to defend the actions of the world historical agent against the 'small-minded moralist.' The first involves defending her against the Kantian accusation that she furthers ethical ends through selfish motives. Hegel's response here is to simply accuse the moralist of misunderstanding ethics: a subjective motive (say, Caesar's ambition) can be ethically justified when it serves objective ends (Rome's).

The second accusation against the world historical agent is more to the point; it concerns the justification of even the immoral actions of great people, for instance, the large-scale massacres perpetrated by Genghis Kahn. We have already seen how Wood treats passages like these. Wood (1990: 229–30) writes:

> The small-mindedness of the moralist. . . [consists] in failing to see that great men have justification for the crimes they commit which transcends the moral and ethical spheres altogether. Here the small-mindedness of moralists consists in the fact that when they consider world historical deeds, they think it is appropriate to make any moral judgments at all.

In defence of his interpretation, Wood leans heavily on passages like the following from the *Lectures*:

> The deeds of the great men who are the individuals of world history thus appear justified not only in their inner significance (of which the individuals in question are unconscious), but also in a secular sense. But from this latter point of view, no representations should be made against world-historical deeds and those who perform them by moral circles to which such individuals do not belong. The litany of private virtues – modesty, humility, charity, liberality, etc. – must not be raised against them.
>
> *(Hegel 1975: 141)*

While would-be defenders of Hegelian amoralism draw attention to the final line of the quote (the prohibition against holding great people accountable for violations of private virtue), Alznauer thinks this passage underdetermines such readings. Where Wood sees this passage as confirming that external ethical evaluations of the world historical agent are invalidated, Alznauer emphasizes Hegel's reference to 'private virtues,' that is, personal traits that are altogether distinct from the public virtues of ethics. Alznauer (2012: 597–8) writes:

> When Hegel says that great individuals should not be criticized from the point of view of 'moral circles to which they do not belong,' he is not speaking of morality or ethics per se, but of the 'private virtues,' and private is not a redundant adjective here. The direct implication is that world-historical individuals can and should be assessed according to their public virtue.

Alznauer goes on to add that public virtue always concerns service to the state and that this helps make sense of why, just a few lines later, Hegel (1975: 141) rejects the 'misunderstood dichotomy between morality and politics.'

While Alznauer's intuitions here are plausible, he acknowledges that his interpretation appears to be in tension with other passages, for instance, one that directly precedes the quote in question. There Hegel (1975: 141) claims that: 'Those who, on ethical grounds (and hence with a noble intention), have resisted what the progress of the Idea of the spirit required, stand higher in moral worth than those whose crimes have been transformed by a higher order into the instrument of realising its will.' This passage is troubling for Alznauer because it seems to recommend precisely the double standard that he is inclined to resist: that there is, for instance, one ethical standard for world historical agents and another for the rest of us. His response is to qualify the sense in which the standard is double. He writes, 'When world-historical individuals are justified, like Caesar, they are justified on ethical grounds broadly considered. When they cannot be justified on ethical grounds, like Genghis Kahn, their world-historical importance does not affect their moral responsibility for their crimes' (Alznauer 2012: 599). In other words, Genghis Kahn is not measured against a double ethical standard but rather two distinct standards. One is moral and refers to present local norms; the other is rational and refers to the norms of the world historical moment, what the progress of history demands. With respect to only the first set of norms is the world historical agent 'guilty.'

This outcome is puzzling given Alznauer's stated ambition. As we saw above, he sets out to show that the actions of the world historical agent 'do not involve any transcendence of the situated ethical point of view' (Alznauer 2012: 585). In light of our analysis, this needs to be modified a bit. The only thing that Alznauer shows is that the world historical agent is justifiably evaluated according to local ethical norms: Napoleon et al. can be held morally responsible by their contemporaries. At the same time, however, such agents transcend the situated ethical point of view in another respect: they act in accordance with a higher rational norm. While it is perhaps a bit awkward for rational and ethical justification to come apart like this, this appears to be Hegel's view and one that both Wood and Alznauer acknowledge.

We should now consider more explicitly what implications this has for how we think about the teleological suspension of the ethical in *Fear and Trembling*.

Implications for *Fear and Trembling*

Let's quickly recap. In the introduction and in the first section, I argued that de silentio introduces the idea of a teleological suspension of the ethical as a move that – by definition – precludes Hegelian justification. While Hegel can understand and endorse the actions of the tragic hero, he can neither understand nor endorse actions that genuinely suspend the ethical.

Next, I sketched a Local Norm Interpretation of the teleological suspension of the ethical that characterized the latter in terms of a commitment to a higher rational end that relativizes the local authority of social norms. On this interpretation, local social norms are associated with Hegel's ethics. Finally, I offered an analysis of Hegel's world historical agent that presented her as both transcending local ethical norms and acting for a higher rational end, in other words (as the Local Norm Interpreter would have it), teleologically suspending the ethical.

The fact that LNI accounts must judge Hegel's world historical agent to have teleologically suspended the ethical is significant because de silentio goes out of his way to reject this possibility. The teleological suspension of the ethical is intended to be the great stumbling block, not just for ethics, but specifically Hegelian ethics. This means that any satisfactory account of the teleological suspension of the ethical must hypothesize a break with something more significant than a local norm; it must mark a break with a universal standard; it must break with the full rational picture that comes at the end of Hegel's philosophy of history. Put more plainly, this means that the actions of the person who performs such an act cannot, in retrospect or in the right company, be justified. Job's status as a knight of faith does not put him in a position to see that, 'Ah, yes, Abraham should definitely kill Isaac.' While a fellow knight of faith like Job may be able to acknowledge that God has a record that indicates child sacrifice is not off-limits, he cannot affirm Abraham's particular call.

Having suggested that the teleological suspension of the ethical must involve a break with a 'universal' standard, an important question looms: in what sense is this standard universal? We should say something about this as well as address another important question raised by the above account.

One important difference between Napoleon and Abraham is that while Napoleon's actions are at least potentially justified (say, on a world historical stage), Abraham's actions require a decisive and irreparable break with public justification. There is no public (not even a late-model Christian one) for whom Abraham's actions are justified. As de silentio clearly (and I think decisively) puts it, 'one knight of faith cannot help the other at all . . . Partnership in these areas is utterly unthinkable' (FT, 7/SKS 4, 163).[7] This does not mean that contemporary readers won't try to justify Abraham – 'Look at all the good that came from his faithfulness!' – just that the goodness of his faith does not depend on such rationalizations. When Hegelian pastors 'understand' Abraham, they precisely *mis*understand him. All this shows us that where the distinction between Kantian and Hegelian accounts of ethics was taken to be most important (namely, a distinction between universal modes of justification and local), the distinction breaks down. Either the person who teleologically suspends the ethical breaks with a universal norm or Hegel already provides us with the conceptual and philosophical resources to understand her. The latter, you will recall, is a possibility that de silentio explicitly sets out to resist.

The next thing to ask is whether this justification gap applies to all people who teleologically suspend the ethical or just those who, like Abraham, suspend the ethical and make the further movement of faith. You might think it is the latter, especially since de silentio suggests that Abraham (as opposed to the merely infinitely resigned) is especially difficult to understand. I think this assumption is misguided. It depends on conflating two different senses of 'understanding' that de silentio trades between: knowledge about faith and having faith.

De silentio makes the distinction between these two senses early on in *Fear and Trembling*'s preface. There he writes: 'Even if someone were able to transpose the whole content of faith into conceptual form [*Begrebets Form*], it does not follow that he has comprehended faith, comprehended how he entered into it [*kom ind i den*] or how it entered into him' (FT, 7/SKS 4, 103). In this passage we see the juxtaposition of the understanding of the philosopher and the understanding of the first-person participant. We can distinguish the two by noting that philosophic understanding involves something like grasping a concept's meaning, while first-person understanding involves experiential and affective elements – the experience of having faith.

In *Fear and Trembling*'s second 'Problema,' de silentio revisits this distinction in the context of explaining the knight of faith's isolation. He writes:

> Thus, even if a person were craven and base enough to want to become a knight of faith on someone else's responsibility, he would never come to be one, for only the single individual becomes that as the single individual, and this is the greatness of it – which I can certainly understand [*forstaae*] without becoming involved in it [*uden at komme ind deri*], since I lack the courage – but this is also the terribleness of it, which I can understand [*fatte*] even better.
>
> (FT, 71–2/SKS 4, 163)

De silentio is clear that the divide between himself (someone who is infinitely resigned)[8] and the knight of faith isn't one of philosophic understanding. Not only does de silentio claim to understand the commitments of faith, it is conceivable that he and the knight of faith share similar religious beliefs. Notice also that de silentio claims that he possesses philosophic understanding without having faith. The wording here – *uden at komme ind deri* – recalls the claim from the preface, that an ability to conceptualize faith does not entail that one has also come into it [*kom ind i den*].[9] This passage also hints at what first-person understanding has that philosophic understanding lacks. In the end, what prevents de silentio from possessing faith is his failure to muster a certain kind of 'courage.' Thus, having faith, as opposed to merely knowing about it, requires that certain motivational conditions are met.

In the 'Preliminary expectoration,' de silentio makes the above distinction in terms of conventional wisdom and faith. He writes, conventional wisdom 'believes that it is enough to know what is great – no other work is needed. But for this reason it does not get bread; it perishes of hunger while everything changes to gold' (FT, 27/SKS 4, 123–4). A few pages later de silentio explains what such wisdom lacks. He writes: 'What is omitted from Abraham's story is the anxiety,' (FT, 28/SKS 4, 124) and 'yet without this anxiety Abraham is not who he is' (FT, 30/SKS 4, 126). Finally, de silentio locates himself with respect to the distinction, writing:

> I for my part have applied considerable time to understanding [*forstaae*] Hegelian philosophy and believe that I have understood it fairly well ...All this I do easily, naturally, without any mental strain. Thinking about Abraham is another matter, however; then I am shattered. I am constantly aware of the prodigious paradox that is the content of Abraham's life, I am constantly repelled, and, despite all its passion, my thought cannot penetrate it [*ikke trænge ind i det*], cannot get ahead by a hairsbreadth.
>
> (FT, 33/SKS 4, 128)

As in the passage from the second 'Problema,' de silentio again expresses an inability to enter *into* faith. Unlike the intellectual demands of understanding Hegel, faith demands a *passion* that 'repulses' and 'paralyzes,' leaving de silentio in a position where he 'can describe [*beskrive*] the movements of faith, but ... cannot make them' (FT, 37/SKS 4, 132).[10] All this suggests that de silentio's claims about the incomprehensibility of Abraham are not meant to establish that the knight of faith is uniquely opaque to the Hegelian philosopher. Once the ethical has been teleologically suspended, the actions of both the infinitely resigned person and of the person of faith are – from the perspective of practical justification – unjustified.[11]

Relatedly, this also means that neither the knight of infinite resignation nor the knight of faith is capable of 'speech.' Insofar as an ability to speak represents an ability to 'express the universal,' anyone who suspends the ethical (not just faithful folk) can be said to lack it. Additionally, there is reason to think that Hegel, working from a similar rationale, denies full-fledged speech to forms of consciousness that predate the end of history. Insofar as speech represents understanding, and full understanding only occurs in Hegel's ideal community, all preliminary 'communities' are, in a certain sense, socially isolated: they are pre-ethical babblers.[12] This provides further support for the contention that the teleological suspension of the ethical is a break with a universal norm. To lack speech in the relevant sense is to lack justification vis-à-vis an absolute and universal standard that goes beyond the norms of a contingent community. It is to be misunderstood by both the common tongue and the world historical innovator.

Conclusion

If 'ethical life' is understood in Hegelian terms, then Kierkegaardian faith is at irreparable odds with *Sittlichkeit*. Not only does the life of faith fall short of the normative criteria posed by Hegel, agents who suspend the ethical cannot even understand each other. Our ability to understand Hegel as a thinker who is committed to morality's universality requirement allows us to broaden our notion of what kinds of accounts *Fear and Trembling* interacts with. While its immediate historical interlocutor is Hegel, we can now appreciate that this does not preclude extending de silentio's critique to non-Hegelian targets who, like Kant, are committed in various ways to the central program of 'morality.' Teleologically suspending the ethical involves, for de silentio, much more than transcending local mores; it involves acting on a reason that cannot, in principle, justify your actions to a third party.

So where does this leave *Fear and Trembling*'s account of faith? You will recall that one of the apparent achievements of the Local Norm Interpretation was to rescue de silentio's account from the thrall of fideism. Are we now back to square one? It is important to remember that not all fideisms are the same. There is an important difference, for example, between an account that suggests faith involves belief in incompatible propositions and one that suggests faith lacks public justification. If we can put to rest the assumption that Kierkegaard (or de silentio) thinks there can be communities of faith in which mutual and complete justification prevails, then we can get on with the task of trying to understand the specific sense in which he thinks faith is unjustified. At best, this chapter hopes to have cleared some ground for the latter project.

Related topics

'Love for humans: morality as the heart of Kierkegaard's religious philosophy,' Sharon Krishek; 'On faith and reason(s): Kierkegaard's logic of conviction,' K. Brian Söderquist.

Notes

1 De silentio is the name of *Fear and Trembling*'s pseudonymous author. See Kemp (2013; 2015) for my thoughts on the relationship between Kierkegaard and de silentio. In short, I think we have no good reason to suspect significant divergence in their views.
2 For more recent discussions of this issue see Tilley (2012) and Johnson (2011).
3 I use the Walsh translation of the passage because Hannay fails to capture the sense in which Kierkegaard modifies 'det Ethiske' with 'det Sædelige,' and the Hongs fail to capture the sense in which 'det Sædelige' is intended as a technical philosophical term. The Hongs translate 'det Sædelige' as 'social morality,' which, to my ears, does not carry the same technical connotations as Walsh's 'ethical life.' The

Danish reads: 'Thi hvis det Ethiske, det Sædelige er det Høieste, og der intet Incommensurabelt bliver tilbage i Mennesket paa anden Maade, end at dette Incommensurable er det Onde . . . saa behøver man ikke andre Kategorier end hvad den græske Philosophi havde, eller hvad der ved en conseqvent Tænkning lader sig uddrage af disse. Dette burde Hegel ikke have lagt Skjul paa.'

4 See especially Hegel's preface, introduction, and section on 'ethical life.'
5 A characteristic example of this is found in the second paragraph of 'Problema I' (FT, 54–5/SKS 4, 148–9).
6 I have chosen to focus on Evans (2006) because, in addition to being high profile, his interpretation is an especially nice example of the LNI. Westphal (1998) and Stern (2012) are other examples. Westphal (2014) may, however, be committed to a slightly different view. In 2014, he appears to claim that the call of faith may require a rational break with all human communities, even apparently 'faithful' ones (see esp. 97). It is not clear to me whether this account (which is closer to the view I will argue for) is a modification of his earlier view (1998) or is the same view developed in more detail.
7 At this juncture, the Local Norm Interpreter gestures at de silentio's limited understanding of faith: he doesn't have faith, so he doesn't understand faith, so he does not see that there actually can be communities in which the actions of Abraham are comprehensible to all. I think this knee jerk move to dismiss de silentio for these reasons is deeply problematic and I argue as much in Kemp (2013; 2015).
8 In Kemp (2015) I argue that, despite some textual confusion, de silentio is best understood as infinitely resigned.
9 This distinction between the two types of understanding also makes sense of de silentio's otherwise contradictory claim that he both understands and doesn't understand Abraham. What de silentio can't understand (or think himself into) is the source of Abraham's motivational strength.
10 I rehearse the same basic argument of the last three paragraphs in Kemp (2015).
11 It is like the difference between an argument that has one logical mistake and one that has two. Neither work.
12 This is particularly apparent in Hegel's 'Jena period' when he writes his *First Philosophy of Spirit* and the *Phenomenology of Spirit*. The view I attribute to Hegel follows from each of two further theses that are developed by Hegel during this period: (1) that thought is essentially mediated by language and (2) that one of philosophy's primary tasks is to introduce the linguistic innovations required to reach full conceptual understanding. As evidence of the first thesis, consider the following passage from the *Phenomenology*'s 'Physiognomy and Phrenology' section:

> Although it is commonly said that reasonable men pay attention not to the word but to the thing itself, yet this does not give us permission to describe a thing in terms inappropriate to it. For this is at once incompetence and deceit, to fancy and to pretend that one merely has not the right word, and to hide from oneself that really one has failed to get hold of the thing itself, that is, the concept. If one had the concept, then one would also have the right word. (Hegel 1977: 198)

The second thesis is part of Hegel's larger project of modifying the German language in order to introduce more adequate concepts that, among other things, overcome the implicit dualisms that plague received terminology. In this regard, Hegel (1977: 23) bemoans, 'To talk of the unity of subject and object, of finite and infinite, of being and thought, etc. is inept, since subject and object, etc. signify what they are outside of their unity.' For more on Hegel's philosophy of language see Forster (2011: 150–77).

References

Alznauer, M. (2012) 'Ethics and history in Hegel's practical philosophy,' *The Review of Metaphysics*, 65, no. 3: 581–11.
Evans, C. S. (2006) 'Faith as the telos of morality: A reading of "Fear and Trembling",' in C. S. Evans (ed), *Kierkegaard on Faith and the Self*, Waco, TX: Baylor University Press.
Forster, M. N. (2011) *German philosophy of language: From Schlegel to Hegel and beyond*, Oxford: Oxford University Press.
Hegel, G. W. F. (1977) *Phenomenology of spirit*, A. V. Miller (trans), Oxford: Oxford University Press.
Hegel, G. W. F. (1975) *Lectures on the philosophy of world history*, H. B. Nisbet (trans), Cambridge: Cambridge University Press.

Johnson, D. (2011) 'Kant, Hegel, and Kierkegaard's supposed irrationalism: A reading of "Fear and Trembling",' in H. Schulz, J. Stewart and K. Verstrynge (eds), *Kierkegaard Studies Yearbook 2011*, Berlin: Walter de Gruyter.
Kemp, R. (2015) 'Johannes de silentio: Religious poet or faithless aesthete?' in K. Nun and J. Stewart (eds), *Kierkegaard Research: Sources, Reception and Resources*, vol. 17 (*Kierkegaard's Pseudonyms*), Farnham: Ashgate.
Kemp, R. (2013) 'In defense of a straightforward reading of "Fear and Trembling",' in H. Schulz, J. Stewart and K. Verstrynge (eds), *Kierkegaard Studies Yearbook 2013*, Berlin: Walter de Gruyter.
Kierkegaard, S. (2006) *Fear and trembling*, C. S. Evans (ed), and J. Walsh (trans), Cambridge: Cambridge University Press.
Stern, R. (2012) *Understanding moral obligation: Kant, Hegel, Kierkegaard*, Cambridge: Cambridge University Press.
Tilley, M. J. (2012) 'Rereading the teleological suspension: Resignation, faith, and teleology,' in H. Schulz, J. Stewart and K. Verstrynge (eds), *Kierkegaard Studies Yearbook 2012*, Berlin: Walter de Gruyter.
Westphal, M. (2014) *Kierkegaard's concept of faith*, Grand Rapids, MI: Eerdmans Publishing Company.
Westphal, M. (1998) 'Kierkegaard and Hegel,' in A. Hannay and G. D. Marino (eds), *The Cambridge Companion to Kierkegaard*, Cambridge: Cambridge University Press.
Wood, A. W. (1990) *Hegel's ethical thought*, Cambridge: Cambridge University Press.

Further reading

Lippitt, J. (2003) *Routledge philosophy guidebook to Kierkegaard and 'Fear and Trembling'*, London: Routledge.
This is a fantastic introduction to *Fear and Trembling* that also interacts with the secondary literature. It includes an entire chapter dedicated to 'suspending the ethical.'

Thomas, M. (2014) 'Teleological suspension of the ethical,' in S. Emmanuel, W. McDonald and J. Stewart (eds), *Kierkegaard Research: Sources, Reception and Resources*, vol. 15 (*Kierkegaard's Concepts*), tome 6, Farnham: Ashgate.
This is a short encyclopaedia style article that clearly and succinctly summarizes what, in general, Kierkegaard means by a teleological suspension of the ethical.

Tilley, M. J. (2012) 'Rereading the teleological suspension: Resignation, faith, and teleology,' in H. Schulz, J. Stewart and K. Verstrynge (eds), *Kierkegaard Studies Yearbook 2012*, Berlin: Walter de Gruyter.
This is a well-argued criticism of some recent and high-profile interpretations of the teleological suspension of the ethical. The article is noteworthy for, among other things, opposing Local Norm Interpretations.

9

AN ETHICS OF HOME AND HOPE: KIERKEGAARD'S EXILE AND HEIDEGGER'S EMIGRANT

Megan Altman

Introduction

Most contemporary philosophers who focus on ethics have tended to ignore or reject the writings of Søren Kierkegaard and Martin Heidegger. There are seemingly plausible and compelling reasons for this. As John Lippitt (2013: 504) points out, Kierkegaard's religious commitments are at odds with secular moral philosophy, and the Dane's great contempt for 'systematizing' tends to make a strange bedfellow for mainstream (Anglophone) moral philosophy. Like Kierkegaard, Heidegger often scoffs at the project of working out an ethics, and he refuses to say anything that might clarify the relationship between his ontology and ethics. However, the reasons for Heidegger's marginal role in ethics are slightly different from those that pertain to Kierkegaard. Heidegger tends to be excluded from the conversation because his ontology of human existence is characterized, incorrectly, as precluding ethics. A particular source of dissatisfaction with *Being and Time*, for instance, results from its supposedly thin account of human relationships. Insofar as the question about authentic human relations is not central to that work, it is tempting for some critics to conclude that Heidegger fails to capture the richness of social phenomena and thereby eliminates, from the outset, the possibility of the interpersonal, intersubjective ethical relation.

While allowing for important differences between Kierkegaard and Heidegger, it is nevertheless instructive to see Heidegger's project of working out an authentic understanding of existence as sharing important features with the Kierkegaardian project of rescuing the life of faith from the Christendom of the 'present age,' that is, nineteenth-century Denmark. This is because the ties that bind these thinkers together tend to threaten taken-for-granted assumptions of much of mainstream ethics. What is of particular interest here is the widespread assumption that 'doing ethics' means finding an absolute, unchanging system of maxims and examining the grounds for regarding certain actions as right (or wrong). The trouble with ethical theorizing, for Kierkegaard, is that impersonal doctrines and pre-given prescriptive principles for action are inappropriate when facing situations that are of the utmost importance to a person's life. In insisting on individual freedom and responsibility, on the ambiguity and contingency of worldliness, and on the importance of undertaking the personal task of making something of the human predicament, Kierkegaard and Heidegger are suspicious of any attempt to defend a particular ethical outlook that would subsume the individual under abstract principles.

While, in recent decades, a number of scholars have convincingly shown that the Kierkegaardian ideal of 'becoming a Christian' has much to offer when formulating a viable moral orientation toward life, few scholars are willing to grant the same for Heidegger. Indeed, commentators on Heidegger's relationship with Kierkegaard tend to claim that his ontologization of the ethico-religious dimensions of Kierkegaard's thought seems to slide into a kind of solipsism and empty decisionism. This critique has been articulated by Karsten Harries (1976), Daniel Berthold-Bond (1991), and Patricia Huntington (1995), who claim that Heidegger's ontologization of Kierkegaard's model of authentic existence entails a 'de-ethicization' that underscores the experience of cosmic displacement and worldly dislocation, but fails to provide a path for reintegration into the world. Where Kierkegaard's 'exilic' (Huntington 1995: 49) view of ethical life considers this estrangement from the world in terms of anxiety and recognizes personal edification or the life of interiority as that which bridges the gap between the exile and the communal world, Heidegger's ontology seems to know nothing of this shift. Hence, these critics argue, true community remains inaccessible for Heidegger's authentic individual, who has been rendered an 'emigrant' irreparably estranged from the ethical (Harries 1976: 668). To be sure, it is unclear why exile is ethically 'better' than emigration, but this is discussed later. For now, it is sufficient to note that these nomadic images bring to the fore questions about conditions necessary for humans to move forward after exile or forced existential isolation.

What is most remarkable is that Heidegger's view of 'ethics,' properly understood as etymologically related to 'dwelling' and 'abode,' seems to offer an existential hope that, much like Kierkegaard's eschatological hope, enables us to experience the highest, holy things in the lowliest, humble places. My argument moves beyond the narrower task of responding to the particular critique put forth by Huntington, Harries, and others, and goes on to offer tentative conclusions about the possibility of finding ethical notions of home and hope in the work of Kierkegaard and Heidegger.

Kierkegaard and Heidegger

There is no question that Kierkegaard had an immense impact on Heidegger. In the 'loose pages' to the young Heidegger's (2001: 137) Frieburg lectures, quotes from Kierkegaard's '*Exercises in Christianity* and *Either-Or, vol. I*' are acknowledged as the guiding 'motto' of the 1921–1922 course *Phenomenological Interpretations of Aristotle: Initiation into Phenomenological Research*. A few years later, in three often cited notes in *Being and Time*, Heidegger (1962: 492n4, 494n6, 497n3) praises Kierkegaard as the thinker 'who has gone the farthest in analysing the phenomenon of anxiety,' who has 'explicitly seized upon the problem of existence' and 'thought through it in a penetrating fashion,' and 'who has seen the *existentiell* phenomenon of the moment of vision with the most penetration.' Time and time again, Kierkegaard appears in the marginalia of Heidegger's work, and it is generally agreed by many Heidegger scholars that Heidegger sees himself as developing specific themes he finds in Kierkegaard's work – for example. the 'today,' the public, anxiety, moods, death, the 'instant' or 'moment of vision,' repetition, and existence (*Existenz*).

What makes this relationship especially messy is that most of Heidegger's published acknowledgements of Kierkegaard's influence come across as backhanded compliments. This is in part because Heidegger was at pains to distance himself from what he regarded as the trendy 'Kierkegaardism' of the day (see Kisiel 1993: 275, 541n2). For example, in his first public reference to Kierkegaard, Heidegger credits Kierkegaard as the source of his notions of the 'today,' averageness, publicness, and everydayness. In the same breath, however, Heidegger (1999: 25; cf. 1984: 190–1) says Kierkegaard's 'presuppositions, approach, manner of execution, and goal were fundamentally different, insofar as he made these too easy for himself. What was basically in question for him, was nothing but the kind of personal reflection he pursued. He was a theologian and stood within the realm of faith, in principle outside of philosophy.'

Insofar as Kierkegaard's thought is limited to the 'regional' mode of experience called 'the religious,' Heidegger's (1962: 333, 359, 363) appropriation of Kierkegaardian concepts involves 'doing violence' to the taken-for-granted assumptions of theology. Heidegger's statement, in a 1920 letter to Karl Löwith, that 'Even Kierkegaard can *only* be theologically unhinged (as I understand theology and will develop in the winter semester)' is followed by the explanation that 'What is of importance in Kierkegaard must be appropriated *anew*, but in a *strict* critique that grows out of *our own* situation' (Kisiel and Sheehan 2010: 104). To clarify, it will be helpful to unpack some technical terms. Heidegger's ambitious project is to revitalize philosophy (and, arguably, Western culture) by explicating the generally tacit and unnoticed all-encompassing background understanding of what it is to be anything in particular. He attempts to loosen the grip of the prevailing 'regional' domains of 'Being' – for example, theology, mathematics, physics, ethics, psychology, and anthropology – that have been passed down in the sediment of our current historical tradition in order to formulate a clearer understanding of what things are in general – that is, an account of the 'Being' of entities in general. To put the same point in Heidegger's technical vocabulary, the philosophical attempt to develop an 'ontology' of entities in general and an account of 'existential' structures of humans should not presuppose anything from the 'ontic' or 'existentiell' levels of experience. For Heidegger, then, to recognize that Kierkegaard holds existential ideas in the service of the existentiell interests of Christianity is to see that he is, at best, an 'unhinged theologian.'

Suffice it to say, the relationship between Heidegger and Kierkegaard is complicated, and examining all of the details in the hope of coming to a definitive account of Kierkegaard's influence on Heidegger is beyond the scope of this paper. In what follows, my aim is to present a rough overview of a number of overlapping themes in their respective inquiries into human existence and authenticity. This general sketch will set the stage for considering the points of contention in the ongoing debate about the viability of ethics for these two thinkers.

Authenticity

Both Kierkegaard and Heidegger are critical of the traditional ideal of achieving 'objective knowledge' of the human situation. In the 'Truth Is Subjectivity' section of *Concluding Unscientific Postscript*, Kierkegaard's pseudonym Johannes Climacus makes some observations that can be seen as central to Heidegger's thought. First, he notes that 'objective reflection' (what Heidegger calls the 'theoretical attitude') tends to bleach out the element of care or involvement the subject has in the object of inquiry. 'The way of objective reflection turns the subjective individual into something accidental,' writes Climacus, 'and thereby turns existence into an indifferent, vanishing something' (CUP 1, 193/SKS 7, 177). To be sure, objective validity has its place in mathematics and science; however, theoretical detachment cannot give me access to what Climacus calls 'subjective truth' – 'the highest obtainable truth for an *existing* individual' (CUP 1, 203/SKS 7, 186).

Such truth is 'subjective,' because it is deeply personal and particular, and not some abstraction that applies to everyone and hence no one in particular. Whereas objective truth is a matter of *what* is known or believed, subjective truth is a matter of *how* one lives. Subjective truth is not so much thought as it is lived *'with the most passionate inwardness'* (CUP 1, 203/SKS 7, 186). Truth, in this regard, is the continuous and burdensome confrontation with the unknowable and unrationalizable dimension of human existence. To live in the full light of the truth of one's existence is terrifying, because it is objectively uncertain and cannot be grasped through reason.

To follow one's own truth requires commitment, risk, and sacrifice, and this is why Climacus says that living truthfully is 'precisely the daring venture of choosing the objective uncertainty with the passion of the infinite' (CUP 1, 203/SKS 7, 186).

Heidegger is in agreement with Kierkegaard that humans are always in some affective orientation toward the world. We inhabit a value-laden world in which certain things can matter for us, and that mattering itself motivates us and carries us forward toward accomplishing certain sorts of things and doing various sorts of things. Though Heidegger (1962: 32) drops the language of 'subject' and 'object,' there is an analogy between Kierkegaard's notion of subjective truth and Heidegger's ontological concept of 'care' (*Sorge*). For Heidegger, our ability to encounter things as *mattering* and *counting* in some way – that is, our ability to distinguish what is relevant from what is not and to discern what is of central importance from what is peripheral – is made possible by the fact that humans are beings that care about their being. 'Care' is Heidegger's technical term for the essential meaning-making structures of human existence, which Heidegger calls '*Dasein*' (literally, 'being-there'). Understood in this way, care 'has nothing to do with "tribulation," "melancholy," or the "cares of life," though ontically one can come across these in every Dasein. These – like their opposites, "gaiety" and "freedom from care" – are ontically possible only because Dasein, when understood *ontologically*, is care' (Heidegger 1962: 84).

Simply put, to be human is to care about what it means to be human. As we live our lives, we care about what our lives amount to. Existence, in this sense, is not a finished product or final state. Rather, and this is another Kierkegaardian hallmark taken up by Heidegger, human 'existence' is the difficult task and ongoing struggle of striving to be human. In the words of Climacus, 'The subjective thinker's task is to transform himself into an instrument that clearly and definitely expresses in existence the essentially human' (CUP 1, 356/SKS 7, 325; cf. Heidegger 1962: 32–3).

Kierkegaard's pseudonym Anti-Climacus frames this task in terms of a tension between two contradictory dimensions that make up humans. To be human, he says, is to be 'a synthesis of the infinite and the finite, of the temporal and the eternal, of freedom and necessity' (SUD, 13/SKS 11, 129). Our human situation is such that we exist as self-contradictory beings torn apart in the tension between, on the one hand, our finite, earthly needs and desires, and, on the other, our ability to grasp that something is at stake in life – something that goes beyond our temporal limits and, hence, reflects our higher, eternal desires and ideals. Understood this way, the tension created by this contradictory set of demands represents the structural issue built into our very existence, and being human is the subjective task of taking a stand on this tension in trying to make something of the human predicament.

In the language of *Being and Time*, the question of *who* Dasein is, is always 'an *issue* for this entity in its very Being' (Heidegger 1962: 67). This distinctive way of 'being-in-the-world' is what Heidegger (1962: 183) calls a 'thrown project': we find ourselves *thrown* into a shared world from a past that saddles us with obligations and commitments of our cultural context, yet we are also *projecting* toward an indeterminate future in taking up some set of possibilities that form a personal identity. This means that there is no definitive or final account of being human. Rather, Dasein is a '*not yet*' (Heidegger 1962: 186), always in the process of self-formation – for example, being a Palestinian widow, a single mother of two, a doctoral candidate with no job prospects, or a tortured poet. For Heidegger, as for Kierkegaard before him, each individual struggles to come to terms with the unsettledness built into the human situation by making a commitment to something in the world that provides content, direction, and focus for their life. In everyday life, however, we arrive at inadequate answers, and we tend to live dispersed and distracted, lacking any real integrity and cohesiveness as individuals.

Heidegger calls this mode of existence 'inauthentic.' The German word for 'authentic,' *eigentlich*, comes from the stem *eigen*, which means 'own' and 'proper.' To speak of authenticity, then, is to refer to what makes a life one's own, where this is understood as 'being responsible' (*Verantwortlichkeit*) in the sense of responding to questions about what is truly worth pursuing in life. A life characterized by inauthenticity, on the other hand, is one that is disowned or unowned. Heidegger and Kierkegaard recognize that, in our struggle to maintain a sense of identity, there is a tendency toward falling into step with the crowd and thoughtlessly conforming to socially approved conventions and norms. In Heidegger's (1962: 165) words, the everyday life of *das Man* (the German *das Man* means the 'they' or the 'one') 'constantly accommodates the particular Dasein by disburdening it of its Being.' Although the 'they' is a *'primordial phenomenon'* that *'belongs to Dasein's constitution,'* Heidegger (1962: 165, 167) is critical of the ways in which the 'they' 'deprives the particular Dasein of its answerability. . . . It can be answerable for everything most easily, because it is not someone who needs to vouch for anything.'

Heidegger's characterization of the way the everyday life of the 'they' tempts us into being inauthentic has clear resonances with Kierkegaard's diagnosis of the public and its principles. For Kierkegaard, people need something concrete in the world to serve as a stabilizing and steadying influence, not some abstraction where anything could do the trick. The trouble is that instead of providing insight into worthy and unworthy purposes in life, the anonymity of the 'public' tends to reflect and reinforce an increasingly empty and futile cultural life. In his polemical essay, 'The present age,' Kierkegaard is especially contemptuous of the dispirited mood of discouragement of nineteenth-century Denmark. The conformism of the present age, according to Kierkegaard, is characterized by the 'abstraction of levelling' achieved by the 'public,' that is, the 'monstrous nothing' prone to endless 'chattering' because it 'dreads the moment of silence, which would reveal the emptiness' (TA, 87, 98/SKS 8, 83, 93). In Kierkegaard's view, calls for social solidarity and genuine community are empty in a world that undermines the individual's ability to develop a moral orientation toward life: 'Not until the single individual has established an ethical stance despite the whole world, not until then can there be any question of genuinely uniting' (TA, 106/SKS 8, 100–1).

To jolt people out of their complacent condition of average everydayness, Kierkegaard and Heidegger try to find something in the human situation that motivates people to take a stand on their lives. Kierkegaard's pseudonym Vigilius Haufniensis points to anxiety as an illuminating mood that places the familiar in an unfamiliar light. Anxiety lets things be in a distinctive way: in withdrawal, in lapsing into nothingness and meaninglessness. The anxiety-laden individual learns 'that he can demand nothing of life, and that the terrible, perdition, and annihilation live next door to every man' (CA, 156/SKS 4, 455). In this experience, all the distractions, evasions, people-pleasing, and constant busyness of ordinary life collapse. We lose any sense of belonging, of familiarity, of feeling at home; hence Heidegger (1962: 233) speaks in this regard of 'not being at home' (*Un-heim-lichkeit*). Heidegger, here clearly indebted to Kierkegaard, says the unsettling experience of anxiety strips away the security of everyday life, robs me of my trust and conviction that my life makes sense, and brings me face to face with the fundamental contingency, vulnerability, and dependency of human existence. As Daniel Magurshak (1985: 181) aptly puts it, 'anxiety is for both thinkers that which places one at a moment of decision about how one should live, about how time itself is experienced.'

For Kierkegaard, our only hope is to get into the right relationship with the power that constituted us. In contrast to the comforting and comfortable God-relationship characteristic of self-styled 'Christians' in nineteenth-century Christendom, genuine Christianity, according to Kierkegaard, is a terrifying and awesome mode of existence that involves the most extreme form of risk, uncertainty, and vulnerability. To be a true Christian is to be totally devoted to the God-man, who is a particular common and fragile person that lived in a particular time and place, but to be related to that person as if he is also the eternal, infinite, all-powerful creator of heaven and earth. To hold these two beliefs together is the greatest paradox. We can see why Kierkegaard's pseudonym Johannes de silentio says that genuine faith 'begins precisely where thought stops' (FT, 53/SKS 4, 147).

Using the biblical figure of Abraham, silentio illustrates the 'paradoxical and humble courage' of the life of faith (FT, 49/SKS 4, 143). As an expression of the infinite and eternal, Abraham is willing to sever his ties to the temporal and finite, and is resigned to sacrificing Isaac. And yet, at the same time, as an expression of the finite and temporal, he accepts his worldly commitments and welcomes Isaac back. For silentio, it is crucial that, at the very same time Abraham resigns the finite, he 'does not lose the finite but gains it whole and intact' (FT, 37/SKS 4, 132). Filled with fear and trembling, Abraham dies to the world and lives in the light of a higher truth: the subjective truth embodied in the solitary individual who stands in 'absolute isolation' before an incomprehensible God (FT, 79/SKS 4, 170). The faithful relationship with God provides Abraham, the individual, with an understanding of the 'eternal validity' underlying all his strivings (FT, 46/ SKS 4, 140); he lives fully in the 'here and now,' living every instant as having an overarching purpose – as eternal, infinite, and free. With a religious conscience, Abraham makes the leap, becomes a knight of faith, and overcomes despair.

Stripped of its religious connotations, Heidegger's ideal of authenticity is a distinctive way of approaching our ontological homelessness (revealed in anxiety). Recall that, for Heidegger, the unnerving experience of anxiety gives us access to a fundamental truth of what it is to be human: no matter how anchored our lives may seem, or how grounded our home in the world may be, homelessness is '*more primordial*' than being at home (Heidegger 1962: 234). This does not mean that, as some commentators have claimed, anxiety separates us from the world. Rather, when the world loses its at-home-ness and familiarity, being at home in the world becomes an issue for us. In this respect, anxiety delivers us over to ourselves as exposed, fragile beings, who are ultimately responsible for the meaning of our lives. Or, as Heidegger (1962: 394) puts it, 'Anxiety liberates him *from* possibilities which "count for nothing" [*nichtigen*], and lets him become free *for* those which are authentic.'

Like Kierkegaard's knight of faith, what is definitive of human authenticity, according to Heidegger, is choice in the form of resoluteness. What is most important about this idea of resoluteness for authentic human being is the fact that its structure displays the underlying temporality of human lived time. Heidegger calls this temporal structure our 'historicity' (*Geschichtlichkeit*). For Heidegger, the phenomenon of historicity has important consequences for our understanding of human relations and community. It means that we can encounter the unfolding of our community not just as something that has passed, nor as calcified tradition, but rather as a vital living '*heritage*' that provides the background of understanding through which we can become concretely human in the first place (Heidegger 1962: 435). In being authentic, Dasein takes over the definitive possibilities of its historical context and resolutely undertakes the project of pursuing those projects. In doing so, authentic Dasein commits itself to being 'steady and steadfast' in its involvements with the world (Heidegger 1962: 369). It frees itself from all incidental possibilities that happen to be currently floating in the 'they,' and it 'simplifies' itself, gaining focus and coherence in its agency (Heidegger 1962: 435). 'The more authentically Dasein resolves,' Heidegger (1962: 435) says, 'the more unequivocally does it choose and find the possibility of its existence, and the less it does so by accident.' Heidegger (1962: 436, 443) suggests that in this way of life we will have a clear-sightedness about who we are, and where we are going.

Consequences for ethics

There appears to be something deeply unsettling about Heidegger's account of resoluteness and Kierkegaard's knight of faith. The criticism, as formulated by Charles Guignon (2000: 92), is that they may be advancing a form of 'decisionism,' which is 'the view that one should make a commitment to something' – such as intellectual or creative activities, some political or moral cause, or religious life – 'with no other basis than the need to make a commitment itself.' What is distinctive about 'commitments' is that they are the sorts of identity-shaping, world-disclosing, and character-building projects that people organize their lives around. They are upbuilding truths (in the Kierkegaardian sense) that transform our first-order moral commitments and play an ineliminable role in how we make sense of our lives. What many critics find troubling about Kierkegaard and Heidegger's notion of commitment is that it fails to capture what is most fundamental about being committed: 'the experience of *answering* a call or *responding* to something outside ourselves, something that makes a demand on us' (Guignon 2000: 92). Kierkegaard's knight of faith responds to God's demand to sacrifice Isaac, but this happens only after he has made the leap of his own accord. And when Heidegger (1962: 345) asks, 'On what basis does Dasein disclose itself in resoluteness? On what is it to resolve?' his answer is, '*Only* the resolution itself can give the answer.' This means that Dasein must go with what resonates in the current situation once it has become resolute. Notice that, without the moral dimension of being called, Kierkegaard and Heidegger's account of authentic individuality could lead to some unappetizing conclusions. If the ideal of authenticity does not necessarily have any moral or political implications, then, one could ask: what is to keep an authentic individual from taking over, as the Nazis did, the racist, sexist, homophobic, cruel and brutish traditions that have been embedded in Western cultures for millennia?[1]

To put it somewhat crudely, it seems that Kierkegaard's knight of faith can be saved from decisionism by the Christian virtues of faith, love, and hope, but no such saving grace is found in Heidegger. Huntington and like-minded commentators present a secular version of this argument. Huntington (1995: 49–50) characterizes Kierkegaard's ethical individual as an 'exile' who is 'separated off from the "crowd"' by virtue of 'intensifying participation in the community.' 'The individual suffers social isolation because,' as Huntington (1995: 50) puts it, 's/he takes seriously the ideas that everyone else merely parrots.' In a similar turn of phrase, Harries (1976: 649) describes Kierkegaard's knight of faith as a 'homeless stranger' who 'has suspended his ties to the world' in order to receive them back in a heightened form. While Kierkegaard's 'exilic' view of ethical life restores, albeit in a transformative way, what anxiety nullifies, critics have a hard time seeing a parallel experience in Heidegger's ontology. They claim that the homelessness of anxiety leaves Dasein with no meaningful signposts or worldly markers with which to reconfigure and reclaim its home. Hence, Harries (1976: 668) argues, Heidegger's authentic individual has been rendered an 'emigrant': 'He lives in this world, but as an outsider, whose thinking prevents him from really belonging to it.'[2]

I sympathize with these objections, and in fact, I find the nomadic images of 'exile,' 'emigration,' and 'homeless stranger' to be quite interesting in this context. A number of questions arise from the claim that being an exile is 'better' than being an emigrant. For instance, if both forms of life are distinguished by the loss of 'home(land),' as the site of the ethical, then why does it matter which is which? The claim that the exile is more likely to reclaim its home is especially curious when we consider that (voluntary) emigration usually includes an element of choice that is denied in exile. Indeed, given that exile is usually a form of punishment, one may wonder how exile provides a picture of the ideal way of life and hints of how it might be formed.

To see why this is so perplexing, let us briefly consider the experience of exile formulated by Holocaust survivor Jean Améry (1980: 42): 'Whoever didn't know it was taught later by daily life in exile that the etymology of the German word for misery [*elend*], whose early meaning implies exile, still contains its most accurate definition.'[3] In this passage from Améry's famous book, *At the Mind's Limits*, we get a glimpse of the concrete realities of human suffering and misery experienced by those who have been irrevocably displaced in the diaspora. Their experiences are haunted by the memories of torture, banishment, and deportation, and they exist 'without God, without history, and without messianic-national hope' (Améry 1980: 94). In contrast to Huntington's (1995: 50) picture of exilic life, Améry's exile is not merely an exceptional outsider who 'takes seriously the ideas that everyone else merely parrots.' Rather, being an exile involves bearing witness to the systematic annihilation of a cultural world of possibilities and carrying on in the wake of such worldly devastation. As Hannah Arendt (1994: 162) sees it, the exile is held captive in 'the abyss that yawns between the "no longer and not yet" of history, between the "no longer" of the old laws and the "not yet" of the new saving word, between life and death.' I do not see how an exile can even hope to flourish in the wake of the destruction of ethical life.

When our traditions have been drained of substantive content, when there is no going back home, where can a community be found? How do 'we,' those who have been disinherited, disenfranchised, and marginalized, find *hope to rebuild* our world? Going back to its etymological roots in the Old English noun, 'hope' refers to 'a piece of arable land surrounded by swamp or marsh,' 'a broad upland valley,' 'a small bay or inlet,' and 'a haven' (Babcock Grove et al. 1976). The word 'hope' contains existential connotations of the experience of a particular, local place of refuge and shelter, an abode that nurtures, preserves, and protects, a bit of hospitable land surrounded by an inhospitable world.[4] Using this conception of hope as tethered to a distinctive place where one can feel at home (or what the Germans call a '*Heimat*'), we might ask whether Kierkegaard and Heidegger can identify conditions for renewing the sense of community that was destroyed in the wake of exile and forced isolation.

Home and hope

Given that hope is one of Christianity's most cherished virtues, it would seem that Kierkegaard's religious commitments would give him an advantage over Heidegger's ontologization of theological concepts. As Clare Carlisle (2013: 434) explains, 'In Kierkegaard's work, the emphasis on responsibility, freedom, and decision is tempered by an insistence on our dependence on God, which demands a response of gratitude, humility, and patience. These virtues of receptivity are right at the heart of his account of spiritual life, and they are thematised in his pseudonymous texts as well as in the edifying discourses.' We can add love and hope to this list of Kierkegaardian virtues of receptivity and suggest ways in which Christian 'works of love' might offer respite and relief for the exile. It seems to me that Kierkegaard's solution is to follow the example of Christ and live in light of Christ's law of love, 'which is greater than faith and hope' (WL, 248/SKS 9, 247). The way to experience the hope of all creation is to live a life of merciful, selfless, agapic love. In Kierkegaard's words, 'Christ's hope is eternity, and Christ is the Way; his debasement is the Way, but he was also the Way when he ascended to heaven' (WL, 248/SKS 9, 247). Kierkegaardian hope, with its teachings of love, self-emptying, humility, and meekness, could offer a path of worldly restoration and renewal for the exile.

However, one must still contend with the fact that Kierkegaard is at pains to remind his readers that Christianity 'takes no place in the world,' and 'Christianity and worldliness will never come to a mutual understanding' (WL, 71, 135/SKS 9, 78, 138). Christianity would no longer be a sacrificial practice if it were tethered to the world. Recalling Kierkegaard's criticism of Christendom, Christianity loses its core when it becomes partners with the world. Christendom is a way of being at peace with the world, but 'worldliness is in itself heavy, ponderous, sluggish, slack, despondent, and dejected, and cannot involve itself with the possible, least of all with the possibility of the good, neither for its own sake nor for the sake of another' (WL, 257/SKS 9, 256). For worldly matters to matter, they must be mediated by the Christian's faithful relationship to God. Given the fact that 'Kierkegaardian faith is primarily about salvation' (Davenport 2008: 176–7) rather than worldly matters, it is not clear whether earthly hope and worldly prospect can be integrated into religious life.[5]

Alternatively, what I find in Heidegger's ontology is a trace of existential hope that resonates with the search for a *Heimat* (a distinctive place where one can feel at home). The key to developing a Heideggerian account of hope is to understand the inescapable place of '*ethos*.' When Heidegger (1993b: 256, 260) was asked to clarify the relationship between his ontology and ethics, he said that the field of philosophy called 'ethics' fails to see that *ethos* 'means abode, dwelling place. The word names the open region in which man dwells.... This dwelling is the essence of "being-in-the-world". The reference in *Being and Time* to "being-in" as "dwelling" is no etymological game.' As this formulation suggests, *ethos* is a distinct way of being where, through one's actions, one *is* what one *does*. As self-making beings, constituting ourselves through our actions, we manifest an *ethos* of a particular sort. For Heidegger, we are inescapably communal beings: we cannot exist independently of a concrete social world in terms of which we come to see what is possible and in which our actions always participate in the common undertakings of that world. Thus, the world is fundamental in shaping our *ethos*.

It follows from considerations of this sort that there is no 'view from nowhere' from which we can say something about the human *ethos* that does not reflect and draw on the actual context from which we speak. To try to answer questions about the human struggle for moral clarity and hope, Heidegger suggests that we must start from our own *ethos*, always remembering that this starting point is subject to criticism in light of conversations with other cultural and historical ways of life (see Heidegger 1962: 41, 44, 213, 434–8; 1971a). In contrast to the otherworldly dimension of Kierkegaardian faith, the appeal of Heidegger's ethics, properly understood in relation to *ethos*, lies in seeing that there is always a trace of hope in the mundane and impoverished regions of human life. Understood as abode and dwelling place, the *ethos* bestows meaning and valorises 'the little things' in everyday life. Even in the humblest, most common spaces (*Raum*)[6] the highest is present. Or, as Heidegger (1971b: 53) puts it, 'At bottom, the ordinary is not ordinary; it is the extra-ordinary, uncanny [*Un-heim-lich*].' Dwelling, in the proper sense of the word, illustrates a principle we saw in *Being and Time's* account of the homelessness of anxiety: being at home includes being estranged. The places where we feel most at home – for example, home town, neighbourhood, regional dialect, cultural values, traditions, and rituals – are the strangest and least familiar.

How does Heidegger's ontological account of dwelling respond to the exilic search for hope to rebuild the sense of community that was lost? To begin to answer this question, we must first ask about the relationship between dwelling and building. In his essay, 'Building, Dwelling, and Thinking,' Heidegger (1993a: 349) develops the etymological connections between 'dwelling' (*baun*) and 'building' (*bauen*), noting that the latter 'also means . . . to cherish and protect, to preserve and care for.' Heidegger moves from building to dwelling to being to protecting and to nurturing. Through these etymologies we see that dwelling must be understood as the cultivation of what comes forth on its own, or the construction of what is to be brought forth, and these are ways of dwelling which in turn take the form of building. The point is that building has a dual aspect: construction and preservation, and I think hope is found in the work of preservation. Just as Kierkegaardian hope is not something we do, but it is something we receive, so too, Heidegger says that receptivity is essential to the work of preservation. Such work involves 'caring for' and 'remaining at peace,' not forcing things, pushing things around, or trying to impose an agenda on things. Rather, the function of humans is to spare these things, to let them be, and to care for them. This sense of existential hope is captured well in Iris Marion Young's (2001: 275) claim that dwelling 'consists in preserving the things and their meaning as anchor to shifting personal and group identity. But the narratives of the history of what brought us here are not fixed, and part of the creative work and moral task of preservation is to reconstruct the connection of the past to the present in light of new events, relationships, and political understandings.'

The activities of preservation of the meaningful things that constitute home are seen in the following examples. Jews preserved the Sabbath in the concentration camps. Dr. Martin Luther King, Jr., appealed to Christian ideals of love and faith, as well as democratic ideals of liberty and equality, to embolden the civil rights protests in Montgomery, Alabama (despite his father's request for him to return to the 'safety' of Atlanta, Georgia) to stand up against racist traditions that have been embedded in Western cultures for millennia. Early Christians in pagan Rome began their celebratory meal together with what is called a collect (*sunagôgê*) and Jews gathered in synagogues. These are ways that people found small, local places (abodes) for collective life, community, in an alien world. Such examples also suggest that the activities of preservation and remembrance contain the glue of community, and this glue binds the marginalized, the dishonourable, and those deemed unworthy of respect.

Admittedly, the central features of Kierkegaard's life of faith mark a drastic difference from Heidegger's ontological notion of dwelling. Whether there can be a reconciliation among the competing views of hope represented here remains to be seen. The upshot of my sketch of home and hope is twofold. First, it offers a roadmap for further inquiry into the relationship between Kierkegaard and Heidegger. Second, and more importantly, it shows how Kierkegaard and Heidegger have something to say to a wide audience about how we can be at home in the world. In light of the ongoing refugee crises in our contemporary world, I think it is of pressing importance to explore ways of reclaiming hospitable habitats for communal life, and I think Kierkegaard and Heidegger can teach us how to undertake this timely task.

Related topics

'Love for humans: morality as the heart of Kierkegaard's religious philosophy,' Sharon Krishek; 'Ethical reflection as evasion,' Rob Compaijen and Pieter Vos.

Notes

1 Alasdair MacIntyre (1998: 139–40; 2008: 39–43) famously levels this criticism at Kierkegaard, while a number of his defenders have made compelling cases against MacIntyre's reading (see Davenport and Rudd 2001). On Heidegger's supposed decisionism, see Jürgen Habermas (1987: 139–41, 149–55) and Herman Philipse (1999).
2 For a more detailed analysis of this argument, see Buben (2016: 127–30, 132, 135, 152n13, 167n9).
3 The German word '*elend*' means 'wretched,' 'miserable,' and, when traced back to its old High Germanic roots – '*alilanti*,' '*elilenti*,' '*elendi*' – it means 'living in a foreign country, banished, alien, outlandish, and captive' (Straube 1904: 49).
4 I am grateful to Kate Bradshaw for bringing this etymological connection to my attention.
5 For example, Jonathan Lear (2006: 102–4) sees structural similarities between Plenty Coup's experience of hope when faced with the cultural devastation of the Crow way of life, and the knight of faith's teleological suspension of the ethical. Whether or not Kierkegaard's Christian views can actually be reconciled with Lear's account is an issue in need of further attention.
6 '*Raum*' can mean 'room' in the sense of room for growth or room for things to take place, but it can also mean 'space' understood in the geographical and geometrical sense.

References

Améry, J. (1980) *At the mind's limits: Contemplations by a survivor on Auschwitz and its realities*, S. Rosenfeld and S. P. Rosenfeld (trans), Bloomington, IN: Indiana University Press.
Arendt, H. (1994) *Essays in understanding 1930–1954: Formation, exile, totalitarianism*, J. Kohn (ed), New York: Schocken Books.
Babcock Grove, P. et al. (eds) (1976) *Webster's third new international dictionary of the English language unabridged*, Springfield, MA: G. & C. Merriam Company.
Berthold-Bond, D. (1991) 'A Kierkegaardian critique of Heidegger's concept of authenticity,' *Man and World*, 24, no. 2: 119–42.
Buben, A. (2016) *Meaning and mortality in Kierkegaard and Heidegger: Origins of the existential philosophy of death*, Evanston, IL: Northwestern University Press.
Carlisle, C. (2013) 'Kierkegaard and Heidegger,' in J. Lippitt and G. Pattison (eds), *The Oxford Handbook of Kierkegaard*, Oxford: Oxford University Press.
Davenport, J. J. (2008) 'What Kierkegaardian faith adds to alterity ethics: How Levinas and Derrida miss the eschatological dimension,' in J. A. Simmons and D. Wood (eds), *Kierkegaard and Levinas: Ethics, Politics, and Religion*, Bloomington, IN: Indiana University Press.
Davenport, J. J. and Rudd, A. (eds) (2001) *Kierkegaard after MacIntyre: Essays on freedom, narrative, and virtue*, Chicago, IL: Open Court Publishing.
Guignon, C. (2000) 'Philosophy and authenticity: Heidegger's search for a ground for philosophizing,' in M. Wrathall and J. Malpas (eds), *Heidegger, Authenticity, and Modernity: Essays in Honor of Hubert Dreyfus*, Cambridge, MA: Massachusetts Institute of Technology Press.
Habermas, J. (1987) *The philosophical discourse of modernity: Twelve essays*, F. G. Lawrence (trans), Cambridge, MA: Massachusetts Institute of Technology Press.
Harries, K. (1976) 'Heidegger as a political thinker,' *The Review of Metaphysics*, 29, no. 4: 642–69.
Heidegger, M. (2001) *Phenomenological interpretations of Aristotle: Initiation into phenomenological research*, R. Rojcewicz (trans), Bloomington, IN: Indiana University Press.
Heidegger, M. (1999) *Ontology–hermeneutics of facticity*, J. van Buren (trans), Bloomington, IN: Indiana University Press.
Heidegger, M. (1993a) 'Building, dwelling, thinking,' in D. F. Krell (ed), *Martin Heidegger: Basic Writings*, New York: Harper Collins.
Heidegger, M. (1993b) 'Letter on humanism,' in D. F. Krell (ed), *Martin Heidegger: Basic Writings*, New York: Harper Collins.
Heidegger, M. (1984) *The metaphysical foundations of logic*, M. Heim (trans), Bloomington, IN: Indiana University Press.
Heidegger, M. (1971a) 'A dialogue on language between a Japanese and an inquirer,' in P. D. Hertz and J. Stambaugh (trans), *On the Way to Language*, New York: Harper & Row.
Heidegger, M. (1971b) 'Origin of the work of art,' in A. Hofstadter (trans), *Poetry, Language, Thought*, New York: Harper Perennial.
Heidegger, M. (1962) *Being and time*, J. Macquarrie and E. Robinson (trans), New York: Harper Collins.
Huntington, P. (1995) 'Heidegger's reading of Kierkegaard revisited: From ontological abstraction to ethical concretion,' in M. Matuštík and M. Westphal (eds), *Kierkegaard in Post/Modernity*, Bloomington, IN: Indiana University Press.
Kisiel, T. (1993) *The genesis of Heidegger's 'Being & Time,'* Berkeley; Los Angeles, CA: University of California Press.
Kisiel, T. and Sheehan, T. (eds) (2010) *Becoming Heidegger: On the trail of his early occasional writings, 1910–1927*, 2nd ed., Seattle, WA: Noesis.
Lear, J. (2006) *Radical hope: Ethics in the face of cultural devastation*, Cambridge, MA: Harvard University Press.
Lippitt, J. (2013) 'Kierkegaard and moral philosophy: Some recent themes,' in J. Lippitt and G. Pattison (eds), *The Oxford Handbook of Kierkegaard*, Oxford: Oxford University Press.
MacIntyre, A. (2008) *After virtue*, 3rd ed., Notre Dame, IN: University of Notre Dame Press.
MacIntyre, A. (1998) *A short history of ethics: A history of moral philosophy from the Homeric age to the twentieth century*, 2nd ed., London: Routledge.
Magurshak, D. (1985) '"The Concept of Anxiety": The keystone of the Kierkegaard-Heidegger relationship,' in R. L. Perkins (ed), *International Kierkegaard Commentary*, vol. 8 (*The Concept of Anxiety*), Macon, GA: Mercer University Press.
Philipse, H. (1999) 'Heidegger and ethics,' *Inquiry*, 42, nos. 3–4: 439–74.

Straube, M. (1904) *Manual of German etymology in its relation to English*, New York: Albright Publishing Company.

Young, I. M. (2001) 'House and home: Feminist variations on a theme,' in N. J. Holland and P. Huntington (eds), *Feminist Interpretations of Martin Heidegger*, University Park, PA: Pennsylvania University Press.

Further reading

Davenport, J. J. (2008) 'Faith as eschatological trust in "Fear and Trembling",' in E. F. Mooney (ed), *Ethics, Love, and Faith in Kierkegaard: Philosophical Engagements*, Bloomington, IN: Indiana University Press.

    This chapter clarifies the contentious issues in Kierkegaard scholarship concerning the transition from ethical resignation to religious faith, and addresses various challenges that arise when trying to think through the relationship between Kierkegaard's eschatological commitments and worldly matters.

Schrag, C. O. (1961) *Existence and freedom: Towards an ontology of human finitude*, Evanston, IL: Northwestern University Press.

    This book provides an account of how Heidegger makes explicit the ontology presupposed by Kierkegaard's reflections on becoming a Christian, and it situates their relationship within the intellectual milieu of nineteenth- and twentieth-century continental philosophy.

Vogel, L. (1994) *The fragile 'we': Ethical implications of Heidegger's 'Being and Time,'* Evanston, IL: Northwestern University Press.

    This book provides a thorough overview of the ongoing discussion about ethics in Heidegger scholarship, which covers topics such as Heidegger's Nazism, moral nihilism, the authority of tradition, and the liberalism/communitarianism debate.

10
LOVE FOR HUMANS: MORALITY AS THE HEART OF KIERKEGAARD'S RELIGIOUS PHILOSOPHY

Sharon Krishek

Introduction

One of the stories that *Fear and Trembling* – probably Kierkegaard's most celebrated and well-known essay – presents, is a story of a youth who fell in love with a princess but could not (for some unknown reason) carry out a relationship with her. In response to this miserable state of affairs, the young man performed what Kierkegaard terms a 'movement of resignation,' which 'transfigured' his love for the princess 'into a love of the eternal being' (FT, 43/SKS 4, 138).

Given the significance of resignation to faith, it might be inferred that in Kierkegaard's view, love for humans does not play an important role in the religious life; rather, what is at stake is 'love of the eternal being,' which is a 'transfiguration' of the former. Hence (it might be claimed), the real object of love is God, not humans. Coupling this with Kierkegaard's reservations regarding romantic love and friendship in his *Works of Love* and with his definition of faith as 'resting transparently' in God in *The Sickness unto Death* (see SUD, 14, 49/SKS 11, 130, 164), more than a few readers of Kierkegaard have concluded that love for humans is marginalized in Kierkegaard's conception of faith.[1] Accordingly, given that for Kierkegaard the good life amounts to the life of faith, he is deemed a philosopher who does not consider love for humans to form an integral part of the desired life.

Careful exegetical work of recent years, however, has defeated quite successfully this problematic conception of Kierkegaard, and many of his present readers would agree that he does affirm love for humans as an integral part of the religious life.[2] In what follows I wish to defend this view further and claim something even stronger. It is not just that love for humans is affirmed by Kierkegaard as a legitimate and an integral part of the religious life – it is a *necessary condition* for the realization of such a life. Namely, one cannot genuinely love God if one does not actively love humans.[3] Hence, morality – as the realm concerned with relationships between humans – lies at the heart of Kierkegaard's philosophy. The thesis of this chapter, then, is that for Kierkegaard, religiosity is conditioned by morality. To demonstrate this, I shall take the following steps.

I begin with a presentation of Kierkegaard's understanding of humans as *disposed by nature* to loving and, more crucially, as dependent for their flourishing on *realizing* this disposition. This interpretation relies on a distinction I take Kierkegaard to (implicitly) make in his *Works of Love*, between a human being's *potential* for loving and her actual fulfilment of this potential. I develop this idea further by turning to Kierkegaard's analysis of the self in *The Sickness unto Death*. The potential for loving, I claim, forms a crucial part of a human being's potential for becoming the self that God intends – namely, *wills* – her to be. If I'm correct in this, then the connection between fulfilling God's will (religiosity) and loving humans (morality) becomes evident. Against this background, and as a final step, I revisit the love story from *Fear and Trembling*. I hope to show that despite its past reputation, this unrequited love story provides yet further evidence for the moral heart of Kierkegaard's religious philosophy.[4]

Human love and human nature

Near the end of his *Works of Love*, Kierkegaard famously declares that 'to love people is the only thing worth living for, and without this love you are not really living' (WL, 375/SKS 9, 368). Whatever it is that 'not really living' amounts to, at the very least it amounts to an undesirable life – a life which is somehow wasted, failing to fulfil its potential. And as 'the only thing worth living for' (without which one is 'not really living') is 'to love people,' it is clear that for Kierkegaard, to 'really live' is conditioned by loving people. But what is the nature of this recommended love?

Kierkegaard draws a clear line between spontaneous love (such as romantic love) and neighbourly love. While the former comes naturally to the lover and is essentially gratifying, the latter is commanded (i.e., not spontaneous), and gratification is not (necessarily) part of its nature. Kierkegaard, somewhat misleadingly, commends neighbourly love as the only genuine love, and expresses reservations regarding romantic love and friendship, condemning them as nothing but self-love. However, he does explicitly affirm spontaneous love as legitimate and even desirable – granted that it be correctly related to neighbourly love, which arguably secures it as genuine (i.e., *not* a form of self-love).

The exact nature of the relation between neighbourly love and spontaneous love is a matter of a scholarly debate,[5] but here it suffices to concede the following uncontroversial three points, which are implied by Kierkegaard's basic distinction: (1) There are correct and incorrect ways of loving; (2) Every human being *can* love correctly; (3) Loving correctly is not easy to achieve and requires a conscious (spiritual, emotional, and moral) effort in order to be fulfilled. Based on this account, it is plausible to suggest that Kierkegaard takes humans to have a *potential* for loving, but a proper *actualization* of this potential does not come naturally to humans and is rather a matter of *work*.

The idea of possessing a potential (i.e., power or capacity) for loving as a part of human nature is also vindicated by the opening deliberation 'Love's Hidden Life and Its Recognizability by Its Fruits':

> Love's hidden life is in the innermost being, unfathomable. . . . Just as the quiet lake originates deep down in hidden springs no eye has seen, so also does a person's love originate even more deeply in God's love. If there were no gushing spring at the bottom, if God were not love, then there would be neither the little lake nor a human being's love. Just as the quiet lake originates darkly in the deep spring, so a human being's love originates mysteriously in God's love.
>
> *(WL, 9–10/SKS 9, 17–8)*

According to Kierkegaard, love is hidden in two ways. First, love is embedded in a person's 'innermost being' and is 'unfathomable.' This is likened to a gushing spring: the unseen 'power' in which the quiet lake (the 'result' of this 'power') originates. The spring is that which brings the lake into existence, and the lake indicates the existence of the spring. I suggest that this characterization demonstrates that love is a power (like the 'gushing spring'), whose existence is discernible only by virtue of the (physical and mental) actions it generates (the 'quiet lake'): these are the works of love. Love is 'hidden,' then, because it primarily exists as a potential and is hence manifested only when it is actualized by actions (which, again, can be either external and palpable, say, physically helping the beloved; or internal and imperceptible, say, thinking good thoughts about the beloved and wishing him well). Love is therefore a power, a potential for acting in a specific way, that of *caring*.[6]

Further, love is hidden in an additional, even deeper, way. Depicting it as 'originating in God's love' while soon afterwards referring to God *as* love,[7] Kierkegaard presents love as rooted in God. This means, I suggest, that according to Kierkegaard love is *essential* to human nature in a two-fold way. First, granted that humans are created in God's image (as Kierkegaard obviously believes they are), then in being thus created they are bestowed with that which is most typical of God's nature. And if most typical of God's nature is loving, then humans are granted the ability to love, and it is *this* ability that makes them akin to God. Hence, in loving they fulfil their *essence* (as God's creatures). This makes love – and this is already the second point – the most significant of all human abilities. After all, by loving, the human being gets an insight from 'within' to God's essence; and if so, to love is to be as intimately connected to God as one can.

It is therefore crucial for humans' relationship with God – as well as for human flourishing ('the only thing worth living for') – to fulfil their potential for loving. This idea is significantly strengthened by Kierkegaard's analysis of the self.

The essential connection between loving humans and being a self

The first paragraph of *The Sickness unto Death*, an essay that Kierkegaard considered as particularly significant,[8] reads as follows:

> A human being is spirit. But what is spirit? Spirit is the self. But what is the self? The self is a relation that relates itself to itself ... the self is not the relation but is the relation's relating itself to itself. A human being is a synthesis of the infinite and the finite, of the temporal and the eternal, of freedom and necessity. ... A synthesis is a relation between two. Considered in this way, a human being is still not a self.
>
> (SUD, 13/SKS 11, 129)

This complicated characterization of the self raises many questions, which I will soon attempt to answer. But to begin with, it should be noted that the opening of this passage – '[a] human being is ... the self' – seems to contradict its ending: '[c]onsidered in this way, a human being is still not a self.' If a human being *is* a self, how is it that under certain conditions (which are, we will see, quite typical) it is *not* a self? I believe this indicates a distinction between two meanings that Kierkegaard attributes to the term 'the self.'

The first meaning of 'the self' is a 'default' self: this is the kind of self that every human *is* simply by virtue of existing (as will be clarified below). The second meaning of 'the self' is a 'destined' self: this is the kind of self that every human *ought* to become, the self that God intends one to be. This gap between the 'is' and the 'ought' immediately brings forth the idea of potential: every human *has the potential* for becoming the self that she ought to be.

However, it is not easy to fulfil this potential to its fullest. Hence, the *actual* self of most humans amounts to only a *partial fulfilment* of their potential. For Kierkegaard, not to actualize one's potential to its utmost – and hence to fail in becoming the self that one ought to be – is precisely the state of despair (which is obviously opposed to the good life). But this begs the question: what is a 'self' to begin with, and what does it mean to have it (partly or fully) actualized?

Simply put, I suggest that 'to be a self' means to be a person with a *particular identity*. In other words, a person's 'selfhood' is that which signifies her as the particular person she is (distinct and distinguished from every other person). Hence, a self is a human being who possesses the quality of selfhood. This (eminently complex and significant) quality is that which makes her a self. For example, S. Kierkegaard's selfhood is that which makes him the self that he is: a person with a specific identity, S. Kierkegaard. The question, then, is what the nature of selfhood *is*. Here it is time to return to Kierkegaard's definition of the self.

Kierkegaard characterizes the human being as a special entity which is both finite and infinite (hereafter: the First Synthesis), both subject to necessity and free (hereafter: the Second Synthesis), and both temporal and eternal (hereafter: the Third Synthesis). He further claims that to be a *self* is to posit these syntheses in a certain relation. Before examining this latter claim, let us clarify the nature of the three syntheses.

Commentators generally interpret the three syntheses as different expressions of one and the same fact regarding human existence. According to this interpretation, the three syntheses typify humans as being both *limited* (this is what 'finite,' 'subject to necessity,' and 'temporal' stand for), and capable of *transcending* the limitations inherent in their existence (this is what 'infinite,' 'free,' and 'eternal' stand for).[9] I agree, but I think that the Third Synthesis conveys another, additional, meaning. I suggest that it expresses not only the idea of limitation and transcendence, but also the idea of potential and actualization. The potential is eternal, its actualization is temporal. What do I mean by this?

In my suggestion, humans are 'eternal' by virtue of possessing a divinely bestowed potential for becoming a particular person, a *self*. Each human is created not only as a person, but rather as a *particular* person: a person with identity, a person with a name. Under the assumption that a person's identity is determined first and foremost by her intrinsic qualities,[10] I take their combination to amount to both universal and particular qualities. Universal qualities (such as rationality and the capacity for loving) are shared by all humans, by virtue of being human. Hence, these qualities are that which makes one a *person* (in *the image of God*). Particular qualities (such as, say, wisdom, kindness, wit) are idiosyncratic (in their specific combination) to a person in her singularity, and hence make her the *particular* person she is. That is, while universal qualities make S. Kierkegaard (for example) a *person*, particular qualities make him *S. Kierkegaard*.

In this context, I take as specifically significant Kierkegaard's characterization of the despairer – who is, after all, someone who fails to become the self that he is intended to be – in terms of someone who 'forgets his name, divinely understood' (SUD, 33–4/SKS 11, 149). Relying on this characterization, I suggest considering the amalgamation of universal and particular qualities as comprising the name that God gives to each and every individual upon creating her. At the same time, being thus bestowed with a name does not entail that a person necessarily lives up to it – she can very well 'forget' it. Hence, I suggest that these qualities (the universal and the particular alike) are inherent in the human being only as a *potential*.

Indeed, a person's 'name' directs her in the course of her life – after all, a potential can be fulfilled to *some extent* without any effort consciously involved. However, it takes much more than simply living in order to fulfil one's potential – one's name – to its utmost, and become the self that God intends one to be (by giving their particular name). Here the significance of the *actualization* of one's potential (which is 'temporal') becomes evident. But first we should ask: how does a person actualize her potential *at all* (even if only by 'simply living')? To answer this question, we have to return to the understanding of the three syntheses as expressing a human's limitedness and the human ability to transcend it.

Human life, her existence 'in the world,' amounts to engaging with the events and people – as well as the constraints and opportunities – that comprise her reality. Now, a major characteristic of a person's reality is that it is finite, bound to necessity, and temporal. A person lives her life, not knowing for how long, facing threats (diseases, wars, accidents) that continually recall her limitedness. Much of what happens to her is not under her control: she needs to face obstacles to her will, and sometimes her will is entirely frustrated. Her interaction with other people also reflects the fact that the gap between willing something and fulfilling it may sometimes be unbridgeable. The experience of living in the world, then, is shadowed by finitude and the limits of necessity.

Nevertheless, this evident limitedness does not exhaust a person's experience of living. Her human (universal/eternal) ability to reason, imagine, and desire make freedom – and the infinitude of possibilities it entails – an essential part of her life. Thus, a person's limitedness is not the last word. The decision of how to *respond* to it is up to her. Reality is limiting, but at the same time it always carries a promise for a change. Hence, it is the responsibility of every person to discern this promise and act accordingly. Such a promise clearly does not eradicate finitude, necessity, and temporality; rather, it emerges between their lines.

Knowing how to read both the lines and what is in between them is far from easy, and it is in *this* context – the unending intertwining of temporality/necessity/finitude and eternity/possibility/infinitude – that one's potential is actualized. A person's potential is actualized via her interactions with others, her responses to adversities and opportunities, her construal of her life out of the materials given to her. And this brings us back to the distinction between the 'default' self and the 'intended' self. After all, every person interacts with other people, responds to situations, and shapes her life. In other words, every person – by virtue of simply living – realizes her potential *to some extent or another*. However, to become the self that one is *intended* to be – that is, to realize one's potential to its utmost – 'simply living' is not enough; one must be living *correctly*.

Living correctly is the opposite of despair. Thus, as Kierkegaard typifies the latter as a state of 'misrelation' between the opposing components of each synthesis – and hence as failing to achieve a state of 'equilibrium' (see SUD, 14/SKS 11, 130)[11] – I take him to mean that *not* to be in despair is to achieve a state of *harmony* between these opposites. In this view, then, to become the self that a person is intended to be, she has to enact her universal *and* particular qualities by balancing between her limitedness and her ability to transcend it.

In the previous section, the idea of humans having, essentially, a potential for loving was introduced. Returning to this idea, we can now further say that enacting this potential is crucial for becoming the self that a person is intended to be. After all, the ability to love forms an important – if not the most important – part of a person's universal qualities (those qualities, recall, that make her akin to God). As 'becoming the self that one is intended to be' is undoubtedly considered by Kierkegaard to be the highest task of human existence (religious and otherwise), it is clear that he must be considering love for humans – the evident way to enact this universal quality – as specifically important. Thus, against the background of the analysis of the self, it is now possible to demonstrate what it takes to actualize *correctly* one's potential for loving.

The actualization of one's potential selfhood (which is, again, comprised of universal qualities, including the ability to love, and particular ones) requires loving people properly. To love properly, the lover has to give shape to her universal capacity for loving by means of enacting her particular qualities. She has to find her unique way of loving, given her temperament, character traits, and other particular abilities. Doing this *correctly* is achieved by her balancing of the limitedness inherent in her existence and her essential ability to transcend it. That is, she has to love in the context of *her* living in the world, in the context of the concrete circumstances of her life (cf. Evans 2004: 170–9; Davenport 2013: 245–6).

A person's love potential, then, cannot be enacted in the abstract. It is not just that her capacity for loving must receive a particular shape (in accordance with her particular qualities), but it can only receive such a shape when acting in the world – which necessarily entails interacting with other people. Becoming the self that one is intended to be, then, is *conditioned* by enacting one's love potential by *properly* interacting with other people. Which means, simply put, that it is conditioned by an active love for humans.

We therefore see that despite focusing on a different issue, Kierkegaard's analysis of the self in *The Sickness unto Death* essentially continues and substantiates the connection he draws between loving humans and living correctly in his *Works of Love*. Love for humans is central – and essential – to the good life.

And indeed, a failure to love is commonly connected with the grim emotional state that we associate with despair. To demonstrate how illuminating Kierkegaard's analysis is for understanding this connection, I wish to make a small detour and look – through Kierkegaardian glasses – at a contemporary short story of a person in despair.

The failure to love is despair: a literary depiction

There are basically two types of despair, and each of these has three stages of intensity ('unconscious despair' is the first, 'weak despair' is the second, and 'defiant despair' is the third). One type of despair can be termed 'despair of detachment (from the world),' which Kierkegaard describes in terms of a person's failure to take seriously the constraints inherent in her situation. The other type of despair can be termed 'despair of confinement (to the world),' which Kierkegaard describes in terms of a person's submission to the constraints inherent in her situation, thus failing to take seriously her ability to transcend them.[12] The following is the story of a despairer of the latter kind.

Ronit, the protagonist of the short story *Omsk* (Arad 2009), is unhappy with her life. At forty-something – after having despaired of finding the perfect man with whom she would have the family she has dreamt of, and having failed in her attempts to conceive a child alone – she decides to adopt a child. The story takes place in Omsk, where Ronit has travelled to fulfil her dream; but alone she comes to Omsk, and alone she will leave it. The story begins with a fantasy and ends with a bad dream: two indirect encounters with reality that reflect Ronit's failed interaction with it. They reflect, in other words, her state of despair.

Ronit's fantasy – walking in the snow with a newborn – reveals her deep unwillingness to consent to the relevant situation she finds herself in: 'Yes, she knows you can't adopt newborns. That it's almost impossible to adopt before they're a year old. Still, she can't give up on her dream: a baby bundled in thick blankets in the snow' (Arad 2009: 367).[13] But there is no snow – it is a stifling Siberian summer – and no newborn. Instead there is a toddler awaiting adoption. His name is Constantine, which Ronit dislikes upon hearing. This insignificant fact (she knows she can simply rename the child), just like the unexpected heat, taints Ronit's long-anticipated joy, making her reserved and suspicious with regard to the whole situation.

Things go from bad to worse when Ronit meets Constantine. The frightened child responds neither to her nor to his surroundings, which makes her believe that there must be something wrong with him. Indeed, the doctor tells her that his behaviour is perfectly normal for a child in his situation, however – given the child's unknown background, as well as his early age – he naturally cannot assure her that it is absolutely certain that there exists no hidden problem with his (mental or physical) health. She therefore declines the adoption, feeling sad 'about the name she chose so thoughtfully' (ibid. 377).

Back at the hotel lobby Ronit meets Martha, a friendly Christian woman from the United States, a mother of four biological children who has come to Omsk with her husband to adopt another child. Ronit patronizes Martha, considering her a simple, boring woman, but when Martha mentions that she had a very difficult day, her attention is captured: 'Maybe they got a defective kid too,' she thinks to herself, 'Maybe all the kids here are defective. A cursed place' (ibid. 380). Martha's troubles, however, turn out to be of a different nature than those of Ronit. She is at a loss as to how to choose among the multitude of needy children. 'We wanted to take the one who would have the hardest time finding a home,' she tells Ronit, but adds: 'Not that I'm judging anyone, God forbid. Not everyone has the strength. But I feel the Lord has given me a lot of strength to help others, and I want to use it to bring good to the world. God forbid, I'm not judging anyone' (ibid.). Returning to her room, this is the first time that Ronit thinks of Constantine:

> She no longer thinks about how nothing goes her way, or about the fact that she won't be a mother at forty-four like she planned. Now she thinks of the baby, who will stay in the institution. Who will forever remain Constantine. She thinks about him and knows she could not raise him. Impossible. She has no husband. No supportive community. No fourteen-year-old daughter, a free au pair. Not to mention God thrown in as part of the deal. God hasn't given her anything. Never has. She has nothing. Nothing to give a boy like that. Those who have, can give. Those whom God has given to.
>
> *(ibid. 381)*

The meeting with Martha affects Ronit in this way because it makes her realize how far her dream of having a child was from reflecting the real nature of parenthood. And given her deluded notion of parenthood, it is not surprising that when encountering the first difficulty with the child she shrinks and backs down. Now, the difficulty is indeed a real one – the fear of raising alone a child who might be unhealthy is not to be dismissed – but it reflects something deeper. Engaging in a relationship of care and love – any relationship, let alone with one's child – entails entering into an insecurity zone fraught with risk, frustration, and pain. Love requires acceding to the unknown, to the insecure, to the risk of loss. But Ronit is unwilling to take this upon herself. Her (unacknowledged) sense of the depth of her failure emerges clearly from the dream that ends the story:

> I'm standing bundled in a fur coat, gloves and a hat. I hold a thick baby blanket. I look inside. The blanket is empty. I want to shout out for help. But then I discover that I'm standing in a huge icy wilderness. All around me is only snow, all the way to the horizon. Not a single living soul.
>
> *(ibid. 382)*

Judging Ronit's state as that of despair is tenable regardless of Kierkegaard's analysis, but it is Kierkegaard's analysis that provides us with the tools to understand the (moral, spiritual, and existential) roots of her emotional emptiness and gloom. In Kierkegaard's terms, her despair amounts to her failure to shape the universal/eternal in her – namely, her potential to love – in accordance with the particular aspect of her nature. After all, Ronit succumbs to that which comes naturally to her: her tendency for self-enclosure, her desire for control, her preference to discuss life rather than live it. The failure to actualize her potential to love is manifested in her failed interaction with the world, that is, in her failure to balance her (real and pressing) limitedness with her ability to transcend it. Hence, she fails to love Constantine. Hence, she despairs.

Revisiting *Fear and Trembling*'s love story

To recap, the thesis that was hitherto discussed is as follows. In my reading, *Works of Love* introduces the idea that each person, by nature, possesses the ability to love. This ability is highly significant, as it makes humans akin to God (whose nature *is* to love). Given only as a potential, however, every person has to actualize this ability, enacting it 'in the world' – that is, in the context of her interaction with other persons. An active love for humans, then, is an integral part of being like God (i.e., in His image), and hence of adhering to God's will.

Further, the connection between loving humans and fulfilling God's will is substantially strengthened by Kierkegaard's analysis of the self in *The Sickness unto Death*. Becoming the self that God intends one to be is presented as the 'formula' for 'resting transparently' in God (see SUD, 14, 49/SKS 11, 130, 164), which is (I suggest) a poetic way to express the desirable state of adhering to God's will. In my interpretation, this desirable state amounts to fulfilling one's potential selfhood, which includes both universal and particular qualities. Among the set of universal qualities that make humans 'like' God, the ability to love arguably brings us the closest – and is therefore most significant. Further, since its actualization depends on the person's way of living in the world – including her relationship with the people surrounding her – the invaluable significance of loving humans is reaffirmed.

Against this background, we can finally return to *Fear and Trembling*'s story of unrequited love, and offer a renewed interpretation of the 'transfiguration' of the heartbroken youth's love for his princess (see the Introduction above). By telling this story, Kierkegaard demonstrates the nature of (what he terms) the movement of 'resignation.' This movement, which amounts (roughly put) to submitting one's will to the will of God, is a necessary condition for faith. Given its significant role as such, it is important to understand the exact nature of the youth's love transfiguration.

> His love for that princess would become for him the expression of an eternal love, would assume a religious character, would be transfigured into a love of the eternal being, which true enough denied the fulfillment but nevertheless did reconcile him once more in the eternal consciousness of its validity in an eternal form that no actuality can take away from him.
>
> *(FT, 43–4/SKS 4, 138)*

I suggest that the emotional and spiritual process that the lover has gone through does not amount (as is often suggested) to a simple replacement of one kind of love (for the princess) with another (for God), but is rather more nuanced than that. In my understanding, the shift that Kierkegaard describes here – from a secular position to a religious one – is rooted in the lover's new understanding of his love for the princess. The young man turns into a knight of resignation when he recognizes his ability to love as forming a part of his nature as 'God's creature.' He becomes a knight, then, upon acknowledging his (eternal) potential for loving.[14]

Hence, 'the love for that princess became for him the expression of an eternal love,' in the sense that he gained a deeper understanding of it as being an actualization of his (divinely bestowed) potential to love. Accordingly, even though 'actuality' prevents a relationship with her, his love for her – being an emotional-spiritual expression of a force that is rooted deeply in his nature – is 'valid.' While it was indeed dependant for its initiation on actuality – that is, the presence of the princess – it is not thus dependant on actuality for its endurance.

Nevertheless, a love for an absent princess cannot be the same as a love for a present princess. In this sense, his love must be 'transfigured.' The meaning of this transfiguration, however, is not that the object of his love is replaced (God instead of the princess). On the contrary, he can keep his love for *the princess* 'alive' through his loving relationship with God. In other words, the nature of this transfiguration is akin to the transfiguration of love in the case of (the beloved's) death. Just as a romantic love for a dead (and hence absent) person is not the same as a romantic love for a living and present beloved – for example, the active love for the former becomes more a work of recollection,[15] and there are no expectations for a joyful future with the beloved – so the knight's resigned love must assume a different character. However, *because* it is a love in the context of *resignation*, its religious basis rather safeguards its endurance. The youth's love for God gives him a context for actively loving the princess, despite her absence. (In the same way, for example, that a person can actively love his dead spouse through his love for their child).

And yet, even in this revised interpretation – which understands the transformation of the knight's love to attest not to a change in the *object* of one's love but rather to a change in love's nature – Kierkegaard is far from presenting the love of resignation as an ideal. While resignation is indeed a necessary condition for faith, it is importantly distinguished from it. Faith necessarily entails resignation, but resignation in itself is not as yet faith. Hence, since for Kierkegaard there are fundamentally only two basic states of existence – faith and despair – it is clear that as long as resignation is *not* faith, it still amounts to despair.[16] Thus, Kierkegaard cannot be considering the state of the resigned lover as desirable, and accordingly he cannot be recommending this kind of attitude (with regard to love for humans) as ideal.

Rather, Kierkegaard explicitly poses as an ideal the love of *faith*, which is characterized by a relationship with a princess who is *present* in the lover's life (see FT, 50/SKS 4, 144).[17] Such an outright convergence between a fulfilled (and happy) love for a human being and the highest relationship with God strengthens yet again the thesis of the present chapter. *Fear and Trembling*, *Works of Love*, and *The Sickness unto Death* – these three pivotal works carry the same message: love for humans is at the heart of faith.[18]

Related topics

'Kierkegaard's post-Kantian approach to anthropology and selfhood,' Roe Fremstedal; 'Kierkegaard, Hegel, and Augustine on love,' Thomas J. Millay.

Notes

1. Well-known examples include Adorno (1940); Buber (2002); and Singer (1987). For a succinct introduction to the history of this problematic reception of Kierkegaard, see Ferreira (2001: 5–7).
2. See the recommendation for further reading at the end of this chapter.
3. And at least in this sense, love for humans is as important as love for God.
4. Two of the three essays that I discuss here are signed pseudonymously: *Fear and Trembling* (Johannes de Silentio) and *The Sickness unto Death* (Anti-Climacus). Kierkegaard's reasons for signing some of his

works pseudonymously are various, and it is controversial whether (and to what extent) it is legitimate to consider these pseudonymous works as faithful to Kierkegaard's 'real' opinions. This exegetical issue, however, is less relevant for the present article. First, as far as *The Sickness unto Death* is concerned there is an agreement among scholars that Kierkegaard took this essay to reflect his own conception of the ideal life (see note 8 below). Second, as far as *Fear and Trembling* is concerned, in the present article I read it in light of the two other essays, in a way that complies with Kierkegaard's more 'authorized' words.

5 See, in this regard, Krishek (2017).
6 Given Kierkegaard's analysis of love as essentially neighbourly, it seems reasonable to assume (as most commentators do) that Kierkegaard understands love to be a form of caring, of wholeheartedly minding the good of the beloved.
7 Kierkegaard's assertion that 'if God were not love' attests that he affirms that God *is* love.
8 See the translators' introduction (SUD, xxiii).
9 See, for example, Davenport (2013: 235); Rudd (2012: 41); Stokes (2010: 64); Walsh (2009: 99–100); Elrod (1987: 109); Roberts (1987: 138–9).
10 But not *only* by them. One's *potential* selfhood amounts to intrinsic qualities, but its *actualization* is determined by one's 'living in the world,' as will be shortly explained.
11 See also Kierkegaard's presentation of the different forms of despair in terms of 'lacking' finitude/necessity or infinitude/possibility (SUD, 30–42/SKS 11, 146–57).
12 For a textual grounding of categorizing the forms of despair in this way, see Krishek (2016).
13 References are to the Hebrew original; translation is by Jessica Cohen and is available as a webpage at: http://www.jewishfiction.net/index.php/publisher/articleview/frmArticleID/244.
14 Such an acknowledgement is, of course, only a necessary condition for becoming a knight, not a sufficient one. For a detailed discussion of resignation and what it requires, see Krishek (2009: ch. 2).
15 See 'The Work of Love in Recollecting One Who Is Dead' (WL, 345–58/SKS 9, 339–52).
16 Despair is a heterogeneous phenomenon. Hence it can qualify as the lot also of those who are more spiritually developed than their other despairing fellows. However, this does not mean that these two kinds of despairers are (morally, existentially, and spiritually) the same. It only means that both of them have not reached the state of complete spiritual health (i.e., faith).
17 For an elaborated discussion of this ideal, see Krishek (2009: ch. 3).
18 This research was supported by The Israel Science Foundation (grant No. 111/16).

References

Adorno, T. W. (1940) 'On Kierkegaard's doctrine of love,' *Studies in Philosophy and Social Science*, 8: 413–29.
Arad, M. (2009) 'Omsk,' in M. Arad (ed), *Short Story Master*, Tel Aviv: Am Oved.
Buber, M. (2002) 'The question to the single one,' in R. Gregor-Smith (trans), *Between Man and Man*, London; New York: Routledge.
Davenport, J. (2013) 'Selfhood and "spirit,"' in J. Lippitt and G. Pattison (eds), *The Oxford Handbook of Kierkegaard*, Oxford: Oxford University Press.
Elrod, J. (1987) 'The social dimension of despair,' in R. L. Perkins (ed), *International Kierkegaard Commentary*, vol. 19 (*The Sickness unto Death*), Macon, GA: Mercer University Press.
Evans, C. S. (2004) *Kierkegaard's ethic of love: Divine commands and moral obligations*, Oxford: Oxford University Press.
Ferreira, M. J. (2001) *Love's grateful striving: A commentary on Kierkegaard's 'Works of love'*, Oxford: Oxford University Press.
Krishek, S. (2017) 'Kierkegaard on impartiality and love,' *European Journal of Philosophy*, 25, no. 1: 109–28.
Krishek, S. (2016) 'The moral implications of Kierkegaard's analysis of despair,' *Religious Studies*, 52, no. 1: 25–43.
Krishek, S. (2009) *Kierkegaard on faith and love*, Cambridge: Cambridge University Press.
Roberts, R. C. (1987) 'The grammar of sin and the conceptual unity of "The Sickness unto Death",' in R. L. Perkins (ed), *International Kierkegaard Commentary*, vol. 19 (*The Sickness unto Death*), Macon, GA: Mercer University Press.
Rudd, A. (2012) *Self, value, and narrative: A Kierkegaardian approach*, Oxford: Oxford University Press.
Singer, I. (1987) *The nature of love*, vol. 3 (*The Modern World*), Chicago, IL: University of Chicago Press.
Stokes, P. (2010) *Kierkegaard's mirrors: Interest, self, and moral vision*, London: Palgrave Macmillan.
Walsh, S. (2009) *Kierkegaard: Thinking Christianly in an existential mode*, Oxford: Oxford University Press.

Further reading

Davenport, J. (2013) 'Selfhood and "spirit,"' in J. Lippitt and G. Pattison (eds), *The Oxford Handbook of Kierkegaard*, Oxford: Oxford University Press.

> This article presents an analysis of selfhood that explains how its achievement is related to the good life, and in its last part connects the former more specifically to love.

Evans, C. S. (2004) *Kierkegaard's ethic of love: Divine commands and moral obligations*, Oxford: Oxford University Press.

> This book argues for a close connection between moral obligation and human flourishing, and defends Kierkegaard's conception of love as providing the moral basis for natural forms of love.

Ferreira, M. J. (2001) *Love's grateful striving: A commentary on Kierkegaard's 'Works of love'*, Oxford: Oxford University Press.

> This commentary on *Works of Love* provides an in-depth reading of this essay and defends Kierkegaard's conception of love as humanistic.

Stokes, P. (2015) *The naked self: Kierkegaard and personal identity*, Oxford: Oxford University Press.

> This book situates Kierkegaard's conception of selfhood within contemporary debates concerning personal identity, arguing that Kierkegaard can significantly contribute to our understanding of both the metaphysical and practical aspects of personal identity.

PART 3

Aesthetics

11
THE ETHICAL LIFE OF AESTHETES

Ulrika Carlsson

Introduction

Judge William is known as one of the key models of the ethical life in Kierkegaard's thought. He outlines his life-view in personal letters to the aesthete, 'A,' in the second part of *Either/Or*, and the epistolary form is significant for a few reasons. First of all, it marks a contrast with the papers of 'A,' to which Victor Eremita deemed it appropriate to append 'as a kind of motto: *ad se ipsum*' – 'to himself' – a phrase found among the aesthete's aphorisms (EO 1, 8/SKS 2, 15). Secondly, this form of address clearly illustrates that the view elaborated is dialectical – shaped by its rejection of another view. Much of the Judge's letters are taken up with characterizing the aesthetic view he rejects, both in general terms and in the particular way in which 'A' supposedly exemplifies it. Yet it is important to keep in mind that these letters are presented as spontaneous comments on the latter's life by the Judge. Kierkegaard does not present them as a response to the aesthetic writings that Eremita has collected for the reader in a separate volume. With the exception of 'The First Love,' the Judge does not refer to any of the papers attributed to 'A,' and – as Joakim Garff (1995: 93) also notes – we have little reason to suppose that he has read them.

All of this entails certain problems for the interpreter. As part of deciding how the aesthetic fares in light of the ethical critique, readers must assess how accurate the Judge's characterizations of both 'A' and the aesthetic life are. It might be that his papers give insights into the aesthetic life (and his own spiritual life) that have been lost on the Judge. Yet in the Kierkegaard scholarship, it is common not only to accept the Judge's critique of the aesthetic life without much question, but also to have such trust in his judgment that when characterizing the aesthetic life, commentators often quote from the Judge's writings rather than from those of 'A,' or paraphrase the Judge's sweeping generalizations. George Pattison, though he engages closely with the 'A' writings in his *Kierkegaard and the Quest for Unambiguous Life*, defers entirely to the Judge when characterizing the aesthetic life. That life, he writes, lacks 'an ethical or a religious dimension: it preoccupies itself only with what can appear on the surface of life, with what can be experienced, enjoyed, or played with, but refuses any serious commitment to anyone or anything' (Pattison 2013: 62). The temptation to rely on the Judge is easy to understand given that he offers far more explicit and succinct definitions of the aesthetic approach to life. But it is a temptation that must be resisted. Before letting the ethical have its say, we should try to describe the aesthetic from the inside, on its own terms. And we must not assume that the Judge is an authority on all of *Either/Or*. Otherwise, there can be no fair judgment as to which of the life-views is better.

In this chapter, I will point out ways in which the Judge's critical characterization of the aesthetic life misses its mark, given what we know as readers of 'A.' Whether this is by Kierkegaard's intention or if it constitutes a failure of the ambitious project of dialogue in *Either/Or* is something to be debated. What is clear is that 'A' is not as superficial a person as the Judge's letters would make us believe. He already voices some of the criticisms of aesthetic living the Judge elaborates in his letters. Moreover, the aesthetic life 'A' is preoccupied with in his studies of operas and works of literature is actually closely intertwined with ethics and religion. And his writings are pregnant with serious challenges to a position like the Judge's, which the latter never thinks to address. Whereas the Judge is concerned with how one should conduct one's life given that one owes that life to God, 'A' is struggling with the question of why he should live at all. Lacking the Judge's religious faith, 'A' seeks some other source of value – an enchantment like Don Giovanni's, a sense of family like Antigone's – and finally tries to devise a method for making even the most accidental features of the world meaningful through poetic recollection.

Who is 'A?'

Although the Judge's letters are supposedly addressed to 'A,' their criticism often seems most suited for Johannes the Seducer. Johannes describes in his journal the strange games he plays with a girl, Cordelia, whom he sees around town. His actions in relation to her are calculated to prompt interesting reactions that he will later recall and enjoy as if they were part of a play he watched. 'I am experiencing with her the emergence of her love,' he writes; 'I myself am almost invisibly present when I am sitting visible at her side. It is like when a dance meant to be danced by two is danced by one person alone. . . . She moves as in a dream, and yet she is dancing with another' (EO 1, 380/SKS 2, 368–9). As an artist paints his beloved, Johannes explains, so he too fashions an image of Cordelia 'in a spiritual sense' (EO 1, 389/SKS 2, 377; translation modified). His 'love' is an infatuation with images and fragments of fantasy.

Now as the Judge describes 'A,' he bears an important resemblance to Johannes. The Judge recalls a story 'A' once told him, about how he had walked up to a girl in the street and handed her a bill of five rix-dollars, the precise amount he had just overheard her say she wished she had (EO 2, 12/SKS 3, 21–2). The Judge regards this incident as the manifestation of a deep problem in his counterpart's character. As he tells 'A,' 'what you wanted was to play the role of fate' (EO 2, 13/SKS 3, 22), to 'experiment' with other people (EO 2, 15/SKS 3, 22; my translation). Because 'A' refuses to actually be engaged in the world, his life has no content (EO 2, 80/SKS 3, 90). What he cares about, according to the Judge, is the quality of his experience. But he does not care whether anything real underlies that experience. This striking similarity between Johannes and 'A,' as the Judge portrays him, has prompted many readers (e.g., Evans 2009: 80; Pattison 2013: 202) to conclude that the diary attributed to Johannes is really written by 'A,' a possibility that Victor Eremita already hints at in his preface. This is also corroborated by 'Rotation of Crops,' where 'A' prescribes precisely the method for enjoying life that Johannes employs. Certainly, Kierkegaard wanted the reader to entertain this possibility very seriously. But if the diary is understood this way, then it functions in the logic of *Either/Or* as the absurd conclusion that calls for rejecting the aesthetic life and condemning the aesthetic persona. That is because the diary presents the aesthetic life in an altogether repugnant way. Much is at stake then, in identifying 'A' with Johannes, and we should be careful not to do so lightly.

Although 'Rotation of Crops' and some of the former's aphorisms and subtitles support this identification, 'The First Love' speaks against it. 'A' offers, in that review of Scribe's *The First Love*, a criticism of the kind of immediate love that is actually the love of an imaginary person rather than a real one. 'She has pathos,' 'A' writes of the protagonist of the play, Emmeline, 'but since its content is nonsense, her pathos is essentially chatter; she has passion, but since its content is a phantom, her passion is essentially madness' (EO 1, 253/SKS 2, 246). She indulges herself in the illusion that 'she loves her cousin Charles, whom she hasn't seen since she was eight years old' (EO 1, 253/SKS 2, 246). When a suitor shows up presenting himself as Charles, she instantaneously loves this man. Yet even if it had been the real Charles, 'A' points out, Emmeline's love would not really have him as its object. She would still be in love with an image she herself has conjured up (EO 1, 255/SKS 2, 248), an image so abstract, it can fit any man (EO 1, 260/SKS 2, 252–3). What 'A' implies here is that he believes in a truer love, just like the Judge does — a love based on the lovers' revealing themselves completely to each other. It is also doubtful whether the kind of behaviour described in the diary is coherent with his other writings, notably 'The Tragic in Ancient Drama Reflected in the Tragic in Modern Drama.' Here 'A' writes with pathos about the importance of attachments to persons, no matter the grief and pain such attachments bring.

To be sure, Eremita asserts in his preface that 'a coherent esthetic view of life can hardly be presented' and that the aesthete's papers 'contain a multiplicity of approaches to an esthetic view of life' (EO 1, 13/SKS 2, 21). This would seem to suggest that 'A' could be the author of the diary even if he elsewhere expresses a view of life radically opposed to that of Johannes. Let us suppose Eremita is right. What kind of coherence is it that the aesthetic view of life lacks? Presumably some kind of logical coherence. The aesthetic life is not based on principles but on desires, inclinations and tastes. Not having their origin in the faculty of reason, these do not answer to the individual's sense of logic, to the principle of non-contradiction.

Nonetheless, if 'A' is supposed to be a person, and if we want to assert that this person is identical with Johannes, then other criteria of coherence come into play, whether Eremita acknowledges this or not. In fact, persons do not usually display logical consistency among their values, desires, emotions and beliefs. (It is not even clear what it would mean for a person to be logically coherent. Is a momentary attraction to another woman logically inconsistent with a man's wedding vow to his wife?) But we sense a kind of organic consistency in persons, a psychological coherence. A fictional character, if he is to be plausible, must have this coherence too; and in his 'First and Last Explanation,' Kierkegaard claims that his pseudonyms have precisely 'psychological consistency' (CUP 1, [625]/SKS 7, 569). We have then to decide whether 'A' would be psychologically consistent if the diary were ascribed to him as his own sincere record of his life rather than a piece of dystopian fiction. What kind of person is 'A?'

Vincent McCarthy (2008: 61) suggests that 'A' suffers from bipolar depression. This certainly seems plausible, and would explain how he can both write with exuberance about *Don Giovanni* and call death the greatest blessing in 'The Unhappiest One.' But this diagnosis cannot ground an identification of 'A' with Johannes. Johannes is a calm and calculating manipulator; if he displays any symptoms of a psychiatric condition, they are those of a sociopath, someone who could not feel deep sympathy for Antigone and the Silhouettes, as 'A' does. The different pieces written by 'A,' then, are better interpreted as articulating different varieties of aesthetic life, which no single person can embody all by himself. This opens up another important possibility in our assessment of the aesthetic life, namely to affirm some of its forms while rejecting others. If the view presented in 'The Seducer's Diary' is neither logically entailed nor psychologically coherent with that of 'The Immediate Erotic Stages' and 'The Tragic in Ancient Drama

Reflected in the Tragic in Modern Drama,' then the repugnant ethos of the diary cannot serve ethicists as a reductio ad absurdum of 'A' and all the life-views he presents.

The ethical inside the aesthetic

Early in his discussion of marriage, the Judge complains that contemporary culture has lost something of great value. 'Our time,' he writes, 'is highly reminiscent of the disintegration of the Greek state; everything remains, yet there is no one who believes in it' (EO 2, 19/SKS 3, 28; translation modified). Thus people have lost faith in marriage as well as the courage required for entering a marriage (EO 2, 26/SKS 3, 34). In this regard, 'A' is a child of his age, in the Judge's estimation.

But 'A' has his own grievances about 'the age.' In the essay on tragedy, which Heinrich Fauteck (1974: 94) reads as a critique of modernity, 'A' complains that aspiration for social status has taken the place of authentic personal aims, so that people only desire that which their neighbours have. 'A' calls this an expression of envy, and thus 'sinful' (EO 1, 22/SKS 2, 31). He goes on to call the times wretched – not for being evil, but for being devoid of passion, to the point where transgressions are committed in such a paltry way they cannot even be called 'evil.' It was different in the times of the Old Testament and Shakespeare, he says, when human beings hated, loved and cursed each other, and meant it (EO 1, 27–8/SKS 2, 36). Worst of all for 'A' personally is that the spirit of the times has infected his soul, so that he too lacks the wholeheartedness of ancient and medieval times. 'I have, I believe, the courage to doubt everything,' he writes; 'I have, I believe, the courage to fight against everything; but I do not have the courage to acknowledge anything, the courage to possess, to own, anything' (EO 1, 23/SKS 2, 32). To arouse his pathos, he must immerse himself in artworks and fictional characters of ages past – their passion inspires him. Even as these melancholy self-reflections bear out some of the Judge's criticisms of 'A,' the latter's self-awareness takes the force out of that criticism. This evidence of agreement in their world views also indicates that the Judge and 'A' could have a more nuanced and productive discussion, as intellectual equals, than the Judge's criticism suggests. As it is, the Judge's letters fail to address 'A.' They, too, could be marked '*ad se ipsum.*'

It is with the essays on tragedy and grief that we should confront one of the key points in the Judge's first letter. According to the Judge, ethical and religious approaches to life preserve the aesthetic element in love in a way that a haphazard aesthetic way of life cannot. Aesthetic love contains gratitude and humility, pregnant in which is a yearning for eternity. 'A first love is humble and is therefore happy that there is a power higher than itself . . . in order to have someone to thank' (EO 2, 43/SKS 3, 60). That urge to give thanks to a higher power, with its implication that love is a kind of miracle or divine grace – something that cannot be accounted for simply by the actions and inclinations of two individuals – is accommodated in the wedding ceremony. It is God who presides over this ceremony, and the fact that the specific features of the ceremony are prescribed by tradition is also significant, according to the Judge. The wedding ceremony 'is not something the lovers themselves thought up in an opulent moment, something they could abandon if they thought of something else along the way' (EO 2, 89/SKS 3, 92). In making their vows, bride and groom create a duty for themselves, and ask God to be their witness in remaining faithful to it. This duty thus exists outside the lovers, and yet it is not a stranger to them but rather like an old friend (EO 2, 146/SKS 3, 144). When this 'friend' speaks, the Judge continues, 'what he says is not something new, but something familiar,' to which the lovers have already assented; 'and when he has spoken the individuals humble themselves under it but are also elevated by it, since they are assured that what he bids them to do is what they themselves wish' (EO 2, 146/SKS 3, 144; translation modified). By binding themselves in this way to each other through God, the lovers gain a positive freedom (EO 2, 67n/SKS 3, 72n).

This discussion of marriage and of the ethical and religious tendencies with which the aesthetic is pregnant is in my view the most compelling part of the Judge's writings. Jon Stewart (2003: 229) has noted that the Judge's treatment of the relation between immediate love and marriage is very Hegelian, and matches the view of marriage Hegel (1967: 111f) outlines in *Philosophy of Right*. But the Judge makes a convincing case about God's importance in the wedding ceremony – because the marriage vows are made before God, they have unusual gravity for the spouses – and this is a radical departure from Hegel's account. The merits of the Judge's view notwithstanding, his argument that the ethical and aesthetic can be combined is dialectically and rhetorically problematic, insofar as it presupposes that 'A' promotes some pure version of aesthetic living and aesthetic values, free of ethical and religious elements.

For a clear counter-example to that presupposition, consider how 'A' proposes to re-write Sophocles' *Antigone* to suit the modern mindset, which is more reflective and individualistic than the ancient. In modern tragedies, it is not some terrible fate imposed on the hero by vindictive gods that derails him. The modern tragic hero plays a more active part in his own undoing. The modern Antigone devotes her life to her father, guarding the secret of his terrible deeds and anxiously dwelling on the question of whether he himself knew what he had done. 'She loves her father with all her soul,' 'A' writes, 'and this love draws her away from herself into the father's guilt' (EO 1, 161/SKS 2, 159). Far from living a life of pleasure and being concerned only with her own experience, the modern Antigone has a deep commitment to her father and sacrifices her own happiness for him. In fact, she feels a duty to her father, a duty that – like the one a bride takes upon herself through her wedding vow – coincides with what she is immediately, emotionally inclined to do.

In removing fate from his modern tragedy, 'A' has not, then, removed all external influence on the heroine. She maintains enough 'substantiality' – ties to family, culture and religion – to experience deep sorrow (EO 1, 153–4/SKS 2, 152). In fact, 'A' denounces modern ethics with its rabid individualism. Every person, he writes, is 'a child of God, of his age, of his nation, of his family, of his friends, and only in them does he have his truth' (EO 1, 145/SKS 2, 144). The modern Antigone illustrates precisely this. It is by loving her father that she feels like herself, and it is this love, too, that leads her to ruin. The ethics 'A' thereby espouses not only harks back to a communitarian society that preceded the Enlightenment, but also anticipates what the Judge will say in his second letter. In the modern Antigone, 'A' celebrates a person who does not create herself from scratch but affirms her place in the world in a way quite similar to what the Judge calls 'choosing oneself.' As the Judge writes, the self the individual chooses 'has a boundless multiplicity within itself inasmuch as it has a history,' a history reaching back through its ancestors. In this history, 'he stands in relation to other individuals in the race and to the whole race, and this history contains painful things, and yet he is the person he is only through this history' (EO 2, 216/SKS 3, 207).

Yet there is an important difference between the ethics of 'A' and the ethics of the Judge, which becomes clear when the Judge goes on. The individual, he writes, 'can give up nothing of all this, not the most painful, not the hardest, and yet the expression for this struggle, for this acquiring, is – repentance. He repents himself back into himself, back into the family, back into the race, until he finds himself in God' (EO 2, 216/SKS 3, 207). Now *Anger* – what the Hongs translate as 'repentance' but might be better rendered 'remorse' – comes up also in the discussion of tragedy provided by 'A.' The Judge and 'A' agree that it is an ethical rather than an aesthetic phenomenon (EO 1, 148/SKS 2, 148). As such, remorse has no place in tragedy, 'A' says (EO 1,

144/SKS 2, 143–4). Instead, the guilt of a tragic hero must always be ambiguous. The modern Antigone wishes her father had not performed those actions that later turned out to be patricide and incest. In loving her father, the modern Antigone feels the painful regret she imagines him having felt about his deeds. To feel his pain is to identify with him; we can say that she regrets herself 'back into family.' But that feeling is not an act of repentance and makes no reference to God. She does not seek God's forgiveness for the essential depravity the Judge would say is hers by virtue of her being a finite human being and an heiress of original sin. She despairs, but the Judge would say that this despair lacks redemptive power, because she does not *will* to despair, and thus doesn't come to 'own herself' through this despair (cf. EO 2, 190, 213/SKS 3, 184, 204).

The modern Antigone then falls short of ethical living as understood by the Judge. But it should be noted that the Judge's conception of ethics is a very peculiar one. Indeed, Noreen Khawaja (2016: 70f) has shown that not only the explicitly religious components, but also the heavy emphasis on reflection, the idea of choosing oneself and the demanding notion of responsibility for oneself are ideas Kierkegaard adopted from Protestantism. With a slightly broader ethics, we could call the modern Antigone not only ethical, but unusually virtuous. Her life is governed by an ethos (in a way that Johannes the Seducer's is not). Her freedom is bound by reverence for other people. And it is in her relationships with other people that she finds meaning in life.

Faith

While calling on 'A' to repent, the Judge also accuses his friend of lacking faith. 'Instead of saving your soul by entrusting everything to God, instead of taking this shortcut, you prefer the endless roundabout way, which perhaps will never take you to your destination,' he writes (EO 2, 14/SKS 3, 23). He goes on to identify depression as the cause of this lack of faith. Is not depression, he asks, 'the defect of the age; is it not that which echoes even in its light-minded laughter; is it not depression that has robbed us of the courage to command, the courage to obey, the power to act, the confidence to hope?' (EO 2, 23–4/SKS 3, 32). Like all depression, this one 'is defiant,' presumably of God (EO 2, 25/SKS 3, 33).

Now if the Judge thinks 'A' lacks faith in God, why should he bother asking 'A' to repent? To repent, after all, is to express remorse for sin and ask forgiveness of God. Repentance thus presupposes faith. A person without religious faith can be remorseful and ask forgiveness of other people, but he will not repent before God. Nor will he consider his entire personality sinful and in need of repentance. The Judge of course does regard 'A' as a sinner, but the question is why he expects a distinctly religious command to be effective when directed at a non-believer. The command is odd from a rhetorical point of view. Perhaps the Judge thinks repentance is a way to gain faith – he does say that when an individual 'repents himself back into the family, back into the race,' he will find himself in God (EO 2, 216/SKS 3, 207). But what can motivate the individual to perform this repentance if not some initial faith in God? He must have some premonition that there is a God who is good, who loves him and to whom he owes everything. Otherwise, he cannot begin to see his depression as defiance and his whole life as a sin in need of forgiveness.

It is well known that Kierkegaard disdained the appeal to evidence in religion. If the believer relies on evidence, then he doesn't need to draw upon resources in himself – courage and pathos – that, for Kierkegaard, are constitutive of true faith (Carr 1996: 238). But this does not mean that the believer doesn't have reasons to believe and to live a religious life. A premonition that there is a good God is such a reason. Whatever its epistemic merits, it will certainly have motivational force for the individual. Indeed, I want to suggest that religious faith is ultimately grounded in some such gut feeling, and that atheism can be explained by the non-believer's lack of such a feeling. To seize upon that feeling and build one's life around it certainly takes courage and passion, especially when one encounters reasons speaking against the existence of a loving God. When asked how a good God could command a man to kill his child, the believer might not find the theoretical resources to give an answer. But his practical, emotional resources can allow him to maintain his own faith in the face of what sounds like counter-evidence to God's goodness.

Kierkegaard liked to speak of the religious life in the most dramatic terms as a life of inner turmoil, and of true faith as something that is achieved only through continuous struggle. In *Fear and Trembling*, Johannes de silentio says that 'the movement of faith is made by virtue of the absurd' (FT, 35/SKS 4, 131); in *Concluding Unscientific Postscript*, God's incarnation in the historical person Jesus is called an 'absolute paradox' (CUP 1, 217/SKS 7, 198). In contrast with the courage and persistence of a 'knight of faith,' it is easy to regard the non-believer as a weakling and coward, or someone too superficial to understand his mistake. But if we want to understand faith, it would be a good idea to try to understand also the lack of faith, and not only from the theist's outside perspective, but from within. On the view I've presented, it is in fact far easier for the believer to persevere in his faith than it would be for an atheist to begin to believe. Without some hunch that there is a good God, it would truly be absurd for the non-believer to kill his child because he was ordered to, or to 'repent' for everything that he is. In fact, it would be impossible to perform these actions in the spirit required. That is not to say that conversion is impossible; but most likely it happens through some transformative experience that causes a gestalt shift in the individual's worldview. Sheer willpower will not do. In commanding 'A' to repent, the Judge is perhaps blind to his own religious presuppositions, unconsciously projecting them onto 'A.' For the Judge, who already believes, repentance makes sense. But the command cannot hope to be obeyed unless 'A' shares the Judge's religious feelings.

Although the idea of a religious gut feeling actually harmonizes well with Kierkegaard's claims that it takes passion to be a true believer, he would probably reject the idea as too aesthetic and Romantic. Nor have I intended to offer an interpretation of Kierkegaard's own theoretical view of faith. After all, we don't have to assume that Kierkegaard was right about faith – even his own faith or that of his fictional characters. At any rate, there is a line from *The Concept of Irony* that is worth keeping in mind when we read the Judge's elaborate denunciations of his interlocutor's life and character:

> It takes courage not to surrender to the shrewd or sympathetic counsel of despair that allows a person to erase himself from the number of the living; but this does not necessarily mean that every sausage peddler, fed and fattened on self-confidence, has more courage than the person who succumbed to despair.
>
> *(CI, 327/SKS 1, 355)*

Meaning

'Rotation of Crops' identifies boredom as the greatest evil human beings have to contend with. All people are boring, 'A' writes, and implies also that all of reality is boring (EO 1, 285/SKS 2, 275). Indeed, boredom is the negative force that has propelled humanity forward (EO 1, 285/SKS 2, 275). Having diagnosed the problem, 'A' proceeds to offer a method for enjoyment that can be employed regardless of how boring one's circumstances are. To avoid boredom, one must harness the creative power of the imagination, forgetting the real world and imagining a more interesting version of it. This entails that value is subjective. Value pertains to experience, not to the world that causes or occasions that experience. Objective reality is reduced to a source of prompts for interesting moods and musings.

In laying out this attitude toward reality, 'A' plays right into the Judge's hands. Outlined in hyperbolic terms that seethe with frustration, even irritation, the approach is so extreme as to make the Judge's critique all but redundant. Though presented in the first person, it reads like a caricature, which could stand on its own as a critique of what it purports to espouse. This also means, as I noted earlier, that we lose any hold we previously had on 'A' as a plausible person. For the ethicist, this is actually not an advantage but a dialectical and rhetorical problem. The strength he takes himself to establish for his position by refuting the aesthetic will turn out to be partly illusory if the aesthete he argues against is a straw-man.

That is, if we take the claims of 'A' at face value. But we could also read the essay with an eye to diagnosing an existential problem that 'A' suffers from, or a mood he is stuck in. Such a reading can actually gain important insights about value in his essay. Boredom may seem like a banal problem, a problem for those who have no real problems. But it would be a mistake to dismiss his concern with boredom, as becomes clear when we see the close connection between boredom and depression. One important symptom of depression is anhedonia, an inability to feel pleasure, which leads to a general lack of interest and motivation. A persistent state of boredom is really a form of depression.

After considering the idea of supplying the general public with enough money to allow them to stop working and spend their days enjoying themselves, 'A' turns to a more elaborate means of eradicating boredom. Now 'A' is no longer concerned with making changes in the external world. Rather he urges us to change how we experience it. He bases his discussion on a distinction between remembering and recollecting. To recollect, he says, is to remember 'poetically'; and as a person recollects, he actually forgets, replacing memories with recollections (EO 1, 293/SKS 2, 282). People generally have little appreciation for the art of recollection, 'A' continues, and 'usually want to forget only the unpleasant, not the pleasant' (EO 1, 294/SKS 2, 283). But in his view, one should recollect, and thus forget, as much as possible; one should, additionally, avoid friendship and marriage, and only deal with people in the passing way that can provide stuff for interesting recollections (EO 1, 295/SKS 2, 284–5).

It is a suggestion that makes us queasy, even if we can't immediately articulate why. In that sense, the suggestion can function as a thought experiment. Indeed, Kierkegaard may be inviting us to draw a conclusion that is similar to the one Robert Nozick (1974: 42) draws from his thought experiment 'the experience machine.' In Nozick's scenario, we are asked to consider connecting our brains to computers that would produce pleasant or interesting experiences for us for the rest of our lives, according to a kind of 'playlist' we ourselves would get to compose in advance. Like the experience machine, the method proposed by 'A' for controlling one's experiences and feelings drives home the fact that most of us care about the reality that underlies our experience, not just the experience itself. Most of us wouldn't opt to live in an illusion, however pleasant, even if once in it, we wouldn't be able to tell the difference.

Nonetheless, these thought experiments are a bit simplistic. Experience relates to reality in a complex way; it cannot simply be a mirror of it. There is a different way to conceive of recollection that maintains the kinship with the Platonic method of acquiring knowledge, fits the description 'remembering poetically' and refers to a psychological phenomenon with great ethical significance. Consider the fact that it is easier to remember a line of thinking if its steps are logically related to one another, just as it is easier to memorize a poem if it rhymes. In such cases, we make use of patterns to grasp a chunk of data – we *recollect* the data. This is similar to our experience and memory of series of events. Time itself is continuous and doesn't have parts with beginnings, middles and ends. Yet in our memory, strings of events become grouped into discrete wholes, which are recalled and retold as coherent stories. When we treat a series of events as one story, our perception of the meanings of individual events is shaped by the story as a whole. A story with a happy ending will make the events leading up to it seem fortuitous in hindsight, even if they didn't at the time of their occurrence. Their true meaning is explained by something that they enabled, something that happened later. This way of making sense of events in time is what is called *narrative*.

As is well known, memories change over time. The process of making sense of past experience is one source of such change, and not just by adding meaning as some separate ingredient. Rather, as a pattern emerges in or is superimposed upon the remembered events, certain aspects will be emphasized at the expense of others. Moreover, data that doesn't fit the pattern may be eliminated altogether, and made-up data that corroborates the pattern may be added. (Hence the phenomenon of legends that we disbelieve because they make *too* much sense.) This means that there is a negative correlation between, on the one hand, the accuracy and complexity of memory, and on the other hand, its intelligibility and coherence. We could say, with 'A,' that remembering and recollecting are at odds with one another.

Though we can make a conceptual distinction between remembering and recollecting, as 'A' does, recollection as I have characterized it is usually an integral *part* of remembering. Organizing events into a narrative need not distort them; it assists us in remembering. Yet 'A' seems to assume a naïve realism in his essay whereby, ordinarily, memories are absolutely true records of the past unaffected by the process of interpreting and understanding. In a similarly misguided fashion, 'A' talks about recollection as an activity under voluntary control that does not naturally aim toward truth. But the activity that fits that description is actually fantasizing, or imagining. And contrary to what 'A' suggests, we are unable to conjure up a fantasy and then simply take it to be true while knowing we ourselves made it up. When fantasy supplants memory, this happens through mental processes of which we are not in control. Self-deception relies crucially on poor self-awareness, on some opacity in the mind, and cannot be achieved in such a studied way. In addition to the implausibility of ascribing 'The Seducer's Diary' to 'A,' it is utterly unbelievable as a piece of first-person writing for this reason: someone inclined to live like Johannes would not document his life that way.

Recollection is not only a source of intelligibility by organizing events into meaningful narratives, it is also a source of pleasure. We read literature partly in pursuit of this pleasure. That is one reason it is appropriate to call recollection 'aesthetic' or 'poetic.' In life, this pleasure often goes unnoticed, perhaps because it is so pervasive. We become aware of it most acutely when it goes away. This can happen as part of severe anxiety or depression, which consist partly in a failure to see meaning in things that happen. At such times, life can feel pointless or chaotic. The individual who has lost the sense that her life makes sense, that what she does fits into a bigger picture, may find herself turning this crisis into a philosophical question: how, if at all, can life in this world be made worthwhile? It's a difficult question to address from within a state of boredom or depression. Perhaps that is why the rotation method suggested by 'A' is such an absolute failure. From within his disenchantment, all enjoyment may seem equally arbitrary, equally illusory. Therefore it does not make sense to distinguish between real experience and a gratuitous indulgence in pleasant feelings. This is not entirely mistaken, since things and events in the world are not inherently meaningful. Meaning is a feature of the way in which our minds interpret our experiences. It is creative, but not thereby unbounded in its freedom. Just like Platonic recollection, it aims to be true to things and events in the world by capturing their essences.

As he lectures 'A' about how one ought to live one's life, the Judge rests in his certainty of the good God who presides over the world and the devoted woman who makes his house into a home. But for someone who finds no meaning in life, who lacks faith in God and whose love was not reciprocated, the Judge's writings on marriage and repentance will not be all that relevant. In grappling with the question of whether life is worth living, 'A' is engaged in a more fundamental ethical inquiry than the Judge. Until we find life meaningful, none of the other questions matter anyway.

Related topics

'Kierkegaard and the desirability of immortality,' Adam Buben; 'Ethical reflection as evasion,' Rob Compaijen and Pieter Vos.

References

Carr, K. (1996) 'The offense of reason and the passion of faith: Kierkegaard and anti-rationalism,' *Faith and philosophy*, 13: 236–51.
Evans, C. S. (2009) *Kierkegaard: An introduction*, Cambridge: Cambridge University Press.
Fauteck, H. (1974) 'Kierkegaards Antigone,' *Skandinavistik*, 4: 81–100.
Garff, J. (1995) *Den søvnløse: Kierkegaard læst æstetisk/biografisk*, Copenhagen: C. A. Reitzel.
Hegel, G. F. W. (1967) *Hegel's Philosophy of Right*, T. M. Knox (trans.), Oxford: Oxford University Press.
Khawaja, N. (2016) *The religion of existence*, Chicago, IL: University of Chicago Press.
McCarthy, V. (2008) 'The case of aesthete 'A' in "Either/Or",' in H. Schulz, J. Stewart and K. Verstrynge (eds), *Kierkegaard Studies Yearbook 2008*, Berlin: Walter de Gruyter.
Nozick, R. (1974) *Anarchy, state and utopia*, New York: Basic Books.
Pattison, G. (2013) *Kierkegaard and the quest for unambiguous life*, Cambridge: Cambridge University Press.
Stewart, J. (2003) *Kierkegaard's relations to Hegel reconsidered*, Cambridge: Cambridge University Press.

Further reading

Carlsson, U. (2013) 'Love among the post-Socratics,' in H. Schulz, J. Stewart and K. Verstrynge (eds), *Kierkegaard Studies Yearbook 2013*, Berlin: Walter de Gruyter.
    This paper interprets the essays on the modern Antigone and the Silhouettes, in light of *The Concept of Irony*, as expressing a disenchantment with the Socratic ethos of freedom, individuality and reflection.
Garff, J. (1995) *Den søvnløse: Kierkegaard læst æstetisk/biografisk*, Copenhagen: C. A. Reitzel.
    Garff takes the aesthetic to represent something fundamental in the private individual Søren Kierkegaard. His reading of *Either/Or* is incisive and free from the burden of preconceptions usually brought to that book.
Harries, K. (2010) *Between nihilism and faith: A commentary on 'Either/or'*, Berlin: Walter de Gruyter.
    Devoting one chapter to each essay in *Either/Or*, this commentary is a great resource for students. Harries situates the book in the history of philosophy and aesthetic theory, while also developing his own view of the relation between the aesthetic, the ethical and the religious.
Pattison, G. (1999) *Kierkegaard: The aesthetic and the religious*, London: PCM.
    This book traces the evolution of Kierkegaard's view of art and aesthetics from his early days as a student. Pattison also shows that Kierkegaard assimilated much of the romantic and Hegelian view of art, so that it is present in his mature philosophy, even if he at times claims to completely reject it.

12
KIERKEGAARD ON NATURE AND NATURAL BEAUTY

Anthony Rudd

Kierkegaard, nature, and the self

In this chapter I will consider Kierkegaard's attitude to the world of nature – that is, the non-human world, the world of rivers and mountains, seas and forests, animals and plants. Kierkegaard was born a generation or so after the great age of Romanticism at the end of the eighteenth and the beginning of the nineteenth centuries, and he was certainly influenced – both positively and negatively – by it. One central theme of Romanticism was the discovery or rediscovery of Nature as a 'moral source' – to use Charles Taylor's (see 1989: chps. 4 and 20) terminology – that is, as a locus of incomparable value in relation to which our lives gain meaning. The experience of the natural world had, for many of the Romantics, a quasi-religious – or indeed, actually religious – significance, as a source of healing, wholeness, and joy. And for many people today, of course, that is still true. We cultivate our gardens, watch birds, or go hiking in the wilderness; and these activities are felt by many of us to *matter*. They are not just enjoyable or health-promoting, but have, beyond that, a deeper spiritual significance. They put us in touch with something that we would be impoverished without.

Kierkegaard is not very often thought of much in this connection. Indeed, he is often supposed to have had rather little to say about non-human nature. His emphasis on subjectivity seems to direct us inwards, rather than outwards, while his critique of the 'aesthetic' life might seem to involve some suspicion of an excessive delight in the sensuous beauty of the natural world. Some have even found his thought 'acosmic,' involving a 'loss of the world' in its focus on human subjectivity (see e.g., Mackey 1986; and, for a useful critique, Piety 1998). Even when – as many recent commentators do – we emphasize what Kierkegaard says about the importance of our relationships with other people, his discussions of love and intersubjectivity, it may still seem that the natural, non-human world is neglected by him. But although natural beauty is not very often made an explicit theme in Kierkegaard's writings, his earliest journal entries (the Gilleleje diary) include eloquent and closely attentive appreciations of natural beauty (see KJN 1, 3–13/SKS 17, 7–18); and passages in his later published works – both pseudonymous and signed – show his continuing sensitivity to nature, and his ability to celebrate its beauty in lyrical prose (e.g., SLW 15–9, 187–9/SKS 6, 22–6, 175–8). Instead of attempting a survey, though, I will focus on one text in particular in which our attitude to nature is a central theme – the 1849 discourses on *The Lily in the Field and the Bird of the Air* (WA, 1–45/SKS 11, 5–48). These three discourses deal, respectively, with the themes of silence, obedience, and joy, and they form a sequence in which each builds on its predecessor(s), so that they culminate with the evocation of the joy that emerges from and with silence and obedience. Such joy is said to involve being 'present to oneself' (WA, 39/SKS 11, 43). In accordance with the text from the Sermon on the Mount on which he is commenting (Matthew 6: 24–34),[1] Kierkegaard insists that we can learn such joy from nature, or the things of nature; 'the lily and the bird are joy because by silence and unconditional obedience they are completely present to themselves in being today' (WA, 39/ SKS 11, 43).

To understand what Kierkegaard is doing in *The Lily*, I think it is helpful to compare it to another book that Kierkegaard published in the same year, *The Sickness unto Death*.[2] *Sickness* is an analysis of the forms of despair, all of which are various ways of failing to be oneself through failing to synthesize the aspects or polarities of one's being – which one can only do through coming to 'rest transparently in the power that established' one (i.e., God) (SUD, 14/SKS 11, 130). *The Lily and the Bird* can be seen as offering a positive counterpart to that analysis by showing us what it means to be present to oneself by 'resting transparently' in God. The joy that is presence to oneself should therefore be seen as the opposite state to the despair that is a failure to be oneself. In *Sickness*, the self becomes whole (becomes fully itself) through relating properly to God. But there is some controversy about where this leaves the relation of the self to other selves – let alone to the non-human world. Some have tried to take up the structure of Kierkegaard's account, while de-theologizing it. They have argued that a committed relation to human, or perhaps non-human, others (or to ideals, causes, etc.) can enable the self to overcome despair in the way Kierkegaard insists that only the God-relation can (see e.g., Habermas 2003; Dreyfus 2008). Others have argued that although the God-relation is the *sine qua non*, there is still an important, though subordinate, role that other relationships can play in constituting or synthesizing the self (see e.g., Davenport 2013; Rudd 2012: ch. 2). But still others have expressed scepticism about this, arguing that for Kierkegaard it is only the God-relationship that really matters for self-constitution (see e.g., Van Stee 2015).

In *The Lily* Kierkegaard asserts that in joy we are present to ourselves through being present to God. But, as we have seen, he also claims that this is something that we can learn from nature. In what follows, I will investigate more closely what connection our relationship to nature, or the things of nature, has to our relating to God, and thus to our relating properly to ourselves. In these discourses there is certainly a powerful sense of nature as a theophany – that is, a revelation of God:

> In nature everything is unconditional obedience. The sighing of the wind, the echoing of the forest, the murmuring of the brook, the humming of the summer, the whispering of the leaves, the rustling of the grass, every sound, every sound you hear is all compliance, unconditional obedience. Thus you can hear God in it, just as you hear him in the harmony that is the movement of the celestial bodies in obedience.
> *(WA, 25/SKS 11, 30)*

But what exactly does this sense of nature as theophany amount to? What is the relation between the joy of presence to oneself and to God, and the joy, emphasized by so many of the Romantics, that we may feel through being present to the natural world – to mountains, rivers, forests – and, indeed, lilies and birds? Does nature play an essential role in mediating God to us? And even if it does, do we take joy *in* the lily and bird, or simply learn from them to take joy in God and in ourselves? (And in asking these questions, we are also, of course, asking how Kierkegaard's conception of nature relates to those of the Romantics.)

'Obedience' in nature and humanity

How is it that we can learn silence, obedience, and therefore joy, from the lilies and the birds? To become 'silent' in Kierkegaard's sense does not involve literally ceasing to speak, but rather, adopting a meditative discipline, in which we learn to set aside our desires, anxieties and preoccupations, and even our own beliefs about what is for the best, so that we can then hear what God asks of us. Considering one who is anxious to pray rightly to God, Kierkegaard says:

> Gradually, as he became more and more fervent in payer, he had less and less to say, and finally he became completely silent. He became silent. Indeed he became what is, if possible, even more opposite to speaking than silence; he became a listener. He thought that to pray is to speak; he learned that to pray is not only to be silent but is to listen. And so it is; to pray is not to listen to oneself speak, but is to become silent, to wait until the one praying hears God.
> *(WA, 11–2/SKS 11, 17–8)*

Similarly, we need to cultivate obedience, which means simply the unconditional willingness to act in accordance with what one 'hears' when one silently listens to God. To develop these virtues is to set aside our egoistical demands to be constantly in control – to speak rather than to listen, to order rather than to obey. In this, we can take the lily and the bird in their simple, unselfconscious harmony with their own natures, and with the wider nature around them, as exemplars and inspirations. But of course, they are 'silent' and 'obedient' in this sense simply because it is their nature so to be. We have the task of *becoming* silent and obedient – it is not something that we are automatically. And, of course, our task is not simply to become as they are, but to become silent and obedient in a properly human way. (I will return to what this might involve shortly.)

Silence and obedience lead to joy, and not just causally, or as a side-effect; rather, to be silently obedient and attentive to God *is* to be freed from one's cares and anxieties and therefore joyful. This we can again see exemplified in the lily and the bird, which are simply present to themselves, without any of the characteristically human anxieties about what the future will bring:

> [T]heir teaching of joy, which their lives in turn express, is quite briefly as follows: There is a today; it *is* – indeed an infinite emphasis falls upon this *is*. There is a today – and there is no worry, none whatever, about tomorrow or about the day after tomorrow. This is not light-mindedness on the part of the lily and the bird but is the joy of silence and obedience ... when, because of silence and obedience, tomorrow does not exist, then in the silence and obedience, today is, it *is* – and then the joy is as it is in the lily and the bird.
> *(WA, 38–9/ SKS 11, 42–3)*

This joy is not to be confused with happiness, which comes and goes as circumstances change. That is the point of joy being unconditional: 'The one whose joy is dependent on certain conditions is not joy itself' (WA, 37/SKS 11, 41). Aware, no doubt, that he might be accused of sentimentalizing or prettifying nature, Kierkegaard readily admits that it is full of pain and suffering. 'Yet the lily and the bird do have sorrow also, just as all nature has sorrow' (WA, 40/ SKS 11, 44); but still, they accomplish 'something that looks almost like a miracle: in deepest sorrow to be unconditionally joyful' (WA, 41/SKS 11, 45).[3] Of course, Kierkegaard is not really concerned with the details of ornithology or botany as such. The lyrical picture of the lilies and birds is there to encourage us to cast all our cares on God. 'Cast all your sorrow upon God, totally, unconditionally, just as the lily and the bird do – then you will become unconditionally joyful like the lily and the bird.... The unconditional joy is simply joy over God' (WA, 42–3/SKS 11, 46). The reality of suffering is not denied; but through it all we can rest in the unconditional joy of knowing that we are loved and sustained by God. This joy is unconditional because the 'condition' that God loves and cares for us is always and necessarily met. Hence the absolute joy, which consists in our being present to ourselves, freed from anxieties about 'tomorrow,' is grounded in joy over God and in our relationship to God.

While these discourses have a lot to say specifically about the lilies and birds, they do of course take them as illustrative of nature as a whole; it is from all of nature that we should learn silence, obedience, and joy. In the discussion of obedience, we are told to 'Pay attention then to nature around you' (WA, 25/SKS 11, 30). Kierkegaard goes on to an extended lyrical evocation of nature (part of which I quoted near the start of this chapter):

> The sighing of the wind, the echoing of the forest, the murmuring of the brook, the humming of the summer, the whispering of the leaves, the rustling of the grass, every sound, every sound you hear is all compliance, unconditional obedience ... the vehemence of the rushing winds, the buoyant flexibility of the clouds, the droplet fluidity of the sea and its cohesion, the speed of light and the even greater of sound – it is all obedience.
>
> *(WA, 25–6/SKS 11, 30)*[4]

The Romantic attention to, and delight in, nature is certainly present in this passage, but what we are to learn from nature is not just about nature in itself; it is about nature's obedience to God. And as the passage continues, Kierkegaard shifts from emphasizing the sensuous immediacy of nature to emphasizing its law-governed order and regularity: 'The rising of the sun on the hour, and its setting on the hour, the shifting of the wind in a flash, the ebb and flow of the tide at specific times, and the agreement among the seasons in their precise alternating – all, all, all of it is obedience' (WA, 26/SKS 11, 30). Indeed, as Kierkegaard continues, nature seems to become absorbed into God: 'In nature everything is nothing, understood in this way: it is nothing but God's unconditional will; the moment it is not unconditionally God's will, it ceases to exist.' (WA, 26/SKS 11, 30). Here nature's dependence on God and 'obedience' to His will is so stressed that its independent being is apparently denied. A little later, the lily and bird are commended for believing '*that everything that happens is unconditionally God's will*' (WA, 26/SKS 11, 31). This apparent assertion of strict theological determinism is striking and – coming from Kierkegaard – surprising. Does he really mean it? 'Everything that happens' would on the face of it include all human action, in which case it would seem that even our sins are willed by God. This is not a very palatable conclusion, although Luther and Calvin, amongst others, were willing to bite this particular bullet; but perhaps Kierkegaard's language allows for the interpretation that God's will for us is that we act freely, so that He doesn't directly will that we sin, but wills not to prevent us from doing so.[5]

This indeed seems to be suggested in a passage where Kierkegaard distinguishes between what happens in nature and what happens in the human sphere. In nature 'it is not only the case – as it is also in the human world – that because God is the Omnipotent nothing happens, not the least little thing, without his will; no, here it is also because everything is unconditional obedience' (WA, 25/SKS 11, 30). Human beings *can* (and do) disobey God, but even that disobedience 'is not capable of doing the least thing without his will, the will of the Omnipotent'

(WA, 25/SKS 11, 30). By contrast, in nature, nothing even tries to disobey; everything is just as God wills it to be. This of course raises the problem of suffering (which, as we noted above, Kierkegaard admits is prevalent in nature) and specifically of animal pain, since on this view it would seem that such suffering must be directly willed by God. Kierkegaard does not really address this issue, though – his concern is not with a theodicy of the animal world, but with what *we* can learn from nature. We should learn absolute obedience; and, just because this doesn't happen naturally for us but has to be an achievement, it is a greater thing for *us* to obey God unconditionally than it is for the lily or the bird.

Kierkegaard is well aware that this demand for obedience is liable to stick in the throats of post-Enlightenment readers attuned to the value of autonomy (and he no doubt enjoys emphasizing it for precisely this reason). But isn't it legitimate to worry that his stress on silence and obedience involves setting aside our rationality and autonomy, and with them our humanity? Kierkegaard himself notes, 'Surely it is speech that distinguishes humanity above the animal and then ... far above the lily' (WA, 10/SKS 11, 16). And, despite the deterministic-sounding remarks I quoted above, he does also assert that '[A] *human being* is placed between these two enormous powers [good and evil] and the choice is left up to him' (WA, 34/SKS 11, 38) – the free will that enables us, if we choose, to be disobedient to God is also a great gift from God. Our task cannot be literally to discard our distinctively human characteristics, to become absorbed into nature by reducing ourselves to a merely animal or even vegetative level. 'But,' Kierkegaard continues, 'because the human being is able to speak, the ability to be silent is an art; and a great art precisely because this advantage of his so easily tempts him' (WA, 10/SKS 11, 16). For Kierkegaard the capacity for speech (reason) and free will really are 'advantages' we have, but they mean that we can go astray – fall into sin and despair – in a way no other creature can. Silence and obedience are therefore ways in which we can discipline speech and freedom; they are not ways to extirpate them. And although they may seem like passive states, silence and obedience are really what Gregory Beabout (2007: 145–6) has helpfully called virtues of 'active receptivity.' They require us to be attuned to, actively listening for, the voice of God. As such they involve what Simone Weil (1973: 105–16, 149) and, following her, Iris Murdoch (1970: 17–9, 22–3, 31–5), have called 'attention.' This certainly involves setting the demands of the ego aside and opening oneself so as to take note of what comes to one from beyond. But to do that is itself a difficult task, one which requires hard and patient work.

We can take Kierkegaard as saying that we should learn from nature, rather than reducing ourselves to it. However, he does seem to take a more radical position when he chides an imagined interlocutor for saying that the lilies and birds are automatically 'obedient' because they can't be otherwise; their 'obedience' is simply making a virtue of necessity. Kierkegaard replies: 'You, too, are indeed subject to necessity. God's will is still done anyhow; so strive to make a virtue of necessity by unconditionally obediently doing God's will' (WA, 30/SKS 11, 34). Here it seems that we cannot do what goes against God's will; we can only choose to be either reluctant or obedient in doing what God wills us to do. Our only freedom lies in the attitude we adopt to what must be. This view seems (disturbingly) reminiscent of the Stoics or of Spinoza (though for them, of course, what attitude we adopt to the determined course of events is itself as determined as anything else). This would seem to significantly diminish the difference between us and merely natural beings. Perhaps what Kierkegaard says can be made consistent with a less deterministic notion – that what is willed by God will be done *eventually*, despite our temporary defiance of it, so that we might as well learn to submit to it now. But Kierkegaard is getting into very deep water here and there are real difficulties in reconciling what he says in this passage with the belief in human freedom that he clearly does want to maintain. Perhaps we can charitably point out that Kierkegaard is not the only thinker to have got into trouble trying to navigate these deep and turbulent waters, and also note that *The Lily* is not a theoretical treatise but an upbuilding discourse with a practical intent. And, again, that intent cannot be that we lose our distinctively human capacities, nor that we adopt a complacent *que sera, sera* attitude of acceptance of whatever happens to be the case. (For example, Kierkegaard himself showed no sign of thinking, 'Well, if the Danish Church is the way it is, then that must be how God wants it to be and I must be obedient to that.') The intent, as noted above, is that we lead our lives with a joyful serenity in and through all our struggles and sufferings.

Nature as revelation: Kierkegaard and romanticism

Kierkegaard does not solve the problem of freedom and determinism in these discourses, and his rhetoric at some points does seem to me to leave too little autonomy or independence to even the world of non-human nature – he is in danger of presenting it simply as a sort of divine puppet-show. Whatever reservations I have about the way in which he does this, the very fact of his presenting the natural world as a theophany – a revelation or showing of God – is of great interest. And this does mark a real point of connection between his thought and that of the Romantics. To quote again a passage I have quoted before: 'every sound, every sound you hear is all compliance, unconditional obedience. Thus you can hear God in it just as you hear him in the harmony that is the movement of the celestial bodies in obedience' (WA, 25/SKS 11, 30). To listen to nature is to hear God speak. This is certainly a familiar thought to the Romantics, as we can see by comparing Kierkegaard to a major Romantic poet and thinker who he certainly hadn't read: Samuel Taylor Coleridge. In an early poem, 'Frost at Midnight,' Coleridge (1996: 44) – imagining his then infant son growing up roaming freely amongst the beauties of nature – assures him:

> so shalt thou see and hear
> The lovely shapes and sounds intelligible
> Of that eternal language which thy God
> Utters, who from eternity doth teach
> Himself in all and all things in himself.

In another poem ('This Lime-Tree Bower My Prison') from the same period, he imagines a friend on a country walk:

> So my friend
> Struck with deep joy may stand, as I have stood,
> Silent with swimming sense; yea, gazing round
> On the wide landscape, gaze till all doth seem
> Less gross than bodily; and of such hues
> As veil the Almighty Spirit, when yet he makes
> Spirits perceive his presence.
> *(Coleridge 1996: 48)*

It is interesting to note that in commenting on these lines in a letter to a friend Coleridge remarked, 'remember I am a Berkelean.'[6] Berkeley's idealism denies the physical world an existence independent of our God-given experience of it, which means that for Berkeley sense experience is indeed the language God uses to communicate directly with us. Of course, Berkeley's theophanic vision is certainly exposed to the same criticism I raised of Kierkegaard's above – it leaves nature itself too thin and insubstantial. Coleridge's Berkelean phase didn't last; shortly after writing these poems he visited Germany and became deeply influenced by Kant and then Schelling. But the poetry doesn't depend on the philosophy; that is, the evoked experience of the natural world as God's self-revelation does not depend on being given one rather than another philosophical articulation. One should note, of course, that the experience of God in or through nature is characterized by Coleridge, as it is by Kierkegaard, as one of joy. But we can now raise the question of whether this experience of joy which they both find in their experience of nature is really joy in nature, or a joy in God which we reach through nature. That is: is nature merely a messenger, a means through which God communicates to us or through which we rise to God? (Or maybe even a ladder we can discard having climbed it?) Or does it have some deeper, more essential role to play? Can the experience of nature itself be a source of healing joy, not merely a reminder of where else to look for it? Kierkegaard does, in *The Lily*, make it very clear that we are not merely to look to (a fancifully anthropomorphized) nature in order to draw moral lessons about the importance of silence and obedience; rather, the beauty of nature itself is something we should delight in and be glad over:

> Surely no one would seriously think that what the lily and the bird rejoice over and comparable things are nothing to rejoice over! Therefore, that you came into existence, that you exist ... that you became a human being; that you can see, bear in mind that you can see, that you can hear, that you can smell, that you can taste, that you can feel; that the sun shines for you and for your sake, that when it becomes weary the moon begins to shine and the stars are lit; that winter comes, that all nature disguises itself, plays the game of stranger, and in order to delight you; that spring comes, that the birds return in great flocks, and in order to give you joy.
>
> (WA, 39–40/SKS 11, 43)

Here the beauty of nature, and the senses that we have to appreciate it with, are seen as gifts of God, and the refusal to delight in them is seen as ingratitude to God. Kierkegaard – here at least – is very far from the asceticism that would see nature as a competitor with God for our affections.[7] To appreciate nature is to relate to God, for it is to react properly to the gift that God has given us. This may be true even if we are not consciously aware of nature as a gift of God. Kierkegaard would think it sad that people don't realize nature is God's gift; but if they still find joy in nature, their attitude is surely better than that of those who disdain it – perhaps especially if the latter do so out of a misplaced devotion to God. (According to Simone Weil [1973: 158–81], the love of the beauty of the world is a form of 'the implicit love of God.') To think that we have to choose between nature and God is, moreover, to think of God as *a* (limited) being – a view which Kierkegaard firmly rejects: 'If God were to speak or were able to speak of himself ... as if he were not the one and only, unconditionally all, but merely also a something of sorts ... then God would have lost himself, lost the idea of himself, and would not be God' (WA, 23/SKS 11, 28). Here again, one might wonder if Kierkegaard is toying with the Spinozistic pantheism which appealed to so many of the Romantics (Coleridge included). I think it is clear that for Kierkegaard the idea of God as 'absolutely everything' is not intended to deny God's transcendence, or to identify God with the creation. But nor is God to be thought of as simply another being alongside the created beings of nature. Nature exists essentially as an expression or revelation of God; if it is properly understood, therefore, it cannot be thought of as alien from – and therefore as potentially *alienating* from – God. Although I have been using the language of 'gift,' it is important to remember that for Kierkegaard, nature is not simply a distinct thing from God, which He gives to us; it is God's way of communicating with us. Nature's relation to God is not a purely external one (as if it were something that He has made, but now exists quite independently of Him, as the product of a human artisan exists independently of its original maker). Rather the relation is an *internal* one, in that nature cannot be properly understood apart from God, cannot be understood except as an expression of God's nature – as a person's gestures or speech are expressive of them.

Kierkegaard also makes it clear that our delight in nature is bound up with delight in our own existence. That we exist at all, that we are human, that we have the senses we do – these are all occasions for rejoicing. Part of what Kierkegaard means by being 'present to' ourselves must surely be this conscious recognition of – and delight in – the most basic aspects of our human nature, which we tend to take for granted in our preoccupation with our more particular struggles, sorrows, and triumphs. But the simple fact of being human, of being embodied and sensuously endowed beings within a world of sensible beauty that we can appreciate and respond to: this is always an occasion for joy, irrespective of whatever else may be going on in our lives.

One might still ask, 'Why bring God in?' Can we not rejoice in nature and in ourselves as parts of nature which can consciously appreciate the nature in which we are, without making reference to God? Certainly, many people find joy and even a sort of healing – a being-made-whole – through their experience of the natural world, or of specific aspects of it (birds and flowers being prominent among them). For some, this is an alternative to religion (or, perhaps we should say an alternative religion). Kierkegaard would certainly resist the idea that we can heal the despair which is the mis-relation of the elements of the self simply through a relation of the self to a nature that was not itself expressive of God. But, of course, for him there is no such nature. Atheism does not simply remove God while leaving our understanding of nature unaffected; if there were no God, then nature itself would be quite different from what theists suppose it to be – and there would be room for serious doubt about whether it could then function as a 'moral source' in Taylor's sense – a locus of deep value and meaning. For it is hard to see how the natural world, construed as it is in 'disenchanted' terms by post-Darwinian philosophical naturalism, could be such a source. As Johannes de silentio observed in *Fear and Trembling*: 'If a human being did not have an eternal consciousness, if underlying everything there were only a wild fermenting power that, writhing in dark passions produced everything, be it significant or insignificant, if a vast, never appeased emptiness hid beneath everything, what would life be then but despair?' (FT, 15/SKS 4, 112). For Kierkegaard, it is only through experiencing nature as a theophany that we can appreciate it for what it really is. So it is misleading to pose the question: 'Can the conflicts in the self be healed only through the self's relating to God, or could a relation to nature (or other people) do the trick?' The beauty of nature and the value of persons – which make them worth relating to – derive from their relation to God and their *participation* in God's goodness, as a Christian Platonist would say.[8]

However, it would also seem that, for Kierkegaard, it is, in part, through our experience of the natural world that we come to recognize God. This isn't through *arguments* (such as the traditional Cosmological or Design Arguments)[9] but through a capacity to see nature as theophanic, as expressive of God.[10] And the point is not simply a developmental one. It isn't just that we *come* to know God through nature, but can thereafter enjoy knowledge of Him without further reference to nature. For the knowledge of God in question is not simply propositional knowledge that we might have acquired in a variety of ways; it is an affective knowledge, which exists through being continually renewed. And as embodied and sensuous beings – or as long as we are embodied and sensuous beings – who do not know God directly, it is at least in part through continuing to experience the world around us as expressive of God that we continue to know and appreciate Him. If we don't experience nature as expressive of God, we don't really – existentially – know God as the Creator, even if we are prepared to assent to the *proposition* that God created the heavens and the earth. Of course, for Kierkegaard there are other ways in which God becomes manifest to us: through Scripture, through the moral life and through our struggles with guilt, sin, and forgiveness. But for Kierkegaard these are not simply different and unrelated ways. Rather, we experience and learn from nature as moral beings who are struggling to develop the virtues of silence and obedience; and *The Lily* discourses are themselves presented as meditations on a passage from the Bible. The Romantic sense of God-in-Nature – perhaps vague, perhaps implicit, perhaps tending towards pantheism – is taken up and rendered more theologically specific by Christianity; but it isn't lost or left behind.

Of course, all manner of objections to Kierkegaard's view of nature could be raised. In particular, it might be said that he is in fact projecting into nature the moral and religious meanings he wants us to find there. A critic could point to his relentless anthropomorphizing of the birds and even the lilies, or indeed to his insistence, in the long lyrical passage I quoted from him above, that the changes of the seasons and all the beauties of nature exist simply 'in order to delight' us. Shouldn't we be learning to look at nature in a more disenchanted, less anthropocentric, more objective light? We should of course distinguish between the surface literary effects that Kierkegaard deploys and his deeper meanings. Engaging as he is, critically but not unsympathetically, with Romanticism, it is natural that he should use Romantic devices such as anthropomorphism, ascribing poignantly human feelings to birds and even plants. Of course he is well aware of what he is doing. But the more serious point is that, for Kierkegaard, realism and objectivism do not go together. That is, in his view, the way to experience nature *realistically*, for what it really is, is not to be dispassionate and detached. The neutral objective gaze of the ideal scientist does, certainly, reveal real and important phenomena. But there are deeper metaphysical truths about nature that can only appear to one who approaches nature in the right spirit – one of emotional attunement, of openness to levels of significance and meaning that are to be found in the natural world.[11] This is one of the enduringly relevant lessons of Romanticism – one that has been echoed closer to our times by, amongst others, Heidegger,[12] counter-cultural neo-Romantics such as Theodore Roszak (1973), 'traditionalists' such as the Iranian philosopher Seyyed Hossein Nasr (1997), and some advocates of 'Deep' Ecology. It seems that they would have Kierkegaard, as well as Coleridge, on their side. And it certainly seems that between them they have made a powerful case that the still dominant objectivist/technological attitude to nature in our culture is not only practically unsustainable but is also one that promotes a singularly joyless form of life.

Related topics

'Beyond Worry? On learning humility from the lilies and the birds,' John Lippitt; 'Kierkegaard on the value of art: an indirect method of communication,' Antony Aumann; 'The ethical life of aesthetes,' Ulrika Carlsson; 'Kierkegaard's transfigurations of the sublime,' Samuel Cuff Snow; 'Kierkegaard's defense of nature and theology against natural theology,' Will Williams.

Notes

1 Kierkegaard had commented on the lily and bird of this passage before – see UDVS, 155–212/SKS 8, 251–307; see also CD, 3–91/SKS 10, 11–98.
2 Kierkegaard published it in 1849, though he had written it in the previous year and then set it aside for a time.

3 This theme of finding joy not only despite, but *in*, suffering is developed at length in 'The Gospel of Suffering' (UDVS, 213–341/SKS 8, 313–421; see also CD, 93–159/SKS 10, 101–66).
4 Presumably the mistake about the relative speeds of light and sound was just a slip of the pen!
5 This is the Thomistic position, according to Elenore Stump (2003: chps. 9 and 13; also see 2010: Part Two).
6 See the 'Editor's Notes' in Coleridge (1996: 307).
7 See, for example, Augustine (2009: 183–4 [X,VI, 8–10]) and Petrarch (1948: 36–46). These texts are, of course, full of ambivalence and make vividly clear just how conflicted both Augustine and Petrarch are in their feelings about nature.
8 That Kierkegaard *was* a Christian Platonist is something I have argued for elsewhere (see Rudd 2012: ch. 2; 2015).
9 Although these may be of value in spelling out some of what is involved in our experience of nature as revealing God.
10 One might think of polytheism as an immature – or as a degenerate – form of this 'natural religion.' To see everything as 'full of gods' is at least closer to the truth as Kierkegaard sees it than the modern 'disenchanted' view of nature – even when that is conjoined with a Deistic hypothesis of its having a divine creator.
11 And, of course, a scientist, qua existing human being, may take this attitude as much as anyone else – and may be inspired to pursue scientific research precisely because of this appreciation of nature. There is nothing in science that contradicts or needs to conflict with this Romantic attunement to the natural world.
12 The contrast between the technological 'enframing' of nature as calculable resource and an open contemplative attitude to it is central to the later Heidegger. See especially Heidegger (1977).

References

Augustine (2009) *Confessions*, H. Chadwick (trans), Oxford: Oxford University Press.
Beabout, G. (2007) 'The silent lily and bird as exemplars of the virtue of active receptivity,' in R. L. Perkins (ed), *International Kierkegaard Commentary*, vol. 18 (*Without Authority*), Macon, GA: Mercer University Press.
Coleridge, S.T. (1996) *Selected poems*, R. Holmes (ed), New York: Penguin Books.
Davenport, J. (2013) 'Selfhood and "spirit,"' in J. Lippitt and G. Pattison (eds), *The Oxford Handbook of Kierkegaard*, Oxford: Oxford University Press.
Dreyfus, H. (2008) 'Kierkegaard on the self,' in E. Mooney (ed), *Ethics, Love, and Faith in Kierkegaard*, Bloomington, IN: Indiana University Press.
Habermas, J. (2003) 'Are there postmetaphysical answers to the question: What is the good life?' W. Rehg (trans), in J. Habermas, *The Future of Human Nature*, Cambridge: Polity Press/Blackwell.
Heidegger, M. (1977) *The question concerning technology and other essays*, W. Lovitt (trans), New York: Harper Torchbooks.
Hossein Nasr, S. (1997) *Man and nature*, Chicago: ABC International Group/KAZI Publications.
Mackey, L. (1986) 'The loss of the world in Kierkegaard's ethics,' in L. Mackey, *Points of View: Readings of Kierkegaard*, Tallahassee, FL: Florida State University Press.
Murdoch, I. (1970) *The sovereignty of good*, London: Routledge.
Petrarch (1948) 'The ascent of Mount Ventoux,' in E. Cassirer, P. Kristeller, and J. Randell (eds), *The Renaissance Philosophy of Man*, Chicago: University of Chicago Press.
Piety, M. G. (1998) 'The place of the world in Kierkegaard's ethics,' in G. Pattison and S. Shakespeare (eds), *Kierkegaard: The Self in Society*, London: Palgrave Macmillan.
Roszak, T. (1973) *Where the wasteland ends*, New York: Anchor Books.
Rudd, A. (2015) 'Kierkegaard's Platonic teleology,' in J. Lippitt and P. Stokes (eds), *Narrative, Identity and the Kierkegaardian Self*, Edinburgh: Edinburgh University Press.
Rudd, A. (2012) *Self, value, and narrative*, Oxford: Oxford University Press.
Stump, E. (2010) *Wandering in darkness*, Oxford: Oxford University Press.
Stump, E. (2003) *Aquinas*, London: Routledge.
Taylor, C. (1989) *Sources of the self*, Cambridge: Cambridge University Press.
Van Stee, A. (2015) 'Selves, existentially speaking,' in A. Rudd and J. Davenport (eds), *Love, Reason, and Will: Kierkegaard after Frankfurt*, New York; London: Bloomsbury Academic.
Weil, S. (1973) *Waiting on God*, E. Craufurd (trans), New York: Harper and Row.

Further reading

Egenberger, S. (2017) 'Schubert: Kierkegaard's reading of Gotthilf Heinrich Schubert's Philosophy of Nature,' in J. Stewart (ed), *Kierkegaard Research: Sources, Reception and Resources*, vol. 6 (*Kierkegaard and His German Contemporaries*), tome 1, Farnham: Ashgate.

Of broader interest than its title might indicate, this chapter is helpful on Kierkegaard's relation to Romantic philosophy of nature in general.

Kirmmse, B. (2016) 'Introduction: Letting nature point beyond nature,' in S. Kierkegaard, B. Kirmmse (trans), *The Lily of the Field and the Bird of the Air*, Princeton, NJ: Princeton University Press.

This is an excellent introduction to a new English translation of the *Lily* discourses.

McDonald, W. (2013) 'Kierkegaard and Romanticism,' in J. Lippitt and G. Pattison (eds), *The Oxford Handbook of Kierkegaard*, Oxford: Oxford University Press.

This chapter is a useful overview of Kierkegaard's relations to Romanticism, focussing on his Danish and German sources.

Pattison, G. (2007) 'The joy of birdsong, or lyrical dialectics,' in R. L. Perkins (ed), *International Kierkegaard Commentary*, vol. 18 (*Without Authority*), Macon, GA: Mercer University Press.

This chapter is an interesting comparison of Kierkegaard with both Hegel and Romanticism.

13
KIERKEGAARD'S TRANSFIGURATIONS OF THE SUBLIME

Samuel Cuff Snow

Introduction

Despite the long and multifaceted history of the interpretation of the sublime from antiquity to modernity, its defining element has remained indisputable: as the seventeenth-century French poet and critic Nicolas Despréaux Boileau declared, it utterly transforms everything it touches. Boileau made this assessment on the basis of his reading and translation of the treatise *Peri hupsous*, or *On the Sublime*, by the presumed author Longinus, the longest-surviving text we have (explicitly) on the sublime, which treats it as a mode of rhetorical speech and a quality of literary works that involves a certain kind of transportation of the listener (or reader) out of herself.[1] Longinus writes that sublime passages 'exercise an irresistible force and mastery' and strike like a 'bolt of lightning' (Longinus 1995: 163); they are timeless and exalt the reader even after 'repeated consideration' (179). Since Boileau's translation of Longinus, the sublime has moved beyond the boundaries of literature and rhetoric and become, alongside beauty, a central category in modern philosophical aesthetics. And yet Longinus' central reflections set the terms for the way the sublime has been broadly understood. Its transformative force is inseparable from the struggle, the pain, the negative element involved in the way it overwhelms or exceeds our ordinary powers of apprehension and action, while still uplifting us in some way. As I will attempt to demonstrate, Kierkegaard can be placed within this tradition of thought on the sublime.

The following is, therefore, an argument for the presence of an absent concept in Kierkegaard's work. What I will identify as the sublime is precisely not *det Sublime* or *Ophøiethed*, the two Danish terms for 'the sublime.' Neither term is employed by Kierkegaard in a way that is consistently germane to modern philosophical aesthetic discourse on the sublime (Pattison 1998: 246–7).[2] (This may explain the scant treatment the sublime has received in Kierkegaard reception.[3]) I will instead take the *Kantian* sublime as a starting point for identifying and analysing certain aesthetic figures in Part One of *Either/Or* as sublime: the *tragic* sublime, embodied by the 'new Antigone,' and sublime *grief*, embodied by 'the silhouettes.' They are *transfigurations* of the Kantian sublime in two senses. First, they share *and* modify certain central features of the Kantian sublime. Second, they represent *transfigurative* experiences.

The Kantian sublime

The sublime in Kant is highly complex. In order to outline its relevance for the following analysis, I will restrict myself to a brief contextualization of the place of the sublime in Kant's aesthetic theory, before elucidating its basic structure and highlighting the features that are relevant to these Kierkegaardian aesthetic figures.

Kant outlines his mature aesthetic theory in the third of his three *Critiques*, the *Critique of the Power of Judgement*. In the *Critique of Pure Reason* Kant developed an epistemological account of the capacity of human beings to observe and know objects of nature in accordance with *heteronomous* laws of nature. In his *Critique of Practical Reason* he justified his view of human beings as moral agents capable of *autonomous* self-determination. In other words, Kant (2000: 80) expounds a view of nature on the one hand, and freedom on the other, as realms which display different modes of causality and can by definition have 'no mutual influence' on one another. Kant (2000: 81) refers to this as the 'great chasm' between nature and freedom, which gives rise to a certain *nihilism*, that is, the apparent impossibility of conceiving how human beings can actualize their freedom in the material world in a meaningful and effective manner. In the third *Critique* he endeavours to bridge this gap. His proposed solution rests on demonstrating that there are certain singular and contingent *forms* of nature for which no universal concept is available, and which appear *immediately* to resemble or harmonize with our own powers of apprehending and acting in the world.[4] They prompt us to *reflect* simultaneously on our relation to these forms and our mode of engaging with them, which expresses itself *aesthetically* in the feeling of pleasure. Such forms qualify as beautiful. Beauty becomes a medium for reflection on the specific place of human beings in the world. As Kant famously remarked, 'beautiful things indicate that the human being fits into the world.'[5] Viewed from this (aesthetic) perspective, the conflict between the autonomy of our freedom and the heteronomy of nature falls away.

The aesthetic category of the sublime in Kant must be understood within this overall critical project. And yet it occupies a unique place in that project. Rather than engendering an immediate awareness of the agreement between us and nature, as in beauty, Kant calls sublime those appearances of nature that are form*less* and *conflict* with our epistemic and moral capacities; in this respect, such appearances are initially 'contrapurposive' (*zweckwidrig*). The 'Analytic of the Sublime,' in his third *Critique*, is Kant's attempt to reconcile nature in its formless and therefore contrapurposive appearances with vital moral meaning.

The reflective aesthetic judgement of the sublime is based on an aesthetic experience in which the subject feels a double conflict. In the first arm of the conflict, it presents either an epistemic threat, in which the sheer magnitude of a natural vista, such as a deep ravine or towering mountain range, overwhelms the subject's sensible capacity to apprehend it (in the 'mathematically sublime'). Or it is an existential threat, in which the destructive (and absolute) might of nature undermines her sense of physical safety (in the 'dynamically sublime'); the classic example here is a shipwreck in a stormy sea.[6] These overwhelming threats exert an existential hold – they 'grip' the subject, as Kant (2000: 152) writes. On the other hand, this engenders the second conflict: The threatening encounter with nature prompts reason to 'step in' and contribute either the idea of infinity (in the first case) or the idea of our freedom (in the second case). These ideas serve as resources for the subject to find orientation and sense despite being initially overwhelmed. In doing so, reason enjoins the imagination (our sensible faculty) with the task of finding a sensible presentation (or image) for its idea of infinity or freedom. Given ideas of reason, for Kant, transcend sensuous experience, they cannot be sensibly presented. And yet the sublime appearance leaves the imagination with no choice but to ceaselessly and 'earnestly'[7] (Kant 2000: 129) attempt to achieve this unfulfillable task, namely, to *present the unpresentable* (cf. Lyotard 1991: 119–28). There is a fundamental incongruence or contradiction between form (presentation) and content (idea). Kant (2000: 156) calls this a 'presentation of the infinite' or a 'merely negative presentation.'

On the basis of the double conflict in which the subject is embroiled, the sublime designates an *affective* state of *self-reflection*. The subject reflects *both* on the relationship between herself and the appearance of nature (expressed in the first arm of the conflict) *and* on her own state of mind in that relationship (expressed in the second arm of the conflict). In fact, strictly speaking the sublime is a predicate of the state of mind into which we are propelled by such appearances (cf. Kant 2000: 129). This involves a twin discovery, in *feeling*, of the subject's finite limits – the inadequacy of the imagination – *and* her capacity to strive to overcome those limits – to provide an image of the unrepresentable. That is what calls for Kant's (2000: 129, 142) identification of the feeling accompanying sublimity as 'negative pleasure' – it is a mixture of 'displeasure' and 'pleasure' and thus 'repulsive' and 'attractive' in equal measure. The aesthetic experience of the sublime is necessarily doubly signified and meaningful only in this way: It is negative insofar as we are assailed from the outside by nature at its grandest and most threatening, and positive insofar as we discover the resources to garner existential meaning and orientation from the encounter. The significance of the aesthetic experience of the sublime in Kant, then, goes one step further than beauty. We could rephrase Kant's famous remark about beauty, quoted above, and say that *sublime* things indicate that the human being is able to fit into the world *even at its most hostile*.

The sublime in Kant expresses that we possess the ideas or principles that can guide us through the most diverse range of encounters and phenomena that can be thrown at us, including the most formless and contrapurposive. We are simultaneously made aware of the need for images (sensible presentations) to supplement the kind of (cognitive and moral) orientation that is able to function in these hostile encounters with the material world. These images are, at the same time, broken images. In Kant, they do not even become images. It is the activity of *image-making* that is brought to mind. We attempt to provide an image and fail. But the attempt continues nonetheless – and continues to fall short. And yet by falling short (repeatedly), we are brought to an even more acute awareness of these ideas (of reason) and their very unrepresentability. We are brought to the limits of our imagination, which allows these ideas to have such an affectively intense influence and palpability. The breakdown of the image indicates the idea which reason is able to provide and according to which we can and ought to act, and thus generates existential meaning and orientation.

The structure of the Kantian sublime provides a lens through which to view the structure and operation of the aesthetic in some of its forms in Kierkegaard's work. The number and variations of the sublime in Kierkegaard are almost as vast as the range of meanings of the aesthetic. An analysis of all of these falls outside the purview of this chapter.[8] What follows here, then, will be a close reading of a selection of the aesthetic figures of Antigone and the silhouettes in order to excavate two distinct shapes of aesthetic experience that can be characterized as sublime.

Applying sublimity to aesthetic (and specifically human) *figures* seems to violate Kant's explicit restriction of the sublime to appearances of nature, or the state of mind occasioned by such appearances. My interpretation, then, departs from the letter of Kant, or reads him against himself. I contend that the sublime designates a state of self-reflection in which we garner sense from an encounter with that which assails our ordinary conception of ourselves as knowers and moral agents in relation to nature as a realm we cognize or act within. This can, however, *also* be an encounter with a human event, such as revolution or war, in which our *animality*, our propensity to violence, is made present to us. In this case, our ordinary (civilized) conception of and relation to ourselves is put into question. Kant can be read as engaging with such an application and extension of the sublime to the non-natural, *political-historical* field in his references to the sublimity of war in the third *Critique* and the 'enthusiasm' of the spectators of the French Revolution in the *Conflict of the Faculties* (Kant 1996a: 301–3), which he describes as 'aesthetically sublime' (Kant 2000: 154; cf. Clewis 2009). The focus on the spectator rather than the actor of the Revolution enables him to extract *meaning* from an event[9] – which he otherwise criticizes as an abrogation of the civil laws of public right (Kant 1996a: 302; 1996c: 300) – that serves reflection on the political-historical question of cultural progress.[10] A reading that connects Antigone and the silhouettes with the sublime, as I do here, takes this one step further. It takes seriously one of the main innovations of Kierkegaard's aesthetics, that is, that he both expounds an aesthetic theory and transposes its central categories into the guiding elements of a way of living. I interrogate the sublime as a form of aesthetic experience that is embodied and lived out and that, in its breakdown, generates ethical-religious meaning.

Kierkegaardian transfigurations of the sublime

The point of departure for *Either/Or*, and indeed for Kierkegaard's work as a whole, is the spectre of nihilism – here, the view that the world is disenchanted and cannot be a source of meaning and orientation (cf. Harries 2010; Rasmussen 2017). The aesthetic in Kierkegaard is, similar to Kant, motivated by the hope to dispel this spectre. In contrast with Kant, however, such nihilism is not resolved but precisely embodied by the aesthetic life-view. The pseudonymous author of Part One of *Either/Or*, the aesthetician 'A,' declares in the opening collection of aphorisms entitled the 'Diapsalmata': 'How empty and meaningless life is' (EO 1, 29/SKS 2, 38).[11] Constantin Constantius, the pseudonymous author of *Repetition*, also attests to the spectre of nihilism when he remarks that without the category of repetition, 'all life dissolves into an empty meaningless noise' (R, 149/SKS 4, 26). One of Kierkegaard's explicit verdicts is that 'A' is not only unable to overcome such meaninglessness, he produces *and* reproduces it. This finds its most damning expression in Part Two of *Either/Or*, where its pseudonymous author, the ethicist Judge William, characterizes the aesthetic mode of existence as a life lived in sheer (or 'total') 'immediacy,' as the pure (unreflective) and unrelenting pursuit of pleasure that shirks personal responsibility and inevitably ends in indifference, boredom and discontinuity. Indeed, this complete self-immersion in sensuous desire goes hand in hand with an absolute commitment to the ideality of the imagination or poetic fantasy. Imaginative fantasy offers an escape from the aesthete's enslavement to his desires. The aesthete discards the external, contingent conditions on which his satisfaction rests, in order to escape them or arbitrarily populate his imaginative world with objects of his possible desire – the 'prey' he snatches and encloses in his 'castle' of 'sorrow' (cf. EO 1, 42/SKS 2, 51). But, according to the Judge, this is merely a pseudo-escape which furthers the aesthete's dependence on his desires and ultimately deepens his melancholy: 'it obviously follows that he who enjoys himself by discarding the conditions is just as dependent on them as one who enjoys them' (EO 2, 191/SKS 3, 185). Only the ethical act of choosing oneself and acquiring the 'eternal validity' of 'personality' can overcome melancholy and secure 'meaning in this life' (EO 2, 190/SKS 3, 184).

Rather than accept the ethicist's judgement of the aesthete, I am going to shed some different light on the aesthetic. I suggest that the failure of the aesthetic to provide meaningful orientation for self-development gestures towards the kind of existential inwardness required for ethical-religious selfhood.[12] This failure can be explained in terms of the incongruence between idea and sensible presentation that is characteristic of the Kantian sublime; in this case, between the ideal *hope* for meaningful selfhood, based on love, and its aesthetic realization. When Kierkegaard intends to highlight the hopelessness of the aesthetic life-view, in melancholy, he unwittingly underscores that the melancholic figure is able to discern precisely what material life denies but which must nonetheless be hoped for within it. The aesthetic figures of Antigone and the silhouettes strive (hope) to live according to their love, which condemns them to devastating forms of despair. Their experiences serve as sublime images of tragic love and grief that gestures beyond their despair to modes of existence governed meaningfully, even ethical-religiously, by love.[13]

The tragic sublime: Antigone

In his essay 'The tragic in ancient drama reflected in the tragic in modern drama,' the third section of Part One of *Either/Or*, 'A' examines the difference between ancient and modern tragedy and their respective conceptions of 'tragic guilt.' In ancient tragedy, guilt lies with both the individual *and* 'substantial determinants' external to the individual, such as fate, the family, and the state (EO 1, 143/SKS 2, 143), and yet external determination is the primary element and the feeling or 'mood' corresponding to this is 'sorrow.' In modern tragedy, by contrast, the rise of reflection and subjectivity has dissolved the objective, substantial determinants of the individual, rendering modern subjects fully autonomous and thus responsible for their actions. The guilt here lies solely with the individual and the prevailing mood is 'pain.' For 'A,' however, this is misguided as it removes the 'aesthetic ambiguity' central to tragic guilt (EO 1, 148/SKS 2, 147).[14] Conceived as the 'sole author' of her deeds, the individual is unable to *distance* herself from her actions and connect herself in her reflection with the social fabric in which her agency is ultimately grounded (cf. EO 1, 145/SKS 2, 144). Moreover, one is unable to feel compassion ('the authentic expression for the tragic') for a protagonist understood to be entirely responsible for her own actions; 'the spectator shouts: Help yourself, and heaven will help you – in other words, the spectator has lost compassion' (EO 1, 149/SKS 2, 148).

'A' therefore re-narrates Sophocles' drama of *Antigone* such that ancient and modern tragic elements are integrated and yield a new protagonist, 'our Antigone,' in order to identify and present the requisite level of ambiguity and indefiniteness in her guilt for reflection on the twin determination and demand of modern subjects. In 'A's retelling, Antigone's dilemma is determined objectively and subjectively, by substantial determinants *and* subjective conditions. Her duty to Creon (and thus the state) is (still) present, as well as her (subjective) love for Haemon.[15] She partakes of (her father) Oedipus' guilt and yet, subjectively, she is forced to bear the weight of this guilt as a secret only she knows. It is a secret that, should she reveal it, would destroy the 'honor and glory of the lineage of Oedipus' (EO 1, 157/SKS 2, 156). Antigone's tragic condition consists in a two-fold love (of Oedipus and Haemon) that is irreconcilable and unrealizable.

Antigone embodies a specific type of aesthetic experience that qualifies for the category of what we can call the *tragic sublime*, in which the double conflict between the subject and nature expressed in the Kantian sublime is *transfigured* and radicalized in the ambiguous, tragic guilt of Antigone.[16] On the one hand, Antigone is caught between her guiltlessness (she is a victim of her father's guilt) and her guilt (she decides to keep his secret). On the other hand, she is torn between her love for her father and her love for Haemon. In both cases, the conflict ends (or persists) tragically, as she is unable to resolve the fundamental contradiction at their heart: She cannot realize her love for Haemon without destroying her love for Oedipus, and vice versa. The gripping and self-reflective nature of the Kantian sublime manifests here in the way Antigone is 'hurled' by the secret into a *self-reflective* relation to both the secret and her two-fold love, which manifests in 'anxiety' (EO 1, 154/SKS 2, 153). It recalls Vigilius Haufniensis's characterization of the 'demonic' in *The Concept of Anxiety*, which grips and holds the individual prisoner suddenly and involuntarily in 'anxiety about the good' (CA, 123–32/SKS 4, 424–33; cf. EO 1, 154–5/SKS 2, 153–4). However, whereas the Kantian sublime precipitates a dynamic 'movement' of the mind, first inhibiting life and then animating the judge's vital faculties, the secret arrests Antigone in 'silence' – her state is 'continually in motion' but leaves her immobile

(EO 1, 158/SKS 2, 156). An end to Antigone's dilemma can only be found in death: 'our Antigone carries her secret in her heart like an arrow that life has continually plunged deeper and deeper, without depriving her of her life, for as long as it is in her heart she can live, but the instant it is taken out, she must die' (EO 1, 164/SKS 2, 162). And yet she continues to live and, tragically, lives a kind of death, just as the members of the society to whom 'A' addresses his story of Antigone (the *Symparanekromenoi*) are buried alive. (The essays on 'The silhouettes' and 'The unhappiest one' are also written for the *Symparanekromenoi*.) Antigone's living death at the hands of her contradictory love is sublime in the way she experiences the full weight of the conflict between her principle of love and her (in)capacity to realize it.

At the same time, her tragic guilt has the indeterminacy required to motivate an engagement with the question of how to move beyond the boundaries of the aesthetic. This can be illuminated on the basis of what we can call, with Kant, the 'formlessness' of the fragmentary outline that 'A' provides of her tragic dilemma. The scene for her struggle is her interior reflective life, which cannot find full exterior expression and thus exceeds the structure of dramatic presentation (Lisi 2016: 169): Her 'outline is so indistinct, her form so nebulous' (EO 1, 154/SKS 2, 152), and 'the stage is inside, not outside; it is a spiritual stage' (EO 1, 157/SKS 2, 155). 'Our Antigone' is a negative presentation of the unrepresentability of her inwardness and thus resembles the contradiction in Kant of the imagination's failing endeavour to find an adequate image for an idea of reason. 'A's reworked version of our Antigone serves as a broken image of existing in love, thereby raising ethical-religious existence as a contrastive point of reference through the way Antigone *wishes* or 'is beginning to want to live altogether spiritually' (cf. EO 1, 146/SKS 2, 146; Harries 2010: 170). This (ultimately unfilled) wish of Antigone's is the negative sensible index of the idea of a spiritual life, the 'mood' of anxiety that remains as the 'only trace of her actuality' (EO 1, 162/SKS 2, 152). Its pathos consists in this tragic guilt, but also in its failure to represent an embodiment of ethical-religious life, which nonetheless indicates the pathos of inward and outward suffering that is expressive of ethical-religious existence (cf. CUP 1, 387–555/SKS 7, 352–504; Cuff Snow 2016; Walsh 2004). Antigone's experience is therefore sublimely *transfigurative* in the way it attunes us to the life-principle of love, both its force and the possible tragedy of its actualization.

Sublime grief: the silhouettes

In his essay 'Silhouettes: psychological diversion,' 'A' builds on his reflections on 'our Antigone.'[17] Rather than tragic guilt, 'A' is concerned in this essay with 'reflective sorrow' or 'grief' – the two terms are translations of the Danish *Sorg* – which has a 'singular nature' that is 'silent, solitary, and seeks to return into itself.' It is 'constantly in motion' and thus requires the medium of 'poetry' because, for 'A,' poetry is capable of depicting temporal sequences, while art can only depict spatial structures. In order to trace reflective sorrow, then, 'A' attends to three literary works and their protagonists, and subjects them to poetic treatment: Marie Beaumarchais from Goethe's *Clavigo*, Donna Elvira from *Don Giovanni*, and Margarete from Goethe's *Faust*. The details of each of the silhouettes' stories are complex, but there are two features they share in common that are of interest for our purposes. The first concerns their content: Each figure is in love and has been (seduced and) deceived by their beloved. 'A' calls attention to the fundamental 'paradox' between deception and love. The paradox is that their love prevents them from accepting that their beloved is deceptive, which condemns them to a state of unrequited love, and yet compels them to reflect on the possibility of deception. Their sorrow is therefore reflective and unending.

The second crucial feature of the silhouettes concerns their form. The interior nature of sorrow, as one of the 'soul's faintest moods,' can only be appreciated through a series of interweaving modifications of these sorrowful characters in order to afford the 'special eye' that is needed to see what is not immediately visible (EO 1, 175/SKS 2, 172). The name 'A' chooses for these literary transfigurations, 'silhouettes' or 'shadowgraphs' (*Skyggerids*), is immediately suggestive of the interrelation of idea and sensible presentation in the sublime. The idea can only be intimated and approached via the shadow it casts. For 'A,' the 'images' he presents serve to reveal an 'interior image [*Billede*]' that is not 'externally perceptible' (EO 1, 173/SKS 2, 170; translation modified). The silhouette serves as a 'form' for a content that is incapable of assuming form. As such, it eludes exterior (artistic) presentation and thus exceeds the framework of beauty: 'Reflective grief does not become visible in the exterior, that is, it does not find its beautiful, composed expression therein. The interior unrest does not permit this transparency . . . it does not have the interest of the beautiful' (EO 1, 177/SKS 2, 175).

The transfiguration of all the literary figures into silhouettes resembles the activity of the imagination in the Kantian sublime as it strives and fails to present the unpresentable – in Kant an idea of reason, in Kierkegaard the paradox or contradiction of their reflective sorrow. It is an enactment of the striving to give the formless form. The silhouettes distinguish themselves from the temporality of suddenness, or 'now-ness,' of the Kantian sublime (Kant 2000: 142; cf. Lyotard 1991: esp. 78–88), as they emerge gradually. And yet within the series of images and their constant reconfiguration, they exert a hold, a hold which is structured at least in part by the conflict between the temporal constraints of certain finite moments (of love and attraction) that burst forth, and the infinite ideality of interior reflection. What is present is a transfiguration of objective sorrow into an uplifting image, an image whose (interior) content constantly withdraws itself – it disappears. Elvira's silent despair, for example, bursts forth 'in a blaze,' becomes 'pictorial' [*malerisk*] and occasions reflection. She is pictorial not in the sense of being simply or *actually* visible, but in the sense that 'the Elvira we *imagine* is visible in her essentiality,' a visibility that is loaded with significance but does not *depict* her despair (EO 1, 193/SKS 2, 189). 'A' reshapes the silhouettes' despair in a fashion that allows their despair to be transfigured into an image for reflection. In the same way that Antigone's tragic silence provided a sublime image of love, the silhouettes are sublime in the way they manifest, in the shadows of their grief, the complexity and force of love.

Conclusion

In the images of Antigone's fatal secret and the silhouettes' paralysing and paradoxical grief, we find an intimation of the hope for spiritual self-realization that these images present insofar as the hope is not fulfilled or exhausted in them. The aesthetic is productive in its failure.

The tension between the aesthetic and the non-aesthetic (necessarily) persists beyond the struggles of these sublime figures. In *Practice in Christianity*, when Anti-Climacus is articulating the requirements of ethical-religious existence, he resorts to a complex account of the way the 'sign of contradiction' of the God-man (PC, 124–7/SKS 12, 128–32) becomes a 'prototype' or exemplary image (*Forbillede*), which calls for 'imitation' rather than 'admiration' (PC, 233–57/SKS 12, 227–49). The object of imitation, however, is an exhibition of that which cannot be exhibited – the contradiction of the God-man *and* suffering as such (PC, 187/SKS 12, 187). The hope for self-realization persists throughout Kierkegaard's work and ultimately remains dependent on (sublime) images. As Adorno (1989: 133) writes, 'for Kierkegaard the original experience of Christianity remains bound to the image. . . . His image goes beyond all art; it is "insignificant from the artistic point of view" and itself an image; it thus restores the aesthetic even as the aesthetic is lost.'

Antigone and the silhouettes represent Kierkegaardian transfigurations of the aesthetic experience of the sublime. Their experiences *transfigure* the interior lives of the figures themselves, in devastating manner, compelling them to various forms of anxiety, despair, and grief. Their experiences also *transfigure* the way in which the principles of love and hope may be viewed and embodied: The tragic anxiety of Antigone and devastating grief of the silhouettes point, in their breakdown, beyond themselves to principles of love capable of grounding ethical-religiously oriented lives.

Related topics

'The ethical life of aesthetes,' Ulrika Carlsson; 'Kierkegaard on the value of art: an indirect method of communication,' Antony Aumann.

Notes

1 James Porter (2015) has explored the degree to which certain authors prior to Longinus can be seen as developing a notion of sublimity. He identifies 'specimens of a multiform sublime tradition' that can be traced as far back as the Pre-Socratics.
2 The Latin-derived *det Sublime* is used only twice in the published works. The term *Ophøiethed* (and its cognates) can be found in various passages and captures a sense of elevation and holiness (Pattison 1998: 246–47). Neither the English term 'sublime' nor any of its cognates features in the cumulative index to the collected English-language edition of Kierkegaard's writings. There is also no entry on the sublime in the recently published, otherwise very exhaustive, multivolume series on key concepts in Kierkegaard's work (Emmanuel, et al. 2013–2016).
3 George Pattison (1998) has compared the Kantian sublime with anxiety in Kierkegaard (see Further Reading). John Millbank (1996) sees a 'sublime discourse' in Kierkegaard that is taken up and furthered in twentieth-century, post-modern French philosophy. Edward Mooney (2007) identified what he calls the 'ethical sublime' in Kierkegaard. For Joakim Garff (2018: 86), Kierkegaard's work, in particular *Practice in Christianity*, can be seen to 'imitate or mimic the sublime by shaking its reader rhetorically' and thus be read in terms of the arresting quality of the Kantian sublime. Ettore Rocca (2017) has brought the (primarily Hegelian) sublime to bear on a reading of boredom and the theory of prudence in 'Rotation of Crops' in *Either/Or*. Finally, Bruce Kirmmse (2000) has investigated Kierkegaard's reference to the 'sublime lie' [*ophøiede Løgn*] by Desdemona at the end of Shakespeare's *Othello* (SLW, 142/SKS 6, 134; CUP 1, 262/SKS 7, 238). For Climacus, 'a sublime lie' involves a 'contrast of form' that contains a 'contradiction' and which is necessary for the communication of central ethical-religious themes. The 'abyss of inwardness' of the knight of faith (Abraham), for example, can only be expressed in 'a deceptive form' (CUP 1, 262/SKS 7, 238).
4 The technical term Kant uses to describe this harmonious relation between the apparent constitution of nature in these appearances and our manner of engaging with it is 'purposiveness' (*Zweckmäßigkeit*). Although one can only fully appraise the aim and possible merit of Kant's project in the third *Critique* by examining both of its halves together, including his teleological theory of the purposiveness of natural organisms and nature as an organic whole, my focus is his aesthetics.
5 Quoted in the editors' footnote in Kant (2000: 380).
6 Hans Blumenberg's (1997) examination of the history of the metaphor of shipwreck in Western discourse since Lucretius serves as a comprehensive and illustrating companion to any overview of the history of the sublime.
7 Although I cannot pursue this here, the 'earnest' (*ernshaft*) occupation of the imagination in the Kantian sublime, as opposed to its playful engagement in Kantian beauty, invites comparison with Kierkegaard's conception of the 'earnest' (*alvor*) occupation of the subject in ethical-religious existence.
8 A full account of the sublime in Kierkegaard would need to take into consideration its presence and operation in other concepts, phenomena and figures, such as anxiety (cf. Pattison 1998), the knight of faith in *Fear and Trembling*, and the 'sign of contradiction' of the God-man, articulated by Anti-Climacus as a 'prototype' in *Practice in Christianity* (see the conclusion to this chapter). And it would also need to consider the way that certain aesthetic figures, images, and concepts can be approached through the lens of *beauty* in Kant, which Ettore Rocca (1999; 2018) has done. One could argue that one finds a 'double aesthetics' (Zelle 1995) of beauty and sublimity in Kierkegaard.
9 Kant actually refers not to the event of the Revolution but the 'event' of the spectators' enthusiasm.

10 Two famous and illuminating attempts to connect Kant's theory of reflective aesthetic judgement with political concerns, in particular the French Revolution, war, and 'enthusiasm,' are by Hannah Arendt (1992: 52–8) and Jean-François Lyotard (2009).
11 I follow Ettore Rocca (2003: 125), who refers to 'A' as an 'aesthetician,' a theorist or philosopher of art. The term 'aesthete' first arose in the late eighteenth century. The aesthetician becomes an aesthete only in Part Two of *Either/Or*, where Judge William says that 'A' not only elaborates aesthetic principles but also attempts to live according to them.
12 In this way, I intend to avoid depicting the aesthetic in Kierkegaard solely from the perspective of its critique and disavowal from an ethical-religious perspective, which has been a common tendency in the scholarship (cf. Carlsson 2013: 243–46).
13 I follow Adorno in this regard, for whom the aesthetic sphere provides a 'schema' of the fundamental elements of ethical-religious existence, that is, non-aesthetic existence. In the 'Diapsalmata,' among other texts, Adorno (1989: 125) finds a series of motives which display the structure and form of *hope* that animates Kierkegaard's work within *and* outside the aesthetic sphere.
14 Indeed, the modern notion of individual autonomy becomes, for 'A,' 'comic,' as it 'places all responsibility on the individual and demands a self-sufficiency that we cannot actually provide' (Lisi 2016: 171).
15 'A' does not actually name the object of Antigone's love, but it can be inferred that he has Haemon in mind, to whom Antigone is betrothed in Sophocles' drama.
16 For more on the connection between the tragic and the sublime, see Billings (2014: 80–8) and Courtine (1993).
17 'A' opens the essay, 'The silhouettes,' with striking imagery of the sublime: the 'vortex,' the 'world's core principle,' which manifests in the chaos and wild, violent disorder of nature, its raging seas and the 'darkness' of the 'night' (EO 1, 168/SKS 2, 166). These passages recall, among others, Kant's remarks that the thought of the end of all time is 'horrifying' and 'frighteningly *sublime* partly because it is obscure, for the imagination works harder in darkness than it does in bright light' (Kant 1996b: 221; italics in original).

References

Adorno, T. (1989) *Kierkegaard: Construction of the aesthetic*, Minneapolis, MN: University of Minnesota Press.
Arendt, H. (1992) *Lectures on Kant's political philosophy*, R. Beiner (ed), Chicago, IL: University of Chicago Press.
Billings, J. (2014) *Genealogy of the tragic: Greek tragedy and German philosophy*, Princeton, NJ: Princeton University Press.
Blumenberg, H. (1997) *Shipwreck with spectator: Paradigm of a metaphor for existence*, S. Rendall (trans), Cambridge, MA: The MIT Press.
Carlsson, U. (2013) "'Love' among the post-Socratics,' in H. Schulz, J. Stewart, and K. Verstrynge (eds), *Kierkegaard Studies Yearbook 2013*: 243–66.
Clewis, R. R. (2009) *The Kantian sublime and the revelation of freedom*, Cambridge: Cambridge University Press.
Courtine, F. (1993) 'Tragedy and sublimity: The speculative interpretation of "Oedipus Rex" on the threshold of German idealism,' in J.-L. Nancy (ed), and J. S. Librett (trans), *Of the Sublime: Presence in Question*, New York: State University of New York Press.
Cuff Snow, S. (2016) 'The moment of self-transformation: Kierkegaard on suffering and the subject,' *Continental Philosophy Review*, 49, no. 2: 161–80.
Emmanuel, S. M., McDonald, W., and Stewart, J. (eds) (2013–2016) *Kierkegaard research: Sources, reception, and resources*, vol. 15 *(Kierkegaard's Concepts)*, London: Routledge.
Garff, J. (2018) 'Kierkegaard's Christian Bildungsroman,' in E. Ziolkowski (ed), *Kierkegaard, Literature, and the Arts*, Evanston, IL: Northwestern University Press.
Harries, K. (2010) *Between nihilism and faith: A commentary on Either/Or*, Berlin; Berlin: Walter de Gruyter.
Kant, I. (2000) *Critique of the power of judgment*, P. Guyer and E. Matthews (eds), and P. Guyer (trans), Cambridge: Cambridge University Press.
Kant, I. (1996a) 'The conflict of the faculties,' in A. Wood and G. Di Giovanni (eds), and M. Gregor (trans), *Religion and Rational Theology*, Cambridge: Cambridge University Press.
Kant, I. (1996b) 'The end of all things,' in A. W. Wood and G. Di Giovanni (eds and trans), *Religion and Rational Theology*, Cambridge: Cambridge University Press.
Kant, I. (1996c) 'On the common saying: That may be correct in theory, but it is of no use in practice,' in M. Gregor (ed and trans), *Practical Philosophy*, Cambridge: Cambridge University Press.

Kirmmse, B. (2000) '"I am not a Christian" – A "sublime lie"? Or: "Without authority," playing Desdemona to Christendom's Othello,' in P. Houe, G. D. Marino, and S. H. Rossel (eds), *Anthropology and Authority: Essays on Søren Kierkegaard*, Amsterdam: Rodopi.

Lisi, L. (2016) 'Tragic/tragedy,' in S. M. Emmanuel, W. McDonald, and J. Stewart (eds), *Kierkegaard's Concepts: Salvation to Writing*, London: Routledge.

Longinus (1995) *On the sublime*, W. H. Fyfe (ed and trans), revised by D. A. Russell, in G. P. Gould (ed), *Aristotle's 'Poetics'; Longinus' 'On the Sublime'; Demetrius' 'On Style'*, Cambridge, MA: Harvard University Press.

Longinus (1995) *On the sublime*, W. H. Fyfe (ed and trans), revised by D. A. Russell, in G. P. Gould (ed), *Aristotle's 'Poetics'; Longinus' 'On the Sublime'; Demetrius' 'On Style'*, Cambridge, MA: Harvard University Press.

Lyotard, J.-F. (2009) *On enthusiasm: The Kantian critique of history*, G. van den Abbeele (trans), Stanford, CA: Stanford University Press.

Lyotard, J.-F. (1991) *The inhuman: Reflections on time*, G. Bennington and R. Bowlby (trans), Stanford, CA: Stanford University Press.

Millbank, J. (1996) 'The sublime in Kierkegaard,' *Heythrop Journal*, 37: 298–21.

Mooney, E. (2007) *On Søren Kierkegaard: Dialogue, polemics, lost intimacy, and time*, Farnham: Ashgate.

Pattison, G. (1998) 'Kierkegaard and the sublime,' in N. J. Cappelørn and H. Deuser (eds), *Kierkegaard Studies Yearbook 1998*: 245–75.

Porter, J. I. (2015) 'The sublime,' in P. Destrée and P. Murray (eds), *A Companion to Ancient Aesthetics*, Chichester: Wiley Blackwell.

Rasmussen, A. M. (2017) 'Self and nihilism: Kierkegaard on inwardness, self and negativity,' in M. Gabriel and A. M. Rasmussen (eds), *German Idealism Today*, Berlin: Walter de Gruyter.

Rocca, E. (2018) 'Analogy and negativism,' in C. Welz and R. Rosfort (eds), *Hermeneutics and Negativism: Existential Ambiguities of Self-Understanding*, Tübingen: Mohr Siebeck.

Rocca, E. (2017) 'Der Unglücklichste/Die Wechselwirtschaft: Die Autonomie des Ästhetischen angesichts der Langeweile,' in M. Kleinert and H. Deuser (eds), *Søren Kierkegaard: Entweder–Oder*, Berlin: Walter de Gruyter.

Rocca, E. (2003) 'The secret: Communication denied, communication of domination,' in P. Houe and G. D. Marino (eds), *Søren Kierkegaard and the Word(s): Essays on Hermeneutics and Communication*, Copenhagen: C. A. Reitzel.

Rocca, E. (1999) 'Kierkegaard's second aesthetics,' in N. J. Cappelørn and H. Deuser (eds), *Kierkegaard Studies Yearbook 1999*: 278–92.

Walsh, S. (2004) 'Standing at the crossroads: The invitation of Christ to a life of suffering,' in R. L. Perkins (ed), *International Kierkegaard Commentary*, vol. 20 (*Practice in Christianity*), Macon: Mercer University Press.

Zelle, C. (1995) *Die doppelte Ästhetik der Moderne: Revisionen des Schönen von Boileau bis Nietzsche*, Stuttgart: J. B. Metzler.

Further reading

Carlsson, U. (2013) "'Love' among the post-Socratics,' *Kierkegaard Studies Yearbook*, 18: 243–66.

Carlsson criticizes the tendency in the secondary literature to dismiss the aesthetic sphere (in particular Part One of *Either/Or*) from the perspective of the ethical and/or religious and argues that the silhouettes present a distinctive and genuine mode of loving that is worthy of serious consideration. Their feminine love is a unique combination of passion and action and displays a devotion to the beloved that renders it more than simply self-love and which is arguably absent in other depictions of love in Kierkegaard's later work, such as in *Fear and Trembling*.

Pattison, G. (1998) 'Kierkegaard and the sublime,' in N. J. Cappelørn and H. Deuser (eds), *Kierkegaard Studies Yearbook 1998*: 245–75.

In this astute examination of the sublime in Kant and anxiety in Kierkegaard, Pattison identifies various points of relevant contact between the two concepts and the ways that what he coins the 'anxious sublime' in Kierkegaard can ground a possible critique of modern culture and urban experience.

Rebentisch, J. (2017) *The art of freedom: On the dialectics of democratic existence*, Cambridge: Cambridge University Press

In Chapter 3 'The ethics of aesthetic existence: Kierkegaard,' Rebentisch reads Kierkegaard's project in *Either/Or* as a critique of aestheticization that reveals, at the same time, the potential for aesthetic existence to be a legitimate and fulfilling life of freedom.

14
KIERKEGAARD ON THE VALUE OF ART: AN INDIRECT METHOD OF COMMUNICATION

Antony Aumann

Introduction

Questions about the value of art are nothing new. Lovers of art have been asked to explain its importance since the time of Plato's *Republic*. We encounter one common line of defence in Kierkegaard's writings. Like many nineteenth-century thinkers, including the leading figures of the Idealist and Romantic movements (Speight 2015; Zuckert 2010), Kierkegaard embraced a 'cognitivist' picture of the arts. He located art's value in its ability to teach or educate – to provide us with cognitive benefits.

Kierkegaard's version of cognitivism has a predictable existentialist twist. He is not as interested as Hegel or Schelling in whether art can express general truths about the spirit of the age. Nor is he as concerned as Kant with whether art manages to provide us with concrete representations of abstract ideas. Kierkegaard focuses his attention on art's ability to teach us about ourselves. Works of art matter to him because they can help us with the project of discovering who we are as individuals.

Despite cognitivism's popularity, it also received pushback in Kierkegaard's day. Some critics complained that what art accomplishes does not exactly amount to teaching. Others conceded that art might manage to teach in some sense, but they objected that it does not do so as well as philosophy or the sciences. The lessons communicated through art, they claimed, are never as clear-cut or well-supported by reasons.

The goal of this chapter is to explain how Kierkegaard turns these objections on their heads. I will argue that he does so by making two moves. First, he maintains that works of art do not teach 'directly' by telling us truths and offering us evidence. Instead, art educates in an 'indirect' fashion by helping us make our own discoveries. Second, the fact that art does not teach in a straightforward manner is not a defect. On the contrary, it is precisely because art teaches indirectly that it teaches better than philosophy and the sciences.

Philosophical objections to cognitivism

To appreciate Kierkegaard's contributions to the cognitivist tradition, we must set them against the backdrop of two well-known challenges. The first challenge is the 'no assertions' objection. It states that, on a traditional view, educating people involves giving them truths they need to know. The problem with most works of art is that they do not try to impart any truths. They do not even make any claims or assertions about the way the world goes. Thus, they cannot be said to teach in the traditional sense.

The second major challenge to the cognitivist view of art is the 'no reasons' objection. It points out that teaching is more than offering people truths. *Real* teaching requires providing people with knowledge. People have knowledge only when they have justifications for what they take to be true. Thus, the deeper problem with works of art is that, even when they do convey truths, they often fail to support them with justifications – that is, reasons, arguments, or evidence.

These two objections have received much attention in contemporary aesthetics. But they are not peculiar to our times. Their pedigree extends back to Plato's (1992: 607d) argument in the *Republic* for thinking art should be banished from the ideal city. They also stand behind the view held by many philosophers in the modern era that art is not as reliable a path to the truth as science (Carroll 2003: 368–9; Kivy 1997: 84–119). Finally, we catch glimpses of the two objections in the reasoning presented by Hegel for his 'end of art' thesis. Despite the educational function art has served throughout history, Hegel claimed, it ultimately must be replaced by philosophy. For philosophy is a more transparent medium for communicating truths (Hegel 1975: 10–1; see Beiser 2005: 286–97; Pattison 1992: 14–6).

It should not surprise us, therefore, that Kierkegaard alludes to these two objections in his writings. At times he even does so sympathetically. Sylvia Walsh (1994: 170–3) calls attention to passages in *Either/Or, Concluding Unscientific Postscript*, and *Works of Love* that characterize art as a deficient teacher, one that fails to present the world as it actually is. Elsewhere Kierkegaard describes a passion for art as a preoccupation with a realm other than our own; it is a flight from reality into fantasy (SUD, 77–8/SKS 11, 191; CUP 1, 387–90/SKS 7, 352–6). In his most critical moments, he appears to agree with Plato: 'the poet is, in a godly sense, the most dangerous of all' (TM, 225/SKS 13, 281). Such passages lead Kai Hammermeister (2002: 130) to conclude, 'Kierkegaard associates the aesthetic more or less with deception and corruption.'

Kierkegaard's cognitivism about the arts

Kierkegaard's negative comments about art should not unduly colour our interpretation. For he usually restricts them to particular kinds of art or specific approaches to art. When we take a holistic look at his writings on the subject, it becomes apparent that he has a positive conception of the role art can play in human life. As noted at the outset, we can think of Kierkegaard as falling in line with the Idealists and Romantics on this issue. However much he disagrees with them elsewhere, he shares their view of the importance of art. He too believes art matters because it has the power to educate us about the world and ourselves.

Hints of Kierkegaard's cognitivist view of the arts appear in his account of Thomasine Gyllembourg's first novel, *A Story of Everyday Life*. He praises the book because it reveals the way life actually is. It offers readers 'an explanation of life or a strengthening of their understanding of it' (TA, 22/SKS 8, 25). To some it is even 'a guide' (TA, 22/SKS 8, 25). Kierkegaard's cognitivism also comes across in what Ettore Rocca (1999) describes as his call for a 'second aesthetics' in which poets express new ideals for living (JP 2, 288–9/SKS 24, 82–3; see also McDonald 2014: 26). Kierkegaard's clearest statements on the value of art, however, occur in the context of his defence of his own attempts at literature. He turns to a literary or poetic format because he considers it the best way to help readers learn. Indeed, when it comes to ethics and religion, good instruction *has to be* artistic (CUP 1, 79, 242–3/SKS 7, 29, 220–1; PV, 43, 54/SKS 16, 25–6, 35; PC, 94, 123, 133–44/SKS 12, 103, 128–9, 137–47; see Aumann 2010). Thus, in the mind of Kierkegaard, the Hegelians have it backwards. Art rather than philosophy or science is the superior way to educate people.

Kierkegaard is an important member of the cognitivist tradition for several reasons. Chief among them is that his version of cognitivism contains a couple of insights that allow him to avoid the objections described in the previous section. His *first insight* is that philosophers often presuppose a narrow view of teaching. They tend to assume that teaching involves imparting truths and supporting these truths with reasons. To use Kierkegaard's terminology, when philosophers talk about teaching, they restrict their focus to the 'communication of knowledge' or 'direct communication.'

If the 'direct' model of teaching were the only one, the standard objections to cognitivism would go through. Art would be an impoverished educator because it seldom follows the 'truth plus justification' pattern. But, and this is Kierkegaard's *second insight*, the direct model is not the only legitimate model. It may reflect the stereotypical way instruction occurs in philosophy or the ideal pursued in the sciences, but it does not capture how instruction happens in art. When works of art teach, they tend to do so *indirectly* rather than directly. They educate us without asserting truths or offering reasons to believe them.

Kierkegaard's writings contain several accounts of art's indirect method of instruction or what he calls 'indirect communication' (JP 1, 267–93/SKS 27, 390–434; CUP 1, 72–80, 242–99/SKS 7, 73–80, 220–73; PC, 123–44/SKS 12, 128–47; PV, 41–56/SKS 16, 23–36). The details of these accounts differ, but the central idea remains the same. Rather than straightforwardly telling us the truth, art indirectly teaches us by empowering us to uncover the truth for ourselves. It provides us with the tools, training, and background resources we need to make discoveries on our own. For this reason, Kierkegaard describes indirect communication as 'the communication of capability' rather than 'the communication of knowledge' (JP 1, 281–90/SKS 27, 404–14). The implication here is that the indirect method does not involve giving people new information to know. Instead, it involves helping people cultivate the ability to learn new things on their own. The aim, as Kierkegaard puts it, is to help the learner 'stand alone' (JP 1, 280/SKS 27, 403; WL, 274–5/SKS 9, 272–3).

To further explain indirect communication, Kierkegaard draws on Socrates's metaphor of midwifery or 'maieutics' (PV, 7–9/SKS 13, 13–15; CUP 1, 80/SKS 7, 80; JP 1, 274–80/SKS 27, 397–403; see also Aumann 2010: 297–305; Daise 1999). The maieutic teacher does not give birth to his or her own knowledge and then pass it along to the learner. He or she rather helps learners 'give birth' to their own knowledge just as the midwife draws the infant from the mother. More perspicuously, the maieutic teacher induces learners to arrive at the relevant lesson on their own rather than straightforwardly telling it to them.

One qualification to this picture deserves our attention. Although Kierkegaard often associates art with indirect communication, he does not identify the two (CUP 1, 251–300/SKS 7, 228–73; see Aumann 2008: 30–57; 2010). He does not reduce art to indirect communication or indirect communication to art. It is possible, he says, to teach indirectly without using artistic means. One prominent example comes from Socrates. His question-asking method counts as indirect communication even though it does not amount to fine art (CUP 1, 277–8/SKS 7, 251–4). For it too prompts learners to reason under their own steam to a conclusion rather than handing it over to them as a finished product. In addition, Kierkegaard claims that some works of art attempt to teach us directly rather than indirectly. They are *didactic* by nature, sometimes even beating us over the head with their theses and badgering us into accepting their points of view (see TA, 34–5, 41/SKS 8, 34–5, 41). Finally, Kierkegaard acknowledges that many artworks do not teach us at all. Some attempt to assist us with the learning process but fail; the tools, training, or resources they offer us are flawed. Other works of art do not even try to help us. They serve as diversions from the task of learning rather than occasions to pursue it. Works of these last two sorts are among the targets of Kierkegaard's negative remarks about art mentioned above.

Artistic methods of indirect communication

There are a number of specific ways in which art teaches us indirectly, according to Kierkegaard. Chief among them is by providing us with cognitive tools we can use to enhance our understanding of our lives. In particular, works of art help us by offering us lenses through which to see ourselves better or prisms through which to view the world around us afresh. These lenses or prisms can focus our attention on considerations we have overlooked. They also have the power to structure our conception of the world in ways we could not have imagined on our own.

Kierkegaard's way of expressing the point is to say works of art can serve as 'mirrors' for ourselves (FSE, 25–6, 40–4/SKS 13, 53–4, 66–70; see Stokes 2009: 111–33). He is most explicit about this way of framing the idea when it comes to his own literary writings. Indeed, as the motto for one of his books, he uses the quotation from Georg Lichtenberg, 'Such works are mirrors: when an ape looks in, no apostle can look out' (SLW, 8/SKS 6, 16). Kierkegaard's idea here is that, if we attend carefully to the stories he gives us, we can see reflections of ourselves in the characters they describe.

Works of art that serve the kind of mirroring function Kierkegaard has in mind may not themselves contain much knowledge. The standard philosophical objections may be right that they offer us little in the way of truth-plus-justification. Thus, Kierkegaard admits in his journals that in many cases of indirect communication 'there is no object' or 'the object drops out' (JP 1, 270–1/SKS 27, 395). What he means here is that there is no piece of knowledge or bit of information conveyed from teacher to learner. Nevertheless, works of art that serve a mirroring function still have cognitive value because we can use them to acquire knowledge about the world and ourselves. In fact, like ordinary mirrors, they may enable us to discover things we would otherwise miss. They may reflect back to us truths about ourselves we are too myopic to see on our own.

Art as mirror of the self

Kierkegaard's idea that works of art can serve as mirrors for ourselves is a fruitful one. Although not always owing to his influence, it is also one that has received attention in contemporary aesthetics (e.g., Danto 1981). Perhaps the most lucid account of the art-as-mirror-of-the-self view occurs in the work of Elisabeth Camp. It is worth taking a moment to explain her view.

Camp (2009) distinguishes between two ways we can see ourselves in the characters we encounter in works of literature. The first, called 'pretense,' involves using our imaginations to transform ourselves into the figures being described. When reading Tolstoy's *Anna Karenina*, for example, I engage in pretense if I contemplate what it would be like to live in Anna's shoes. I mentally pull myself out of my own situation and put myself into hers. In the most radical version of this exercise, I strip off all my character traits – everything that makes me who I am. I replace them with the traits Tolstoy has given Anna. I attempt to think, feel and experience the world exactly as she does.

Camp's second way of seeing ourselves in literary characters is 'metaphorical seeing-as.' It brings us closer to the idea Kierkegaard has in mind. Instead of putting myself in Anna's shoes so I can understand *her life*, I use Tolstoy's description of Anna to help me understand *my own life*. Her story becomes a pattern for structuring and organizing my own. I come to see my troubles in terms of her troubles and my choices in terms of her choices. As a result, my image of myself becomes 'transfigured,' to use Arthur Danto's word. I gain a new picture of who I am. New aspects of my identity come to the forefront and new connections between moments in my life solidify. It may become apparent, for example, that like Anna I too can be driven to fits of jealousy when my goals are threatened, or that I too have pursued romantic love to the detriment of my own well-being.

David and Bathsheba

Kierkegaard provides us with several of his own examples of metaphorical seeing-as. One of the most revealing occurs in *For Self-Examination*, where we find his rendition of the story of David and Bathsheba (FSE, 37–9/SKS 13, 64–5). The outlines of the story are well-known. Although King David has many wives, he becomes smitten by the beautiful Bathsheba, who is herself already married to another. Unable to resist her charms, David has Bathsheba brought to the palace so he can sleep with her. As part of the cover up for his adultery, he arranges for Bathsheba's husband, Uriah, to be moved to the front lines of a battle where the fighting is fierce and he is soon killed.

God sends the prophet Nathan to help David see the error of his ways. But rather than coming right out and admonishing David, Nathan offers him a parable. It is a tale about a rich man who must prepare a meal for a traveller. In a fit of selfishness, the rich man decides to forgo slaughtering any of his own many animals for the feast. Instead he seizes his poor neighbour's one and only ewe lamb, which the neighbour has loved and treated like a daughter.

On Kierkegaard's retelling of the Biblical account, David becomes enamoured with Nathan's tale. He praises its literary richness and offers Nathan advice about how to make it more interesting. But then Nathan utters the famous words – '*thou* art the man' – and David's perspective shifts. He suddenly sees himself as the metaphorical target of the parable. The rich man's actions and his callous insensitivity to how his greed harms the less fortunate become a lens through which David sees himself. They focus his attention on his own selfishness with Bathsheba and his own insensitivity to the suffering of Uriah. With his sins in view, David repents.

Beyond literature

Kierkegaard, like Camp, focuses on literature when making his case for the cognitive value of art. He is less sanguine about other types of art. Following a nineteenth-century trend, his comments about the revelatory powers of painting and sculpture in particular are negative (EO 1, 49–57/SKS 2, 57–65; EO 2, 133–9/SKS 3, 132–7; see Fried 2002: 141–66; James 2008). But I believe it is a mistake on Kierkegaard's part to downplay the power of painting and sculpture. They too can provide us with lenses or prisms that help us restructure our vision of ourselves. They too can work as mirrors that reflect back transfigured images of our lives – images that afford us new ways to conceive of who we are.

Consider one of Caravaggio's final paintings, *The Denial of Saint Peter* (1610). It depicts a scene found in all four gospels from the last day of Jesus's life. After Jesus is betrayed and arrested, Peter follows him into the courtyard of the high priest. Over the course of the evening, three people accuse Peter of belonging to Jesus's group of disciples. Peter denies the charge each time. He thereby fulfils Jesus's prophesy that he would be denied thrice before the cock crowed.

In *The Denial of Saint Peter*, Caravaggio paints one of the accusations. He has close-cropped three figures – an indicting servant girl, an inquiring soldier whom the girl has summoned, and Peter himself – so each appears at half-length. The light is cast so that the girl and the soldier are in the dark. We barely see the questioning finger of the soldier or the two pointing fingers of the servant girl. Instead, Caravaggio highlights Peter's indignant scowl along with his hands, which he has folded inward toward his chest as if to say, 'Who me?'

The power of the painting lies in its ability to communicate more than just Peter's physical appearance. As explained by Keith Christiansen (2017), the curator of the exhibit at the Metropolitan Museum of Art in New York where the painting hangs, Caravaggio 'probes with unparalleled poignancy a dark world burdened by guilt and doom.' He has rendered Peter's outward visage in such a way that it provides a window into his inner mental state. We see in Peter's defiant facial expression an anticipation of his coming remorse.

When we contemplate Peter's emotional state, our mirror neurons fire, leading us to empathize with his distress. The terror-cum-regret that overcame him washes over us as well. These powerful emotional tremors pave the way for associated memories. We find ourselves thinking of moments when we too have denied the ones we love in order to save ourselves. In this way, Caravaggio sheds light not only on the life of Saint Peter but on our lives as well. His painting works as a mirror that reflects back on us viewers the truth about who we are. Thus, we discover in Peter's denial of Jesus our own failings, just as David saw his failings in the sins of the rich man from Nathan's parable.

Art, science, and philosophy

I have been expanding on Kierkegaard's cognitivist view of the arts. In particular, I have been elaborating on what he means when he says that art teaches us indirectly rather than directly. But there is another feature of Kierkegaard's view that deserves attention. He does not merely maintain that art's mode of instruction is *different* than the one we typically find in philosophy and the sciences. He also holds that art's mode of instruction is *better*.

Kierkegaard here inverts another popular line of thinking. Many philosophers have held that insofar as art teaches at all it does so in a *deficient* manner. It would be better if artists were more straightforward about their lessons – if they came right out and told us what we needed to know and gave us clear reasons for why we should believe them. Indeed, this is why Hegel held that the messages communicated in works of art ultimately need to be clarified and justified by philosophy and the sciences. Kierkegaard's insight is that Hegel and like-minded thinkers have it backward. Art is not held back by its indirect method of instruction but is better because of it. Art's indirectness, in other words, is not a defect but a virtue. It is something that makes art's mode of instruction *superior* to that provided by philosophy and the sciences.

Kierkegaard provides several defences of this claim (see Aumann 2010; Tietjen 2013: 49–60). One of the most prominent is that art's indirect approach is *pedagogically* superior to more direct approaches. It is simply a more effective way to help people learn. Kierkegaard's argument here revolves around two claims. First, an indirect method of teaching is better than a direct method because it requires learners to become more actively engaged in the learning process. In line with contemporary educational theory, Kierkegaard maintains that a lesson is more likely to hit home and stick with people when they have to discover it for themselves than when it is handed to them. In Kierkegaard's language, learners are less likely to end up with 'rote understanding' this way (PV, 41–55/SKS 16, 23–36; CUP 1, 72–80, 277–8/SKS 7, 72–80, 251–4; TDIO, 37–8/SKS 5, 416).

Second, although there are several ways to undertake the indirect method of instruction, artistic ways are often the best. The reason is that artistic instruction is more responsive to our nature as human beings (PV, 54/SKS 16, 35). In particular, it better accommodates the fact that we are not computers or robots who process ideas in a strictly logical way. Our passions, emotions, and imaginations all play roles in our decision-making processes. The value of art over philosophy and the sciences is that it has the ability to engage us on *all* these levels. Art addresses 'the whole person,' as the popular phrase has it. Appreciating the force of this claim requires a detour through Kierkegaard's account of human nature.

Kierkegaard on human nature

The centrepiece of Kierkegaard's view of human nature is that we are not purely rational creatures. Proof of this claim lies in the kind of errors we commit. If we were purely rational, Kierkegaard avers, incoming information would always perfectly translate into action and belief (CUP 1, 22/SKS 7, 30; SUD, 92–6/SKS 11, 205–8). We would always do what we took to be good and always believe what appeared to us to be true. Thus, any mistakes would be the result of a lack of education. We would do evil only because we did not yet know what the good really was. So too, we would believe falsehoods only because we had not yet been taught what was actually true. All sin, to put the point how Anti-Climacus does, would be a matter of ignorance (SUD, 95/SKS 11, 207).

But this is not how things go. Our problem as human beings is not always a lack of knowledge or education (CUP 1, 242, 249–50/SKS 7, 220, 226–7). We sometimes fail to do what we take to be right or intentionally do what we know is wrong (SUD, 90/SKS 11, 203; TDIO, 100/SKS 5, 467; see Kosch 2006: 170–1). In addition, we find ourselves believing what deep down we are aware is false or failing to believe what in a sense we recognize is correct. These possibilities – weakness of the will, radical evil, and self-deception – all show that we are not purely rational creatures. Other faculties play a role in our decision-making and belief-forming processes.

Passion

To be a human being, for Kierkegaard, is also to be a passionate being (TA, 61–9/SKS 8, 59–66; CUP 1, 33, 130–1, 311/SKS 7, 39, 122–3, 283–4; see Evans 2009: 21–2; Walsh 1994: 200–2). In other words, a genuinely human existence is one that involves *caring* about things. It is a matter of taking things to be of significance and regarding them as worth structuring our lives around. We are passionate in the relevant sense, Johannes Climacus says, if we are willing to take risks for things, venture for them, or pursue them at great cost to ourselves (CUP 1, 200–4/SKS 7, 183–6).

To say we are passionate beings is not to say we are all already properly passionate. The problem with many of us is that we do not have enough passion. Indeed, Kierkegaard often complains that his age is a tepid one (TA, 68/SKS 8, 66). 'What our age needs is pathos,' he writes in his journals, 'just as scurvy needs green vegetables' (JP 3, 428/SKS 20, 119). Climacus goes so far as to say that most people have forgotten what it is to be passionate and thus have forgotten what it is to be human (CUP 1, 242/SKS 7, 220).

Contrary to some readings (e.g., Dreyfus 1999), Kierkegaard does not recommend that we be passionate about just any old thing. Although he does suggest caring about something is better than caring about nothing, he believes the object of our cares matters (CUP 1, 201/SKS 7, 184; JP 3, 427/SKS 18, 217). For instance, he laments that some people place too much emphasis on abstract reflection (CUP 1, 249/SKS 7, 226–7). He chastises others for being preoccupied with mundane worldly affairs (SUD, 48/SKS 11, 163; CD, 124/SKS 10, 135). Perhaps Kierkegaard's favourite whipping boy, however, is the person who obsesses over what 'the crowd' thinks, something he believes ought not to concern us at all (PV, 106–12/SKS 16, 86–92; UDVS, 95–6/SKS 8, 199–200).

In Kierkegaard's mind, what we ought to care about are ethical and religious matters. We ought to devote ourselves to doing the good, loving our neighbour, and abiding by God's will (UDVS, 24–30/SKS 8, 139–48; WL, 44–60/SKS 9, 51–67). Relatedly, we should care about developing our identities in an ethical and religious direction. We should focus our attention on the goal of becoming ideal versions of ourselves (CUP 1, 130/SKS 7, 122; EO 2, 178/SKS 3, 173–4; see Stokes 2009: 63–4).

Emotion

Kierkegaard does not just advocate for the importance of passion in the sense of *care* or *devotion*. He also regards passion in the sense of *emotion* or *feeling* as a crucial component of human nature (Furtak 2005: 45–51; Strelis 2013; Evans 2009: 113). In fact, one of the mistakes Kierkegaard harps upon is the attempt to bracket our emotions from our inquiries (CUP 1, 32–4, 350–1/ SKS 7, 38–40, 320–1). Under the sway of the Platonic tradition, he thinks we often attempt to approach issues from a dispassionate point of view (CUP 1, 253/SKS 7, 230). In part this means we try not to let our own personal interests and agendas – our 'passions' in the first sense of the term – interfere with our judgments about what is right or true. But it also means we try to keep our emotions out of it. We aim to think and reason with an even-keeled or placid disposition.

Kierkegaard has two problems with our pursuit of this sort of objectivity. First, he maintains that being completely dispassionate and disinterested is impossible. We never approach anything with perfect neutrality. Indeed, it is a fundamental feature of human consciousness that we are always in some way 'interested' in the issues we think about (JC, 170/SKS 15, 57; see Stokes 2009: 47–60). We always approach them against the backdrop of pre-existing concerns and so we always possess a variety of emotional attitudes toward them (EO 2, 164/SKS 3, 161; see Ferreira 1991: 125–7).

Second, Kierkegaard believes that to the degree it is possible to become dispassionate, doing so is often a mistake. As Rick Furtak (2005: 48–50; 2008: 59–66; 2015: 228–9) has shown, Kierkegaard embraces a perceptual theory of the emotions according to which our emotions can help us see the world *better*. They can serve as lenses that focus our attention. In particular, they can put in sharp relief the value or significance of what we encounter. Kierkegaard goes so far as to say that 'fundamentally all understanding depends upon how one is disposed toward something' (JP 4, 354/SKS 23, 24–5). As such, 'a person's inner being . . . determines what he discovers and what he hides' (EUD, 60/SKS 5, 70).

Imagination

One final faculty Kierkegaard discusses is the imagination. He identifies it as our ability to see possibilities or make images of possibilities (SUD, 31/SKS 11, 147; see Frances 2014; Grøn 2002). Of particular importance for Kierkegaard is the role the imagination plays in helping us come up with possible ways to live. Included under this umbrella is possible ways we can think, reason, feel, and care. Thus, our imagination shapes and delimits what we can do with all our faculties. It is 'the capacity *instar omnium* [for all capacities]' (SUD, 31/SKS 11, 147). As we read in *The Sickness unto Death*, 'When all is said and done, whatever of feeling, knowing, and willing a person has depends upon what imagination he has' (SUD, 31/SKS 11, 147).

Kierkegaard's respect for the power of imagination leads him to worry about its misuse (Söderquist 2016: XIV; Stokes 2009: 75). For instance, Anti-Climacus notes with consternation how many of us get caught up in fantasies about ourselves. We let ourselves be seduced by stories about who we are that are loftier (or lower) than the facts allow. Those of us who succumb to such illusions are said to suffer from 'the despair of infinitude' (SUD, 30–3/SKS 11, 146–8). This phrase is meant to capture the idea that we have failed to ground our identity in the finite realm of the actual world.

Just as often, however, Kierkegaard thinks we err on the opposite side. We go astray not because of an excess of imagination but because of a lack of imagination. In the most troubling case, we become small-minded about our own possibilities (SUD, 33–5/SKS 11, 149–51). We wrongly restrict our sense of what we can do with our lives to what society tells us. We confine our vision of whom we might become to the options the media or the public deems acceptable. As a result, we fail to pursue paths that might be more appropriate for us as unique individuals.

The pedagogical superiority of art

With Kierkegaard's view of human nature in hand, we are in position to appreciate his argument for the pedagogical superiority of art. His guiding insight, once again, is that teachers ought to use a mode of instruction that is responsive to our nature as human beings. He concedes that if we were purely rational creatures, it might be appropriate to engage us on an entirely rational level (PV, 53–4/SKS 16, 35). It might be fitting to adhere to the ideal of direct communication and offer us only theses and justifications. For we could be counted on to transform this information into right action and right belief. As it happens, though, we are not purely rational creatures. Passion, emotion, and imagination also play important roles in our decision-making and belief-forming processes. Therefore, we need a mode of instruction that engages us on all these levels as well.

It is here that fine art comes into play. Works of art are powerful educators, for Kierkegaard, because they do not engage us only on a rational level. They help us to imagine what it would be like to occupy perspectives other than our own, as we see with Tolstoy's *Anna Karenina*. Works of art also evoke powerful emotions in us and these emotions focus and refine our view of the world. They disclose aspects of it we would miss if we remained dispassionate. Moreover, because art conveys ideas in an emotional medium, these ideas become embedded in our minds. They sink in more deeply than they would if they had been conveyed prosaically. This is why Caravaggio's painting, *The Denial of Saint Peter*, has such staying power. The vision of life it affords lingers in our minds because it reaches us on an affective level. Finally, because art engages our imaginations and emotions, it also moves our passions. The parable Nathan offers David shows how, more effectively than the street corner evangelist's harangues, art can make us care in new ways about new things (PV, 41–53/SKS 16, 23–36; BA, 16/SKS 15, 101–2; see Aumann 2010: 317–24).

We can now see why Kierkegaard regards Hegel's view as backwards when it comes to art. The very features of art that led Hegel to say it was an ineffective guide compared to philosophy and science are what make it so potent in Kierkegaard's mind. Art's engagement with our passions and emotions is not a reason to be suspicious of its ability to teach us. Quite the opposite. It is precisely why art is the superior mode of instruction.

Related topics

'Kierkegaard on nature and natural beauty,' Anthony Rudd; 'Kierkegaard's post-Kantian approach to anthropology and selfhood,' Roe Fremstedal; 'Kierkegaard: the dialectical self and the political,' Shoni Rancher.

References

Aumann, A. (2010) 'Kierkegaard on indirect communication, the crowd, and a monstrous illusion,' in R. L. Perkins (ed), *International Kierkegaard Commentary*, vol. 22 (*The Point of View*), Macon, GA: Mercer University Press, 295–324.

Aumann, A. (2008) *Kierkegaard on the need for indirect communication*, Ph.D. Dissertation, Bloomington, IN: Indiana University.

Beiser, F. C. (2005) *Hegel*, London: Routledge.

Camp, E. (2009) 'Two varieties of literary imagination: Metaphor, fiction, and thought experiments,' *Midwest Studies in Philosophy*, 33, no. 1: 107–30.

Carroll, N. (2003) 'Aesthetics and the educative powers of art,' in R. Curren (ed), *A Companion to the Philosophy of Education*, Oxford: Blackwell, 365–83.

Christiansen, K. (2017) *The Denial of Saint Peter*. Retrieved from <http://www.metmuseum.org/art/collection/search/437986> [accessed December 17, 2017].

Daise, B. (1999) *Kierkegaard's Socratic art*, Macon, GA: Mercer University Press.

Danto, A. C. (1981) *The transfiguration of the commonplace: A philosophy of art*, Cambridge, MA: Harvard University Press.

Dreyfus, H. L. (1999) 'Kierkegaard on the Internet: Anonymity vs. commitment in the present age,' in A. Hannay, C. Tolstrup, and N. J. Cappelørn (eds), *Kierkegaard Studies Yearbook 1999*, Berlin: Walter de Gruyter.

Evans, C. S. (2009) *Kierkegaard: An introduction*, Cambridge: Cambridge University Press.

Ferreira, M. J. (1991) *Transforming vision: Imagination and will in Kierkegaardian faith*, Oxford: Oxford University Press.

Frances, M. B. (2014) 'Imagination,' in S. Emmanuel, W. McDonald and J. Stewart (eds), *Kierkegaard Research: Sources, Reception and Resources*, vol. 15 (*Kierkegaard's Concepts*), tome 3, Farnham: Ashgate.

Fried, M. (2002) *Menzel's realism: Art and embodiment in nineteenth-century Berlin*, New Haven, CT: Yale University Press.

Furtak, R. A. (2015) 'Love as the ultimate ground of practical reason: Kierkegaard, Frankfurt, and the conditions of affective experience,' in A. Rudd and J. J. Davenport (eds), *Love, Reason, and Will: Kierkegaard After Frankfurt*, London: Bloomsbury, 217–42.

Furtak, R. A. (2008) 'Love and the discipline of philosophy,' in E. F. Mooney (ed), *Ethics, Love, and Faith in Kierkegaard*, Bloomington, IN: Indiana University Press, 59–71.

Furtak, R. A. (2005) *Wisdom in love: Kierkegaard and the ancient quest for emotional integrity*, Notre Dame, IN: University of Notre Dame Press.

Grøn, A. (2002) 'Imagination and subjectivity,' *Ars Disputandi*, 2, no. 1: 89–98.

Hammermeister, K. (2002) *The German aesthetic tradition*, Cambridge: Cambridge University Press.

Hegel, G. W. F. (1975) *Aesthetics: Lectures on fine art*, T. M. Knox (trans), 2 vols., Oxford: Oxford University Press.

James, D. (2008) 'The significance of Kierkegaard's interpretation of Don Giovanni in relation to Hegel's philosophy of art,' *British Journal for the History of Philosophy*, 16, no. 1: 147–62.

Kivy, P. (1997) *Philosophies of arts: An essay in differences*, Cambridge: Cambridge University Press.

Kosch, M. (2006) *Freedom and reason in Kant, Schelling, and Kierkegaard*, Oxford: Oxford University Press.

McDonald, W. (2014) 'Aesthetic/aesthetics,' in S. Emmanuel, W. McDonald and J. Stewart (eds), *Kierkegaard Research: Sources, Reception and Resources*, vol. 15 (*Kierkegaard's Concepts*), tome 1, Farnham: Ashgate.

Pattison, G. (1992) *Kierkegaard: The aesthetic and the religious: From the magic theatre to the crucifixion of the image*, London: Palgrave Macmillan.

Plato (1992) *Republic*, G. M. A. Grube (trans), Indianapolis, IN: Hackett Publishing Company.

Rocca, E. (1999) 'Kierkegaard's second aesthetics,' in N. J. Cappelørn and H. Deuser (eds), *Kierkegaard Studies: Yearbook 1999*, Berlin: Walter de Gruyter.

Söderquist, A. S. (2016) *Kierkegaard on dialogical education: Vulnerable freedom*, Lanham, MD: Lexington Books.

Speight, A. (2015) 'Philosophy of literature in the nineteenth century,' in N. Caroll and J. Gibson (eds), *Routledge Companion to Philosophy of Literature*, London: Routledge, 30–9.

Stokes, P. (2009) *Kierkegaard's mirrors: Interest, self and moral vision*, London: Palgrave Macmillan

Strelis, A. (2013) 'The intimacy between reason and emotion: Kierkegaard's "simultaneity of factors",' *Res Philosophica*, 90, no. 4: 461–80.

Tietjen, M. A. (2013) *Kierkegaard, communication, and virtue: Authorship as edification*, Bloomington, IN: Indiana University Press.

Walsh, S. (1994) *Living poetically: Kierkegaard's existential aesthetics*, University Park, PA: Penn State Press.

Zuckert, R. (2010) 'The aesthetics of Schelling and Hegel,' in D. Moyar (ed), *The Routledge Companion to Nineteenth Century Philosophy*, London: Routledge, 165–93.

Further reading

Aumann, A. (2018) *Art and selfhood: A Kierkegaardian account*, Landham, MD: Lexington Books.
  This work, which builds on the present chapter, brings Kierkegaard's views into dialogue with contemporary philosophical discussions about the value of art and the nature of art appreciation.

Jothen, P. (2014) *Kierkegaard, aesthetics, and selfhood: The art of subjectivity*, Farnham: Ashgate.
  This text presents Kierkegaard's views on aesthetics through the lens of his religious and especially his Christian commitments.

Pattison, G. (1992) *Kierkegaard: The aesthetic and the religious: From the magic theatre to the crucifixion of the image*, London: Palgrave Macmillan.
  A seminal analysis of Kierkegaard's views on art that helpfully situates them against the historical backdrop of Romantic and Idealist aesthetics.

Söderquist, A. S. (2016) *Kierkegaard on dialogical education: Vulnerable freedom*, Lanham, MD: Lexington Books.
  This monograph traces the role art plays for Kierkegaard in encouraging the exercise of our freedom, placing special emphasis on the power of stories to help us shape ourselves.

Walsh, S. (1994) *Living poetically: Kierkegaard's existential aesthetics*, University Park, PA: Penn State Press.
  An influential study of the aesthetic dimensions of selfhood in Kierkegaard's writings, in particular exploring the sense in which identity-formation is poetic for Kierkegaard.

Westfall, J. (2007) *The Kierkegaardian author: Authorship and performance in Kierkegaard's literary and dramatic criticism*, Berlin: Walter de Gruyter.
  This book unpacks Kierkegaard's aesthetics by providing detailed commentaries on his often-neglected works of literary and dramatic criticism.

15
DELEUZE ON KIERKEGAARD

Andrew Jampol-Petzinger

Introduction

In this chapter I want to present three ways in which the French philosopher Gilles Deleuze reads Kierkegaard as what I am calling an 'aesthetic' philosopher, with the intention of ultimately justifying the appropriateness of this nomination. Deleuze, who may be known as a devoutly atheistic philosopher in the manner of Nietzsche, may seem a strange pairing for Kierkegaard. And yet, if one looks through his work, one finds that Kierkegaard's name comes up quite frequently and, in particular, that there is a kind of Kierkegaardian influence at play in the normative and existential themes of the French philosopher's work. A shared focus that exists for Kierkegaard and Deleuze on the topics of concreteness, the limits of rationality, and the problem of philosophical speech places these two well within one another's company in terms of their general philosophical orientation. I want to suggest, in what follows, that Deleuze's attribution of a kind of aesthetic character to Kierkegaard's thought is ultimately justified, but perhaps not quite in the sense that has traditionally been suggested: I would like to follow an interesting line of interpretation that Deleuze presents, to the effect that the theological dimension of Kierkegaard's work does not so much conceal as manifest a kind of undecidable tendency between the religious domain and the aesthetic domain.[1] Where Deleuze chooses to speak of the creative, generative power of a fundamentally aesthetic, atheistic Nature, Kierkegaard chooses to speak of an 'absolutely different' God who solicits the powers of change and becoming in the person of faith, and invites her to a kind of self-abnegating gratitude for the fortuitousness of existence. I want to suggest that, from a certain perspective, the difference between a religious and an aesthetic outlook may ultimately be undecidable and possibly irrelevant, once one expands past the domains of traditional metaphysics. And, following Deleuze, I want to suggest that Kierkegaard's thought may bear the imprint of this undecidability, so that any attempt at a rigorous distinction between the two does little more than account for a difference of tone, rather than an irreconcilable difference of approach between the two conceptions of normativity and philosophical authorship. This may seem strange to the general reader, on account of the way in which Kierkegaard himself distinguishes between a so-called aesthetic domain and a religious domain, where the latter is seen as markedly superior to the former. But a closer consideration of the nature of aesthetics and of the most crucial elements of the religious will show that they share important similarities in their essential features.

I've chosen three dimensions of Deleuze's reading of Kierkegaard to look at in terms of this aesthetic character. First, I look at Deleuze's suspicion of the supernatural, in order to see why the vocabulary of religious, non-aesthetic existence proves superfluous on Deleuze's account, given the inadequacy of Kierkegaard's understanding of nature and aesthetics in his pseudonymous works. After this, I will discuss Kierkegaard's form of authorship and follow Deleuze's (1994: 5) understanding of Kierkegaard as a 'philosoph[er] of the future' relying upon a certain aesthetic sensibility of his reader for his philosophical authorship. Finally, I will argue for a kind of aestheticism intrinsic to the mode of being that Kierkegaard counts as distinctively religious and involving the supra-ethical principles of religious faith; and reciprocally, I will argue that a Kierkegaardian conception of faith is invaluable to a Deleuzian notion of art. We will see that it is not only informative to understand Kierkegaard's Christianity from the perspective of a certain aestheticism, but also useful to understand art from the perspective of Kierkegaardian belief.

Nature and supernature

To introduce the aesthetic principles of Kierkegaard's work, it will first be helpful to establish some common ground between Kierkegaard and Deleuze. One of the most interesting points of coincidence between these philosophers has to do with the concept of repetition, which plays an outsized role in their work given the relative rareness of this topic in the preceding history of philosophy. Deleuze, for his part, discusses the concept of repetition extensively, often in reference to Kierkegaard, in his early lectures *What is Grounding?*, as well as in his 1968 *Difference and Repetition* and *The Logic of Sense* (cf. Deleuze 2015: 72–8; 1994: 5–11; 1990: 300–1). Kierkegaard, of course, discusses the concept of repetition in his pseudonymous book *Repetition*, as well as in the long set of notes written in reply to the critic J. L. Heiberg (R, 299–319/SKS 15, 63–83), although references to the concept are otherwise scattered throughout his early pseudonymous works (e.g., CA, 17–9/SKS 4, 324–7; CUP 1, 284–5/SKS 7, 259–60; JC, 171–2/SKS 15, 58).[2] Part of the importance of this concept, for both philosophers, has to do with a difference highlighted between certain rationalistic approximations of the concept of repetition, in which repetition amounts to little more than a recurrence of some previously existing object or identity now returned, and a properly 'spiritual' or true repetition, which coincides with the highest aspirations of the existing individual, and involves a movement towards the absolute novelty and unpredictability of the future (cf. R, 149/SKS 4, 25; Deleuze 1994: 24). In *Repetition*, Kierkegaard writes: 'When the Greeks said that all knowing is recollecting, they said that all existence [*Tilværelsen*], which is, has been; when one says that life is a repetition, one says: actuality [*Tilværelsen*], which has been, now comes into existence [*bliver nu til*, or "becomes"]' (R, 149/SKS 4, 25). And in *The Concept of Anxiety*, he writes: '[T]ranscendence separates repetition from [one's] former existence by such a chasm that one can only figuratively say that the former and the latter relate themselves to each other as the totality of living creatures in the ocean relates itself to those in the air and to those upon the earth' (CA, 17/SKS 4, 324). In other words, for Kierkegaard repetition does not stand for an external repetition of what has already been, but instead the emergence of an absolute novelty that corresponds to a movement or change in the repeating individual. Deleuze (1994: 24), for his part, similarly separates repetition into two types:

> The first repetition is repetition of the Same, explained by the identity of the concept or representation; the second includes difference, and includes itself in the alterity of the Idea, in the heterogeneity of an 'a-presentation.' One is negative occurring by

default in the concept; the other is affirmative, occurring by excess in the Idea. One is conjectural, the other categorical. One is static, the other dynamic. One is repetition in the effect, the other in the cause. One is extensive, the other intensive. One is ordinary, the other distinctive and singular.

In this paragraph, Deleuze distinguishes between repetition understood as the mere recurrence of an identical object over time, and a repetition that is instead a function of the individuality of the object and which therefore exempts it from being understood conceptually or from having a 'type' that can recur across time. True repetition, on Deleuze's account, is intrinsic to the absolute singularity of an object – there is a repetition 'in place,' so to speak – on account of the way in which certain objects or ways of being escape both the vanishing of non-being as well as the generality of a shareable identity. Consequently, repetition is the proper sort of existence belonging to what is undeniably distinct without for that matter vanishing into nothingness.

Yet speaking of Kierkegaard's very attractive conception of repetition, Deleuze (1994: 11) is sceptical of the adequacy of his framework for representing its true nature:

> Where will [repetition] be better protected against generalities, against mediation? Is repetition supernatural, to the extent that it is over and above the laws of nature? Or is it rather the most natural will of Nature in itself and willing itself as *Physis*, because Nature is by itself superior to its own kingdoms and its own laws? Has Kierkegaard not mixed all kinds of things together in his condemnation of 'aesthetic' repetition: a pseudo-repetition attributable to general laws of nature and a true repetition in nature itself; a pathological repetition of the passions and a repetition in art and the work of art?

Here Deleuze's claim is not that Kierkegaard fails to oppose the limited conception of repetition which consists in the mere repetition of sensible habit (that is to say, one that occurs merely as a matter of our organic tendency to acquire patterns of behaviour and reaction), or which understands repetition as a mere function of nature as governed by the universality of law. Rather, Deleuze's argument is that Kierkegaard elides or confuses two *distinct* frameworks within the terms 'aesthetic' and 'natural,' so that the superiority of a Natural world governed essentially by principles of aesthetic or gratuitous creation is overlooked. In other words, when Kierkegaard insists upon the necessity of a supra-aesthetic or a supra-natural conception of repetition, he unnecessarily invokes the conceptuality of the supernatural domain, when it would have been, if not necessary, certainly more informative to insist upon the *essentially* natural and *essentially* aesthetic character of this conception of repetition. And why is this domain a distinctively natural and aesthetic domain of repetition? It is distinctively natural and aesthetic because, on Deleuze's account, both nature in its purest form and art in its highest ideal are fundamentally matters of *singularity* or *novelty* beyond the domain of familiarity. Speaking of the work of art, for example, he writes that all apparent, phenomenal, and identical repetition should be known as little more than an 'effect' of deeper, more unknowable repetition:

> Perhaps this repetition at the level of external conduct echoes, for its own part, a more secret vibration which animates it, a more profound, internal repetition within the singular. This is the apparent paradox of festivals: [t]hey do not add a second and a third time to the first but carry the first time to the 'nth' power. . . . Monet's first water lily which repeats all the others. . . . The repetition of the work of art is like a singularity

without concept, and it is not by chance that a poem must be learned by heart. The head is the organ of exchange, but the heart is the amorous organ of repetition. (It is true that repetition also concerns the head, but precisely because it is its terror or paradox).

(Deleuze 1994: 1–2)[3]

Here the absolute singularity of the work of art – rather than invoking the mere organic reactivity of the passions or the mundanity of mere habit (cf. R, 170/SKS 4, 44; CA, 149/SKS 4, 448) – involves a kind of novelty or resonance that links it to the singularity of all other works of art and even the singularity of natural objects in their aesthetic character, 'repeating them in advance' through its very novelty.

On the natural side of the equation, Deleuze invokes a point that he draws from his contemporary Pierre Klossowski, who writes in his *Sade, My Neighbor* of Nature being 'subject to her own laws' in everyday experience, but itself a lawless creative and destructive force in its proper existence. For Klossowski, nature is generative of forms and entities that tend to persist in their identities – obeying rules and principles intrinsic to their character and propagating themselves with a regularity that takes the form of law. A human being, for example, will tend to follow certain apparent laws of behaviour, bringing about a persistence of her own identity as well as a persistence of the human species more generally through propagation. Nature in itself, on the other hand, is condemned to perennially suffer these law-governed forms, remounting to its own primordial power only through whole cloth destruction of such forms in order to make space for the novel creation which is its proper expression. Nature, consequently, is perennially re-captured by the diverse forms and modes that it creates, despite its own tendency towards a kind of gratuitous and unforeseeable creation that gives nature a kind of aesthetic identity. In this sense Nature in its proper form – beyond the empirical, regular modes in which it appears – is essentially superior to law, creative out of pure excessiveness and in that sense a repetitive power like the artwork that repeats through singularity rather than through generality (Klossowski 1991: 84–7).[4]

Deleuze's view is that the Kierkegaardian conception of nature, as well as art, as ultimately governed by a regularity that the religious domain is supposed to exceed, is misguided. When Kierkegaard denounces art and nature in this sense – that is, when he distinguishes sharply between the regularity of the material, phenomenal world and a kind of spiritual repetition (R, 306/SKS 15, 72) – Deleuze's claim is that Kierkegaard confuses *empirical* nature for Nature as it exists in itself, and confuses pathological repetition in an aesthetic personality for the irreducibility of the work of art. Consequently, Kierkegaard's search for a supernatural order beyond the domains of habit and morality fails to recognize both Nature as a creative and destructive force sharing all the characteristics of an affirmative, *aesthetic* process of production, and art as an essentially uncategorizable, disruptive phenomenon.

In this sense, when Deleuze criticizes Kierkegaard for his supernatural orientation towards repetition, it is not so much to say that Kierkegaard invokes something *other* than aesthetic and natural repetition – rather it is in order to point out that Kierkegaard's invocation of a supernatural repetition relies upon a vocabulary of what is supposed to exceed the empirical natural world and pathological aestheticism, without justifying the particular choice of the vocabulary as *un*-natural and *non*-aesthetic. Is what exceeds the regularity of nature 'super-natural,' Deleuze asks, or is it 'hyper-natural' (a term he does not use) in its excessiveness (as much as in its excessiveness with respect to the moral world)? I claim, following Deleuze, that an alternative account of the sensuous domain that follows upon the regularity of nature and habit entails the possibility of a rigorously aesthetic reading of the religious domain. Having discovered and thematized what I am calling the 'hypernatural' aesthetic world of repetition, we are invited to consider its similarity to the supposedly non-aesthetic, non-natural, spiritual domain. As Deleuze (1994: 96) writes, 'we have too often been invited to judge the atheist from the viewpoint of the belief or the faith that we suppose still drives him ... not to be tempted to the inverse operation – to judge the believer by the violent atheist by which he is inhabited.'

The logic of sense: philosophy as art

To the proposal of an alternate terminology and conceptuality for thinking about Kierkegaard's religious domain, Deleuze adds a second aesthetic element to his interpretation of the former's work: a recognition of a fundamentally *sensuous* character of Kierkegaard's mode of authorship. Here the primary point of reference for Deleuze's (1994: 8) thinking is his way of understanding works of art in general:

> Kierkegaard and Nietzsche are among those who bring to philosophy new means of expression. . . . In all their work, *movement* is at issue. Their objection to Hegel is that he does not go beyond false movement – in other words, the abstract logical movement of 'mediation.' They want to put metaphysics in motion, in action. They want to make it act, and make it carry out immediate acts. It is not enough, therefore, for them to propose a new representation of movement; representation is already mediation. Rather, it is a question of producing within the work a movement capable of affecting the mind outside of all representation; it is a question of making movement itself a work, without interposition; of substituting direct signs for mediate representations; of inventing vibrations, rotations, whirlings, gravitations, dances or leaps which directly touch the mind.

Deleuze (1994: 9) continues: 'When Kierkegaard explains that the knight of faith so resembles a bourgeois in his Sunday best as to be capable of being mistaken for one, this philosophical instruction must be taken as the remark of a director showing how the knight of faith should be *played*.' In other words, as with the function of the work of art to affect the reader directly, the specific 'casting' or choreographing of Kierkegaard's work produces a set of signs or sensible phenomena, ultimately referring themselves to the aesthetic sensibility of the reader for their interpretation.[5] In Kierkegaard's composition of the multiple prologues to *Fear and Trembling*, for example, a movement of the eye (one could imagine this specifically as a shot in a storyboard) modifies the entire character and content of the depiction; and it does so in a way that is not reducible to a theoretical description of the differences between the one version and the other.[6]

In *The Logic of Sense*, Deleuze describes this manner of 'showing' or pointing towards existence as a means of undermining abstruse reasoning, which Kierkegaard does in his illustrations of concrete human situations, as 'humour'; and it is unsurprising that Kierkegaard appears here as a representative of the 'humorous' mode of philosophical authorship. Here, Deleuze distinguishes between what he calls an 'ironic' art of ascent (best represented by Socrates, whose irony moves the reader from the particularity of the case in question towards the transcendent principles on which it is supposed to depend), and the 'humorous' art of descent, according to which a philosopher moves from abstract principles of philosophical thought *back down* towards the phenomena of material existence that bypass or undercut the authority of abstract thought. Describing Diogenes the Cynic as such a humorous philosopher, Deleuze (1990: 135) writes:

> Every time we will be asked about signifieds such as 'what is Beauty, Justice, Man?' we will respond by designating a body, by indicating an object which can be imitated or even consumed, and by delivering, if necessary, a blow of the staff. . . . Diogenes the Cynic answers Plato's definition of man as a biped and featherless animal by bringing forth a plucked fowl. And to the person who asks 'what is philosophy?' Diogenes responds by carrying about a cod at the end of a string.

What does it mean, in this case, to describe Diogenes as a representative of the 'humorous' mode of philosophizing? It means that for Diogenes, the method of showing – of pointing towards reality and of using the irreducibility of fact to undermine the abstraction of reflection – counts as a valid mode of philosophizing, and not one ultimately just translatable back into philosophical argumentation. When, for example, the Stoic philosopher responds to a student who asks 'what is Beauty?' with a blow from his staff, the blow is not supposed to be interpreted as a way of *saying* that 'we ought to focus on existence here and now' in a different manner. Rather the blow of the staff is itself a kind of argument, or – to put it otherwise – it asserts a different sort of claim upon the interlocutor than the register of the question 'what is Justice?' so that referring to the concreteness of reality is necessary to establish its priority. In some of his earliest published comments on Kierkegaard, Deleuze (2015: 62–3) writes that in Socrates 'it is life which must submit itself to thought, it is reasonable, philosophical life [but] on the contrary, in Kierkegaard life cannot deny itself, cannot submit itself to the order of reason. . . . Thenceforth it is thought which submits itself to the categories of life.' In other words, for Deleuze, Kierkegaard's philosophical writing is not intended to interact with one's intellectual apprehension so as to demonstrate the validity or viability of his viewpoint. Rather, it is intended in the manner of a work of art: it directly affects the reader as if it were an object of concrete experience, undermining our abstract reflection and compelling our personal reaction to the reality that is expressed there.

Kierkegaard's own similarities to Diogenes – to whom he refers at the opening of *Repetition* – in this respect seem to go without saying. Kierkegaard's multiple solicitations of the reader in his individuality, his use of pseudonyms that elicit a response to their type rather than to the mere content of what they say, and even the assertive way he uses 'I' in order to bypass the impersonality of philosophical thought (JP 6, 177/SKS 22, 136) – all this attests to the way Kierkegaard's authorship undercuts or circumnavigates the rationalistic medium of traditional philosophical reflection. It is this tendency to point towards or 'monstrate' existence that places Kierkegaard within what Deleuze calls a theatrical, 'artistic' mode of philosophizing: rather than simply illustrating or dramatizing philosophical points, Kierkegaard produces a sensible content that affects the reader directly, through a kind of higher sensibility or immediacy. This is what Deleuze means by Kierkegaard's 'theater of humor and of faith': the aesthetic character of the latter's work undercuts the reflective function of its content in order to affect the reader directly. For Deleuze, Kierkegaard's work – even in his signed writings – can be considered aesthetic in the broad sense of eliciting such a sensible encounter with the reader, and bringing about its effects in this way, rather than merely invoking the intermediary of an illustration having a philosophical content.[7]

Faith as performance: the aesthetics of existence

Finally, in addition to the aesthetic elements I have already highlighted here, there is the closeness, on Deleuze's account, of Kierkegaard's ideal of religious belief to a kind of *theatrical* or *aesthetic* self-perception. In *The Logic of Sense* Deleuze speaks, in a different context, of the ethical ideal of Stoicism in terms of its similarity to a kind of acting, in that the sage, living under the influence of necessity and material causes, nonetheless distinguishes himself by being capable of duplicating the concrete fact of what happens in a kind of incorporeal will. On Deleuze's account, material conditions that follow a certain kind of causal necessity are always doubled by a kind of immaterial, discursive reflection of that materiality, so that for every concrete, specific set of facts on the material level there is another, related, conceptual schema he calls the 'event' of this materiality. So while it may be the inexorable sequence of physical causes that brings about a specific clash of human bodies and swords, 'fighting a war' – the indeterminate, non-specific sense of what is going on – occurs at the level of an incorporeal event. Deleuze's reflection on the nature of the Stoic sage in this case is that although he recognizes the set of causes that necessitate the concrete state of affairs that he lives, nonetheless – at the immaterial level – he identifies with this necessitated state of affairs through a will which takes the corresponding event as its object. In this sense, the inexorable flow of effects that makes one's life a forgone conclusion in one domain, is experienced and lived on a personal level as a kind of task or destiny, so that rather than alienating the individual from her or his life, what happens is instead profoundly appropriated in that individual's will. The behaviour of the sage is not unlike that of an actor: instead of mimicking or pretending to behave in a certain manner that is not his own, a good actor takes the given or necessitated sequence of events that he can discern and identifies himself with this behaviour at an intended moment in time. The actor finds his freedom not in changing or controlling the script of what happens, but rather in appropriating or making his own the sequence of behaviours that are ineluctably given. Thus the ethical ideal of the Stoic sage can itself be understood as a kind of existential acting. Neither controlling the events of his life (as if he were free in his behaviour and depended upon nothing), nor passively carrying out the inexorable set of events, the sage identifies with the set of events that have been given to him to perform; it is his distinction to carry this out as his *own* particular life.

And there are numerous places in Deleuze's work where the peculiar 'performative' conception of life – one which nearly eliminates the distinction between ethics and aesthetics, to the extent that the highest practical task given to an individual is to perform or act out the story given to her – is presented as an appropriate schema for understanding the Kierkegaardian conception of faith as an ideal of non-despair and a kind of affirmation of one's dependent existence.[8] In *A Thousand Plateaus*, for example, Kierkegaard's tax-collecting knight of faith is presented as a kind of ideal of this life-affirmative subject-type – one who inhabits so perfectly the life or role that has been given to him that the gap between the role and the identity he assumes is reduced virtually to zero. Deleuze (1987: 279; 1990: 152) describes the knight's way of behaving as a kind of 'being . . . everybody' (*tout le monde*, meaning literally 'the whole world'), which is to say that the knight of faith learns an impersonal appreciation for his life that is proper to the Stoic ideal. The knight of faith, like the Stoic sage, identifies so fully with the set of events that are given to him in his everyday life that even the smallest fact contains all the beauty of a work of art. Like the protagonists of Virginia Woolf's *Mrs. Dalloway* or James Joyce's *Ulysses*, nothing more than a day in the life of an unremarkable individual is necessary in order to find – as Deleuze (1990: 152) puts it – 'the splendor of the "they" (*l'on*) . . . or of the fourth person,' by which he means the aestheticization of the small life that is given to one. In this sense, faith – which seems to enable the individual to inhabit more deeply, and even more joyfully, the finite world that had been renounced in ethical subjectivity – functions as a kind of aesthetic inhabitation or aestheticization of the ineluctable life that has been given to oneself (on the knight as 'heir to the finite,' see FT, 40–1, 50/SKS 4, 135, 144).

This dimension of aesthetics in religious faith is reduplicated, furthermore, on Deleuze's account, in the value of religious vocabulary for a comprehension of aesthetic phenomena themselves. In his reflections on film (in his books *Cinema I* and *II*), in his discussions of painting and literature in *What Is Philosophy?*, and in his literary reflections in *A Thousand Plateaus*, Deleuze invokes the Kierkegaardian concept of faith in order to understand something essential about specifically modern aesthetic sensibility. But what is it about modern art that so immediately invokes a religious belief, and a kind of religious immediacy for Deleuze?

Deleuze's (1989: 168; see also 1990: 260) claim is that it is the fundamental preoccupation of modern art to present the necessity of a 'faithful' kind of engagement with a world become impossible, intolerable, or otherwise unliveable. In Deleuze's *Cinema* books, for example, he describes the condition of film-making following World War II, in which the primary concern of the protagonists presented is not to accomplish a particular task or overcome some narrative obstacle, but rather to orient themselves in a familiar but now uninhabitable world for which they no longer have appropriate prepared reactions. Here a market no longer attended, a bombed-out square, a school that has been turned into a hospital, even the very insanity of a world that is supposed to exist normally after the catastrophe of war, stages the dispossession of the individual of her rational or prescriptive capacity to engage with the surrounding world. Deleuze's observation, in this connection, is that the fundamental interest of modern cinema is to present the challenge of a subjectivity forced back upon alternative modes of engagement or encounter with what one no longer has a rational capacity for engaging. In Roberto Rossellini's *Europe '51*, for example, the conflict of the film centres upon the protagonist's life after the senseless death of her son. The familiar coordinates of her world having disappeared, she is now presented in her capacity to see the terrible mundanity and suffering that surrounds her. Like a newly born saint, she wanders the landscape in a mode of compassionate urgency, struggling to realize an inhabitable world through her selfless encounters with others. Similarly, in *Stromboli, Land of God*, the protagonist Karin is confronted by dual impossibilities that her rational account is forced to sketch: she can neither leave the tiny island that has become her home after the war, nor can she continue to live there surrounded by the brutality of the island. Fleeing across Stromboli's volcanic terrain, she collapses in despair and cries out, in the final shot of the film, for God to save her.

This elimination or forced abdication of a predictable and organized response to the world (the blockage of a way forward in a familiar direction) solicits a novel faculty of 'belief,' for which the task of living *in* the impossible situation is presented for itself. Just as Abraham walks towards the place where he will sacrifice Isaac while sustaining an impossible view on the world – 'I will sacrifice Isaac; I will keep Isaac' – so here is the abdication of the understanding in relation to the world an opportunity for the kind of faithful, affirmative engagement that Abraham manifests, where the intellectually impossible is held in place for the sake of an emergence of an unknown possibility (FT, 58/SKS 4, 152–3).

Such a conception of film as essentially staging a kind of faithful engagement with the world is not the only invocation of this concept, however. Speaking of Francis Bacon's form of engagement, as a creating artist, with the world around him, Deleuze (2003: 61-2; Sylvester 1987: 91) describes a faithful or optimistic orientation towards the world as characteristic of non-figurative art more generally:

> Bacon says that he himself is cerebrally pessimistic; that is, he can scarcely see anything *but* horrors to paint, the horrors of the world. But he is nervously optimistic, because visible figuration is secondary in painting, and will have less and less importance. . . . But why is it an act of vital faith to choose 'the scream more than the horror,' the

violence of sensation more than the violence of the spectacle? The invisible forces, the powers of the future – are they not already upon us, and much more insurmountable than the worst spectacle and even the worst pain? Yes, in a certain sense. . . . But in another sense, no. When, like the wrestler, the visible body confronts the powers of the invisible, it gives them no other visibility than its own. It is within this visibility that the body actively struggles, affirming the possibility of triumphing. . . . It is as if combat had now become possible.

This emphasis on the 'possible,' and the abdication of the intellectually known horrors in favour of a kind of struggling engagement with the world, and particularly the refusal of despair that is itself endemic to artistic production corresponds to a kind of Kierkegaardian element intrinsic to modern art.[9] What we see here is a conception of art as a form of engaged struggle, beyond the domain of intellectual apprehension, for the conquest of a possibility or the appearance of an unexpected novelty. In this, modern art manifests something of the undecidability I am claiming exists between the religious and aesthetic domains. Here it is not just that the knight of faith, living his everyday life in the mode of a tax collector, is engaged in all the struggles of the actor to affirm and play his role with perfect accuracy. We also see that the aesthetic character of religious faith is carried over in the faith of aesthetic creation, where the making of art is fundamentally equated with an act of imagining new possibilities of life in an otherwise inhospitable world – with a kind of struggle against despair, and belief in the possibilities of the future. The life of the artist, as much as that of the religious person, invokes all the optimism of a faith, if only in the generativity and possibility of the unknown to bring forth new forms of existence.

Conclusion

Deleuze's work has much to say about the importance of Kierkegaard for his own conception of art. But Deleuze also seeks to introduce, into an understanding of Kierkegaard, something of the gratuitousness of aesthetic creation, and to ask after the essentially aesthetic core of religious ways of being and even the concepts associated with religious discourse. From this, what we see is that when these philosophers move beyond the domain of rational accounting and seek to disclose the forces beyond empirical existence, we find a kind of ambiguity between the domains of art and religion. And for both thinkers, it is then that the rejuvenation of life before the horrors of an intolerable world becomes possible.

Related topics

'Imagination and belief,' Eleanor Helms; 'Kierkegaard on the value of art: an indirect method of communication,' Antony Aumann; 'Kierkegaard on nature and natural beauty,' Anthony Rudd.

Notes

1 For some of the more central accounts of Kierkegaard as a fundamentally 'aesthetic' thinker, see Pattison (2014); Mackey (1971); and Walsh (1994).
2 For an overview of the concept of repetition in Kierkegaard, see Kemp (2015); Crites (1993); and Eriksen (2000). The latter draws some very Deleuzian conclusions about the centrality of becoming for this concept.
3 Deleuze here is likely invoking Kierkegaard in affirming that repetition is an affair of 'the head . . . precisely because it is its terror or paradox,' which paraphrases *Philosophical Fragments*: 'The paradox is the passion of thought' (PF, 79/SKS 4, 242).

4 Both Klossowski (2007: 11) and Deleuze (1990: 260–3) draw heavily upon Nietzsche as supposing the essence of the Natural world to be very nearly aesthetic in character. See for example Nietzsche (2009: 36): 'The *work of art* and the *individual* is a *repetition* of the *primal process* in which the world came into being, so to speak, a ripple within the wave.'
5 In *Proust and Signs*, Deleuze (2000: 41, 11) describes art in profoundly Kierkegaardian terms, as involving signs of 'absolute and ultimate Difference' and 'transmit[ting] a kind of imperative [to interpret].' Kierkegaard refers to God as the 'absolutely different' at PF, 44/SKS 4, 249.
6 In *A Thousand Plateaus*, Deleuze and Guattari (1987: 281) describes Kierkegaard as 'acting astonishingly like a precursor to cinema.' And he calls Kierkegaard 'a director before his time' in *Difference and Repetition* (Deleuze 1994: 8).
7 Kierkegaard describes all his pseudonymous writings, with the exception of those by Anti-Climacus and H. H., as aesthetic (cf. SUD, xxii; JP 6, 186/SKS 22, 169).
8 On the concept of faith as a kind of acceptance and affirmation of dependency see, for example, Podmore (2011). On the (lack of) distinction between the ethical and the aesthetic in Deleuze, see Surin (2011).
9 See Deleuze's and Guattari (1994: 177) description, in *What is Philosophy?*, of art as a matter of 'the possible as aesthetic category ("the possible or I shall suffocate"),' where he paraphrases Kierkegaard's comments in *The Sickness unto Death*: 'When someone faints, we call for water, eau de Cologne, smelling salts; but when someone wants to despair, then the word is: Get possibility, get possibility, possibility is the only salvation' (SUD, 38–9/SKS 11, 154).

References

Crites, S. (1993) '"The blissful security of the moment": Recollection, repetition, and eternal recurrence,' in R. L. Perkins (ed), *International Kierkegaard Commentary*, vol. 6 (*Fear and Trembling* and *Repetition*), Macon, GA: Mercer University Press.
Deleuze, G. (2015) *What is grounding?* A. Kleinherenbrink (trans), Grand Rapids, MI: &&& Publishing.
Deleuze, G. (2003) *Francis Bacon: The logic of sensation*, D. W. Smith (trans), Minneapolis, MN: University of Minnesota Press.
Deleuze, G. (2000) *Proust and signs: The complete text*, R. Howard (trans), Minneapolis, MN: University of Minnesota Press.
Deleuze, G. (1994) *Difference and repetition*, P. Patton (trans), New York: Columbia University Press.
Deleuze, G. (1990) *Logic of sense*, M. Lester (trans), New York: Columbia University Press.
Deleuze, G. (1989) *Cinema II: The time-image*, H. Tomlinson and R. Galeta (trans), Minneapolis, MN: University of Minnesota Press.
Deleuze, G. and Guattari, F. (1994) *What is philosophy?* H. Tomlinson and G. Burchell (trans), New York: Columbia University Press.
Deleuze, G. and Guattari, F. (1987) *A thousand plateaus*, B. Massumi (trans), Minneapolis, MN: University of Minnesota Press.
Eriksen, N. (2000) *Kierkegaard's category of repetition: A reconstruction*, Berlin: Walter de Gruyter.
Kemp, R. (2015) 'Repetition,' in S. M. Emmanuel, W. McDonald, and J. Stewart (eds), *Kierkegaard Research: Sources Reception and Resources*, vol. 15 (*Kierkegaard's Concepts*), tome 5, Farnham: Ashgate.
Klossowski, P. (2007) *Such a deathly desire*, R. Ford (trans), New York: State University of New York Press.
Klossowski, P. (1991) *Sade, my neighbor*, A. Lingis (trans), Evanston, IL: Northwestern University Press.
Mackey, L. (1971) *Kierkegaard: A kind of poet*, Philadelphia: University of Pennsylvania Press.
Nietzsche, F. (2009) *Writings from the early notebooks*, R. Geuss and A. Nehamas (eds), Cambridge: Cambridge University Press.
Pattison, G. (2014) *Kierkegaard: The aesthetic and the religious*, London: Palgrave Macmillan.
Podmore, S. (2011) *Kierkegaard and the self before god: Anatomy of the abyss*, Bloomington, IN: Indiana University Press.
Surin, K. (2011) '"Existing not as a subject but as a work of art": The task of ethics or aesthetics?' in N. Jun and D. Smith (eds), *Deleuze and Ethics*, Edinburgh: Edinburgh University Press.
Sylvester, D. (1987) *The brutality of fact: Interviews with Francis Bacon*, New York: Thames and Hudson.
Walsh, S. (1994) *Living poetically: Kierkegaard's existential aesthetics*, University Park, PA: Pennsylvania State University Press.

Further reading

Jampol-Petzinger, A. (2019) 'Faith and repetition in Kierkegaard and Deleuze,' *Philosophy Today*, 63, no. 3: forthcoming.
    This article broadly accounts for Deleuze and Kierkegaard's shared interest in the theme of repetition and argues for an interpretation of Kierkegaardian faith in terms of Deleuze's notion of repetition as a form of self-overcoming.

Justo, J. M. (2012) 'Gilles Deleuze: Kierkegaard's presence in his writings,' in J. Stewart (ed), *Kierkegaard Research: Sources, Reception and Resources*, vol. 11 (*Kierkegaard's Influence on Philosophy*), tome 2, Farnham: Ashgate.
    This article contains probably the most systematic account of Kierkegaard's appearance in Deleuze's work, including references to shifts in Deleuze's views over time.

Surin, K. (2011) '"Existing not as a subject but as a work of art": The task of ethics or aesthetics?' in N. Jun and D. Smith (eds), *Deleuze and Ethics*, Edinburgh: Edinburgh University Press.
    This chapter is a discussion of the difficult (if not undecidable) distinction between the concepts of aesthetic normativity and ethical normativity in Deleuze's work. It is central for an understanding of the aesthetic dimension of a non-rational ethical normativity.

Walsh, S. (1994) *Living poetically: Kierkegaard's existential aesthetics*, University Park, PA: Pennsylvania State University Press.
    This book is a classic aesthetic interpretation of Kierkegaard, describing his conceptions of religious and ethical living as fundamentally aesthetic in nature.

PART 4

Philosophy of religion and theology

16
KIERKEGAARD'S EXISTENTIAL MIMESIS

Wojciech Kaftanski

Introduction

My aim in this chapter is to introduce the reader to the complexity of mimesis in Kierkegaard by both emphasizing important features of the discussion present in the literature and contributing my own position on a particular aspect of the problem. After offering general technical insights into mimesis as a concept, I will present three interpretive lenses that have been used to analyze the phenomenon in question in Kierkegaard's work. I then argue for a particular conceptualization of mimesis I find in Kierkegaard that I term 'existential' and characterize it as indirect, intention-oriented, 'non-comparing,' and concerned with ends rather than means.

Conceptual and linguistic remarks

Identifying the different philosophical meanings attributed to mimesis is a challenging task. Since its conceptual formulation in the dialogues of Plato, it has carried different connotations depending on the period and context (Gebauer and Wulf 1995: 31; Potolsky 2006: 1–2). Furthermore, individual thinkers do not have one specific understanding of the word. No translation of the term into any vernacular is capable of exhausting its meaning. Mimesis can designate 'emulation, mimicry, dissimulation, doubling, theatricality, realism, identification, correspondence, depiction, verisimilitude, resemblance' (Potolsky 2006: 1). It qualifies the distinction between real and unreal, original and copy, true and untrue (Gebauer and Wulf 1995: 1–8).

In this chapter I will rely heavily on the conceptualization of mimesis offered in Stephen Halliwell's (2002) work. Of the five facets of mimesis Halliwell distinguishes, I choose three that are pertinent to the way mimesis is operative in Kierkegaard's writings. They are imitation, representation, and emulation. This threefold classification of mimesis does not restrict its meaning but rather emphasizes its complexity and broadness. Consequently, when I refer to mimesis in this chapter, I do not simply mean imitation, but rather use the word in a broad sense that encompasses the aforementioned three facets of mimesis.

The Danish language does not offer a direct translation of the Greek *mimesis* into a noun. The key Danish term in this context is *Efterfølgelse*, which is a translation of the Latin term *imitatio*, itself the translation of *mimesis*. *Efterfølgelse* is used for instance in the title of the Danish editions of Thomas à Kempis' *De imitatione Christi*. The famous Danish Dictionary *Ordbog over det danske*

Sprog (Society for Danish Language and Literature: 1918–1956) situates *Efterfølgelse* predominantly in the Christian tradition that portrays Christ as the ideal and example for imitation. The term can be literally translated into English as 'following after.' Its usage as the equivalent for 'imitation' decreased in modern Danish on account of other words such as *Efterligne*, which would be literally translated into English as 'likening after.' Kierkegaard uses both words, but it is *Efterfølgelse* that is most common in his work. The frequency of his employment of various mimetic terms, with special emphasis on *Efterfølgelse*, increases considerably in his output from 1848 to 1855. However, Kierkegaard's mimetic vocabulary is impressive and far wider than has been acknowledged in the literature.[1]

Scholarly approaches to mimesis

Kierkegaard's writings

I propose three categories of approaches to mimesis in Kierkegaard in the relevant literature, namely: Kierkegaard's writings, Kierkegaard's library, and contemporary debate. To the first category I ascribe Marie Mikulova-Thulstrup (1962), Bradley Rau Dewey (1968), and M. Jamie Ferreira (2001). These scholars, apart from breaking the ground for a systematic consideration of mimesis in Kierkegaard, tacitly established 'standards' for future discussion. Typical of their approach is a reading of mimesis as either tantamount to imitation, or of imitation as divorced from mimesis. Second, by focusing their research almost exclusively on Kierkegaard's production, they appraise the subject 'from the inside' as a homogeneous and continuous notion.

Mikulova-Thulstrup's (1962) reading of imitation in Kierkegaard presupposes a unity of Kierkegaard's thought, literary production, and personal development. For Mikulova-Thulstrup, on the one hand, Kierkegaard is either not interested in the phenomenon of imitation *per se*, or is somehow dismissive of it. It is predominantly the necessity of addressing the message embedded in the Gospels that leads Kierkegaard to engage with imitation. On the other hand, imitation, properly understood as the imitation of Christ, is a conceptual response to his consideration of mysticism and asceticism, both linked with the social and religious phenomenon of *imitatio Christi*. For Mikulova-Thulstrup, the imitation of Christ requires suffering, dying to the world, martyrdom, and grace. Although Christ is presented to us as a salvific figure of the Redeemer and the Pattern for Christian existence, we should ultimately only attempt to imitate the latter. Mikulova-Thulstrup (1962: 272) contests the universality of Christ's example, indicating that Christ cannot work as the Pattern for everyone, because that would imply merely undertaking 'external' imitation of Christ by non-Christians.

Such a complex and contentious approach sets a hermeneutical horizon of problems that subsequent thinkers will have to deal with. Among them are (1) the question whether the imitation of Christ is demanded from all Christians, and only Christians; (2) the problem of the relationship between Christ as the Pattern and Christ as the Redeemer; and (3) the relationship between grace and one's efforts in being or becoming a genuine Christian represented in self-denial and spiritual training.

Dewey (1968) holds that true Christian life is 'the life of imitation' that integrates the two dimensions of imitation in Kierkegaard: religious and ethical. The imitating self is the subjective and passionate *I* of the single individual that struggles with the offensiveness and attraction of Christ. Dewey sets imitation in Kierkegaard in contrast with two mistaken types of imitation: slavish and facsimile. On the one hand, genuine imitation defies 'slavish adherence to one set pattern' (Dewey 1968: 107) and guards against a facsimile imitation by securing a qualitative difference between Christ and the single individual. On the other, it disagrees with the idea of the imitating self as being 'propertyless,' a misreading of the ideal self Dewey attributes to ascetic imitation cultivated in the Middle Ages. Moreover, he finds the phrase 'the imitation of Christ' more pertinent to the medieval take on the problem and misrepresentative of imitation in Kierkegaard, and intentionally chooses 'following Christ' by focusing on the etymology of *Efterfølgelse*. Dewey's (1968: 145) appraisal of the imitation of Christ is less masochistic than Mikulova-Thulstrup's, as 'one is not commanded *per se* to suffer.'

Ferreira (2001) sees imitation in Kierkegaard primarily as ethical regulation. Both imitation and its object boil down to concrete acts in Kierkegaard. Addressing the relation between the Pattern and the Redeemer, she says that 'we are called on to ... follow the example [Christ] set in his human nature. Kierkegaard sees Christ as the prototype in meeting earthly needs' (Ferreira 2001: 82). Ferreira returns to mimesis in her reading of the imitation of Christ, but, for the most part, implicitly. She considers representation, emulation, and performance as important aspects of the imitation of Christ. By performing an ethical act, we make Christ present in the concrete here and now; therefore, what is being brought about is a particular understanding of ethics as loving the other, where the theological dimension of the imitation of Christ is read through the lens of ethics. In stark contrast to Mikulova-Thulstrup, the demand to imitate Christ is universal, and seeking suffering is morally wrong and should be avoided (Ferreira 2001: 36, 237).

Kierkegaard's library

Sylvia Walsh (1994; 2009), Joel D. S. Rasmussen (2005), and Christopher Barnet (2011) attempt to understand imitation in Kierkegaard by going beyond his oeuvre and considering the body of works found in Kierkegaard's own library.

Walsh (1994: 236) reads imitation in Kierkegaard in relation to Christ as the prototype, whose life 'has fully expressed the ideal' of human selfhood. She expands her initial Platonic understanding of the ideality of Christ (Walsh 1994: 237) by considering two complementary traditions, Christian and philosophical (Walsh 2009: 139–41). The former tradition has both biblical and patristic roots, and was especially developed in the Middle Ages by men such as Bernard of Clairvaux, Francis of Assisi, Thomas à Kempis, and Johannes Tauler; it emphasizes obedience, self-giving, and suffering in the Christian life. The philosophical take on the problem stems from the works of Kant and Schleiermacher, where Christ is understood as either a human universal or God-consciousness actualized in human perfection. In that vein, Christ is understood as the prototype for human existence in a more general sense, not as a direct prototype for individual human perfection. The imitation of Christ requires what Walsh calls 'the dialectic of inversion,' which is based on the idea that 'the essentially Christian is always the positive which is recognizable by the negative' (JP 4, 407/SKS 24, 458), and which emphasizes that our likeness to Christ means in fact our unlikeness. Moreover, the imitation of Christ is in fact unattainable for humans unless constantly aided by grace. Walsh attempts a systematic presentation of several types of suffering in relation to the imitation of Christ: non-Christian and Christian, innocent and guilty, Christ-like and human-like. These distinctions reinforce the conclusion that Christ is not an all-round pattern for imitation – as his experience of suffering is different from ours, and vice versa (Walsh 2009: 134–7).

Rasmussen (2005) locates imitation in Kierkegaard in a context of intellectual debates throughout the history of philosophy, theology, and art. Ultimately, imitation in Kierkegaard is understood as a synthesis of the three readings of mimesis: the classical and neo-classical, the medieval tradition of *imitatio Christi*, and the Romantic. It is the latter reading that Kierkegaard is most concerned with. On the one hand, Kierkegaard writes of the imitation of Christ in order to criticize the Romantic ideal of 'originality' and unconditional autonomy in creativity, which results in the non-concreteness and abstractness of human existence (aesthetic dimension), as well as contempt for the real world (ethical dimension) (Rasmussen 2005: 109, 122–4, 137–8). On the other hand, Kierkegaard subscribes to the Romantic downplaying of mimesis and criticizes a natural human propensity to imitation. The genuine type of mimesis has both poetic and religious dimensions, which he calls 'religious poetics,' and it requires the involvement of imagination in the imitation of Christ. However, genuine imitation is different from mere admiration, as it demands personal involvement and humility; it is also paradoxical and complemented by Christ's forgiveness.

Barnett (2011) sees imitation in Kierkegaard as both influenced by, and a development of, *imitatio Christi*. Kierkegaard's take on the imitation of Christ has its sources in the works of various Pietists, in movements such as Halle Pietism and *Brødresocietet*, and in *Erbauungsliteratur*. Although Barnett identifies both Christological and Socratic elements in the variety of pietistic resources, it is the kenotic nature of Christ that is the actual object of imitation for Kierkegaard. Although one may will to imitate Christ, the will suffers from human imperfection, and needs to be aided by Christ's grace.

Contemporary debate

William Schweiker (1990) and Patrick Stokes (2010) read imitation in Kierkegaard in relation to three types of resources: Kierkegaard's oeuvre, the texts of Kierkegaard's contemporaries, and the current philosophical debates on human selfhood and agency. Schweiker situates imitation in Kierkegaard in a broad current debate on mimesis. He engages Kierkegaard's thought in order to address contemporary criticisms of mimesis that render a human being subservient to abstract and 'totalizing' notions such as 'God,' 'ideal,' and 'original,' but also divorce an individual from something greater, and hence leave her feeling lost and abandoned. Mimesis should be understood in accordance with Paul Ricoeur's concept of 'figuration' that seeks to generate new meanings through interpretation rather than establishing a relation between original and copy. Schweiker (1990: 171; cf. 137) interprets mimesis in Kierkegaard as deeply qualifying human selfhood and 'a way of authentic existence.'

Explaining the mimetic dimension of human selfhood in Kierkegaard, Schweiker turns to the Bible but goes beyond the *imitatio Christi* of the New Testament to the *imago Dei* of the Old Testament. He notices that, on the one hand, the self has a mimetic task of the imitation of Christ; on the other, *imago Dei* indicates that the human self is *already* in an imitative relationship to the Ideal. The self is mimetic in Kierkegaard, as it 'always comes to be relative to another' (Schweiker 1990: 136), but it also needs to be understood in relation to a set of configurations of human existence, namely the stages of existence. So understood, a self is not a substance, nor a simple given, but a mimetic task of turning 'prefigured human existence [into] a concrete refiguration of life' (Schweiker 1990: 159).

Stokes (2010) investigates imitation in Kierkegaard in relation to the role it plays, together with imagination and reflection, in the process of becoming of the human self. Human selfhood is mimetic because it involves creating a vision of oneself in the future, a value-laden image of one's would-be self, and resembling that image in real life. The 'becoming' of the self is predicated on an individual's ability to (1) form an alternative self, which is the self one wants to become, and (2) exercise agency over that process of imagination and reflection. To be a genuine self, it has to come back to itself in that reflection from the realm of imagination. Although the formed image of the ideal self is imaginary, the change within the self is not simply imaginative, but is realized in the life of the actual individual. Moreover, imagination goes beyond what is given and actual, but it is limited by what is truly possible for the self and can be imitated in real life.

That act of 'translat[ing] our imaginative activity into action' (Stokes 2010: 81) is part of our daily practice and, understood as an obligation, has a moral dimension. It is the fact that we are personally invested in these images, what Stokes (2010: 90) calls 'being interested in' them, that makes these images into real possibilities for the self. Being interested in the ideal self, means locating in the vision itself 'an immediate, decisive phenomenal sense of self-involvement [that Stokes calls] the experience ... of being directly *claimed* by the imagined image' (Stokes 2010: 90). Inability or failure to recognize the demand of the image is assigned to the imitator-admirer who does not wish to be personally involved with the image-ideal. In contrast, the true imitator resembles and, hence, becomes what she admires.

The prototype

Plurality of mimetic models

One important facet of mimesis in Kierkegaard is imitation understood as that which interrelates an imitator and an object of imitation, which he calls a prototype. In that sense, imitation rendered as a movement that occurs between the imitator and the prototype represents what Gebauer and Wulf (1995: 61) characterize as acting according to a model.

Kierkegaard's understanding of imitation as a movement is dialectical. On the one hand, the imitator tries to conform their life to the prototype, which is the movement from the imitator towards the realm of the prototype. On the other hand, imitation is 'mak[ing] an attempt to place "the prototype" into actuality,' which is the movement from the ideal to the actual (JP 2, 335/SKS 24, 14). Accordingly, imitation is then a double-movement that 'engages' two spheres: the sphere of the imitator and the sphere of the prototype.

Scholars in the field have rightly pointed to the fact that Christ is the model for imitation in Kierkegaard. This is especially true in the context of Kierkegaard's deliberation on what it means to be a genuine Christian. However, upon close inspection of Kierkegaard's thought, we see that the uniqueness of Christ in that regard does not mean his singularity. In fact, the thinker often speaks of more than one prototype. He names particular persons as prototypes such as 'the tax collector,' 'the woman who was a sinner' (JP 2, 321/SKS 22, 244), Job (EUD, 109/SKS 5, 115–6), and Socrates (PV, 125/SKS 16, 105; cf. Kaftanski 2017). And he explicitly attributes the predicate of a prototype to entities such as 'the lily and the bird' (JFY, 186/SKS 16, 233–4). I call these imitative models 'external,' in the sense they are presented as external to the imitator.

If one understands 'prototype' in Kierkegaard in a broad sense as an ideal that an individual should internalize, one can also identify in his authorship what I call 'internal' imitative models. They are universal structures of the human self. Kierkegaard focuses on the tension between human ideality and actuality. Of Kierkegaard's internal mimetic models, I consider here 'the ideal picture of being a Christian.'

'The lily and the bird'

Kierkegaard's engagement with the first mimetic model comprises a considerable part of his signed writings. *The Lily of the Field and the Bird of the Air* discusses 'what it is to be a human being and what religiously is the requirement for being a human being' (WA, 3/SKS 11, 10), and suggests that the answer is to be found in 'the lily and the bird.' To be a genuine self, which in Kierkegaard means to become such a self, we need to learn silence, obedience, and joy. These three characteristics of genuine selfhood we learn from the lily and the bird, Christ's 'assistant teachers' (CD, 9/SKS 10, 21) appointed to that role by the Gospels (JFY, 186/SKS 16, 233–4).

Kierkegaard says: 'Pay attention to the lily and the bird; . . . If you live as the lily and the bird live, then you are a Christian,' and quickly adds, 'which the lily and the bird neither are nor can become' (CD, 9/SKS 10, 21).

This is a puzzling statement. First, if the general intention of the teacher is that the student becomes what the teacher is (EUD, 156/SKS 5, 156) and, second, if the lily and the bird are not Christian, and will never be, how can the 'lily and the bird' actually teach us how to live a genuine (Christian) life? Seen from another angle, the lily and the bird can teach us silence, as they are 'the silent teachers,' obedience, as they are 'the obedient teachers,' and joy as they are 'the joyful teachers of joy;' but can they teach us how to be Christians, or even human beings for that matter, if neither of these is what they are or can become?

The prototypical role of the lily and the bird in the context of Christian existence – which as such illustrates something important about Christ the prototype – is paradoxical and limited, for two reasons. First, they are not considered as *the* prototype by Kierkegaard, but as *a* (derivative) prototype whose role exhausts itself in pointing beyond itself. Second, as Pattison (1989: 385–6) suggests, the lily and the bird do not represent the realm of the human, but of nature; the former is characterized by freedom, while the essence of the latter is its outer form.

The key to understanding their roles of teacher and prototype is that, as was noted, the lily and the bird teach obedience by being 'obedience' themselves. This is, however, a peculiar type of obedience, as it is pre-reflective and involuntary. Being part of the natural world, they do not possess spirit, soul, or consciousness. Their obedience is therefore something that is part of their nature from which they cannot deviate. Their willingness to do X seems to be at odds with the human endeavour to will the same; the latter requires freedom.

A close analysis of Kierkegaard's treatment of the lily and the bird as a prototype of Christian existence exposes us to a certain hidden problem pertinent to his consideration of the imitation of Christ, and possibly to a more general philosophical problem inherent to *imitatio Christi*. The qualifications and limitations we ascribe to the lily and the bird in the context of their prototypical role for genuine human existence resemble those we ascribe to Christ. Just as the lily and the bird have a different nature from humans, so has Christ. Moreover, neither the lily and the bird, nor Christ, can become or be Christians. What seems to escape scholars who analyze the inherent conundrum of the imitation of Christ, such as what in Christ should be imitated (deeds, intentions, virtues), is the fact that Christ is *not* a Christian.

'The ideal picture of being a Christian'

The above-stated problem becomes more palpable if we agree to take imitation to signify representation, which is one of the key facets of mimesis. In that sense representation means both a process and a product of that process. It is valuable to use the example of painting to illustrate these two dimensions of representation. Representational painting is an act through which the painter aims to represent the object they paint. The painting is what we arrive at via the act of painting; it is then an effect or a product of imitation.

In representational painting we assume a correspondence between the painting and the painted object, the model. If a painter paints an object, let's say a fruit, the painting itself should have an essential reference to that object; this is so, because we assume a certain correspondence between the painting and the fruit. Hence, if the painting presented a person, we would question the effect of the painter's work. One cannot simply take a fruit as a model and paint a person. Returning to our problem of the imitation of Christ, if Christ is not a human being, let alone a Christian, we cannot presume that the imitation of Christ will make humans or Christians of us.

Kierkegaard identifies this problem in his work and tries to address it. He observes that the nature of Christ is different from the nature of every human being by noting the fact that Christ does not 'experience' the existential dimension of human becoming. Akin to the nature of the lily and the bird, his nature is predetermined, and, if that is the case, Christ should not be assumed as the model for Christian existence of becoming. Contrary to Christ who 'is,' humans 'become.' Kierkegaard attempts to solve this problem by introducing a new type of a prototype in his posthumously published *Armed Neutrality*, namely 'the ideal picture of being a Christian,' which he calls 'the middle terms':

> Jesus Christ, it is true, is himself the prototype [*Forbillede*] and will continue to be that, unchanged, until the end. But Christ is also much more than the prototype; he is the object of faith. In Holy Scripture he is presented chiefly as such, and this explains why he is presented more in being than in becoming, or actually is presented only in being, or why all the middle terms are lacking – something that everyone has indeed ascertained who, even though humbly and adoringly, has earnestly sought to order his own life according to his example.
>
> *(PV, 131/SKS 16, 113)*

The missing link in the equation of imitation is 'the middle terms,' which for Kierkegaard represent 'the ideal picture of being a Christian.' The picture is an internal model for imitation, a type of a prototype that satisfies the complexity of human being and becoming. Kierkegaard regards the picture as the most important part and task of his authorship (PV, 129/SKS 16, 111). 'The ideal picture of being a Christian' is presented in *Armed Neutrality* with the purpose of redefining the relationship 'between thinking Christianity and being a Christian' (PV, 130/SKS 16, 113). Its role is to draw attention to what has been abolished in religious reflection on the human condition, which is the decisive dialectic qualification of being a Christian – the fact that a human being never truly is, but is becoming.

The relation between the two, 'the ideal of being a Christian' and Christ, is complex. One does not exclude or complement the other, but they remain in tension. The ideal we find in Christ is complete and unchangeable, while 'the picture' is dynamic and open. '[T]he ideal picture of being a Christian [rendered] . . . in relation to Christ as the prototype. . . [is] a human interpretation' (PV, 132/SKS 16, 114). From this we learn important features of the mechanism of imitation in Kierkegaard. 'The picture' is not a theological or exegetical concept derived from the Bible. On the contrary, it is a theoretical construct established by Kierkegaard. 'The ideal picture of being a Christian' equips Kierkegaard with means to discuss and communicate the ideal of human becoming; hence, it 'makes' becoming a Christian 'possible.'

Kierkegaard's novel appraisal of both the imitator – a self in the process of becoming – and his new reading of the model for imitation – the plurality of prototypes – requires a different conceptualization of the relation between the two, which I term existential mimesis.

Existential mimesis

While putting forward the idea of Kierkegaard's existential mimesis, I am using the term 'existential' to qualify his account of genuine human existence as essentially influenced by mimesis. Kierkegaard explores a variety of interrelated mimetic concepts. His interest in that regard is not solely in imitation understood as a form of a distinctive similarity between an imitator and a model. For instance, while speaking of the imitation of Christ, Kierkegaard claims that it means to represent Christ in two senses: in one's daily life through 'works of love,' but also by 'putting on Christ' in a sense akin to dressing in borrowed clothes, something we do not own (JP 2, 322/SKS 22, 391). In both senses, we are talking about a performative dimension of the life of a genuine Christian. Moreover, as indicated in the previous section, the customary reading of the imitation of Christ is very problematic; it cannot really mean imitation understood as (a degree of) similarity. Quite the reverse, Christ is absolutely different from human beings, and that difference is, paradoxically, the negative Kierkegaard is looking for in the imitation of Christ. As I will elaborate in the following sections of this chapter, Kierkegaard employs in his writings a conceptualization of mimesis that has four features: it is indirect, intention-driven, 'non-comparing,' and concerned with ends rather than means.

Indirect and intention-driven mimesis

To understand the indirectness of mimesis that is implied here, it is important to see a certain underlying way of asking and answering questions about the imitation of Christ in Kierkegaard that has plagued the scholarship. Asking 'Can we imitate Christ?' which is typically followed by distinguishing what in Christ can or cannot, should or should not, be imitated, presupposes a direct type of imitation in both the question and the answer. Some scholars look for a sense of similarity between Christ and humans while identifying Christ's human nature as the actual object of imitation. In that sense every human can imitate Christ's deeds, as they result from his human nature. Others point to the inseparability of the two natures in Christ to suggest a reading of Christ as the Pattern in a more general sense, for example, as a model of suffering.

Kierkegaard envisages a different dynamic that governs the relation between the imitator and its model(s). His conceptualization of mimesis is not about correspondence and similarity. Moreover, although tangible and concrete ethical acts are at stake in the imitation of Christ, for instance, it is the performer's intentions behind them that are the real object of imitation, not the acts themselves. In my argumentation for the indirect and intention-driven imitation, I first return to the problem of the prototypes and show how the puzzle forces us to think differently about mimesis; I then refer to a distinction between the imitation of means and ends and show how it addresses the puzzle of mimesis.

Kierkegaard presents imitative models dialectically linking imitation and obligation. On the one hand, he exposes us to a plurality of imitative models that do not correspond to us directly or isometrically, and then he emphasizes the obligation of imitation. As I have shown, the lily and the bird and Christ, who are not Christians and are not in one-to-one relations to us, cannot be considered direct objects of imitation. Yet we are not relieved from the obligation to imitate them. On the other hand, Kierkegaard considers some potential candidates for direct imitation, such as the apostles, martyrs, Church Fathers, or Doctors of the Church, but then he clearly guards against imitating them (JP 3, 185/SKS 22, 57). This dialectical conundrum, I suggest, indicates that we should look for a different type of relationship with the imitative models.

I claim that what Kierkegaard has in mind is a type of mimesis that is indirect in the sense that it is more concerned with the understanding of the purpose, environment, and meaning of the imitated action or object than merely with their exhaustive capturing and representing. I find it useful to refer to the discernment between imitation of means and intentions (goals and ends) in human behaviour in empirical psychology.[2] The former is concerned with the detailed representation of elements of perceived behaviour; it is considered to be of a lower order than the imitation of intentions, as it often misses the actual reason for the performed action, inhibits innovation, and restricts agency.

Existential mimesis in Kierkegaard is closer to the imitation of intentions, often called 'goal emulation' in the relevant literature. Hence indirect and intention-driven mimesis in Kierkegaard is not about copying the means, or even the results in some cases, but it is rather about grasping the intentions behind the imitated objects or actions, and representing them through (often) completely different means. Let's take obedience to illustrate that dynamic. If obedience is that which needs to be imitated by a genuine Christian, we should consider the fact that Christ's obedience to the Father, and the lily's obedience towards its creator, are achieved by different means – they can also be understood as different objects, such as different types of obedience. On the one hand, we should be like the lily and the bird – 'naturally' obedient to Christ. On the other hand, that obedience must be expressed through our will.

Existential mimesis confronts and accommodates the two spheres of human existence, the immediate – which represents the ideal of nature – and the reflective – which represents the human capacity to imagine and will. Pure reflection does not satisfy indirect mimesis, as one can simply entertain an idea of following after Christ. Indirect mimesis requires immediacy after reflection, which is, among other things, represented in one's 'decision to choose' (UDVS, 219/SKS 8, 321) to be oneself and follow Christ, and which allows for a certain openness and inventiveness in the realization of that undertaking.

That openness and inventiveness of indirect mimesis is contained in Kierkegaard's allegorical presentation of faith as a pilgrimage from 'The Gospel of Suffering.' He reinforces this metaphor by juxtaposing it with other mimetic images of followers as strangers and pilgrims. Answering the eponymous question of the text, 'What Meaning... [Is] There ... in the Thought of Following Christ[?],' Kierkegaard points out (in an invocative prayer) that Christ '[himself] once walked the earth and left footprints that we should follow' (UDVS, 217/SKS 8, 319). What it means to imitate Him is not clearly defined; we are left with an allegorical image of a track on the ground. A path, a track, or a pattern cannot be directly followed or imitated for the very reason of what it is. It is not a prescription (or suggestion on the other hand), but 'guidance' (UDVS, 217/SKS 8, 319).

Existential mimesis takes place in the absence of the one followed, although it starts with a vision of the prototype. Analogously, the Disciples of Christ only started following Him after his death. To follow Christ is, for Kierkegaard, 'to walk by oneself and to walk alone' (UDVS, 220/SKS 8, 322). Such mimesis is radically different from a direct type of imitation where the model is at hand.

Comparison

Kierkegaard offers a paradoxical account of authentic Christian existence. On the one hand, a Christian seeks likeness with Christ, despite the fact that human nature is absolutely different from the nature of Christ. On the other hand, an authentic Christian existence requires seeking dissimilarity from other human beings despite their shared human nature. This is succinctly articulated in a journal entry from 1852: 'What must be emphasized is the following of Christ – and I must remain as I am in my unlikeness to others' (SKS 25, 22). That unlikeness or heterogeneity (*Ueensartethed*) refers to a negative type of imitation based on the phenomenon of comparison (the root of the Danish word for comparison, *Sammenligning*, is *ligne* which means to liken oneself) that is one of Kierkegaard's main interests in mimesis.

Kierkegaard introduces his conceptualization of comparison to explain what he means by 'not being like others.' In one of his concluding works, *The Moment*, he redefines spirituality through the lens of difference: 'Spirit is precisely: not to be like the others' (TM, 344/SKS 13, 408). Here being like others entails comparison because to know what others are and whether one is indeed like others, we have to engage our ability to reason and recognize in order to eventually find correspondence between the others and ourselves. There is also an important link between comparison and the theological-spiritual realm shared between human beings and God. At stake here is the fact that comparison is not a value-neutral notion, but one that represents a negatively valued imitative practice or inclination. By imitating others, who likewise imitate others, we compromise our individuality. On the other hand, we also redirect our attention from the inner of our being to the outer. We become what we are not, or rather, we become someone else.

Our mimetic relation with God does not have the same dimension of comparison for Kierkegaard. Because God is in His nature absolutely different from anything there is but God, our relation to God does not make us into a God (although at stake is a form of human divinization), but rather instructs us to secure our difference. Consequently, drawing upon the fact that we are both created in the image of God and that we are becoming that image, our task is to become ourselves; this will occur by upholding that spiritual realm in us, namely difference.

However, comparison has to be comprehended in a dialectical manner, because not being like others may be in fact motivated by what it tries to avoid, namely, mimeticism. In 'The Tax Collector,' Kierkegaard discusses two levels of harmful or negative imitation. In that work we have the tax collector whom God justifies and the Pharisee who leaves the temple accused by God. Interestingly, the latter is the one who claims that he is not like the tax collector, but it is he who is 'the hypocrite who deceives himself and wants to deceive God' (WA, 127/SKS 11, 263). The Pharisee's claim of being different from another is in fact based on his adhering to 'the criterion of human comparison' (WA, 129/SKS 11, 265). It is so because he uses other people as his point of reference in evaluating his spiritual condition. In contrast, the tax collector casts his gaze down, and does not look either towards the sky, or to the sides; being before God, he is too humble to look up, and not interested in looking sideways. Abstaining from a horizontal gaze, he secures the intimacy of 'standing by himself'; looking downwards and 'staying far away,' the tax collector admits his sin and relies on God's mercy.

The second type of comparing imitation is the one performed or acted out by shrewd readers of the story. Although they 'have chosen the tax collector as their prototype, [they] resemble the Pharisee' (WA, 127/SKS 11, 263). This is to say that in their choice to be like the tax collector, they imitate the attitude of the Pharisee; they become contaminated with comparison and 'sanctimoniously say, "God, I thank you that I am not like this Pharisee"' (WA, 127/SKS 11, 263). These readers of the biblical story are also guilty of making their faith into a meaningless performance; with exaggerated gestures they mimic the behaviour of one they condemn, the Pharisee, and in fact condemn themselves.

Conclusion

In their respective approaches to mimesis, whether limited to Kierkegaard's authorship, or seeking points of reference among his contemporaries and beyond, scholars have focused on imitation as the main understanding of mimesis. I have demonstrated that it is useful to read imitation in Kierkegaard in the context of its mother concept, mimesis, because such a reading discloses the complexity of Kierkegaard's affair with the phenomenon in question. Kierkegaard is aware of the intrinsic problems of the imitation of Christ, such as the issue of the suitability and compatibility between prototypes and imitators. I have highlighted his attempts to resolve these issues via novel approaches to mimesis that define it as indirect and intention-driven. According to Kierkegaard, authentic existence can be both threatened and enhanced by mimesis in our daily lives; we need to be aware of, and guard against, our propensity to imitate others and instead seek non-comparing difference from them in order to secure genuine existence.

Related topics

'Kierkegaard on nature and natural beauty,' Anthony Rudd; 'Beyond worry? on learning humility from the lilies and the birds,' John Lippitt.

Notes

1 He uses a variety of terms to refer to the broad mimetic sphere in his corpus, such as *Ligne* (likeness, and to liken, to resemble), *Lighed* (compare), *Sammenligning* (comparison), *Eftergjøre* (going and doing after), *Efterabelse* (aping or parroting), *mimisk* (mimic or mimical), but also *Fordoblelse* (redoubling), *Reduplikation* (reduplication), *Dobbelt-Reflexion* (double-reflection), *Dobbelthed* (doubleness or duplexity), *Dobbelt-Bevægelse* (double-movement), *Billede* (image or picture), and *Forbillede* (prototype, model, type, pattern). For an example where several mimetic terms are used in a short passage, see JP 2, 335/SKS 24, 14.
2 It is difficult to ultimately settle differences between imitation, emulation, mimicry, copying, and so forth. Donald (2005) distinguishes between mimicry, imitation, and mimesis. Mimicry is directed to the means of reduplicated action; imitation is concerned with the ends and purpose of the imitated action. Mimesis, builds upon the other two, engages the reflective faculty of the performer ('it is reflective and potentially self-supervisory' [Donald 2005: 288]), and takes the audience into account. We find a more nuanced distinction between mimicry and imitation in Tomasello and Carpenter (2005), who distinguish between an imitation of means and an imitation of intentions (in ends) behind performed actions in relation to the phenomenon of imitative learning.

References

Barnett, C. B. (2011) *Kierkegaard, pietism and holiness*, Farnham: Ashgate.
Dewey, B. R. (1968) *The new obedience: Kierkegaard on imitating Christ*, Cleveland, OH: Corpus Book.
Donald, M. (2005) 'Imitation and mimesis,' in S. Hurley and N. Chater (eds), *Perspectives on Imitation: From Neuroscience to Social Science*, vol. 2 (*Imitation, Human Development, and Culture*), Cambridge, MA: Massachusetts Institute of Technology Press.
Ferreira, M. J. (2001) *Love's grateful striving: A commentary on Kierkegaard's Works of Love*, Oxford: Oxford University Press.
Gebauer, G. and Wulf, C. (1995) *Mimesis*, D. Reneau (trans), Los Angeles: University of California Press.
Halliwell, S. (2002) *Mimesis and the history of aesthetics*, Princeton, NJ: Princeton University Press.
Kaftanski, W. (2017) 'The Socratic dimension of Kierkegaard's imitation,' *Heythrop Journal*, 58, no. 4: 599–611.
Mikulova-Thulstrup, M. (1962) 'Kierkegaard's dialectic of imitation,' in H. A. Johnson and N. Thulstrup (eds), H. R. Harcourt (trans), *A Kierkegaard Critique*, New York: Harper & Brothers.
Pattison, G. (1989) 'Eternal loneliness: Art and religion in Kierkegaard and Zen,' *Religious Studies*, 25, no. 3: 379–92.
Potolsky, M. (2006) *Mimesis*, London: Routledge.
Rasmussen, J. D. S. (2005) *Between irony and witness: Kierkegaard's poetics of faith, hope, and love*, New York: T. & T. Clark.
Schweiker, W. (1990) *Mimetic reflections: A study in hermeneutics, theology and ethics*, New York: Fordham University Press.
Society for Danish Language and Literature (1918–1956) *Ordbog over det danske Sprog*, vols. 1–28, Copenhagen: Gyldendal.
Stokes, P. (2010) *Kierkegaard's mirrors: Interest, self, and moral vision*, London: Palgrave Macmillan.
Tomasello, M. and Carpenter, M. (2005) 'Intention reading and imitative learning,' in S. Hurley and N. Chater (eds), *Perspectives on Imitation: From Neuroscience to Social Science*, vol. 2 (*Imitation, Human Development, and Culture*), Cambridge, MA: Massachusetts Institute of Technology Press.
Walsh, S. (2009) *Thinking Christianly in an existential mode*, Oxford: Oxford University Press.
Walsh, S. (1994) *Living poetically: Kierkegaard's existential aesthetics*, University Park, PA: Pennsylvania State University Press.

Further reading

Abrams, M. H. (1958) *The mirror and the lamp: Romantic theory and the critical tradition*, Oxford: Oxford University Press.

This book provides readers with important conceptualizations of mimesis in the arts, literature, theology, and philosophy that Kierkegaard converses with.

Kaftanski, W. (2014) 'Kierkegaard's aesthetics and the aesthetic of imitation,' in H. Schulz, J. Stewart, and K. Verstrynge (eds), *Kierkegaard Studies Yearbook 2014*, Berlin: Walter de Gruyter.

This article complements the religious reading of imitation in Kierkegaard by accounting for its aesthetic dimension in Kierkegaard's corpus.

Stan, L. (2014) 'Imitation,' in S. Emmanuel, W. McDonald, and J. Stewart (eds), *Kierkegaard Research: Sources, Reception and Resources*, vol. 15 *(Kierkegaard's Concepts)*, tome 3, Farnham: Ashgate.

This entry presents imitation in Kierkegaard in relation to the *imitation Christi* and addresses the various ways that imitation appears predominantly in his signed writings.

17
BECOMING A SUBJECT: KIERKEGAARD'S THEOLOGICAL ART OF EXISTENCE

Peder Jothen

Introduction

One challenge in understanding Kierkegaard's thought is that the varied voices of his authorship defy easy categorization. He is not simply a philosopher or a theologian; he is not merely an ethicist or a poet. His writing reveals all of these perspectives as well as many more. Indeed, he blurs the boundaries between these intellectual categories, thereby critiquing the 'pure' categories of thinkers such as Kant and Hegel. But such disruption can mean a reader has a dizzying time finding a lens to enter into and wrestle with his thought.

That said, arguably what stitches Kierkegaard's thought together is his articulation of the twists and turns through which one becomes a 'true' self. His authorship throughout claims that 'truth is subjectivity' (CUP 1, 189/SKS 7, 173). He poetically envisions an account of actualizing an ideal possibility of subjectivity within one's existence. Two clear issues come to the fore within this theme. One issue concerns the teleological ideal that reveals true subjectivity. The other issue is how one forms oneself into this true subject. When seen in tandem, they frame Kierkegaard's authorship as deeply intertwined with ontological thought.[1]

Writing within a decidedly Christian context, Kierkegaard addresses these issues by articulating an account of subjectivity oriented in the *Imitatio Christi*. Christ is thus the ideal image of selfhood, meaning one must mimetically exist through this biblically revealed way of being. As for the second problem, he stresses how the existential actualization of this ideal requires practice, creativity, and intentionality; it is also a never-ending process. It demands that the human capacities of the imagination, passion, and will are rightly oriented towards God, oneself, and the world. But as such a process, an important lens to understand subjectivity is as an aesthetic act: in short, 'to exist is an art' (CUP 1, 351/SKS 7, 321).

For Kierkegaard, rather than such arts as painting, poetry, and music, the highest artistic endeavour is the practice of an existence directed at true selfhood.[2] This existence is theological, as it requires the acknowledgement of one's sinful nature, rightly imagining and choosing Christ as one's subjective possibility, and passionately desiring this ideal. But it is also aesthetic, as one sees one's existence as a creative, productive act and uses creative capacities such as the imagination and desire in the process. It requires linking Christian subjective possibility and one's existing, embodied form in an act of subjective creation. Kierkegaard thereby paints a picture of subjectivity through an aesthetic vision of human development.

Understanding subjectivity as an art reframes the interpretive confusion about Kierkegaard's view of art and aesthetics. His authorship offers numerous qualifications about the existential importance of art. Through his various authorial masks, he asks whether Christ would want to sit and have his portrait painted amidst the injustices of the world (PC, 255/SKS 12, 247), whether Christian poetry is possible (WL, 49/SKS 9, 56), and he describes how music is the demonic (EO 1, 65/SKS 2, 71). Yet, surprisingly, echoing Augustine's *uti/frui* distinction, when understood in light of becoming a subject, his thought reveals how art can offer a means of subjective awakening and self-reflection. For Augustine, art is a sign of God; one must then see art in light of God (*uti*) rather than lose oneself in the enjoyment of the artwork (*frui*).[3] Likewise for Kierkegaard, art itself is not the problem; rather, it is how one relates to a particular artistic object amidst becoming a true subject that becomes the subjective task.

In fact, his authorship exemplifies the use of artistic means to awaken the demands of subjectivity in a reader. On the one hand, he wrote provocative, indirectly communicative, pseudonymous texts that ask a reader to question the beliefs and desires that animate their existence. On the other, he wrote a series of hopeful, upbuilding Christian discourses to encourage a reader to enter into this way of subjectivity. Both were aimed at leading a reader into the faith-rooted, passionate attempt to form a self-to-God relationship that should define one's identity and actions. Both used allegories, irony, humour, metaphor, and a variety of aesthetic devices as tools directed at this end.

Detailing this link between art and existence amidst the art of subjectivity means offering a close reading of a particular example. In *Practice in Christianity*, writing as Anti-Climacus, Kierkegaard describes the existential development of a youth, one that is an allegory about life being an examination. God is the examiner, asking 'whether one will in truth be a Christian or not' (PC, 186/SKS 12, 186). Being young, the youth is ignorant of subjectivity and lacks the proper direction for his passion and thought. By the end of his life, though he develops morally, his ideal is a human-created image of subjective possibility rather than Christ, meaning he never becomes a true self.

That said, the youth's story offers an account of how relating to material art shapes one's subjectivity. The threefold relational form of the youth's imagination, will, and passion shape how he relates to art and thus his ethical formation. These capacities are interrelated and interdependent, as formation depends on the proper inward relationship between the capacities expressed outwardly in moral action. Specifically, the youth's imagination perceives and inwardly *grasps* an existential ideal received either through visual art or his own imagination as the first condition of development. The imagination makes the image into a mentally held image of subjective perfection. The will *chooses* to strive to become the image as the second, and decisive, condition. Though decisive, without passionate self-interest, he would not strive to existentially become the image. It is only through passion-filled love that he *moves* towards redoubling the image.

In the process, Anti-Climacus asks a reader to imagine one's existence in light of the youth's story. There are then two dimensions to the allegory: (1) as a literary, aesthetic production and (2) as a provocative call into true subjectivity. As an artful, imaginative thought experiment, it speaks to the use of capacities that humans use to relate to art but also to existence. In its wider context, the story provokes a reader into recognizing Christ as the ideal existential subject. Finally, it reveals how art can awaken and shape human subjectivity. As such, it offers clarity on the intertwining of selfhood and art within Kierkegaard's thought.

True subjectivity: Christ

The first issue in understanding Kierkegaard's art of existence is to detail his vision of the ideal subject. As the image of true subjectivity, Christ is decisive for human becoming in three ways. The first is as the historical, incarnational gift of God's very being. This element of Christ emphasizes the *past* moment of God's action to free humans from the clutches of human sin. In Christ's very nature, as both God and man, humans are made right with God independent of any human action or work; by becoming human, God shows the depth of divine love for humanity, a love expressed most fully in the atonement provided by Christ's death and resurrection.

The second element relates to each human *present*. In the idea of Christ (as God/man), each person receives the condition that enables humans to rightly use their reason within subjectivity. In *Philosophical Fragments*, Kierkegaard describes how humans lack the condition to understand truth because of the reality of sin; the Socratic aphorism to 'know thyself' is not possible. Only God, being sinless, gives humans an awareness of the existential reality of being human (as sinners) as well as what humans should be (as saints). To do so, God becomes human, because 'in order to put the learner in possession of it, he must be man. This contradiction is the object of faith and is the paradox, the moment' (PF, 62/SKS 4, 264). In short, as a paradox, Christ sets a limit to human reason and self-generated ideas of subjective possibility. One cannot rationally understand Christ; Christ is then an object of faith as a type of passionate trust, rather than reasoned comprehension.

Finally, as a third dimension, Christ's life becomes each person's *future*, as in the imitative ontological model that God calls each person to become. To imitate is to redouble (*Fordoblelse*); one's duty is to become Christ's double. 'Christ came to the world with the purpose of saving the world, also with the purpose . . . of being *the prototype*, of leaving footprints for the person who wanted to join him, who then might become an *imitator*, this indeed corresponds to "footprints"' (PC, 238/SKS 12, 231–2). Christ is the true form of humanity. Through this connection between truth and subjectivity, religious truth is not propositional but existential. It is existential in that it shapes one's lived, daily, meaningful activities as a particular person in a particular context. It shapes one's very being, pointing to the ontological dimensions within Kierkegaard's argument.

Though it includes deontological elements such as the love commandment, Christ serves a teleological purpose.[4] He is the measure and telos of one's being, and thereby the basis for good action. But Christian truth, rather than being merely a set of epistemological creeds, should transform one's existence, as in loves, actions, and thoughts. One *lives* it, rather than merely knows it, unifying being and existing, thereby making one into a subject: responsible, loving, neighbour-focused. It means having a form that exists through, by, and with Christ-like love (as *Works of Love* describes).

The Bible is primary in this revelation. Kierkegaard stresses that 'the Holy Scriptures are the highway signs: Christ is the Way,' meaning the Bible is not to be read literally as in an historical transcript (JP 1, 84/SKS 20, 105). Rather, it is the means to hear about God's action in Christ and the truth about the human condition. The Bible is also a love letter from God, directed at each person as a particular individual. And as a love letter, its primary theme – the reality of freedom from sin through faith in Christ – is clear and does not require special skills, teachers, or books for a hearer to understand. Indeed, what matters in reading the Bible is hearing the call to become a true subject. It reveals a diagnosis of the human sickness and its cure in Christ that makes true mimesis an actual possibility for a self (see Jothen 2014: ch. 3).

Yet, other works of art can also reveal, at least partially, this paradoxical God and Christian subjectivity. When understood through a sin-consciousness, art can provide a means to reflect on the shape of one's life. For instance, Kierkegaard links Thorvaldsen's sculptures of Christ and the apostles in Copenhagen's Vor Frue Kirke to upbuilding in his *Discourses at the Communion on Fridays*. And Kierkegaard remarks on music by noting 'My favorite hymn: "Commit Thy Ways Confiding,"... selected today!' (JP 6, 346/SKS 23, 478). Art matters for existence when used as such; certainly, art can be misused to celebrate sensual love and materialism, but it can also be a part of becoming true as well.

Subjectivity as mimetic movement

In the task of actualizing this subjective ideal within one's life, the youth's story from *Practice in Christianity* offers further depth to this argument. For one, it clarifies the role of art (here visual art) as a means of awakening self-reflection about subjectivity. It also details the importance of how one uses the imagination, passion, and will in relation to existential ideals. It thereby reveals the aesthetic dimensions within human existence.

The youth's ideal

The story begins by focusing on images and perfection. The youth's imagination perceives an 'image of perfection,' either of a historical figure or one self-generated (PC, 186/SKS 12, 186). Anti-Climacus suggests two image types that form the nexus of self-formation. The first is historical. Prior to this story, Anti-Climacus discusses a child who sees images of Napoleon, William Tell, and the crucified Christ. All three images are of historical figures, and thus have an actuality of being, meaning they depict a once living being. The second form comes from the imagination. Not being rooted within human history, it is merely a mental image, though like the historical image, it too is perceived through the imagination.

In either case, the aesthetic matters: whether a visual or imaginative image, the youth discovers an idea of subjective perfection that imaginatively becomes his 'perfect (more ideal) self' (PC, 187/SKS 12, 186). This ability to turn a visual image into a mental representation of perfection shows the power of images: they can stimulate self-awareness. The youth uses a visual image to establish an existential standard by which to evaluate his existence. Indeed, through the image, he becomes self-aware of his need to develop and grow as a moral agent.

However, there is a problem with the youth's ideal: it is merely an imaginative representation. Thus, it exists only 'in the imagination's infinite distance from actuality' (PC, 186/SKS 12, 186). Content-wise, his image is too perfect. Christian perfection is living like Christ in the material world despite human fallibility and sin, a form of existence that requires *actually* suffering and loving others. Imitating, rather than thinking about imitating, is existentially determinative; it is also an essential component of Christ's image. Taking a swipe at Hegelian Idealism, Anti-Climacus' point is that to *imagine* giving away all of one's possessions or leaving a well-paying job to work for justice is not the same as *doing* it. Imitation requires both; one knows the true image but relates to it by existing through it in imitating Christ. As such, the youth has not discovered the true ideal.

The youth's imagination

Holding up this account of imagistic formation is the imagination as the means to perceive, and thus relate to, a visual image. 'Every human being possesses to a higher or lower degree a capability called the power of the imagination (*Indbildningskraften*), a power (*Kraft*) that is the first condition for what becomes of a person' (PC, 186/SKS 12, 186). In order for the youth to develop the self-consciousness that he is not fully formed, he must have some image of a subjective possibility that reveals what he is not yet, should be. Having this power of perception, the youth's imagination *grasps* such a possibility of selfhood. It is the 'first condition' and foundational capacity for self-formation.

Kierkegaard's account of the imagination develops in relation to thinkers such as Kant and Hegel, who view the imagination as a free and productive capacity. The key definition of the imagination is from Anti-Climacus' *The Sickness unto Death*. Here, he sees the imagination as the capacity '*instar omnium* [for all capacities]' that 'infinitizes' because 'whatever of feeling, knowing, and willing a person has depends upon what imagination he has, upon how that person reflects himself – that is, upon imagination' (SUD, 30–1/SKS 11, 146–7). Any thought, emotion, or choice is thus dependent upon the imagination.

Ethically, imaginative activity enables a person to develop the self-consciousness needed to become responsible for becoming a subject. Everyone is born unaware of selfhood possibilities, whether as a vocation (e.g., pilot, baseball player) or as a worldview (e.g., Christian, hedonist). Through the imagination, one can 'try out' types of selfhood in relation to one's self-identity, a task Anti-Climacus calls infinitization. Infinitization has two dimensions. In the first, the imagination holds the range of subjective possibilities that one could define oneself through, as in a sports hero or brilliant professor; the second stresses the imaginative awareness that one is not just a material body, but spiritual as well. In the process, infinitization enables self-conscious reflection about the type of being one wants to be.

As infinitization's first dimension, imaginative possibility is vital to selfhood as it makes one responsible for self-formation. 'To lack possibility means either that everything has become necessary for a person or that everything has become trivial' (SUD, 40/SKS 11, 155). The activity of imagining possibilities of selfhood is itself necessary, for 'possibility is for the self what oxygen is for breathing' (SUD, 40/SKS 11, 155). Yet this imaginative ability, a component of human freedom, is not total. Because of sin, a true image of human possibility is needed, revealed by God from beyond temporality and sin. Humans must recognize the limits to such imaginative reflection. One must develop a sin-consciousness as such.

The second dimension of infinitization enables a self to see itself as both physical and spiritual. Humans have bodies but also have an infinite, spiritual essence: 'A human being is spirit. But what is spirit? Spirit is the self' (SUD, 13/SKS 11, 129). Through imagining oneself as being spiritual, one sees oneself as greater than the material world; one thereby becomes self-conscious about the existential consequences of choices about relating to others and God. In short, one is both theological, an infinite creature created in God's image, and aesthetic, a finite body.

This awareness of being infinite carries within it, however, the impact of human sin. Each person is anxious regarding the act of choosing a possibility of selfhood to redouble.[5] Consequently, a self may use the imagination to flee from making any existential choice, doing so in two possible ways. One, the imagination *endlessly* imagines such possibilities, meaning one exists 'in the fairyland of the imagination' (CUP 1, 357/SKS 7, 326). Imaginative flight avoids the actuality of acting towards others, and neglects seeing oneself as thrown into a web of relationships (e.g., father, sister, lover, leader, friend) that demand one's attention.

Second, the imagination is easily led astray by the world, as it is full of beautiful, sexy, and shocking images that turn one into an admirer rather than an imitator. The world is an aesthetic paradise, turning one into an admirer that 'forgets [oneself] ... and precisely this is what is beautiful, that he forgets himself in this way in order to admire' (PC, 242/SKS 12, 235). To admire is to lose oneself in something other than a true subjective image, meaning one has stopped caring about subjectivity.[6] Indeed, the imagination is a *creative* capacity. A person can use the imagination to imagine numerous possibilities of selfhood that lack a connection to material reality, say of becoming Superman. The normative *content* of the image is self-created, arising out of a mistaken account of the authority of human reason to come up with such truth.

This possibility of the misuse of the imagination returns us to the youth. His ideal arises in relation to an actual, historical figure or an imaginatively created image, rather than Christ. It may have been an icon of a famous person he saw in a shop window, such as Napoleon, that he then turns into the mental representation of perfect selfhood. Or it may be a portrait of Hegel, as in a visual image that moves him from Hegel the actual person to Hegelian Idealism. Unlike the image of Christ, which is 'diametrically opposite to perfection (ideality),' Hegelianism affirms the human capacity to create its own ideal possibility of selfhood, one that arises out of the seeming purity of the intellect (PC, 187/SKS 12, 187). A final possibility that the youth reveals is to self-create his own subjective ideal. Here, the image would have a 'thought-actuality,' as it is merely imaginary, not tied to actuality and therefore lived existence. This fantastical, imaginative purity, however, gives it a persuasive power.[7]

No matter whether historical or idealistic, the youth uses his imagination to mis-imagine. Rather than recognizing these subjective possibilities as imperfect ones, he's imaginatively intertwined his existence within them. What's more, the youth is content to merely imagine these possibilities, to live within the imagination, rather than his actual daily existence. He exists within a fantasyland, one distant from the demands of actually relating, loving, and suffering for others. He is enraptured with the imagination that is 'in itself more perfect than suffering in actuality' (PC, 187/SKS 12, 187). Nonetheless, conceptually, the imagination is a foundational capacity that *grasps* the content for ethical formation. Though the youth 'has not watched his step, has not paid attention to where he is' by not imagining Christ as his image, the imagination makes him aware of the importance of thinking beyond his time and place (PC, 189/SKS 12, 188). The imagination is thus vital for subjectivity.

The youth's will

The will's capacity to choose serves as the second condition for ethical formation: in freely choosing an image to redouble, one takes responsibility for subjectivity. Thus, the will intends to actualize the ideal within the sensual, aesthetic world. Yet, though 'decisive,' the will is interdependent, as choice depends upon the imagination to grasp a visual and mental image of possibility, and passion to move the self towards imitating the image. More to the point, developing the Kierkegaardian will shows the necessity for each individual to choose a subjective possibility, an act which opens one to God's actions. Because of sin, Kierkegaard establishes limits to human responsibility, as the true content of choice is divinely revealed and the act of imitation is governed by God's grace. Subjectivity is both theological and aesthetic.

Kierkegaard's idea of the will exhibits elements of both Augustinian-infused Protestantism and Kantian Modernism. It has continuity with Augustine's bonded will as either sinful *cupiditas* or converted *caritas*, and Kant's free will that connects *a priori* freedom and *a posteriori* volition as a kind of causality.[8] Anti-Climacus' account of the will stresses that it is both free and bound. The youth exemplifies this tension. As free, the youth can choose to exist based on a particular image of selfhood. Indeed, the very purpose of life 'is to *will* to be, to *will* to express the perfection (ideality)' amidst one's everyday life (PC, 190/SKS 12, 189). Therefore, for Kierkegaard, choice is decisive. The will's capacity to choose a particular ideal account of selfhood, imaginatively held, turns this ideal into the teleological image that orients self-formation; one chooses to become it within one's existence. But one can never choose the true image (Christ) independently of Christian revelation nor move towards it without grace, exemplifying the bound dimension. Only through God is there a prototype, meaning the youth misunderstands human freedom if he strives to become a self based on his own ideas.

Further, as one can never be a true Christian because of sin, God's grace is needed to enable a self to continue to strive to become true despite never succeeding. Such a dialectical tension leads one to despair without divine assistance. To move beyond despair requires the recognition that true selfhood only comes from God: 'The formula that describes the state of the self when despair is completely rooted out is this: in relating itself to itself and in willing to be itself, the self rests transparently in the power that established it' (SUD, 14/SKS 11, 130). On this account, to will to be 'itself' is to rightly will to be the self that God created: dependent, both sensual and spiritual, and sinfully misrelating these two dimensions.

As such, Kierkegaard's ethics is nonsensical without God as giver; his ethics is a theological ethics. The truth that matters for selfhood, including the knowledge of sin (from *The Sickness unto Death*) as well as Christ (from *Philosophical Fragments*), comes not from reason but divine revelation. God reveals the paradoxical moral exemplar (the lowly Christ in *Practice in Christianity* and *Works of Love*), giving each person the potential to exist rightly relating to God and then others and oneself. Divine action gracefully opens the possibility of restoring humanity to a state that predates sinful existence, to the self as originally created in the divine image. To will to be 'itself' is to acknowledge sin and have one's centre in God, as 'the power that established [the self]'; this always requires divine activity: only God as creator can restore fallen creation.

Yet, unlike his Lutheran forebears, Kierkegaard stresses human willing as a necessary component of formation. Behind an existential choice is the recognition that the possibility of true selfhood only comes with an active movement to passive willing. God's decisiveness provides the condition that makes the choice of the image of Christ possible. Therefore, only because God gifted Christ to creation does one have the possibility to become a Christian agent; yet a self must *actively* choose and strive to practice a state of *passive* dependence on God.

This idea of gift affirms the true image of moral perfection as the loving and suffering Christ. To will truthfully is to focus one's intentions towards becoming like Christ through the *Imitatio Christi*. Choosing Christ's image is a grace-filled act. Climacus writes that in learning existential truth, an 'assisting love but also a procreative love' are given by the divine teacher to a learner (PF, 30/SKS 4, 237). God's grace assists, in a manner similar to the ideas of prevenient or operative grace, in guiding the self in its willing. These forms of grace are prior to human willing; they detail God's activity in lovingly laying the foundations for a self to willingly choose Christ. What matters is the active *choice* of a mental image that both truthfully assesses human capacities (i.e., dependent, limited, sinful) and passively opens itself up to God's grace.

Such a choice is not made by the youth. Rather than choosing the true ideal given through Christian revelation, the youth wills something opposed to true existence and thus is deceived by the imagination. 'Look, there is a youth who has let himself be enticed by his imagination to go out too far,' to choose a false ideal (PC, 189/SKS 12, 188–9). He thereby wills a mental image opposed to the ethical demands of actuality. As visual or imagined, it is an ideal that is far removed from Christian truth. Yet, though his choice is untrue, Anti-Climacus suggests that any choice is better than no choice. 'In a certain sense the youth's imagination has deceived him, but indeed, if he himself *wills*, it has not deceived him to his detriment, it has deceived him into the truth; by means of a deception, it has, as it were, played him into God's hands' (PC, 190/SKS 12, 189). Even if the image is flawed, choosing makes one responsible for selfhood. The reflexive act of trying to become a certain type of person can be a stage on life's way. It also emphasizes God's grace as supporting one's life.

Unfortunately, the youth's wilful enthusiasm towards his image only intensifies the power of his non-Christian image. Though God constantly supports him during his willing, the youth suffers as he holds onto this flawed image, even when he is unable to become his image. As a consequence, his will moves him away from the suffering caused by this failure by participating further within the imaginative purity of his perfect image. The youth is not cognizant of his dependence on divine governance; his will is trapped willing merely a human-created subjective possibility.

The youth's passion

Neither imagining nor willing actualizes the possibility of selfhood as the content that determines one's existential form of life. Rather, passion *moves* a self towards imitating an image, thereby shaping how one exists. For instance, the youth's passion is about love, as his love for an ideal image of selfhood drives his attempt to live out this possibility in his life. It is passion as being interested in some thing or idea that causes actions in the aesthetic, sensual world. Within subjectivity as truth, the true object of passion is Christ, and to be interested in Christ then makes one into an imitator of Christ.[9] Though the youth loves a flawed image, his story reveals the importance of passion as the primary cause behind subjective becoming.

Passion [*lidenskab*] has various meanings for Kierkegaard, including emotion, energy, and concern. Within subjectivity, the vital dimension of passion is as self-interest.[10] Self-interest here is not a form of ethical egoism or hedonism; rather, it is about being an interested self. To be interested in something is transformative. Climacus puts it this way: 'Ethically the highest pathos is the pathos of interestedness (which is expressed in this way, that I, acting, transform my whole existence in relation to the object of interest)' (CUP 1, 390/SKS 7, 356). One's existential being changes and develops based on what one is interested in and how one relates to this object or idea.

Passion is an inward mode of relating. 'At its highest, inwardness in an existing subject is passion' (CUP 1, 199/SKS 7, 182). Kierkegaard views existence as moving from the inner self outward, with a correlative understanding that one's particular inner relation to God is incommensurable externally (see *Fear and Trembling*). Universal ethical laws only go so far within self-formation; one's external actions may not correspond with one's inner motivation.[11] In contrast to Kantian free will or Hegelian Idealism, it is not pure knowledge but rather desiring to become true (as in willing Christ's subjectivity as one's own) that is existentially formative. The inner world of desire, moodiness, and emotion becomes the fertile ground that causes ethical action.

Thus, passion is one part of the three-fold structural form of subjectivity. It is not an object or idea but rather a mode of relating to existence: God and the world, mental ideas, and sensible things. Christianity essentially communicates a non-objective truth – the uncognizable, paradoxical Christ; rather than a truth to be merely known, Christianity is an interested truth that transforms one's being through this very interest. Doing so is subjective in terms of both the means – a particular individual passionately relating to God as a particular individual – and also the end – forming as a particular Christian subject. 'Christianity is spirit; spirit is inwardness; inwardness is subjectivity; subjectivity is essentially passion, and at its maximum an infinite, personally interested passion for one's eternal happiness' (CUP 1, 33/SKS 7, 39). With the interrelatedness of truth and passion, relating passionately to Christianity is itself the form of truth as it determines the thoughts, desires, and external actions within one's existence. In sum, Christian truth is about being a Christian subject, one who embodies Christ in the world through thought, choice, and love. It is a truth that determines how one exists. As measured by human time, Christian passion is then 'infinite' as it is a concern as long as a person can be concerned: unto death. Eternal happiness is not yet – always a future hope for an existing self.

Within ethical formation, passion is an immediacy that is reflectively aware, and thus beyond the immediacy of natural impulses like erotic love. Rightly forming the passion is dependent upon thought, for ethical and religious passion must be directed by human understanding in order for a self to develop rightly. For example, take faith. In seeing the offensive, paradoxical God-man as the promise of God's love, reason falters and halts as it tries to comprehend Christ. Faith then is a 'happy passion': 'when the understanding steps aside and the paradox gives itself,' it forms a third thing: faith (PF, 59/SKS 4, 261). This type of thought-formed passion is the proper means of relating to God, oneself, and the world.

In becoming a true subject, one moves beyond natural desires (e.g., the erotic) and beyond reasonable knowledge to a life decisively shaped by trust (as faith) and the love of the paradoxical divine, a love guided by the example of Christ. This never-ending, impassioned, relational movement is at the centre of Kierkegaard's art of existence. Consequently, rather than deliberating over consequences or the justifications for action (e.g., 'What Would Jesus Do?'), this passionate self acts, just as Christ did, without concern for the rationality of a choice, theories of justice, or moral deliberation. Christ acted, and did not deliberate over *why* he acted. And like Christ, who willed to suffer for others, to become a true self is to understand the consequences of becoming like Christ: being seen as a fool, banishing selfish love to live with the poor, and looking beyond worldly differences. Knowing these sacrifices, a Christian strives to imitate Christ anyway.

While passion (which is intertwined with thought) must move beyond natural immediacy through reflective thought, it gives thought *interest*, a focus leading a self to seek to *exist* as (and thus become) the imagistic ideal of selfhood that the imagination holds. 'The subjective thinker as existing is essentially interested in his own thinking, is existing in it. Therefore, his thinking has another kind of reflection, specifically, that of inwardness, of possession, whereby it belongs to the subject and no one else' (CUP 1, 73/SKS 7, 73). Passion allows one to possess this truth, meaning truth becomes subjective as one embodies this truth.

This logic makes passion vital to rightly relating to God amidst human epistemological limits. There is an abyss that reason cannot go beyond: God as absolutely different. Any attempt at clear knowledge of God is a fantasy, as 'the understanding certainly cannot think it, cannot hit upon it on its own' (PF, 47/SKS 4, 252); yet, we crave such knowledge. Here the will returns. Ethical and religious passion relate to the will, but in a manner that is beyond simplistic choice. The Trinitarian God cannot be understood rationally; instead, one must choose to believe in a logical impossibility (e.g., Christ), using passion to relate to this truth. In the process, a self is changed, for if confident certainty is not possible, only relating to Christian truth through passionate interestedness in being this truth matters.

Thus a passionate relation existentially unifies the theological and aesthetic dimensions of each person. One must know Christ and God to the point where one is faced with the choice of atheism, agnosticism, or a passionate mode of relating to God. Passionate self-interest, intertwined with imaginatively grasped thought and the will, enables a self to become a Christian. At its highest, passion is faith, a matter of trust in God's promise.[12] It integrates and shapes a continuity within a self between the theological and aesthetic dimensions of existence.

These themes are evident in the youth's life, as his passion has two dimensions – the aesthetic and the theological. Within aesthetic passion, there are two types, one that pushes him towards a visual and mental image of subjective possibility and the other that holds onto this image despite any suffering or difficulty grasping the image. The will emboldens the youth's passion and vice versa. Yet, passion enables the choice in the first place as love moves the youth towards choosing the ideal image grasped by the imagination. This love has such a hold that it makes him sleepless.

'He becomes infatuated with this image, or this image becomes his love, his inspiration, for him his more perfect (ideal) self' (PC, 187/SKS 12, 186). Through passion, his will develops the clarity to choose. Love pulls the will towards the image, demands its attention and a decision about its value.

The second type of passion is one that refuses to let go of the desired object, despite any suffering associated with it. The youth 'perseveres, and by persevering in this way he is strengthened, as one is strengthened in suffering – now he loves that image of perfection twice as much' because of suffering for it (PC, 191/SKS 12, 190). The act of having chosen it only intensifies the love and vice versa. The will and passion 'persevere' together, thereby strengthening the youth's focus on the image. In fact, his passionate intensity prevents him from recognizing it as a false, humanly derived image of subjectivity.

Yet, despite this misrecognition, the theological – God's love – grounds the youth's movement, thereby showing the role that grace plays throughout self-formation. His suffering is made palatable through God's love. 'Now he is probably able to bear it – yes, he must be able to, since Governance does it with him – Governance, who is indeed love' (PC, 191/SKS 12, 190). Divine love supports the self in its willing, despite the fact that the self may will untruth.

As such, Christian subjectivity is about a passionate relationship to the world and God, as human passion and divine grace both are essential to Kierkegaard's account of self-formation. The youth's passion pulls him towards a visual or mental image of subjectivity grasped by the imagination, which he then wilfully chooses. It also leads him to strive to form his existence around the subjective content of this image. Even though his choice is flawed, God's love supports him in its movement. In these instances, passion connects the visual and mental to the actual relations in his life. His passion is the direct cause of his actions in the world, and thus a vital component of his formation as a subject, and it helps him integrate the theological and aesthetic dimensions of existence.

Conclusion

In Kierkegaard's art of subjectivity, Christian truth is decisively non-propositional in nature. Christianity, rather than merely a set of epistemological creeds, transforms one's existing being, as in loves, actions, thoughts, habits, and rules. It makes one into a particular kind of being: a true subject. To relate to Christian truth is thereby about knowing intertwined with doing, about being and acting. It is decidedly existential in determining how one exists within one's daily life, yet also in the imaginative self-reflection in which one acknowledges an evaluative, teleological ideal that shapes how one exists.

As mimetic, it requires one to artfully use the relational capacities of the imagination, the will, and passion to unify one's existing form with Christ's subjective content. Doing so re-forms one's existence, linking one's actions with divine truth.

But this task requires practice; it requires seeing one's subjectivity as an artistic task. To creatively reshape one's identity, ideas, and actions towards the true measure and end of subjectivity becomes then the highest form of artistic practice. Other art forms can aid this process, if one sees them as secondary activities, parts of the whole that one is becoming. Art then can awaken a self to ideas of subjectivity, both in its teleological and existential elements. And (for Kierkegaard) in the end, supported by God, one *becomes* a particular type of being, one is made into a subject: responsible, loving, neighbour-focused, Christ-like. This act of self-production, ever rooted in divine love and grace, is the art of existence; it is an existence oriented towards becoming a true subject.

Related topics

'Kierkegaard on the value of art: an indirect method of communication,' Antony Aumann; 'Kierkegaard's existential mimesis,' Wojciech Kaftanski; 'The passion of Kierkegaard's existential method,' Lee C. Barrett.

Notes

1 Paul Tillich (1951: 164), in his *Systematic Theology*, writes about the intertwining of philosophical and theological thought as partners in the ontological project, as 'only artificial barriers can stop the searching mind from asking the question of the being of God, of the gap between man's essential and existential being, of the New Being in the Christ.'
2 Kierkegaard uses *poesis* to delimit this idea, derived from the Greek *poieo*, meaning 'creation, production' (see Jothen [2014: ch. 1]; Walsh [1994]).
3 See Küpper (2012) for a longer explication of this idea.
4 For debates about typing Kierkegaard's ethics, see Davenport (2001); Evans (2004); Ferreira (1991); Jothen (2014).
5 See Kierkegaard's *The Concept of Anxiety*, as well as *The Sickness unto Death*.
6 With this view, Kierkegaard critiques the Kantian (1952: §10–1) idea of aesthetic judgment as disinterested contemplation.
7 Kierkegaard is responding to the German Romantic tradition. See Kierkegaard's *The Concept of Irony*, as well as Bernstein (2003) and Bowie (2003).
8 See Jackson (1998) for this account of the Kierkegaardian will.
9 For a variety of accounts of passion in Kierkegaard see: Evans (1992); Ferreira (1991); Roberts (1998).
10 Kierkegaard frequently uses *pathos* as synonymous with passion. Pathos, from the Greek, meaning 'suffering,' 'feeling,' and 'emotion,' conveys the idea that passion has a desirous, emotive element.
11 Though Kierkegaard has a much lower opinion of the power of reason and lacks a systematic, coherent conception of the soul, this view is analogous to Aristotle's idea of virtue from *Nicomachean Ethics*. Kierkegaard owned Trendelenburg's *Elementa logices Aristotelicae*. There are also clear correlations with Luther's (1989) *Freedom of a Christian*.
12 There is a much closer connection among the words *belief*, *trust*, and *faith* in Danish than in English. In Danish, all three share the root *tro*.

References

Bernstein, J. M. (2003) *Classic and Romantic German aesthetics*, Cambridge: Cambridge University Press.
Bowie, A. (2003) *Aesthetics and subjectivity: From Kant to Nietzsche*, London: Palgrave Macmillan.
Davenport, J. J. and Rudd, A. (eds) (2001) *Kierkegaard after MacIntyre*, Chicago, IL: Open Court.
Evans, C. S. (2004) *Kierkegaard's ethic of love: Divine commands and moral obligations*, Oxford: Oxford University Press.
Evans, C. S. (1992) *Passionate reason: Making sense of Kierkegaard's Philosophical Fragments*, Bloomington, IN: Indiana University Press.
Ferreira, M. J. (1991) *Transforming vision: Imagination and will in Kierkegaardian faith*, Oxford: Oxford University Press.
Jackson, T. (1998) 'Arminian edification: Kierkegaard on grace and free will,' in A. Hannay and G. D. Marino (eds), *The Cambridge Companion to Kierkegaard*, Cambridge: Cambridge University Press.
Jothen, P. (2014) *Kierkegaard, aesthetics, and selfhood*, Farnham: Ashgate.
Kant, I. (1952) *Critique of judgement*, J. C. Meredith (trans), Oxford: Oxford University Press.
Küpper, J. (2012) '"Uti" and "frui" in Augustine and the problem of aesthetic pleasure in the Western tradition (Cervantes, Kant, Marx, Freud),' *MLN*, 127, no. 5: S126–55.
Luther, M. (1989) *Martin Luther's basic theological writings*, Timothy Lull (ed), Minneapolis, MN: Fortress Press.
Roberts, R. C. (1998) 'Existence, emotion, and virtue: Classical themes in Kierkegaard,' in A. Hannay and G. D. Marino (eds), *The Cambridge Companion to Kierkegaard*, Cambridge: Cambridge University Press.

Tillich, P. (1951) *Systematic theology*, vol. 1, Chicago, IL: University of Chicago Press.
Walsh, S. (1994) *Living poetically: Kierkegaard's existential aesthetics*, University Park, PA: The Pennsylvania State University Press.

Further reading

Jothen, P. (2014) *Kierkegaard, aesthetics, and selfhood*, Farnham: Ashgate.

This book expands and deepens the argument about the interconnectedness in Kierkegaard's thought between ethics, theology, and aesthetics. It examines key passages from both the indirect (1843–1846) and direct (1849–1851) periods of authorship that focus on music, visual art, and poetry amidst the task of becoming a Christian.

Pattison, G. (1992) *Kierkegaard: The aesthetic and the religious*, New York: St. Martin's.

This text describes the tensions between artistic endeavours and being religious in Kierkegaard's thought. Pattison argues that Kierkegaard views art as a distraction amidst the attempt at becoming Christian.

Walsh, S. (1994) *Living poetically: Kierkegaard's existential aesthetics*, University Park, PA: The Pennsylvania State University Press.

Walsh looks at the way Kierkegaard's various authorial methods are unified in the attempt to lead one to a religious existence. Aesthetic devices such as pseudonymity, irony, and direct/indirect communication all serve this end within his authorship.

18
ENGENDERING ATONEMENT: KIERKEGAARD ON THE CROSS

Deidre Nicole Green

Introduction

Kierkegaard's Christian theology of imitation, sacrifice, and martyrdom can be seen as consistent with the potential of atonement theory to stimulate an obsession with death and suffering, which feminist theologians find objectionable. At the same time, his writings draw upon the lived experience of women to offer non-violent, joyful, and relational forms of atonement. The resources in Kierkegaard's thought for a feminist theological approach to atonement are critical because, as feminist theologians point out, if Christians' primary hermeneutic to understand the atonement is through the violence of the cross, then violence comes to define the imaginary and set the agenda for Christian imitation. While this situation is harmful for everyone, it renders women especially vulnerable (Streufert 2006: 65; Ray 1998: 21). The risk here is that, given the traditional patriarchal structure of society and its attendant androcentric atonement theories, women's sacrifice can amount to bearing the costs of structural injustice in a way that renders their sacrifice invisible to its beneficiaries while also diminishing their personhood. By contrast, Kierkegaard's female figures transform *imitatio Christi* into graceful endeavours to receive redemption, redirecting attention towards modes of relating that foster mutual becoming.

Employing the narratives of Sarah from the apocryphal Book of Tobit and the woman who was a sinner [*Synderinden*] from the Book of Luke, Kierkegaard engages these women to accentuate that atonement is a work of mutual receptivity: Sarah demonstrates the humble acceptance of another's willingness to die on her behalf, suggestive of human receptivity to Christ, while the woman who was a sinner exemplifies Christ's receptivity to humanity. Both stories convey Christ's desire for reconciliation and a need for each individual's willingness to take risks in order to be redeemed. Combined, the two women affirm the totality of atonement as that which heals human frailty and innocent suffering and overcomes and eradicates volitional sin. Illuminating Kierkegaard's perspectives on atonement, these women make apparent Christ's open invitation to redeem each individual despite her inherent fragility and inevitable fallibility. Through these Kierkegaardian models of atonement, women offer unique examples of imitating Christ and accepting his atonement without the inclusion of their own sacrificial deaths or physically destructive behaviours, manifesting instead mutual responsiveness free of an economic demand for reciprocity. As such, Kierkegaard holds forth a portrait of Christian life as a peaceable and profound connectedness among human beings, as well as between humanity and God, which also encourages human flourishing.

Furthermore, drawing from women's experience to find 'God's hidden presence' proves crucial given that the theological tradition has largely denigrated women. Feminist theologians seek to redirect attention to the 'forgotten and ignored elements of Christian tradition that highlight the power of women as agents and recipients of God's love' (Thompson 2006: 80). By turning to women to envision atonement, Kierkegaard illuminates agentic and non-violent modes of relating to God and the other, highlighting gentleness on the human side of reconciliation with the divine that relies upon mutuality without devolving into masochism. It thereby restores the full range of human modes of relating to the God-relationship.

Imitation and the cross

The problematic of imitation as a work draws attention to the need for multiple models of Christian love. Averring that Christ's atonement is necessary because his 'death is the coming-into-being of grace' (KJN 8, 151/SKS 24, 153), Kierkegaard cautions against allowing concern with imitation to overshadow atonement:

> I must now watch out, or better said, God will surely watch out for me, so that I'm not led astray by staring much too one-sidedly at [Christ] as Exemplar. This is the dialectical moment that corresponds to [Christ] as gift, as that which is given us (to recall Luther's distinction). But dialectical as I am by nature, I always look at where the passion of the dialectical moment directs me as if the complementary idea just didn't exist – and then that element takes precedence, and strikes me most forcefully.
>
> *(KJN 5, 348–9/SKS 21, 337)*

Here, Kierkegaard considers his own propensity towards relying on human imitation over the divine grace of atonement to be a personal weakness. To try to gain salvation by works denigrates the atonement: 'to want to build your salvation on any work whatsoever, daring to come before God with such things – this is the most repulsive of sins, it holds [Christ's] atonement in contempt' (KJN 6, 120/SKS 22, 123). Without negating the requirement for imitation, Kierkegaard privileges grace as absolutely indispensable. In this context, love for Christ appears not as rigorous mimesis, but as humble acceptance of the free gift he offers.

For Kierkegaard, the essential rigour of imitation within Christianity functions positively to attune a person to the need for grace, which Christ alone can provide. The atonement is a comfort when one inevitably falls short in one's striving to follow Christ – it makes hope in an eternal happiness possible amid constant reminders that one is steeped in sin (KJN 8, 473–4/SKS 24, 467). Reconciling the tension between these two aspects of Kierkegaard's thought, salvation as task and salvation as gift, Reidar Thomte (1949: 175) asserts that his understanding of Christ as pattern is 'essentially grounded in his conception of Christ as the atoner for sin.' Atonement thus receives primacy over example. Furthermore, Christ's atonement remains inimitable and therefore separate from the issue of imitation. Kierkegaard is emphatic that the atonement is not an example for human beings for several reasons: first, to make Christ's death into a task for imitation is to reduce him to a historical person; second, Christ is uniquely identified as the atoner and with the atonement (KJN 5, 295/SKS 21, 284); and third, Christ alone resists every temptation while being tested in every way (WA, 121–2/SKS 11, 257–8), including having the actual experience of Godforsakenness rather than just seeming to do so (WA, 121–2/SKS 11, 257). Each of these modalities emphasizes Christ extending grace to be received over against presenting an example to follow.

As much as he privileges the salvific efficacy of Christ's atonement over human works, Kierkegaard takes pains to relativize the sacrifice symbolized by the cross rather than lionize it as exclusively expressing Christ's love. He maintains that love was uniformly manifest at every point in Christ's life: it was 'totally present in the least things as in the greatest' and 'equally present in every moment, not greater when he expired upon the cross than when he let himself be born' (WL, 100/SKS 9, 104). Balancing Christ's birth by a mortal woman with his willingness to suffer death at the hands of violent men as equally embodying love pushes toward less necrophilic and more fecund ways to conceive of Christian life.[1] Sallie McFague (1982: 9) underscores the importance of such juxtaposition, stating that when one aspect of the divine excludes others it becomes an idol, such that 'what ought to be seen as *one* way to understand our relationship with God has become identified as *the* way.' By making Christ's life a locus of salvation equal in import to the atonement, as well as a standard of loving relationship for human beings in a way that atonement is not, Kierkegaard retains the centrality of atonement without celebrating masochism. Further, by recognizing Christ's life and death as dual instantiations of love, he echoes feminists who argue that although the practice of love may at times require mortal sacrifice, sacrifice should never be considered the sole model of redemption (Streufert 2006: 285).

Even more strongly, Kierkegaard decries the cruelty of the cross, questioning its virtue. In his journals, he reflects that the sight of the crucifix does not inspire or edify in any way; rather, it strikes one as abhorrent. Kierkegaard writes that when the sight of the dying Christ is taken as paradigmatic, it is 'scarcely upbuilding or edifying.' Observing that there is virtually nothing uplifting about seeing an innocent, holy being suffer so greatly at the hands of a corrupted world, he clarifies that both of these components are troubling, namely viewing Christ's innocent suffering as exemplary and the depravity that leads human beings to impose suffering on the innocent. Retaining the belief that the atonement effected within this suffering edifies, Kierkegaard reflects that 'at the same time that he repels me, as if he were saying, What do you and I have in common[?] – at the same time, he draws me to himself in the atonement' (KJN 4, 115–6/SKS 20, 115).[2] While the fact of the suffering does not build up, the resulting union between Christ and an individual does. Moreover, the cross provides a potent reminder of humanity's absolute need for a redemptive relationship with Christ.

The cross bears the capacity to drive humanity to Christ insofar as it serves as the sign of humanity's potential for extreme violence. Kierkegaard holds that all human beings ought to see themselves as part of the crowd that jeers at the crucifix, complicit in perpetrating Christ's death (CD, 172/SKS 10, 184). The upshot of its inherent violence, then, is that the cross reminds human beings of their sin and their resultant need for the atonement promised by it; it is precisely the awareness of personal sin that impels an individual toward God. According to Kierkegaard, one can have hope to overcome evil just because 'every one of its assaults merely leads us closer to God.' Kierkegaard is emphatic that 'in the atonement it is precisely the consciousness of sin that leads us closer to God' (KJN 4, 207/SKS 20, 207). Accentuating the potential of the cross to draw the believer into closer intimacy with Christ, he anticipates the insight of Leonardo Boff (2001: 72) who claims that the cross is simultaneously an 'indictment of the wickedness of the person who caused [Jesus'] death' and the 'symbol of love stronger than death.' For Kierkegaard, the cross is an indictment upon the world insofar as it serves as a synecdoche for the fact that 'love was not loved' (WA, 172/SKS 12, 287). Yet, divine love proves itself to be indestructible and beckons humanity toward a reconciliation that does not require further violence.

Beyond helping one to recognize sin and the need for redemption, atonement can be upbuilding insofar as it allows Christ to identify and stand in solidarity with the sufferer. Here, Kierkegaard focuses on Hebrews 4: 15, which states, 'We have not a high priest who is unable to have sympathy with our weaknesses, but one who has been tested in all things in the same way, yet without sin.' At least in this context, Kierkegaard elevates the cross for only one reason: since Christ was placed on a cross instead of on a throne, he is completely capable of empathizing with a human being, that is, he can put himself in her place (WA, 118/SKS 11, 254). This substitution that Christ performs on behalf of human beings is threefold: Christ puts himself in the place of both one who suffers and one who is tempted, and also stands in the place of sinners (Rae 2010: 102). Significantly, Kierkegaard prioritizes empathic suffering together in solidarity over and above more traditional notions of penal substitution. Murray Rae (2010: 103) comments that both here and in Kierkegaard's further discussion of the issue, the emphasis is 'placed not at all upon the punitive aspect of the satisfaction but entirely upon the compassion of the Saviour who bears for us the cost of sin.' Lee C. Barrett (2013b: 16–7) further explains that, for Kierkegaard, rather than being a 'perverse exercise in divine masochism,' the suffering of Christ on the cross was the 'price that God had to pay in order to be in fellowship with toxic humanity.' Divine love is epitomized in the self-abasement that unifies God with sinners (Barrett 2013b: 16), rendering Christ's substitution – in which he suffers the punishment that justice would impose on sinful human beings so that they do not have to – primarily a matter of divine identification with the plight of humanity, rather than the placation of God's wrath.

Reimagining atonement

Even when conceptualizing substitution in more traditional terms, Kierkegaard characterizes it in terms of maternal care and protectiveness. Constructing atonement in ways traditionally considered feminine while drawing on the concept of covering, Kierkegaard compares Christ to a mother hen.[3] He writes, 'Just as the mother hen, concerned, in the moment of danger gathers her chicks under her wings, covers them, will rather lose her life than deprive them of this hiding place,' in the same way Christ 'hides your sin' (WA, 185/SKS 12, 299). Fleshing out the analogy, Kierkegaard explains that Christ is so 'concerned, infinitely concerned in love' that he 'lost his life precisely in order to ensure you a hiding place under his love' (WA, 185–6/SKS 12, 299–300). But unlike a hen that covers her chicks with her wings, Christ hides others *with his death* (WA, 186/SKS 12, 300). Insistent that through his death Christ literally overlays human sin 'with his *holy body*' (WA, 185/SKS 12, 299), Kierkegaard signals a stark contrast between Christ and this feminine figure, who covers in a way that requires effort and self-extension for the sake of the other yet without suffering violence. In this way, he signals that imitation, perhaps especially for women, neither demands nor idealizes self-destructive behaviour, yet it does require acts of love.

The analogy invites Christians to understand the death of Jesus not exclusively as expiation but also as the 'embodiment of the risk to love' (Streufert 2006: 75). Proposing maternal sacrifice as a hermeneutic of the cross, Mary J. Streufert (2006: 73) contends that 'continued life, transformation, and nonviolence – ultimately reflect maternal sacrifice.' She elaborates that 'restorative wholeness of relationship, both with God and with neighbour, redeems' and that as the heart of both life and the gospel, it is relationship that saves (Streufert 2006: 75). Through this maternal metaphor, Kierkegaard lifts up the covering of Christ over and above the carnage of the cross. 'He gave himself for the whole world as a hiding place, also for you, just as for me' (WA, 187/SKS 12, 301). Kierkegaard's use of a mother-child relationship to depict his conception of covering is compelling because it conveys a loving gesture that is both non-reciprocal and inimitable and which therefore can only be received in humility. Furthermore, the image emphasizes the gift character of Christ's offering, illustrating a relationship established through volition that is motivated by mutual desire instead of compulsion, wrath, or debt.

The use of maternal imagery is significant since for Kierkegaard, maternal love encourages becoming. On Kierkegaard's view, Christ's provision of a hiding place protects a person from justice, and just as importantly, from herself, thereby buffering the Christian against inauthentic and sinful ways of being even in her self-relation. Shielding a person from justice, herself, and the torturous memories of her sin, God through Christ further aids an individual in becoming 'a changed, a different, a better person – to remain in my hiding place, forgotten by justice and by that person I detest' (WA, 187/SKS 12, 301). Although Kierkegaard depicts Jesus as providing satisfaction for divine justice, Barrett (2013a: 317) holds that he favours examining the ways in which Christ's atonement can transform an individual's existence. Just as Christ offers himself to every single individual in the world (WA, 187/SKS 12, 301), he also offers each individual the possibility to become her own authentic self. This feminine image used to communicate truths about atonement, including that it works to protect from violence rather than to engender the enactment of it, that little more can be done by human beings than to humbly accept it, and that it facilitates becoming a self within relation, sets the stage for more concrete characters who embody these aspects of atonement within the Kierkegaardian corpus.

Christ's receptivity: the woman who was a sinner

Kierkegaard's examples of Sarah and the woman who was a sinner afford two models that, instead of lifting up the violence of the cross, show how the cross draws the believer into closer intimacy with Christ. In both of these narratives as drawn upon by Kierkegaard, profound lessons of atonement are taught while death is neither necessitated nor actualized (Streufert 2006: 69). In these women's narratives, as with the mother hen analogy, atonement manifests as nurturing the other, physical and emotional intimacy, wholeness, and reconciliation. Sarah teaches that to be redeemed is to be loved and the woman who was a sinner teaches that to be redeemed is to love. For Kierkegaard, this desire to be loved by God and to love God is definitive for what it means to be Christian (JP 4, 431–2/SKS 26, 22). Forgiveness and redemption become existential modes for these two women, and through Kierkegaard's particular use of their stories, his readers are taught how to likewise embody forgiveness and redemption. Both narratives make clear that redemption is a 'profoundly this-worldly affair, though it implies a radical transformation of our conception of and place in the world' (Ray 1998: 132). Atonement brings about intimacy with Christ not only through suffering in solidarity while striving for eternity but also by making possible earthly joy that emanates from special bonds with other human beings.

The woman who was a sinner models intimate devotion to Christ by risking social damnation for reconciliation to Christ; in so doing, she prefigures Christ's willingness to suffer for the sake of atonement. Echoing Christ's own words in the biblical text by asking his readers to truly see and learn from this woman (WA, 152/SKS 12, 264), Kierkegaard asserts that by entering the house of Simon the Pharisee without invitation and silently anointing Christ's feet, the nameless woman known only by her sinful status makes herself 'indispensable to the Savior' (WA, 143/SKS 11, 279). She provides a model of redemption that Christ is unable to reveal on his own by inserting herself into a patriarchal context in which she is met with disdain and ridicule, judged unworthy of Christ. In this way, she embodies Kierkegaard's contention that no power drives a person to risk terror like love does (EUD, 71/SKS 5, 80). The woman prefigures Christ's willingness to suffer the abjection of atonement, as well as rejection by those he loves, out of his love for them and God. By disregarding the fact that others do not want her to be reconciled to Christ, the woman embodies one feminist theologian's contention that, invariably, 'to live out the kingdom of God on earth places one in an ethic of risk' (Streufert 2006: 75).

In this regard, she prefigures Christ who also knowingly upsets the social order through his life and death. Yet negative responses to his being and message do not restrain Christ; likewise, the danger of eliciting unfavourable reactions does not restrain the woman who demonstrates great love toward him.

In pointing out that had she been concerned with becoming worthy, the woman would have never approached Christ, Kierkegaard highlights that she 'decides to go immediately, in her unworthiness.' Her sense of her own depravity makes her acutely aware that she is incapable of redeeming herself. It is her feelings of unworthiness that prove determinative for her (WA, 155/SKS 12, 268). Here, Kierkegaard makes plain that neither imitation nor reconciliation should be hindered by a need to achieve a certain standing before God. Instead, the humility born of a recognized relationship with the divine other drives her choices. Relating to the divine out of her need, rather than her merit, the woman embodies the Kierkegaardian motif that to need God is a human being's highest perfection (EUD, 303/SKS 5, 297). Rather than being a source of shame that enervates her, her lack of self-sufficiency is the very thing that strengthens her resolve to urgently draw herself into relationship with Christ.

Kierkegaard notes that it is her uncommon sorrow that makes her into a saint rather than a sinner (WA, 152/SKS 12, 264–5). Through his depiction of this woman, Kierkegaard illustrates his contention that an 'authentic sinner' has the authority to proclaim Christianity, something she shares only with God and an apostle. Understanding that she is a sinner, she makes repentance her sole concern. Although this sinner experiences despair from a human perspective, 'Christianly he is saved, for he is a believer; humanly repentance is his only passion, but the Atonement is his consolation.' The sinner is comparable to a starving person who voraciously consumes bread, 'so the hunger of repentance within him devours the Atonement; just as it is a matter of life or death to the hungry man if he does not get food, so it is life and death to him if he does not hear the Atonement' (JP 6, 88/SKS 27, 464–5). One's acknowledged inability to redeem oneself engenders a desperation that can only be alleviated through Christ's redemptive death.

The woman's superfluous self-offering typifies Christian atonement, yet remains distinct by sacrificing through non-violent means. On Kierkegaard's reading, because tender reconciliation is her sole objective, the woman generously 'squanders' her ointment from a worldly perspective (WA, 155/SKS 12, 269). Her extravagant love foreshadows the love of Christ manifest in atonement on a Kierkegaardian view by virtue of the fact that Christ suffers more than would be required to engender equality and sympathy with human beings (WA, 117/SKS 11, 253). Identifying her affectionate gesture with Christ's culminating act of charity, Kierkegaard opines that 'if there is discussion of love's work ... then there is ... only one work ... you know at once who it is about, about him, about Jesus Christ, about his atoning death, which hides a multitude of sins' (WA, 186/SKS 12, 300). Barbara E. Reid (2002: 117) speaks to this parallel when she claims that the woman's care prefigures Christ's atonement: her pouring of the expensive ointment because of love prefigures Jesus pouring out his blood for those whom he loves. Christ's actions and identity are so bound up with those of this woman that, according to Reid (2002: 117), to misperceive the woman and her behaviour is to misperceive Jesus.

This story proves especially constructive for a Kierkegaardian notion of atonement. The narrative centres around a woman who has lived inauthentically by choosing sin over love and has suffered alienation from self and society as a result. Redemption for her is a story of becoming: transitioning from being identified with sin by other human beings to being identified as love by the divine. The nameless woman changes her relationship to both by exchanging her unidentified sin and social invisibility for authentic selfhood and sociality. In so doing, she transforms herself and sets herself free. Redemption appears in the form of receiving as much as in the form of sacrificing; what is gained is a new and profound relationship with God, self, and the neighbour. Likewise, in the atonement Christ not only makes the authenticity of others possible, he further offers his own model of becoming an authentic self (KJN 9, 203/SKS 25, 201). Because Christ embodied prophecy about the atonement, he was thereby 'the scriptures brought to life' (KJN 6, 165/SKS 22, 166); in other words, he realized his God-given identity by making the abstract concrete. Becoming an authentic self through his life and atonement, Christ makes possible authentic selfhood and relationship for all others. This woman likewise becomes an authentic self by entering into a conciliatory relationship with Christ and appropriately embodying aspects of atonement.

The act of receiving is an inextricable component of gaining authentic selfhood, since selfhood, like salvation, is a matter of both task and gift (Barrett 2013b). This is in part because receiving from an external other allows forfeiting shame in favour of forgiveness. As she transforms her relationship to others in this way, the woman avoids masochism, instead demonstrating an embodied and non-destructive form of service that is both volitional and self-initiated, resulting in reconciliation. In a way that resonates with feminist perspectives on religious sacrifice, Kierkegaard employs an image that does not participate in self-destructive modes of sacrifice; instead, the figure he regards as prototypical for Christians performs a kenosis of service.[4] The woman sinner demonstrates that she is both limited and powerful: not arrogating sacrifice to herself in superhuman ways, she simply makes faithful movements that evince her gracious willingness to be redeemed in loving relation with the other with the full understanding that because Christ alone is 'unconditionally capable of everything' (WA, 156/SKS 12, 269), atonement is something that ultimately can only be received.

Appropriation is key to Kierkegaard's use of this narrative: in his analysis, the woman anointing Christ's feet completely understands that Christ is speaking metaphorically about her when he tells the story of the two debtors who are forgiven equally for drastically different debts, and she fully internalizes his message. Kierkegaard implies that readers should likewise realize that he is speaking to them, encouraging a notion of atonement free of violence or self-destructive forms of sacrifice for every human individual. Reconciliation necessarily entails the risk inherent in relationships, yet this risk remains minimal relative both to its potential results and to whom the risk is for, namely Christ who is 'grace and the giver of grace' (WA, 143/SKS 11, 279). Although the woman came to Christ with 'her sin and sorrow,' she left with 'forgiveness and joy' (WA, 157/SKS 12, 270). Ultimately, her risk amounts to sacrificing sin and alienation for wholeness and mended relation. As Barrett (2013a: 318) explains, for Kierkegaard, to believe in the atonement is to 'abandon the project of cherishing one's guilt,' elaborating that it is the 'yearning for forgiveness' that 'draws the heart to the crucified one.' Kierkegaard wants his readers to appreciate the same thing that he expressed in his personal writings: that receiving the gift is incredibly difficult; the joy that only emanates from the divine is attained as a person realizes her own incapacity and accepts restitution from another on her behalf. Paradoxically, it is only by recognizing one's lack that one can fully become oneself in one's full authenticity.

Human receptivity to Christ: Sarah

For Kierkegaard, Sarah of Tobit indicates how authentic selfhood connects to the willingness to receive the gift of someone else's mortal risk in hopes of bringing about joyful love. Having lost seven different would-be husbands to a demon who kills each man she tries to marry on her wedding night (FT, 102–4/SKS 4, 191), Sarah faces a despair not unlike the woman sinner. Kierkegaard characterizes her as a person 'so unhappy that the things of this earth and earthly advantage … lost their attraction' and who 'deeply, grieved, thought of suicide' (WL, 123/SKS

9, 126). Elaborating on her pathos in *Fear and Trembling,* Johannes de silentio focuses on her willingness to let yet another man, Tobias, with whom she is in love and who knows about her curse, risk the grim fate of her past loves in hopes of marrying and surviving. In his treatment of this apocryphal story, silentio valorises the willingness of Sarah to let another risk death on her behalf with the hope that her curse could be overcome and joyful love could finally be obtained.[5] He privileges the exemplariness of Sarah, who allows someone to die on her behalf, over and above Tobias who ventures dying for her, ultimately proclaiming Sarah to be the hero (FT, 104/SKS 4, 193). Hugh Pyper (2011: 121) comments that for silentio, it is Sarah's 'humble acceptance' of another's willing sacrifice that is the 'truly courageous act.' Echoing silentio, Pyper (2011: 119) elucidates that Sarah's role involves agency: she reveals an active will to love and be loved, as well as to be joined together in an unbreakable union.[6]

Although Tobias is the more obviously Christological figure, Sarah reveals the connection between atonement and human frailty. She is unable on her own to make love possible and therefore requires an external in-breaking. In enumerating Sarah's commendable traits and actions, silentio shows that atonement not only defeats sin but heals the human deficiency and affliction for which one is not culpable, punctuating the Christian attributes required in order to be amenable to one's own healing. He exclaims, 'what love for God it takes to be willing to let oneself be healed when from the very beginning one in all innocence has been botched ... a damaged specimen of a human being!' (FT, 104/SKS 4, 193). Another translation emphasizes the fact that this impairment occurs 'through no fault of one's own' (Kierkegaard 1986, 129/SKS 4, 193). The Danish reads 'uden Skyld' – without guilt or blame – emphasizing the fact that this impairment is not one's own fault. Exculpating her for her own anomalous predicament, silentio is definitive that to be placed outside the universal from the beginning, whether by nature or historical circumstances, is the beginning of the demonic, for which the individual cannot be blamed (FT, 106/SKS 4, 194). Unlike the woman who was a sinner, her plight is not the result of her own sinful choices, yet she still needs another external to herself to make joyful love possible, since according to Kierkegaard, no matter how strong a person is, the enemy within is one that she can never conquer on her own (EUD, 18/SKS 5, 27–8). Sarah's story clarifies that to need to work interdependently to bring about one's own redemption reveals strength rather than weakness.

For Kierkegaard, ethical maturity entails that Sarah takes the responsibility for letting her beloved endanger himself. Silentio notes that a poet would concentrate on Tobias' courage to risk his life willingly in such obvious danger (FT, 103/SKS 4, 192). Yet, for him, Tobias' action is a matter of obligation rather than being supererogatory, and to overlook Sarah's lionhearted humility is to miss the crux of the story (FT, 103–4/SKS 4, 192–3). Analogously, Christ provides atonement because he was foreordained to do so (KJN 9, 203/SKS 25, 201), while human beings must exert themselves toward volitional acceptance of it. In this light, one is attuned to how difficult it is not just for Christ to offer the atonement and its resultant grace, but also for human beings to receive both of these. To defend his stance that Sarah is the heroic one, silentio articulates that 'the great mystery [is] that it is far more difficult to receive than to give' (FT, 104/SKS 4, 193). Sarah's arduous task is to allow another to do for her what she cannot do for herself in order to make her life whole. Moreover, she offers a model of sacrifice that resists an easier path of relegating herself to death in favour of the struggle to receive full life, even when this struggle involves forfeiting the delusion of being able to realize salvation in isolation from others. The ethical maturity she evinces in actively allowing someone to die for her resolves the problem of passivity in purely self-sacrificial models of love.

Ultimately, the human role in atonement is to sacrifice sorrow in favour of joyful love. Willing to be redeemed, Sarah evinces Christian love by not regarding herself as so far away from perfection so as to be disqualified from love, which would actually expose her as an unloving and self-concerned person (EUD, 74/SKS 5, 81–2). A person who truly loves neither excludes herself from happiness nor makes herself the cause of her happiness; instead, turning away from self, she becomes happy about love (EUD, 74/SKS 5, 82). This turn further encourages the sacrifice of one's sorrow. Exhorting his readers to make this sacrifice in totality, Kierkegaard enjoins: 'one is to cast away *all* sorrow; if one does not cast away *all* sorrow, then one … does not become joyful, to say nothing of unconditionally joyful.' There is only one right place to cast this sorrow and that is upon God because to cast it elsewhere means that one does not unconditionally rid oneself of it. Instead, it returns somehow, 'often in the form of even greater and more grievous sorrow' (WA, 42/SKS 11, 46). Sarah's part in her own redemption is to release her curse and the inauthentic identity built around it. Foregoing the human tendency to deceive, manipulate, and circumvent the aspect of herself that makes her a liability in her own eyes, Sarah allows her beloved both to see her full vulnerability and to take it upon himself. In relationship to Christ, such resolve proves especially brave since Kierkegaard describes Christ as one who experienced all human sorrow more grievously than any human being and therefore understands all of a person's sorrow even better than she does. More than an end in itself, this knowledge serves as a means to take away an individual's sorrow and offer her rest (CD, 266/SKS 10, 282). This exchange reciprocates love between the one who sacrifices sorrow and the one who makes that sacrifice efficacious by offering joy in its stead.

Reciprocal love ought to characterize a person's relation to Christ over against maintaining her own intrinsic suffering or assuming violent affliction. As George Pattison states, the heart of Christian imitation is not so much a matter of resembling the external pattern of his life but of one's internal orientation to the other, both human and divine. He writes that 'imitation is not just a matter of religious exercises but of a basic commitment to a life lived in and as love.' By virtue of this commitment, the requirements of love will not always be self-evidently religious, but from Kierkegaard's perspective they must 'always be rooted in the relation to God given in Christ' (Pattison 2012: 170). Rather than embodying and perpetuating a cycle of violence, Sarah and the woman who loved much associate themselves with Christ in loving reciprocity. Pattison (2012: 155) elaborates that the 'nothingness manifested in the figure of the weeping sinful woman is, at the same time, and yet more fundamentally, also an expression of a virtuous circle of love: of her total love for the Saviour and of his totally accepting love for her.' Humble reception and non-destructive forms of sacrifice typify the way that relation to Christ and atonement effect a mutually responsive dynamic of love that expands Christian existence.

Kierkegaard presents Sarah's story in a way that expresses the perpetual cyclicality of a person's loving relation to Christ through the atonement by directing attention to the fact that she lets another risk death for her not once, but multiple times. For Kierkegaard, the atonement, understood as the power by which Christ provides a new start for an individual (Watkin 2010: 214), is the 'most profound expression of repetition' (R, 313/SKS 15, 78). In Sarah's case, the consummate repetition only comes after several unsuccessful attempts at receiving redemption. Correlatively, Kierkegaard suggests a hypothetical repetition of Christ's performance of the atonement in order to poignantly portray the love that Christ's offering embodies. Imagining that if somehow the atonement proved incomplete, Christ would suffer again for those needing redemption, he writes that Christ would 'rather lay down his life once again in order to procure by his death a hiding place for you than have you deprived of the hiding place' (WA, 186/SKS 12, 300). Sarah's continual readiness to allow another to die for her mirrors the unceasing availability of Christ's atonement. Although the hypothetical willingness of Christ to repeat atonement envisioned by Kierkegaard proves unnecessary, the process of becoming an authentic self through the atonement and a perpetual openness to the divine other does not. Selfhood is realized through the intimate association with Christ and his atonement effected by repeatedly participating in the ritual of communion, which commemorates the self-giving death of Christ (WA, 186–8/SKS 300–2). What Kierkegaard incisively points his readers towards is that not only performing the works of love in relation to the neighbour, but also receiving the gift of atonement, requires rigorous effort. The work of acceptance in appropriating salvation as gift just *is* salvation as task.

Conclusion

A Kierkegaardian notion of atonement informed by feminist theology would concentrate on the immanence of the concrete and embodied relationality between the self and the beloved that may assume the risk of violence or other negative consequences from others but without unnecessarily or zealously enacting it. Atonement, as provided by God, cannot be earned, yet requires the individual to accept it by resisting the urge to resign herself to a life of tragedy and alienation. This framing resonates with the insight of liberation theologian Virgilio Elizondo (1983: 66), who accentuates that through Christ, God experiences the rejection of the world's non-persons, sharing in their suffering while affirming their struggle against suffering. He further explains that Jesus never gave up on the possibility of love and forgiveness so that 'he triumphed over violence without giving in to violent ways'; by means of this tenacious love, he opens up the possibility of new creation that is based on active non-violence rather than passivity or violence (Elizondo 1983: 77–8). The notion of atonement teased out from Kierkegaard's use of female figures, read in light of his emphasis on the gentleness of the divine response to humanity effected through the atonement and his downplaying of the violence of the atonement, engenders the possibility of Christian reconciliation outside an economy of destructive self-sacrifice and within the realm of vitality, communion, and flourishing. Through its demand for the sacrifice of estrangement and the suffering that accompanies it, atonement within a Kierkegaardian framework brings the struggle for selfhood amid human frailty, sin, and injustice to its culmination in the establishment of new relationships to Christ, self, and other human beings, including those that are most beloved.

Related topics

'Conscience, self-deception, and the question of authenticity in Kierkegaard,' Claudia Welz; 'Love for humans: morality as the heart of Kierkegaard's religious philosophy,' Sharon Krishek.

Notes

1 Although Kierkegaard's earlier writings assume that reconciliation includes receiving back one's beloved in the present, he never seems able to integrate this belief into his own life; perhaps as a result, his later writings increasingly fixate on the abject suffering of Christ on the cross and the sort of imitation that requires similar forms of suffering. Further, Kierkegaard's Christian writings come to focus more on a form of salvation that points toward the eternal and ethereal at the exclusion of the temporal and mundane. Yet, although Kierkegaard uses the terminology of 'dying to' increasingly in his late writings, he mainly refers to dying to the world, a term that describes shedding inauthentic forms of selfhood in order to realize one's true self in Christ.
2 For a contemporary account of a similar view of atonement, see Davis (2014).
3 Note that the Hebrew word for atonement is *kaphar*, meaning 'to cover' (Brown, Driver, and Briggs 2008: 497–8).

4 Stephen T. Davis and C. Stephen Evans (2009: 313–5) hold that kenosis is a valid theological option for Christians, advocating for a moral kenosis in which masters act as servants. They hold up Christ's act of washing his apostles' feet as a 'mini-kenosis.' What makes kenosis compelling is the religious power inherent in such an act of love and humility.
5 Significantly, Luther's (1960: 345; cited in Pyper 2011: 116) preface to Tobit in the Bible of 1534 comes across as more dismissive of Tobit than silentio is, describing it as a 'delightful, devout comedy' about adversities to family harmony that ends with a hopeful resolution.
6 Pyper notes that Luther described Sarah in language that could have influenced Kierkegaard, whether directly or indirectly. In *Table Talk*, Luther (1912: § 697, 338; cited in Pyper 2011: 119) describes Sarah as 'one who comes out on top,' yet he sees the story as describing a comedy concerned with the domestic economy and women's place within it. This makes silentio's treatment of the story even more impressive insofar as his reading valorises the woman not for domestic relations, but for the courage and humility to be saved by another who, as I have suggested, symbolizes Christ.

References

Barrett, L. C. (2013a) *Eros and self-emptying: The intersections of Augustine and Kierkegaard*, Grand Rapids, MI: Eerdmans Publishing Company.
Barrett, L. C. (2013b) 'Kierkegaard on the atonement: The complementarity of salvation as a gift and salvation as a task,' in H. Schulz, J. Stewart and K. Verstrynge (eds), *Kierkegaard Studies Yearbook 2013*, Berlin: Walter de Gruyter.
Boff, L. (2001) *Passion of Christ, passion of the world*, Maryknoll, NY: Orbis Books.
Brown, F., Driver, F. R., and Briggs, C. A. (2008) *The Brown-Driver-Briggs Hebrew and English lexicon*, Peabody, MA: Hendrickson.
Davis, R. W. (2014) 'The authority of God and the meaning of the atonement,' *Religious Studies*, 50, no. 4: 405–23.
Davis, S. T. and Evans, C. S. (2009) 'Conclusion: The promise of kenosis,' in C. S. Evans (ed), *Exploring Kenotic Christology: The Self-Emptying of God*, Vancouver: Regent College Publishing, 313–21.
Elizondo, V. (1983) *Galilean journey: The Mexican-American promise*, Maryknoll, NY: Orbis Books.
Kierkegaard, S. (1986) *Fear and trembling*, A. Hannay (trans), London; New York: Penguin Books.
Luther, M. (1960) 'Preface to the Book of Tobit [1534],' in *Luther's works*, vol. 35 (*Words and Sacraments I*), E. T. Bachmann (ed and trans), Philadelphia, PA: Muhlenberg.
Luther, M. (1912) *Dr Martin Luthers Werke Kritische Gesamtausgabe: Tischreiden 1–6*, vol. 1, Weimar: Hermann Böhlhaus Nachfolger.
McFague, S. (1982) *Metaphorical theology*, Philadelphia, PA: Fortress Press.
Pattison, G. (2012) *Kierkegaard and the theology of the nineteenth century: The paradox and the point of contact*, Cambridge: Cambridge University Press.
Pyper, H. (2011) *The joy of Kierkegaard as a Biblical reader*, Sheffield: Equinox Publishing.
Rae, M. (2010) *Kierkegaard and theology*, London; New York: T. & T. Clark International.
Ray, D. K. (1998) *Deceiving the devil: Atonement, abuse, and ransom*, Cleveland, OH: Pilgrim Press.
Reid, B. E. (2002) '"Do you see this woman?": A liberative look at Luke 7: 36–50 and strategies for reading other Lukan stories against the grain,' in A. J. Levine and M. Blickenstaff (eds), *A Feminist Companion to Luke*, London: Sheffield Academic Press, 106–20.
Streufert, M. J. (2006) 'Maternal sacrifice as a hermeneutics of the cross,' in M. Trelstad (ed), *Cross Examinations: Readings on the Meaning of the Cross Today*, Minneapolis, MN: Augsburg Fortress, 63–75.
Thompson, D. A. (2006) 'Becoming a feminist theologian of the cross,' in M. Trelstad (ed), *Cross Examinations: Readings on the Meaning of the Cross Today*, Minneapolis, MN: Augsburg Fortress, 76–90.
Thomte, R. (1949) *Kierkegaard's philosophy of religion*, Princeton, NJ: Princeton University Press.
Watkin, J. (2010) 'Repetition,' in J. Watkins (ed), *The A to Z of Kierkegaard's Philosophy*, Lanham, MD: Scarecrow Press.

Further reading

Green, D. N. (2015) 'Sacrifice,' in S. Emmanuel, W. McDonald and J. Stewart (eds), *Kierkegaard research: Sources, reception, and resources*, vol. 15 (*Kierkegaard's Concepts*), tome 5, Farnham: Ashgate.

This entry in an encyclopaedia of important concepts in Kierkegaard's writings succinctly describes the various uses of the notion of sacrifice within his corpus.

Søltoft, P. (2000) 'To let oneself be upbuilt,' in H. Schulz, J. Stewart and K. Verstrynge (eds), *Kierkegaard Studies Yearbook 2000*, Berlin: Walter de Gruyter.

In this essay, the author argues both that relationships that are mutually upbuilding constitute a type of indirect communication free of deception, and that universal human needs necessarily involve both the receiver and the communicator in the process.

Welz, C. (2008) 'Love as gift and self-sacrifice,' *Neue Zeitschrift für Systematische Theologie und Religionsphilosophie*, 50, nos. 3–4: 238–66.

In this essay, the author discusses religious sacrifice and its relationship to love in Kierkegaard's thought, and includes a response to contemporary feminist critiques of self-sacrifice.

19

ON FAITH AND REASON(S): KIERKEGAARD'S LOGIC OF CONVICTION

K. Brian Söderquist

Introduction

One of the most consistent themes in Kierkegaard's authorship is an insistence that religious life, especially the Christian version he was familiar with, is not to be understood. For him, it seems there is no conceptual analysis of Christianity that does not distort it and detract from how it ought to be viewed: namely, as an ardent, life-governing commitment the individual will never fully understand, or be able to explain or defend. Kierkegaard keeps a steady eye on the existential difficulties this lack of understanding gives rise to. In different voices and different ways, he reiterates that it can be intellectually unpalatable, even offensive, to be asked to accept the claims that ground Christian religious life. Rather than alleviate the tension religious life engenders, however, his works direct the individual away from justification of religious beliefs and right back to the troubled passions that arise precisely because she cannot justify them. And, often, Kierkegaard pushes even harder: Not only is it misguided to try to defend beliefs, it is also 'extraordinarily stupid' (SUD, 87/SKS 11, 200). Throughout his works, his starting assumption is that Christian religious life is foolishness when measured with the wisdom that otherwise governs our common worldview.[1]

But one might ask if Kierkegaard's talk about the foolishness of religious life is *too* convincing. If religious beliefs are inconsistent with what one otherwise takes to be reasonable, defensible, and intellectually satisfying, why would a reflective, critically educated person – like Kierkegaard himself – ever opt for religious life at all? Upon what is religious conviction then based? Can one ever give good objective arguments for it? Can one even give good subjective reasons for it? If so, what sorts of reasons are they? In short, why does anyone initiated into our intellectual culture ever risk her life on something so incredible? It is with questions like these in mind that Kierkegaard's reflections on religious conviction may be most interesting. I would like to suggest that his most discerning insights have to do with the existential conditions that might lead an individual to become convinced that she ought to live a life of faith even though it can seem indefensible to her. The question here is not so much about Kierkegaard's place in classic debates about faith and reason, or about his view of the ultimate rationality of a life of faith.[2] Instead, the question is about what gives rise to a religious conviction in the first place. One of the most provocative aspects of Kierkegaard's analysis is his suggestion that our most profound convictions arise from an interplay of factors that lie deeper than sound argumentation. In fact, as he sees it, conviction does not arise as the result of objectively defensible arguments at all; rather, when reasons seem needed, they are pulled together to justify deeper intuitions. Most crucially, he argues that the only kind of religious conviction that can withstand the assault of the understanding is one grounded in subjective religious experience; the only 'proof' is what he calls the *argumentum spiritus sancti*, the 'proof of the holy spirit' (KJN 6, 105/SKS 22, 108).

This chapter charts the basic movements of this strange kind of proof. I begin with a brief review of Kierkegaard's lifelong campaign against attempts to secure religious conviction via objective argumentation, as if it emerged in the same way as do convictions about natural science or history. I then turn to his account of the psychological moods and emotions that condition belief and to his suggestion that genuine conviction arises only when driven by a desperate longing for existential comfort. Finally, I suggest that Kierkegaard's logic of religious conviction includes both active and passive movements: it follows from an active choice to live a life of faith coupled with a passive reception of the testimony of an odd kind of witness, the 'witness' of spirit. Like mystical experience, this spiritual testimony might be utterly persuasive to an individual who has experienced it, but it cannot be imparted to anyone else, nor explained in the same way one explains most other kinds of human experience. It is to this inner, spiritual experience that Kierkegaard points as the basis of conviction, inexplicable as it is.

Kierkegaard's arguments against arguments

Kierkegaard's starting point is an insistence that faith is foolishness (e.g., PF, 52, 102/SKS 4, 255, 299; EUD, 83/SKS 5, 90; CUP 1, 213–9/SKS 7, 195–200; cf. 1 Cor. 1: 23). On this matter, he is in closer agreement with Enlightenment critics of religion – and even later critics such as Nietzsche or Freud – than with traditional defenders of it. But unlike those critics, he makes his critique in the name of faith. For Kierkegaard, the problem with the apologetic impulse within a person is that it tempts her to believe that her faith will be strengthened by good explanations. As he sees it, that's simply not true. He wants to make it clear that *understanding* faith is the *problem*, not the solution, precisely because our deepest convictions about religious matters are never grounded in explanation or good arguments.

From one end of his authorship to the other, he directs his reader away from objective demonstrations and proofs and toward inward, subjective territory and, ultimately, toward the possibility of a 'spiritual proof.'

While Kierkegaard's suspicion of defending religious commitment is present from the outset of his authorship (Hughes 2014: 9–45; Söderquist 2017), *Fear and Trembling* provides some of the most striking examples. Far from offering a defence of religious faith, this text paints a picture of faith so unattractive that the book might be read as an indirect argument for why one should *never* embrace it. Pseudonym Johannes de silentio, who makes it clear that he lacks faith, observes Abraham with fascination and horror as he acts upon a religious conviction that is wholly incomprehensible to him: Abraham is absurdly willing to kill his son but absurdly confident that his son will survive to become the father of nations. Judged with reasonable intersubjective standards, Abraham 'believed the preposterous' (FT, 20/SKS 4, 117); 'human calculation was out of the question' (FT, 35/SKS 4, 131).[3] De silentio concludes that the only explanation for Abraham's absurd willingness to kill his son is that he let go of the kind of reason we use to understand our world: He 'left one thing behind, he took one thing along: he left behind his worldly understanding and took along his faith' (FT, 17/SKS 4, 113). For a shrewd fellow like de silentio, this is all terribly disturbing: 'to be able to lose one's understanding and along with it everything finite, for which it is the stockbroker, and then by virtue of the absurd, to get the same finitude back again – that appalls me' (FT, 36/SKS 4, 131). In the end, and to de silentio's great consternation, he gets no further than bafflement. And, crucially, the reader is left with de silentio's questions: Upon what is Abraham's conviction based? For what reasons might a person opt for the life of faith described in such dubious terms? What speaks for this absurd risk?

In the *Concluding Unscientific Postscript*, Kierkegaard's polemic against the attempt to understand faith continues. Large sections of this book – written by Johannes Climacus, another pseudonym who claims to be an 'outsider' to faith (CUP 1, 16/SKS 7, 25) – are devoted to criticizing the misguided attempt to understand and justify Christianity historically and logically, that is, 'objectively' (e.g., CUP 1, 214, 218–23/SKS 7, 196–7, 199–203). Like de silentio, Climacus observes that a life governed by a reliance on logical 'certainty' or empirical 'probability' is at odds with a life governed by trust in a God, whose existence can never by proven. But more clearly than we see in de silentio, Climacus reveals the emotional tension he himself experiences because of this philosophical void. Even earnest defences of the orderliness and apparent design of the universe will lead to existential distress as much as it leads to comfort. Climacus writes: 'I observe nature in order to find God, and indeed I see omnipotence and wisdom, but I see much else too that troubles and disturbs. The sum total of this is objective uncertainty' (CUP 1, 203–4/SKS 7, 186–7).

Elsewhere in the authorship, the personal cost of trying to justify one's own life-governing beliefs is even more apparent. Kierkegaard suggests that the person of faith will never be free from an aspiration to defend her way of life to herself because she innately desires to justify why she lives the way she does. She will be inclined to turn to reasons when her convictions falter and she will want to remind herself about why she lives as a believer (cf. FSE, 68/SKS 13, 90). And at times, she will be intellectually offended at her own religious convictions and feel compelled to admit to herself the absurdity of her own beliefs. A journal entry captures neatly the internal conflict. Kierkegaard writes that the faithful person

> grasps it as duty of character that he must not insist upon comprehension. But then comes the conflict. To be willing to believe something one can't comprehend is blind obedience, obscurantism, stupidity, etc. This means that the world will make the believer anxious with the fear of other human beings, and instill in him the vanity that he'll also be able to comprehend it. There's the conflict.
>
> *(KJN 6, 38/SKS 22, 42)*

This impulse to understand Christianity leads a person away from discovering that the real existential issue will never be resolved through an investigation of the 'objective' problem of 'Christianity's truth' (CUP 1, 214/SKS 7, 196). Rather, Christianity must be taken as a lived response to the deep subjective problem of existential homelessness; it is about the possibility of finding an abiding 'happiness' (CUP 1, 15–7/SKS 7, 24–6).

Desperate longing

Other works go further in this direction, underscoring that religious conviction is not first and foremost about reason or the lack of it. For Kierkegaard, concern, need, and longing for the divine must be included in the equation. In *The Sickness unto Death*, this troubled concern is explicitly called a prerequisite for faith. Though we again find a caustic polemic against trying to grasp what cannot be grasped (SUD, 87, 96–104/SKS 11, 200, 209–16), Anti-Climacus's primary aim is to engage the reader in dialogue about her own inner misalignment, her ambivalence about her own fundamental projects, and the abiding sadness deep within her soul. He presupposes that just under the surface of everyday awareness, the modern individual experiences herself as someone fragmented, fractured, misaligned, imperfect, incomplete, splintered, or cracked. Something is not quite right inside, even if it's difficult to say exactly why, or to explain what external factors could be the cause. And he assumes that alongside a hushed sorrow in the soul, there is also a latent hope for a cure, which, when circumstances become tight enough, will reveal itself more clearly. Religious conviction is not centred on the rational persuasiveness of doctrinal propositions; it is not about good or bad arguments. For Kierkegaard, concern, need, and longing for the divine precede reasonable arguments. This desperation is the psychological wellspring of faith. Putting it succinctly, he writes: 'this is the first requirement of faith – despair – and within it an intense longing for the religious' (SUD, 110/SKS 11, 192; see also EUD 136/SKS 5, 139; EO 2, 83–4/SKS 3, 87–8; Cappelørn 2007; Hughes 2014: 9–45). A passage from his journals written alongside *The Sickness unto Death* describes the confusion that arises when this fundamental despair and longing is left out of the discussion of faith:

> The great catastrophe is that, quite smoothly, Xnty has become a thought project for shrewd minds and speculators who have absolutely nothing to do with real Xnty. It is no longer solace for an illness that no human wisdom can alleviate, solace for the anguish and pain of the consciousness of sin, solace that is meant only for those who suffer. What would we think of a medicine if, by some strange mistake, it were made the object of analysis for a chemist rather than a remedy for an ill person for whom it was intended? And what if the chemist then discovered that it wasn't a remedy at all – and he even made the mistake of saying: I myself am not sick.
> (KJN 6, 40–1/SKS 22, 44)

For Kierkegaard, Christianity is meant to be a cure for a spiritual illness and it is on these terms that it must be judged and understood.

Conviction and reason(s)

Kierkegaard's logic of religious conviction, then, begins negatively: it presupposes an intellectual uncertainty, a sorrow in the soul, and an accompanying desire for a remedy to an illness (Law 1993: 24–34; Pattison 2002: 35–64; Theunissen 2005: 43–4, 85–6). But even if a person is aware of her silent desperation, it is not obvious that religious faith is the cure. How does Kierkegaard think religious conviction arises from the abyss? What reasons are there for choosing religion over other possible existential cures?

Kierkegaard answers that there are no 'reasons,' at least not if reasons are taken to mean objective arguments that will appeal to and satisfy the understanding. In a particularly and perhaps uncharacteristically straightforward journal entry, he describes the relationship between arguments and conviction, inverting the order one might expect:

> All this talk about world history, arguments, and proofs for the truth of Xnty must be eliminated. There is only one proof: that of faith. If I'm genuinely convinced of something (and this is a mode of inwardness on the way to becoming spirit), then I'll always value my conviction higher than the arguments for it. Conviction *sustains* argument: argument doesn't sustain conviction. . . . It can't possibly be the case that a person holds back his convictions while pushing forward with arguments. No, one's conviction . . . that's what is decisive. One can speak semi-humorously about reasons: if you really want reasons, I'll happily give you some. Do you want 3 or 5 or 7? How

many do you want? But I can say nothing more profound than this: *I* believe. This suffices, this is the positive saturation point, just as when a lover says 'I love her' and talks neither about loving her more intensely than others love their beloveds, and still less about his reasons.

(KJN 6, 104–5/SKS 22, 107–8)

Kierkegaard's logic of conviction acknowledges that good arguments don't lead a person to change her mind; and convictions don't arise as the result of a deliberate search for sound reasons. As he sees it, our convictions orient us in the world first, and we find reasons to defend that worldview when pressed to do so. Of course a person *can* find reasons to support her convictions and 'defend' herself against her own critical voices, but that move is superficial: as long as she remains within the discourse of defence, her best arguments will leave her cold.

Kierkegaard's psychological observations here anticipate some of the conclusions of William James's study of religion, *The Varieties of Religious Experience*, published a couple of generations after Kierkegaard. James's extensive analysis of reports of subjective religious experiences leads him to conclude that religious convictions are based on psychological intuitions found at a deeper level than the one at which scholarly argumentation operates. He argues that while it's a 'splendid tendency' that existential concerns, feelings, and desires, are banished from rational systems like natural science, our deep convictions are nonetheless intimately and inextricably bound up with more profound concerns. And ultimately, any arguments that fail to harmonize with them will remain unconvincing:

[If] we look on man's whole mental life as it exists, on the life of men that lies in them apart from their learning and science, and that they inwardly and privately follow, we have to confess that the part of it of which rationalism can give an account is relatively superficial. It is the part that has the *prestige* undoubtedly, for it has loquacity, it can challenge you for proofs and chop logic, and put you down with words. But it will fail to convince or convert you all the same if your dumb intuitions are opposed to its conclusions. If you have intuitions at all, they come from a deeper level than the loquacious level which rationalism inhabits.

(James 1982: 73)

James describes a kind of comic contradiction that appears for anyone initiated into our contemporary academic culture. A disciplined rational ideal governs our methodical scholarly investigations and colours our workplace consciousness – but deeper intuitions govern our lived existence. Scholarly debates are an apparently serious matter during academic conferences but, if Kierkegaard and James are right, the conclusions of those arguments do not lead us to change our deepest convictions when we return home. When our arguments are challenged, we simply retool and find better ones to justify what we already take to be right.

In a later discussion in *The Varieties of Religious Experience*, James argues, like Kierkegaard, that when it comes to religion – or to any of the things that matter most to us like human relationships or political values – the pattern is the same. Below the surface of reason, 'dumb intuitions' and feelings arbitrate what we believe:

[T]he logical reason of man operates in this field of divinity exactly as it has always operated in love, or in patriotism, or in politics, or in any other of the wider affairs of life, in which our passions or our mystical intuitions fix our beliefs beforehand. It finds arguments for our conviction, for indeed it has to find them. It amplifies and defines our faith, and dignifies it and lends it words and plausibility. It hardly ever engenders it; it cannot now secure it.

(James 1982: 432)

Here James points to feelings and 'mystical intuitions' as the principal ground of religious conviction and, as we will see, this can be helpful when interpreting Kierkegaard's position. But there is another element in Kierkegaard's logic of conviction that ought to be treated first, namely, what he takes to be the first movement out of the negativity of existential despair: the *choice* to live a life of faith. A commitment to faith is a prerequisite for a genuine conviction; it is the *active* element in Kierkegaard's active-passive dialectic of conviction.

The will to believe

The importance of the movement of the will is indicated throughout Kierkegaard's authorship and has been widely discussed. For him, it seems faith is always partly a matter of volition, within the subject's own power. For faith to become vital, an individual must actively appropriate the demands made by her religion; she must resolve to risk her life on something intellectually absurd, to live 'as if' there were a God upon whom she could rely (Pattison 1997). We find examples in the *Postscript*, where Climacus compares the choice of risking one's life on Christianity to Socrates' choice to live 'as if' he had an immortal soul. Socrates doesn't know if he has an immortal soul, but he lives 'as if' he has; he 'invests his entire life' in it, Climacus writes (CUP 1, 199–204/SKS 7, 182–7).

We see this choice to live 'as if' Christianity were true reflected in *The Sickness unto Death*, too, when Anti-Climacus underscores that a 'will' to live a spiritual life is one of the conditions for better spiritual health (SUD, 14, 131/SKS 11, 130, 242). In his inventory of various ways one can be despairingly misaligned with oneself and one's God, he underscores that a mere understanding of the malady will never bring about a cure. In addition to a consciousness of one's illness, one must resolve to make the movement to seek relief. One must make a move 'from having understood something to doing it' (SUD, 93–6/SKS 11, 205–8). This movement of will *is* an act of faith, he says (e.g., SUD 82/SKS 11, 196).[4]

We find the centrality of volition articulated especially clearly in another section of the journal passage I cited earlier, which was written alongside *The Sickness unto Death*. Kierkegaard describes conviction as a process that begins with a choice:

This is how my development, or anybody's development, proceeds: Perhaps we begin with some reasons, but these are in the background. Then we choose. With the weight of responsibility, before God, a conviction is formed within us, with God's help. Now we have the positive element. Our convictions can't be defended or proven with arguments, which would be self-contradictory because reasons remain in the background. No, from here on the matter becomes personal, a matter of personality. One can only defend one's conviction ethically, personally, i.e., with regard to what one is prepared to sacrifice for it and the degree to which one refuses to be scared away from maintaining it.

(KJN 6, 105/SKS 22, 108; cf. WA, 34–5/SKS 11, 38–9)

Passages like these, which celebrate the active commitment to faith in the absence of good reasons, have played a major role in the reception of Kierkegaard's thought and it is possible to sense his influence in many of the debates in the philosophy of religion in the twentieth century.[5] But Kierkegaard's discussion of choice is only part of the story. Conviction involves more than an active commitment. Just as essential to Kierkegaard's logic of conviction is the *passive* element. We cannot actively and autonomously *convince* ourselves that something is good or right simply because we commit to it. In fact, much of Kierkegaard's authorship is a reaction to the haunting impossibility of autonomously *creating* one's own paths, values, and personal identity. In the end, despair itself shows the futility of self-creation (cf. SUD, 67–74/SKS 11, 181–7). Here, too, in his logic of conviction, autonomy finds limits. An inner conviction, as Kierkegaard sees it, is dependent upon the *reception* of something that the subject cannot give herself: a confirmation of her choice. It is the result of a dialectical process with both active and passive elements: the active choice to open oneself to the possibility of an inner, utterly private and incommunicable confirmation, what one might call, with James, a 'religious experience.'

Receiving confirmation

In the journal entry cited above, Kierkegaard proposes that a person of faith chooses to live a religious life without being compelled by 'reasons'; but he also indicates that choice is only one element in the formula. In the wake of choice, he writes, 'with the weight of responsibility, before God, a conviction is formed within us, with God's help.' Note the passivity implied in this 'with God's help.' This passive element – which can be received only if one actively and even strenuously holds oneself open to it – represents the boundary of autonomy in an act of faith. And this receptivity is crucial to conviction. In fact, a received confirmation is the only kind of 'proof' one could ever have about the reality of the divine or about the obligation to live a religiously governed life: 'There is only one proof for the truth of Xnty,' he writes, 'the inner proof, *argumentum spiritus sancti*' – the witness or testimony of the holy spirit (KJN 6, 105/SKS 22, 108). The conviction engendered by this kind of private proof is beyond what the subject can autonomously create for herself. And the private nature of this proof also limits what she could appeal to or argue for in a public forum. On this aspect of faith, Kierkegaard might be inclined to agree with Schleiermacher (1996: 9), who writes:

> The matter of religion is so arranged and so rare that a person who expresses something about it must necessarily have had it, for he has not heard about it anywhere. Of all that I praise and feel as its work there stands precious little in holy books, and to whom would it not seem scandal or folly who did not experience it himself?

Perhaps this is why there is so little direct discussion in Kierkegaard's authorship about how to understand this 'spiritual proof.' His entire authorship points toward and even circles around this liberating, redemptive experience – this 'proof of the holy spirit' – but as far as I can see, he never describes this positive element in the same kind of detail that he describes negative, despairing ways of life. Of course, this 'spiritual proof' is not within Kierkegaard's power to provide or guarantee. At most he can point to the promises of deliverance implied in the religious text he is most familiar with, the New Testament. Perhaps this is why he is largely content to dwell with the negative: to invite the individual to remain aware of a possible lacuna within her soul as he describes the intellectually offensive movements toward faith. We see examples of this pattern in many of his edifying discourses.

Kierkegaard's early discourse 'Strengthening in the Inner Being,'[6] for example, is a meditation on the need for spiritual witness when, during periods of disillusionment or crisis, the understanding demands an explanation. More specifically, it explores the longing for inner confirmation (*bekræftelse*) in the face of existential questions about one's ultimate purposes, a longing that arises when an apprehension or concern (*en bekymring*) awakens in a person's soul 'about what meaning the world has for him, and he for the world' (EUD, 86/SKS 5, 93). Kierkegaard points out that the circumstances that give rise to this existential crisis are many. It might be occasioned by the grief and despondency of 'cruel misfortune,' or by disillusionment in the wake of the death of one's God: when one's 'eyes continually read an invisible handwriting in everything, indicating that it is all emptiness and illusion' (EUD, 94–5/SKS 5, 99–100). This deep concern may announce itself when one feels betrayed by one's closest friends or family or when, like Abraham, it seems as if trials are sent by God to lead one into damnation (EUD, 96–8/SKS 5, 102–4). This concern can even arise in the face of inexplicable good fortune – when 'life is a dance' and 'every dream is fulfilled' – precisely because the fortunate person knows better than anyone that she has done nothing to deserve it (EUD, 88–93/SKS 5, 94–9). In short, Kierkegaard suggests that when a person reflects seriously and earnestly about the mystery of her own existence and her role in the world, she inevitably seeks to assure herself of 'a coherence in everything'; she 'extorts an explanation from creation, demands a testimony' from it (EUD, 86/SKS 5, 93). Interestingly, the 'explanation' that the soul earnestly longs for is *never* given, at least not in the form that would satisfy her craving to understand. Kierkegaard notes that this deep concern 'is not calmed by more detailed or more comprehensive knowledge' about the world; 'it craves knowledge *of another kind*.... It craves an explanation, a witness, but *of another kind*,' namely a witness from the only being who could possibly give such a strange assurance, God (EUD, 86–8/SKS 5, 93–4; my emphasis). And because 'God is Spirit, and thus can give witness only in spirit,' this witness must be given in 'the inner being'; 'Any external witness for God, if such a thing could be conceived, could just as well be a deception' (EUD, 86–7/SKS 5, 94). The discourse ends with Kierkegaard calling attention to the boundaries of subjective autonomy. He writes that 'no one can provide this confirmation himself.' Indeed, as the biblical Paul indicates, this is 'because the witness itself is a *gift* from God' (EUD, 98/SKS 5, 104; my emphasis).

We find a similar pattern in an early discourse that takes a personal approach to the traditional problem of evil: Why would a good God allow me or those I love to suffer so much misery? Here Kierkegaard focuses on the inevitable desire for explanation in the face of personal loss. And as we saw in the discourse on spiritual confirmation, the crucial movement for the subject is to passionately embrace the longing for a divine explanation: the one who struggles to understand 'sits there idly with his loss; but still he is not idle, for he ruminates; and still he is not passive, for he ponders an explanation' (EUD, 394/SKS 5, 376). And, just as we saw earlier, an explanation that could satisfy the understanding is never given. There is no explanation for why things happen the way they do or what greater meaning her loss might have. Instead, we read that if she actively chooses to listen with openness, something else happens: she herself is changed in the experience, she is given an 'assured spirit' (EUD, 396/SKS 5, 378). She receives no explanation (*forklaring*), but she is changed in such a way that she can receive comfort; she is 'transfigured' (*forklaret*) (EUD, 400/SKS 5, 380).[7]

In both of these discourses, we see a movement that points toward the possibility of conviction. The individual experiences a crisis of the understanding, and she remains there, without explanation. If a longing for wholeness becomes her fundamental concern, it can lead to the desperate decision to open herself to the possibility of experiencing a divine confirmation, despite how intellectually unattractive it is. Here the individual reaches the limits of autonomy in the matter, and we reach the limits of what Kierkegaard will promise. Religious experience is an individual matter.

What does 'religious experience' mean?

There has been some debate among Kierkegaard scholars about the degree to which this private 'spiritual testimony' ought to be understood as a kind of mystical experience. Of course, a wide range of different experiences can fall under the general heading 'mysticism.' This could include the ecstatic experiences of authors often associated with the mystical tradition such as Meister Eckhart, Johannes Tauler, and Jakob Böhme. Kierkegaard himself studied several of them and knew of others indirectly (Florin 2002; Mulder 2005; Piety 2017; Šajda 2008; 2009). This exceptional sort of experience is described by those who have it as powerful, even overwhelming, and it often brings with it an undeniable assuredness of the reality of the experience. Other phenomena on the spectrum of religious experience are more continuous with ordinary consciousness. The 'testimony of spirit' Kierkegaard speaks of might just as well indicate a conviction developed from personal experience over time (Cappelørn 2007; Pattison 1997: 78; 2002: 56–64). This kind of experience, which James (1982: 70) calls a 'chronic sense of God's presence,' is less dramatic or exceptional, but is still often characterized by the subject as a 'reality'; in fact, it is said to be just as real as the experiences of ordinary empirical consciousness. In virtually all these cases, James (1982: 72–3) concludes that the result of religious experience is a deep and abiding conviction:

> Such is the human ontological imagination, and such is the convincingness of what it brings to birth. Unpicturable beings are realized, and realized with an intensity almost like that of an hallucination. . . . They are as convincing to those who have them as any direct sensible experiences can be, and they are, as a rule, much more convincing than results established by mere logic ever are. One may indeed be entirely without them; probably more than one of you here present is without them in any marked degree; but if you do have them, and have them at all strongly, the probability is that you cannot help regarding them as genuine perceptions of truth, as revelations of a kind of reality which no adverse argument, however unanswerable by you in words, can expel from your belief.

A similar subjective and experiential interpretation of Kierkegaard's concept of the 'testimony of the holy spirit' would help explain why a person might embrace the decision to live a religiously governed life in the face of her own deep uncertainties and intellectual misgivings about that choice. This might be the *logos* behind even Abraham's absurd faith. As Louis Dupré (1998: 38–9) writes,

> Religious disclosure is truth that, in its essentials, refuses to submit to external criteria. . . . Precisely in following the very course of consciousness in time, experience acquires its unique purchase on truth – namely that it is, and becomes, *my own* experience. It hereby endows truth, on whichever level acquired, with some form of *practical indubitability* that, though not warranting freedom from error, nevertheless secures incontrovertible evidence.

If Dupré is right, this 'religious disclosure' is impressive to those that experience it. That being said, an emphasis on a private spiritual proof probably disqualifies it as philosophical evidence, which must insist on demonstrations of universality. As Johannes Climacus writes in the *Postscript*: 'The testimony of spirit for a Christian is different from all other (universally defined) activities of mind' (CUP 1, 610/SKS 7, 554). Dupré (1998: 36–7) sums it up like this: a spiritual witness enables a believer to accept the veracity of religious claims, 'but such an idea is not likely to satisfy the philosopher. . . . Religious discourse . . . does not appear to possess the kind of impartial, universally accessible quality that philosophy demands of truth.' And as Kierkegaard himself goes to great lengths to underscore, this personal experience, however convincing, does not rid the soul of a longing for understanding. It seems that the tension that arises from the desire to explain or understand one's own beliefs in intellectually satisfying ways will always accompany a person who chooses to risk her life on faith. Such is religious life.

A strength or a weakness?

One might ask, however, if this insistence on the ultimate inexplicability of conviction should be taken as the strength of Kierkegaard's account, or its weakness? Or perhaps both? It might indeed be a strong psychological account of the issue from the perspective of the individual who experiences the intellectual offensiveness of her own religious commitments – and for Kierkegaard, the first-person perspective is the only one fully relevant here. An individual who takes Kierkegaard's position could agree with, and even embrace, virtually any objection to the objective reasonableness or general coherence of the religious tenets by which she lives. She could be as adamant about the problems of religion as a Nietzsche or a Freud, but still choose the inner strife of religious life because of a conviction based on a 'spiritual witness.' The position could be summarized like this: 'Living a religiously governed life is objectively absurd, and you will never grasp it in terms that the understanding will be satisfied with, but if you've experienced a 'spiritual proof,' you'll be convinced that it is the right way for you, nonetheless.'

At the same time, if indeed religious conviction is strongest and deepest when grounded in private spiritual experience, which cannot be imparted from one person to another, it seems to be beyond the territory where public debate will be efficacious. This seems to be a tacit admission that – from the subject's perspective – the measures of reasonableness or rationality she employs when assessing scientific and scholarly matters – that is, 'objective' matters – are not operative in the same way when it comes to religious conviction. And it is far from obvious that the logic of religious conviction is coherent with the logic of science and scholarship, even though she lives by both. And, as Dupré notes, anyone who takes this kind of Kierkegaardian position should at least be willing to admit, with Kierkegaard, that this causes internal problems: 'daily apostasies,' demonstrate that the distance between these two logical spheres 'cannot be stretched indefinitely' (Dupré 1998: 32–3).

Related topics

'Imagination and belief,' Eleanor Helms; 'Christian epistemology and the anthropology of sin: Kierkegaard on natural theology and the concept of "offense,"' Karen L. Carr; 'Varieties of existential uncertainty,' Rick Anthony Furtak.

Notes

1 In my reading, Kierkegaard is not an apologist (cf. Gouwens 1996: 67–74; Law 1993: 71–123). Throughout his authorship, he is overwhelmingly critical of the inclination to defend Christianity in terms that make it more palatable. I tend to agree with scholars who suggest that Kierkegaard's position is best described as 'anti-rationalist' (Buben 2013; Carr 1996). For an interpretation that softens Kierkegaard's criticism of apologetics, see Evans (1998).
2 For more on this debate about faith and reason, see Ferreira (1991); Helms (2017); Westphal (2014).

3 In this chapter, some of the quoted English translations of Kierkegaard have been slightly modified.
4 In *Practice in Christianity*, Anti-Climacus simply writes: 'faith is a choice' (PC, 141/SKS 12, 144). See also WL, 200–1/SKS 9, 199; PC, 96, 127, 134, 159–60/SKS 12, 104, 131, 138, 163–4; WA, 21/SKS 11, 26.
5 See, for example, Rudolph Bultmann, who suggests that faith is a matter of 'decision' or 'resolve' to 'appropriate the meaning' of the crucifixion. For him the ultimate question asked by the New Testament is whether or not we are 'willing to believe it' (Bultmann 1984: 15, 20, 28, 36, 39–40). See also Gouwens (1996: 100–5); Pattison (1997: 75); Thonhauser (2013).
6 The word translated by the Hongs as 'strengthening' (*bekræftelse*) is loyal to the English wording of the biblical passage in focus in Kierkegaard's discourse. See Ephesians 3:16 in the NRSV, where Paul writes: May God 'grant that you may be strengthened in your inner being with power through his Spirit.' In Kierkegaard's time, the Danish translation of this same passage used the word *bekræftes*, which can mean both 'to receive confirmation' and 'to be strengthened.' Kierkegaard plays on this ambiguity.
7 In Danish, the line reads '*istedenfor at faae en Forklaring af Gud, blev [han] forklaret i Gud*' (EUD, 400/SKS 5, 380).

References

Buben, A. (2013) 'Neither irrationalist nor apologist: Revisiting faith and reason in Kierkegaard,' *Philosophy Compass*, 8, no. 3: 318–26.
Bultmann, R. (1984) *New testament and theology*, S. M. Ogden (trans), Philadelphia, PA: Fortress Press.
Cappelørn, N. J. (2007) 'Longing for reconciliation with God: A fundamental theme in "Friday Communion Discourses," fourth part of "Christian Discourses",' in N. J. Cappelørn and H. Deuser (eds), *Kierkegaard Studies Yearbook 2007*, Berlin: Walter de Gruyter.
Carr, K. (1996) 'The offense of reason and the passion of faith: Kierkegaard and anti-rationalism,' *Faith and Philosophy*, 13, no. 2: 236–51.
Dupré, L. (1998) *Religious mystery and rational reflection*, Grand Rapids, MI: Eerdmans Publishing Company.
Evans, C. S. (1998) *Faith beyond reason*, Edinburgh: Edinburgh University Press.
Ferreira, M. J. (1991) *Transforming vision: Imagination and will in Kierkegaardian faith*, Oxford: Clarendon Press.
Florin, F. (2002) 'Was Kierkegaard inspired by medieval mysticism? Meister Eckhart's "Abgeschiedenheit" and Kierkegaard's "Udsondring",' *Kierkegaardiana*, 22: 172–90.
Gouwens, D. (1996) *Kierkegaard as religious thinker*, Cambridge: Cambridge University Press.
Helms, E. (2017) 'On Climacus's "against reason thesis": A challenge to Westphal,' *Faith and Philosophy*, 34, no. 4: 471–88.
Hughes, C. (2014) *Kierkegaard and the staging of desire*, New York: Fordham University Press.
James, W. (1982) *The varieties of religious experience*, New York: Penguin Books.
Law, D. (1993) *Kierkegaard as negative theologian*, Oxford: Clarendon Press.
Mulder, J. Jr., (2005) *Mystical and Buddhist elements in Kierkegaard's religious thought*, Lewiston, NY: Edwin Mellen Press.
Pattison, G. (2002) *Kierkegaard's upbuilding discourses*, London: Routledge.
Pattison, G. (1997) '"Before God" as a regulative concept,' in N. J. Cappelørn and H. Deuser (eds), *Kierkegaard Studies Yearbook 1997*, Berlin: Walter de Gruyter.
Piety, M. G. (2017) 'Søren Kierkegaard,' in W. J. Abraham and F. D. Aquino (eds), *Oxford Handbook of the Epistemology of Theology*, Oxford: Oxford University Press.
Šajda, P. (2009) 'Kierkegaard's encounter with the Rhineland-Flemish mystics: A case study, Kierkegaard's reception of Johannes Tauler,' in N. J. Cappelørn and H. Deuser (eds), *Kierkegaard Studies Yearbook 2009*, Berlin: Walter de Gruyter.
Šajda, P. (2008) 'The patriarch of German speculation who was a "Lebemeister": Meister Eckhardt's silent way into Kierkegaard's corpus,' in J. Stewart (ed), *Kierkegaard Research: Sources, Reception and Resources*, vol. 4 (*Kierkegaard and the Patristic and Medieval Traditions*), Farnham: Ashgate.
Schleiermacher, F. (1996) *On religion*, R. Crouter (trans), Cambridge: Cambridge University Press.
Söderquist, K. B. (2017) 'Socrates and the blessed fall of Athens: Kierkegaard on negativity as the way toward religious authenticity,' in A. Burgess and W. McDonald (eds), *Acta Kierkegaardiana*, vol. 7 (*Kierkegaard and Classical Greek Thought*), Nitra; Toronto: Central European Research Institute of Søren Kierkegaard & Kierkegaard Circle.
Theunissen, M. (2005) *Kierkegaard's concept of despair*, B. Harshaw and H. Illbruck (trans), Princeton, NJ: Princeton University Press.

Thonhauser, G. (2013) 'Choice,' in J. Stewart (ed), *Kierkegaard Research: Sources, Reception and Resources*, vol. 15 (*Kierkegaard's Concepts*), Farnham: Ashgate.

Westphal, M. (2014) *Kierkegaard's concept of faith*, Grand Rapids, MI: Eerdmans Publishing Company.

Further reading

Harries, K. (2010) *Between nihilism and faith*, Berlin: Walter de Gruyter.

Primarily a study of *Either/Or*, this book looks at the conditions for the possibility of meaning in a secularized world haunted by nihilism. Along with Kierkegaard, Harries asks what makes life meaningful after the death of God and a loss of faith in Enlightenment reason.

Nymann Eriksen, N. (2000) *Kierkegaard's category of repetition: A reconstruction*, Berlin: Walter de Gruyter.

This book investigates the absence of ethical guidelines as a negative prerequisite of Kierkegaardian faith. Nymann Eriksen provides an especially sensitive reading of the philosophical issues in Kierkegaard's edifying work and puts them in dialogue with the thought of Nietzsche and Heidegger.

Pattison, G. (1997) *Kierkegaard and the crisis of faith*, London: SPCK.

This small work focuses on Kierkegaard's critique of the thought of modernity, with chapters that focus on his assessment of Enlightenment and post-Enlightenment social structures, science and scholarship.

20
COMING TO AN UNDERSTANDING WITH THE PARADOX

Mark A. Wrathall

Christianity is insanity because it is incommensurable with any finite why. But then what good is it? Answer: be silent, it is the absolute.

Anti-Climacus

Christianity is not a doctrine but an existence-communication.

Johannes Climacus

Climacus's puzzle

Kierkegaard's pseudonymous author Johannes Climacus seems to commit himself to each of these claims:

(1) A contradiction is incomprehensible and thus can't be believed.
(2) A Christian believes in the God-man.
(3) The God-man is a contradiction.

Together, those claims entail:

(4) Christianity is incoherent – it believes in something that can't be believed.

How can one be a Christian if Christianity is, as Climacus insists, 'the essentially incomprehensible' (CUP 1, 562/SKS 7, 511)? I'll refer to this as Climacus's puzzle.[1]

Theologians who want to avoid the conclusion usually deny the third premise. Denying this typically takes the form of explaining how a single person can be at one and the same time both fully divine and fully human – that is, showing that a single individual can coherently have all the necessary attributes of a human being and of God.[2] But there are other, less orthodox, options. One might opt, for example, for Nestorianism and argue that Christ was in fact two people – a human person and a divine person. I'm not going to talk about these traditional theological approaches to the problem.[3]

Kierkegaard rejected theological solutions to the problem and, indeed, seemed to embrace the conclusion. For instance, in notes that date to the period when he was composing the *Postscript*, he wrote:

> Christianity does not want to be understood – but the rude speculator does not want to understand this. He cries incessantly: 'From the standpoint of the eternal, there is no paradox.' Christianity entered into the world not to be understood but to be existed in. This cannot be expressed more strongly than by the fact that Christianity itself proclaims itself to be a paradox. If the horror in the beginning of Christianity was that one could so easily take offense, the horror now – the longer the world exists – is that Christianity, aided by culture, abundant knowledge, and objectifying, can so easily become sheer nonsense. The longer the world continues, the more difficult it becomes to become a Christian.
>
> *(CUP 2, 53)*

The paradox that Kierkegaard alludes to here is, of course, the contradiction implicit in the God-man (premise 3): 'Christianity, in its principal doctrine and at every point proclaims itself as a paradox. Christianity's teaching, that God was man, was an individual human being, lived a certain number of years in time, ate and drank, this is certainly the most terrible paradox that can be presented to an existing person' (CUP 2, 53). The reason it gets harder to become a Christian the longer the world continues is that familiarity breeds neglect. Through long acquaintance, we get accustomed to the peculiarity of Christian doctrines and stop really paying attention to them. Soon, the contradiction of the God-man no longer seems remarkable, and little by little a patina of intelligibility encrusts Christian doctrines and smooths over the crevices and gaps. But this process is for Kierkegaard a source for alarm since he believes that the incomprehensibility of Christianity is vital to making the movements of faith.

What are we to make of Kierkegaard's apparent embrace of the incomprehensibility of Christianity?

Relativizers, bullet-biters, and disambiguators

Daniel Watts (2016) has helpfully catalogued three different general approaches to Kierkegaard's embrace of paradoxes like this, although Watts didn't explicitly address this particular paradox. His concern is the related paradox involved in Kierkegaard/Climacus writing and thinking about matters that he claims lie beyond the limits of thought. But I've found Watts' taxonomy very helpful in working through Climacus's puzzle.

One group – the 'relativizers' – responds to Kierkegaard's embrace of paradox by trying to dissolve the appearance of contradiction. What seems to be a contradiction, they argue, is only a contradiction from a certain perspective. From another perspective, it is not contradictory at all. And it is not a strict contradiction from any perspective. For instance, when dealing with the paradox of the God-man, C. Stephen Evans (1992: 88; my emphasis) argues that interpreters who take the paradox as a strict contradiction 'confus[e] the idea of believing a logical contradiction with the very different notion of believing something which *appears to be* logically contradictory.' The incarnation of God appears to be contradictory from the perspective of human reason (Evans 1992: 89), but that need not mean that it is in fact a logical contradiction. And so, following Evans' lead, one might resolve Climacus's puzzle in the following way:

(1) A contradiction is incomprehensible and thus can't be believed.
(2) A Christian believes in the God-man.
(3) The God-man appears to be a contradiction from the perspective of human reason.
(4) From the perspective of human reason, Christianity appears to be incoherent.

Evans thus concludes that Kierkegaard is committed only to 'the claim that [the incarnation] is something human reason can never master or comprehend.' But that is consistent with believing that the (mere) appearance of contradiction could be dispelled for a supra-human reason, and that Christianity could 'be known to be true by revelation' (Evans 1992: 90). The upshot of the relativizer's reading of this argument is to establish limits within which human reason must restrict itself, and beyond which one is free to believe that a higher truth lies.

Watts calls a second type of response 'bullet biting.' For bullet-biters, the relativizing move is shown up as empty the moment we try to say something about the truth that lies beyond the limits of thought. They thus accept the conclusion of the original argument form, together with all the consequences that flow from it. Once we bite the bullet and accept that the core teaching of Christianity is irredeemably self-contradictory, we will see that everything Climacus and Kierkegaard say about the paradox is sheer nonsense, a kind of joke, utter gibberish. Ultimately, Climacus has no alternative but to fall silent and the discerning reader will, with any luck, recognize that the whole point of the exercise

> is not to 'prove' the superiority of Christianity or even to show us in a theoretical way that the absolute paradox makes a kind of sense as *supra rationem* which is lacking in garden variety nonsense, but rather to help us realize existentially what it means to become a Christian, and to see that the only valid concept which we can form about Christianity is that it defies conceptualization.
>
> *(Allison 1967: 459–60)*

Other bullet-biters object that even this interpretation doesn't bite the bullet hard enough – it still thinks that it 'means' something to become a Christian. On Conant's reading, for instance, the final illusion to be dispelled is the thought that there is something *there* of which one cannot speak. 'There is no particular *thing* that cannot be said. The "what" in what cannot be said refers to nothing' (Conant 1989: 244). Kierkegaard's 'teaching cannot be stated' because 'there is no "it" to state, i.e., no "doctrine" ... to expound' (Conant 1989: 266). The bullet-biters put a lot of stock in the fact that Climacus, nearing the end of the *Postscript*, notes that 'what I write contains an additional notice to the effect that everything is to be understood in such a way that it is revoked' (Kierkegaard 2009: 522/SKS 7, 562). This revocation, Conant (1989: 266) claims, is 'a silence that looms in the wake of the realization that one's voice can speak while saying nothing.' The bullet-biters are right to emphasize that Kierkegaard's ultimate aim is the 'existential realization of Christianity.' They're also right that he thinks the definitive features of Christian existence defy any coherent discursive articulation. There is a great deal about Christianity, on Kierkegaard's account, that can't be spoken. But the bullet-biters are committed to a further claim – namely, that there is no distinctive content to being a Christian. That would mean that there's no difference between being a faithful Christian (i.e., the existential realization of Christianity) and being an unbeliever.

In contrast to relativizing and bullet biting, Watts himself advocates an approach he calls 'disambiguating.' While Watts doesn't really define what he means by disambiguating in general, he discusses at some length a particular case of a disambiguating approach. As I noted above, the incomprehensibility that was the focus of Watts' article is the paradox involved in Kierkegaard's apparent commitment to thinking beyond the limits of thought. We saw that the relativizer embraces the paradoxical idea that there is some limit beyond which rational thought cannot go, but holds out the prospect that there is nevertheless a perspective other than that of human reason from which one could understand whatever it is that is beyond the limit of thought. The bullet-biter insists that the very idea of a limit of thought is incoherent, and that, in trying to talk about the limit, 'our voice speaks while saying nothing.' And if we're saying nothing, the bullet-biter concludes, we really ought to lapse into silence. Watts (2016: 95) suggests instead that the idea of thought itself might be systematically ambiguous between thinking as a form of disinterested contemplation, and thinking as a kind of deliberation 'about your own individual existence *in concreto*, as one for whom the issue of what you are – or, rather, who you are becoming – is inescapable.' The second kind of thinking – Watts calls it 'ethico-religious thinking' – guides me in the existential decisions I make about who to be and how to live. It also enables me to recognize that the first kind of thinking – disinterested contemplation (or what Watts calls 'aesthetic-intellectual thought') – is ill-suited for guiding me in my existential decisions, precisely because of its disinterested and impersonal mode of representing situations. On Watts' account, then, when Climacus posits that a Christian existence can be suitably thought of as lying beyond the limits of thought, he doesn't mean there is something about which thought *cannot* think. He means instead that the second kind of deliberation (ethico-religious thinking) should recognize the unsuitability and inadequacy of disinterested contemplation when it comes to certain topics, such as death, sin, faith, and freedom. Such topics so profoundly 'challenge our understanding of what it essentially means to be human' that to contemplate them in a disinterested and dispassionate way is precisely to misunderstand them (Watts 2016: 96). Thus, Watts (2016: 99) concludes that 'Christianity is suitably represented *in an ethico-religious way* as incapable of being suitably represented *in an aesthetic-intellectual way.*'

I would put the point in this way: Christianity is the sort of thing that we can only properly understand when we sense immediately and directly the challenge it poses to our everyday, predominantly self-interested, mode of life. When thinking about Christianity in a disinterested, theoretical fashion, it's easy to rationalize away the incommensurability of Christian life with conformist submission to public norms. Intellectual thought thus can be used to shield us from experiencing the existential challenge that Christianity presents to everyday life. It's at this point that 'ethico-religious deliberation' enters the scene. Upon reflection, I might recognize that Christianity threatens everyday forms of existence precisely because it reveals something genuine and true about my individual condition – something that's obscured by intellectual and theoretical thought. I might be unable to communicate this insight because it can't be couched in the vocabulary of general or disinterested thought, but – and this is Watts' point – that recognition itself counts as thoughtfully deliberating beyond the limits of (disinterested) thought.

Climacus offers a parable of the judgment day that helps illustrate Watts' insight:

> It is indeed possible, after all, that Christianity is the truth; it is after all possible that some day there will be a judgment which hinges on the relation of inwardness to Christianity. Suppose someone stepped forward who had to say, 'I have indeed not believed, but I have so honoured Christianity as to employ every hour of my life in pondering it.' Or suppose someone came forward of whom the accuser had to say, 'He has persecuted the Christians,' and the accused replied, 'Yes, I admit it; Christianity has set my soul aflame, and I have wanted nothing else than to root it from the earth, precisely because I perceived its tremendous power.' Or suppose there came someone of

whom the accuser had to say, 'He has renounced Christianity,' and the accused replied: 'Yes, it is true, for I saw that Christianity was so great a power that if I gave it one finger, it would take all of me and I could not belong to it wholly.' But now suppose that, finally, a snappy *privat-docent* came along, with quick and busy step, and spoke as follows: 'I am not like those three; I have not only believed but gone so far as to explain Christianity, shown that what the Apostles propounded and was appropriated in the first centuries is only true to a certain degree, and shown on the other hand how, in the speculative understanding, it is the true truth, for which reason I must beg a suitable remuneration for my services to Christianity.'

(Kierkegaard 2009: 194/SKS 7, 211)

In other words, we are to imagine that four individuals stand at the judgment bar of God. None of the first three became a Christian in mortality. One of them went so far as to persecute Christians. But each of them in their own way recognized the deep significance that Christianity has for their particular existential situation, the import it would have on their specific life plans. The fourth individual believed Christianity in a detached, theoretical way, and believed it insofar as it could be supported by reason and evidence. Climacus poses the question: 'Which of these four positions would be the most terrible?' And he answers: 'no one's position would be as embarrassing as that of the *privat-docent*s' (Kierkegaard 2009: 194–5/SKS 7, 211).

The moral of the story is: as long as my approach to Christianity is preoccupied with keeping straight the noetic structure of my beliefs, or with making Christian doctrines intelligible and plausible, I will miss the point. It is only in an awareness of the extreme demands that Christianity places on how I live now – even if I respond to that awareness by rejecting Christianity – that I start to sense its true significance. I grasp the meaning of Christianity when it challenges me as an individual to act, and to act in a way that is indexed to me and my time and situation in all its specificity – and that immediate motivation to act is precisely the content that gets elided in disinterested thought.

Now what are the implications of a disambiguating approach for the paradox of the incarnation? How does this help us with Climacus's puzzle? I take the key insight of Watts' (see 2016: 97–8) disambiguating approach to Kierkegaard to consist in this: we need to carefully distinguish between the doxastic and the existential – between what's relevant to the formation of opinions or beliefs on the one hand, and on the other what's relevant to the motivation of actions or to the creation of a coherent, distinct, style of living.[4]

The adoxalist disambiguation

Taking my cue from Watts, then, I'd propose that the key move in Climacus's resolution of the puzzle is to recognize that the second premise is ambiguous. If 'belief' is understood as a doxic state – as a taking-to-be-true – then Climacus would hold it to the standards of rationality that govern beliefs in general. Within that domain, Climacus endorses the principle of non-contradiction (see PF, 108/SKS 4, 304; more on this below) and insists that Christians have an obligation to be rational in their beliefs. Climacus, for instance, insists that

> someone who is truly a Christian ... may well have understanding (yes, he must have, in order to believe against understanding); he is able to use it in all other connections, use it in his association with others...; he will be well able to see the point of all objections, indeed, to advance them himself as well as any, for otherwise a higher understanding would begin to look suspiciously like the promotion of stuff and nonsense....

Nonsense, therefore, he cannot believe against the understanding, as one might fear, for the understanding will precisely see nonsense for what it is and prevent him from believing it.

(Kierkegaard 2009: 475–6/SKS 7, 516)

Given his commitment to the importance of reason in the domain of belief formation, Climacus ought to endorse the following argument:

(1) A contradiction is incomprehensible and thus can't be believed.
(3) The God-man is a contradiction.

Therefore,

(5) It is not the case that (2) a Christian believes in the God-man.

And yet, having just asserted the Christian's obligation to be rational, Climacus reiterates that the Christian believes in the face of reasons: 'he believes against the understanding, and here too uses the understanding – to make sure that he believes against the understanding' (Kierkegaard 2009: 476/SKS 7, 516). How do we make sense of this distinction Climacus draws between 'believing nonsense' and 'believing against the understanding?' It's tempting at first glance to think the distinction lies in the content of these beliefs – to think, that is, that we can distinguish between nonsense on the one hand, and ideas that are contrary to all understanding on the other. The bullet-biters argue persuasively that this is a distinction without a difference. Instead of drawing the distinction in terms of their respective content, Climacus's approach is to distinguish the attitudes themselves. 'Belief' is ambiguous, and can refer either to a cognitive state or attitude of holding-to-be-true, or to a practical stance of trust or reliance. A 'practical stance,' as I'm using the phrase, refers to a disposition that involves perceptual and affective components – the ability to pick up relevant information, and the tendency to be moved by it in a characteristic way – as well as active components – being ready or poised to respond to the environment. To reduce the risk of confusion, I'll refer to belief in this latter sense – belief as a practical stance – as 'faith.' The distinction Climacus relies on, in other words, is between 'believing nonsense' (which no one should do) and 'having faith that is contrary to the understanding' (which is an attitude at the very core of Christian existence).

Finding in Kierkegaard's writing the distinction between a cognitive notion of 'belief' and faith as a practical disposition is complicated by the fact that Kierkegaard's Danish has just one word – *tro* – that must do double duty to express both. But he signals in a variety of ways that he understands Christian faith in pragmatic, not cognitive, terms. For instance, Climacus explicitly draws a distinction between '*Troen* . . . in the direct and ordinary meaning,' that is, belief, and '*Troen* . . . in the wholly eminent sense' – faith; merely because one 'accepts that God exists,' Climacus notes, it doesn't follow that one has faith (PF, 87/SKS 4, 285–6; translation modified).[5] Anti-Climacus argues that 'the whole of Christianity turns on this, that it *must* be believed (*troes*) and not comprehended (*begribes*)' (SUD, 98/SKS 11, 210; translation modified). Of course, when we have in mind belief in a cognitive sense rather than faith in a pragmatic sense, it makes no sense to say I believe something that I don't comprehend. To believe that *p* is to hold *p* to be true, and that can't be done if one can't even comprehend *p*. Part of the reason Kierkegaard emphasizes paradox, contradiction, and absurdity, then, is to force us away from a focus on belief, and to turn us toward acquiring a practical stance of faith: 'If all attempts to comprehend can just be shown to be self-contradictory, then the matter will fall into proper perspective, then it will be clear that whether one will believe (*troe*) or not must be left to faith (*Troen*)' (SUD, 98/SKS

11, 210). The absurd, the contradictory, the paradoxical will frustrate an effort to arrive at belief in the cognitive sense. But once one gives up on striving for a cognitive belief (which requires comprehension), one can take up the 'proper perspective' on the matter, with a view to seeing whether it can sustain a style of life.

Anti-Climacus explains that 'the concept "faith" (*Tro*) is an altogether distinctively Christian term' (PC, 81/SKS 12, 91). In the Christian concept of faith, the opposite of faith is not 'doubt' but 'being offended' (PC, 81n/SKS 12, 91). Here again, Kierkegaard shifts the discussion out of a cognitive register (where believing that *p* is opposed to doubting that *p*), and into a practical register (where having faith in or reliance on a person is, at its outermost extreme, opposed by taking offense at that person). One stands at the threshold of the domain of Christian existence when one stands before 'the offense κατέξοχήν [in an eminent sense]' – namely, 'that an individual human being is God.' The God-man offends because he 'conflicts with all (human) reason' (PC, 26/SKS 12, 40). Confronting the paradox 'is like standing at the crossroad ... one turns either to offense or to faith' (PC, 81/SKS 12, 91). The question whether to doubt or believe, to hold not true or hold true, is not at issue. The decision is how to live, and the paradox 'direct[s] people (individual persons) to the ethical, the religious, the existential' rather than to speculation and worries about objective warrant (PC, 81n/SKS 12, 91).

Climacus sheds light on how to think about the relation between Christian faith and belief with an example 'drawn from lesser life-situations' (Kierkegaard 2009: 475/SKS 7, 515). The example is that of an idiosyncratic man – 'a man who arranges his life in a special way' on the basis of his intimate acquaintance with himself. The consistent implementation of this peculiar style of life, Climacus explains, is laughable or ludicrous to everyone (including the man himself), but he sticks with it all the same because it suits him and his idiosyncratic preferences, habits, abilities, faults, etc. Such a man can, in conversation with others, calmly listen to their opinions and see perfectly well why others find it unintelligible – indeed, comic – to live in the way he does. But, Climacus concludes, 'he will then go home quite calmly and pursue this life-plan as conceived according to his own acquaintance with himself (*Kjendskab til sig selv*)' (Kierkegaard 2009: 475/SKS 7, 515; translation modified). Now, Climacus emphasizes that this example has 'no analogy to the sphere of the paradox-religious' (Kierkegaard 2009: 475/SKS 7, 515) – because, I take it, the style of life of the man in the example is not unintelligible *in principle*, whereas a life centred on the contradiction of the God-man is. Still, the example provides vital insight into Climacus's resolution of the puzzle: the Christian's embrace of the God-man is to be located, not in her beliefs, but in the way she arranges and carries on her life. If her practical stance on life functions well, she will be unconcerned with the unintelligibility of her efforts to provide a discursive account of that life to others.

The Christian is thus distinguished from others not primarily in terms of what she believes (understood as a takings-to-be-true). She is distinguished instead by the content of her faith – that is, 'belief' understood as an impassioned, interested, deeply subjective 'life-plan' or 'movement of existence' that is centred on God. Because he distinguishes belief from faith, Kierkegaard would endorse the argument presented earlier in this section, concluding that

(5) It is not the case that (2) a Christian *believes* in the God-man.

But he would immediately follow up this argument with the observation that, nevertheless,

(6) the Christian has faith in the God-man.

Disambiguating (6) from (2) in this way allows Kierkegaard to be committed to an *adoxal* faith – that is, a faith that is antithetical to belief or that draws its strength from the failure of beliefs to give us an appropriate existential stance for perceiving and responding to the world.

Being a Christian is not defined by one's belief states about the God-man. As a movement of existence, faith is to be sought, not in one's occurrent beliefs or in what one says, but in one's stance toward and movement through the world and in the way one is solicited to act by the situations one encounters.

The conjunction of (5) and (6) might well sustain one in accepting that (4) Christianity is incoherent, but not because there is a strict contradiction between (5) and (6). Rather, it is incoherent to the extent that we can't understand how belief and faith can function so independently of one another. Let's take a closer look at this issue.

Adoxalism and the skills model of faith

The adoxalist disambiguation of faith and belief saves the Christian from one source of incoherence by insisting it is not the cognitive question of the beliefs one holds, but the practical question of one's style of life or movement of existence that determines whether one has faith. It does not matter whether one *believes* that Jesus is the God-man — in fact, one *can't* believe that, because one can't believe a contradiction. 'Someone with abundant imagination and feeling,' Anti-Climacus explains, 'could go and think that he believed that this particular human being was God,' but that is only because he lacks 'a developed conception of God' (PC, 83/SKS 12, 93). If one truly grasps what the Christ is – one who is fully both man and God, then 'one cannot *know* anything at all about *Christ*'; 'He is the paradox, the object of faith, exists only for faith' (PC, 25/SKS 12, 40). As the paradox, moreover, historical understanding 'can never digest or convert [him] into an ordinary syllogism' (PC, 30/SKS 12, 44) – that is, belief in the God-man can admit of no rational support.

What does count as having faith is being oriented in the right way by the God-man toward life. When we are preoccupied with beliefs and knowledge about the God-man, with proofs and demonstrations of his divinity, this leads to a lack of practical understanding of him: 'we really do not care to find out in a deeper sense what it is he does,' Anti-Climacus complains. 'Even less do we try with the help of God and according to our humble capacities to imitate him in doing the right, the noble, the sublime, the true. What that is, we really do not find out' (PC, 36/SKS 12, 49).

But the spectre of incoherence remains. First of all, there is the performative incoherence of Christian religions, which typically put a great deal of emphasis on orthodoxy, on argumentative demonstrations of the truth of their beliefs, on learning creeds and doctrines, on catechizing children and converts. These discursive practices don't sit well with an adoxal approach to faith. Not surprisingly, then, Kierkegaard is dismissive of many of the discursive practices of Christendom as distractions that keep us from ever having to make the movements of faith: 'Christendom has abolished Christianity' (PC, 36/SKS 12, 49).[6] Moreover, he argues that it is a fundamental mistake to take the scriptures as offering evidence or warrant for belief formation, as if they were in the game of proving propositions and giving reasons for belief:

> One can 'prove' only that it [i.e., the God-man] conflicts with reason. The proofs for the divinity of Christ that Scripture sets forth – his miracles, his resurrection from the dead, his ascension – are indeed only for faith, that is, they are not 'proofs.' Neither do they want to prove that all this is in complete harmony with reason; on the contrary, they want to prove that it is contrary to reason and consequently is the object of faith.
>
> *(PC, 26/SKS 12, 41; translation modified)*

But even in insisting that the scriptures are not in the business of proof, and in refusing to accommodate Christianity to the demands of reason, Anti-Climacus still accepts as legitimate certain types of discursive practice. We can consider here also Kierkegaard's 'autonomous' writings – upbuilding discourses, scriptural meditations, and even philosophical works. He is, at the end of the day, deeply committed to presenting arguments in favour of a particular way of construing the God-man and our relationship to him.[7] How are we to square that with an adoxal view of faith? To understand this, we need to say something more generally about the relationship between practical understanding and discursive knowledge.

Kierkegaard's (2009: 478/SKS 7, 518; see also 318–9/346) view of the proper role of discourse in Christianity is pithily expressed in the epigram to this chapter: 'Christianity is not a doctrine but an existence-communication (*Existents-Meddelelse*).' The Danish word for communication – '*Meddelelse*,' like the etymologically related German word '*Mitteilen*' and the etymologically unrelated English word 'communication' all mean literally 'to share with,' 'to take a share in,' or 'to take part in along with' another. An 'existence-communication' uses language in such a way that the communication of propositional contents is incidental to the main point, which is co-orienting the communicants to the world so that they are able to share and take part in a particular practice or form of life. An existence-communication succeeds when the hearer of the communication is not allowed to become 'a spectator.' Existence-communication opens up for the hearer the possibilities that determine the speaker's existence, so that she can experience what it is like to be the speaker (Kierkegaard 2009: 301/SKS 7, 327–8). An existence-communication of a Christian form of life is thus one that so orients the hearer to the world that she immediately experiences in a Christ-like way the people and situations she encounters, and is solicited by the suffering and needs of others to perform acts of love. In this respect, one can think of the aim of Christianity as developing in Christians a certain skill for existing. The challenge for the existence-communicator is to use language (and other communicative resources) to initiate others into this skilful mode of being in the world.

A skill involves acquiring, maintaining, and improving bodily stances and dispositions – dispositions both to discern the relevant features of a given situation, and to act in response to those features in a way that will sustain the agent's maximal grip on the situation as she pursues her aims. With many skills – and especially with complex skills – there is often a mismatch between what a highly skilled agent is disposed to do, and what she can correctly think or say about how she should act. Skills involve an understanding that is 'not "discursive"' – meaning 'it cannot be explained in non-indexical terms' (Stanley and Williamson 2016: 715). That is, if a skilful agent's understanding were to be made explicit, this would often necessarily have to take the form of expressions like 'in *this* situation, do *this now*' (for instance, 'when the football is moving like *this* at *this* spot on the field with *those* players moving like *that*, kick it like *this*'). There is considerable disagreement on what follows for the role of propositional knowledge in acquiring skills and guiding skilful action once one grants that expert understanding involves a heavy dose of non-discursive understanding.[8] But everyone at least seems to agree that it is unnecessary – indeed, a recipe for failure – to insist that one acquire a comprehensive propositional understanding of a practice before, and as a condition of, engaging in that practice.

There are several constraints on what we can expect of a discursive understanding of a skill domain. Skilful expertise requires, in addition to whatever knowledge is propositionally specifiable, bodily dispositions and perceptual capacities to pick up the relevant situational features and to execute the bodily movements called for by the various situations one might encounter. This limits what discursive practice can achieve in contributing to skilful activity (either by initiating a beginner, or coordinating and guiding more skilful practitioners). Words and gestures and expressions in general might help to orient us to the task at hand by guiding us to the right angle of approach. But being told by an expert, for instance, how to balance on a bike or how to bend the flight of a football is never going to make someone an expert at those skills. (And that's assuming that experts in those skills in fact know what they're doing when they perform those skills; see, for example, Dreyfus 2014: 85.)

Talk also can be used to draw our attention to what's truly significant in the situation. But the acquisition of the ability to discern the significant features of a situation on one's own – in many cases that is an ability we only acquire *after* developing the skills to act. Because the acquisition of skills is often a prerequisite to developing the discriminatory capacities and tastes that allow an agent to discern the relevant aspects of a domain, and because the ability to discern features is a prior condition of understanding the words that refer to those features, a discursive practice alone can't initiate one into a skill domain. Even non-discursive expressions will fail if the hearer is unable to discern the feature indicated by an indexical, and until she develops the skill, she may well lack that ability. Sooner or later, to acquire a skill, we have to learn what cannot be learned through discursive practices alone, and that requires us to act, to get to work, to experiment and practice until we learn to see what an expert sees and to respond as an expert responds.

Thus, one upshot of recognizing Christian faith as a kind of expertise – as the ability to respond skilfully, fluidly, and appropriately to the needs of others in a Christ-like manner – is that we need not worry about our inability to offer a coherent discursive account of the God-man who is the paradigm and focus of the practice of faith. We need not worry about this, because skilful expertise by its nature resists discursive articulation.

Coming to an understanding with the paradox

For the faithful practitioner of Christianity (as for the idiosyncratic man discussed above), it doesn't matter how absurd, ludicrous, or contradictory their mode of existence is when described discursively. What matters is its success or failure as a practice. One who successfully engages in the practice of Christianity, Climacus explains, 'come[s] to an understanding with the paradox.' Climacus states:

> we do not say that he is supposed to understand the paradox but is only to understand that this is the paradox. We have already shown how this occurs. It occurs when the understanding and the paradox happily encounter each other in the moment, when the understanding steps aside and the paradox gives itself, and the third something, the something in which this occurs (for it does not occur through the understanding, which is discharged, or through the paradox, which gives itself – consequently *in* something), is that happy passion to which we shall now give a name, although for us it is not a matter of the name. We shall call it *faith*.
>
> (PF, 59/SKS 4, 261)

The medium in which the paradox 'gives itself' to us is not the doxastic medium of the understanding. It's the praxic medium of faith. And note that Climacus does not say that paradox is dissolved – it is 'received,' or taken up and incorporated into a style of living. The paradox becomes the most important feature of our world because it attunes us to everything else around us. 'When the believer has faith,' Kierkegaard noted, 'the absurd is not the absurd – faith transforms it, but in every weak moment' – that is, every moment in which our skills start to fail us and we slip back into discursive reflection and deliberation – 'it is again more or less absurd to him' (JP 1, 7).

To the extent that discourse is in the service of a practical engagement with the world (that is, it is discourse as existence-communication) it fails not by delivering false or contradictory propositions, but by weakening one's ability to act in faith, by interfering with one's fluid course of purposive activity. In assessing a football manager's discursive practice on a training pitch, it is of only incidental interest whether she inculcates true discursive beliefs in her players. Her primary concern is to guide them into the optimal stance to develop and exercise their skills. Similarly, in assessing the scriptures or Kierkegaard's own discursive practice, including his insistence on the incomprehensibility of Christian doctrine, the primary question is not whether they produce true beliefs. We should ask instead how well they are designed to guide someone to expertise in the practice of Christianity.

According to the reading I'm proposing, the point of Climacus's puzzle, and the *Fragments* and the *Postscript* more generally, is precisely to redirect the reader away from a concern with belief formation and toward the task of developing an adoxal faith. As Eric Kaplan has argued persuasively, to understand the argument in the *Postscript*, we have to remember that Climacus is a character in a dramatic work.[9] (The drama-to-philosophy ratio is quite low, but it is nevertheless a significant feature of the work – a fact reinforced when Kierkegaard (2009: 527/ SKS 7, 569), in his own voice, intervenes at the very end of the *Postscript* to explain his use of pseudonymous authors: 'What is written is indeed therefore mine, but only so far as I have put the life-view of the creating, poetically actualized individuality into his mouth in audible lines.') When dealing with a dramatic work, Kaplan (2017: 90) notes, in order 'to evaluate what the character says we have to form an opinion of what sort of person he is.' So, who is Climacus? He is a thirty-year-old man who, we discover, finds it hard to commit to and follow through on any existential project. He tells us that, after six years of 'brilliant inactivity' as a student – time spent 'loafing and thinking, or thinking and loafing' – he found himself sitting on a park bench, smoking a cigar, and reflecting to himself:

> You are getting on, I said to myself, and are becoming an old man without being anything, and without really taking on anything.... And what are you doing? Here my soliloquy was interrupted, for my cigar was finished and a new one had to be lit. So I smoked again, and then suddenly this thought flashed through my mind: You must do something.
>
> *(Kierkegaard 2009: 156/SKS 7, 171)*

Having thus resolved to throw himself actively into existence, Climacus finds himself an indeterminate amount of time later once again sitting on a bench, this time in a graveyard. Hidden from view, he sees what he describes as 'the most affecting scene I have ever witnessed' – a grandfather and grandson, weeping over the grave of their respective son and father, fearing that his eternal soul has been lost through his embrace of Hegelian philosophy. Climacus is so moved by observing this event that he sets out immediately to do something. Well, actually, it takes him four years to get around to doing something – but he eventually comes to the decisive moment, and sits down to write a book[10] explaining 'the dubious relation between a modern Christian speculation and Christianity' (Kierkegaard 2009: 202/SKS 7, 219).

The motivating thought that informs the entire book is this: speculation misunderstands and diminishes faith, and the misunderstanding 'might indeed lie in the fact that, in all this knowledge, one has forgotten what it is to *exist*.' This is Climacus's 'main thought,' and he ventures that existential forgetfulness is the 'whole tendency of the age' (Kierkegaard 2009: 203/SKS 7, 220; see also 209/226). 'Speculation' in this passage refers to Hegelian philosophy. But Kierkegaard's concern is not limited to Hegelian approaches to religion. His target is anyone who, like Hegel (1986: §564), 'cannot rest satisfied with the plain pictures of faith, but rather [feels] duty bound to proceed to thought – at first, to reflective understanding, but ultimately to conceptual thought.' Hegel (2007: §573) dismisses religious thinkers who 'avoid any difficulties that emerge in their conception of God's relation to the world, by confessing that this relation contains for them a contradiction which they do not understand at all.' Such '*faith*,' Hegel (2007: §573) notes acerbically,

> means no more than a refusal to advance to a determinate representation, to get more involved in the content. That men and classes of uncultivated intellect are satisfied with indeterminate representations is appropriate; but when a cultivated intellect and an interest in reflective study is willing to put up with indeterminate representations in what is acknowledged to be a higher and the highest interest, then it is hard to tell whether the mind really takes the content seriously.... If factual claims are advanced and the facts are thoughts and concepts, then it is indispensable to understand such things.

Speculative philosophy, for instance, refuses to rest content with a religion in which 'faith is based on the *witness of the spirit*'[11] and 'sets itself against conceptual reason' (Hegel 1986: §573). Without a 'systematic,' 'reflective,' and ultimately 'conceptual' understanding in which God is 'correctly and determinately grasped in thought,' Hegel (1986: §564) explains, 'human beings know nothing of God.'

Hegel's core commitment to systematic, reflective, conceptual thought is precisely what Kierkegaard thinks leads speculative philosophy to misunderstand religious life. While Climacus singles out speculative philosophy for special criticism, he sees the widespread enthusiasm for Hegel amongst his contemporaries as just the latest iteration of a broader tendency toward what he calls 'objectivity' about religious life. Objectivity is itself best understood as an existential style – one whose primary commitment is to forming true beliefs about the objective world. Objective truth is a truth that is factually demonstrable to any rational observer. As a result, the objective search for truth proceeds disinterestedly and dispassionately. It aims at certainty and (like Hegel in the passage above) is thus loathe to act without a discursive understanding of itself, its aims, its principles. When gripped by objectivity, we feel an almost irresistible impulse to 'proceed from life to thought' – to try to capture in the medium of a noetic structure what it means to have a particular form of existence or way of life. But translating a life into a structure of beliefs surreptitiously brings with it an obligation: beliefs are the kind of thing that ought to be supported by reasons, and objectivity is subject to the demand that it establish and secure the objective truth of those beliefs.

The irony of Climacus as a dramatic figure is that his commitment problem is the result of his sharing to some degree in the modern addiction to objectivity. Whilst he portrays himself as being moved to rescue society at large from a misplaced objectivity, in reality his aim is much more personal. He ultimately writes the book as an attempt to overcome his own objective urges and throw himself more faithfully and passionately into existence. He confesses this openly in the appendix to the book, just before revoking what he has written. He writes:

> the whole book is about myself, solely about me. 'I, Joh. Cl., now thirty years old, born in Copenhagen, a plain, ordinary human like most, have heard tell of a highest good in prospect, which is called an eternal happiness, and that Christianity wants to bestow it on one on condition of adhering to it. Now I ask, how do I become a Christian?' I ask solely for my own sake.
>
> *(Kierkegaard 2009: 520/SKS 7, 560)*

He has pursued this question by forcing himself to confront his objective impulse toward thought and rational understanding with a very particular kind of paradox – one that can't be solved rationally, but one that can't be ignored either. Climacus calls such an experience – an experience of being unable to rationally grasp the meaning of a phenomenon, but also unable to turn away and quit trying to come to grips with it – the 'crucifixion of one's understanding' (see Kierkegaard 2009: 468, 472–3, 505/SKS 7, 508, 513, 545). Only an irresolvable contradiction at the heart of his most important concern – the promise of eternal happiness in this worldly existence – could nail Climacus's reason to the cross. This is a high-stakes affair: if it turns out that his hope is centred on something irremediably absurd and paradoxical, that will either provoke despair or teach him to see himself and his world in a whole new light.

The struggle with the paradox, Climacus humorously notes, breaks the back of the understanding 'which does indeed give it a singular kind of suppleness' (PF, 50/SKS 4, 254). When the understanding takes offense at having its back broken, and objects that the paradox is an absurdity, the paradox replies: 'Now, what are you wondering about? *It is just as you say, and the amazing thing is that you think that it is an objection*' (PF, 52/SKS 4, 256; my emphasis). The paradox, Climacus continues, has 'the effrontery to call the understanding a clod and a dunce who at best can say "yes" and "no" to the same thing, which is not good theology' (PF, 53/SKS 4, 256). The paradox is meant to force the understanding to withdraw from the field – to persuade us to stop doing theology, because if one persists in trying to understand the God-man using the resources of reason, one will inevitably contradict oneself. Later, Climacus returns to the same theme. In discussing the challenge that believers face when confronted by the paradox of the God-man, he reminds us of the reproach that Christ directed at his followers, saying 'So, then, you love only the omnipotent one who does miracles, not the one who abased himself in equality with you.' Climacus follows up that reproach by saying: 'But here I shall stop. Even if I were a better dialectician than I am, I would still have my limits. Because at bottom, an unshakable insistence upon the absolute and absolute distinctions is precisely what makes a good dialectician. This is something we in our day have completely disregarded by canceling and in canceling the principle of contradiction' (PF, 108/SKS 4, 304). What Climacus is saying, in other words, is that even the best dialectician encounters her limits when having to understand how the God-man could be both omnipotent and abased. It is the combination of her respect for the principle of non-contradiction and her love for Christ as *both* omnipotent and abased that should compel her to stop trying to understand the paradox. For reason to make sense of the contradiction, it will have to affirm one side and deny the other – it will have to, for instance, love the god, not the one who abased himself as a man. If you want to stay true to the God-man, Climacus is saying, you'll need to know your limits, and know when to stop philosophizing, because there is no getting around the fact that the God-man is a contradiction.[12]

The moral of the story, then, is that an insistence on having coherent, well-founded beliefs as a prerequisite to engaging in Christian practices will prevent one from ever getting started on the path of faith. The paradox of the God-man plays a pivotal role in turning us away from the discursive practice of belief examination and justification, and toward the existential task of living a worthwhile life. Climacus wants us rigorously to hold on to the principle of non-contradiction precisely because then, when confronted with the strict paradox of the God-man, we will experience the extreme tension that forces us to stop thinking and philosophizing and theologizing and, for God's sake, finally make an existential commitment.

Anti-Climacus emphasizes this point in *Practice in Christianity*: 'The God-man is the sign of contradiction.' He continues:

> And only the sign of contradiction can do this: it draws attention to itself and then it presents a contradiction. There is a something that makes it impossible not to look – and look, as one is looking one sees as in a mirror, one comes to see oneself, or he who is the sign of contradiction looks straight into one's heart while one is staring into the contradiction. A contradiction placed squarely in front of a person – if one can get him to look at it – is a mirror; as he is forming a judgment, what dwells within him must be disclosed. It is a riddle, but as he is guessing the riddle, what dwells within him is disclosed by the way he guesses. The contradiction confronts him with a choice, and as he is choosing, together with what he chooses, he himself is disclosed.
>
> *(PC, 126–7/SKS 12, 131)*

What is the choice I face when confronted by the paradox of the God-man? He asks me to choose: do I want an eternal God (for which reason alone suffices)? The merely temporal teacher of love (in whom reason can find no cause of offence)? Or both – finding the eternal in the temporal, and the abased in perfect conformity with the infinite? For that, faith alone will suffice – but only because Christian faith is not a cognitive state, it is a practical stance of being disposed by the God-man.[13]

Related topics

'Christian epistemology and the anthropology of sin: Kierkegaard on natural theology and the concept of "offense,"' Karen L. Carr; 'Logic, language, and existential knowledge,' Melissa Fox-Muraton; 'On faith and reason(s): Kierkegaard's logic of conviction,' K. Brian Söderquist.

Notes

1. Anti-Climacus, the most fully Christian of Kierkegaard's pseudonymous authors, is an important corroborating witness to Climacus's claims. He also endorses each of these claims – perhaps most concisely in the prayer that 'in our day especially is so appropriate' (see SUD, 129n/SKS 11, 240).
2. For a concise overview of many different strategies for dealing with the problem of incoherence, see Hill (2017).
3. I also pass in silence the 'dialethic' alternative of denying the first premise. Kierkegaard would not accept it. I discuss this further below.
4. Of course, what is relevant to the formation of beliefs may also prove relevant to the motivation of actions. But the significance of a fact or a belief for other beliefs is not identical with its significance for action.
5. Thanks to Dan Watts for calling this passage to my attention.
6. This is in part because of its preoccupation with 'demonstration' of the truth of Christian doctrines. It is only 'unbelief' (i.e., a lack of faith), Anti-Climacus insists, that 'invents demonstrations' (PC, 29/SKS 12, 43).
7. Bullet-biters, of course, dismiss all of this as utter nonsense. If there is a way to find meaning in Kierkegaard's discursive practice, consistent with his rejection of reason and objectivity as providing a means to arrive at faith, then this would be manifestly a more charitable approach than bullet biting. After all, Climacus anticipates and explicitly rejects the bullet biting interpretation of Christianity: 'Furthermore, to say that Christianity is empty of content because it is not a doctrine is only chicanery. When a believer exists in faith, his existence has enormous content, but not in the sense of a yield in paragraphs' (CUP 1, 380/SKS 7, 346).
8. For a variety of positions on the question whether propositional thought interferes with skilful action or enhances it, see Stanley and Williamson (2016); Montero (2016); and Dreyfus (2014).

9 Many of the insights in what follows are owed to Kaplan (2017).
10 The reader is meant to recognize the irony of the fact that Climacus's grand, decisive action consists in writing a book – a book, moreover, that he ends up revoking.
11 For Kierkegaard on the witness of the spirit, see K. Brian Söderquist's contribution to this volume.
12 Because Evans is oriented toward belief rather than faith, he misses the force of these passages. He takes them to show that the God-man can't be a strict contradiction, since it's not good theology to accept a strict contradiction (see Evans 1992: 100).
13 I am grateful to many people for their helpful comments and responses to earlier drafts of this paper. I'd like to express particular appreciation to Dan Watts, Eric Kaplan, Sophie Archer, Beatrice Han-Pile, Adam Buben, Patrick Stokes, Aaron Reeves, Teppo Felin, and all the participants at the conference on *The Phenomenology of Religious Life,* held at Corpus Christi College, Oxford, on June 9, 2018.

References

Allison, H. E. (1967) 'Christianity and nonsense,' *The Review of Metaphysics*, 20: 432–60.
Conant, J. (1989) 'Must we show what we cannot say?' in R. Fleming and M. Payne (eds), *The Senses of Stanley Cavell*, Lewisburg, PA: Bucknell University Press.
Dreyfus, H. L. (2014) *Skillful coping*, M. A. Wrathall (ed), Oxford: Oxford University Press.
Evans, C. S. (1992) *Passionate reason: Making sense of Kierkegaard's Philosophical Fragments*, Bloomington, IN: Indiana University Press.
Hegel, G. W. F. (2007) *Philosophy of mind*, W. Wallace and A. V. Miller (trans), revised by M. Inwood, Oxford: Oxford University Press.
Hegel, G. W. F. (1986) *Enzyklopädie der philosophischen Wissenschaften im Grundrisse: Dritter Teil: Die Philosophie des Geistes* [1830], *Werke*, vol. 10, Frankfurt: Suhrkamp.
Hill, J. (2017) 'Introduction,' in A. Marmodoro and J. Hill (eds), *The Metaphysics of Incarnation*, Oxford: Oxford University Press.
Kaplan, E. L. (2017) 'Kierkegaard and the funny,' *UC Berkeley*. Retrieved from <https://escholarship.org/uc/item/2np978rn>
Kierkegaard, S. (2009) *Concluding unscientific postscript to the 'Philosophical Crumbs,'* A. Hannay (trans), Cambridge: Cambridge University Press.
Montero, B. G. (2016) *Thought in action*, Oxford: Oxford University Press.
Stanley, J. and Williamson, T. (2016) 'Skill,' *Noûs*, 51: 713–26.
Watts, D. (2016) 'Kierkegaard and the limits of thought,' *Hegel Bulletin*, 39: 82–105.

Further reading

Buben, A. (2013) 'Neither irrationalist nor apologist: Revisiting faith and reason in Kierkegaard,' *Philosophy Compass*, 8, no. 3: 318–26.
  This paper uses a comparison with Pascal to support the anti-rationalist reading of Kierkegaard.
Carr, K. L. (1996) 'The offense of reason and the passion of faith: Kierkegaard and anti-rationalism,' *Faith and Philosophy*, 13: 236–51.
  This paper provides an illuminating discussion of the contrast between the 'irrationalist,' the 'anti-rationalist,' and the 'supra-rationalist' interpretations of Kierkegaard.
Dreyfus, H. L. (2017) *Background practices*, M. A. Wrathall (ed), Oxford: Oxford University Press.
  This is a collection of essays that show the fusion of existentialism and a skills-based pragmatism. Chps. 12 and 13 are especially relevant to the present topic.
Wrathall, M. A. and Londen, P. (2019) 'Anglo-American existential phenomenology,' in I. Thomson and K. Becker (eds), *The Cambridge History of Philosophy 1945–2015*, Cambridge: Cambridge University Press.
  This paper offers a concise overview of a *Gestaltist* and non-discursive account of skilful action.

21
KIERKEGAARD'S DEFENSE OF NATURE AND THEOLOGY AGAINST NATURAL THEOLOGY

Will Williams

Introduction

In the nineteenth century, Søren Kierkegaard found himself the inheritor of a culture in Denmark that was a product of the Protestant Reformation as well as of the philosophical and scientific developments that followed it. Kierkegaard was a Lutheran in Lutheran Denmark, and he was convinced of the truthfulness of Lutheranism, although he was extremely unhappy with how it had been received and instantiated by the established Church of Denmark. Kierkegaard says, including himself in the criticism of his culture, 'Lutheran doctrine is excellent, is the truth. With regard to this excellent Lutheran doctrine, I have but one misgiving. It does not concern Lutheran doctrine – no, it concerns myself: I have become convinced that I am not an honest soul but a cunning fellow' (FSE, 24/SKS 13, 52). Kierkegaard believed that his culture, and by extension European Christendom, had taken advantage of Protestant theology in order to warp it and to relieve themselves of the burden of living holy lives that were faithful to Scriptural requirements and expectations.

Nature as delight and danger

One area in which Kierkegaard identified great vulnerability in his culture was the concept of nature. Kierkegaard loved nature and was known to frequent various parks and forests in the vicinity of Copenhagen. He wrote frequently and joyfully about nature and of its capacity to calm the soul and direct our attention to the power and majesty of God. For example, consider some entries from Kierkegaard's journals:

> Trees carry on the most pleasant, the most refreshing conversation, and although all the leaves talk away at the same time (in spite of all the rules of etiquette), it is not at all disturbing; instead it lulls the external senses and awakens the inner ones.
> *(JP 3, 256/SKS 18, 48)*

> The heath must be particularly adapted to developing vigorous spirits; here everything lies naked and unveiled before God, and here is no place for a lot of distractions, those many odd nooks and corners where the consciousness can hide, and from which

earnestness often has a hard time recovering vagrant thoughts. Here consciousness must come to definite and precise conclusions about itself. Here on the heath one must truly say, "Whither shall I flee from thy presence?"

(JP 3, 257/SKS 19, 201; see Psalm 139: 7)

[A]nd when I go out under the arch of heaven, behold the myriad stars – I do not feel at all alien in this enormous world – for, truly, it is my Father's. Nor do I feel abandoned on the crossroad of life and in the misery of life, for I am always under my Father's eye.

(JP 3, 263/SKS 20, 378)

Kierkegaard was concerned that as the population grew in the nineteenth century and became more centred in cities that it was losing important contact with nature and, therefore, with an important testimony of the character and majesty of God: 'Really, we need to live more with nature if for no other reason than to get more of an impression of God's majesty. Huddled together in the great cultural centers we have as much as possible abolished all overwhelming impressions – a lamentable demoralization' (JP 3, 264/SKS 24, 477). One of Kierkegaard's favourite Scripture passages to reflect on within his authorship is the Matthew 6 passage of the lilies of the field and the birds of the air, which Kierkegaard treated perhaps most famously in Part Two of his *Upbuilding Discourses in Various Spirits* (UDVS, 155–212/SKS 8, 251–307).

Even so – and perhaps surprisingly – Kierkegaard is sharply critical of the increasing fascination with natural science in his culture, including within Christian theology. Strikingly, he says, 'Ultimately all corruption will come from the natural sciences' (JP 3, 242/SKS 20, 63; italics removed). He believes that the interest in natural science is an expression of an arrogating desire to appropriate the authority of ethics and theology, eventually leading toward 'the establishment of natural science in the place of religion' (JP 3, 251/SKS 23, 27). My goal is to clarify Kierkegaard's relationship to nature and in what ways it is seen as helpful and unhelpful for Christian faith and theology. Kierkegaard loved nature and loved faithful Christian theology, but he saw the rise of natural theology in Protestantism, particularly as it drew heavily from the advancements of natural science, as a threat to both as a source of edification for the believer.[1]

Two corruptions of nature

Romanticism: the direct relation to nature as the ethical

Despite Kierkegaard's love of nature, he sees it as vulnerable to corrupting ideas from at least two quarters in his culture. First, under the influence of Romanticism, some may see nature as a source of ethical guidance and seek wisdom from nature. Kierkegaard considers this belief to be a category mistake and criticizes A. P. Adler for succumbing to it: 'Adler's dizziness is apparent also in his careless, loose thinking and believing that greatness will prevail even if wrong and injustice also occur, and the best proof of this dizziness is his constant appeal to analogies from nature, for nature simply is not the ethical; nature allows rain to fall on good and evil alike, but the ethical makes the qualitative distinction' (JP 3, 263). Nature does not make ethical distinctions and cannot be used, simply and directly, as a source of understanding for moral guidance or for the concept of holiness. Instead, by alluding to Jesus' teaching in Matthew 5: 45 that God makes natural provision like sun and rain for all of humanity, including the good and evil alike, Kierkegaard depicts nature as a provision from God that generally functions as a gracious context or backdrop within which humans must act and choose. That nature at times sends blessing on the wicked (such as gravity, oxygen, sunlight, etc.) is an indication to Kierkegaard that nature cannot function as a sure guide to ethical discernment. To think so, as he accuses Adler of believing, would be to think mistakenly that God could be accessed directly in nature. Rather, as Kierkegaard's pseudonym Johannes Climacus puts it: 'In paganism, the direct relation is idolatry.... Nature, the totality of creation, is God's work, and yet God is not there, but within the individual human being there is a possibility (he is spirit according to his possibility) that in inwardness is awakened to a God-relationship, and then it is possible to see God everywhere' (CUP 1, 246–7/SKS 7, 224). Nature offers us, not direct ethical instruction, but an occasion for possibly opening up to the Creator of nature, who has given us ethical instruction through the Scriptures and the prophets. Nature offers us, not God directly, but a possibility of awakening to a God-relationship.

Natural science: distractions of content and of mode of existing

The second possible source of corrupting our reception of nature – and here is where I will direct most of my attention – is natural science. The achievements of natural science were captivating to many in Kierkegaard's day, and that included Kierkegaard himself, who read about scientific developments and discoveries with interest and admired the accomplishments of natural scientists in Copenhagen. In his early twenties, Kierkegaard even considered entering a career in natural science (JP 5, 20–4/SKS 17, 18–21). In the end, though, he decided against this course for his life: 'I have been enthusiastic about the natural sciences and still am, but I do not think that I will make them my principal study. The life by virtue of reason and freedom has always interested me most, and it has always been my desire to clarify and solve the riddle of life' (JP 5, 22/SKS 17, 21). While natural science may promise to solve many riddles for Kierkegaard's curious mind, even at an early age he suspects that the riddle of life itself will not essentially be found down that path as it frequently gets lost in details and fails to see the whole. Aside from a few great lights in natural science who had great depth of perception, Kierkegaard judged many successful natural scientists to 'know a great many details and have discovered many new ones, but nothing more. They have merely provided a substratum for others to think about and work up' (JP 5, 22/SKS 17, 20).

Extending this characterization of the natural sciences, Kierkegaard considers them to be not just incidentally tending towards myopia but also essentially a distraction from ethical-religious requirements. He writes:

> A physiologist takes it upon himself to explain all mankind. The question here is, first and foremost, *principiis obsta* [resist the beginnings]: What do I have to do with this. Why should I need to know about afferent and efferent nerve-impulses, about the circulation of blood, about the human being's microscopic condition in the womb. *The ethical has tasks enough for me.* Do I need to know the digestive process in order to eat? Do I need to know the processes of the nervous system – in order to believe in God and to love men?
>
> (JP 3, 240/SKS 20, 60)

Kierkegaard's concern was in living a life, not in increasing conceptual accuracy about the mechanical processes of life-living. One may object, 'But advancing scientific knowledge will save lives and extend lifespans! Surely this is an earnest matter about which ethicists should be concerned.' Kierkegaard is unimpressed by this argument. He says, 'The ethicist says with enthusiasm: In a certain sense all medical science is a jest. The fun of saving a man's life for a few years is merely fun – earnestness is to die blessed' (JP 3, 246/SKS 20, 66–7). While his culture is earnestly invested in how science may save lives, Kierkegaard replies with the sobering observation that we all nevertheless die anyway, and while extending life a few years is good fun, it would be a mistake to believe that science is solving anything here. It is merely a delaying tactic. Every doctor's patient, including the doctor himself, will finally die. In the end, the truly earnest concern – the one with infinite rather than merely finite consequences – is to die reconciled to God, having served Him faithfully. To have all of the benefits of medicine but to lose that would be a dark irony. As Jesus put it, 'For whoever would save his life will lose it, but whoever loses his life for my sake and the gospel's will save it. For what does it profit a man to gain the whole world and forfeit his soul?' (Mark 8: 35–6, ESV).[2]

For Kierkegaard, then, pursuing the curiosities of natural science is a distraction from the ethical-religious tasks that we have under God. But Kierkegaard believes its distractions are not only in content but also in mode of existing. Encountering the greatness of nature, he believes, moves us to a state of wonder, overwhelmed by the greatness of God. But the scrutiny of scientific investigation – parsing and detailing and rationally reflecting – cultivates an entirely different posture than worship and amazement and tempts us into thinking that we can control and understand. This mode of existing may be suitable for provoking sceptical philosophical reflection on the nature of ethical commands, but it is not a way of existing that characterizes immediate obedience to such commands. He writes:

> I shall ask again: I wonder if I am not weakening my whole ethical passion by becoming a natural scientist? And I wonder if, with all this diverse knowledge of analogies, of abnormalities, of this and that, I do not lose more and more the impress of the ethical: the *you shall*, it is *you* yourself . . . even if heaven and earth collapse, YOU SHALL. I wonder if it is not a way of providing myself with a lot of sly evasions and excuses. I wonder if my gaze is not turned away from the most important thing by letting myself begin with physiology, instead of assuming the whole of physiology and saying: Begin.
>
> *(JP 3, 240–1/SKS 20, 60)*

Later, he says:

> If there were anything by way of the natural sciences which would help define spirit, I should be the first to get hold of a microscope, and I think my perseverance would equal anyone's. But when by qualitative dialectic I easily perceive that, qualitatively understood, in 100,000 years the world will not have advanced one single step, I shall do the very opposite, preserve my soul and not waste one single second of my life on curiosity. . . . I certainly do understand that it is God who has given man the kind of acuteness with which he makes discoveries by means of instruments and such, but it is also God who has given man the reason by which . . . he might perceive the self-contradiction inherent in [the endeavour] . . . thus man ought devoutly and humbly to renounce curiosity, renounce the kind of equanimity which is required for microscopic research and rather pray to God and relate himself to him only through the ethical.
>
> *(JP 3, 247/SKS 20, 68)*

In addition to promoting a disposition of equanimity, curiosity, and supposed objectivity, Kierkegaard also thinks that an accent on the achievements of the sciences and on understanding those achievements cultivates pride, dividing up people into hierarchies of education or intelligence rather than uniting them in their common humility and need for God. Kierkegaard believes that the differences among human beings, which are many, are all relative and frequently quantitative distinctions which ultimately matter not at all in comparison with the infinite qualitative distinction that divides us from a holy and eternal God (e.g., JP 5, 417/SKS 20, 251–3; SUD, 126–7/SKS 11, 237–8). To divide people by accentuating those finite distinctions cultivates the illusion that some of us really are a bit further along than others, a superior class in our culture, knowledge, spiritual maturity, etc., which distracts from the more fundamental Christian truth that, for example, 'all have sinned and fall short of the glory of God' (Romans 3: 23, ESV). Kierkegaard writes:

> From the natural sciences a tragic distinction will spread between the simple folk who believe simply and the learned and half-learned – who have looked through a microscope. No longer as in the old days shall one confidently dare to speak about the one and undivided highest and address all, all, all men, regardless of whether they are black or green, have big heads or little ones – we must first see if they have brains enough – to believe in God. If Christ had known about the microscope, he would have examined the apostles first.
>
> *(JP 3, 248/SKS 20, 71)*

Believing through faith will become the poor man's way of relating to God, while the intelligentsia have the advantage of confidence and surety through their knowledge of scientific facts. A right approach to nature, then, would unite humanity through wonder at beauty and greatness, while a wrong one, he believes, accentuates our prideful desire to edge our neighbour out for praise and accomplishment in quantitative knowledge.

Natural science and Socratic ignorance

In resisting the curiosity of natural science in favour of obedience under the ethical-religious, Kierkegaard saw himself as following the example of Socrates, who maintained a pure focus on the ethical and refused to be distracted by questions of the ontology of nature or the latest developments in astronomy.[3] Kierkegaard writes:

> The hypocrisy is namely this – that natural science is supposed to lead to God ... Tell [the natural scientist] that any man has all he needs in his conscience and in Luther's *Small Catechism*, and the natural scientist will look down his nose. In an imposing way he wants to make God into a coy beauty, a devil of a fellow, whom not everyone can understand – stop, the divine and simple truth is that no one, absolutely no one, can understand him, that the wisest of men must humbly take his stand on THE SAME as does a simple man. – Herein lies the profundity in Socratic ignorance – truly to *forsake* with TOTAL PASSION all curious knowledge, in order in all simplicity to be ignorant before God, to forsake this show (which, after all, is something between man and man) of making observations by way of the microscope.
>
> *(JP 3, 243/SKS 20, 64)*[4]

Further, Kierkegaard believes that many of the assumptions of natural science could not withstand Socratic scrutiny. For example, Kierkegaard observes the progressive and additive nature of science. While many of his day saw this as evidence that such science is triumphant, carrying history forward into progress, he considered this as evidence that it was always revising itself, including the revocation of former conclusive pronouncements, in the quest for a final truth that it, by its nature, can never attain. Kierkegaard writes, 'Do an experiment using Socrates' simple question: "Does natural science know something or does it not?" It can answer neither Yes nor No, for the whole secret of it is that it is almost and as good as and not very far from and almost, just as if it knew something' (JP 3, 248/SKS 20, 70). Kierkegaard believes that the natural sciences make a pretense of knowing something that they at best can only approximate, and at times they simply must use rhetorical flourish to distract from their own ignorance. For him, natural science is a quantitative and approximative exercise that must necessarily founder on explanations for qualitative developments. At times, natural science admits its inability and confesses some questions to be a miracle: 'a miracle that consciousness comes into existence, a miracle that the idea becomes mind, that mind becomes spirit (in short, the qualitative transitions)' (JP 3, 244/SKS 20, 65). In order to save face, natural science must make promises of being just on the cusp of solving these miracles, perhaps with just a little more funding and research: 'Therefore it wants to conjure up an appearance, as if it nevertheless could almost, as good as, as it were, for the most part, just about – explain the miracle' (JP 3, 245/SKS 20, 66). In other words, natural science makes rhetorical claims of its offering certainty, but it is always in motion and never quite arrives at the certainty it promises. In response, Kierkegaard says, '*The only certainty is the ethical-religious*. It declares: Believe – you shall believe' (JP 3, 245/SKS 20, 66).

Natural theology: natural science's invasion into ethics and theology

Kierkegaard's understanding is that natural science in his day was not content simply to be about the tasks of natural science.[5] The problem, as he says, is 'that natural science is supposed to lead to God' (JP 3, 243/SKS 20, 64). In other words, as he understands it, it is as if the natural science of Kierkegaard's day had more or less consciously internalized some of the motives and drives of natural theology, aspiring to explain more than a strict scientific method permits. It is as if one of the justifications for why one should engage in natural science in the first place is a sort of ethical, theological, and spiritual payoff, aiding in the advancement of all European culture to its consummation. However he may object to it, Kierkegaard believes that, at least as his culture was then constituted, natural science and natural theology implied one another. This situation was welcomed by natural theology,[6] which, for its part, desired the authority, cultural cachet, and implied factual certainty that natural science lent to it.

As Kierkegaard saw it, natural science continually overflowed its banks into both ethics and religion. In ethics, Kierkegaard objected firstly to the rationalization of ethics, which is entirely the wrong mode of existing for ethical obedience. He remarks on the vast difference between a young girl in love and a calmly reasonable and knowledgeable man objectively lecturing on the nature of love:

> But if an extremely cold and calculating fellow calmly told the young girl: I shall explain to you what love is, and if the girl confessed that everything he said was absolutely correct, I wonder if she would choose his miserable common sense instead of her treasure. I wonder if the young girl would not say to him, 'What you say is quite right; I, too, can understand it very well, and yet there is one thing which I do not understand. I do not understand how you can speak so calmly and coldly about this, something which affects me so deeply. Obviously we must not be talking about the same thing, since the effects are so very different.'
>
> (JP 3, 239/SKS 20, 59)

Kierkegaard continues,

> It is easy to see that one loses out by choosing reason when this so-called reason (enlightenment, speculation, etc.) puts something in place of faith and immediacy. But even when reason seemingly would provide the same thing, only in a different form, it is still a great loss. Here it is a question of choice. One can choose not to let himself be chilled by reason, can choose to hold on to rapture and enthusiasm, in faith and in confidence.
>
> *(JP 3, 239–40/SKS 20, 59)*

One does not become a better lover by listening to cold lectures on loving, he thinks. Kierkegaard also detects the sway of the natural sciences in the tendency of ethics in his day to move toward the rationally calculative[7]: 'In our time it is the natural sciences which are especially dangerous. Physiology will ultimately extend itself to the point of embracing ethics. There are already sufficient clues of a new endeavor – to treat ethics as physics, whereby all of ethics becomes illusory and ethics in the race is treated statistically by averages or is calculated as one calculates vibrations in laws of nature' (JP 3, 240/SKS 20, 59–60). In addition to his objections that the calculative mode is all wrong for ethics and his scepticism that such things could be calculated with mathematical precision in the first place, Kierkegaard is also objecting to the invasion of the natural sciences into ethics because he thinks that it causes the subject – the human self – to fall away and be replaced by chemical and biological processes. As he says, 'The conflict between God and "man" will therefore culminate in the withdrawal of "man" behind natural science' (JP 3, 252/SKS 25, 186). It weakens the self in abstraction precisely when a self is being called upon to respond ethically and narrates human action in terms of physical determinisms. While in our day, we may be more likely to excuse bad behaviour due to genetic predisposition, Kierkegaard has his own version:

> Imagine the most infamous criminal who has ever lived and suppose that physiology at the time had on its nose the most wonderful pair of spectacles there ever was so it could now explain the criminal, that the whole thing was a natural necessity, that his brain was too small, etc. – how horrible this exemption from subsequent indictment in comparison with Christianity's judgment upon him, that he will go to hell if he does not repent.
>
> *(JP 3, 242/SKS 20, 62)*

The natural sciences invade religion with similar results. Indeed, Kierkegaard seems to think that the culture of Christendom would much prefer natural science to traditional Christianity such that this 'invasion' is actively welcomed. Taking a swipe at Schleiermacher's notion of Christian consciousness, Kierkegaard criticizes his supposedly Christian culture: '[T]he world ... wants to market a new culture-consciousness, a Christian diffusion, therefore a Christian consciousness, – and it probably will make natural science its religion' (JP 3, 251/SKS 24, 315). Kierkegaard believes that Christendom had grown complacent through years of taking Christianity and grace for granted, which allowed doubts to creep up from all quarters, such as the academic criticism being levelled against the reliability of the Scriptures in his day. Now many in Christendom no longer saw the traditional faith as a sure foundation and went looking for more solid and certain grounding in the sciences and natural theology. Theology, Kierkegaard believes, no longer wants to be a matter of conviction, passion, and faith but a science with scientific certainty! Kierkegaard observes the irony:

> [T]heological scholarship is ... eager to be a science, but then it loses the game here, too. If the whole thing were not so serious, it would be extremely comical to consider theology's painful situation, which it certainly deserves, for this is its nemesis for wanting to be a science. ... The joker is and remains scientific theology. It is actually in real trouble and with the help of the natural sciences it will get into trouble more and more. For scientific theology is without faith, without open confidence before God, without a good conscience in the presence of Holy Scripture.
> (JP 3, 252–4/SKS 25, 186–7)

'Scientific theology,' as he describes it, far from an aid to Christian faith, is in fact symptomatic of a sickly faith that wishes to gain the apparent surety of science *instead* of being a venture of personal commitment and trust. For Kierkegaard, scientific theology is the way out of Christianity for Christendom.

Nature and Christian faith

Returning to a consideration of nature more broadly, one sees that Kierkegaard is not critical of nature and its role in telling of the majesty of God. He loves nature and recommends it. But he is very critical of certain ways of relating to and understanding nature that are common in his culture, notably the tendency to understand nature primarily through the lens of natural science. Nature is not the problem, and indeed nature may hold some solutions to these problems if it cultivates in us the passions of faith, and if it is acknowledged that the role and powers of nature are limited to what is suitable to claim for them. For example, traditionally Romans 1: 18–32 has been a *locus classicus* for promoters of natural theology, claiming it as Pauline justification for their enterprise. Verses 19–20 (ESV) state, 'For what can be known about God is plain to them, because God has shown it to them. For his invisible attributes, namely, his eternal power and divine nature, have been clearly perceived, ever since the creation of the world, in the things that have been made. So they are without excuse.' Clearly, nature reveals God's attributes, not only special revelation via the Scriptures or the prophets. Kierkegaard does not deny this, but neither does he claim that such passages grant *carte blanche* for any unrestrained conclusions of natural theology. After all, Paul limits his claims to 'what can be known about God is plain to them' – not anything whatsoever – and the entire passage immediately follows verse 17, which states, 'For in [the gospel] the righteousness of God is revealed from faith for faith, as it is written, "The righteous shall live by faith"' (Romans 1: 17, ESV). No arguments of natural theology looking to the following verses may abrogate that it is *by faith* that the righteous live, fully and finally. Faith trumps and perhaps informs whatever conclusions natural theology may come to by the power of its own reasoning, and Kierkegaard preserves this distinction and priority.

In 1848, Kierkegaard publishes *Christian Discourses* under his own name. While he does not often engage the Romans 1 passage in his writing, Part Four of *Christian Discourses*, entitled 'Discourses at the Communion on Fridays,' does include some engagement with it in chapter VI. Here, he praises God for revealing Himself in nature, but one will note that he does not let natural revelation win the day in terms of how we know of God and His character. In his opening prayer, note how Kierkegaard frames our knowledge of God in the open expanse of nature versus in the particularity of a local church celebrating communion. I quote the prayer in full:

> Great are you, O God; although we know you only as in an obscure saying and as in a mirror, yet in wonder we worship your greatness – how much more we shall praise it at some time when we come to know it more fully! When under the arch of heaven I stand surrounded by the wonders of creation, I rapturously and adoringly praise your greatness, you who lightly hold the stars in the infinite and concern yourself fatherly with the sparrow. But when we are gathered here in your holy house we are also surrounded on all sides by what calls to mind your greatness in a deeper sense. You are indeed great, Creator and Sustainer of the world; but when you, O God, forgave the sin of the world and reconciled yourself with the fallen human race, then you were even greater in your incomprehensible compassion! How would we not, then, in faith praise and thank and worship you here in your holy house, where everything reminds us of this, especially those who are gathered here today to receive the forgiveness of sins and to appropriate anew reconciliation with you in Christ!
>
> (CD, 289/SKS 10, 311)

God is great in creating the vast and beautiful universe; He is greater in his atonement of sin and reconciliation of humans to Himself. Note that Kierkegaard chastens epistemological overconfidence, such as he believes is found in the natural sciences and natural theology of his day, by alluding to Paul's 'now we see through a glass, darkly' (1 Corinthians 13: 12, KJV). He gives pride of place to the particularities of the Christian gospel – Christ's atonement and its representation in the Lord's Supper – which are known through revelation and confessed by faith.

Later, Kierkegaard invokes the Romans 1 argument that God's 'eternal power and divine nature' are revealed in nature, but he also suggests that this is not sufficient for Christian confession. While God's power can be known through nature's direct manifestation, God's mercy cannot be and is only seen through faith. He says, 'Everyone, *marveling*, can see the signs by which God's greatness in nature is known, or rather there actually is no sign, because the works themselves are the signs. For example, everyone can of course see the rainbow and must marvel when he sees it. But the sign of God's greatness in showing mercy is only *for faith*; this sign is indeed the sacrament' (CD, 291/SKS 10, 313). Seeing a rainbow and marvelling at it has a universal access, and this says something about the majesty of the Creator. But one cannot see the rainbow as a sign of God's mercy unless one knows and believes that it was given to Noah as a promise that God would never destroy mankind like this again, which is a story known only in particularity through the revelation of Scripture (see Genesis 6: 5–9: 17). Kierkegaard continues, 'God's greatness in nature is *manifest*, but God's greatness in showing mercy is a *mystery*, which must be believed. Precisely because it is not directly manifest to everyone, precisely for that reason it is, and is called, the *revealed*. God's greatness in nature promptly awakens *astonishment* and then *adoration*; God's greatness in showing mercy is first an occasion *for offense* and then is *for faith*' (CD, 291/SKS 10, 313). One sees that Kierkegaard preserves Paul's prioritizing of faith over the manifestation of God through creation. Faith is not a lesser way of knowing God, beneath the supposed certainty and universality of philosophical syllogisms or scientific observations; it is the higher, greater, and more intimately particular way of knowing him. As Kierkegaard sees it, to abandon the passion of faith for the arguments of objective rationalism is trading down, not trading up. Indeed, mere reflection on nature, even if done in the correct way that emphasizes astonishment and wonder over the equanimity of rational parsing, still falls short of the gospel and its mercy for sinners. Kierkegaard concludes, 'Out there the stars proclaim your majesty, and the perfection of everything proclaims your greatness, but in here [in your holy house] it is the imperfect, it is sinners who praise your even greater greatness!' (CD, 295/SKS 10, 317).

Conclusion

Kierkegaard received the wonders of nature as a gracious gift from God. They held beauty and delight for him, as well as stimulating his mind and providing the occasion to reflect on the power of their Creator. Unfortunately, because of how it was received by his nineteenth-century Danish culture, he believed that nature also held many temptations away from ethical clarity and religious health. Nature offered humanity the occasion of 'possibility' (CUP 1, 246/SKS 7, 224), and we could fail to live up to the opportunity. Under Romanticism, nature became the possibility of a category mistake wherein one attempted to relate to God directly by reading the ethical immediately off of the face of nature. Under the influence of natural science, one replaced wonder at the whole of nature with the measuring of stamen length and soil acidity, humility with the cold confidence of quantifying human existence, and the adventurous risk of praising an infinite God who dwells in mystery with a supposed scientific certainty that a rationally guaranteed truth is almost – almost – at hand, perhaps with just a little more funding. Kierkegaard did not thank the proponents of natural theology for coming to the aid of Christian faith through such means. Indeed, he believed that it hindered faith since it cultivated the wrong manner of existing and made promises it could not sustain. Further, he thought that the arguments of natural theology implied disdain for Scripture and special revelation, touchstones of Protestant Christianity, since it grounded itself on pride in its clever proofs rather than humbly accepting the testimony of the Word. What he thought the flagging faith of the nineteenth century required was not more supposedly objective proofs but more repentance, humility, and worship. As Kierkegaard says, 'To stand on one foot and prove the existence of God is altogether different from falling on one's knees and thanking him' (JP 2, 531/SKS 19, 219).[8] What was needed, he thought, was not more theorizing about the processes of nature but more personal exposure to it in order to be overcome by its – and God's – immensity. Then, through the eyes of faith and aided by divine revelation, one may perhaps come to see the mercy offered to us in Christ.

Related topics

'Kierkegaard on nature and natural beauty,' Anthony Rudd; 'Christian epistemology and the anthropology of sin: Kierkegaard on natural theology and the concept of "offense,"' Karen L. Carr.

Notes

1 The amount of scholarly literature addressing Søren Kierkegaard and natural theology is somewhat light, and this is probably because Kierkegaard did not publish much on the subject. Many of his most insightful comments on the matter are found in his journal entries, many of which are addressed here. Nevertheless, I argue that Kierkegaard is important to read on this issue for a couple of reasons. First, Kierkegaard is an influential thinker, and his influence on the subject of natural theology may be felt through those who have received him. For example, Karl Barth's rejection of natural theology is well known and has a decisive influence on modern theology. It also is Kierkegaardian in many ways, since for both men the critique of natural theology was made in defence of Christianity against arrogating cultural and political movements that sought to use natural theology to redefine or gain leverage over traditional Christian theology. Kierkegaard's influence on Barth's thought is widely acknowledged, especially in his *Der Römerbrief*, where Barth defines his theological system by invoking the Dane's infinite qualitative difference between God and humankind (Schwöbel 2000: 20). I believe there is

more work that needs to be done to determine the degree to which Barth may have been influenced by Kierkegaard in his critique of natural theology. Second, Kierkegaard is imaginative, and his argument may provide intellectual resources for philosophers and theologians who are looking for models of appreciating nature other than the frequently rationalizing examples of natural theology. Kierkegaard may fuel the intellectual imagination for a different way forward.

2 Also implied in Kierkegaard's argument is the critique that a life lived in obsessive pursuit of the promises of science in order to wring out a few more years of living is not a life that is predisposed to fulfil the Christian duty to be willing to be martyred for the gospel and so to die early (e.g., Matthew 16: 24; 24: 9; Romans 14: 8–9; Hebrews 11: 35–40). Furthermore, to cling to life in this way is not very Socratic either, as indicated by Socrates' arguments in the *Crito* that it is disgraceful for one to be willing to surrender one's ideals and virtues in order to eke out a few more years of life. On the influence of Socrates on Kierkegaard's arguments here, see below.

3 As Kierkegaard puts it, 'Yet I am happy at this point to remember Socrates "who gave up astronomy and the study of heavenly things as something which did not concern man"' (JP 2, 220).

4 One sees that, for Kierkegaard, Socratic ignorance implies more than an epistemological posture alone. For him, Socratic ignorance is always a posture aimed at Christian faith. Kierkegaard's pseudonym Anti-Climacus even attributes 'a kind of fear and worship of God' to be Socrates' own motivation for his method of ignorance and so can speak of 'a Socratic, God-fearing ignorance, which by means of ignorance guards faith against speculation' (SUD, 99/SKS 11, 211). Here, 'ignorance' is no insult but a tactic of practiced epistemological humility, which provides space for a life of faith. A little Socratic ignorance, Kierkegaard believes, is just what is required in the face of the pretensions and speculations of natural theology.

5 One exception to this is the psychological work of Carl G. Carus, whom Kierkegaard compliments for restraining his conclusions and refusing to turn his insights into something arrogating regarding the realm of religion. Kierkegaard says, 'At all decisive points [Carus] makes unqualified room – for the miracle, for the creative power of God, for the absolute expression of worship, and says: This no one can grasp, no science, neither now nor ever. Then he communicates the interesting things he knows' (JP 3, 249/SKS 20, 71). That discipline and restraint is admirable for a worker who acknowledges the limits of his field and knowledge – not just for today, as if perhaps tomorrow the miracle will be exposed, but perpetually since he does not pretend that psychology is capable of achievements beyond the powers of its method. I argue that Kierkegaard's criticisms of the natural sciences and the tendency to try to explain all of human experience via reduction to its fundamental mechanical elements are, more precisely, criticisms of their use and of the vast unjustified hope that his culture placed in them. Kierkegaard is not opposed to natural science as such, as long as it is humble enough to remember the limits of its powers and purposes.

6 Natural theology in the nineteenth century was 'natural' because it relied on evidence that was 'taken from direct observation of the natural world (including the human body), or from observations made in the increasingly specialized settings of science' (Eddy 2013: 100). In addition to arguments in natural theology such as teleological and cosmological arguments, Eddy (2013: 113) argues that the importance of natural science to nineteenth-century natural theology has been underappreciated in most histories of the period.

7 In picking up on the tendency of ethics in his day toward the quantitative and the rationally calculative, Kierkegaard is anticipating developments that would flower, for example, in Utilitarianism, where the ethically correct procedure is that which produces the greatest happiness for the greatest number of people, both of which are categories that depend on the quantification of human experience for its calculations. Kierkegaard was certainly familiar with one precursor to Classical Utilitarianism, David Hume (1711–1776), who advocated for a notion of social utility against a traditional religion-based ethic, and, while Kierkegaard did not live long enough to encounter the arguments of J. S. Mill (1806–1873) on Utilitarianism, he was aware of Jeremy Bentham (1748–1832), at least second-hand through the writings of I. H. Fichte (1796–1879) (JP 3, 685–6/SKS 24, 244).

8 As Mulder (2009: 51) puts it, 'Faith and demonstrative reasoning are the operations of, if you will, different organs of the person. The former is the one thing needful, and the latter does not help us acquire it, for Kierkegaard.'

References

Eddy, M. D. (2013) 'Nineteenth-century natural theology,' in R. R. Manning, J. H. Brooke, and F. Watts (eds), *The Oxford Handbook of Natural Theology*, Oxford: Oxford University Press.

Mulder, J. Jr., (2009) 'Kierkegaard and natural reason: A Catholic encounter,' *Faith and Philosophy*, 26, no. 1: 42–63.

Schwöbel, C. (2000) 'Theology,' in J. Webster (ed), *The Cambridge Companion to Karl Barth*, Cambridge: Cambridge University Press.

Further reading

Evans, C. S. (1992) *Passionate reason: Making sense of Kierkegaard's Philosophical Fragments*, Bloomington, IN: Indiana University Press.

Chapter 5 of this work includes an insightful discussion about natural theology in Kierkegaard's thought. Specifically, it considers and evaluates critiques from Kierkegaard's pseudonym, Johannes Climacus, regarding the argument from design and the defensibility (or not) of proofs for the existence of God.

Holmes, S. R. (2012) 'Divine attributes,' in K. M. Kapic and B. L. McCormack (eds), *Mapping Modern Theology: A Thematic and Historical Introduction*, Grand Rapids, MI: Baker Academic.

This work is an excellent primer on the major *loci* and themes of modern theology. Chapter 3 includes a treatment of natural theology after Kant, locating the discussion around Karl Barth and his historical influences. Kierkegaard is not mentioned, unfortunately.

Manning, R. R. (2013) 'A perspective on natural theology from continental philosophy,' in R. R. Manning, J. H. Brooke, and F. Watts (eds), *The Oxford Handbook of Natural Theology*, Oxford: Oxford University Press.

This chapter addresses Kierkegaard only in passing, but it offers a useful primer of several themes within natural theology from a perspective that locates Kierkegaard within the framework of continental philosophy.

Mulder, J. Jr., (2010) *Kierkegaard and the Catholic tradition: Conflict and dialogue*, Bloomington, IN: Indiana University Press.

This work treats Lutheran Kierkegaard in relation to the Catholic tradition. Given the traditional Catholic interest in natural reason and natural theology, these topics are addressed as they relate to Kierkegaard's claims, especially in chapter 1. Mulder is forthright when he sides with Catholicism against Kierkegaard, but his admiration for the Dane is clear. Those interested in natural theology and the surrounding issues should find this treatment to be pertinent, even if their interests are broader than specifically Catholic ones.

Posch, T. (2014) 'Nature/natural science,' in S. Emmanuel, W. McDonald, and J. Stewart (eds), *Kierkegaard Research: Sources, Reception and Resources*, vol. 15 (*Kierkegaard's Concepts*), tome 4, Farnham: Ashgate.

This volume addresses significant concepts and terms in Kierkegaard's writings, and Posch's entry is a brief but helpful overview of Kierkegaard's treatment of nature and natural science. It does not address natural theology per se, but it touches on relevant themes.

PART 5

Philosophy of mind

22
CONSCIOUSNESS, SELF, AND REFLECTION

Patrick Stokes

Introduction

The nature of consciousness has been among the most heavily trafficked topics in philosophy over the last century. Kierkegaard is rarely invoked even as an historical forerunner to these debates. However, as I will argue in this chapter, Kierkegaard is not merely an interesting influence on major figures in phenomenology – he is also someone with philosophically interesting things to say to contemporary philosophers about the nature of consciousness, selfhood, and ethical experience.

Using Kierkegaard in this way carries inherent risks of distortion. Even if one does not agree that Kierkegaard shouldn't be read as a philosopher at all (a view put forward by, for example, Turnbull 2011), trying to bring Kierkegaard into dialogue with later philosophers can lead to misleading or plain anachronistic mis-readings of Kierkegaard. Yet if it's done carefully, this sort of reading can also genuinely open up our understanding of Kierkegaard's thought *and* make useful contributions to live philosophical questions. In this case, his 'answer' to a question that has troubled phenomenology for almost a century – whether self-awareness is given in consciousness, or achieved via reflection – turns out to be a paradoxical, yet illuminating, 'both.'

Ego and anonymity

An ongoing disagreement in phenomenology and philosophy of mind is whether consciousness is egological or anonymous. The question here is roughly whether consciousness presents itself intrinsically as being the consciousness *of someone*, or whether instead the 'owner' of an experience can only be inferred, not directly intuited from consciousness. Put differently, the issue is whether experience necessarily contains a *sense of self*, or not.

Egological views are particularly associated with Husserl's mature understanding of the 'transcendental ego,' but survive in more subtle forms in contemporary phenomenology. Dan Zahavi (2005; 2014) is a key contemporary proponent of an influential egological view, holding that all consciousness contains a 'minimal self' that exists as a function of the inherent 'what-it's-likeness' of experience. The claim here is not that we directly observe some sort of Cartesian soul in our experience, but that 'reflective self-awareness presupposes a primitive pre-reflective self-awareness as its condition of possibility' (Grunbaum and Zahavi 2013: 226). The first-person character of experience, that it always presents itself as experience *for* someone, suffuses all experience with an inherent self-referentiality.

The non-egological, anonymous view of consciousness denies this. Just as Hume (1985) denied that we encounter anything called 'myself' in introspection, the non-egological approach holds that consciousness contains no implicit subject of experience. Your consciousness doesn't contain anything that picks it out as specifically *your* consciousness. Proponents of versions of this view include Jean-Paul Sartre (1969), Aron Gurwitsch (1940), and Husserl himself at an earlier stage.

As you can see, this is a fairly stark dividing line. For proponents of egological accounts, every moment of your experience involves some extra sense or property of 'for-me-ness.' On non-egological accounts, by contrast, there simply is no such invariant property of for-me-ness (Dainton 2008). That it's *you* having the experience of reading these words, and not, say, Napoleon, is something we can only show via inference ('I can't be Napoleon, because this book I'm reading is about Kierkegaard, and Napoleon died on Kierkegaard's eighth birthday, well before he'd written anything!'). For the egological account, consciousness is always *self*-consciousness in some sense. For non-egologists, however, self-consciousness or self-awareness is something intermittent, something that only happens when we're thinking about ourselves as an *object* of thought, not just the *subject*. Self-consciousness is a 'generally unactualized, but always actualizable' potential (Schear 2009: 99).

Kierkegaard doesn't phrase his discussions of consciousness in terms of its anonymity or personality. In fact, Kierkegaard says relatively little, at least explicitly, about consciousness at all. Perhaps this is down to his preference for using philosophically infused versions of commonplace, everyday Danish words such as 'inwardness' (*inderlighed*) and 'passion' (*lidenskab*) instead of technical terms. The Danish word for consciousness, *bevidsthed*, is a latecomer, first appearing in the early nineteenth century as a Danification of the German philosophical term *Bewusstheit* (Stokes 2013b). Yet whichever terms are used, self-consciousness and self-awareness are clearly crucial features that run throughout his work. For Kierkegaard, speaking in personae as different as Anti-Climacus and Judge William, to be a self is to be aware of oneself in a particular way. Crucially, he seems to both identify consciousness with *self*-consciousness, and make consciousness *constitutive of* selfhood, as in a vital passage from *The Sickness unto Death*:

> Generally speaking, consciousness – that is, self-consciousness – is decisive with regard to the self. The more consciousness, the more self; the more consciousness, the more will; the more will, the more self. A person who has no will at all is also not a self; but the more will he has, the more self-consciousness he has also.
>
> *(SUD, 29/SKS 11, 145)*

Earlier, in *The Concept of Anxiety*, Vigilius Haufniensis wrote that self-consciousness is:

> The most concrete content that consciousness can have . . . so concrete that no author, not even the one with the greatest power of description, not the one with the greatest powers of representation, has ever been able to describe such a single self-consciousness, although every single human being is such a one.
>
> *(CA, 143/SKS 4, 443)*

Note the implications of these passages: consciousness *is* self-consciousness, and each of us *is* self-consciousness.[1] To understand selfhood, then, we need to understand both what consciousness is, and how, according to Kierkegaard, selfhood emerges from consciousness. To that end, we need to look at Kierkegaard's most sustained explicit treatment of consciousness, with an eye to the question of whether self-consciousness is a given feature of consciousness (as in egological accounts) or a product of reflection (as in anonymity accounts).

The structure of consciousness

Around 1843–44, Kierkegaard begins writing *Johannes Climacus, or De Omnibus Dubitandum Est*. He ultimately abandons the work, which remained unpublished during his lifetime. The first part of the text is told in third-person narrative, and recounts the intellectual development of Johannes Climacus, 'author' of both *Philosophical Fragments* and the *Concluding Unscientific Postscript to 'Philosophical Fragments.'* It explores how Climacus comes to work through, in his characteristically sceptical way, the claim of the Hegelian era that modern philosophy begins with doubt. The final few pages of the book, however, are very different. All narrative and character disappear, and we are instead given a short discussion of the structure of consciousness, at once both rich and schematic, like a conceptual plan that Kierkegaard never fleshed out.

According to Climacus (assuming this part of the work is in his voice or at least tracks his views), consciousness needs to be distinguished from mere 'sense perception' or 'experience,' 'for in consciousness there is more' (JC, 169/SKS 15, 56). This 'more' is sufficiently cognitively complex in nature that the consciousness of children is not properly qualified *as* consciousness (JC, 168/SKS 15, 54). So what is the 'more' that differentiates sentience from consciousness? Is this more egological, or does consciousness remain anonymous?

Climacus's account of consciousness begins from the question of how doubt is possible, of '*doubt's ideal possibility in consciousness*' (JC, 166/SKS 15, 54). In a discussion that foreshadows some key twentieth-century discussions of consciousness – particularly Sartre's (1969) account of consciousness as a capacity for the negation of the given – Kierkegaard recognizes that to doubt is to disrupt the immediacy of our relationship to the world we perceive through our senses. Insofar as we can ask questions like 'Really?,' 'Is that true?,' 'How do we know that?,' and so on, we break any straightforward connection between how the world spontaneously appears to us and how we reflectively judge it to be. Categories of reflection are 'always *dichotomous*. . . . In reflection, they touch each other in such a way that a relation becomes possible' (JC, 169/SKS 15, 56). In other words, it is through reflection that ideality (the realm of concepts) and actuality (the material world of direct experience) can be brought into relation to one another.

But reflection does not take place merely on paper, so to speak. Reflection is dichotomous, but 'If there were nothing but dichotomies,' Climacus tells us, 'doubt would not exist, for the possibility of doubt resides precisely in the third, which places the two in relation to each other' (JC, 169/SKS 15, 57). For doubt to occur, something has to both posit a relationship between the two elements *and* call that relationship into question ('Ah, it's raining – no wait, is that sound I hear rain on the roof, or something else?'). Doubt thereby shows that consciousness is not merely *dichotomous*, but always *trichotomous*: it contains three terms, the two relata *and* that which posits the relationship between them either as holding or as dubious.

Crucially, though, what does this positing isn't to be understood as a sort of third *entity*. We're not to picture consciousness as *itself* a sort of conscious being, a mediating between actuality and reality. Instead consciousness is described as the 'medium' for this 'collision':

> Ideality and reality therefore collide; in which medium? In time? That is indeed an impossibility. In eternity? That is indeed an impossibility. In what then? In consciousness; there is the contradiction.
>
> (JC, 171/SKS 15, 58)

'Consciousness,' we're told, 'emerges precisely through the collision, just as it presupposes the collision' (JC, 171/SKS 15 58). And so Climacus tells us, consciousness is always *mediacy*: there is no immediate access to actuality, as all our experience is always already the mediation of ideality and actuality. If consciousness could remain in immediacy, 'there would be no consciousness at all' (JC, 167/SKS 15, 55) and no possibility of truth or falsity, and so no possibility of doubt (JC, 167/SKS 15, 54–5). Immediately everything is true yet everything is not true; truth can only arise as a *question* in mediated thought. Or to put this somewhat difficult thought another way, the very possibility of truth or falsehood, and so of doubt, only arises in consciousness, not in either concrete reality or propositional ideality themselves. If I hear a sound and think 'is that rain?' I'm already raising a question that mediates the sound I hear and the concept 'rain,' and without that mediation the question of which of the propositions 'it is raining' or 'it is not raining' are true can't appear. So for Kierkegaard the question of a *pure immediacy* never really arises. All consciousness is already mediated, already conceptualized. If consciousness is the actuality of reflection, then all consciousness is already – in some way and to some extent at least – reflective in character.

Tellingly, the structure of consciousness outlined in these pages is isomorphic with the structure of selfhood offered in other texts. In *The Sickness unto Death*, the self is a 'third' that emerges in a reflexive relation between dichotomous elements such as body and mind, finitude and infinitude, and so forth – a structure that appropriates Luther's claim that humans are composed of body, soul, and spirit (Luther 1956: 303). For Anti-Climacus, selfhood is not something *added to* that dichotomy, but is instead a sort of emergent property *of* that dichotomy, a state that the dichotomy attains when it achieves a particular form of self-reflexivity.

If that isomorphism between Kierkegaard's accounts of selfhood and consciousness holds, and so if consciousness is likewise an emergent property of reflection, we might seem already to be in non-egological consciousness territory. Consciousness is a relation between ideality and reality that is reflexive – or to borrow the language of *Sickness unto Death*, it is 'a relation that relates to itself' (SUD, 13/SKS 11, 129, translation modified). There's no additional ego posited here. But there's still more to the picture of consciousness in *Johannes Climacus*: consciousness is further defined or qualified as *interestedness*.

'The interesting' (*det Interessante*) is a significant category in Kierkegaard's aesthetic writings (Koch 1992), though it also plays a somewhat ambiguous role, with 'the interesting' representing a sort of transitional category from aesthetic immediacy to ethical self-awareness (cf. Stokes 2010: ch. 1). 'Interest' and its cognates play an important part in the Climacan writings, climaxing with the 'infinite, passionate interest' in eternal happiness that drives the *Postscript*. In *De Omnibus Dubitandum Est*, Climacus calls attention to the word's Latin roots: *inter* + *esse*, 'between being' or 'being between.' That of course gels with the description of consciousness as something that emerges from the collision of ideality and reality, something that has its existence 'in between' these two elements.

But the choice of the word 'interest' suggests something more than *mellemvaerelse* (between-being or middle-being), a term which Kierkegaard also uses (CUP 1, 264/SKS 7, 240). Climacus contrasts the interestedness of consciousness with the 'interestlessness' (*interestløs*) of forms of discourse such as mathematics, aesthetics, and metaphysics (JC, 170/SKS 15, 57). These purely 'objective' forms of discourse are interest-less precisely because they don't involve the subject who is inquiring into them. The content of a mathematical problem is the same whether it's you, me, or Napoleon thinking about it. But if consciousness is interestedness, then consciousness, it seems, *does* involve us; it does in fact contain some sort of reference to the conscious subject. But *what sort* of reference?

Viewed through the lens of the egological vs anonymous consciousness debate, Kierkegaard it seems could still go either way: either consciousness involves an implicit sense of ourselves as a being involved in what we experience, or our interest (and thus consciousness) emerges reflectively. Either we're implicitly self-aware all the time, regardless of what we're thinking about, or we're only self-aware in those moments when we're reflecting on ourselves, that is, thinking *about* ourselves as a topic of interest. Both options present problems, however. If consciousness is intrinsically interested, and this interest is not a matter of overt thematization, how can it be the case that infants and non-human animals aren't fully qualified as conscious? Surely they experience themselves as involved in the world just as much as human adults do? On the other hand, if we're only self-aware when we're thinking about ourselves as objects of interest, then it seems we're only intermittently conscious – and so, per *The Sickness unto Death*, only intermittently selves.

To try and nail down what Kierkegaard's position is here, let's turn to consider what it means to *not* be self-aware for Kierkegaard, using another contemporary debate as our frame of reference: immunity to error through misidentification.

Thinking I-thoughts

If self-awareness is the sort of *given* property suggested by thinkers like Zahavi, a sense of 'mineness' or 'for-me-ness' built automatically into all experience, Climacus's insistence that the consciousness of children isn't properly qualified as consciousness makes no sense. Anti-Climacus's claim that consciousness can be a matter of degrees ('the more consciousness, the more self; the more consciousness, the more will' [SKS 11, 145/SUD, 29]) will also come to look, if not unintelligible, at least suspect. The alternative, it seems, is to say that consciousness – not mere sentience, but self-awareness – is a matter of thinking *about* the self: we are conscious when we are thinking thoughts about the subject 'I.' If that's true, we're not really conscious most of the time. We're sentient, but we're only conscious, *self*-conscious, when explicitly thinking what we might call 'I-thoughts.'

Now, something like that might seem quite in keeping with the overall thrust of Kierkegaard's thought. Indeed, one of the most incisive strands of criticism of Kierkegaard is precisely that the form of life he recommends is self-absorbed to the point of solipsism. There have been various such criticisms (e.g., Adorno 1989) and defences (e.g., Ferreira 2001), but perhaps the most persistent is that offered by Kierkegaard's fellow Dane, K. E. Løgstrup, who charges that Kierkegaard's ethics are so excessively self-reflective that they take the moral agent out of the world of concrete action altogether. For Kierkegaard, as Løgstrup reads him, we become the persons we are through reflecting on ourselves and our eternal status. That however leads to a state Løgstrup calls 'obsessiveness' (*indkredsene*, 'encircling' rumination) that cuts us off from the sphere of ethical action in self-absorption. In thinking obsessively about ourselves and our eternal salvation, we end up focusing on ourselves instead of the others we should be acting for in the world. 'Never before,' Løgstrup claims, 'has ethics so shut itself in and so shut out the world as it has in Kierkegaard's thought' (Løgstrup 1968: 63).

Yet it is telling that when Kierkegaard compares self-awareness with its opposite, which he calls being 'absent-minded' (*distraite*, which could also be translated 'distracted'), the examples he gives us go well beyond 'not-thinking-I-thoughts.' The figure of Salomon Soldin (1774–1837), the Copenhagen bookseller, author, and publisher, is instructive here as both an example and a caricature. Climacus repeats stories about Soldin's legendary absent-mindedness, including the quip that 'When he was going to get up in the morning, he was not aware that he was dead' (CUP 1, 167/SKS 7, 155). One time, according to Climacus, a customer impersonated

Soldin's voice when he wasn't looking, causing Soldin to turn to his wife and say 'Rebecca, is it I who is speaking?' (CA, 51/SKS 4, 356).[2]

Part of the reason this Soldin story is funny is precisely because it violates a fairly basic intuition: namely, that we cannot be mistaken about who I-thoughts refer to. We assume that 'A person cannot think an I-thought without knowing and understanding that she is thinking something about herself' (Grunbaum and Zahavi 2013: 224), what is known in the literature as immunity to error through misidentification or IEM.[3] That is, while I can be mistaken about the *content* of my self-regarding thoughts, I cannot be mistaken in ascribing these thoughts to myself. Someone once insisted to me she remembered the Cyclone Tracy disaster, until she realized that Cyclone Tracy occurred several years before she was born. What she actually remembered, in all likelihood, was a TV miniseries about the cyclone made in the 1980s. She was wrong about *what* she remembered, but she *could* not have been wrong that it was *she* who had the putative memory.[4] There is a more complicated story to be told here about predication de se and de dicto, but examples like false memory make clear enough for present purposes how IEM operates, and jokes like the Soldin vignette make it clear in negative outline by presenting absurd violations of it.

But it's far from clear that what it is that's missing in Soldin's case would be supplied by his thinking thoughts like 'I, Soldin, am speaking now.' On some higher-order thinking accounts of consciousness he *must* be thinking something like that *on some level*, but even in these cases it seems that such a thought will be more implicit than overt or thematized. Moreover, for Climacus, we can violate IEM *even when* we're thinking propositionally true I-thoughts. A key claim in the *Postscript* is that we can think about our own death, for instance, without realizing that in a deeper sense it really is *our own* death that we're thinking about:

> for me, *my* dying is by no means something in general; for others, my dying is some such thing. Nor am *I* for myself some such thing in general; perhaps for others I am some such thing in general. But if the task is to become subjective, then every subject becomes *for himself* exactly the opposite of some such thing in general.'
> (CUP 1, 167/SKS 7, 154–5)

We can think thoughts like 'I'll die someday' and yet do so in such a way that 'the statement itself does not contain in itself the consciousness of that which the statement directly declares' (CUP 1, 170/SKS 7, 157). We can think this thought in a way where I treat the object of impending death as being fully identical with the self doing the thinking – a subjectively transformative experience – or we can do so in a *non-interested* way that treats 'I will die someday' as just a more localized version of 'everyone will die someday' (see, for example, Stokes 2013a). What's missing in Soldin, in the absent-minded systematic philosophers Climacus loves to puncture, and in *most* of us much of the time, is not simply a matter of thinking *about* oneself on a propositional level, but thinking *in a particular way*.

Subjective reflection

Kierkegaard is highly ambivalent about reflection, a concept that he understands and evaluates in a number of different ways across his writings. In *De Omnibus Dubitandum Est*, as we've already seen, reflection is presented as a necessary condition of consciousness, and thereby of selfhood. No non-reflective being can become a self, and no being for whom such reflection is impossible can interrogate the question of its own selfhood in any case. Yet while reflection is a necessary condition of attaining selfhood, it is clearly not, for Kierkegaard, a sufficient one.

In reading Kierkegaard it is easy to assume that the aesthetic, the immediate, and the unreflective are coterminous: to be an aesthete is to lack reflective insight and thereby be stuck in the immediate economy of desire and satisfaction. Heiko Schulz defines immediacy in Kierkegaard in its anthropological sense as 'a form of existence, in which the actualization of a person's affective, conative and cognitive powers is restricted to certain conditions on the first level of the synthesis that constitutes a human self.' In its ethical sense, immediacy refers to the lack of 'a reflectively (and also: volitionally) mediated conception of his or her own self *as such*' making the immediate person 'someone who interprets the meaning of his or her own existence inadequately, namely by exclusively invoking aesthetical categories (wish-fulfilment, fate, happiness or misfortune etc.) without mediating it by means of what Judge William and de silentio call the ethical or "the universal"' (Schulz 2003: 73–4). In other words, the aesthete is immediate simply because she never stops to reflect 'Hang on: *should* I be living for my own pleasure like this?' – a lack of reflection that also stops her from attaining a deeper ethical understanding of herself and her relation to the world.

Yet there are, as Paul Cruysberghs notes, echoing Anti-Climacus, no purely immediate, totally unreflective human beings. It may be that 'reflection grants the self its proper identity,' but even the most immediate aesthete is 'characterized by a minimum of self-reflection' whereby he or she distinguishes him or herself from the external world (Cruysberghs 2003: 12). Indeed, one can be 'immediate' and yet *highly* reflective. The first part of *Either/Or* is given over to describing various forms of aesthetic existence, none of which rises to the level of ethical, self-integrated personhood – yet many of which are, as Andrew Cross (1998) notes, highly reflective indeed. Johannes the Seducer, the culmination of *Either/Or*'s journey through aesthetic life-views, is if anything *hyper*-reflective, someone who ruminates over every detail of experience and recollection on progressively more 'meta' levels. Johannes is virtually a model of the sort of obsessive figure that Løgstrup decries, except that he obsesses about seduction instead of his own moral status. The absent-minded professors of the *Postscript* are likewise highly reflective, yet cut off from their own concrete existence by the *nature* of that reflection.

This problem scales up dramatically: in *Two Ages* we're told that the pathology of the whole present era is precisely that it is an 'essentially reflecting' age, a condition that allows ethical action to be indefinitely deferred. As Shakespeare's Hamlet puts it, 'the native hue of resolution is sicklied o'er with the pale cast of thought,' whereby 'enterprises of great pith and moment . . . lose the name of action' (Act III sc. 1). Reflection, as Kierkegaard is keenly aware, is all too often a cryptic mechanism for evasion, whereby the imperative to act is pushed back for further consideration 'tomorrow' (SUD, 94/SKS 11, 206). Reflection is necessary for ethical action, but on its own not sufficient.

The reason we're able to use reflection to defer action in this way is that reflection 'has the notable quality of being infinite' (CUP 1, 112/SKS 7, 109). You can't stop reflection reflectively; left to its own devices, reflection will simply run on forever. Reflection can only be stopped by the reflector 'willing to stop the infinity of reflection' through an act of 'resolution . . . for only in that way can reflection be stopped' (CUP 1, 113/SKS 7, 109–10). This, as Cruysberghs (2003: 23) notes, 'seems to suggest at least that this subject has a certain autonomy, a certain freedom over against his own reflections.' But this is troubling: it seems to disconnect reflection and will, such that we can't make sense of our resolutions by reference to the reflection that proceeded them. If reflection can go on forever then decision, it seems, will always be at least partly irrational. There is always another thought to think, always another angle to consider – so in that sense resolution is not the outcome of deliberation but its brute, non-rational interruption.

Up to this point, we seem to have identified three interconnected problems that attend at least a straightforward reading of Kierkegaard's discussion of consciousness, subjectivity, and reflection:

- 'The self *is* reflection' (SUD, 31/SKS 11, 147; emphasis added), and depends upon self-consciousness for its existence – but if consciousness and self-constitution consists in thinking 'I-thoughts,' then it seems we are only intermittently conscious or selves (call this our *ontological problem*).
- If we are only selves when we are thinking I-thoughts, and we are enjoined to become and remain self-conscious selves, then we are enjoined to be thinking about ourselves at all times, which would drastically impair our capacity to attend to others and act selflessly for their sake (call this our *ethical* problem).
- Reflection cannot be stopped except by act of will, so reflection cannot instigate action – instead it must be stopped for the sake of acting, which makes it seem as if action is troublingly disconnected from rational deliberation (call this our *agential problem*).

One answer to the ontological problem is to appeal to the temporality of the first-person perspective. If selves only exist when we're thinking I-thoughts, then *for myself* the ontological problem never arises: anytime I ask whether I am a self, I am already thinking I-thoughts. Conversely, if I am not thinking I-thoughts, I am a fortiori not thinking about the ontological problem. Attention to the temporality of the first-person perspective in Kierkegaard does, I think, answer a number of important problems about the temporality of selfhood, despair, and salvation in Kierkegaard's work (see especially ch. 6 of Stokes 2015). But it will not answer the sort of question a metaphysician of personal identity is interested in here – a diachronic question about the persistence of selves across time,[5] not Kierkegaard's first-personal question of whether *I am a self now*. Nor will this approach answer the ethical and agential problem for us.

However, an answer to all three problems might lie in the specific *way* in which the self is figured in thought. Not all reflection is the same – and Climacus indicates that some forms of reflection might be self-reflexive without being I-thoughts. If that's true, then self-consciousness and self-constitution, though not automatically given in all moments of consciousness, might nonetheless become pervasive and persistent.

Climacus draws a distinction between 'objective reflection' which seeks 'to disregard the subject,' and 'subjective reflection' for which 'truth becomes appropriation, inwardness, subjectivity, and the point is to immerse oneself, existing, in subjectivity' (CUP 1, 192/SKS 71, 176). While Climacus insists that objective reflection that seeks 'objective truth' takes the thinker 'away from the subject' and thereby makes both truth and subjectivity 'indifferent' (CUP 1, 193/SKS 7, 177), the opposite is true of subjective reflection:

> Subjective reflection turns inward toward subjectivity and in this inward deepening will be of the truth, and in such a way that, just as in the preceding, when objectivity was advanced, subjectivity vanished, here subjectivity as such becomes the final factor and objectivity the vanishing. *Here it is not forgotten, even for a single moment, that the subject is existing.*
>
> (CUP 1, 196/SKS 7, 180; emphasis added)

What does 'not forgetting for a single moment' involve? On a non-egological view of consciousness, it would presumably mean thinking I-thoughts about the subject's existence at all times – something we plainly don't do. On an egological view, it would involve an automatically given sense or awareness that the subject is constantly existing – which would contradict Kierkegaard's insistence that we can be absent-minded or led astray by objective reflection. Yet there might in fact be a third way here, one that steers around these problems.

Thinking ourselves into every moment

Return for a moment to thinking one's own death as a paradigm instance of a type of reflection in which both a subjective (self-regarding) and objective (self-excluding or self-effacing) approach is possible. We can think our death as *our* death, or merely as the death of an I-in-general with which we do not subjectively identify. In his non-pseudonymous discussion of the thought of death in the discourse 'At a Graveside,' Kierkegaard tells us we must think death into every moment. As Merold Westphal notes, this cannot simply mean that whenever I am asked what I am thinking about, I can truthfully reply 'my death and immortality' (Westphal 1996: 109–10). That would be both psychologically impossible and, as in our ethical problem identified above, a recipe for just the sort of self-absorption Løgstrup diagnoses in Kierkegaard's ethical writings. If we are to make the idea of 'thinking my death into every moment' credible, then my death has to somehow be part of every thought without every thought being *about* my death on the level of propositional content. There has to be some sense in which my death is psychologically present when I'm thinking about *anything* or doing *anything*. As Climacus puts it:

> But if the task is to become subjective, then for the individual subject to think death is not at all some such thing in general but is an act, because the development of subjectivity consists precisely in this, that he, acting, works through himself in his thinking about his own existence, consequently that he actually thinks what is thought by actualizing it, consequently that he does not think for a moment: Now, you must keep watch every moment – but that he keeps watch every moment.
>
> *(CUP 1, 169/SKS 7, 156–7)*

Watchfulness is an interesting illustration here: in a state of vigilance our watchfulness is not *itself* the object of our thought, but what we are attentive to and what we think about in such a state expresses the need for vigilance; hence Levinas' claim that insomnia is a kind of vigilance without an object, a state of sheer attention to being as such (Levinas 1978: 61–3). Likewise, thinking death into every moment is, as Climacus puts it here, an act of attention – but not one that necessarily makes my death *itself* the *object* of my attention, but part of the non-thematized content of my consciousness.

Kierkegaard's thought is in fact pervaded by claims of this sort.[6] His use of mirror metaphors often points to instances where our own relationship to something is to be found not in the propositional content of what we are thinking about, but in the *way* in which we think about it, the non-thetic content of our thought. In *For Self-Examination*, we are told that to 'be alone with' Scripture, to read Scripture in the right way, is to see oneself in the 'Mirror of the Word' – a mirror which does not contain oneself on the propositional level. The stories told in the New Testament do not contain us or address us by name, but we are, for Kierkegaard, to read them as being *about* us nonetheless, as making demands upon us directly. This point is also made in *Works of Love*: 'beside every word in the holy books a disturbing notice in invisible writing confronts [the reader] that says: go and do likewise' (WL, 46/SKS 9, 53).

Because Scripture imposes demands, my own involvement in it is implicit in the experience of reading it: 'What the prophet Nathan added to his parable, "You are the man," the Gospel does not need to add, since it is already contained in the form of the statement and in its being a word of the Gospel' (WL, 14/SKS 9, 22). The problem is that most of us, at least most of the time, *are* in the same position as King David: we need explicit thematizations like 'You are the man' or 'The tale is told of you' (SLW, 478/SKS 6, 440) or '*You* will die, not just you-in-general.' But the implication seems to be that we shouldn't need them. Thus, a kind of unthematized reflexivity in consciousness, 'for-you-ness,' is not a sheer given as in egological accounts of consciousness, but something we are enjoined to achieve. We are to think our own relation to the normatively engaging world in which we find ourselves, and our own position as finite, mortal beings (and, theologically viewed for Kierkegaard, as sinners whose only hope is via grace) *without* needing to constantly think overt I-thoughts.

If we can achieve such a state, we will have answered all three of the problems outlined above:

- The *ontological problem* is solved in that we can be self-conscious and thus selves through implicit self-awareness and thus without thinking explicit I-thoughts; hence we are self-conscious even when we're not explicitly thinking *about* ourselves on the propositional level.
- The *ethical problem* is solved in that even though our consciousness has ourselves and our status as morally enjoined beings present in its non-thematized content, its intentional object in moments of ethical engagement will be other people and their needs. We can act for the sake of the other, without thinking *about* ourselves, while remaining self-conscious.
- The *agential problem* is solved by considering that when we call reflection to a halt, we do so not via an act of brute, irrational decision; rather, the act of ending reflection is *itself* suffused with reasons. Subjective reflection calls itself to a halt in order to act, but because it does so on the basis of an unthematized recognition of the urgent need to act, its decision is not simply disconnected from reflection and the space of reasons.

Conclusion

We started this chapter by asking whether, in modern terms, Kierkegaard's account of consciousness is egological or anonymous. What we've found is that Kierkegaard occupies a third position, distinct from both of these modern contenders. Instead of self-awareness being an automatically given condition of consciousness, or a function of overt self-reflection (that only exists during the moments when we're actively thinking about ourselves), Kierkegaard suggests that a constant sense of self-awareness is an *achievement*. On Kierkegaard's view, reflexivity is both *proper to* consciousness and something that must be brought about through our own efforts of a particular type. This, as we've seen, allows Kierkegaard to avoid certain problems that either an egological or anonymous view would generate. This is not to suggest that Kierkegaard's own view doesn't create problems of its own – no doubt it does. But it also demonstrates that on matters of self, consciousness, and subjectivity, Kierkegaard remains not merely a historical pioneer, but a worthy ongoing interlocutor.[7]

Related topics

'Kierkegaard's post-Kantian approach to anthropology and selfhood,' Roe Fremstedal; 'The Kierkegaardian self: convergences and divergences,' Jack Mulder, Jr.; 'Ethical reflection as evasion,' Rob Compaijen and Pieter Vos.

Notes

1 One could rightly object here that we're comparing statements from two different pseudonyms. That should, indeed, stop us from drawing any hasty conclusions here. However, it's noticeable the extent to which Anti-Climacus and Vigilius Haufniensis both overlap philosophically – see the somewhat embryonic account of selfhood as a synthesis in *The Concept of Anxiety* that emerges fully formed in *The Sickness unto Death* – and play a similar function in Kierkegaard's writings. Both are as close to 'didactic' in their approach as Kierkegaard lets his pseudonyms become; there is a great deal of direct philosophical and theological assertion in both, but little of the playful ironizing of Climacus or the deliberate limitations of Judge William and Johannes de silentio.
2 Kierkegaard gets this wrong, in fact: Soldin's wife was named Hanne, not Rebecca.
3 There is a considerable literature on IEM, but see, for example, Shoemaker (1968) and Pryor (1999).
4 It is also possible to be wrong *that* someone remembers something rather than simply imagining it. But it is not possible to be wrong that it is *I* who has the experience of either remembering or imagining.
5 From that perspective, the problem of selves only existing while we're thinking I-thoughts is a problem about reidentification: few metaphysicians accept the idea that entities can cease to exist, come back into existence, and still be the same entity, so if we are only selves when we're thinking I-thoughts, each new I-thought brings with it a wholly new self.
6 This is the central topic of Stokes (2010).
7 Much of this material was presented at the 2017 Utech Seminars at the Hong Kierkegaard Library, St. Olaf College, Minnesota. My thanks to Gordon Marino and Eileen Shimota for the invitation and to attendees for their helpful feedback.

References

Adorno, T. W. (1989) *Kierkegaard: Construction of the aesthetic*, Minneapolis, MN: University of Minnesota Press.
Cross, A. (1998) 'Neither either nor or: The perils of reflexive irony,' in A. Hannay and G. D. Marino (eds), *The Cambridge Companion to Kierkegaard*, Cambridge: Cambridge University Press, 125–53.
Cruysberghs, P. (2003) 'Must reflection be stopped? Can it be stopped?' in P. Cruysberghs, J. Taels and K. Verstrynge (eds), *Immediacy and Reflection in Kierkegaard's Thought*, Leuven: Leuven University Press, 11–24.
Dainton, B. (2008) *The phenomenal self*, Oxford: Oxford University Press.
Ferreira, M. J. (2001) *Love's grateful striving: A commentary on Kierkegaard's Works of Love*, Oxford: Oxford University Press.
Grunbaum, T. and Zahavi, D. (2013) 'Varieties of self-awareness,' in K. W. M. Fulford (ed), *The Oxford Handbook of Philosophy and Psychiatry*, Oxford: Oxford University Press.
Gurwitsch, A. (1940) 'A non-egological conception of consciousness,' *Philosophy and Phenomenological Research*, 1, no. 3: 325–38.
Hume, D. (1985) *A treatise of human nature*, New York: Penguin Books.
Koch, C. H. (1992) *Kierkegaard og 'Det interessante': En studie i en æstetiske kategori*, Copenhagen: C. A. Reitzel.
Levinas, E. (1978) *Existence and existents*, A. Lingis (trans), Pittsburgh, PA: Duquesne University Press.
Løgstrup, K. E. (1968) *Opgør med Kierkegaard*, Copenhagen: Gyldendal.
Luther, M. (1956) *Works*, vol. XXI, St Louis, MO: Concordia House.
Pryor, J. (1999) 'Immunity to error through misidentification,' *Philosophical Topics*, 26, nos. 1-2: 271–04.
Sartre, J.-P (1969) *Being and nothingness*, Hazel E. Barnes (trans), London: Routledge.
Schear, J. (2009) 'Experience and self-consciousness,' *Philosophical Studies*, 144, no. 1: 95–105.
Schulz, H. (2003). 'Second immediacy: A Kierkegaardian account of faith,' in P. Cruysberghs, J. Taels and K. Verstrynge (eds), *Immediacy and Reflection in Kierkegaard's Thought*, Leuven: Leuven University Press, 71–86.
Shoemaker, S. (1968) 'Self-reference and self-awareness,' *Journal of Philosophy*, 65, October: 555–67.
Stokes, P. (2015) *The naked self: Kierkegaard and personal identity*, Oxford: Oxford University Press.
Stokes, P. (2013a) 'Death,' in J. Lippitt and G. Pattison (eds), *The Oxford Handbook of Kierkegaard*, Oxford: Oxford University Press.
Stokes, P. (2013b) 'Consciousness,' in S. Emmanuel, W. McDonald and J. Stewart (eds), *Kierkegaard Research: Sources, Reception and Resources: Kierkegaard's Concepts*, tome I (*Philosophy*), Farnham: Ashgate.
Stokes, P. (2010) *Kierkegaard's mirrors: Interest, self, and moral vision*, London: Palgrave Macmillan.

Turnbull, J. (2011) 'Saving Kierkegaard's soul: From philosophical psychology to Golden Age soteriology,' *Kierkegaard Studies Yearbook 2011*: 279–02.
Westphal, M. (1996) *Becoming a self: A reading of Kierkegaard's Concluding Unscientific Postscript*, West Lafayette, IN: Purdue University Press.
Zahavi, D. (2014) *Self and other: Exploring subjectivity, empathy, and shame*, Oxford: Oxford University Press.
Zahavi, D. (2005) *Subjectivity and selfhood: Investigating the first-person perspective*, Cambridge, MA: Massachusetts Institute of Technology Press.

Further reading

Løgstrup, K. E. (1997) 'Settling accounts with Kierkegaard's "Works of Love",' in A. MacIntyre and H. Fink (eds), *The Ethical Demand*, Notre Dame, IN: University of Notre Dame Press.

    A summary of Løgstrup's ethical critique of Kierkegaardian ethics, which he attacks as excessively self-absorbed.

Stokes, P. (2010) *Kierkegaard's mirrors: Interest, self, and moral vision*, London: Palgrave Macmillan.

    An exploration of both the nature of self-reflexivity in Kierkegaard's thought, and his account of moral vision.

Westphal, M. (1996) *Becoming a self: A reading of Kierkegaard's Concluding Unscientific Postscript*, West Lafayette, IN: Purdue University Press.

    An important reading of the *Postscript* that connects it to larger themes of self and consciousness in Kierkegaard.

23
CONSCIENCE, SELF-DECEPTION, AND THE QUESTION OF AUTHENTICITY IN KIERKEGAARD

Claudia Welz

Introduction

What does it mean to be 'authentic'? This question will here be investigated *via negativa*, taking an indirect route via the opposite of authenticity, namely self-deception. While authenticity is linked to being true to oneself, self-deception is associated with lying to oneself. Conscience – derived from the Latin word *con-scientia* – is a 'knowing-with' oneself that testifies to one's thoughts and feelings as well as to one's actions and decisions in relation to others. Being accused by one's own conscience can be so painful that we may desire to delete the self-knowledge that conscience provides against us. Yet, we would thereby deceive ourselves, since we cannot simply forget the knowledge we have with (or against) ourselves. According to Kierkegaard, self-deception involves blinding oneself and turning away from possible insight. How can we prevent or cure self-deception, so that we may live authentically, if this is possible at all?[1]

Conscience

To start with, let us see how conscience is described in Kierkegaard's writings. Particularly three aspects need to be taken into account: conscience as (1) an inner witness, (2) a power of judgment, and (3) as the experience of a call that conveys an ethical demand.

(1) Kierkegaard's idea of conscience as a witness within oneself goes back to Paul's Letter to the Romans (2: 15). When one's thoughts accuse and excuse one, 'bad' conscience manifests the self as a site of conflict, revealing the gap between who one is and who one ought to be: 'I myself at a distance from me myself' (Hart 2009: 130). In 'An Occasional Discourse' in *Upbuilding Discourses in Various Spirits*, we read that conscience 'is no third person' (UDVS, 131/SKS 8, 230), but rather a kind of partner in dialogue. However, Kierkegaard also establishes the identity between oneself and one's inner voice or collocutor, because one's conscience is not a separately existing counterpart as another person is: 'you and conscience are one' (UDVS, 131/SKS 8, 230). Conscience mirrors one's self-relation intellectually in critical reflections and affectively in unintended feelings.

In addition, conscience is an indicator of one's relation to God. According to *Works of Love*, 'to relate to God is precisely to have conscience' (WL, 143/SKS 9, 145). This sounds as if the God-relationship itself grants that one has conscience and listens to its voice. Can the voice of conscience, then, diverge from the voice of God? In Kierkegaard's view, we cannot take for granted that it is God speaking through conscience; yet in order to find out whether this is the case we need to be attentive to what it 'says.' In a note from 1848, Kierkegaard has jotted down that conscience and its 'burdensome thoughts' make sure that 'in all eternity it is impossible to forget' what it communicates (KJN 5, 27/ SKS 21, 23). Negative feelings, like anxiety and guilt, unrest and insomnia constitute what Kierkegaard in 1851 called the 'constraint' and 'oppression of conscience' (KJN 8, 211/SKS 24, 213). In *Judge for Yourself!* (1851–1852), he describes the mental states presupposed by Christianity: 'the struggle of an anguished conscience, fear and trembling' (FSE, 201–2/SKS 16, 247).

Kierkegaard here draws on the Lutheran tradition, taken up and modified by Heidegger in *Being and Time* (1927) where anxiety works as a *principium individuationis* and conscience calls *Dasein* away from falling-prey to the world of its concern, summoning the individual to seize its own possibilities of being and becoming (cf. Heidegger 2001: 322). While Kierkegaard connects 'bad' conscience to wrongdoing and sin (in the sense of misrelating to God), Heidegger detaches being from doing and develops a non-religious and trans-moral understanding of 'guilt' that boils down to finitude: one's leeway in decision-making is diminished with every choice one makes (cf. Welz 2008: 154–78; 2011: 277–83). Heidegger is thus, in contrast to Kierkegaard, not interested in the normative distinction between 'good' and 'bad' conscience. Both of them affirm the impossibility of escaping from oneself. Kierkegaard views the self, its peace of mind or agony of soul *sub specie aeternitatis*: 'In eternity there are plenty of rooms; there is exactly one for each one, because where there is conscience, and this is and must be in everyone, there is in eternity a solitary prison or a delightful room of eternal happiness' (UDVS, 134/ SKS 8, 233). The self is forced to face itself in the judgment of its conscience.

(2) Like Kant, who in *The Metaphysics of Morals* (1797) considers conscience to be the consciousness of an inner court,[2] Kierkegaard assumes that conscience is a power of judgment. Who operates as judge? Insofar as it is one's own conscience that contains the judgment, the judge is always oneself, yet insofar as internalized norms play a role, others can also speak through conscience, and in the last instance it is God who passes judgment on the human being. In a journal entry from 1851, Kierkegaard admits that conscience is 'one of life's greatest inconveniences' and asks whether it would help to 'form a group' to make the task a bit easier for oneself (KJN 8, 402/SKS 24, 396). The answer is: 'with a group it is good-bye to conscience: when it comes to conscience, one cannot be 2 or 3, or Møller Brothers and Company' (KJN 8, 402/SKS 24, 396) because one cannot delegate one's own responsibility to others.

While Kierkegaard was aware of the phonetic similarity between the German words *Gewissen* and *Gewissheit* (KJN 6, 191–2/SKS 22, 192), he was also aware of the danger that the certainty of conscience might lead one astray in degenerating into self-righteousness. In his dissertation *On the Concept of Irony*, he refers to Hegel's famous sentence, in the *Philosophy of Right* (1821), that if conscience is only formal subjectivity, it is on the verge of slipping into evil (Hegel 2003a: §139, 261; see CI, 227/SKS 1, 270). How, then, can we know whether our judgment is correct? Does conscience have to comply with a social consensus? Kierkegaard follows Hegel, who stresses the universal in the particular, and who, in the posthumously published lectures on the *History of Philosophy* (1837), defined conscience as the idea of common individuality (*die Vorstellung allgemeiner Individualität*) and of a self-assured spirit that is at the same time general truth (Hegel 2003b: 491; see CI, 224/SKS 1, 268). This implies that the individual is obliged by norms that are valid for everyone. However, simply following the majority does not, of course, guarantee that one's moral 'compass' points in the right direction. Therefore, Kierkegaard also reckons with the infinitizing work of the imagination through which the finite subject can envision a life without end in which it has to live eternally with the consequences of its temporal acts.

Furthermore, Kierkegaard introduces the thought of 'God's voice delivering judgment in stillness' (TDIO, 11/SKS 5, 393), which, for him, is the highest authority. According to the discourse 'On the Occasion of a Confession,' in *Three Discourses on Imagined Occasions* (1845), every human being must present an account for his or her life before God. In the same vein, the aforementioned occasional discourse from 1847 reminds us that 'the most pernicious of all evasions' is to, hidden in the crowd, want to 'avoid hearing God's voice as a single individual, as Adam once did when his bad conscience fooled him into thinking that he could hide among the trees' (UDVS, 128/SKS 8, 228). No one can circumvent God's judgment. In no. VI of his 'Discourses at the Communion on Fridays' (1848), Kierkegaard also mentions the problem of self-condemnation. He addresses all those who might condemn themselves: 'whether it was something terrible that so weighed upon your conscience that your heart condemned itself – God is greater!' (CD, 293–4/SKS 10, 315). Hence the punishing voice of conscience does not have the last say. In this regard Kierkegaard is a good Lutheran.[3]

(3) While conscience 'speaks' unexpectedly and is experienced passively, listening to its call and paying heed to it is an activity. Being conscientious in the sense of having an active conscience involves sensitizing oneself to the ethical demand that lies in the call of conscience, rendering an account for one's deeds, and becoming one with oneself. As Kierkegaard wrote in one of his notebooks, there is no other human skill or capacity that requires such lengthy and demanding schooling as conscientiousness, which is not a natural quality, but needs to be cultivated: 'eternity, where every hum. being is to be judged, will first and foremost require that every hum. being has acquired a conscience' (KJN 5, 239/SKS 21, 230). One cannot create one's conscience, but one has the duty to sustain it by being attentive to the voice of the inner judge.

For Kierkegaard, 'the accounting of eternity' is the same as 'the voice of conscience' that speaks to the single individual regarding 'whether he ... has done good or evil' (UDVS, 128–9/SKS 8, 228). However, it happens that the one called upon tries to hide in the masses or 'completely deafens his conscience – his conscience, since he does not get rid of it; it still is his or, rather, he belongs to it' (UDVS, 129/SKS 8, 228). The voice of conscience can be 'outvoted' in this earthly life; yet Kierkegaard asserts that in eternity it must be heard 'because the single individual has become the eternal echo of this voice' and is responsible before God for all actions and omissions (UDVS, 129/SKS 8, 229).

Instead of wanting to place one's own guilt and responsibility on someone else, every human being has to learn to become one with him- or herself by shouldering the blame. As the 'inner court' of conscience comprises both the judge and the accused, experiences of 'bad' conscience are ambiguous: on the one hand, they establish a certain distance to oneself, the guilty one, who desires to evade the ethical demand conveyed by its call; on the other hand, they strengthen the personal unity with oneself as the responsible one who nonetheless accepts the ethical demand. Rejecting the responsibility for oneself and one's comportment by not wanting to be the person one is would amount to deceiving oneself about oneself.

Self-deception

If self-deception means that one is caught in a self-made illusion, one cannot escape it as easily as one entered into it. Only in retrospect or from a third-person perspective does the phenomenon of self-deception appear as such. In *A Literary Review* (1846), concerning Thomasine Gyllembourg's anonymously published novel *Two Ages*, Kierkegaard states that people do not seem to have 'a Socratic fear of being deceived by themselves' (TA, 10/SKS 8, 14). He quotes Plato's dialogue *Cratylus*, 428d, where Socrates says that 'the worst of all deceptions is self-deception' and asks rhetorically whether it is not a terrible thought that 'the deceiver is always present and never stirs from the spot' (Plato 1926: 151; cf. SKS K8).[4] For Kierkegaard, self-deception is a common social – and sometimes even collective – phenomenon. If one does not fear self-deception as Socrates did, one is not safeguarded against it because one lacks self-critical scepticism towards one's own opinions. Kierkegaard detected self-deception in everyday situations that concern all of us, and his analyses are still topical. Self-deception is a key term in his psychology and theological anthropology, surfacing in his entire authorship. He emphasizes three aspects of self-deception, namely (1) self-created ignorance about oneself, (2) dishonesty in vital relations to others, which reacts upon oneself, and (3) performative self-contradictions.

(1) How can one become or remain artificially ignorant of something one knows? Self-inflicted ignorance is self-deceptive if it is 'an intentional not-wanting-to-know-that-one's-will-is-in-conflict' – which presupposes that one *has* some awareness of what one does not want to know (Hügli 1989: 69). In the first section of *The Sickness unto Death*, part C.B.a, Anti-Climacus explains that despair is a universal sickness, yet most people do not realize that they are sick. That is why they are 'altogether secured in the power of despair,' and only 'when the enchantment of illusion is over, when existence begins to totter, then despair, too, immediately appears as that which lay underneath' (SUD, 40/SKS 11, 159). Thus, one has actively brought forth and maintained ignorance about oneself, and therein lies a *will to ignorance*, which obscures one's self-understanding (cf. Grøn 1997: 129–32, 218–9). It is not a coincidence that Kierkegaard uses active verb forms in order to underline the resistance towards reaching clarity of mind: the despairing one 'may try to keep himself in the dark about his state' with the help of amusements, work, and busyness, or 'he may even realize that he is working this way in order to sink his soul in darkness and does it with a certain keen discernment and shrewd calculation' but nonetheless, 'he is not, in a deeper sense, clearly conscious of what he is doing' (SUD, 42/SKS 11, 163). The intellectual opacity that blocks self-knowledge is traced back to 'a dialectical interplay between knowing and willing' (SUD, 42/SKS 11, 163).

Accordingly, in the second section of the book, part A, chapter 2, despair before God is described as sin, and sin counts as self-deception grounded in the corruption of the will (SUD, 72/SKS 11, 208). While Socrates believed that human beings refrain from doing what is right because they have not understood what is right, Kierkegaard shows that they cannot do what is right because they *do not want* to understand (SUD, 71/SKS 11, 207). He tellingly depicts how the will lets some time pass, and the intellect becomes dimmer until 'knowing has come over to the side of willing and admits that what it wants is absolutely right' (SUD, 71/SKS 11, 207). In this case one's unwillingness comes to manipulate one's thoughts. Here Kierkegaard has anticipated ideas later developed by Nietzsche and Freud, who understand forgetting and repressing as part of the process of self-deception (cf. Welz 2018). When considering the fate of biblical Job and discussing how to bear grievous loss, Kierkegaard in his discourse 'The Lord Gave and the Lord Took Away; Blessed Be the Name of the Lord' (1843) outlines the possibility that someone 'mendaciously' tries 'to defraud the good once bestowed on him – as if it had never been splendid, had never made him happy…, as if there were strength in falsehood' (EUD, 117–8/SKS 5, 123).

However, in struggling to preserve one's soul, success and profit can become just as threatening as loss and failure. We can lose ourselves in self-complacency and false security, thereby overestimating ourselves and acting ruthlessly in relation to others. In the aforementioned discourse 'On the Occasion of a Confession,' Kierkegaard sees 'selfishness,' 'self-admiration,' and 'self-confidence' as huge temptations (TDIO, 39/SKS 5, 417). In all three attitudes one is self-centred without noticing that one is betraying oneself.

(2) This brings us to the next form of self-deception, which is modelled upon deceiving others: dishonesty. Vigilius Haufniensis, the pseudonymous author of *The Concept of Anxiety*,

directly mentions 'dishonest self-deception [*uredeligt Selvbedrag*]' (CA, 97/SKS 4, 438) as one of the expressions (or masks) of the demonic; of freedom that is lost through human beings making themselves unfree. Here it becomes conspicuous that dishonesty, if it has ever been a strategy to deceive others, ends up in a confusion where the deceiver primarily deceives and damages him- or herself. Correspondingly, Kierkegaard's journal entry on 'The Dialectic of the Ethical and the Ethical-Religious Communication' (1847) discloses the confusion of modern times in terms of dishonesty: not as a deliberate deception, but as self-deception. The latter must not be mistaken for hypocrisy: 'A real hypocrite is a rare sight in these times, for a real hypocrite is a man of character' (JP 2, 290/SKS 27, 415). The difference between the self-deceiver and the hypocrite is that the hypocrite 'can give himself good account of his dishonesty,' while 'the self-deceived person is bewildered,' though never blamelessly so (ibid.). Kierkegaard argues that modernity lacks 'naivety' and 'primitiveness' in the sense that one lives one's life without getting an actual impression of oneself, that one always compares oneself with others, does away with the category of individuality, and puts the generation in its place. His diagnosis of the times runs as follows:

> There is nothing more dangerous than the thief passing himself off as a police-man, nothing more dangerous than a radical cure miscarrying and contributing to the disease, nothing more dangerous than being stuck in something and saying: Now I will make a desperate extreme effort to get loose – and then by this attempt proceeding to get all the more stuck.
>
> (JP 2, 291/SKS 27, 416f)

Kierkegaard highlights not so much the confusion of thought itself as the fact that one presumptuously conceals one's confusion from oneself. Self-reflection alone cannot cure this, since it is also contaminated by the sickness of self-deception, which invades all relations in which a person is involved. Self-deception can, for instance, be accompanied by the flight into anonymity, by not wanting to be oneself as an identifiable person before other persons. If a person speaks and acts as 'they' do and hides behind others, he or she loses his or her own voice. The opposite extreme is the dominance of the first-person perspective at the expense of others: the 'I' is, so to speak, centre stage, and hears only itself speaking. In his *Concluding Unscientific Postscript*, Kierkegaard warns: 'let us never forget that interiority without outwardness is the most difficult interiority, in which self-deception is easiest' (CUP 1, 406/SKS 7, 369). Solitude promotes self-deception if it implies a solipsistic mis-relation to others. When we shut ourselves away and are no longer interested in an exchange of ideas with others, we miss out on our chance to self-correct.

Stages on Life's Way shows that a person's self-deception can even consist in proudly dismissing self-deception. Frater Taciturnus describes God's 'intervention' in the course of life. Taciturnus does not want community 'with what is cosmeticized or self-deluding [*det Selvbedragerske*]' but states about himself: 'I have become a prisoner in the appearance I wanted to conjure up. I have indeed acted shabbily toward a human being.... Governance has made me captive. The idea of my existence was proud; now I am crushed' (SLW, 224/SKS 6, 326). God – who in the above quote appears as *Styrelsen*: the principle that governs the run of events without being addressable as a person on a par with other human beings – has not prevented Taciturnus's self-deception, but placed him in situations in which he finally had to relinquish his pride. In *Works of Love*, Kierkegaard makes it clear that a human being cannot deceive God: 'in relation to God a person can deceive only himself' (WL, 235/SKS 9, 236). If we think we can manipulate God He remains 'silent' and, seemingly, does not react at all; the situation changes only if we ourselves change. We cannot fool God. On the contrary, God reveals human dishonesty in relation to Him, or a person reveals him- or herself by way of performative self-contradictions.

(3) This is the third point of interest: self-deception can be debunked by the voice of what Kierkegaard calls a 'subtle' conscience, which expresses a person's innermost convictions in one way, while the same person shows the very reverse in the way in which (s)he is acting in the social world. In these performative self-contradictions, we manoeuvre ourselves into a special kind of double bind: we are scrupulous and far too submissive to the voice of conscience, while we at the same time make every effort to ignore it. In the final chapter of the *Postscript*, Kierkegaard claims that 'a downright unscrupulous person' is rarely seen, 'but a subtle conscience is not rare . . . in the agonizing self-contradiction of simultaneously having to explain away a responsibility and remaining unaware of doing it' (CUP 1, 604/SKS 7, 549). A conscientious person knows his or her obligation, but (s)he might trivialize it and pretend not to know that (s)he is irreplaceable in meeting that obligation. This attempt to lighten one's load is most certainly unsuccessful, leading into a vicious circle where one only moves deeper into the opposite of what was intended.

Furthermore, one can cheat oneself through ostentatious gestures towards others, which only cover the disproportion between one's subjective decisions taken in 'interiority' and their display in the 'exteriority' of the intersubjective sphere. To Kierkegaard, Magister Adler is a glaring example of such a contradiction between 'the inner' and 'the outer world.' According to *The Book on Adler* (1844–1846), Adler burned his Hegelian manuscripts in order to show that he had broken with Hegel's philosophy. He remained a Hegelian, but the contradiction was hidden from him (BA, 102/SKS 15, 258). Doubting the value of Adler's symbolic action and the urge to give such a blatant external expression to an inner decision, Kierkegaard made fun of him: 'Hegelian philosophy actually explains away the revelation. Adler solemnly maintains that he has had a revelation and then, *à la Hegel*, instructively explains that a revelation actually is unthinkable, but does not notice the discrepancy himself' (BA, 102–3/SKS 15, 259). Adler was ridiculed because of the obvious but overlooked contradiction between his grand gesture and the attitude it expressed. He deceived himself 'unconsciously' (BA, 100/SKS 15, 257).

Kierkegaard gives another example of a performative self-contradiction in the drunkard who has decided not to drink again. He does not need to solemnly throw bottle and glass out of the window and break them into pieces in order to demonstratively step into total abstinence. He needs only to stop drinking, even if the bottle and the full glass remain right in front of him (BA, 101/SKS 15, 257–8). This example, which touches upon the problem of addiction, might remind us of the motto sometimes employed in the treatment of alcohol or drug abuse: *fake it till you make it*! (or, in social psychologist Amy Cuddy's 2012 TED talk version: *fake it till you become it*!). While still addicted, drug-dependent persons are encouraged to live as if they were already 'clean.' In this way, one hopes to create new habits that at some point will prove victorious. What does this imply for a possible prevention of or cure for self-deception? In returning to this question, another one arises: if there is a genuine, truthful, honest mode of existence for human beings, unadulterated by self-deception, what does it look like? Let us assume that it can come under the heading of 'authenticity' and ask, again, what it means to be 'authentic' under the present circumstances? After all, a pure lack of self-contradiction is not yet a sign of authenticity.

Authenticity

'Authenticity' concerns an object's genuineness in relation to its source, prototype or original. This use of the word corresponds to the Latin term *authenticum*, which during the Middle Ages designated the original manuscript as opposed to the reproduced copy, the *exemplarium* (Dehs 2012: 12). Speaking of things, the term 'authentic' is used either in the strong sense of being of undisputed origin or authorship, or in a weaker sense of being an accurate representation; when attributing 'authenticity' to human beings, the question arises what it is 'to be oneself, at one with oneself, or truly representing one's self' (Varga and Guignon 2014: Introduction).

The current interdisciplinary discussion is moving away from an essentialist understanding of authenticity, which focuses on a certain quality inherent in things or persons (cf. Vannini and Williams 2009). There is a tendency towards hermeneutic approaches that stress the interpretation of authenticity as a dynamic product of concrete processes of interaction and communication in specific situations. Further, phenomenological approaches that define authenticity as an affective, cognitive, and narrative experience of congruence with one's (culturally shaped) ideas of the 'true self' and the corresponding values are in vogue. However, it is controversial whether authenticity is to be primarily regarded as a normative ideal or more pragmatically as a motivational force in social relations. Another issue concerns the relation between 'authenticity,' 'autonomy,' and 'sincerity': What are the similarities and differences between these notions (cf. Golomb 1995: 7–17; Varga 2011)?

Even though Kierkegaard managed fine without the concept of 'authenticity,' which first came into circulation long after his death, he found his own formulations for the matter at hand. In Kierkegaard's authorship, the authentic is shown indirectly through the inauthentic, via a detour through negativity. Among the antonyms of authenticity is self-deception. As we have already seen, self-deception is, in *The Sickness unto Death*, described as despair or, theologically, as sin. This sickness of the spirit comes to the fore either as the weakness of not wanting to be oneself or the defiance of insisting upon being oneself. As Varga and Guignon (2014: section 3.1) rightly point out, Kierkegaard's suggestion that each of us is to 'become what one is [*at vorde det man saadan uden videre er*]' (CUP 1, 130/SKS 7, 122) is linked to his criticism of modern society, of 'massification' and hollowness. Since Kierkegaard defines selfhood in relational terms, the task of authentically becoming what one is can be fulfilled only in relation to someone or something outside oneself, something which bestows one's life with meaning. Here Kierkegaard's normative framework and his Christian premises become apparent: he refers to a network of relations, among which the God-relationship has a foundational character in bearing and sustaining all other relations. As references to our common humanity are bound to our being-created by God, a secular version of Kierkegaard's account that would focus exclusively on certain ontological structures would, in his view, throw the baby out with the bathwater.

Kierkegaard characterizes self-deception and its antithesis with the aid of three semantic fields within which authenticity is paraphrased as (1) purity of heart, (2) honest earnestness, truthfulness, and sincerity, and (3) the trustworthiness of the one who loves faithfully.

(1) The first-mentioned form of authenticity is 'the purity of heart to will one thing,' which is portrayed in contradistinction to 'doublemindedness' (UDVS, 24/SKS 8, 138). The most challenging task is perhaps the task of becoming 'simple-minded,' willing not more than just one thing, namely the good. According to Kierkegaard's *Upbuilding Discourse* 'On the Occasion of a Confession,' purity of heart is not acquired by reading many scholarly books, but by kneeling down and praying to God (UDVS, 26/SKS 8, 140). Thereby human beings become similar to the One in whose image they are created (Gen. 1: 27–8). The following private prayer in a journal entry from the year 1850 confirms this attitude:

> you, O Holy Spirit, when you dwell in a hum. being, you dwell in something that is infinitely inferior: You, Spirit of Holiness, dwell with uncleanness and infection; you, Spirit of Wisdom, with foolishness; you, Spirit of Truth, with self-deception! Oh, continue to dwell [here]; and you, who do not conveniently search for the desirable dwelling that you would surely seek in vain; you, who yourself, in creating and giving rebirth, make your own dwelling place—o, continue to dwell [here], that one day you

might be pleased with the dwelling place you yourself have prepared for yourself in my infected and foolish and deceitful heart.

(KJN 7, 29/SKS 23, 17–8)

The person praying expresses that his heart is not pure, and that he needs God's Holy Spirit to transform it, so that his heart will some fine day once again resemble its creator. The inauthentic here pertains to one's alienation from one's origin, which lies in the unequivocally good: in God, who—metaphorically speaking—is light without darkness. No human being can avoid taking a stance on existential ambiguities. One's position depends on the criterion or standard chosen for one's being and doing. If one oscillates between light and dark, good and evil, one risks obscuring one's self-knowledge in order to justify one's divisiveness. In this context, to be authentic does not mean that one always chooses what is right, but rather that one is capable of admitting one's flaws.

Remarkably, Kierkegaard does not identify purity of heart with the goodness of one's heart. Instead of speaking of kindheartedness, he only speaks of the heart's longing, yearning, and craving for the good. Further, the good is not defined in terms of content. Kierkegaard is not telling us *what* is good, but gives us only an indication of the formal features of the good: it is that which does not contradict itself. The good is experientially given in a way that denies all ambivalence: in wholeheartedness. By contrast, self-deception is connected to opacity and duplicity, which exclude a wholehearted commitment to one thing alone. Kierkegaard's formal definition of the good, however, contains an open question; that is why a person's authenticity depends upon an ongoing search for the good. Kierkegaard here invites us to embark on the quest for that which can only be reached in a noble simplicity of heart. 'The good' is thereby nothing more and nothing less than a teleological term that can help the bewildered to re-orient themselves.

(2) Another form of authenticity we can find in Kierkegaard is what he calls 'an honest earnestness that lovingly maintains the tasks' (FT, 94/SKS 4, 208). This earnestness involves truthfulness and sincerity. But what, exactly, does that mean? If the authentic is that which cannot lie or play-act, that does not disguise or distort itself, and that is without any hidden agenda or intrigue – like nature, which is just what it is, without guile (cf. Dehs 2012: 7) – the question is to what degree such a description of authenticity matches human beings who first have to discover who they are, what they can do, and how they want to become. Unlike trees, bushes, and flowers, people can tell a lie, they do pretend, and they often have ulterior motives. In becoming ourselves, we have to appropriate ourselves, and at least a part of our life story is influenced by the ways in which we present ourselves to others, for instance when applying for a job or looking for a partner. Here we may ask whether there is a correspondence between the inner and the outer, between thinking and acting: are we what we think we are, and do we act as we say we do?

Kierkegaardian 'honest earnestness' is, nota bene, related to certain 'tasks.' It stands for a type of authenticity that involves conscientiousness. It does not necessarily centre around perfect self-presentation, but rather pays attention to the way in which someone performs his or her tasks: are they maintained 'lovingly'? If one focuses on the tasks and how they are performed, one might run into the problem that not all work is done properly. This situation can become a test: how does one relate to the fact that one has not lived up to the demands—by glossing over it or by being sincere in truthfully admitting regrettable neglects? Unfortunately, we do not always act according to our own convictions. As long as reality is such a long way from ideality, we have to accept our own imperfections, fragility, and failings. Yet confessing what went wrong is one thing, and being content with it is another. The 'honest earnestness' Kierkegaard has in mind implies that we resist self-satisfied self-laudation and instead try to improve ourselves and carry out our duties, not least the duty to love one's neighbour as oneself (Lev. 19: 18; Matt. 19: 19), which Kierkegaard accentuates in *Works of Love*.

(3) A third form of authenticity is the trustworthiness of someone who loves another. Kierkegaard juxtaposes being 'trapped in a self-delusion [*hildet i et Selvbedrag*]' to having loved 'faithfully' (SLW, 244/SKS 6, 356). It is important to realize that fidelity in relation to another is intertwined with trustworthiness. It is difficult to build trust if one is not willing to demonstrate the constancy and stability that is part and parcel of maintaining oneself in a love that is firm and strong. Translating authenticity into trustworthiness, one can see oneself as the responsible author of one's actions. This corresponds to the etymology of authenticity: *authentikós* is derived from *authéntes*, 'originator,' and related to *autos*, '(one)self.' In the course of the history of language, the meaning of the authentic has become equivalent to that which takes its authority from itself (Dehs 2012: 25).

Nonetheless, we need to take into account that human beings can lose control over their lives and thereby also the authority required for self-determined, autonomous actions, rational deliberations, and the capacity to decide for oneself according to self-chosen guidelines. If we can come to corrupt ourselves so easily by finding excuses for faithlessness, unreliability, and betrayal, how realistic is the thought that there is a cure for self-deception? If God is the only one we cannot fool, is He then also the only one who can help us—or how can we help ourselves and each other in the struggle against self-deception?

Conclusion

Let us finally return to the motto *fake it till you make it* or *fake it till you become it* (Cuddy 2012). At first sight, this motto seems diametrically opposed to authenticity, regardless of whether we understand authenticity as (1) being faithful to one's creator in wholeheartedly wanting the good; (2) being what one professes or is reputed to be, thus being truthful and sincere, or (3) being true to oneself in burgeoning as the reliable and loving person one is to become. These are features that are hard to fake.

Yet Kierkegaard advocates a thought compatible with the motto: in *Works of Love*, Socrates is called 'that rogue' who has done 'the greatest beneficence' towards another person by trying to 'deceive the other into the truth' (WL, 276–7/SKS 9, 274–5). Could we, based on this thought, turn Kierkegaard against Kierkegaard and claim that even if a person cannot normally trick *another* into the truth, it is possible to deceive *oneself* into the truth with the help of a double-movement that dissolves the self-deception? To succeed in this endeavour one must 'outwit' the deceiver in oneself by making the self-deception transparent, and thereby diminishing its impact. The attempt to cheat one's deceitful heart (i.e., to live *as if* it were possible to get rid of one's self-deception, thus *faking it*), might lead to a change in actuality (i.e., to the disclosure of one's self-deception, which will move one closer to a life in truth, until one can *make it*). But still, insofar as self-deception is not only a psychological problem of a solitary person or a social problem between a plurality of persons, but also a religious problem between God and human beings and a 'sin' in Kierkegaard's eyes, it can probably not be solved solely by a paradoxical strategy that aims at deceiving the deceiver. After all, the deceiver operating in self-deception is identical with oneself.

By contrast, to be authentic means to be clear about one's own feelings, desires, and convictions, and to be ready to openly express one's stance in the public arena (Guignon 2008: 288). If we concede that authenticity is a goal more than a given fact, we can freely confess that we here and now also live in inauthenticity and untruth. An authentic life in truth can be actualized only to a certain degree. Since none of us is capable of effectively warding off self-deception, and since it is never easy to see through a 'subtle conscience,' we should, in any case, be cautious in criticizing self-deception in *others*. As Henrik Ibsen's play *The Wild Duck* (1884) illustrates, exposing others' life-lies can result in tragedy (cf. Landweer 2001).[5]

While authenticity and the sincerity of delivering on one's words can entail 'languages of personal resonance' that lie beyond the scope of Kantian autonomy (Taylor 1992: 90) in guiding moral agents to follow only those sources *outside* them that resonate *within* them (Taylor 1989: 510), it is crucial to also see the danger of a notion of authenticity that aims at a correspondence between one's inside and outside: it may suggest that non-alienated relations are to be found only where one somehow 'fits in' with a given community or consorts with an idea of the 'true self.' In contrast to the misunderstanding that social 'resonance' is tantamount to consonance or harmony, it must be emphasized that it involves a genuine response that does not just echo others, thereby reinforcing identities, but that also indulges in a dialogue with those who are different and may therefore contain dissonance (Rosa 2017: 312–3, 316). Kierkegaard, however, surpasses purely psychological and sociological considerations by discussing the question of authenticity in the horizon of infinity. While it is easy to say what authenticity is not, it is hard to pinpoint what it actually is. Kierkegaard has chosen to circumscribe the phenomenon in terms of having cultivated one's conscience. The latter can be regarded as an interface of aesthetic, ethical, and religious aspects of his existential approach (Welz 2017).

In summary, it can be said that 'authenticity vs. self-deception' is not a conceptual opposite, but a way that possibly leads us to a 'purity of heart.' Kierkegaard does not offer a solution to the existential problem of inauthenticity, but provides, rather, a 'melody' in gesturing towards future self-transfiguration in faith.[6] Thus, to conclude, let us once more consider his 1850 prayer. It teaches us how to deal with ambiguities in a gentle and thoughtful way. Instead of accusing others or making them miserable with lamentations, Kierkegaard turns to the One who is exalted above and superior to human pettiness: God's 'Spirit of Truth' that can dwell in places we would never expect it to be, even 'with self-deception' (KJN 7, 29/SKS 23, 17–8). Instead of resigning in the face of human mendacity, including his own, he opens his heart to the One who alone can cleanse it. Thereby the acknowledged inauthenticity is already surmounted, secretly transformed.

Related topics

'Love for humans: morality as the heart of Kierkegaard's religious philosophy,' Sharon Krishek; 'Agency, identity, and alienation in *The Sickness unto Death*,' Justin F. White.

Notes

1. I discuss the ideas in this chapter in greater detail in Welz (2015).
2. Cf. Kant (1963: §13, A 99): 'Das Bewußtsein eines *inneren Gerichtshofes* im Menschen ("vor welchem sich seine Gedanken einander verklagen oder entschuldigen") ist das *Gewissen*.'
3. Cf. Welz (2011: 268–71, 278), where I refer to a number of quotes by Luther (1889: 152), such as, 'ynn den gewissen wil er [Gott] alleyn seyn unnd seyn wort alleyn regieren lassen, da soll freyheyt seyn von allen menschen gesetzen.'
4. See also the journal entry KJN 2, 169/SKS 18, 183 as well as SLW 302/SKS 6, 444 and CUP 1, 344/SKS 7, 351, where Kierkegaard references this line.
5. The Ekdal family, whose everyday life is based on dreams, illusions, and lies, is not healed when the truth (that Hjalmar is not the biological father of Hedvig) is revealed; rather, the family collapses. Hjalmar wants to leave his wife Gina and rejects his daughter Hedvig, who then commits suicide. Does this confirm the famous words of one of the protagonists, Doctor Relling: 'Rob the average man of his life-illusion, and you rob him of his happiness at the same stroke' (Ibsen 1907: 372)? Strictly speaking, it is

not an unbearable truth that breaks Hedvig, but rather her father's self-centred reaction to its disclosure (Pahuus 1995: 81). Hjalmar suspects Hedvig has never truly loved him, while Hedvig, in fact, renounces her life for him, wanting to prove her love (cf. Ibsen 1907: 391; Pahuus 1995: 82, 211). Gregers, who wanted to free Hjalmar from his falsehood, thereby also wanted to 'find some cure' for his own 'sick conscience' (Ibsen 1907: 312). Sadly, he did not live up to his own ideals of living in truth. He turned out to be a different person than he claimed to be.

6 Thanks to Brian Söderquist for expressing this thought!

References

Cuddy, A. (2012) 'Your body language may shape who you are,' *TED Talk*. Retrieved from <https://www.youtube.com/watch?v=Ks-_Mh1QhMc> [accessed February 18, 2018].
Dehs, J. (2012) *Det autentiske: Fortællinger om nutidens kunstbegreb*, Copenhagen: Vandkunsten.
Golomb, J. (1995) *In search of authenticity from Kierkegaard to Camus*, London: Routledge.
Grøn, A. (1997) *Subjektivitet og negativitet: Kierkegaard*, Copenhagen: Gyldendal.
Guignon, C. (2008) 'Authenticity,' *Philosophy Compass*, 3: 277–90.
Hart, J. G. (2009) *Who one is: Book 2: Existenz and transcendental phenomenology*, Dordrecht: Springer.
Hegel, G. W. F. (2003a) *Grundlinien der Philosophie des Rechts oder Naturrecht und Staatswissenschaft im Grundrisse. Mit Hegels eigenhändigen Notizen und den mündlichen Zusätzen*, E. Moldenhauer and K. M. Michel (eds), Frankfurt am Main: Suhrkamp.
Hegel, G. W. F. (2003b) *Vorlesungen über die Geschichte der Philosophie I*, E. Moldenhauer and K. M. Michel (eds), Frankfurt am Main: Suhrkamp.
Heidegger, M. (2001) *Being and time*, J. Macquarrie and E. Robinson (trans), Oxford: Blackwell.
Hügli, A. (1989) 'Pseudonymity, sincerity and self-deception,' in B. Bertung (ed), *Kierkegaard—Poet of Existence*, Copenhagen: C. A. Reitzel.
Ibsen, H. (1907) *An enemy of the people; The wild duck*, New York: Scribner's.
Kant, I. (1963) *Die Metaphysik der Sitten* in *Immanuel Kant: Werke in sechs Bänden*, vol. IV: *Schriften zur Ethik und Religionsphilosophie*, W. Weischedel (ed), Darmstadt: Wissenschaftliche Buchgesellschaft.
Landweer, H. (2001) 'Selbsttäuschung,' *Deutsche Zeitschrift für Philosophie*, 49, no. 2: 209–28.
Luther, M. (1889) *D. Martin Luthers Werke: Kritische Gesamtausgabe (Weimarer Ausgabe)*, vol. 8, Weimar: Hermann Böhlau.
Pahuus, M. (1995) *Selvudfoldelse og selvhengivelse: livssynet hos Henrik Ibsen og Henrik Pontoppidan*, Aalborg: Aalborg Universitetsforlag.
Plato (1926) *Cratylus, Parmenides, Greater Hippias, Lesser Hippias*, H. N. Fowler (trans), Cambridge, MA: Harvard University Press.
Rosa, H. (2017) *Resonanz: Eine Soziologie der Weltbeziehung*, Berlin: Suhrkamp.
Taylor, C. (1992) *The ethics of authenticity*, Cambridge, MA: Harvard University Press.
Taylor, C. (1989) *Sources of the self: The making of the modern identity*, Cambridge, MA: Harvard University Press.
Vannini, P. and Williams, J. P. (2009) *Authenticity in culture, self, and society*, Farnham: Ashgate.
Varga, S. (2011) 'Self-realization and owing to others: A morality constraint?' *International Journal of Philosophical Studies*, 19: 71–82.
Varga, S. and Guignon, C. (2014), 'Authenticity,' *Stanford Encyclopedia of Philosophy*. Retrieved from <https://plato.stanford.edu/entries/authenticity/> [accessed December 7, 2017].
Welz, C. (2018) 'Self-knowledge and self-deception: Existential hermeneutics and psychoanalysis,' in C. Welz and R. Rosfort (eds), *Hermeneutics and Negativism: Existential Ambiguities of Self-Understanding*, Tübingen: Mohr Siebeck.
Welz, C. (2017) 'The voice of conscience, Kierkegaard's theory of indirect communication, and Buber's philosophy of dialogue,' in H. Schulz, J. Stewart, and K. Verstrynge (eds), *Kierkegaard Studies Yearbook 2017*, Berlin: Walter de Gruyter.
Welz, C. (2015) 'Samvittighed, selvbedrag og autenticitet hos Kierkegaard,' in M. Pahuus, J. Rendtorff, and P. Søltoft (eds), *Kierkegaard som eksistentiel fænomenolog*, Aalborg: Aalborg Universitetsforlag.
Welz, C. (2011) 'Das Gewissen als Instanz der Selbsterschließung: Luther, Kierkegaard und Heidegger,' *Neue Zeitschrift für Systematische Theologie und Religionsphilosophie*, 53, no. 3: 265–84.
Welz, C. (2008) 'Keeping the secret of subjectivity: Kierkegaard and Levinas on conscience, love, and the limits of self-understanding,' in C. Welz and K. Verstrynge (eds), *Despite Oneself: Subjectivity and Its Secret in Kierkegaard and Levinas*, London: Turnshare.

Further reading

Lippitt, J. (2015) 'Forgiveness and the rat man: Kierkegaard, "narrative unity" and "wholeheartedness" revisited,' in J. Lippitt and P. Stokes (eds), *Narrative, Identity and the Kierkegaardian Self*, Edinburgh: Edinburgh University Press.
  This chapter is a discussion of authenticity, understood in terms of wholeheartedness vs. ambivalence.

Welz, C. (2015) 'Self-deception,' in S. M. Emmanuel, W. McDonald, and J. Stewart (eds), *Kierkegaard Research: Sources, Reception and Resources*, vol. 15 (*Kierkegaard's Concepts*), tome 6, Farnham: Ashgate.
  This chapter discusses how Kierkegaard uses the concept of self-deception in his writings.

Welz, C. (2011) 'Puzzles of self-deception and problems of orientation: Kierkegaard and the current debate in the philosophy of psychology,' in H. Schulz, J. Stewart, and K. Verstrynge (eds), *Kierkegaard Studies Yearbook 2011*, Berlin: Walter de Gruyter.
  This chapter relates Kierkegaard's approach to self-deception to other approaches in the philosophy of mind and psychology.

24
IMAGINATION AND BELIEF

Eleanor Helms

Introduction

In everyday conversation, we are likely to think of imagination and belief as opposed. Imaginary beings, like unicorns and hippogriffs, are the ones I *don't* believe in. At times, as we might expect, Søren Kierkegaard treats imagination as an escape from reality or a tool for ignoring the tasks of an existing individual. It might seem that a movement toward faith must be away from imagination. I will show, however, that faith for Kierkegaard is a continuation of imaginative activity rather than a turn in a new direction. For Kierkegaard, building on German Idealism and anticipating the work of phenomenologists like Maurice Merleau-Ponty, belief of any kind takes place within an implicit teleological structure in all experience, or what Merleau-Ponty calls an 'intentional arc' (2012: 137). (Here 'intention' is used in the broad, phenomenological sense of an activity of attention or consciousness. It need not be voluntary.)

While Kierkegaard refers to imagination throughout his authorship, I will focus on *Either/Or* and *The Concept of Anxiety*. In both works, the arbitrary power to imagine is placed within a wider context of the ability to see, which means to recognize what is actual as continuous with what is possible and in that way as part of a larger whole. The most basic belief in existing objects, according to Merleau-Ponty, requires such a synthesis. I will show that Kierkegaard similarly describes existence as a relation of appearances, anticipating later phenomenological analyses in ways that are not yet fully appreciated. Both Kierkegaard and Merleau-Ponty conclude that imagination is deceptive when it lacks a convergence toward unity with other appearances. Images that are continuous with other appearances, by contrast, motivate belief. By understanding Merleau-Ponty's later account of how these structures are at work in perception, we can better understand the relationship between imagination and belief in Kierkegaard.

Perception and belief in Merleau-Ponty's phenomenology

Writing over a century after Kierkegaard, Merleau-Ponty (2012: 315) makes the very Kierkegaardian observation that in perception 'we are never enclosed within appearance.' We instead interpret each appearance as part of a context, relying on elements of a wider situation that includes memory and expectation to make sense of what we see. Ordinarily, for example, we take a plate seen from the side to be circular rather than elliptical, even though the shape that immediately appears in our visual field is an ellipse. Any distortion of these appearances – such as changes in shape as we move around the object – make sense within a whole, as fluctuating around a norm (316). The stable way in which we experience reality in and through such distortions shows that we do not normally take appearances at face value but instead treat them *as* aspects of a whole.

Merleau-Ponty wonders how determinate objects ever successfully crystallize out of the flux of experience. What does it mean to believe something is really there rather than just looking like it is? 'Reality,' writes Merleau-Ponty, 'is not one privileged appearance that would remain beneath the others; it is the framework of relations to which all appearances will conform' (313).[1] I arrive at a conclusion about what something 'is' by welding different appearances together (e.g., 'It's Chartres') (344). Merleau-Ponty notes that confidence in the objective world (in a reality underlying appearances) depends on the synthetic, unifying activity of an observing subject: 'Things and instants can only be linked together to form a world through this ambiguous being that we call "subjectivity," and can only become co-present from a certain point of view and only in intention' (348). Each snapshot of experience is incomplete, though we do not generally notice any gaps because we anticipate future fulfilments. We 'see,' or seem to see, more than is immediately in front of us.

In contrast with mere illusions, which present a single aspect or façade, 'The real lends itself to an infinite exploration, it is inexhaustible' (338). Merleau-Ponty echoes Kierkegaard's well-known insistence that what is known by faith cannot be known in other ways (e.g., conceptually):

> The perceiving subject must, without leaving his place or his point of view in the opacity of sensing, tend toward things whose key he does not hold in advance, and whose design [*projet*] he nevertheless carries within himself, he must open up to an absolute Other that he prepares from deeper within himself.
>
> *(340)*

Apart from the question of religious belief, Merleau-Ponty shows that even for ordinary perception there is no single invariant in an object that motivates belief in its existence. Interacting with an object as existing means that the many ways in which it appears (and can appear) converge toward one thing we call the 'object.'

On the other hand, since a plate seen from the side *looks* like an ellipse, what stops us from taking it to be so? What would happen if someone lost contact with, or confidence in, that wider invisible context and instead took appearances at face value? Merleau-Ponty concludes that the 'ambiguity' of ordinary experience (that is, that it can be interpreted in different ways) opens the door to deceptions and illusions. Discussing real patients, Merleau-Ponty considers how different physical and psychological pathologies can occur given the basic structure of foreground (appearance) and background (context) established by phenomenology. Most importantly, in summarizing comments from people suffering from hallucinations, he notes that such appearances tend to be discontinuous with the rest of experience. For example, a patient who suffers from paranoia might claim that something is poisoned for her but not for others, as if she has lost faith in a shared world (2012: 356–7). Such isolation of appearances is possible, argues Merleau-Ponty, because of the basic structure described above: the real world is *never* presented in its completeness but instead as aspects that hint at a whole. Since all experience includes gaps to be filled in, it is not really strange that we can fail to fill them in or relate them in such a way as to overlook a contradiction. In fact, what comes to seem remarkable is that we connect them so effortlessly most of the time. Why should we be surprised, after all, if someone takes something that *looks like* an ellipse to *be* an ellipse?

We never fully cancel the basic relatedness of experience, however. Merleau-Ponty finds that while people are understandably unwilling to dismiss how things look, they do not believe in isolated appearances with the same confidence they have in those that converge with others. By examining cases where experience lacks a projective or teleological level of convergence and showing the corresponding change in belief, Merleau-Ponty establishes the underlying importance of an intentional arc for belief in reality. In the following sections, I will show that continuity among appearances is likewise a central theme in Kierkegaard's work and has similar consequences for belief.

Pull it together: the Judge's critique

In *Either/Or*, Judge William (the pseudonym known as 'B') critiques 'A' for his reluctance to become any one thing, and an overactive imagination seems partly to blame (EO 2, 162/SKS 3, 159–60). He treats life as a masquerade, where 'every disclosure is always a deception' (EO 2, 159/SKS 3, 157). Rather than committing to a vocation or marriage, 'A' lives on his own terms, even avoiding reading books from beginning to end at the risk of having an experience planned by someone else (EO 1, 299/SKS 2, 288). He maintains control with the help of a method he describes as a variant of 'crop rotation,' or changing his inner perspective in arbitrary ways by controlling what and how he remembers (EO 1, 292/SKS 2, 282) – that is, by isolating the present. With the help of this method, he sets appearances free from reality ('one lets its reality [*Realitet*] run aground on this' (EO 1, 299/SKS 2, 288)), abandoning the relation to an original (EO 1, 300/SKS 2, 289). Like the pathological cases discussed by Merleau-Ponty, 'A' treats each appearance as isolated, though for 'A' (perhaps unlike the cases above) there is at least some element of conscious choice involved. While we might call this kind of free variation just 'imagination,' or even daydreaming, 'A' reserves the term 'imagination' [*Phantasi*] for something even lower in his estimation: a more passive fixation on appearances. He criticizes a tendency (which he attributes to young women) to attend to one's own superficial appearance or to be deceived by that of others. For example, one part of the writings associated with 'A' includes a diary produced by 'Johannes' (arguably a pseudonym for 'A') recounting his seduction of Cordelia, where he concludes in a description of her that 'imagination is the natural cosmetic of the fair sex [*Phantasi er det smukke Kjøns naturlige Sminke*]' (EO 1, 395/SKS 2, 382). He similarly describes a naïve character (Emmeline) in a play he reviews (*The First Love*, by Scribe, discussed further below) as taken in by her imagined portrait of her lover, which then leads her to mistake another character for him (EO 1, 260/SKS 2, 252–3). Like 'A,' Emmeline focuses on an arbitrary element, in this case whether the person possesses a certain ring (EO 1, 270/SKS 2, 262). The difference between 'A' and those he critiques as taken in by passive imagination [*Phantasi*] is that A controls the appearances rather than being fooled by them or producing them unreflectively. In contrast to his own mastery of every situation, 'A' describes Emmeline as the one taken in [*har den hende til Bedste*] (EO 1, 271/SKS 2, 263). Yet he elsewhere describes imagination more positively as a latent power: Cordelia has 'imagination [*Phantasi*], spirit, passion – in short, all the essentials, but not subjectively reflected' (EO 1, 343/SKS 2, 332). In characters who are weaker and less mature in 'A's' estimation (like Emmeline and Cordelia), imagination isolates appearances, cutting them free from reality, but fails to do so in a controlled way.

In both the deliberate and passive instances, imagination is 'aesthetic' in the broad sense of concerning how things appear. It might seem natural, then, to associate imagination with Kierkegaard's aesthetic first stage, in contrast with the higher religious stage, as George Pattison has argued (1991).[2] On this interpretation, Kierkegaard has a poor view of art and imagination, inherited from Kantian idealism, which in turn leads him to choose the term 'aesthetic' to describe inauthenticity in general and to emphasize, according to Pattison, the 'ultimate failure (as he saw it) of art in the face of religion' (1991: 142). Others have argued instead for the importance of imagination even at higher stages, including for philosophical truth (Carlsson 2016), recognizing moral obligations (Stokes 2010), acquiring moral motivations (Wietzke 2013), 'edifying' and 'upbuilding' the human subject (Walsh 1994), and even for faith (Ferreira 1991a; 1991b). David Gouwens also shows how different kinds of imagination employed by characters train the reader to understand Kierkegaard's writing, proposing further that imagination is important for relating to one's ideal self (1982; 1993). Still others have steered imagination toward aesthetics in the narrower, more concrete sense of providing a philosophy of art, arguing for a 'theological aesthetics' (Stoker 2010) and the importance of religious art (Gregor 2009).

My view is that the structure of imagination itself creates a basic momentum toward synthesis in the higher stages but is also, unfortunately, an effective tool for undermining that movement. That is, imagination has a teleological [*teleologiske*] component that can be fulfilled – or not. Since works of art are the objects of experience that rely most conspicuously on (1) sensory appearances, (2) background concepts, and (3) an implied or anticipated unity of appearances with context (all of which are emphasized by Kant in the *Critique of Judgment*), they reveal the teleological structure of *all* appearances (including ordinary perception) particularly well. Kierkegaard often turns to art, especially literary works (and, following Aristotle, the differences between comedy and tragedy), to clarify the teleological structure of consciousness and experience in general. He invents his own fictional characters ('imaginary constructions' [*Experimenter*]) to clarify the various ways in which the teleology inherent to what appears can be (or fail to be) recognized. So while we can certainly draw conclusions about aesthetics in the sense of a philosophy of art, as well as imagination's role in failures of selfhood, we do not want to miss the ways in which Kierkegaard's discussions disclose the role of imagination and appearances ('aesthetics' in a broad sense) in the higher stages of selfhood and faith. Imagination [*Phantasi*] needs development, but it also – perhaps for the first time – reveals the direction in which such development is needed.

The character of 'A,' the aesthete, embodies one set of ways in which imagination can be a danger – that is, can undermine the teleological direction of appearances toward reality and belief. The Judge critiques 'A's' use of imagined possibilities to escape life and effectively dissolve his own existence into a multiplicity:

> You continually hover above yourself, but the higher atmosphere, the more refined sublimate, into which you are vaporized [*forflygtiget*], is the nothing of despair, and you see down below you a multiplicity of subjects, insights, studies, and observations that nevertheless have no reality [*Realitet*] for you but which you very whimsically utilize and combine to decorate as tastefully as you can the sumptuous intellectual [*Aandens*] palace in which you occasionally reside. No wonder that existence [*Tilvaerelse*] for you is a fairy tale.
>
> *(EO 2, 198/SKS 3, 192)*

While Judge William also makes use of imagined scenarios, he warns that 'imaginary constructions in thought' [*Tanke-experimenter*] are something he finds difficult and even risky, especially with respect to marriage as something he cares deeply about: 'I find it difficult to imagine [*at tænke*] myself loved by anyone else' (EO 2, 193/SKS 3, 187). He elsewhere asserts that 'imaginary construction' [*Experiment*] undermines belief and tends toward scepticism, calling imaginary construction 'equivalent to sophistry in the realm of knowledge' (EO 2, 253/SKS 3, 241). In describing how A does this, the Judge suggests that the problem is not liking fiction or having a vivid imagination but taking a single aspect of reality and isolating it. For example, the Judge accuses A of taking a single 'stolen glance' as 'a motif for your aimless fantasy [*Phantasi*]' (EO 2, 7/SKS 3, 17), and characterizes appeals to the imagination [*Phantasi*] alone as a cheap tactic of an author who 'curries a reader's favor' (EO 2, 188/SKS 3, 182). He associates imagination with deception, as when the Judge accuses 'A' of letting the one he seduces produce her own image of him while he remains hidden (EO 2, 233/SKS 3, 222). In each case, imagination deals in mere appearances. The Judge wants to convince 'A' instead of the reality [*Realitet*] of love (EO 2, 192/SKS 3, 186).

The Judge further emphasizes the importance of continuity for any life in his description of an engraving. He writes:

> There is an engraving that portrays Cain murdering Abel. In the background, one sees Adam and Eve. Whether the engraving itself is valuable I am unable to decide, but the caption has always interested me: *prima caedes, primi parentes, primus luctus* [the first killing, the first parents, the first sorrow]. Here again the first has a profound meaning, and here it is the first itself that we contemplate, but it is still more with respect to time than to content, since we do not see the continuity with which the whole is established by the first. (The whole must naturally be understood as sin propagating itself in the race.)
> (*EO 2, 40–1/SKS 3, 47–8*)

The viewer is joined with the 'firsts' in the engraving, but that relationship cannot be represented in the engraving. The Judge associates sin itself with lack of continuity, moreover: 'The first sin, if by this we think of Adam and Eve's fall, would itself steer thought more to the continuity, but since it is the nature of evil not to have continuity, you will readily perceive why I do not use this example' (EO 2, 41/SKS 3, 48). He later says that a healthy life, by contrast, is extended 'in hope and in recollection, and only thereby does his life gain true and substantive continuity' (EO 2, 142/SKS 3, 140).

The Judge associates 'A's' denial of continuity in his own life with illusions. In 'The Balance between the Aesthetic and the Ethical' he insists that an inner teleology [*indre Teleologi*] requires movement and change if this claim (that something has its teleology in itself) is not to *itself* become an illusion [*Illusion*] (EO 2, 274/SKS 2, 260). The Judge concludes that 'A's' life lacks such an inner telos and so instead must settle for an external point of view, as when one marries for extrinsic reasons (EO 2, 64–5/SKS 3, 69–70). The Judge characterizes this external perspective as not merely superficial and arbitrary but as an illusion [*Illusion*] (EO 2, 78–9/SKS 3, 82–3), as imaginary or faked [*fingerede*] (EO 2, 56/SKS 3, 62), and as an experiment [*Experiment*, or 'imaginary construction'] (EO 2, 15/SKS 3, 24).

Just as for Merleau-Ponty, the Judge associates continuity with the ability to unify appearances. He accuses 'A' of clinging to 'visible symbols' (EO 2, 140/SKS 3, 139) and fixating on the word 's e e' [*s e e*]: 'you are very adept at spacing it, at endowing it with an infinite reality' even though the meaning of the symbols, meaningless in themselves, 'depends on the energy, the artistic bravura – which are indeed also a natural genius – with which they are executed' (EO 2, 140/SKS 3, 139). 'A' treats the visible components as if they have eternal significance; the Judge reminds him it is their relationship to the whole that gives them meaning, namely, the 'unity of hope and recollection' (EO 2, 143/SKS 3, 141).

Merleau-Ponty's analysis of appearances and perception clarifies why belief in existing things requires basic confidence in a world and horizons that extends beyond one's field of vision – that is, that appearances 'arc' toward a centre rather than standing on their own. Merleau-Ponty's analysis sheds light on the Judge's characterization of the lack of stability in 'A's' life as a lack of faith [*Tro*] (EO 2, 14/SKS 3, 23). In accusing 'A' of being preoccupied with possibility ('you are the epitome of any and every possibility' (EO 2, 17/SKS 3, 25)), the Judge shows that selfhood and faith in the world are a certain relationship *among* possibilities rather than a willed commitment to just one. The Judge concludes his letter to 'A' by reminding him of the importance of hope in the future and recollection of the past. These temporal horizons allow movement without treating each variation as a new object that appears from nowhere. In keeping with Merleau-Ponty's intimation that perception requires trust, the Judge describes faith as a relation to the world, claiming 'I would lose the whole world only when I lost this faith' (EO 2, 276/SKS 3, 262).

Moving quickly past the perceptual levels, however, interpreters more often draw conclusions about the importance of practice over theory (e.g., Howland 2017; Berthold 2006), such as by cultivating a kind of personal openness or a humble attitude of the will (Evans 1989; Carr 1996). Wessel Stoker, after rightly emphasizing the importance of teleology and movement for marriage in *Either/Or*, draws a normative conclusion for art: it should have a functional relation to existence (2010: 185–6, 194). A phenomenological reading takes Kierkegaard to mean something more far-reaching: imaginative activity reveals the teleological structure of all experience. Appearances aim beyond themselves, and our implicit grasp of whether and how they do determines whether or not we believe in them.

Yet Kierkegaard and the pseudonyms do often characterize imagination as aimless and arbitrary rather than unifying. According to Judge William, 'A' creates 'an ideal image [*et idealt Billede*]' that hides his own reality and, lacking inner teleology, can be conjured up 'in any direction' (EO 2, 202/SKS 3, 195). In light of such criticisms, I suggest it is not images (appearances) or imagination that are the problem. Instead, a phenomenological understanding of perception would lead us to expect that what is missing is a certain (teleological) relation among the images. We do in fact find the Judge claiming that 'A' ignores or outright thwarts teleological convergence in his own life:

> You are like a woman in labor, and yet you are continually holding off the moment and continually remaining in pain. If a woman in her distress were to have the idea that she would give birth to a monstrosity or were to ponder just what would be born of her, she would have a certain similarity to you. Her attempt to halt the process of nature would be futile, but your attempt is certainly possible, for in a spiritual sense that by which a person gives birth is the *nisus formativus* [formative striving] of the will, and that is within a person's own power.
>
> (EO 2, 205–6/SKS 3, 198)

Every human, claims the judge, has a natural need to form a life-view (EO 2, 179/SKS 3, 175). The fascination with arbitrary things comes from trying to avoid a centre toward or around which one could develop, which he accomplishes mainly by constructing an ideal image [*et idealt Billede*] of himself for others and then shattering the image, 'which makes you start all over again' (EO 2, 202/SKS 3, 195).

Yet 'A's review of *The First Love*, I argue below, suggests that the natural movement toward wholeness is already at work at the most basic level of doubt and belief (that is, in real identity through changes in time), even if the whole personality is not yet involved. The Judge is inviting 'A' into a space in which present actions have implications for the future and rely on the past. In contrast to some readings of Kierkegaard (Howland 2017: 109), any resolution of the tensions within *Either/Or* will be not only practical and personal but imaginative – that is, a mental act of drawing together appearances as part of a whole.

Belief and illusion in *The First Love*

While *Either/Or* has been foundational for debates about selfhood and agency (Kosch 2006), the centrality of illusion to the work – especially 'A's' review of *The First Love* – has received less attention. Passages on wholeness seem to make good enough sense when taken to be about committed action and will, as when 'A' describes literary work as 'a production out of nothing' (EO 1, 236/SKS 2, 230). Yet the review of *The First Love* shows the importance of what surrounds a work for its meaning, observing that 'strange forces seem to produce what a person believes belongs to himself' (EO 1, 237/SKS 2, 231), including the occasion for writing (in this case, a play that 'A' wants to review). He clarifies that the occasion, while not the work itself, is 'the tenuous, almost invisible web in which the fruit is suspended' (EO 1, 235/SKS 2, 229). He then goes on to say, 'Without the occasion, nothing at all actually occurs, and yet the occasion has no part at all in what occurs' (EO 1, 238/SKS 2, 231–2). The occasion as a background context plays a similar role to the world in general in Merleau-Ponty's analysis, as the background of reality in which meaningful action occurs.

So what elements of *The First Love* has 'A' taken as an occasion? The play has illusion as its theme: Emmeline suffers from childish illusions as well as her simplistic mental image of Charles (discussed above), and Charles, while in some ways more mature, has a deep confidence in his own powers of deception ('mystifying'), which 'A' describes as an illusion about his own talent (EO 1, 250–1/SKS 2, 244). Like 'A' himself (in the Judge's opinion), the characters' motives are arbitrary, lacking any deep guiding principle. Emmeline blindly follows her self-imposed rule that one loves only once, which 'A' describes as a 'numerically qualified thesis' (EO 1, 254/SKS 2, 247), observing that the character development, if we can call it that, is accidental (EO 1, 255/SKS 2, 248). As mentioned above, Emmeline shows herself throughout to be preoccupied with superficial appearances, with a tendency to accept things she reads in an undigested way. She thinks Charles changes because he no longer confides in her, which 'A' describes as 'one of her ideas from novels' and, more concretely, as above, because he no longer has the ring (as if Emmeline were an obedient genie (EO 1, 270/SKS 2, 262)). At least in the context of the review, 'A' demonstrates the ability the Judge thinks he lacks: he recognizes identity through superficial changes by showing disdain for the characters who fail at it.

So in emphasizing the inner teleology of love that transforms first love within marriage without destroying it, the Judge merely extends 'A's' own observations about the play *The First Love* (EO 2, 60/SKS 3, 66). He describes the transfiguration of love in the higher ethical and religious spheres (EO 2, 56/SKS 3, 62). In marriage, he claims, there is a synthesis of the initial moment of first love with earlier and later time, even eternity: 'It is in the instant, sound and powerful; it points beyond itself, but in a deeper sense than the first love, for the abstract character of first love is precisely its defect, but in the intention that marriage has, the law of motion is implicit, the possibility of an inner history' (EO 2, 61/SKS 3, 67).

Identity through change is 'A's' own idea, now re-packaged as a criticism of 'A's' lifestyle. In fact, 'A's' review ends with an exercise in isolating and juxtaposing appearances – in this case, a literal process of opening and closing one's eyes. 'A' envisions looking at each actor in turn, overlaying images present with those held in mind to form a composite by repeating the movements 'so quickly that they become almost simultaneous in the moment' (EO 1, 278/SKS 2, 269–70). He contrasts sketching, where 'the art is to transform oneself into a surface,' with the stage, which must produce many contradictory surfaces at once (EO 1, 279/SKS 2, 270). Just as 'B' urges, 'A' recognizes the importance of putting things together, though here in a contrived way.

Have we not arrived back at a practical problem, perhaps that 'A' knows what to do but fails to accomplish it or apply it to himself? 'A' considers and rejects this option in the 'Diapsalmata':

'What should I do? Be active in the world, people say. Should I then communicate my sorrow to the world, make one more contribution to prove how pitiable and wretched everything is...?' (EO 1, 35/SKS 2, 44). The world looks one way to 'A' whether or not he acts on it. (And if 'A' is indeed the seducer, acting on his views is not his problem.) The Judge introduces him to another way things could look, emphasizing what endures invisibly:

> Perhaps you have forgotten, just as I have, most of the contents of my previous letters. If so, I wish that you may be able, as I am, at any time and in any variable mood to give an account to yourself of the thought and the development. Like the flower that comes year after year, the expression, the presentation, the wrappings are the same and yet not the same, but the attitude, the development, the position are unchanged.
> (EO 2, 337/SKS 3, 317)

The kind of continuity the Judge describes is organic: a perennial flower. While 'A' celebrates the power of remembering and forgetting (EO 1, 292/SKS 2, 282), 'B' finds comfort in what remains the same no matter what. Just as for Merleau-Ponty, reality is a background we count on in and through appearances rather than something held explicitly in mind. The Judge describes faith (or what 'A' lacks) as an ability to see in a new way: 'With this faith, I see the beauty of life.... The beauty I see is joyous and triumphant and stronger than the whole world. And this beauty I see everywhere, also there where your eyes see nothing' (EO 2, 276/SKS 3, 262).

Continuity and faith in *The Concept of Anxiety*

In *The Concept of Anxiety*, the pseudonym Vigilius Haufniensis's discussions of continuity are concerned more directly with religious faith. As we would expect from the discussion above, Haufniensis describes faith as embodying a continuity of possibilities in contrast with 'the sudden' (CA, 129–32/SKS 4, 430–3). In addition to recognizing continuity (or not), Haufniensis describes higher-level attitudes a person can take toward their own powers. Whereas 'A' was already aware of the context (occasion) as an invisible part of what appears, the imagined characters in *The Concept of Anxiety* realize their ability to attend to horizons beyond what appears – that is, to nothing – which becomes the basis for anxiety. Just as the occasion has real significance for a literary work, the 'nothing' that surrounds experience can have real consequences for individuals: 'This may be expressed by saying that the nothing that is the object of anxiety becomes, as it were, more and more a something' (CA, 61/SKS 4, 366). In anxiety, an individual realizes that events 'signify' [*betyder*] beyond themselves (CA, 76/SKS 4, 380) and yet, as a mere possibility, what the present signifies is, as of now, 'nothing' (CA, 77/SKS 4, 380). Objects for consciousness have an inherent temporal relation to past and future (CA, 89/SKS 4, 392). As relations or horizons rather than independent objects, however, the past and future are not strictly 'there' and can more readily be doubted. Nevertheless, they belong to the arc of consciousness. In describing faith as the antidote to anxiety, Haufniensis is describing a synthesis in which the present and its horizons are posited as a unity rather than isolated or denied.[3]

Haufniensis is wary of some kinds of continuity as well, which brings its own kind of anxiety. The other kinds of anxiety remind us that we ought not to be too attached to one idea. In addition to being a unifying power, faith is also a 'willingness to be vulnerable to a voice not my own' (Westphal 2008: 150). Haufniensis rejects sameness, leading some commentators to say that maturity and faith would mean accepting the dissolution of the self (Rumble 1995). Yet the mixture of praise and suspicion of continuity makes sense if Haufniensis is rejecting superficial sameness in favour of trust in the promise of a deeper identity. In this way, '[a]n adherent of the most rigid orthodoxy may be demonic' (CA, 139–40/SKS 4, 440). While we might think of sudden changes as the 'demonic,' Haufniensis is here saying that staying in one place can reveal just as much discontinuity with one's context and imply a similar lack of inner unity. Even more surprisingly, the dogmatist lacks 'certitude' [*Vished*] (CA, 140/SKS 4, 440). But even this charge makes sense if faith is always a confidence in *even more* than what has already appeared. The more understanding one achieves, the more concerned one can become about its loss (CA, 101/SKS 4, 403). One might cling to the certainty one has out of fear there is nothing beyond what is already given.

Once again, Haufniensis's description of faith anticipates Merleau-Ponty's account of objective reality, even calling the way each moment surpasses itself an 'ambiguity' [*Tvetydige*] (CA, 89/SKS 4, 392). In addition to confidence in a centre of orientation that does not directly appear, Merleau-Ponty similarly emphasizes the movement of consciousness and the need to be open to the new:

> The acquired, then, is only truly acquired if it is taken up in a new movement of thought, and a thought is only situated if it itself assumes its situation. The essence of consciousness is to provide itself with one or many worlds, to make its own thoughts exist *in front of* itself like things, and sketching out these landscapes and abandoning them indivisibly demonstrates its vitality. The structure 'world,' with its double moment of sedimentation and spontaneity, is at the center of consciousness.
>
> *(2012: 131)*

Merleau-Ponty describes a patient, by contrast, who cannot grasp narrative structures and for whom life has no horizons (133–7).[4] His life lacks an intentional arc, which would project past and future as part of the present situation, and he is unable to entertain possibilities like going for a walk or playing: 'To play is to place oneself momentarily in an imaginary situation, to amuse oneself in changing one's "milieu." The patient, however, cannot enter into a fictional situation without converting it into a real situation' (136). Something similar can happen to all of us when we are tired: 'then my "world" of thought becomes impoverished and is reduced even to one or two obsessive ideas' (132). Kierkegaard anticipates Merleau-Ponty by embodying different 'pathologies' imaginatively, that is, through imaginary construction, organizing them systematically as 'stages.'

Both philosophers conclude that perception is more than what is immediately visible. Perceived objects include a richness of possibility that, as non-sensory, can fail to be recognized even when the senses and raw imagination work well. Yet imagination, as the power of possibility and therefore of continuity, is needed to go beyond the strictly visible. By showing the similarity in the relation of appearances to reality for the two thinkers, I have shown how each invokes the teleological direction of imagination toward belief.

Conclusion

If we read too quickly, Kierkegaard's exhortations toward existence begin to sound like nothing more than self-help reminders to act on ideals and pursue dreams in reality. While useful, such advice would hardly require pseudonyms or other forms of indirect communication: these are goals we already like and accept. Rather, Kierkegaard's work discloses the hidden background of experience we take for granted, as well as the doubts, denials, and illusions made possible by these invisible horizons. Reading Kierkegaard in light of Merleau-Ponty's later analyses of perception suggests that language of 'existence' in Kierkegaard may be about mental activities and the unity of consciousness rather than the value of practice over theory. Kierkegaard might be urging something more like narrative unity in one's life (Rudd 2007; 2012), for example, while recognizing the danger of forcing a simplistic story (Lippitt 2007; 2015; Helms 2015). Or he might be motivating conceptual transitions with the help of imagination (Ferreira 1991a; 1991b: 57–84). These activities are theoretical in the sense of mental and conceptual, although of course any change in perspective is likely to make a practical difference as well.

A phenomenological view also has implications for how to read Kierkegaard's work as a whole, following Haufniensis's encouragement to look for underlying continuities: 'It is easy to sketch the various views that are possible and at various times have been actual. This may be of significance, because the diversity of the views may lead to a definition of the concept' (CA, 119/SKS 4, 421). Such an interpretive strategy would be holistic, in contrast with the view, for example, that Kierkegaard's work 'culminates . . . in the subject's self-revocation, an awkward suspension of the act of communication, arrested in mid-performance' (Rumble 1995: 319). Nevertheless, it is surely true, as Joakim Garff has argued, that we cannot take anything Kierkegaard says at face value (1998: 99). However, if Kierkegaard's pseudonyms present aspects of a whole – variations around a centre that does not itself appear – Kierkegaard's project is not disrupted by taking the scenic route through revocations, irony, or other elements sometimes named as leaving the reader to her own devices (e.g., Westfall 2009). Rather than isolated images whose integrity fails on a closer look (like hallucinations), what we find is a remarkable consistency in Kierkegaard's writings, including among the pseudonyms, underlying their many differences.

I have argued that Kierkegaard's account of imagination and belief goes beyond their role in the aesthetic stage as well as specific conclusions about art and its relation to real life. Nevertheless, works of art do often rely more conspicuously on implicit context, making art and aesthetic categories useful for clarifying activities of consciousness that may otherwise go unnoticed. In *Stages on Life's Way* Frater Taciturnus shows how intense passion in a play appears comic unless the hero is self-aware, marking the difference between comedy and tragedy (SLW, 421/SKS 6, 393). Taciturnus claims the reader's consciousness transcends the characters': a hero may die while readers are nevertheless aware the hero has triumphed in an ethical sense. The author trusts readers to recognize an (invisible) ideal according to which the hero has triumphed despite outward appearances, which occurs when elements of the play are taken to signify something that is not directly presented but that alters our understanding of *all* its events. Discussions of comedy and tragedy in *Either/Or* show how concepts relate to action in just the way Aristotle thought – that is, teleologically, as the implicit whole to which the action belongs.

In the same spirit, Merleau-Ponty observes that none of the pathologies he analyzes have the last word. Even false appearances are never entirely closed off from the rest of consciousness: 'I never fully become an object in the world; the fullness of being of a thing is always lacking for me, my own substance always runs away from me through the inside, and some intention is always sketched out' (2012: 168). For Kierkegaard, too, each of the imaginary constructions is incomplete and, on its own, unstable. While the intentional arc can be denied (as with 'A's' reluctance to move beyond first love), it remains as a possibility for which anxiety may be the only reminder. Imagination, rather than being an obstacle to faith and deeper selfhood, becomes our link to what is beyond immediate appearances. Kierkegaardian faith depends on this ability to recognize a richness in experience that is not strictly or immediately 'there.' Rather than being a call to will something or feel something, faith may be a call to see something in this richer sense. As Haufniensis puts it, 'life is rich enough, if only one understands how to see. One need not travel to Paris and London; besides, this would be of no help if one is unable to see' (CA, 74/SKS 4, 378).

Related topics

'The ethical life of aesthetes,' Ulrika Carlsson; 'Varieties of existential uncertainty,' Rick Anthony Furtak; 'Kierkegaard's experimenting psychology,' William McDonald.

Notes

1 There are debates within Kant studies and in the phenomenological tradition about the differences between 'reality,' 'existence,' and 'actuality' that I do not take a position on here. Briefly, 'reality,' 'existence,' and 'actuality' are distinct categories among Kant's 12 concepts of understanding. Kant associates reality with sensory content, which means it could admit of degrees, while existence would be all or nothing (Schwarz 1987). In context, it seems that Kierkegaard uses both the words 'existence' [*Tilværelse*] and 'reality' [*Realitet*] for that which is not merely illusory, or what Merleau-Ponty calls 'reality.' I expect further study might reveal differences in Kierkegaard's use.
2 Wessel Stoker describes the association between Romantic imagination and avoiding commitment (2010: 182), citing *The Concept of Irony*. He also goes on, however, to describe B as presenting an 'ethical aesthetics' in the second part of *Either/Or*, and Kierkegaard himself as establishing a 'theological aesthetics' (Stoker 2010: 187–94).
3 Patrick Stokes (2011) examines the unity of the self through memory and imagination in relation to Kierkegaard's concept of 'contemporaneity,' which I have not discussed here. I have focused instead on relationships of appearances as they enable us to identify an object as the same over time. While there is certainly an implicit reference to the self who does the remembering and imagining, self-reference is not sufficient for recognizing a particular object as the same.
4 Merleau-Ponty's account calls to mind Kierkegaard's critiques of Hans Christian Andersen's *Only a Fiddler* in *From the Papers of One Still Living*. Kierkegaard objects to 'developments' in the main character's (Christian's) life that are unrelated to and unmotivated by other incidents.

References

Berthold, D. (2006) 'Live or tell,' *Philosophy and Literature*, 30, no. 2: 361–77.
Carlsson, U. (2016) 'Kierkegaard's phenomenology of spirit,' *European Journal of Philosophy*, 24, no. 3: 629–50.
Carr, K. (1996) 'The offense of reason and the passion of faith: Kierkegaard and anti-rationalism,' *Faith and Philosophy*, 13, no. 2: 236–51.
Evans, C. S. (1989) 'Does Kierkegaard think beliefs can be directly willed?' *International Journal for Philosophy of Religion*, 26: 173–84.
Ferreira, M. J. (1991a) 'Kierkegaardian transitions: Paradox and pathos,' *International Philosophical Quarterly*, 31, no. 1: 65–80.
Ferreira, M. J. (1991b) *Transforming vision: Imagination and will in Kierkegaardian faith*, Oxford: Clarendon Press.
Garff, J. (1998) 'The eyes of Argus: "The Point of View" and points of view on Kierkegaard's work as an author,' in J. Rée and J. Chamberlain (eds), *Kierkegaard: A Critical Reader*, Oxford: Blackwell: 75–102.
Gouwens, D. (1993) 'Understanding, imagination, and irony in Kierkegaard's *Repetition*,' in R. Perkins (ed), *International Kierkegaard Commentary*, vol. 6 (*Fear and Trembling* and *Repetition*), Macon, GA: Mercer University Press, 283–308.
Gouwens, D. (1982) 'Kierkegaard on the ethical imagination,' *The Journal of Religious Ethics*, 10, no. 2: 204–20.
Gregor, B. (2009) 'Thinking through Kierkegaard's Anti-Climacus: Art, imagination, and imitation,' *The Heythrop Journal*, 50, no. 3: 448–65.
Helms, E. (2015) 'The end in the beginning: Eschatology in Kierkegaard's literary criticism,' in J. Lippitt and P. Stokes (eds), *Narrative, Identity, and the Kierkegaardian Self*, Edinburgh: Edinburgh University Press, 113–25.
Howland, J. (2017) 'The explosive maieutics of Kierkegaard's "Either/Or,"' *The Review of Metaphysics*, 71, no. 1: 106–35.
Kosch, M. (2006) '"Despair" in Kierkegaard's "Either/Or,"' *Journal of the History of Philosophy*, 44, no. 1: 85–97.

Lippitt, J. (2007) 'Getting the story straight: Kierkegaard, MacIntyre and some problems with narrative,' *Inquiry*, 50, no. 1: 34–69.

Lippitt, J. (2015) 'Forgiveness and the Rat Man: Kierkegaard, "Narrative Unity" and "Wholeheartedness" Revisited,' in J. Lippitt and P. Stokes (eds), *Narrative, Identity, and the Kierkegaardian Self*, Edinburgh: Edinburgh University Press, 126–43.

Merleau-Ponty, M. (2012) *Phenomenology of perception*, D. Landes (trans), London: Routledge.

Pattison, G. (1991) 'Kierkegaard: Aesthetics and "the aesthetic,"' *British Journal of Aesthetics*, 31, no. 2: 140–51.

Rudd, A. (2012) *Self, value, and narrative*, Oxford: Oxford University Press.

Rudd, A. (2007) 'In defence of narrative,' *European Journal of Philosophy*, 17, no. 1: 60–75.

Rumble, V. (1995) 'To be as no-one: Kierkegaard and Climacus on the art of indirect communication,' *International Journal of Philosophical Studies*, 3, no. 2: 302–21.

Schwarz, W. (1987) 'Kant's categories of reality and existence,' *Philosophy and Phenomenological Research*, 48, no. 2: 343–6.

Stoker, W. (2010) 'The place of art in Kierkegaard's existential aesthetics,' *Bijdragen: International Journal for Philosophy and Theology*, 71, no. 2: 180–96.

Stokes, P. (2011) 'Uniting the perspectival subject: Two approaches,' *Phenomenology and Cognitive Science*, 10: 23–44.

Stokes, P. (2010) *Kierkegaard's mirrors: Interest, self, and moral vision*, London: Palgrave Macmillan.

Walsh, S. (1994) *Living poetically: Kierkegaard's existential aesthetics*, University Park, PA: Pennsylvania State University.

Westfall, J. (2009) 'Ironic midwives: Socratic maieutics in Nietzsche and Kierkegaard,' *Philosophy and Social Criticism*, 35, no. 6: 627–48.

Westphal, M. (2008) *Levinas and Kierkegaard in dialogue*, Bloomington, IN: Indiana University Press.

Wietzke, W. (2013) 'Practical reason and the imagination,' *Res Philosophica*, 90, no. 4: 525–44.

Further reading

Furtak, R. (2018) *Knowing emotions: Truthfulness and recognition in affective experience*, Oxford: Oxford University Press.

This new book offers an account of layers of value in experience at the level of perception and sensory experience.

Hanson, J. (ed) (2007) *Kierkegaard as phenomenologist: An experiment*, Evanston, IL: Northwestern University Press.

Essays in this collection examine similarities and differences between Kierkegaard's work and that of phenomenologists including Edmund Husserl, Martin Heidegger, Emmanuel Levinas, and Jacques Derrida.

Zuckert, R. (2007) *Kant on beauty and biology*, Cambridge: Cambridge University Press.

Zuckert develops Kant's teleological view in the context of both art and purposes in nature, including the relation between appearances and belief in existence.

25
AGENCY, IDENTITY, AND ALIENATION IN *THE SICKNESS UNTO DEATH*

Justin F. White

> I am much of what my parents and especially my grandparents were – inherited stature, colouring, brains, bones (that part unfortunate), plus transmitted prejudices, culture, scruples, likings, moralities, and moral errors that I defend as if they were personal and not familial.
>
> (*Wallace Stegner, Angle of Repose*)

> There is another woman in me, I'm afraid of her – she fell in love with that man, and I wanted to hate you and couldn't forget the one who was there before. The one who is not me. Now I'm real, I'm whole.
>
> (*Leo Tolstoy, Anna Karenina*)

Introduction

In *The Sickness unto Death*, Kierkegaard describes selfhood as an achievement, specifically claiming that the self's task 'is to become itself' (SUD, 29/SKS 11, 146). Potentially about this sort of task, Kierkegaard writes in a journal entry from December 3, 1854, 'to become human or to learn what it means to be human does not come that easily' (JP 2, 278/SKS 26, 362).[1] But how can one become who or what one already is, and what sort of achievement is it? Contemporary philosophy of agency commonly assumes that not all desires or movements that occur in us are equally ours.[2] Fleeting, incomprehensible desires and muscle spasms, for example, seem to happen to us and not be things we do. But what makes some desire or action uniquely an agent's own or, more technically, internal to the agent or one with which the agent is identified? Or, conversely, when can we dismiss desires or actions as not the agent's own, as external or alien? Sometimes our bodies move in ways that are clearly not up to us, as with a muscle spasm. But what about unbidden and potentially unwelcome desires? Or beliefs and dispositions inherited through upbringing? It is not obvious whether beliefs we inherit from parents or culture without consciously endorsing them are internal to us. Nor is it straightforward how to interpret Anna Karenina's attributing her actions to 'another woman in me,' someone who 'is not me' (Tolstoy 2000: 412). The mere fact that someone experiences an action or desire as external could seem to resolve the issue: if she experiences it as alien, it happens to her and she does not do it. Yet there are reasons to dig deeper.

We are conglomerates of traits, desires, and beliefs – some inherited, some actively acquired, some with hybrid ancestry – and we are tasked with integrating these different aspects into a coherent whole or self. As we adopt, winnow, and shape these components, we can find ourselves doing things that seem foreign to us. But what does it mean when desires or actions are experienced as alien or external? Kierkegaard's accounts of the structure of the self and of selfhood as a task suggest several ways we can be alienated from desires, actions, or, more generally, our selves. As 'the contemporary philosopher who argues most thoroughly for the task-oriented nature of self-constitution' (Lear 2011: 4), Christine Korsgaard and her notion of practical identity make sense for analysing the task of becoming oneself. Furthermore, Kierkegaard's treatment of selfhood – as aspirational and, if undertaken well, appropriately grounded in one's facticity (i.e., the concrete facts of one's situation) – suggests how consciously endorsed identities can guide (or fail to guide) our agency. Having a practical identity involves striving to inhabit adopted roles by aligning our actions with relevant normative demands, but also sometimes embracing and consciously adopting identities already tacitly guiding our engagement with the world.

This chapter has two guiding lines of inquiry. First, what does it mean to achieve selfhood and how can the notion of practical identity illuminate or be illuminated by this question? Second, how can this analysis clarify the experience of not being oneself, whether resulting from self-deception, self-ignorance, or the potentially frustrating gap between who one is and who one wants to be?

Desires (and actions) of one's own and the possibility of alienation

Both Kierkegaard and Harry Frankfurt describe processes through which we become ourselves (Kierkegaard) or make desires our own (Frankfurt). Frankfurt (1988) thinks reflective self-evaluation that leads to the formation of higher-order desires (desires about desires) is unique to persons. By identifying with a desire and wanting it to lead to action, we make it internal and make ourselves morally responsible for resulting actions. By contrast, if we wish we didn't have a desire or wish it didn't lead to action, it becomes external to us. Because we are not fully behind the wheel in such cases – whether passively observing or actively working against the desire – we are not fully responsible for resulting actions. Frankfurt (1988: 63) uses the example of someone overcome with emotion:

> In the course of an animated but amiable enough conversation, a man's temper suddenly rushes up in him out of control. Although nothing has happened that makes his behavior readily intelligible, he begins to fling dishes, books, and crudely abusive language at his companion. Then his tantrum subsides and he says, 'I have no idea what triggered that bizarre spasm of emotion. The feelings just came out of me from out of nowhere, and I couldn't help it. I wasn't myself. Please don't hold it against me.'

Kierkegaard's discussion of despair in *The Sickness unto Death* has similar concerns. In despair, one fails to become oneself either by failing to see (or hiding from the fact) that one is responsible for one's self or by failing to (1) adequately acknowledge and engage with one's facticity or (2) live in light of the fact that one is not reducible or limited to one's facticity.

Engaging with both Frankfurt and Kierkegaard, Mark Wrathall (2015) argues that Kierkegaard's conception of subjectivity as an achievement is more successful than Frankfurt's hierarchical model at explaining how acts and, by extension, a life can be an agent's own. Frankfurt's initial account, as Gary Watson (2004) indicates, fails to explain why some higher-order desire uniquely speaks for the agent. Wrathall (2015: 429) thinks that what is missing is 'some prior vision of who I am or ought to be which guides me in my identifications, some prior sense of self with which my choices can resound.' This vision serves as the basis for reflective self-evaluation as I sift through desires in order to forge a coherent identity (Wrathall 2015: 429, 438, 441). For Kierkegaard, the thought of immortality focuses 'my attention on the style of personality that *is* (or that *I want to be*) essential to being me' (Wrathall 2015: 438; emphasis added). As Wrathall describes it, my sense of self involves a vision of who I am or ought to be. My claim is that, for Kierkegaard, proper selfhood involves a vision of who I am *and* (not 'or') who I ought (or want) to be. Agents failing to properly attend to either aspect fall short of ideal selfhood/agency.

When my body moves or I experience a desire, those are both mine in some sense – they are not anyone else's (see Frankfurt 1988: 60). But it seems justifiably intuitive to distinguish robust actions from muscle spasms and, more controversially, out-of-character actions from those that align with one's core values. Similarly, unbidden and unwelcome desires seem differently, presumably less, mine than desires I have cultivated and happily entertain. However, pinning down what differentiates these can be difficult. Typically, examples of externality are those in which one falls short of one's ideals – one experiences alienation when acting in uncharacteristically bad ways. The tendency to distance the agent *qua agent* from bad actions seems problematic, however, because agents also act in uncharacteristically virtuous ways. Yet even though people deflect praise in various ways – 'I just did what anyone would have done,' for example – I suspect we are less likely to consider uncharacteristically virtuous actions as external. Admittedly, this could just make us suspicious of the tendency (both in the literature and in everyday experience) to see uncharacteristically vicious actions as external. However, the structure of the self, as Kierkegaard understands it, offers another explanation for this asymmetry. Because we are existentially grounded but also drawn to be different than we are, practical identities rightly appeal to descriptions that may not (yet) fit our behaviour. When seeking to change, we may find ourselves alienated from actions that are still consistent with our current character.[3]

The significance of claims to not have been oneself depends on the way in which one does not consciously identify with (or see oneself as inhabiting) some identity, whether those are roles such as parent or teacher, or traits such as being patient or ambitious. This sort of claim could arise out of genuine self-ignorance, motivated self-deception, or out of a conscious effort to try to change oneself. First, I could be self-ignorant, unaware of the sort of person I am. If I inaccurately think of myself as a patient person, I could see impatient actions as instances when I am not myself (even if they occur regularly). Over time, however, it may be hard to describe this as mere self-ignorance. When I try to hide certain truths or facts about myself from myself, I enter the territory of self-deception and/or active repression. Rather than face unpleasant truths about myself, I could in some way convince myself that that is not who I really am. Finally, I could purposefully reject an identity I am trying to leave behind. I could be aware of my tendency to lose my temper and consciously identify as a patient individual, striving to make it the case. These different possibilities suggest that even if we are imperfect judges of ourselves, mere scepticism about the accuracy of self-judgments is a simplistic general approach to claims to not have been oneself.

For Kierkegaard, integral selfhood involves proper grounding in one's facticity and aspiring within or beyond it. Falling short in either way is problematic. A Kierkegaardian analysis of practical identity – including the complex relationship between who we aspire to be and who we find ourselves being – yields different types of alienation.[4] In the despairs of infinitude and possibility, one is inadequately grounded in one's finitude/necessity; in the despairs of finitude and necessity, one fails to appreciate one's infinitude/possibility – the capacity to aspire and to want to be different. This analysis also shows why repression and wishful thinking can lead to troubles in one's agency. Of Freud's Rat Man, J. David Velleman (2006: 346) says, '[He] chose to regard his hatred as foreign because he was afraid of letting it into his emotional life, even though doing so was his only chance of domesticating it. All of us are like the Rat Man at least to this extent, that we feel threatened by various emotions that would introduce conflict into our lives.' By isolating his hatred as foreign, the Rat Man makes it less likely that he can control it (see Lippitt 2015: 132–3). For Kierkegaard, because the self is necessity *and* finitude, but also possibility *and* infinitude, good agency takes account of one's necessity and finitude (including unruly desires), but as possibility and infinitude, it also incorporates, develops, and builds on its facticity.[5]

Selfhood and varieties of despair

Practical identities involve both what Kierkegaard calls externalities (including contingent roles) and the infinite, or the naked self (see SUD, 53–5/SKS 11, 168–71 for a discussion of the relationship between 'externalities' and the 'naked abstract self'). Externalities are crucial to but not exhaustive of who we are. We can strive or aspire to become different. Aspiration could sound like the problematic despair in which one wants to be someone else, but aspirational agency is not only compatible with but necessary to the task of becoming oneself. Different kinds of despair result when agents fail to integrate either aspect of practical identity. On a conceptual level, we can either (1) fail to account for the normative or aspirational dimension of human agency or (2) underappreciate the extent to which the contours of identities and, by extension, agency are not entirely under the agent's active, self-conscious control. The self as simultaneously something one already is and an achievement to which one aspires illuminates the grounded and dynamic nature of practical identity.

Becoming oneself and various ways of falling short are central to Kierkegaard's treatments of despair in *The Sickness unto Death* and anxiety in *The Concept of Anxiety*. He begins *The Sickness unto Death* with an infamously complex description of the structure of the self:

> A human being is spirit. But what is spirit? Spirit is the self. But what is the self? The self is a relation that relates itself to itself or is the relation's relating itself to itself in the relation; the self is not the relation but is the relation's relating itself to itself.
> (SUD, 13/SKS 11, 129)

The human being, as spirit or self, is a relation to and thus responsible for the synthesis of apparently contradictory factors. These factors, which Kierkegaard calls 'moments,' include the pairs of infinitude/finitude and possibility/necessity.[6] The pairs 'are meant to point (respectively) to a constraint and that in virtue of which the constraint is not total or determining' (Kosch 2006: 200). The synthesis 'is the activity of integrating the givenness of oneself with the set of goals or view of life one has taken up – forming one's concrete embodiment into some ideal shape . . . but also tailoring the ideal to the unchangeables of personal history, social situation, physical and psychological nature, and so on' (Kosch 2006: 201).

It could seem that to become oneself, one should simply accept one's station – including one's characteristics, dispositions, preferences, and social roles. But *becoming* oneself is not passively accepting one's facticity. One becomes who one is by taking up the accidents of one's existential situation with the understanding that those accidents do not exhaust one's self.

Kierkegaard's initially puzzling task thus highlights how human agency is grounded in but not reducible to one's facticity.

As Wrathall (2015: 426) describes the synthesis, 'the fundamental human condition is one in which, within our overall mental economy, there are contradictory or incompatible moments – that is, we all possess attitudes, affects, and aims which impel us to move in a way that, in certain key moments of our lives, will frustrate or cancel out the way other attitudes, affects or aims incline us to be moved.' The goal of selfhood is to forge 'a consistent and coherent identity that can encompass the whole of my particular attitudes and affects' (Wrathall 2015: 429). To do this, 'I need a clear sense of the subject I want to be so that this can serve as a background against which to perform the reevaluation' (Wrathall 2015: 429). A clear sense of who I want to be is crucial. But for the aspirational element of selfhood to function well, I also need a sense of who I am. Put differently, effective aspirational agency depends on one's existential situation. Wrathall (2015: 429) picks up on this when he claims, 'There must be some prior vision of who I am or who I want to be which guides me in my identifications, some prior sense of self with which my choices can resound.' For Kierkegaard, my vision of myself (and my self) involves who I am *and* who I want to be. Both aspects are necessary. And even if they are entwined, we must not reduce 'who I am' to 'who I want to be.' Wrathall highlights the aspirational dimension of practical identity – the subject I want to be determines the criteria according to which I evaluate the elements of my self – but if that aspirational self-conception is inadequately connected to my facticity, I am in despair.

Kierkegaard describes two types of despair, that is, different ways to fall short of selfhood: (1) 'despair considered without regard to its being conscious or not, consequently only with regard to the constituents of the synthesis' (for convenience, Despair$_1$) and (2) 'despair as defined by consciousness' (Despair$_2$) (SUD, 29, 42/SKS 11, 146, 157). In Despair$_1$ one element of the synthesis is over- or underemphasized (see Davenport 2013: 236). In Despair$_2$ the individual fails to take responsibility for the synthesis, whether by failing to see or hiding from the responsibility. Alastair Hannay (1997: 332) describes despair for Anti-Climacus as 'wanting to be rid of the self' (see SUD, 19–21/SKS 11, 134–7). One can want to be rid of one of the two elements of the synthesis – not making the self a synthesis of *both* elements (Despair$_1$) – or want to be rid of the responsibility for the synthesis (Despair$_2$). In this section, I focus on the Despair$_1$ arising in the syntheses of (1) finitude/infinitude and (2) necessity/possibility.

Despairs of finitude/infinitude

Kierkegaard writes, 'The self is the conscious synthesis of infinitude and finitude that relates itself to itself, whose task is to become itself, which can be done only through the relationship to God' (SUD, 29–30/SKS 11, 146).[7] In the synthesis, 'the finite is the limiting and the infinite the extending constituent' (SUD, 30/SKS 11, 146). Becoming a self is an ongoing process of moving away from and coming back to oneself (SUD, 30/SKS 11, 146). One finds oneself with moments of finitude – a body, dispositions, social expectations, language, and so forth – and with moments of infinitude – wishing, aspiring, imagining, and seeking to stretch or go beyond that finitude. Wrathall (2015: 425) thus divides the moments into those that volatilize the self – taking one beyond one's concrete patterns of existence – and those that bring one back to the facts of that concrete existence.

The despair of infinitude is closely related to imagination, 'the rendition of the self as the self's possibility' (SUD, 31/SKS 11, 147). Imagination includes distinct possibilities but also the capacity for possibility, that the self can be different than it has been. Possibility is crucial to human agency, but in the despair of infinitude, the individual goes too far and loses touch with the moments of finitude that characterize one's existence. Infinitude's despair is 'the fantastic, the unlimited. . . . The fantastic is generally that which leads a person out into the infinite in such a way that it only leads him away from himself and thereby prevents him from coming back to himself' (SUD, 30–1/SKS 11, 146–7). By aspiring to things that are not (yet) adequately connected to his existential situation, and willing things quixotically beyond the possibilities afforded him, the self – seen as pure, untethered possibility – 'is . . . infinitized, but not in such a manner that he becomes more and more himself, for he loses himself more and more' (SUD, 31/SKS 11, 147).

By contrast, Kierkegaard describes despair of finitude as reductionism or narrowness because the individual is reduced (or reduces oneself) to qualities, characteristics, or roles (SUD, 33/SKS 11, 149). Limited to moments of finitude, one fails to see and act beyond a narrow interpretation of who one is, becoming 'a number instead of a self, just one more [person], just one more repetition of this everlasting *Einerlei* [one and the same]' (SUD, 33/SKS 11, 149). Content to play out the script for one's roles – without thinking about how to make them one's own – life becomes cozy and comfortable: 'it is far easier and safer to be like the others, to become a copy, a number, a mass man' (SUD, 34/SKS 11, 149). Observers may not regard it as despair, but because selfhood involves synthesizing the finite *and* the infinite, if one does not venture beyond this narrowness, one risks losing oneself (SUD, 34–5/SKS 11, 149–51). But if despair is to want to be rid of the self, despair of finitude seems especially well-suited for avoiding self-responsibility.

Despairs of necessity/possibility

For Kierkegaard, both possibility and necessity are essential to the task of becoming oneself: 'Insofar as [the self] is itself, it is the necessary, and insofar as it has the task of becoming itself, it is a possibility' (SUD, 35/SKS 11, 151). In the despairs of possibility/necessity, however, necessity or possibility is overemphasized to the detriment of the other. Hubert Dreyfus (2008: 15) describes despair as 'The feeling that your life isn't working and, given the kind of person you are, it is impossible for things to work out for you.' It is impossible for things to work out because the self involves necessity *and* possibility, and the person in despair fails to properly attend to both.

In the despair of possibility, one has lost touch with one's own necessity. The self 'runs away from itself in possibility, it has no necessity to which it is to return. . . . Eventually everything seems possible, but this is exactly the point at which the abyss swallows up the self' and the individual becomes a mirage (SUD, 35–6/SKS 11, 151). The self lost in possibility lacks 'the power to obey, to submit to the necessity in one's life, to what may be called one's limitations' (SUD, 36/SKS 11, 152). In such cases, 'the tragedy is not that such a self did not amount to something in the world,' but 'that he did not become aware of himself, aware that the self he is is a very definite something and thus the necessary. Instead, he lost himself, because this self fantastically reflected itself in possibility' (SUD, 36–7/SKS 11, 152). Because the self is both its possibility and its necessity, selfhood and effective willing requires awareness of one's necessity. By refusing to acknowledge his limitations, he appears free, and Kierkegaard admits that he has some sort of self-mastery – 'the self is its own master, absolutely its own master, so-called' (SUD, 69/SKS 11, 183). But the mastery is 'so-called' because 'on closer examination . . . it is easy to see that this absolute ruler is a king without a country, actually ruling over nothing' (SUD, 69/SKS 11, 183).

In despair of necessity, by contrast, the individual lacks or does not see possibility. When this happens, everything becomes necessary (the determinist/fatalist) or everything becomes trivial (the philistine-bourgeois). The determinist, the fatalist, has lost his self 'because for him, everything has become necessity' (SUD, 40/SKS 11, 155). Regardless of role – 'whether alehouse keeper or prime minister' – this individual lacks imagination and thus 'lives within a certain compendium of experiences as to how things go, what is possible, what usually happens' (SUD, 41/SKS 11, 156). In this way, Kierkegaard thinks such an individual has lost God and one's self. These losses are connected because 'God' means that everything is possible and if one lacks (fails to see or runs from) possibility, one falls short of selfhood (SUD, 40/SKS 11, 155–6). Hannay describes this with the image of the thorn in the flesh, some limiting aspect of oneself (necessity in Kierkegaard's sense). One could accept the thorn as part of the 'definite thing' that one is and then 'humble oneself under this weakness' before God, for whom everything is possible (see Hannay 1997: 345). In despair of necessity, however, by identifying oneself completely with the thorn, one fails to incorporate the truth that 'with God everything is possible,' that there are various ways to take up the thorn in the flesh.

Instead, in this type of despair, I hold the thorn apart from myself. I want to be myself before God, but I do not want the thorn to be part of myself. Rather than own up to the weakness and humble myself under it, I try to keep it apart from myself. But in so doing, I end up holding on to the thorn (SUD, 77–8/SKS 11, 191–2). If I were to better own up to my necessity, I could better arrange my life to integrate the moments of my self. But instead of acknowledging the thorn as part of my self, I reject it and thereby ensure that it will continue to affect my existence, likely in ways not under my control.

In addition to despair in relation to the synthesis (Despair$_1$), Kierkegaard discusses despair in relation to consciousness (Despair$_2$). Despair$_2$ can take various shapes depending on one's awareness of being a self – of being responsible for the synthesis – and one's response to that awareness (see SUD, 47–74/SKS 11, 162–87). Selfhood is more than the synthesis of elements. It involves one's relationship to the synthesis and the capacity to shape it. However, not everyone is aware that they are spirit, having the freedom and responsibility to shape the synthesis, or, more colloquially, to shape their lives (SUD, 26–7/SKS 11, 142–3). But if one is unaware of being responsible for the synthesis, one is less likely to see one's hand in the shaping of one's life or to see one's actions as expressing oneself. And if one becomes aware that one is spirit, one may still ignore or run from that responsibility.

Despair, then, depends on a problematic self-synthesis or on one's awareness of being responsible for oneself and the response to that awareness. It can go unnoticed by the external observer and even the agent herself. Just as the knowledgeable physician 'does not have complete confidence in what a person says about his condition,' the physician of the soul knows that self-assessments about despair are unreliable: 'He knows what despair is; he recognizes it and therefore is satisfied neither with a person's declaration that he is not in despair nor with his declaration that he is' (SUD, 23–4/SKS 11, 140).

Practical identities and alienation

Instead of mere scepticism, however, Kierkegaard provides resources to analyze the significance of claims to not have been oneself. For Korsgaard (1996: 101), a practical identity is a 'description under which you value yourself, under which you find your life to be worth living and your actions to be worth undertaking.' These identities 'give rise to reasons and obligations. Your reasons express your identity, your nature' (Korsgaard 1996: 101). She notes that 'practical identity is a complex matter and for the average person there will be a jumble of such conceptions' (Korsgaard 1996: 101). But more than just different conceptions, I would add, the structure of practical identities involves two dimensions – one more a matter of facticity and another more a matter of our aspirational capacities. And alienation from (or despair related to) either of these dimensions leads to different ways of being alienated from our practical identities.

Korsgaard (1996: 101) often describes practical identities as roles or characteristics: 'You are a human being, a woman or a man, an adherent of a certain religion, a member of an ethnic group, a member of a certain profession, someone's lover or friend, and so on.' Of the despairing individual, Kierkegaard writes, 'He is a university graduate, husband, father, even an exceptionally competent public officeholder, a respectable father, pleasant company, very gentle to his wife, solicitude personified to his children' (SUD, 63–4/SKS 11, 178). Although describing roles as 'externalities' could make them seem to be obstacles to selfhood, good selfhood involves the agent taking up 'his concrete self or his concretion' along with its 'necessity and limitations' (SUD, 68/SKS 11, 182). When Kierkegaard emphasizes that the self is distinct from externalities, his point is that externalities do not exhaust the self (SUD, 53/SKS 11, 168–9).

Practical identities are often ongoing pursuits, with finite, grounded components and infinite, aspirational components. 'Trying to be a parent' can refer to efforts (a) to have a child or (b) to care for one's child. Thus, although being a parent involves having a child, one can still fall short at being a parent by not meeting the relevant constitutive standards.[8] So understood, practical identities capture the aspirational and grounded dimensions of human agency.

This two-pronged approach to practical identity (exemplified by Kierkegaard's account of selfhood) explains different ways desires and actions can appear as foreign. A spasm is clearly external to the agent, even if the forces causing the movement are internal to the agent's body. But other cases require more nuance. Desires and actions can appear as foreign when they go against a consciously endorsed practical identity. How Frankfurt's temper-afflicted individual sees himself likely affects whether the rise of passion appears as an intrusion, even if the passion is deeply rooted in his self. But actions departing from one's typical engagement with the world can also lead to disorientation. When working to align actions with a consciously endorsed but not yet effectively grounded practical identity, one could act in ways inconsistent with one's character or psychology.

If the self is a synthesis between the selves we want to be (infinitude/possibility) and the selves already shaping our engagement with the world (finitude/necessity), alienation can take various forms. We can be unaware of inherited social expectations or of the extent to which certain dispositions, cares, and values guide us until others point them out or we experience conflict between competing obligations. Sometimes it takes subsequent regret for us to realize how we value features of our lives. In such experiences, we could realize we are different than we assumed (cf. Hannay 1997: 333).

When discussing despair as defiance, Kierkegaard describes someone who, becoming conscious of an infinite self, desires complete control over his concrete self: 'he does not want to put on his own self, does not want to see his given self as his task – he himself wants to compose his self by means of being the infinite form' (SUD, 68/SKS 11, 182). He has achieved some self-consciousness, but by seeing himself purely as an infinite self (detached from its facticity), that self 'is so far from successfully becoming more and more itself that the fact merely becomes increasingly obvious that it is a hypothetical self' (SUD, 69/SKS 11, 183). He fails to acknowledge or incorporate his finitude/necessity (facticity) into his self-conception, holding it apart from himself (SUD, 77–8/SKS 11, 191–2). However, he could feel alienated from his facticity when his desires or actions flow from his 'given self.' He rightly grasps that he is not limited to his characteristics and roles, but he goes amiss by divorcing his possibilities from his facticity. In terms of practical identities, he understands that he has some control over the roles that guide his life, but his ability to act effectively is impeded by his ignorance of or refusal to see how some practical identities guide his actions even if he does not consciously endorse them.

In despair of finitude, when one sees oneself purely in terms of inherited norms and pre-established roles, one is alienated from the aspirational element of practical identity. One sees the identity primarily as acting in certain pre-established ways, instead of as an ongoing and dynamic pursuit. There are different ways to be a (good) teacher, for example. But the way one is absorbed in the role and one's alienation from possibility impede the ability to take up the identity in other than predefined ways. One could do this consciously – saying 'I want to be a good teacher and these are things good teachers do' – or somewhat unconsciously – absorbing rules and practices by observation or through pedagogical training but without sifting through them to determine the sort of teacher one wants to be or how to best use one's unique capabilities as a teacher.

To think through the different problematic self-syntheses in these types of alienation, let's return to Frankfurt's (1988: 63) example of the temper-afflicted individual who 'fling[s] dishes, books, and crudely abusive language at his companion.' The individual sees the emotion and actions as 'a bizarre spasm' and not as his own. But different ways of fleshing out the scenario show distinct ways the individual could experience the emotion as foreign and thus different senses of the claim to 'not have been himself.'

In the first version, imagine he sees himself as cool tempered, even-keeled, and immune to emotional excess. When he senses tides of emotion rising, he works to calm them or at least divert their course. Having aspired to become this way after studying Stoic philosophy, this self-conception is central to his conscious identity. There is only one problem with his self-conception. It's inaccurate. While it is true that he tries to stem perceived tides of rising emotion, he lacks self-awareness. Even though his actions are (often) clearly guided by (in this case unfounded) emotions, because of his self-ignorance, he does not see his actions as being guided by emotions (well-grounded or otherwise). Because his reaction contradicts his carefully cultivated self-conception, he experiences it as foreign.

In the second version, imagine he is aware of his tendency to emotional outbursts. The behaviour has led to trouble before. Despite this self-awareness, however, he does not subjectively identify with the tendency or the associated actions. He sees it consistently occurring in him but not as expressing who he is. Because he sees it as a spasm over which he lacks control, rather than seeking to change, he (perhaps bitterly) resigns himself to it as part of his life.

Although the agents in both versions experience the emotions as alien and their agency seems compromised, the experiences are different. In the first, self-ignorance leads him to overlook emotions and actions that run against his (inaccurate) self-conception. In the second, his fatalistic view of his lack of control leads him to see the actions as his, but not in a way that allows him to change. He relates to his self-synthesis as a sort of bystander (SUD, 55/SKS 11, 170–1). Patrick Stokes (2015: 185) describes the naked self as 'teleologically enjoined to take *responsibility* for the human being that it is, becoming a fully conscious and responsible ethical agent, but which is nonetheless on some level distinguishable from the *human being* it identifies with.' Identification is complex and becoming oneself is difficult because *who we are* involves *how we see ourselves* and *who we want to be* but also *how we are*, and these various elements do not always happily coincide.

Achieving selfhood and dynamic human agency

By understanding practical identity as both aspirational and grounded in one's facticity, the process of becoming oneself (or effective human agency generally) is illuminated. Effective aspirational agency must be grounded in one's facticity, which requires some self-awareness, but (at least in most cases) effectively taking up one's facticity also involves aspiration. One could aspire to be a better parent. But being a better parent is aspirational as it involves continually seeking to respond well in new situations. Effective human agency, then, involves taking up one's facticity in a way that recognizes both freedom and responsibility for one's self.

Achieving selfhood is a delicate balance 'between the need to recognise and accept our natures as having their own stubborn realities; and the need to take active responsibility for their shaping' (Rudd 2012: 244). Or as John Davenport (2013: 238) says approvingly of John Elrod's (1975) interpretation of Kierkegaard: 'existential freedom operates within the limits of an individual's facticity.' One becomes oneself within inherited parameters. If, as Stegner (1971) suggests, much of who we are comes from our parents (and family, friends, teachers, communities, and so on), our task is to take up and respond to the possibilities afforded us by the complex inheritance of genetics, culture, education, society, and the like.

The world of action is shaped by self-conscious, aspirational identities – I want to be a good parent, teacher, or scholar, and identify with those roles – but also by identities that can escape my conscious awareness – being ambitious, arrogant, or insecure. I could be guided by considerations of what a good son would do even if that identity does not appear in my conscious deliberations. I more effectively direct my actions when these components align. If self-conception and aspirations are insufficiently grounded in facticity, aspirational agency loses traction. Perhaps counter-intuitively, my agency improves as I acknowledge and embrace the ways in which my self and my life are not (entirely) up to me. In the other direction, I also miss an important aspect of robust human agency by living my identities in pre-packaged ways.

Good human agency requires awareness of one's necessity but without limiting oneself to the necessity. Although some passages of *The Sickness unto Death* place 'freedom' opposite 'necessity' in the self, more often 'possibility' rather than 'freedom' is opposed to 'necessity' (Davenport 2013: 238). Moreover, in the work as a whole, selfhood involves both possibility and necessity. Unmoored from necessity, freedom is fantastic willing. Self-ignorance creates problems because a poor grasp of one's self or one's being in the world makes it hard to change or reinforce aspects of oneself to allow for a coherent way of being in the world. Someone like Frankfurt's individual who experiences his outbursts as external will regularly succumb to aspects of himself that he does not recognize or identify as his own rather than guide them in self-directing ways. We see this in Kierkegaard's discussions of fantastic willing in *The Sickness unto Death* and anxiety experienced as fate in *The Concept of Anxiety*. In anxiety as fate, even when actions flow from the agent in some significant way, one does not see oneself as the source of the actions and so still experiences them passively, as external to oneself. Similarly, in the despair of possibility, one detached from one's facticity is less able to effectively engage with the possibilities before one.

What emerges is a more modest sense of agency. Much of the necessity that shapes our lives came (or comes) to us in ways that were (or are) not up to us. But we can develop that necessity in different ways. Anthony Rudd (2015) describes Kierkegaard's position as a paradox involving the self-shaping of Sartre and the self-acceptance of Schopenhauer. If holding these elements together is a paradox, that's appropriate because Kierkegaard thinks that the self is a synthesis of contradictory elements. Both contradictory elements are essential to selfhood but neither exhausts human agency, so it is a problem to reduce the self to either element alone. He describes an individual with 'no consciousness of a self that is won by infinite abstraction from every externality, this naked abstract self, which, compared with immediacy's fully dressed self, is the first form of the infinite self and the advancing impetus in the whole process by which a self infinitely becomes responsible for its actual self with all its difficulties and advantages' (SUD, 55/SKS 11, 170). The selfhood dynamic between the naked self and the fully dressed self requires awareness of the self's externalities and of the ways in which we must submit to our necessity.

But understanding that we are more than those externalities and necessity allows us to better pursue our possibilities, including becoming and sometimes changing ourselves. As grounded beings, genuine possibilities must be grounded in our facticity; as aspirational beings, our practical identities stretch beyond our current dispositions and situations. Even if much of who we are is inherited, then, given the sort of selves we are, working through that inheritance is complex and we can find ourselves alienated from our facticity and our aspirations in the process. But, given the creatures (or selves) we are, we distort our natures in both theory and practice if we try to do otherwise.

Related topics

'The ethical life of aesthetes,' Ulrika Carlsson; 'Conscience, self-deception, and the question of authenticity in Kierkegaard,' Claudia Welz.

Notes

1 Jonathan Lear (2011: 3) begins *A Case for Irony* with this passage. In the entry, Kierkegaard attributes the view to Socrates, but he seems to endorse it.
2 See Harry Frankfurt's (1988) 'Identification and Externality,' for example.
3 This possibility does not mean that the asymmetry is always justified. Kierkegaard is keenly aware of our self-serving natures, which can also explain some claims to 'not have been oneself.' In short, although this is not the focus of this chapter, there is a Kierkegaardian case for suspicion about judgments that uncharacteristically vicious actions are external. (Thanks to Patrick Stokes for help articulating this point.)
4 This is, in part, because who we are depends on how we think of ourselves and who we want to be.
5 Kierkegaard's use of 'necessity' does not align with typical use of necessity as a contrast to contingency. There are contingent facts that figure into my necessity in the Kierkegaardian sense. My height or the proportion of fast- and slow-twitch muscle fibres in my legs would typically be thought to be contingent features of my existence. But they are part of my necessity in the way they set limitations on my athletic ability, for example.
6 See Wrathall (2015: 425) for a helpful discussion of Kierkegaard's moral psychology in terms of the relationships between the moments.
7 Hubert Dreyfus (2008) thinks that Jesus shows that both sets of factors (infinite and finite) are essential and embodies of the equilibrium between them. By committing to an identity-defining project, that equilibrium becomes possible. Responding to Dreyfus, Alastair Hannay (2008: 54) argues that Jesus functions as an example of an actual way of life presented as a pattern to be imitated.
8 Lear (2011) describes this dynamic with the concept of irony.

References

Davenport, J. (2013) 'Selfhood and "spirit,"' in J. Lippitt and G. Pattison (eds), *The Oxford Handbook of Kierkegaard*, Oxford: Oxford University Press.
Dreyfus, H. (2008) 'Kierkegaard on the self,' in E. Mooney (ed), *Ethics, Love, and Faith in Kierkegaard*, Bloomington, IN: Indiana University Press.
Elrod, J. (1975) *Being and existence in Kierkegaard's pseudonymous works*, Princeton, NJ: Princeton University Press.
Frankfurt, H. (1988) *The importance of what we care about*, Cambridge: Cambridge University Press.
Hannay, A. (2008) 'Kierkegaard on commitment, personality, and identity,' in E. Mooney (ed), *Ethics, Love, and Faith in Kierkegaard*, Bloomington, IN: Indiana University Press.
Hannay, A. (1997) 'Kierkegaard and the variety of despair,' in A. Hannay and G. D. Marino (eds), *The Cambridge Companion to Kierkegaard*, Cambridge: Cambridge University Press.
Korsgaard, C. (1996) *The sources of normativity*, Cambridge: Cambridge University Press.
Kosch, M. (2006) *Freedom and reason in Kant, Schelling, and Kierkegaard*, Oxford: Oxford University Press.
Lear, J. (2011) *A case for irony*, Cambridge, MA: Harvard University Press.

Lippitt, J. (2015) 'Forgiveness and the Rat Man: Kierkegaard, "narrative unity" and "wholeheartedness" revisited,' in J. Lippitt and P. Stokes (eds), *Narrative, Identity and the Kierkegaardian Self*, Edinburgh: Edinburgh University Press.

Rudd, A. (2015) 'Kierkegaard's Platonic teleology,' in J. Lippitt and P. Stokes (eds), *Narrative, Identity and the Kierkegaardian Self*, Edinburgh: Edinburgh University Press.

Rudd, A. (2012) *Self, value, and narrative: A Kierkegaardian approach*, Oxford: Oxford University Press.

Stegner, W. (1971) *Angle of repose*, New York: Penguin.

Stokes, P. (2015) *The naked self*, Oxford: Oxford University Press.

Tolstoy, L. (2000) *Anna Karenina*, R. Pevear and L. Volokhonsky (trans), New York: Penguin.

Velleman, J. D. (2006) *Self to self*, Cambridge: Cambridge University Press.

Watson, G. (2004) 'Free agency,' in G. Watson (ed), *Agency and Answerability*, Oxford: Oxford University Press.

Wrathall, M. A. (2015) 'Trivial tasks that consume a lifetime: Kierkegaard on immortality and becoming subjective,' *Journal of Ethics*, 19: 419–41.

Further reading

Callard, A. (2018) *Aspiration*, Oxford: Oxford University Press.

Callard examines aspiration, the process by which we acquire values and through which we become a certain kind of person, as a distinctive form of agency. Without an adequate understanding of aspiration, problems emerge in theories of practical rationality, moral psychology, and moral responsibility, respectively.

Lippitt, J. (2013) 'Kierkegaard and moral philosophy: Some recent themes,' in J. Lippitt and G. Pattison (eds), *The Oxford Handbook of Kierkegaard*, Oxford: Oxford University Press.

This chapter explores the connections between Kierkegaard and recent moral philosophers, focusing on the relationship between Kierkegaard and narrative-based views of personal, specifically practical, identity. It then uses the example of self-forgiveness and the notions of wholeheartedness and ambivalence to refine our understanding of narrative unity.

Van Stee, A. (2015) 'Selves, existentially speaking,' in A. Rudd and J. Davenport (eds), *Love, Reason, and Will: Kierkegaard after Frankfurt*, London: Bloomsbury.

This paper uses Kierkegaard and Frankfurt to think through the structure of existential selves. It explores the apparent resemblances between their views – including the way they both emphasize our relations to what we love as we constitute ourselves – but also the way in which their different aims lead them to different characterizations of the structure of the self.

PART 6

Anthropology

26
KIERKEGAARD'S POST-KANTIAN APPROACH TO ANTHROPOLOGY AND SELFHOOD

Roe Fremstedal

Historical introduction

The term 'anthropology' refers both to various views regarding human nature, and to the different academic disciplines that study human beings. The first of these has a very long history, although the term 'anthropology' first appeared in 1501. Regarding the second, anthropology first became an academic discipline in the late 18th eighteenth century, and gradually became institutionalized in the first half of the nineteenth.[1] From its inception, the discipline of anthropology was divided into two very different fields of study. Contemporary physical anthropology (biological anthropology) goes back to the physiological anthropology of Ernst Platner of the late eighteenth century, a discipline that included not only anatomy but also ethnography and empirical psychology (including the relation between mind and body, a topic that was also relevant to philosophical anthropology). Kant's pragmatic anthropology, by contrast, contributed to the philosophical anthropologies of the nineteenth century as well as to the existential and phenomenological anthropologies of the twentieth (Louden 2011: 67, 81). Kant describes the difference between (Platner's) physiological anthropology and his own pragmatic anthropology by claiming that the former concerns 'what *nature* makes out of the human being,' whereas pragmatic anthropology concerns what *man* 'as a free-acting being makes of himself, or can and should make of himself.'[2] The former sees human beings as objects shaped by nature, whereas the latter emphasizes (1) what we *actually* make out of ourselves, (2) what we can *potentially* make out of ourselves, and (3) what we *ought* to make out of ourselves.

Philosophical anthropology in the nineteenth century was not only concerned with the study of human nature in general and the relation between mind and body in particular; it was also concerned with the evolution of humanity.[3] In addition to this, nineteenth-century anthropology discussed the relation between different academic disciplines extensively, particularly the relation between the humanities and (natural) sciences (Orth 1997; Marquard 1971). Like the German '*Wissenschaft*,' the Danish term '*Videnskab*' includes not only science but also the humanities and anthropology. Kierkegaard argues that science essentially differs from ethics and

319

religion. Science concerns explanatory and descriptive questions, whereas ethics and religion concern normative questions in the wide sense of how we should live our lives (KJN 9, 187f./SKS 25, 187).[4] Kierkegaard assumes that Christian theology goes beyond philosophy and science by relying on divine revelation. Christian anthropology in particular differs from philosophical anthropology by presupposing divine revelation and central dogmas of faith (cf. KJN 2, 117, 120/SKS 18, 125f.).

Kierkegaard can be seen as contributing to the nineteenth-century discourse on anthropology by distinguishing between philosophical and theological anthropology on the one hand, and between science, ethics and religion on the other.[5] His influential account of human nature and selfhood is also reminiscent of nineteenth-century anthropology. Kierkegaard develops an existential approach to anthropology which focuses on what it means to be an embodied human being and to become a self. He is concerned with what is common to all humans, at least potentially, rather than what is idiosyncratic to different individuals, groups, or historical epochs.

In the nineteenth-century context, these issues belong to philosophical (and theological) anthropology. Even though Kierkegaard rarely uses the term 'anthropology,' he is familiar with both nineteenth-century philosophical and theological anthropology, and frequently deals with anthropological issues in his work.[6] For these reasons, I will follow earlier scholarship in referring to Kierkegaard's anthropology, while acknowledging that this anthropology is closely connected to philosophical and theological psychology (cf. Nordentoft 1972; Theunissen 2005). I will also follow Theunissen (2005: 122n) in attributing *The Sickness unto Death* to Kierkegaard, although he published it under the pseudonym Anti-Climacus. Kierkegaard shares Anti-Climacus's views and ideals, but he does not claim to live up to them (KJN 6, 127/SKS 22, 130). For this reason, I assume that the content of *The Sickness unto Death* represents (or overlaps with) Kierkegaard's own views and ideals, although these ideals are highly demanding and difficult to live up to.

Method – phenomenology, dialectics, negativism

Part One of *The Sickness unto Death* gives a phenomenological description of despair, one which is reminiscent of the account given in Hegel's *Phenomenology of Spirit*, while also anticipating twentieth-century phenomenology. Like Hegel, Kierkegaard describes, analyzes, and criticizes various forms of consciousness (or self-experience) on their own terms in a dialectical and teleological progression. Like Heidegger (and Sartre), Kierkegaard not only emphasizes historicity and the relational nature of the self (Welz 2013), but also views immediate self-referentiality, *Jemeinigkeit* (mineness), as constitutive of consciousness. At the same time, however, Kierkegaard introduces a normative ethical teleology that breaks with twentieth-century phenomenology (Stokes 2010: 55–60). Although he does not claim to be scientific, he nonetheless provides a systematic analysis of despair. Despair and related phenomena are described from the first-person perspective in a reflective, methodical, and systematic manner that partially anticipates twentieth-century hermeneutic phenomenology (cf. Welz 2013).

Part Two of *The Sickness unto Death* goes beyond the philosophical anthropology in Part One by analysing the kind of despair and sense of selfhood that we experience when we become conscious of existing before God. Whereas Part One criticizes various forms of despair on their own terms, Part Two criticizes them on Christian grounds (Grøn 1997).

Perhaps the most original element in Kierkegaard's account lies in his *negativistic* approach to selfhood. *The Sickness unto Death* indicates that we only understand selfhood negatively through its failure, through despair. Because the never-ending task of 'becoming oneself' presupposes the possibility of failure (despair), becoming oneself is a recurrent problem. Indeed, despair is considered a universal problem affecting all individuals. To get a proper understanding of selfhood, therefore, we need to approach it indirectly by focusing on how despair is overcome.[7]

Human nature as a synthesis

Following earlier works such as *The Concept of Anxiety*, *The Sickness unto Death* views human nature as a *synthesis of opposites*. These opposites are described as soul and body, freedom and necessity, infinitude and finitude, eternity and temporality. In general terms, the first pole of the synthesis deals with our possibilities and our ability to be free by transcending limitations. The second pole, by contrast, deals with the constraints that limit freedom. Both of these poles are constitutive of human nature; therefore, we cannot identify exclusively with either our freedom or our given character (Rudd 2012: 31–4).

Kierkegaard introduces the concept 'facticity' as that which not only limits freedom but also makes it possible. This concept (together with the related idea of choosing oneself) represents one of Kierkegaard's most important contributions to modern European philosophy (Fremstedal 2014: ch. 3). Facticity involves always already being situated in a particular situation. We are always already particular embodied human beings, with specific histories, who are born into, and entangled in, particular traditions and particular communities. Facticity then refers to the very limits – and possibility – of human freedom, as represented by embodiment and a given (non-circumventable) historical and social context (TA, 77f., 96/SKS 8, 75, 91; KJN 4, 90/SKS 20, 90, see also CI, 281/SKS 1, 316; SUD, 36/SKS 11, 152).

Kierkegaard emphasizes the *interplay* between freedom and facticity (whereas earlier philosophical anthropology focused on activity and passivity in human beings). We choose ourselves in particular situations, which involve constraints that limit our freedom. As a result, there is a fundamental tension between facticity and freedom, which is constitutive of our human nature. This tension will develop into despair that exaggerates either facticity or freedom, unless facticity and freedom are reconciled (Rudd 2012: 48f.).

Table 26.1. Types of despair in *The Sickness unto Death*

	Inauthentic – non-conscious despair	Authentic I – conscious of despair	Authentic II – conscious of despair before God
Passivity or weakness	Despair of finitude; Despair of necessity	Despair in weakness: Despair over (1) something earthly, (2) the earthly, or (3) oneself	Despairing over one's sin; Despairing over the forgiveness of sin (offense)
Activity or defiance	Despair of infinitude; Despair of freedom	Defiance – demonic despair	In despair to dismiss Christianity

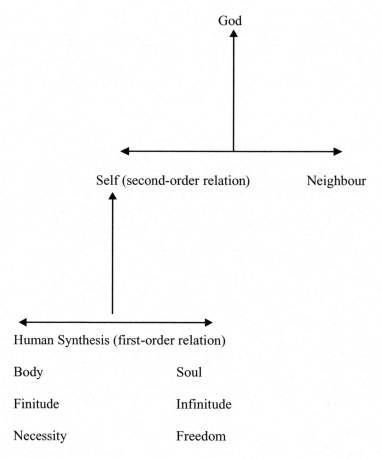

Figure 26.1 The Self and Alterity

Inauthentic (non-conscious) despair and self-deception

Kierkegaard approaches human self-realization *negatively* by studying despair, understood as a deficient form of human agency that involves double-mindedness. He distinguishes between two basic types of despair that need not be recognized consciously. The 'despair of necessity' lacks possibility (and the closely related 'despair of finitude' lacks infinity) (SUD, 33–42/SKS 11, 149–57). This type of despair denies that it is free or capable of transcending facticity. For example, a person could give up the hope of breaking a self-destructive pattern of behaviour such as excessive drinking. This type of despair gives up on life and takes a fatalistic and careless attitude towards existence. It views itself as a suffering victim, entirely in the hands of fortune. It does not try to realize itself, since it lacks the proper awareness of itself and what is involved in the task of becoming a self. It is unwilling to accept the freedom and responsibility that necessarily comes with human existence.

By contrast, the 'despair of possibility' lacks necessity (and the closely related 'despair of infinitude' lacks finitude) (SUD, 30–7/SKS 11, 146–53). It collapses by overemphasizing freedom and self-creation. It regards facticity as a mere hindrance to freedom, instead of something that makes freedom possible. It absolutizes freedom, understood negatively as freedom from limitations. As a result, freedom itself becomes abstract, fantastic and empty, since it is disconnected from the situation in which it finds itself and does not allow positive freedom to realize anything specific or concrete. Neither does it allow criteria for choosing between different possibilities or alternatives, which means that it results in arbitrariness, since all possibilities are equally valid *and* invalid.

This type of despair wants to *create itself*, without any restrictions, in order to get rid of the constraints of the present situation. This implies, however, wanting to be someone else than the person one actually is (Grøn 1997: 119ff.). The agent is therefore *double-minded* or in despair, since he is split between who he is (actuality) and who he wants to be (ideals). He is stuck in a hopeless situation, in which ideals and reality cannot be reconciled, something which epitomizes despair more generally (cf. SUD, 18/SKS 11, 133f.). The despair of possibility (futilely) wants possibility without necessity, whereas the despair of necessity (futilely) wants necessity without possibility.[8]

Taken together, these forms of despair represent the basic forms of *inauthentic* despair (SUD, 29–42/SKS 11, 145–57), a novel type of despair introduced by Kierkegaard in order to explain self-deception or bad faith. This type of despair is controversial because it need not be consciously experienced as despair by the person who is (supposedly) in despair, although it can be diagnosed from outside. Kierkegaard says that it is not authentic despair, but Theunissen (2005) questions whether it is despair at all. I believe it could nevertheless involve despair, if despair is subject to formal and objective constraints that go beyond subjective experience, just as *eudaimonia* involves such constraints. Not all forms of happiness qualify as *eudaimonia*; we can feel happy without being *eudaimon* by lacking the necessary virtues or external goods. Put differently, we might feel happy (and show no sign of authentic despair) yet be in inauthentic despair.

Eudaimonists see virtue as constitutive of eudaimonia, whereas Kierkegaard sees wholeheartedness as constitutive of proper selfhood (spirit). An agent without wholeheartedness is therefore double-minded or in despair, even if he or she fails to realize it. Since despair can be hidden or unacknowledged, Kierkegaard thinks that it is much more widespread than is usually assumed. Indeed, he thinks it is universally self-inflicted yet also possible to overcome (Fremstedal 2014; 2016). Still, despair is not merely a psychological phenomenon or something we can experience or suffer (e.g., a feeling of hopelessness). Despair always involves an *act* whereby we actively despair by giving up hope and courage. We typically suffer a loss or despair over an event, and then attribute infinite significance to it (Grøn 1997: 153).[9] Still, the person in despair may or may not be consciously aware of giving up hope and courage. Moreover, inauthentic and authentic despair seem to be ideal types that actual cases of despair resemble to varying degrees. Although despair generally involves some opacity or self-deception, there is normally some level of self-awareness involved as well. This means that very often the despairing person has at least a dim idea of his or her state (Westphal 2014: 243). Nevertheless, Kierkegaard tells us he deals with inauthentic despair 'abstractly, as if it were not the despair of any person,' whereas authentic despair concerns various actual cases of despair (SUD, 151).

Authentic (conscious) despair and selfhood

For Kierkegaard, the self is not a substance but a self-relating process, in which I relate both to the human synthesis and to the divine and human other (Stokes 2015: 145). The self is therefore conceived of in *relational* and intersubjective terms. My self-relation is (at least implicitly) intertwined with my relation to God and other human beings, so that 'a discord in any' relation 'prevents the others from taking their proper form' (Davenport 2013: 239n). Becoming myself, therefore, requires not only the right self-relation but also a proper relation to God and one's neighbours.

The Sickness unto Death distinguishes selfhood from human nature. Human nature has a latent *potential* for selfhood, but the (actualized) self is neither the human synthesis nor one of its poles (such as the soul) (SUD, 13/SKS 11, 129).[10] Instead, the self is a reflexive self-relation that relates actively to the human synthesis by forming *second-order volitions*. More specifically, selfhood requires not only self-consciousness but volitional identification with some first-order motives and alienation from others (Davenport 2012: 117). For instance, I identify with my desire to take care of my son and alienate myself from my desire to oversleep. The self is then only a self insofar as it presides over itself, or exercises self-relation, by forming second-order volitions (Westphal 2014: 238).

In addition, the term 'self' is used in different senses. On the one hand, it represents an *ideal identity* – identified with spirit – that actively overcomes despair at every instant. This is the self we are supposed to become, something that represents a never-ending task that is highly demanding (more on this in what follows). On the other hand, it represents an actual self that consciously despairs.[11] Indeed, one only becomes a self by relating to oneself, recognizing that one is in despair, and by forming second-order volitions. Whereas inauthentic despair recognizes neither selfhood nor despair (as problems or tasks to be dealt with), authentic despair is aware of both. Yet authentic despair lacks the transparency and wholeheartedness that makes it possible to overcome despair by existing before God.

Part Two of *The Sickness unto Death* deals not only with religious faith that overcomes despair, but also with despair that is conscious of existing before God, which I will examine in further detail below. *The Sickness unto Death* thus provides a *typology* of despair. Kierkegaard describes a dialectical progression of various forms of conscious despair that involve more and more self-consciousness, selfhood, and volition. The self is intertwined with self-consciousness and volition, so that intensified (second-order) volition goes together with intensified self-consciousness and selfhood. Except for the ideal self, this process of intensification also involves an intensification of despair that moves increasingly further from faith (SUD, 101/SKS 11, 213). At its most extreme, despair does not seek help, or forgiveness, but it wants to remain as despair even when it is aware of existing before God (SUD, 108–10/SKS 11, 220–2).

Kierkegaard takes all despair to be dominated by either weakness or defiance, that is, either by passivity or activity (SUD, 47/SKS 11, 162). The 'despair in weakness' does not want to be itself, whereas 'defiance' desperately wants to be itself. The former despairs over a loss or a misfortune, something that is described as 'despair over something earthly' (SUD, 50ff./SKS 11, 165ff.). This despair can develop into despair over 'the earthly' in general if one does not accept the loss, but sees it as fatal by attributing decisive importance, or infinite value, to it (SUD, 60/SKS 11, 175). Nevertheless, in a general sense, despairing over 'the earthly' implies despairing over oneself, that is, viewing oneself as too weak to overcome or accept the relevant loss. Then one is stuck in a desperate situation in which one cannot cope with the loss or realize oneself (SUD, 60ff./SKS 11, 176ff.). The problem, though, is not so much the initial loss or misfortune, as it is our response towards the loss because we relinquish all hope and courage (Grøn 1997: 153).

At the other extreme, we have the 'defiant,' or 'demonic,' who desperately wants to be himself (SUD, 71–4/SKS 11, 184–7). This creature initially strives to be himself by creating himself, something that he fails to do which leads him to conscious despair. In this situation, the defiant, or demonic, gives up hope that despair can be overcome, because he thinks that it is too late for any improvement. He rejects all help to overcome despair and takes pride in despair and victimhood by identifying with it. He is highly conscious of despair, focusing all his attention on it, while refusing to share or communicate this problem with anyone (the state of 'inclosing reserve,' *Indesluttethed*).

The defiant, or demonic, feels offended by existence, hates it, and rebels against it with rage and malice. He sees himself as the big typo in God's creation which demonstrates just how bad an author God is (SUD, 73f./SKS 11, 186f.). Still, scholars disagree over whether he pursues evil only because it is evil, or because he has a perverse understanding of the good. This is not only an exegetical question, but also a question of whether despair and *acedie* represent counter-examples to the influential view that intentional action is always prompted by something that appears good in some respect.[12]

Nevertheless, even defiance involves some weakness and vice versa. Accordingly, Kierkegaard claims that weakness and defiance are both involved in all forms of despair (SUD, 20, 49/SKS 11, 135f., 165).[13] The 'despair of weakness' does not want to be the self it is, whereas the defiant 'desperately wants to be . . . a self that he is not (for the will to be the self that he is in truth is the very opposite of despair)' (SUD, 20/SKS 11, 136). None of them wholeheartedly wants to be themselves as they are, since they value – or identify with – something they are not. And neither hope to overcome despair. As a result, they find themselves stuck in intolerable situations (cf. SUD, 18, 37/SKS 11, 133f., 153).

Overcoming despair – wholeheartedness, ethics, religion

There is always a tension in the human synthesis between our freedom and its limits, between activity and passivity, defiance and weakness. This tension results in despair (double-mindedness) unless I manage to shape my (practical) identity in a coherent manner. In order to reconcile freedom and facticity, I need not only second-order volitions, but also something that shapes and *unifies* selfhood. A unified self requires a final end, or a ground project, that I am fully committed towards in a non-instrumental manner. If I am only partially, occasionally, or conditionally committed to some project or end, then I cannot shape my whole identity, and thereby avoid despair or double-mindedness. A coherent self, one which reconciles freedom and facticity, requires unconditional commitment to one ground project rather than several conflicting ones. Only unreserved commitment to one ground project always makes it possible to shape my identity and to coordinate other projects and different roles. Without such an underlying commitment or character, my identity would lack coherence or unity, since the different roles and projects I engage in (e.g., parenting and espionage) need not then be mutually compatible even in principle (Rudd 2012: 45, 139f., 187f.).

Kierkegaard describes the process of shaping one's identity dialectically as a process of breaking with *and* returning to finitude or facticity (as alienation *and* reconciliation). It involves both negative freedom (from first-order states) and positive freedom (realized in an ideal self). Kierkegaard writes: 'the progress of becoming [oneself] must be an infinitely moving away from oneself in the infinitizing of the self, and an infinitely coming back to itself in the finitizing process' (SUD, 30/SKS 11, 146). First, one has a specific (traditional or conventional) identity by virtue of being a particular individual in a specific historical and social context. Second, the self distances itself completely from this identity by being negatively free and by imagining different possibilities and ideals. Finally, it returns to finitude by realizing ideals in reality (cf. PC, 190/SKS 12, 189). Instead of just contemplating different possibilities, the self acts in the world by being fully committed to one project. In doing this, the self both breaks with its given (traditional or conventional) identity and returns to it, by taking it over and reforming it in light of its commitments.

But not just any unconditional commitment will do. Although some aspects of life can be morally insignificant or indifferent (*adiaphora*), Kierkegaard denies that our characters or basic attitudes toward life can escape morality insofar as we are free and responsible beings. Moreover, 'Purity of heart,' Part One of *Upbuilding Discourses in Various Spirits*, argues that it is impossible to be wholeheartedly immoral, since (objective) immorality is parasitic on (objective) morality (and even immoral action may be prompted by something that seems good). For this reason, Kierkegaard concludes that immorality (or evil) involves double-mindedness or despair, whereas morality facilitates wholeheartedness. A coherent self then requires unconditional moral commitment, not just occasionally (in deeds) but consistently at the level of character. Only by willing the good unconditionally can we will one thing and avoid despair (UDVS, 24/SKS 8, 139f.).[14] The choice then stands between willing the good categorically *and* willing it only partially (or conditionally). Morality requires the former, whereas the aesthetes seem to settle for the latter by prioritizing sensuousness and inclination over morality, at least occasionally (Fremstedal 2015b).[15]

Nevertheless, we must distinguish between Christian and non-Christian ethics in this context. *The Concept of Anxiety* argues that non-Christian ethics collapse internally because of human guilt and sin (CA, 16ff./SKS 4, 323ff.). Insofar as it fails to live up to its own standards, non-Christian ethics involves despair that is split between the ideals it sets out to achieve and their worldly realization. Christian ethics, by contrast, involves not only consciousness of sin, but also divine (and human) forgiveness of sins. Christian ethics relies on divine assistance, whereas non-Christian ethics relies on human willpower (Fremstedal 2014).

Theological and philosophical anthropology

Philosophical anthropology differs from theological anthropology (KJN 2, 117, 120/SKS 18, 125f.) insofar as the former relies on human experience and mere reason, whereas the latter presupposes divine revelation. Like other Christian anthropologists, Kierkegaard emphasizes the dogma of original sin and that man is created in the image of God.[16] Kierkegaard rejects Ludwig Feuerbach's claim that 'theology is anthropology' (SKS K7, 363), because it implies a reduction of theology (and theological anthropology) to philosophical anthropology. Feuerbach thinks God is created in the image of man, whereas Kierkegaard assumes the opposite (cf. JP 3, 119/SKS 26, 285).

Part Two of *The Sickness unto Death* develops a Christian anthropology that focuses on the *theological self* that is aware of itself as existing before God. Here Kierkegaard identifies despair with sin, and interprets it as an unwillingness to be oneself before God that involves an element of self-deception. Despair before God takes three forms:

(1) the sin of despairing over one's sin,
(2) the sin of despairing over the forgiveness of sin (offense), and
(3) the sin of dismissing Christianity.

The person guilty of the first form of despair gives up hope and courage because of their own sin. The person guilty of the second form gives up because they take offense at divine forgiveness, since they assume they are beyond forgiveness. Finally, the third rejects Christianity altogether by denying the incarnation. These forms involve an increased sinfulness and despair, insofar as they move increasingly further away from faith (SUD, 101/SKS 11, 213).

Kierkegaard takes the self to be established by God, so that any conflict in the human synthesis reflects itself (implicitly) in the relation to God. Despair is contrasted with Christian faith, which involves an unconditional (second-order) will to be oneself before God in which 'the self rests transparently in the power that established it' (SUD, 131/SKS 11, 242). Transparency here appears to involve an openness to God and other human beings that is aware of the relational nature of the self, and which affirms it by being unconditionally committed towards Christian ethics, while recognizing the human tendency towards sin, despair, and self-deception. The Christian believer humbly accepts himself as a sinner who is forgiven by God (Westphal 2014: ch. 12).

Still, we may be tempted to ask whether the theological anthropology in Part Two of *The Sickness unto Death* is implicit in the philosophical anthropology of Part One. The concept of infinitude, for instance, may resemble divine infinitude. Yet, *The Sickness unto Death* interprets infinitude in the human synthesis only as the unlimited (Greek, *ápeiron*) that is dialectically dependent upon its opposite (finitude) (SUD, 35/SKS 11, 151). The attempt to abstract infinitude from finitude therefore leads to the 'despair of infinitude.' *The Sickness unto Death* seems to presuppose that God creates us, but Part One only assumes that defiance, the phenomenon of desperately wanting to be oneself, indicates that the self does not constitute itself normatively (SUD, 14/SKS 11, 130). The self despairs because it is confronted with constraints on selfhood that are not self-imposed (e.g., one's facticity). These constraints are external to the will, so the agent cannot set all the rules of its existence autonomously, nor the rules for setting the rules (SUD, 68f./SKS 11, 182f.).

In *The Sickness unto Death*, the philosophical anthropology of Part One results in despair that prepares the transition to Christian anthropology in Part Two. It then seems that philosophy can help us to 'seek the leap as a desperate way out' (CUP 1, 106/SKS 7, 103) because Christianity fits human subjectivity completely (CUP 1, 230/SKS 7, 210). Christian faith solves the pre-Christian problem of despair, but it cannot be reduced to philosophical anthropology, since it has its own perspectives and language. Indeed, pre-Christian philosophical standards (e.g., first ethics) are valid, yet not sufficient, because they collapse internally by leading to despair.

Despair is only overcome by Christian faith in a wide sense that appears to include hope and charity. Christian hope takes the form of 'hope against hope,' as hope in a (humanly) hopeless situation (FSE, 81–3/SKS 13, 102–4). Indeed, Christian hope only becomes an extant possibility when everything breaks down because of despair (JP 2, 247). Christian hope is a divine gift that, if accepted, overcomes human (pre-Christian) despair. Nevertheless, hope involves not so much wishfulness as expectancy of good for oneself and one's neighbour alike (WL, 260/SKS 9, 259). Without a God that makes everything possible (SUD, 71/SKS 11, 185), there is nothing that secures hope or prevents despair.

Conclusion

Like Kant, Kierkegaard is a forerunner of twentieth-century existential and phenomenological anthropology. Kierkegaard's approach to anthropology shares some basic features with Kant's pragmatic anthropology. First, both sketch a normative non-naturalistic anthropology that includes teleology, ethics, and religion. Second, both emphasize what is common to all humans, rather than what is specific to various groups and nationalities. More specifically, both are concerned with human actuality, possibilities, and (objective) ideals. For Kierkegaard, the past seems to represent the actual, the future the possibilities, and the present the moment in which the self relates to the whole by taking full responsibility for itself (cf. Stokes 2015: 163). In the nineteenth-century context, Kierkegaard's analysis of historicity and contingency is reminiscent of the German historicism that was part of the nineteenth-century discourse on anthropology after Herder. It is particularly by introducing the concept of facticity and richer notions of historicity and selfhood, that Kierkegaard's account goes beyond Kant's anthropology, and offers an account that anticipates twentieth-century phenomenology and existentialism (Fremstedal 2014: ch. 3).

The Sickness unto Death represents perhaps Kierkegaard's most important contribution to anthropology, moral psychology, and theories of selfhood. Kierkegaard's approach is original particularly because it involves a negativistic phenomenology (Grøn 1997) and a typology of despair that covers everything from non-conscious despair to demonic despair. Kierkegaard's views on anthropology and selfhood have been highly influential, particularly in continental philosophy and theology. Rudd (2012) and Davenport (2012), however, show that they are also relevant to debates on practical identity and narratives in Anglophone philosophy after MacIntyre and Frankfurt.

Related topics

'Kierkegaard's experimenting psychology,' William McDonald; 'Conscience, self-deception, and the question of authenticity in Kierkegaard,' Claudia Welz; 'Agency, identity, and alienation in *The Sickness unto Death*' Justin F. White; 'The Kierkegaardian self: convergences and divergences,' Jack Mulder, Jr.

Notes

1 The term 'anthropology' is more established in continental philosophy and Kantianism than in analytic philosophy. In the early twentieth century, anthropology was re-established as a philosophical discipline in Germany, something that lead to theoretical controversies regarding vagueness, empiricism, scientism, reductionism, and reification (cf. Marquard 1971; Orth 1997; Honenberger 2015). It is beyond the scope of this paper to discuss these controversies in great depth. Nevertheless, I will say that Kierkegaard's existential approach to anthropology cannot be easily dismissed, since it posits vital questions regarding our very existence, identity, and self-understanding. In this respect, Kierkegaard's anthropology differs strongly from scientific studies of man as an object. Still, one may discuss whether Kierkegaard's work is best described in terms of anthropology, psychology, or selfhood.
2 Kant (Akademieausgabe 7:119) quoted from Louden (2011: 67). To some extent, this chapter also draws on Fremstedal (2014; 2015a; 2015b; 2016).
3 Still, philosophical anthropology is not only supposed to give knowledge about human nature (as one topic among others), but it also sees human beings as the locus of all possible understanding, including the understanding of nature in science. Nineteenth-century philosophical anthropology therefore focuses not only on the experience of the human being but also on how all science, and other human activities, rely on human experience. Instead of merely focusing on the nature of man, anthropology focuses on the problem of experience in general, our total 'encounter with and understanding of the world' (Orth 1997: 522). For an analysis of Kierkegaard's view of human experience and consciousness in general, see Stokes (2010: chps. 2–4).
4 Even if *Videnskab* includes normative legal theory, political theory, and economics, it may still not include ethical normativity. Nevertheless, *The Concept of Anxiety* describes ethics as a *Videnskab*, something that is unusual for Kierkegaard (see CA, 16f./SKS 4, 323–5).
5 In addition, the 'Interlude' of *Philosophical Fragments* argues that contingent truths, in historical and empirical disciplines, differ essentially from necessary truths (e.g., 2 + 2 = 4). The 'Interlude' argues that it is not only the future that is contingent but also the past. History, both future and past, involves transitions from possibility to actuality that cannot be predicted or fully comprehended, since it is based on free agency that contingently intervenes in the world by actualizing some possibilities, while annihilating others. For instance, the king decides that Denmark is allied with France, not England. It is not only history itself that is fundamentally contingent, however, but also our interpretation of it. *Philosophical Fragments* suggests that we should relate to the past just as we relate to the future, namely by forming historical beliefs (PF, 76f./SKS 4,276). History is construed by agents, freely deciding to form one belief over another, selecting one interpretative possibility over others. Of the different possibilities, one is actualized and the others annihilated. Forming beliefs results from acts of will, in which we decide to interpret history in one way instead of another (something that can be supported by reasons to varying degrees). Historical knowledge, then, represents the beliefs and interests of historical agents that take part in society; it does not involve a disinterested ahistorical spectator without presuppositions (Fremstedal 2015a).
6 'Anthropology' is spelled both with and without the letter 'h' by Kierkegaard. There are sixty-two occurrences in the Danish electronic edition (which covers almost all of Kierkegaard's corpus), although fifty-one of these are from the commentaries. It is often the case that some important terms and names occur more frequently in the commentaries than in the primary sources, however, partially because

the latter presuppose context. Important material can therefore be implicit and somewhat hidden to modern readers. Nevertheless, Kierkegaard's familiarity with the nineteenth-century discourse on anthropology is indicated not only by his own account but also by his references to anthropology. For different overviews, see JP 7, 6 (on theological and philosophical anthropology); JP 1, 13–7; http://sks.dk/zoom/search.aspx?zoom_sort=1&zoom_xml=0&zoom_query=ant*ropologi* (2018/21/02).

7 This is the central, negativistic thesis of Theunissen (2005) and Grøn (1997).
8 Kierkegaard describes these conflicting elements, which are constitutive of despair, as conflicting wills: '[E]veryone in despair has two wills, one that he futilely wants to follow entirely, and one that he futilely wants to get rid of entirely' (UDVS, 30/SKS 8, 144). The Danish word for despair, *Fortvivlelse*, is even based on the numeral two (*tvi*), just like the German *Verzweiflung* is based on *zwei*.
9 Inauthentic despair normally refers to a form of consciousness that speaks about itself and claims to be free of despair, typically by claiming to be safe and content (Grøn 1997: 127ff.). There is a conflict between what inauthentic despair says and what it shows, between what it intends and what it achieves, that makes it possible for the observer to conclude that it misinterprets the situation. This misinterpretation results from a complex interplay between cognition and volition, in which we tend to deny problems to ourselves, so that we do not even realize our state of despair. For these reasons, inauthentic despair implies self-deception and a volitional failure rather than a mere cognitive one. Although all forms of despair involve some self-deception, inauthentic despair involves a particularly strong form of it that denies its state of despair and its need to be improved or cured (Grøn 1997; Fremstedal 2016).
10 Kierkegaard's account of human nature seems either to be a form of broadly Aristotelian hylomorphism or a two-aspect account of body and mind. See Davenport (2013: 234).
11 For the distinction between ideal and actual self, see Stokes (2015: 178–80; cf. EO2, 259/SKS 3, 246f.). Stokes (2015) argues that the self only exists in the present, whereas the human being is temporarily extended. Stokes also discusses the relation between practical and metaphysical identity in this connection.
12 For the influential view that we always act under the guise of the good (*sub specie boni*), see, for example, Louden (2011: 115–20).
13 Davenport (2013: 238n) says that 'the way one wills to be oneself or not is [...] also a way of willing to be what God created one to be or not.'
14 Davenport (2012: 98f., 122ff.) argues that moral standards represent an objective basis outside of first-order states that makes it possible to shape our identity coherently, without being at the mercy of the contingencies of time. Rudd (2012: 91ff., 112ff.) argues that the idea of the good is needed (at least regulatively) if we are to shape and improve ourselves in a substantially rational manner. For we cannot assume that we are unable to make ourselves better or worse, by standards external to our will, unless we think that instrumental rationality suffices and let non-rational cares and commitments dominate.
15 Nevertheless, wholeheartedness requires not only a unified identity, which appears to take a temporal and narrative form, but also a naked self that takes unconditional responsibility for its whole life in the present. It is controversial whether the narrative reading of Kierkegaard, defended by Davenport (2012) and (Rudd 2012), can account for the naked self that takes complete responsibility for itself in the present (Stokes 2015: 167). It seems that unless the self takes full responsibility for itself, it cannot fully endorse itself reflectively or accept itself completely. Without full acceptance, or unconditional willingness to be itself, the self is in despair, because it is split between actuality (that it does not fully accept or endorse) and ideals (that it identifies with). To despair is 'to lose the eternal' (JP 1, 346), since 'the eternal' represents the present in which the self should take responsibility for its whole life.
16 See, e.g., Kierkegaard's notes on Christian anthropology from H. N. Clausen's lectures (KJN 3, 18–82/SKS 19, 23–84). For Kierkegaard's views on original sin and *imago Dei*, see Fremstedal (2014); Nordentoft (1972: chps. 4 and 6).

References

Davenport, J. (2013) 'Selfhood and spirit,' in J. Lippitt and G. Pattison (eds), *The Oxford Handbook of Kierkegaard*, Oxford: Oxford University Press, 230–51.
Davenport, J. (2012) *Narrative identity, autonomy, and mortality: From Frankfurt and MacIntyre to Kierkegaard*, London: Routledge.
Fremstedal, R. (2016) 'Kierkegaard and Nietzsche: Despair and nihilism converge,' in K. K. Mikalsen, E. Skjei and A. Øfsti (eds), *Modernity – Unity in Diversity? Essays in Honour of Helge Høibraaten*, Oslo: Novus, 455–77.

Fremstedal, R. (2015a) 'Kierkegaard's use of German philosophy: Leibniz to Fichte,' in J. Stewart (ed), *A Companion to Kierkegaard*, Oxford: Wiley-Blackwell, 36–49.
Fremstedal, R. (2015b) 'Kierkegaard's views on normative ethics, moral agency, and metaethics,' in J. Stewart (ed), *A Companion to Kierkegaard*, Oxford: Wiley-Blackwell, 113–25.
Fremstedal, R. (2014) *Kierkegaard and Kant on radical evil and the highest good: Virtue, happiness, and the kingdom of God*, London: Palgrave Macmillan.
Grøn, A. (1997) *Subjektivitet og negativitet: Kierkegaard*, Copenhagen: Gyldendal.
Honenberger, P. (ed) (2015) *Naturalism and philosophical anthropology: Nature, life, and the human between transcendental and empirical perspectives*, London: Palgrave Macmillan.
Louden, R. L. (2011) *Kant's human being: Essays on his theory of human nature*, Oxford: Oxford University Press.
Marquard, O. (1971) 'Anthropologie,' in J. Ritter (ed), *Historische Wörterbuch der Philosophie*, vol. 1, Basel: Schwabe, 362–74.
Nordentoft, K. (1972) *Kierkegaards psykologi*, Copenhagen: Gad.
Orth, E. W. (1997) 'Philosophical anthropology,' in L. Embree et al. (eds), *Encyclopedia of Phenomenology*, London: Kluwer, 522–5.
Rudd, A. (2012) *Self, value, and narrative: A Kierkegaardian approach*, Oxford: Oxford University Press.
Stokes, P. (2015) *The naked self: Kierkegaard and personal identity*, Oxford: Oxford University Press.
Stokes, P. (2010) *Kierkegaard's mirrors: Interest, self, and moral vision*, London: Palgrave Macmillan.
Theunissen, M. (2005) *Kierkegaard's concept of despair*, Princeton, NJ: Princeton University Press.
Welz, C. (2013) 'Kierkegaard and phenomenology,' in J. Lippitt and G. Pattison (eds), *The Oxford Handbook of Kierkegaard*, Oxford: Oxford University Press, 440–63.
Westphal, M. (2014) *Kierkegaard's concept of faith*, Grand Rapids, MI: Eerdmans Publishing Company.

Further reading

Davenport, J. (2013) 'Selfhood and spirit,' in J. Lippitt and G. Pattison (eds), *The Oxford Handbook of Kierkegaard*, Oxford: Oxford University Press, 230–51.
    This entry gives a useful overview over Kierkegaard's account of spirit, selfhood, and human nature.
Rudd, A. (2012) *Self, value, and narrative: A Kierkegaardian approach*, Oxford: Oxford University Press.
    This work shows the relevance of Kierkegaard for contemporary debates on selfhood, practical identity and narratives.
Westphal, M. (2014) *Kierkegaard's concept of faith*, Grand Rapids, MI: Eerdmans Publishing Company.
    This work gives a useful overview over Kierkegaard's pseudonymous authorship by focusing on Kierkegaard's concept of religious faith. Chapter 12 deals with selfhood and despair in *The Sickness unto Death*.

27
IMAGES OF THE CLOSED SELF IN *THE SICKNESS UNTO DEATH*

Anna Louise Strelis Söderquist

The challenge of fundamental change

The Sickness unto Death lays down a striking sequence of images of the closed self in order to capture the workings of despair. By tracing these images, we see that Anti-Climacus, the pseudonymous author of the work, has consistently depicted the self as tending toward closedness in the face of the dawning awareness of its *given* potential. Anti-Climacus paints in pictures increasingly intense states of despair characterized by a rejection of givenness, including the dependency it entails, and by attempts to withdraw to an autonomous position of self-positing and self-creation. An analysis of these images shows that progressively closed modes of being correspond to increased awareness of dependency, such that a person retreats in equal measure to the degree of exposure. However, the analysis also reveals that with the escalation of despair and self-enclosure, a person nevertheless takes essential steps forward. With an optical illusion of sorts, the self simultaneously withdraws *and* moves closer to the point where fundamental change becomes possible. This dance revealed by images – closed-open, withdrawing-advancing, climbing-descending – sheds light on the vulnerability that resides in the call to become one's given self; and it does so especially by highlighting the playful exploration the self makes of that very vulnerability. In brief, Anti-Climacus's picture show ultimately stages the self's play with the possibility of openness.

The present inquiry, exploring vulnerability and our resistance to receiving help, also offers an interpretation of a key concern of *The Sickness unto Death*, namely the difficulty of having faith in the doctrine of atonement (*at troe på Forsoningslære*). Notably, for Kierkegaard, the challenge of faith always has existential stakes, with the focus on how one lives and whether one wills or dares to face the possibility of change. This holds true for *The Sickness unto Death*, where Anti-Climacus's treatment of the central issue of the forgiveness of sins aims at drawing attention to existential symptoms of despair. If Anti-Climacus is right, we all know something about that haunting feeling from nowhere that begs a person to acknowledge that something is amiss. Acknowledgement is a first step in the spiritual possibility of 'having faith,' which I interpret here as 'openness.' Faith interpreted as openness includes consciously facing up to despair and being receptive to help in overcoming it. As a fundamentally different mode of being, openness also entails an essential turn towards one's divine and given potential; in this, according to Kierkegaard, we also receive help, as the self's becoming comes not from a person's own efforts in self-moulding, but rather from attuning oneself to a call deep within that originates from beyond oneself.

A note about form and content in *The Sickness unto Death*

Considering the form of *The Sickness unto Death*, which often receives treatment either in terms of its classifications of the self or of its theological assumptions, the present focus on imagery may need explaining. Does the work itself, appearing far from aesthetic in form, invite treatment in terms of its aesthetic or literary features? The text, as commentators have rightly observed, is rather formal, and, despite Anti-Climacus's own stated intentions, perhaps even too 'scientific' for the subject matter treated. It reads rather like a catalogue of diseases (Possen 2003: 109). Why not pursue Kierkegaard's aesthetic portrayals of despair where they take full dramatic form, as they do in Part One of *Either/Or*? Kierkegaard himself explains in his notes on *The Sickness unto Death* that this particular project would simply have gotten too large if each characterization of despair needed to be sketched poetically. He preferred to keep it compact; as he writes, 'dialectical algebra does it better' (SKS 20, 366a; see also SUD, 82/SKS 11, 196).[1] If the poetry that works upon our imagination in relation to despair lies elsewhere in Kierkegaard's works, perhaps, one might think, we would do better to examine it there.

However, what we receive from *The Sickness unto Death* depends on how we approach it, and a close look at its imagery highlights an existential import Anti-Climacus seems to have intended. After all, in the preface, Anti-Climacus invites his reader to receive the discourse as though 'a physician speaks at the sickbed,' by which he emphasizes the 'ethical aspect' of religious existence in its 'relation to life' (SUD, 5/SKS 11, 117). Take a look at the setting: the sickroom, a most vulnerable situation. This is not an intellectual battleground where equals fight to persuade or refute one another. Rather, contrasted with the 'scholarly remoteness' of such a '"disinterested" scientific approach,' the sickroom is a personal space, and when we engage the physician, we do so not as an intellect, but as a deeply concerned human being (SUD, 5/SKS 11, 117; translation modified). The spiritual matters at hand, Anti-Climacus continues, demand that one 'risk wholly being oneself, an individual human being, this specific individual human being, alone before God' (SUD, 5/SKS 11, 117; translation modified).

The feat *The Sickness unto Death* accomplishes with its use of imagery is to allow the hidden to come forth such that it seizes the imagination with individualizing power. Anti-Climacus's task is to describe hidden workings of the spirit, seldom indicated directly in life – not to ourselves, not amongst friends, not often by philosophers or theologians. He pauses at times to suggest possible fictional plots that would elucidate the self's closedness (*Indesluttethed*), but he pursues them no further.[2] *The Sickness unto Death* generally avoids external, detailed, fictional portrayals of despair's inner workings, for as Anti-Climacus reveals at the close of Part One: 'With despair it is like the troll in the fairy-tale who disappears through a crevice no one can see' (SUD, 73/SKS 11, 186; translation modified). Lower forms of despair, he clarifies, 'in which there is really no inwardness' can, even must, be portrayed externally in order to indicate them (SUD, 72/SKS 11, 186); but 'the more spiritual the despair becomes,' the more inward, the more hidden (SUD, 73/SKS 11, 186). Then, the author's job becomes subtler: He must describe movements entirely internal, altogether invisible to the eye. Anti-Climacus proves himself up to the task of elevating hidden despair to the level of conscious and individualizing self-reflection, and he does so by literary means, namely through the imagery of the closed self, a leitmotif throughout the diagnosis of despair.

The human ladder of despair

As we trace the thematic image of the closed self in *The Sickness unto Death*, we follow Anti-Climacus in his diagnoses of increasing forms of conscious despair. In both parts of *The Sickness unto Death*, the scale of increasing despair has three levels, so that we climb a ladder with three rungs twice.[3] In Part One, beginning with immediacy, we follow the despair of a person living without consciousness of a divine call; in Part Two, we trace similar steps, now within a person who is indeed conscious of dependency but who finally rejects it totally. As we proceed, the greater the intensity of despair, the more closed the self becomes – though it nevertheless steps up the ladder of despair.

We should keep in mind Anti-Climacus's claim early in the analysis that the self's 'assignment' (*Opgave*) is 'to become itself, which can be done only through the relationship to God' (SUD, 29–30/SKS 11, 146; translation modified). As an avoidance of this calling, despair in its many forms manifests as self-enclosure, as a movement away from being-in-relation.[4] In fact, *The Sickness unto Death*'s 'closed self' imagery first designates a person closed off from his or her own self.[5] This begins in Part One with a description of the immediate person, someone, for Anti-Climacus, who lives unreflectively, simply 'desiring, craving, [and] enjoying' life as 'one' does (SUD, 51/SKS 11, 166). As such, one passively suffers fate as good or bad fortune; when despair strikes, it comes from the outside and *happens to one*. Notably, this despair does not evoke the question of neglecting a deeper calling (see SUD, 52/SKS 11, 166–7). A person rather identifies entirely with outward qualities and aptitudes, leaving unattended any deeper question about the self.

Anti-Climacus here provides the first of three door-related images: '[T]he whole question of the self in a deeper sense becomes a kind of false door [*blind Dør*] with nothing behind it in the background of his soul' (SUD, 56/SKS 11, 171; translation modified).[6] From then on, a person becomes occupied in the world, forgetting himself in his work, in social engagements, in a 'cause,' or even in family duties. Thus engaged, the immediate person avoids the 'ludicrous' thoughts occasionally sprouting up that might lead to deeper reflection, 'fearing that what he has in the background might emerge again. Little by little, he manages to forget it' (SUD, 56/SKS 11, 171). Unaware of what is 'going on behind him' (SUD, 61/SKS 11, 175–6), this person ends up not having a self at all (SUD, 56/SKS 11, 171). In the background of the soul lingers a secret, and to avoid confessing it to oneself, one throws oneself into earthly concerns.

Next, Anti-Climacus describes the despair of someone more self-aware, who sees the downfall in attaching 'such great significance to the earthly' when in neglect of the self, but who now despairs over this avoidance (SUD, 61/SKS 11, 176). Aware but afraid of something that needs tending to in the recesses of the self, one comes almost to a kind of self-hatred (SUD, 62/SKS 11, 177). In this state, a person avoids exposure by taking cover under a contempt for immediacy. After all, it is immediate and sentimental people who, like children, indiscriminately blurt out their inner lives, while more reflective persons have the decency to restrain themselves (see SUD, 63/SKS 11, 177–8). Thus, to steer clear of the vulnerable position of dialogue and openness, the self uses its power to keep a handle on itself. Anti-Climacus designates this continued avoidance of vulnerability with 'the closed person' (*Indesluttede*). The image describing this state of despair goes as follows: 'That false door [*Blinddør*] mentioned previously [in the lower form of despair], behind which there is nothing, is here a real door, but a carefully closed door [*en virkelig, men rigtignok omhyggelig lukket Dør*], and behind it sits the self, so to speak, watching itself, preoccupied with or filling up time with not willing to be itself, and yet still self enough to love itself' (SUD, 63/SKS 11, 177; translation modified).

Note the following evolution contained in Anti-Climacus's imagery. On the one hand, growing self-awareness leads to increased self-enclosure but, on the other, closing in with self-love represents a 'significant step forward' or 'progress' (*Fremskridt*) (SUD, 61/SKS 11, 176). Doubtless, the love of self can become tangled in itself, leading to the illusion of self-creation; this entanglement, despair as defiance, then points to the need for losing the self in order to gain the self (see SUD, 67/SKS 11, 181). But first, Anti-Climacus links the present form of despair to the need one *rightly* feels for solitude (SUD, 64/SKS 11, 178), not in order to suggest salvation lies in closing oneself off from others, but rather, to show solitude, proper self-care, and self-awareness as coexisting where self-transformation becomes possible. Solitude, however, is not synonymous with closedness. Ultimately, overcoming despair involves facing despair's hiddenness within the self, which demands openness. As Anti-Climacus writes, 'this is precisely the path you should follow: you must go through with this despair of the self to get to the self' (SUD, 65/SKS 11, 179; translation modified). Revealed here is an ambiguous interplay between open and closed ways of being.[7] Anti-Climacus underlines the progress in despair's escalation, relaying that 'simply because this despair is more intensive, it is in a certain sense closer to salvation' (SUD, 62/SKS 11, 177). At the same time, he designates openness as the key: 'any moment the despair is held open, there is also the possibility of salvation' (SUD, 62/SKS 11, 177; translation modified). As we shall see, everything depends, at despair's highest and most vulnerable point, on whether a person releases his grip on himself in order to gain himself.

Finally, with the highest rung of despair in Part One, Anti-Climacus describes an inner movement of defiantly willing to be self-creator. Here, despair is neither side-tracked in some external worry, nor shipwrecked on the shore of self-loathing, but sits at the root of despair in neglecting one's calling. However, despairing, this person fears the vulnerability contained in opening up – even if to the possibility of becoming oneself. Such a person 'does not want to put on his own self, does not want to see his assignment [*Opgave*] in his given self [*i det ham givne Selv*]' (SUD, 68/SKS 11, 182; translation modified). To avoid the loss of control implied in openness, defiance takes the form of wanting to rule over oneself, to create oneself; a person shuts out any interference from a deeper calling, 'severing the self from any relation to a power that has established it' (SUD, 68/SKS 11, 182). Here, with the final of three images playing on the metaphor of the door, Anti-Climacus portrays a concealment that constructs an inner world exclusively for its self-project, an enclosure (*Indelukke*) with no exit, 'what could be called an inwardness with a jammed lock [*er gaaet i Baglaas*]' (SUD, 72/SKS 11, 186).[8] *Baglaas*, literally 'locked from behind,' suggests a person who has by some trick managed to lock herself in while leaving the key on the outside.[9] In the illusive safety of self-enclosure, this person can close her ears to any sign of a calling.

When despair has become thus self-entangled, the remedy, as we saw, is openness, but the closed person defiantly seeks self-control and retreats from the vulnerability and apparent passivity this openness entails. Note carefully, 'holding oneself open' is anything but passive. Openness in the form of letting go takes immense ability and strength, not to mention courage; but such ability, strength, and courage one receives as gifts, not as the result of autonomous efforts. By opening to the 'eternal,' 'the self has the courage to lose itself in order to win itself' (SUD, 67/SKS 11, 181). Alas, such imperceptible though essential movements of courage all too often get taken for passivity in the world.

The divine ladder of despair

As we accompany Anti-Climacus into Part Two of *The Sickness unto Death*, we again climb three rungs of a ladder of increasing despair, now with emphasis on unfolding 'before God.' In the course of life, a person sometimes experiences how suddenly a new light can appear and illuminate everything quite differently. Anti-Climacus captures the transformation in awareness of despair as follows: 'The progression in consciousness we have been concerned with up to now is within the category of the human self, or the self that has man as its criterion. But this self takes on a new quality and specification by being the self that it is directly before God' (SUD, 79/ SKS 11, 192; translation modified). Baring oneself before God endows a person with an ability in self-perception previously dormant. In other words, a divine light lends a new appearance to despair. As we approach the ladder in Part Two, Anti-Climacus relies on a traditional Trinitarian schema of the divine, tracing the individual's self-perception in relation first to God, then to Christ, and finally to the Holy Spirit.

Existing 'before God' means an individual becomes conscious of the closed position of autonomy, of self-law and self-positing, and becomes aware of the open position of listening for the self's calling as posited by something or someone other than oneself. This person admits – though only in a hushed whisper within the self – to being closed off from listening to what is willed for the self (see SUD, 81–2/SKS 11, 196). To clarify the meaning of 'transparency before God' and to provoke recognition, Anti-Climacus again points his reader towards inner phenomena. He writes: 'God is not something external like a policeman. What must be noted is that the self has a conception of God and yet does not do what God wants, that the self is disobedient' (SUD, 80/SKS 11, 194; translation modified). 'God,' in this context, is not an object to be grasped by the intellect, just as 'obedience' is not a doctrine to consent to or reject. Rather, one shall imagine an inner voice, like one's conscience, which one recognizes as true, but nevertheless ignores. As such, not only does despair neglect the given self (*givne Selv*) with its given assignment (*Opgave*), but through an act of wilful ignorance, it also covers over its consciousness of this neglect (see SUD, 90, 94/SKS 11, 203, 206–7). Anti-Climacus here treats Socrates' skirting of the issue of wilful ignorance (that anyone could wilfully choose the bad), with the implication that even pagans are capable of covering up a lie to oneself.[10] Certainly, Socrates himself knew the phenomenon of conscience, as he often mentions a personal *daimon*, a divine or spiritual sign that would appear to him as a warning, preventing him from wrongdoing (see, e.g., Plato, *Apology* 31d, 40a–c; *Phaedrus* 242c; and *Theages* 128d). With the image of a self before God, Anti-Climacus invites each of us to recognize an internal movement of shirking what we are called to do, not by some external force chasing after us with the 'cane of duty,' but by an internal source that knows what the self needs.[11]

Just as the imagery of the closed self in Part One made use of the metaphor of the door, that of Part Two proceeds within a metaphor of war. Despite growing self-clarity, despite progress, the tendency continues towards closedness, now a strategic tactic in battle. As Anti-Climacus suggests, *before God* a person becomes aware of the possibility of opening up, but looks upon all talk of 'repentance and grace not only as empty and meaningless but also as its enemy, as something against which a defense must be made most of all, just as the good defends itself against temptation' (SUD, 109/SKS 11, 221). Notably, by incorporating wartime imagery, Anti-Climacus emphasizes the self's inner movements of defence and guardedness. Next, he associates this wartime imagery with the images of self-enclosure from Part One, as despair shuts in as though in a fortress: The self 'closes itself up within itself, indeed, locks itself inside one more inclosure [*Indelukke*],' and, 'aware of having burned the bridge behind it and of thereby being inaccessible to the good and of the good being inaccessible to it,' the self waits 'listening only to itself' and 'having dealings only with itself' (SUD, 109/ SKS 11, 221).[12] The text thus suggests that as we begin opening up to our suffering, allowing light to shine on the self's inner workings, we instinctively move to protect ourselves – we go on the defensive.

The next rung of the ladder of despair viewed under divine light describes perhaps the most powerful, universal, and relatable fear of vulnerability. Now with emphasis on the self's relation to *Christ*, the despairing person's awareness includes the possibility of reconciliation. However, he becomes overwhelmed when implored 'to accept the help that is offered to him': the possibility is 'too exalted for him,' he despairs over it (SUD, 85/SKS 11, 199; translation modified). Anti-Climacus here draws on the tradition of understanding Christ as love. Standing before the look of love is harder than it sounds; for, it entreats us to accept ourselves as the loving look values us in our uniqueness.[13] Anti-Climacus invites us to recognize that a compassionate look overwhelms us precisely because it contains a demand. Love dares us to live up to our particularity, that is, to be ourselves as divine love sees us. Before this challenge – to be the unique self one is before the look of love – we see the human tendency to retreat defensively to the fortress. The person faced with such compassion, Anti-Climacus continues, 'cannot wrap his mind around it, because he cannot remain confident [*faae sin Frimodighed*] in the face of it ... it is as if it were about to choke him' (SUD, 85–6/SKS 11, 199; translation modified). In brief, the look of Christ invites a person to surrender to love, an almost inconceivable requirement.[14]

To further the difficulty, the look of love calls for an acknowledgement of the misguided tendency to seek control when we feel lost at sea. That is, love, which shows how far astray we drift, simultaneously requires that we cease our furious paddling and, instead – have faith. In a journal note illuminating this challenge, Kierkegaard likens love's nearly impossible demand to the situation of the Israelites, who, bitten by serpents sent as punishment for their rebellion, were told they could survive simply by looking at the copper serpent erected on Moses' staff (Numbers 21: 6–9). He writes: 'To believe in the atonement is this: bitten by serpents, while the bite is still painful, tempting people to think only of the pain or at any rate of whether it's possible to have the serpents killed – even right then, to have faith' (SKS 20, 104a). How daunting it is to let go of what hurts us, and especially, to stop trying to control the pain. Yet, just that, the love that acknowledges our pain encourages us to stop nursing our wounds, to give up our habit of self-medicating and instead to seek help. Taking our injury into our own 'controlling' hands can assume many forms: building walls, keeping others at a distance, avoiding re-injury, or simply pouring ourselves into tasks that give the semblance of control and restore the feeling of mastery. In contrast to this reliance on willpower, by acknowledging dependency, a person is asked simply 'to have faith' (*at troe*). In other words, when at a loss, the movement of faith means entrusting ourselves to somebody else's hands. Kierkegaard's analogy suggests the tendency to run deeper into our hurt selves rather than risk such unknown ventures; but it also points towards a healing that involves faith interpreted as openness. In the lines that follow, he acknowledges how difficult, even rare, it is to find this kind of faith: 'Not everyone who is bitten by serpents can come to a decision to have faith in the atonement or find the grace to do so' (SKS 20, 104a). Doubtless, faith is a monumental challenge, an effort often resisted with all one's might.

Continuing the metaphor of war, Anti-Climacus likens the stance of defiance before the look of love to being on the defensive in a 'brawl.' To throw off the demand entailed in the offer threatening to suffocate her, a person declares: 'No, there is no forgiveness of sins, it is impossible' (SUD, 114/SKS 11, 226). 'Offended' by the enormity of the task, in despair, she opposes herself to love; and though, by virtue of opposing it, she turns to face what is calling her, the individual does so by withdrawing in retreat (SUD, 125/SKS 11, 236).

As the imagery suggests, the question put to us by standing before Christ is whether we will allow love to conquer us, to render us transparent to ourselves, to tear the self's enclosure open. The look of love urges the despairer to let go of false comforts, such as defiance, self-assertion, and even self-destruction. The look of love makes us suffer our pride and need humility; and, above all, the look of love shows the despairing self that it is not self-sufficient, but in need of help. Before Christ, the difficulty entails allowing oneself to be vulnerable. The look of love, Anti-Climacus shows, is a challenge for openness. At war, however, the closed self's efforts are concentrated in defending against intrusion.

Finally, at the highest rung of despair, treated in the text's concluding section, the closed self rejects the possibility of any assistance, of any way out of despair through the teachings of openness, which it altogether throws off in a denial of the *Holy Spirit*. The Holy Spirit, synonymous with grace, represents an appeal from beyond oneself to accept help in undergoing fundamental transformation. Grace is a winged visitor, with movements as imperceptible as breath, and whose wordless message says one is not alone in facing one's task (*Opgave*); further, known only by being experienced, grace is a reassurance that *one is able* in the task of becoming oneself. Such offers of assistance, which are made precisely at the site of exposure, the closed self cannot bear. Addressed at the most raw and vulnerable inner depths, the self lashes out like a frightened and cornered animal in a desperate last attempt to retain its independence and to avoid its assigned task. Anti-Climacus thus concludes his use of wartime imagery: This height of despair unfolds as 'a war between man and God,' where the tactics finally switch from defensive to offensive (SUD, 125/SKS 11, 236). The despairing self now steps forward as the aggressor in open and offensive warfare.

Significantly, continuing the thematic interplay of open and closed modes of being, Anti-Climacus again lays emphasis on the self's forward movement (*Fremskridt*) in meeting its opponent. As before, the escalation through increasing levels of despair represents progress. In this 'positive form of being offended' (SUD, 125/SKS 11, 236), although the despairing self 'digs down ever more deeply into itself, thus moving further away, yet in another sense it comes closer, becoming more and more decisively itself' (SUD, 125/SKS 11, 236). Although the self only rushes out of its enclosure to declare the possibility of grace 'as untruth and a lie,' still, it comes closer (SUD, 125/SKS 11, 236). Furthermore, this highest intensity of despair manifests not only as another step on the ladder, but also as an essential turning point. Having moved through all levels of despair, we stand at a crossroads: *Either* we cling to despair and close deeper into ourselves *or* we let go in daring to hold ourselves open.[15]

Faith interpreted as openness

With the above analysis of images of the closed self in *The Sickness unto Death*, we have seen despair as a fear of vulnerability and openness; we have also seen, perhaps unexpectedly, increasing despair manifesting as a playful exploration of that vulnerability, as a venturing towards the possibility of openness.

The present chapter, like *The Sickness unto Death* itself, has dealt primarily with the sickness, though, by interpreting faith as openness, there have been hints along the way of the potential cure.[16] Before concluding, then, it is worth turning briefly towards the possibility of healing, which at the very least is suggested by Anti-Climacus's text. Let us, then, trace one last image.

At the start of Part Two, before tackling the escalation of despair before God, Anti-Climacus writes that a person may have a 'profound religious need'[17] and may love 'God who is his only consolation in his secret anguish,' but still, 'he loves the anguish, he will not let go of it [*den vil han ikke slippe*]' (SUD, 77/SKS 11, 192; translation modified). As the image of holding on to pain suggests, even where an inner dialogue has expressed a longing for release and for relationality, out of fear we keep ourselves isolated in our suffering. Meanwhile, as Anti-Climacus shows, we perform a self-deception that might go unnoticed without the efforts that bring our states of despair to the level of conscious reflection. Anti-Climacus's analysis reflects this strange paradox: Closing oneself in with suffering, one simultaneously manages to avoid facing it in reality, 'here in time' (SUD, 78/SKS 11, 192). The despairer, Anti-Climacus suggests, 'dimly understands that he is required to let go [*at slippe*] of this anguish, that is, in faith to humble himself under it and take it on as having to do with the self'; and yet, 'he wants to *hold it away from himself*, which means precisely *keeping a tight hold on it*' (SUD, 78/SKS 11, 192; translation modified and emphasis added). Herein lies the self-deception: One keeps a tight grip on pain, but this show of strength is only an alibi; in one's inner recesses, the real work of despair aims at keeping the pain away.

With this image, Anti-Climacus shows that letting go of despair means first taking it on – in faith. In other words, when we open up at our most vulnerable point, we finally have the possibility of facing up to a torment too much to bear alone. The question then becomes whether we are willing to receive help in letting go; for, as we saw earlier, 'any moment the despair is held open, there is also a possibility of salvation.'

The same year Kierkegaard published *The Sickness unto Death*, 1849, he described in his journal the individual's relation to Christ. We shudder, he suggests, at the thought of coming too near this divine help, for it implies standing exposed in our vulnerability, without reprieve, without hiding. However, 'as soon as he has yielded entirely, his most blessed comfort will be having Christ with him at every moment – his savior and atoner' (SKS 22, 80). In these lines, we encounter a most hopeful notion: namely, as soon as we make the decision and find the grace to yield, not in small and timid doses, but utterly and completely, so swiftly do we receive comfort and aid, guidance and assurance. However, everything depends on this open yielding. Though human life knows endless forms of suffering, the possibility of healing from despair is also given to us, but faith first.

Related topics

'On faith and reason(s): Kierkegaard's logic of conviction,' K. Brian Söderquist; 'Consciousness, self, and reflection,' Patrick Stokes; 'Conscience, self-deception, and the question of authenticity in Kierkegaard,' Claudia Welz.

Notes

1 Notably, the same decision was made for *The Concept of Anxiety* (1844), published five years before and anticipating *The Sickness unto Death* (see CA, 113n, 128/SKS 4, 415n, 429).
2 We are, for example, asked to imagine a demonic tyrant with a great need to confide his secret torment; he repeatedly does so almost against his will, only to suffer so badly from the slip that he murders his confidants one after another (SUD, 66–7/SKS 11, 180–1). One can imagine the tyrant Periander in a similar pattern of bad faith, as he is described in SLW 323–8/SKS 6, 301–5.
3 In this context, the ladder metaphor is mine, though Kierkegaard plays with it elsewhere, as in *Philosophical Fragments*, where Johannes Climacus uses *Opadstigen* and *Nedadstigen* (*Stige* means 'ladder') in the question of whether one meets God through ascent or descent (see PF, 29–31/SKS 4, 235–8). Significantly, the name Johannes Climacus could refer to the seventh-century saint, John Climacus (author of *The Ladder of Divine Ascent*; *klimax* is Greek for 'ladder'), who preached that one comes to God one rung of virtue at a time (see Lowrie 2013: 166–7).
4 On the relational self in *The Sickness unto Death*, see C. Stephen Evans's (1997) essay 'Who is the other in *Sickness unto Death*? God and human relations in the constitution of the self.' Evans argues for the significance of relationality not only with a divine power, but also among humans.
5 In his essay, '"Before God" as a regulative concept,' George Pattison (1997: 77) sheds light on the phenomenon of 'transparency' as called for in *The Sickness unto Death*'s 'formula' for faith, noting in particular the call for becoming transparent not only to God, but also to oneself before God. Pattison also emphasizes the individual's appropriation of revelation in the relation to God.

6 Just like the term 'false door' in English, a *blind Dør* or *Blinddør* in Danish refers to a door (usually an artistic representation, as on a tomb) not meant to function like a real door, that is, a door that does not open or lead anywhere. Quite strikingly, when seeking etymological clarity on the usage of the term *Blinddør* in the *Ordbog over det danske Sprog*, the comprehensive historical dictionary of the Danish language from 1700 to 1950, one is directed nowhere other than its use by Kierkegaard in *The Sickness unto Death*.

7 The connection between closedness and openness was already made in *The Concept of Anxiety* with the twin concepts of 'the closed' (*Indesluttede*) and 'the unfreely disclosed' (*ufrivilligt Aabenbare*) (see CA, 123, 127/SKS 4, 424, 428).

8 Once again, when consulted on the term *Baglaas*, the *Ordbog over det danske Sprog* cites this very sentence in Kierkegaard as originating the metaphorical usage of the phrase *gaaet i Baglaas*; it refers to a person or situation that has, by its own doing, become 'frozen' or unable to function.

9 A similar trick appears in the pseudonymous work, '"Guilty?"/"Not Guilty?"' when a locked box is fished up from the bottom of Lake Søborg; upon being forced open, the key is discovered inside, along with a handwritten manuscript (later published by its finder); the strange feat of the locked-in key is explained thus: 'closedness [*Indesluttetheden*] is always turned inward [*indadvendt*] in that way' (SLW, 189/SKS 6, 177; translation modified).

10 For an enlightening treatment of this section, see David Possen's (2010) essay 'The exemplarity of Socrates in *The Sickness unto Death*.'

11 This image comes from Wilhelm in *Either/Or*, who suggests that a relationship's absolute commitment can be more like a graceful 'orchestra director's baton' than an 'unpleasant policeman's stick' beating a protestor into submission (EO 2, 145/SKS 3, 143).

12 *The Concept of Anxiety* also emphasizes this monological nature of the demonic, again in its treatment of the closed person (*Indesluttede*): 'monologue is precisely [the closed person's] speech, and therefore we characterize a closed person by saying that he talks to himself' (CA, 128/SKS 4, 429; translation modified). Implied is that closedness tends toward monologue, while openness entails breaking the silence and coming into dialogue.

13 Pattison (1997: 84) emphasizes the challenge of transparency before God as requiring that one accepts to regard one's existence 'with an almost unimaginable value in its quite unique individuality.'

14 Pattison (1997: 84) frames this difficulty thus: 'This immense passivity, vulnerability and wounded openness calls for an orientation of the self that is quite alien to the mainstream of Western philosophical thought about the self and is certainly in profound tension with the post-Enlightenment pursuit of autonomy.'

15 For Alastair Hannay (2004: 5), in his 'Introduction' to *The Sickness unto Death*, this crossroads is also key for transformation: '[T]he cure is simply not available until one reaches a point where continued denial of one's dependence upon God is an act of open defiance. Only then does the alternative – open acknowledgement of that dependence – become possible.'

16 Commentators have noted that Anti-Climacus leaves the cure, if *The Sickness unto Death* deals with the diagnosis, for this work's companion volume, *Practice in Christianity*, also penned by Anti-Climacus (Possen 2003: 111–2; Cappelørn 2004: 95–124).

17 On the theme of innate longing for God in Kierkegaard, see Niels Jørgen Cappelørn's (2007) lovely essay 'Longing for reconciliation with God.'

References

Cappelørn, N. J. (2007) 'Longing for reconciliation with God: A fundamental theme in "Friday Communion Discourses," fourth part of "Christian Discourses",' in N. J. Cappelørn, H. Deuser, and K. B. Söderquist (eds), and K. B. Söderquist (trans), *Kierkegaard Studies Yearbook 2007*, Berlin: Walter de Gruyter.

Cappelørn, N. J. (2004) 'The movements of offense toward, away from, and within faith: "Blessed is he who is not offended at me",' in R. L. Perkins (ed), and K. B. Söderquist (trans), *International Kierkegaard Commentary*, vol. 20 (*Practice in Christianity*), Macon, GA: Mercer University Press.

Evans, C. S. (1997) 'Who is the other in "Sickness unto Death?" God and human relations in the constitution of the self,' in N. J. Cappelørn and H. Deuser (eds), *Kierkegaard Studies Yearbook 1997*, Berlin: Walter de Gruyter.

Hannay, A. (2004) 'Introduction,' in Alastair Hannay (trans), *The Sickness unto Death: A Christian Psychological Exposition for Edification and Awakening*, New York: Penguin Books.

Lowrie, W. (2013) *A short life of Kierkegaard*, Princeton, NJ: Princeton University Press.
Pattison, G. (1997) '"Before God" as a regulative concept,' in N. J. Cappelørn and H. Deuser (eds), *Kierkegaard Studies Yearbook 1997*, Berlin: Walter de Gruyter.
Plato. (1997) *Complete Works*, J. M. Cooper (ed), Indianapolis, IN: Hacket Publishing.
Possen, D. (2010) 'The exemplarity of Socrates in "The Sickness unto Death",' in N. J. Cappelørn, H. Deuser, and K. B. Söderquist (eds), *Kierkegaard Studies Yearbook 2010*, Berlin: Walter de Gruyter.
Possen, D. (2003) 'Anti-Climacus and the "physician of souls,"' in P. Houe and G. D. Marino (eds), *Søren Kierkegaard and the Word(s): Essays on Hermeneutics and Communication*, Copenhagen: C. A. Reitzel.

Further reading

Holm, K. (1993) 'Anti-Climacus – og Kierkegaard,' in B. Bertung, P. Müller and F. Norlan (eds), *Søren-Kierkegaard-Selbskabets populære skrifter*, vol. 21 (*Kierkegaard-pseudonymitet*), Copenhagen: C. A. Reitzel.

In this article, we encounter a perspective on Anti-Climacus as a tragic poet, as an opening towards the divine, who, after the manner of the unhappy poet of *Either/Or*, has the unique ability of expressing his inner anguish such that it reaches the listener's ear as beautiful music.

Podmore, S. (2009) 'Kierkegaard as physician of the soul: On self-forgiveness and despair,' *Journal of Psychology and Theology*, 37, no. 3: 174–85.

Podmore's article treats both Kierkegaard and Anti-Climacus as 'wounded healers,' embodying the despairing poet-existence described in *The Sickness unto Death*, the despair of writing instead of being. Through familiarity with the sickness, they may prescribe a cure both for themselves and the reader, namely through faith interpreted as self-surrendering recognition of acceptance before the holy other.

Possen, D. (2004) 'The works of Anti-Climacus,' in R. L. Perkins (ed), *International Kierkegaard Commentary*, vol. 20 (*Practice in Christianity*), Macon, GA: Mercer University Press.

Possen portrays a pseudonym who poetically reinterprets Christian dogma in the form of a phenomenological interpretation of human existence, leaving the rich possibility for a reader to recognize him- or herself in its descriptions. A key feature is the self's tendency to interpret itself as self-creating rather than given.

Sponheim, P. R. (2017) *Existing before God: Søren Kierkegaard and the human venture*, Minneapolis, MN: Augsburg Fortress.

Sponheim's monograph introduces readers to a unique Kierkegaard by choosing *The Sickness unto Death* as a pivotal work for analysis. In his close reading, Sponheim offers a theologian's existential interpretation of key categories of Christian thought in Kierkegaard's work.

28

THE KIERKEGAARDIAN SELF: CONVERGENCES AND DIVERGENCES

Jack Mulder, Jr.

Introduction

In 1 Thessalonians 5:23 (NRSV), the apostle Paul closes his letter with a blessing to its recipients. It reads: 'May the God of peace himself sanctify you entirely; and may your spirit and soul and body be kept sound and blameless at the coming of our Lord Jesus Christ.' This distinction between soul, body, and spirit has not been lost on the wider Christian tradition. Martin Luther (1956: 303) made this distinction in his commentary on the *Magnificat* (Luke 1: 46–55) where he claims that spirit is that by which we are 'enabled to lay hold on things incomprehensible, invisible, and eternal.' The 1997 *Catechism of the Catholic Church* (§367) notes, following the above passage, that 'sometimes the soul is distinguished from the spirit... "Spirit" signifies that from creation man is ordered to a supernatural end and that his soul can gratuitously be raised beyond all it deserves to communion with God.' Søren Kierkegaard also distinguishes between spirit, soul, and body. His famous concept of 'self' is also termed 'spirit' in a famous passage we will reflect on below. This concept is, in my view, the centrepiece of his philosophical and theological anthropology. In this paper I will discuss Kierkegaard's concept of self, or spirit, and put it into conversation with some philosophical and theological voices that, I hope, will help make clear how and where Kierkegaard's view diverges from and converges with these important figures.

A Kierkegaardian self

In a famous (because rather tortuous) passage, Kierkegaard, through Anti-Climacus,[1] the pseudonymous author of *The Sickness unto Death*, writes,

> A human being is spirit. But what is spirit? Spirit is the self. But what is the self? The self is a relation that relates to itself or is the relation's relating to itself[2] in the relation; the self is not the relation but is the relation's relating to itself. A human being is a synthesis of the infinite and the finite, of the temporal and the eternal, of freedom and necessity, in short a synthesis. Considered in this way, a human being is still not a self.... The human self is such a derived, established relation, a relation that relates to

itself and in relating to itself relates to another.... The formula that describes that state of the self when despair is completely rooted out is this: in relating to itself and in willing to be itself, the self rests transparently in the power that established it.

(SUD, 13–4/SKS 11, 129–30)

This is a difficult passage, to be sure, but there are some elements we can isolate. For one thing, the self is in some sense both a project and a reality. We *are* selves, but the self is not a piece of metaphysical furniture; it is a relation whose dynamic *relating* is fundamental to its very existence. A self requires a 'psychical-physical synthesis,' a concept that recalls a soul-body composite, though is more complex than that (SUD, 25/SKS 11, 141),[3] but the self is not the same thing as the synthesis. The synthesis, or relation, must relate to itself, and then, through relating to itself, relate to God.

This is nicely illustrated in a journal entry Kierkegaard titles 'What is required in order, with true blessing, to observe oneself in the mirror of the word' (KJN 8, 431–2/SKS 24, 425–6). There, we learn that there is 'preparation' required for this observation; that first one must, in some sense, know oneself already. Only then can one come to know oneself in the mirror of God's word. Kierkegaard writes, 'Paganism demanded: Know yourself. Xnty says: No, this is something preliminary: Know yourself – and see yourself in the mirror of the Word in order to know yourself properly. No true self-knowledge without God-knowledge, or before God. Here, to stand before the mirror is to stand before God' (KJN 8, 431/SKS 24, 425–6).

The self's project thus has two parts: it must relate to the *fact* of its existence and it must relate to the *source* of its existence. There are plenty of ways this relation can fail (these are the varieties of despair), but most fundamentally all of these have to do with not wanting to be the self one is ultimately intended by God to be. Anti-Climacus doesn't always help the reader in this regard, since he classifies types of despair under two major headings: in despair *not* willing to be oneself and in despair willing to be oneself (SUD, 14/SKS 11, 130). This apparent discrepancy can be resolved with the help of a distinction from Kierkegaard's discourse 'To Need God Is a Human Being's Highest Perfection.' There Kierkegaard makes a distinction between the 'first self' and the 'deeper self' (EUD, 314/SKS 5, 306–10). This distinction helps us to make sense of Anti-Climacus's varieties of despair, since when the self *proudly* wishes to be itself, the 'first self' wishes to let the roar of inconstancy drown out the 'deeper self' (EUD, 314/SKS 5, 306). However, when the first self submits to the deeper self they can then relate to God (EUD, 316–7/SKS 5, 308–9).

It may be instructive to discuss how the 'psychical-physical synthesis' (*sjelelig-legemlig Synthese*) (SUD, 25/SKS 11, 141) differs from the 'relation' invoked in *The Sickness unto Death* and from the relationship between the first and deeper selves.[4] In 'To Need God,' when things are going well, the first self submits to the deeper self and 'they are reconciled and walk on together' (EUD, 316/SKS 5, 308). This, says Kierkegaard, is still only the condition for coming to know oneself, since then one must further understand that one needs God and in this thought is to be found the human being's perfection (EUD, 317/SKS 5, 309–10). In my view, the first and deeper selves have more to do with the proper ordering of one's inner life than with Anti-Climacus's still fairly descriptive understanding of the self in the opening pages of *The Sickness unto Death*. What this shows us is that there is indeed more to do once the first and deeper selves are reconciled, but the synthesis itself is not the relation that, once it has related to itself, can then relate to God. No, the synthesis is an ontological *fact* about what there is. A human being *is* a psychical-physical synthesis; there is no need for it to *become* a synthesis, and being a synthesis is not a success for it, the way that the reconciliation of the first and deeper selves is.

This will help us understand the figures with whom Anti-Climacus's concept of the self will be in dialogue in what follows. First, we will discuss a bit of the Aristotelian-Thomistic view of the body-soul composite. Next, we will look into John Locke's discussion of personal identity and consciousness with a view to some differences between Kierkegaard and Locke. Finally, we will consider the self's relation to God, where we will briefly consider some texts from St. John of the Cross for a comparison.

The psychical-physical synthesis

There are tasks on the way to becoming a self, on Anti-Climacus's view. A self is not something static that someone just is, though it will also be a misunderstanding to suggest that a self carries no ontological or metaphysical commitments with it. In this section, I want briefly to discuss some of the minimal ontological requirements for the self and then reflect a bit on how the creature's ontological indebtedness to God is characterized.

It is well known that Aristotle and St. Thomas Aquinas had some similar things to say about the soul. Aristotle (1984: 412b5–9) famously wrote that 'we can dismiss as unnecessary the question whether the soul and body are one: it is as though we were to ask whether the wax and its shape are one, or generally the matter of a thing and that of which it is the matter.' There is no question for an Aristotelian of a separated soul floating free in an eternal realm of ideas. Nor is the soul merely the life of what would otherwise be a merely existent, but not living, body. As Aquinas (1999: 21–2) comments on a passage from Aristotle near the previously cited one, 'We must not think, therefore, of the soul and body as though the body had its own form making it a body, to which a soul is super-added, making a living body; but rather that the body gets both its being and its life from the soul.' On this account, we cannot even speak of a body at all without the soul, since 'when seeing is removed, the eye is no longer an eye, except in name – no more than the eye of a statue or of a painted figure' (Aristotle 1984: 412b20–2). Thus a human corpse without a soul is not properly a body, but a heap of stuff for Aristotle and Aquinas.

This is a classic hylomorphic account of the soul, and John Davenport (2013: 234–5) rightly associates a hylomorphic account with the 'first-order' synthesis of *The Sickness unto Death*. Nevertheless, Davenport (2013: 234) argues that Anti-Climacus's account is ultimately a 'rejection of both Aristotelian hylomorphic and substance-dualist accounts of persons . . . Dualist accounts hold that the mind, "soul," or "psyche" is the self (which is also contingently attached to a human body), while hylomorphic accounts hold that the self is that substantial form that is individuated by informing or making function a particular body in a certain segment of space.' Now Davenport is aware that the issue is a bit more complicated than this, but it's worth pointing out that Aristotle himself did not seem to have much demonstrated interest in what we now call the 'self' (at least in his extant works). There is, after all, some work to do in metaphysics by way of getting clear on what sorts of building blocks come together to make a human animal and then later a self, and it is the former project that seemed to have captured Aristotle's interest so far as we can tell.[5]

Where it concerns Aquinas and others with his Christian convictions, the issue gets more complicated. For not only is there the biblical distinction we mentioned earlier between body, soul, and spirit, but there are key Christian theological distinctions that involve persons that go quite beyond the matter of an individual soul or nature.[6] Indeed, this goes beyond a point for doctrinal reflection, since much of the Christian mystical tradition would be difficult to understand without some (at least nascent) notion of self as opposed to body, soul, or their composite.[7] Moreover, it is not at all clear, and is in fact controversial, whether Aquinas held that human *persons* survive their deaths along with their (separated) souls or not (Aquinas argued that an intellective soul would be naturally incorruptible).[8] Many in the Catholic tradition more recently have been working within a broadly Thomistic vein to develop a more phenomenological account of the self that often converges on Kierkegaard's account considerably (see Furnal 2016). Davenport can hardly find this surprising, but Anti-Climacus's view can only be a *rejection* of hylomorphic accounts if these accounts, and that of Anti-Climacus, are incompatible accounts *of the same thing*, namely, the human *self*; and it is not clear that they are.

The question of whether Kierkegaard rejects hylomorphic accounts or merely develops a differing, if complementary, concept can be seen to relate to more significant issues as they concern Kierkegaard's anthropology. George Pattison (2008: 160–1) writes

> Kierkegaard never denies that human beings are creatures, but it is scarcely possible to think of him defining this creatureliness in terms of some essence: the human being is not an individual substance of a rational essence, but a being in dynamic and temporally charged ecstatic dependence on God, a dependence that first becomes actual in the individual's concern for the good.

It is certainly true that the Kierkegaardian self, or spirit, first becomes actual in the individual's ethical subjectivity and thus the very young cannot be said to have a self or a God-relationship in this technical sense. But the idea that some children are not possessed of this relationship to God *before God* is hardly a new issue for philosophers and theologians who opt for a hylomorphic account of the human animal.[9]

A still more significant issue ought to be noticed, namely, that once an Aristotelian view migrated into Christian territory, Christian theologians and philosophers needed to reckon with the fact that God can create but must also conserve in existence each thing that exists. Thus, for Aquinas, although the soul itself may be naturally incorruptible, it is not independent of God's active giving of being to everything that exists.[10] Anti-Climacus himself notes the dependence of not just the self but the whole world on God. He writes 'you do not see God's omnipotence – and yet it is just as fully certain that he, too, is working, that one single moment without him and then the world is nothing' (PC, 155/SKS 12, 159). For Aquinas (1981: I.8.1), 'since God is very being by His own essence, created being must be his proper effect; as to ignite is the proper effect of fire. Now God causes this effect in things not only when they first begin to be but as long as they are preserved in being ... God is in all things, and innermostly.'

Pattison and other interpreters (see Hampson 2001: 263) may wish to differentiate Kierkegaard's view from the idea that being is communicated from God to beings so that the beings are self-existent substances, and there is something to that reading. But I would say two things in response. First, Pattison may be right that the Kierkegaardian self is a 'dynamic and temporally charged ecstatic dependence on God,' but for Aquinas everything is. Why would it be surprising that so, too, is the spirit? At bottom there must still be something that is created from which this relation that relates to itself and to God springs, and this is the entity that we have been calling the human animal. Second, my own view (see Mulder 2010: esp. ch. 3 and 7 and 2015: 159–60) is that on this issue, Kierkegaard simply emphasizes different elements at different times, perhaps never finally reaching consistency.

Now it's true that Anti-Climacus tells us that a human being is *more* than just a psychical-physical (or in other thinkers, body-soul) synthesis, but rather 'a synthesis of the infinite and the finite, of the temporal and eternal, of freedom and necessity' (SUD, 13/SKS 11, 129). Indeed, as John D. Glenn, Jr. (1987: 8) writes, that 'the "finitude" of the Kierkegaardian self does not mean merely its bodily character, but its involvement in actual situations, particularly as this entails a tendency to be absorbed in restrictive social roles.' To that extent, in what Glenn calls its 'specific elaboration' Anti-Climacus's account may have more in common with Sartre or Heidegger than an Aristotelian-Thomistic account of the body and soul. But while the method and focus are clearly different, it is not at all obvious, or so I maintain, that Anti-Climacus's account is a flat-footed rejection of an Aristotelian-Thomistic account. And that may leave the door open to many interesting conversations.

The relation's relating to itself

In the previous section, we discussed some of the metaphysical issues that would concern Anti-Climacus's 'psychical-physical synthesis.' We put that Kierkegaardian concept in conversation with an Aristotelian-Thomistic account and found that there may be more to talk about than some interpreters seem to suggest. In this section, I want to discuss a bit of the next step in the journey to selfhood for Anti-Climacus: the relation's relating to itself. As we've noted, there needs to be a creature that relates to itself and then to God. We pointed to the synthesis of the 'finite and the infinite, of the temporal and the eternal, of freedom and necessity' (SUD, 13/SKS 11, 129) as that creature. But certain writers pointed out that what is really significant about Anti-Climacus's (and Kierkegaard's) view of the *self* is that it is *dynamic*.

Indeed, the Kierkegaardian self is dynamic; it presupposes some metaphysical furniture, but it is not itself metaphysical furniture. The self is a task, almost a verb, for Anti-Climacus. So while, as we've argued, his account is not inconsistent with a body-soul composite, the self clearly is not the same thing as one. The relation of *The Sickness unto Death* is one that relates to itself as an individual and then to God. As Merold Westphal (1987: 42; my emphasis) writes, 'This self-relation is, in the first place, self-consciousness. The self as a synthesis of, for example, the temporal and the eternal, is a self not by virtue of being such a synthesis but by virtue of being *aware* of such a synthesis.' In this section, I want to consider this awareness of oneself in Anti-Climacus alongside the work of John Locke.

For Locke, the self, too, must be differentiated from a body, or a soul, or a body-soul composite (he never fully commits himself to either the existence or non-existence of a soul). In his famous *Essay Concerning Human Understanding*, Locke attempts to distinguish some categories from each other so that we can come to an understanding of what a self is. For Locke, we must first realize that a mass of matter is not the same as a plant or animal. Thus, the identity of a mere 'mass of matter' is 'only the cohesion of particles of matter any how united,' whereas the identity of an oak tree is found in 'an organization of those parts as is fit to receive and distribute nourishment, so as to continue and frame the wood, bark, leaves, &c., of an oak, in which consists the vegetable life' (Locke 1959: 443). The identity conditions for a plant are then 'an organization of parts in one coherent body, partaking of one common life' and this common life can continue throughout an exchange of material particles throughout the life of the plant. The case, Locke says, is similar in the case of animals and indeed in the case of human animals. This is what Locke (1959: 444) means when he says that we are talking about the *same man*[11] when we are talking about 'a participation of the same continued life, by constantly fleeting particles of matter, in succession vitally united to the same organized body.' Locke also goes to some length to say that we will not find the *same man* merely by asking after an immaterial soul. Locke (1959: 445) thinks this will get us into trouble with knotty issues of transmigration of souls and, in any event, he writes, 'I think nobody, could he be sure that the *soul* of Heliogabalus were in one of his hogs, would yet say that hog were a *man* or *Heliogabalus*.'

None of this has gotten us to Locke's concept of a person or a self yet. The key, for Locke, to the concept of a person (which non-human animals are not) is the idea of consciousness, but more, self-consciousness. Locke (1959: 450–1) writes 'it being the same consciousness that makes a man be himself to himself, personal identity depends on that only.' An important impetus for Locke's treatment of this issue is the concern that, when the person is resurrected in the Last Judgment (for Locke was a Christian), her rewards and punishments be doled out fairly. But that couldn't happen if someone were punished for actions she could not consciously remember having performed. Thus, for Locke, consciousness is the key to this forensic notion of personhood, and indeed, consciousness of one's past actions (memory, too, plays a role here). Locke (1959: 451) writes 'For as far as any intelligent being can repeat the idea of any past action with the same consciousness it had of it at first, and with the same consciousness it has of any present action; so far it is the same personal self.' Without consciousness of my past actions, I cannot be said to be the same *person*[12] as the one who committed them, and with that consciousness, I am culpable for those actions, for this consciousness includes a self-consciousness that it was I who did them.

There are certain features of Locke's account that are rather unattractive, though. He was forced to concede that a kind of Jekyll and Hyde case was quite possible so that we could, in theory, have 'two distinct incommunicable consciousnesses' acting at different times in one body and then we would have two persons. Moreover, he also conceded that the opposite case was theoretically possible, namely, that if one consciousness could act, by intervals, in two different bodies, we would have one person in two bodies (Locke 1959: 464).

Also, Locke's theory is often thought susceptible to the 'brave officer' paradox from Thomas Reid (see Jolley 1999: 120). Here, a brave officer captures a standard from the enemy and can also remember being flogged as a child. Later, he becomes a general. The general can remember capturing the standard, and the officer can remember the flogging, but the general cannot remember the flogging. If identity is tied too closely to personal memories and their retention, it looks like Locke will have to say that general is the same person as the officer and the officer is the same person as the child, but the general is not the same person as the child (Jolley 1999: 120). Stokes (2015: 30–1) argues that there is a way, at least partially, to salvage Locke's account by focusing on the appropriation of memories and not the mere having of them, but even then, Stokes himself (2015: 45) wants to argue that Kierkegaard's account has some virtues over Locke's, especially as it concerns the relevance of recollection (as opposed to mere memory).

Indeed, a Kierkegaardian account may hold out some other forms of promise here that may be worth considering. Remember that Anti-Climacus's account of the synthesis, because it is not *merely* about the relation of body and soul, but also about infinitude and finitude, freedom and necessity, and temporality and eternity, gives us some more anchors for the self. Indeed, Davenport (2013: 236) glosses Glenn to include 'actual situations of history and culture,' which seems plausible if we read this as part of the finitude of which the synthesis is composed.

In an important journal entry of 1846, Kierkegaard describes what he calls 'the dialectic of community or society' in three steps. First, the particulars (such as citizens) are thought lower than the relation (as in a single limb of the body to the body itself). Second, the particulars are individually equal to themselves and to the relation (as in the case of love, where 'each is something for itself but the need for the relation is the same for both'). Finally, the highest form of community, says Kierkegaard, is when the particulars that relate to each other are 'individually higher than the relation,' when an individual relates 'first to God and then to the community, but this former relation is the highest, so long as he does not slight the latter' (KJN 2, 261/SKS 18, 283). What cannot be denied about this passage is that, for Kierkegaard, the individual's relation to God is paramount. But that does not mean that the community is lost, and indeed, it cannot be slighted.

In his review of the novel *Two Ages*, Kierkegaard also discusses the relationship individuals have to one another when things are going well. He writes 'When individuals (each one individually) are essentially and passionately related to an idea and together are essentially related to the same idea, the relation is optimal and normative. Individually, the relation separates them (each one has himself for himself), and ideally it unites them' (TA, 62/SKS 8, 61). We can make a suggestion here that goes beyond what Kierkegaard himself actually says, but that seems plausible given other claims to which he is committed. For Kierkegaard, the task of relating to God in faith is never over, and what occurs in faith is that the 'self in being itself and in willing to be itself rests transparently in God' (SUD, 82/SKS 11, 196). That is, the faithful self is the self done right. But to be the self I am 'primitively intended' to be (SUD, 33/ SKS 11, 149), I must continually recollect and revisit the new and changing conditions in which I find myself and the 'actual situations of history and culture' that Davenport and Glenn have invoked. Only then am I in a position to relate, through the relation to myself, to God.[13]

In doing all this, I don't just relate to my body, but to my community, time, place, and culture. These are part of the story of the self that I must come to grips with in order to *become* an individual self who then relates to God. So part of what Kierkegaard can say to Locke is that the relation that relates to itself is not merely the memory of the self's individual actions, and the self is not necessarily diluted according as the memories of these fade. Rather, Kierkegaard's self also takes in the larger network of the body, the community, the culture, and history in order then to relate to God, who in any case is the site of our rest in whatever state we come to him, so long as we rest transparently in God, open to and humbled by his will for us.

The relation to god

A key insight from many theistic traditions, but particularly common in the Christian tradition, is the one St. Augustine (2008: 43) famously expresses in his *Confessions*, where we read 'you [i.e., God] were more inward than my most inward part and higher than the highest element within me.' What I take it Augustine means by this is that the movement inward is itself a movement to God, not because we humans are finally God, but because we humans are, finally, nothing and the truth of our existence can only be found outside of it. We have seen Kierkegaard also emphasizing that there is no self-knowledge without God-knowledge (KJN 8, 431/SKS 24, 425–6). But this is about more than just knowledge, as anyone who thinks about Augustine's claim for more than a passing moment would have to admit. For in faith we rest transparently *in* God, the power that established us. In some ways Kierkegaard might be seen as extending the way in which God is in all things 'innermostly' as we saw in Aquinas even to the non-substantialist self he posits. Even within the most intimate (and, we might have thought, private) reaches of ourselves, we must leave the self to find the self, for it is found in God.

Despite Kierkegaard's charges against what he calls 'mysticism' (see Mulder 2005: ch. 1), the mystical tradition is replete with discussion of this relation, but what is significant at this stage of our discussion of Kierkegaard's self is the notion of *transparency*. Resting transparently in the power that established the self (God), includes this finding of the self *in* God. The transparency that Anti-Climacus invokes makes a great deal of sense with a metaphor invoked by Kierkegaard in the signed discourses. In the upbuilding discourse 'One Who Prays Aright Struggles in Prayer and is Victorious – in that God is Victorious,' Kierkegaard writes that God can 'imprint' himself in a person only when she has become nothing. Kierkegaard goes on to say, 'When the ocean is exerting all its power, that is precisely the time when it cannot reflect the image of heaven, and even the slightest motion blurs the image; but when it becomes still and deep, then the image of heaven sinks into its nothingness' (EUD, 399/SKS 5, 380).[14] This seems a particularly clear example of transparency when the self is resting in God.

A metaphor from one of the Christian tradition's most daring mystics, namely, St. John of the Cross, comes to mind for comparison. In *The Ascent of Mount Carmel* 2.5, John imagines the soul as a window that ought to be wiped clean of smudges so as to reflect the sun's rays. He writes 'If the window is totally clean and pure, the sunlight will so transform and illumine it that to all appearances the window will be identical with the ray of sunlight and shine just as the sun's ray' (St. John of the Cross 1973: 117). John will be even more daring (as is his wont) and claim that the 'soul is God by participation' (1973: 117).[15] Admittedly, John's language rings oddly with Kierkegaard's characteristic emphasis on the 'qualitative contradiction' between being God and being an individual human being (PC, 125/SKS 12, 130), but that is not at stake here.[16] Naturally, the human creature is ontologically distinct from God, but on the level of the self, even Kierkegaard will talk of a unity (*Eenhed*) between the divine and the human after redemption (JP 1, 773/SKS 27, 234). For John, there are several sites of this union (will, intellect, and memory). For Kierkegaard, the union may be more restricted, though the will seems to be a place to start (see Mulder 2005: 131).

While gravity has now replaced John's (1973, 583) Aristotelian analogy of a rock falling toward its centre, namely, the centre of the earth, he follows this case, in *The Living Flame of Love* 1.12, to say that 'the soul's center is God' and that when it has reached God it will 'know, love, and enjoy God will all its might.' To be sure, John has a more systematic view of how one enters into union with God than Kierkegaard ever gives us. Nevertheless, in this chapter, we have seen how, according to Kierkegaard, for the self to be what it is primitively intended to be, it must relate to its created being. When finally it is at rest, it finds its true self, paradoxically, outside of itself where it is given to itself by God, and rests transparently in the power that established it.

Conclusion

Kierkegaard's self is a remarkably fruitful concept both in its own right and for the sake of the many paths of dialogue it opens up with great philosophical and spiritual insights of the past. In this paper, I've tried to show how that concept can open up a field for dialogue with the Aristotelian-Thomistic tradition (and ultimately Catholic-Protestant dialogue), how it may have resources for improving upon John Locke's influential view of the self, and how it can converse with the likes of St. John of the Cross (and others) from the mystical tradition. This chapter mostly points to further ways each of these topics can be developed, but I hope it has shown some of the depth and breadth of this concept in Kierkegaard's work.

Related topics

'Christian epistemology and the anthropology of sin: Kierkegaard on natural theology and the concept of "offense,"' Karen L. Carr; 'Coming to an understanding with the paradox,' Mark A. Wrathall.

Notes

1 Kierkegaard himself makes it clear that the pseudonym Anti-Climacus is not used so much as a fictional persona articulating views Kierkegaard doesn't hold, but rather to give a sharp critique with which Kierkegaard seems largely in agreement. Nevertheless, the pseudonym was used so as not to give the appearance that Kierkegaard himself was exempt from the critique (see KJN 6, 369–70/SKS 22, 365–6).
2 This is a small modification of the Hongs' translation that reads 'relates itself to itself' and 'is the relation's relating itself to itself' (SUD, 13/SKS 11, 129). For more on why this translation should be preferred, see Michelle Kosch (2006: 202n33). Similar instances in the quoted passage are also modified accordingly.
3 It remains somewhat controversial just what exactly Kierkegaard's metaphysical commitments are here. See the dispute between Turnbull (2011) and Rudd and Stokes (2013).
4 In an otherwise very helpful discussion, Christopher Barnett seems at one point to suggest that the synthesis Anti-Climacus is talking about that would then need to relate to God is the synthesis of this first self and deeper selves. He writes 'according to Kierkegaard, the self is actually an interplay (or synthesis) of two opposing selves – a "first self" that derives its orientation from the external world and a "deeper self" that calls [the first self] back from the external' (Barnett 2013: 107). When Barnett claims

that the synthesis is of the first and deeper selves, I would merely contend that this is true of the *relation* to the synthesis, and not the synthesis itself. Rather, the synthesis itself is merely the minimal ontological requirement for acquiring a self. The relation springing from the synthesis must relate harmoniously to itself (including the first and deeper selves) and then to God, but the self is not the synthesis.

5 Davenport (2013: 234) follows Elizabeth E. Morelli (1995) in holding that the hylomorphic account seems to be a correct view of the *human being* according to Anti-Climacus, but not a correct view of the human *self*. This seems fine as far as it goes, though Anti-Climacus does tell us that the 'human being is spirit' which in turn is 'self' (SUD, 13/SKS 11, 129). Consequently, I'll just use 'human animal' for the distinction.

6 For instance, consider that the Trinity for Christians is generally understood to be three persons in one substance, and further that Christ is only, and only ever has been, one *person* but nevertheless has two natures. For Christians, the Council of Constantinople (381) rejected the heresy of Apollinarianism (which held that the divine person took the place of the rational human soul), and so insisted that Christ has a human soul with which, as it later became clear at the Council of Ephesus (431), his divine *person* is not identical. Perhaps Christians with physicalist leanings who reject the notion of a soul would simply claim that, instead of a human soul, Christ possesses whatever counts for full humanity in addition to his divinity, but in any case, Christ is not understood to be a human *person* for the great majority of Christians who follow Ephesus in rejecting Nestorianism. On some interesting implications of these views on Christ's person, see Alfred J. Freddoso (1986).

7 As an example, I would refer the reader to St. Bernard of Clairvaux's (1987) text *On the Steps of Humility and Pride*.

8 See Aquinas (1981: I.75.6) for his account of the incorruptibility of the soul. See Patrick Toner (2012) for a view on the question of the person surviving death in Aquinas.

9 Otherwise, Aquinas' (1995: 5.3) article in *On Evil* on whether those who die with only original sin (such as unbaptized infants) experience the pain of hell would make no sense (for Aquinas, they experience natural happiness but not the supernatural happiness that they never knew they were missing).

10 Aquinas (1981: I.75.6, reply to objection 2) notes the difference between the soul having a potentiality toward non-being (which it doesn't) and God still being always able to withdraw being from the creature (which he can).

11 Despite its gender exclusivity, Locke's term 'same man' here is the one he uses and may pay some dividend for keeping us focused on his text and terms.

12 Patrick Stokes (2015: 31) explains that, for Locke, 'Self' and 'Person' 'are co-referent terms (corresponding roughly to a first-person and a third-person perspective on the same object, respectively.)'

13 There would also need to be a role for the consciousness of sin and forgiveness, as in the movement to faith glimpsed in *Concluding Unscientific Postscript* (CUP 1, 583–4/ SKS 7, 530–2).

14 See Becker (2012: 11) for more on this metaphor and how it relates to Meister Eckhart.

15 We needn't focus overmuch on the question of a soul as opposed to a body. My own view is that John is clearly talking about something like the self even if he is not making as clear a distinction as Kierkegaard later does.

16 Kieran Kavanaugh notes of John of the Cross, that the union with God for him will have to be 'situated on a plane distinct from the ontological' (John of the Cross 1987: 91n5).

References

Aquinas, St. T. (1999) *On human nature*, T. S. Hibbs (ed), Indianapolis, IN: Hackett Publishing Company.

Aquinas, St. T. (1995) *On evil*, J. A. Oesterle and J. T. Oesterle (trans), Notre Dame, IN: University of Notre Dame Press.

Aquinas, St. T. (1981) *Summa theologica*, vol. 1, Fathers of the English Dominican Province (trans), Allen, TX: Christian Classics.

Aristotle (1984) *The complete works of Aristotle*, vol. 1, J. Barnes (ed), Princeton, NJ: Princeton University Press.

Augustine, St. (2008) *Confessions*, H. Chadwick (trans), Oxford: Oxford University Press.

Barnett, C. (2013) 'The mystical influence on Kierkegaard's theological anthropology,' in R. Králik et al. (eds), *Acta Kierkegaardiana*, vol. 6 (*Kierkegaard and Human Nature*), Slovakia: Kierkegaard Society in Slovakia & Kierkegaard Circle.

Becker, H. (2012) 'Mirroring God: Reflections of Meister Eckhart's thought in Kierkegaard's authorship,' in H. Schultz, J. Stewart, K. Verstrynge and P. Sajda (eds), *Kierkegaard Studies Yearbook 2012*, Berlin: Walter de Gruyter, 3–24.

Bernard of Clairvaux (1987) 'On the steps of humility and pride,' in G. R. Evans (trans), *Bernard of Clairvaux: Selected Works*, Mahwah, NJ: Paulist Press.
Catholic Church (1997) *Catechism of the Catholic Church*, 2nd ed., Washington, DC: United States Conference of Catholic Bishops.
Davenport, J. (2013) 'Selfhood and "Spirit,"' in J. Lippitt and G. Pattison (eds), *The Oxford Handbook of Kierkegaard*, Oxford: Oxford University Press, 230–51.
Freddoso, A. J. (1986) 'Human nature, potency and the incarnation,' *Faith and Philosophy*, 3: 27–53.
Furnal, J. (2016) *Catholic theology after Kierkegaard*, Oxford: Oxford University Press.
Glenn, J. D., Jr. (1987) 'The definition of the self and the structure of Kierkegaard's work,' in R. L. Perkins (ed), *International Kierkegaard Commentary*, vol. 19 (*The Sickness unto Death*), Macon, GA: Mercer University Press.
Hampson, D. (2001) *Christian contradictions: The structures of Lutheran and Catholic thought*, Cambridge: Cambridge University Press.
John of the Cross, St. (1987) *John of the Cross: Selected writings*, K. Kavangaugh (ed), New York: Paulist Press.
John of the Cross, St. (1973) *The Collected Works of St. John of the Cross*, K. Kavanaugh and O. Rodriguez (trans), Washington, DC: Institute of Carmelite Studies.
Jolley, N. (1999) *Locke: His philosophical thought*, Oxford: Oxford University Press.
Kosch, M. (2006) *Freedom and reason in Kant, Schelling, and Kierkegaard*, Oxford: Oxford University Press.
Locke, J. (1959) *An essay concerning human understanding*, vol. 1, New York: Dover Publications.
Luther, M. (1956) *Luther's works*, vol. 21, P. Jaroslav (trans), St. Louis, MO: Concordia.
Morelli, E. (1995) 'The existence of the self before God in Kierkegaard's "The Sickness unto Death",' *Heythrop Journal*, 36: 15–29.
Mulder, J., Jr. (2015) 'Grace and rigor in Kierkegaard's reception of the Church Fathers,' in J. Stewart (ed), *A Companion to Kierkegaard*, Oxford: Blackwell.
Mulder, J., Jr. (2010) *Kierkegaard and the Catholic tradition: Conflict and dialogue*, Bloomington, IN: Indiana University Press.
Mulder, J., Jr. (2005) *Mystical and Buddhist elements in Kierkegaard's religious thought*, Lewiston, NY: Edwin Mellen Press.
Pattison, G. (2008) 'Philosophy and dogma: The testimony of an upbuilding discourse,' in E. F. Mooney (ed), *Ethics, Love, and Faith in Kierkegaard*, Bloomington, IN: Indiana University Press.
Rudd, A. and Stokes, P. (2013) 'The soul of a philosopher: Reply to Turnbull,' in H. Schultz, J. Stewart and K. Verstrynge (eds), *Kierkegaard Studies Yearbook 2013*, Berlin: Walter de Gruyter, 475–93.
Stokes, P. (2015) *The naked self: Kierkegaard and personal identity*, Oxford: Oxford University Press.
Toner, P. (2012) 'St. Thomas Aquinas on punishing souls,' *International Journal for Philosophy of Religion*, 71: 103–16.
Turnbull, J. (2011) 'Saving Kierkegaard's soul: From philosophical psychology to golden age soteriology,' in H. Schultz, J. Stewart and K. Verstrynge (eds), *Kierkegaard Studies Yearbook 2011*, Berlin: Walter de Gruyter, 279–02.
Westphal, M. (1987) 'Kierkegaard's psychology and unconscious despair,' in R. L. Perkins (ed), *International Kierkegaard Commentary*, vol. 19 (*The Sickness unto Death*), Macon, GA: Mercer University Press.

Further reading

Davenport, J. (2013) 'Selfhood and "Spirit,"' in J. Lippitt and G. Pattison (eds), *The Oxford Handbook of Kierkegaard*, Oxford: Oxford University Press, 230–51.

This chapter is a particularly helpful exposition of Kierkegaard's concept of the self, especially as it relates to other key writings of Kierkegaard's.

Mulder, J., Jr. (2005) *Mystical and Buddhist elements in Kierkegaard's religious thought*, Lewiston, NY: Edwin Mellen Press.

This discussion of Kierkegaard's dialectic and authorship argues that Kierkegaard can be understood in conversation with the mystical tradition (despite his protests to the contrary), and places him in conversation with figures in that tradition and the contemporary Buddhist tradition.

Stokes, P. (2015) *The naked self: Kierkegaard and personal identity*, Oxford: Oxford University Press.

This book puts Kierkegaard's work on the self and personal identity in conversation with the Lockean tradition and with more contemporary discussions of personal identity.

29
KIERKEGAARD AND THE DESIRABILITY OF IMMORTALITY

Adam Buben

Introduction

Kierkegaard has a great deal to say about immortality in his various writings. This is perhaps not very surprising since he is, after all, an author thoroughly engaged with religious matters. To raise the question of the desirability of immortality, however, is not necessarily to participate in a religious discussion. Inspired by centuries of fantasy and science fiction literature,[1] and further incited by both recent technological advances and optimistic prognostications about near future developments, a cottage industry made up mostly of secular analytic philosophers debating the merits (or lack thereof) of immortality, however it might be attained, has blossomed in the last few decades. Despite his somewhat different pedigree, this chapter will consider the ever-growing number of attempts to insert Kierkegaard into these debates. It turns out that his views on not only immortality, but also on boredom and what makes life of any length worth living are especially helpful for responding to 'immortality curmudgeons' (Fischer 2013: 337). The most prominent of these curmudgeons is Bernard Williams, who argues that an immortal of consistent character would necessarily become profoundly bored, and it would not even take very long for it to happen. When it comes to this and other related claims, Kierkegaard and his pseudonyms offer a number of reasons to think that Williams and like-minded pessimists are mistaken. But before considering what Kierkegaard has to say, and what others have to say about Kierkegaard, it will be important to have a strong sense of why some think immortality would not be so great.

Boredom and identity

Long before Williams put 'the "necessary boredom" thesis' (Fischer 2009: 86) on the philosophical map, Arthur Schopenhauer (1958: 491) succinctly captured the main worry under consideration here: 'the rigid unalterability and essential limitation of every individuality as such would, in the case of its endless duration, inevitably and necessarily produce ultimately such great weariness by its monotony, that we should prefer to become nothing, merely in order to be relieved of it.' Williams attempts to flesh out this point with the help of his chosen literary touchstone, *The Makropoulos Case* (by Karel Čapek), which depicts a woman who is able to 'freeze' the aging process and prolong her existence indefinitely via periodic consumption of a special potion. In his retelling of the story, Williams claims that after 300 years spent at the age of 42, the woman finds her existence tedious and declines another dose of the potion. He explains that 'her trouble was, it seems, boredom: a boredom connected with the fact that everything that could happen and make sense to one particular human being of 42 had already happened to her' (Williams 1993: 82). The dilemma that Williams begins to set up in this passage is that in a life that goes on too long, one of two things must happen – either a person will maintain his or her identity, but become bored, or, in order to fend off boredom, this person will have to surrender his or her identity.

But what does 'identity' mean here? It primarily means 'character' and it is largely bound up with the pursuits, projects, and goals, or what Williams calls 'categorical desires,'[2] with which one associates oneself. If my current categorical desires, and thus my identity or character, have to be abandoned in order to prevent future boredom, then it simply does not make sense for *me* to want such a future. The hypothetical future person, however engaged and enthusiastic, that results from taking on different categorical desires would not quite be me. Williams (1993: 83) states,

> It should clearly be *me* who lives forever. . . . The state in which I survive should be one that, to me looking forward, will be adequately related, in the life it presents, to those aims I now have in wanting to survive at all. . . . Since I am propelled forward into longer life by categorical desires, what is promised must hold out some hopes for those desires.

This identity condition might seem easy to ridicule at first glance. Surely, we do not become entirely new people after major upheavals such as failed marriages, career changes, or losing one's faith.[3] Looking a little closer, however, Williams' point is about why we want to survive, about what would propel us forward into an immortality that we can actually hope for right now. If I want to go on living at this moment in order to be with my spouse, then the prospect of 'playing the field' as a divorcée is not something that would be able to motivate me. In a sense, I would have to become a different person in order to want such a future.

This explains one half of Williams' dilemma, but what about the idea that a person of consistent character would simply run out of interesting experiences and ways to find life worth living after only a few hundred years? The length of time here is surely debatable, but if Williams can make a compelling case that *some* finite number of years would do the trick, then genuine immortality (in which destruction is impossible) begins to look very unattractive. His line of argument is roughly the same as Schopenhauer's. The limitations inherent in maintaining a consistent character will not allow for an unlimited amount of categorical desires. As soon as I have certain categorical desires, they preclude many others, and while some might be compatible with and even give rise to new ones, it seems to be the nature of categorical desires to exhaust themselves one way or another (often simply by realizing the object of one's desire). In fact, Williams (1993: 87) cannot imagine a single categorical desire 'guaranteed to be at every moment utterly absorbing.' Given such limitations, it seems impossible to avoid the 'the threat of monotony in eternal activities' (Williams 1993: 88). Thus, it appears that whichever horn of the dilemma gores you, it does not make much sense to hope for immortality.

The importance of repetition

Since Williams' seminal discussion, there have been quite a few challenges levelled at his argument. Some very good ones concern his rather strict understanding of identity that does not seem to allow for even the sort of shifting interests that we often see in lives of ordinary duration, and others poke holes in the idea that one would eventually (and permanently) run out of new projects to pursue (see e.g., Chappell 2007; Wisnewski 2005). Perhaps the best known of these challenges, however, comes from John Martin Fischer, who suggests that even if we eventually ran out of novel categorical desires, Williams gives us no compelling reason to think that all of our existing categorical desires are necessarily exhaustible. In fact, Fischer thinks, many of the activities we enjoy and look forward to the most are of the indefinitely repeatable variety. He wonders if 'some of the proponents of the "necessary boredom" thesis tend to attend solely or primarily to the self-exhausting pleasures (and associated activities),' and adds, 'but once it is seen that there are also repeatable pleasures, the prospects of a certain sort of immortality are not nearly so grim' (Fischer 2009: 86).[4] While it may be true that working on a PhD was only meaningful and motivating until it was completed, and that it is not an endeavour I would like to take on again, the same cannot be said of discussing the *Star Wars* universe and 'the pleasures of sex' (Fischer 2009: 85).

Of course, even sex (and sex of the most appealing or amusing assortment) could get old if this was one's only interest and one overindulged, but it is consistent with my character that I have a number of coexisting interests of the repeatable sort. If I engage each of them only periodically, and not at the same time, it seems possible that my life might be propelled forward indefinitely as I eagerly anticipate each new opportunity to participate in one of my favourite activities. Thus, even without a renewable source of pleasures or activities of the 'self-exhausting' variety, it seems that the boredom horn of Williams' dilemma can be avoided. Furthermore, because none of the repeatable interests are necessarily 'out of character,' it would seem that Fischer has successfully dodged the identity horn as well. So far so good, but it is at this point that Kierkegaard is first brought into the conversation concerning the desirability of immortality.

Fischer, making relatively little distinction between Kierkegaard and his pseudonyms, introduces him as a prime example of someone who might have doubts about the value of repeatable pleasures when it comes to shutting down immortality curmudgeons. He does this based on the 'Rotation of Crops' essay from *Either/Or*, in which the aesthete 'A' considers something like Fischer's own approach to fending off boredom (albeit not in relation to immortality) by rotating experiences in such a way that things remain interesting (or fertile, to stick with the crops metaphor). After mentioning a few claims from early in the essay about how boring (and susceptible to boredom) humans are, Fischer (2009: 88) accuses Kierkegaard of 'underestimating the repeatable pleasures' because 'even with the rotation method "A" finds life boring.' The problem, as I have laid it out in Buben (2015), is that 'A' never really comes to the conclusion that Fischer attributes to him. In fact, by the end of the essay he says that, 'for many people, this method is an excellent means of stimulation' (EO 1, 300/SKS 2, 288). 'A' certainly sees the dangers of boredom and recognizes the common tendency of human beings to end up bored, but he seems to be fairly enthusiastic about the prospects of the rotation method for combatting tedium, provided that it is properly grasped.

Unlike Fischer, who focuses on what 'A' would call the 'vulgar, inartistic rotation' of the 'extensive' external activities one might participate in (EO 1, 291/SKS 2, 281), 'A' recommends a variation in internal attitudes toward whatever one might be doing. One way of putting this is that 'the eye with which one sees actuality must be changed continually' (EO 1, 300/SKS 2, 288). Even if the range of external activities available to a person is somewhat limited, it seems that there is 'rich material for amusement' (EO 1, 300/SKS 2, 289) of perhaps unlimited variety once these activities are multiplied by the countless moods and attitudes that can be brought to bear on them. An entertaining example of this internal attitudinal rotation involves 'A' running into an acquaintance on a number of occasions and being forced to listen to his extremely boring little philosophical lectures over and over again. From an ordinary perspective this might seem like a kind of torture, but 'A' is able to endure and even enjoy these encounters by coming to appreciate something about them that has nothing to do with the most obvious element of the activity (i.e., the content of the lectures). A change in outlook allows him to take immense pleasure in watching beads of sweat roll down the man's face as he speaks (EO 1, 299/SKS 2, 288). Now maybe the element of callousness in this story is a bit off-putting, but this pseudonym's attention to even such minute and inessential nuances gives the impression that Kierkegaard might provide far more resources than obstacles to someone fighting against the necessary boredom thesis. 'A' may not be as enthusiastic about the sort of external repetition Fischer encourages, but the robust sense of internal rotation he advocates suggests that it was Fischer (2009: 89), not Kierkegaard, who 'ignored the possibility of a range of pleasures' that might offer even greater 'reason to embrace immortal life.'

Meaning beyond rotation

While I think Fischer's negative assessment of 'Rotation of Crops' misses some of its most important elements, I also hold that 'A' would ultimately take Fischer's side against Williams. Interestingly, Iain Thomson and James Bodington (2014: 255), in their assault on the attractiveness of immortality, agree with Fischer's analysis of 'Rotation of Crops,' but claim that he ought to take more seriously 'what the aesthete learns from the implosion of [his] strategy.' As I have explained, however, there is no reason to think that 'A' believes the rotation method implodes, and so it is unclear what he could have learned from its failure. Setting aside this fairly straightforward problem with their account, what Thomson and Bodington seem to be getting at is a common reading of Kierkegaard's early pseudonymous works taken as a whole, according to which a fatal flaw in the aesthetic way of life (boredom, allegedly, in this case) leads one to the ethical realm in search of something more reliably meaningful. Unfortunately for Thomson and Bodington, there is another complication for their account of what Kierkegaard is up to. Another notable reading, this time of *Either/Or* specifically, points out that no such fatal flaw (boredom or otherwise) is lamented in the massive aesthetic part of the book. While it is true that the second part, written by the pseudonym Judge William, offers a critique of the aesthetic way of life from the ethical perspective, there is no indication that such a critique would move a dyed-in-the-wool aesthete like 'A' (any more than his defence of the aesthetic way of life moves the ethicist judge).[5]

Let us say for the sake of argument, however, that the Thomson and Bodington story about the progression through the stages or spheres of existence is viable. Playing it out to its conclusion, the ethical sphere also ends up having a fatal flaw, 'and the implosion of the ethical leads to the "religious" sphere of existence, in which one puts one's unconditional faith in God, who can work miracles to resolve the otherwise irresolvable contradictions that make life absurd and lead us to despair' (Thomson and Bodington 2014: 255). Once the account arrives at the need for miracles in order to make existence enduringly meaningful, Thomson and Bodington feel comfortable side-lining Kierkegaard since (as I acknowledged at the outset) the question of the desirability of immortality is more of a secular question motivated by technological progress. This bracketing suggests that Kierkegaard will not 'be of much help' (Thomson and Bodington 2014: 255) to anyone who disagrees with their curmudgeonly suppositions, but I, once again, feel that Kierkegaard has a bit more to offer.

In Buben (2015), I provide a couple of additional reasons to think that Kierkegaard can contribute to the conversation without having to rely on any explicitly religious doctrines. First of all, I wonder how the alleged progression through the stages might be affected if contemporary technological developments and near-future speculation were taken into consideration. If advancing to the ethical stage is supposed to be motivated largely by the inability of the aesthetic stage to provide one with durable meaning, my contention is that this 'progress' could be rendered unnecessary if technology makes personal immortality possible in the here and now. The problem with repeating, at appropriate intervals, what one personally finds pleasurable across a finite life is not to be found in the pleasurable activities themselves, but in the finitude; the ethical (exemplified by the commitment of marriage) offers a merely temporary individual the opportunity to be part of a tradition or community, which at least seems permanent in comparison with the individual experience. As Ian Duckles (2011: 228; cf. EO 2, 211/SKS 3, 203; Watkin 1990: 66, 71–2) explains, 'Judge William rejects the aesthetic because it ties the individual to finitude while the ethical connects the individual to the infinite and eternal.'[6] If one were able to maintain and enjoy one's personal proclivities indefinitely, then there just would not be as much pressure to lose oneself in the ethical, let alone move on to the religious.[7]

Now I do not want to make too much of this point, because Kierkegaard (unlike most of his pseudonyms) is ultimately a Christian thinker, and the notion of spending all eternity alternating ordinary worldly activities does not sound exactly like what Jesus or Paul were preaching. However, there is still another way that Kierkegaard might support the prospects of immortality in the here and now without having to get overtly religious. I think Kierkegaard identifies at least one project/categorical desire that is perpetually compelling, even without the benefit of rotation. In both his own name and via pseudonyms, Kierkegaard claims that the task of self-reflecting, and tinkering on oneself based on what the reflecting reveals, is something that cannot be completed or otherwise disposed of so long as one lives. Although our other more specific motivations might come and go (and eventually evaporate entirely, if Williams is right), there is no clear temporal limit to this one. According to the short discourse 'At a Graveside,' when it comes to this project it does not matter 'whether one is granted a lifetime to complete it well or only a brief time to have begun it well' (TDIO, 96/SKS 5, 464). The prospect of continual progress, and the ever-present concern that one might (even after long periods of sustained success) make mistakes and fail to be the sort of person one wants to be, especially given constantly shifting circumstances, provide precisely the sort of 'momentum in life' (TDIO, 83/SKS 5, 453) that Williams would demand from an inexhaustible categorical desire.[8]

In *Concluding Unscientific Postscript to 'Philosophical Fragments,'* Johannes Climacus builds on these ideas when he says, 'the way of the ethical becomes exceedingly long. . . . The more profoundly one makes it, the more one has to do'; it lasts 'as long as life lasts' (CUP 1, 162–3/SKS 7, 150, 152). The ethical, in this context, is concerned with the cultivation of subjective selfhood – a personal determination and appropriation of ideals and actions that is to be distinguished from the kind of easy and uncritical 'doing what one does' that people often fall into (cf. Possen 2011: 122; CUP 1, 131–3, 144/SKS 7, 123–5, 135). This issue will be of great interest in the next section, but for now it must be emphasized that while proper subjectivity is deemed necessary, throughout Kierkegaard's writings, for the sake of a genuinely religious life, trying to cultivate it is not described as an exclusively religious task. It is a task for anyone who seeks a consistent and responsible sense of self. However, even if Thomson and Bodington (2014: 255) were too quick to remove Kierkegaard from the not-so-religious conversation about the desirability of immortality, they would still likely argue that 'we have no way of knowing that truly immortal beings might not eventually exhaust [the] meaning' of the supposedly perpetual project he recommends to us.[9] Neither Climacus nor Kierkegaard would deny that someone could feel that such meaning has been exhausted, but they would certainly deny that anyone must or should feel this way: 'To be finished with life before life is finished with one is not to finish the task at all' (CUP 1, 164/SKS 7, 152).

Immortality as a thought experiment

In fact, fears of boredom or other disenchantment with an immortal existence might be a sign of a personal shortcoming. While Kierkegaard turns out to be extremely helpful when it comes to defending immortality from those who think it would sap the meaning from life, Mark Wrathall makes the case that he also launches an offensive campaign against the motivations and character of the immortality curmudgeons themselves. This campaign begins right where we left off in the previous section, with Climacus explaining the importance of becoming a subjective thinker. As an aid in this becoming, he suggests a few topics to ponder – which Wrathall calls 'thought experiments' – that are especially helpful for cultivating subjectivity. Among these topics is 'what it means to be immortal' (CUP 1, 171/SKS 7, 158).[10] People (philosophers and theologians especially) often get wrapped up in discussing the issue of immortality objectively, for example, by providing arguments for or against the possibility that humans in general might live on forever. Climacus, unsurprisingly, redirects the inquiry and claims that each individual should instead ask 'how he, existing, is to conduct himself in expressing his immortality, whether he actually does express it, and for the time being is content with this task, which can easily be sufficient for a person's lifetime, since it is to be sufficient for an eternity' (CUP 1, 177/SKS 7, 163). But what exactly does it mean to express one's immortality?

Wrathall (2015: 435–6) provides a compelling analysis of what Climacus seems to have in mind:

> to imagine myself as living an immortal life requires me to determine whether my character is centered on something that will be eternally worthwhile – an aim worth pursuing forever, an affect worth having forever, and so on. . . . I need to find in my personality and my individual way of pursuing meaning something that provides a normative distinction that I can embrace eternally.

The thought experiment Climacus provides here involves answering the very personal question, 'Am *I* suited for immortality?' (Wrathall 2015: 434). It just does not matter much whether or not immortality is possible if one is not capable of a sustainably meaningful existence (cf. CUP 1, 176/SKS 7, 162). It also does not matter much (at least not at this point in Climacus' discussion) what this 'eternally worthwhile' something might be. What does matter is that a negative answer to this question about being 'suited for immortality' is not an indictment of the prospects of immortality itself, but rather a pessimistic statement about the quality of one's own existence and the value of the projects that define it.

For a healthy, coherent, and flourishing individual, thorough imaginative projection of life into the indefinite future would provide no reason to think that growing tired of oneself is inevitable. If, on the other hand, imagining oneself as immortal sounds terribly boring or otherwise horrible, as it does to someone like Williams, then one has an impoverished sense of who one is or could be. Again, in Wrathall's (2015: 436–7) words,

> Suppose, for example, that I think the thought of immortality and realize that I find intolerably boring the prospect of endlessly repeating the activities that now give structure to my life . . . what does my inevitable boredom show me about my character or personality? . . . Kierkegaard would suspect that those who are persuaded by 'inherently unsuited for eternity'-type arguments are confessing to a kind of despair. . . . [Such arguments] are persuasive to the degree they convince me that, within some finite time limit, I will no longer be able to tolerate being who I am. . . . I learn whether I am well disposed enough toward who I am that I could imagine projecting myself forward indefinitely.

Thinking about the meaning of immortality in this personal manner 'is one way to exercise my capacity for reflective self-evaluation' (Wrathall 2015: 440), which I have already argued is a task meant to last however long life does, according to both Kierkegaard and Climacus. In addition to this broader purpose, the thought experiment more specifically suggests a way to detect flaws in how one attributes meaning to life that might go undetected if simply carried out over the course of an ordinary human lifespan. Just as Nietzsche does with his eternal recurrence scenario, Climacus' treatment of immortality advances more exacting criteria for determining what constitutes a meaningful existence (Wrathall 2015: 437; cf. Nietzsche 2001: §341).

Risk and value

Thus far, the possibility that boredom would set in has been the primary worry about immortality under consideration in this chapter. Although Kierkegaard seems well positioned to dispel this particular worry, immortality curmudgeons have raised a number of other potential concerns. There is simply no way to discuss them all here, but given what has been said up to this point, it seems there is at least one other nay-saying argument to which Kierkegaard has a ready response. This is the argument that what makes life so precious and meaningful is the constant danger of losing it. In a life without death, the meaning-laden risks we take in each course of action would go missing. Take, for example, the decision to run into a burning building in order to save someone. What makes this decision so significant (for the rescuer at least) is the fact that the rescuer is risking his or her own life. Contrary to what summer movie ticket sales might tell us, and obviously leaving aside the means of rescue, it is simply less remarkable when Superman saves someone than it is when a more fragile person does so. Martha Nussbaum (1994: 227–9), A.W. Moore (2006: 326–7), Todd May (2009: 50), and Samuel Scheffler all offer versions of this risk argument. For instance, Scheffler (2013: 97) says that 'in a life without death, the meaning of' many concepts currently associated with a good life 'would be called into question,' including 'health, gain, safety, security, and benefit.' Lacking concerns about health and safety, just to focus on a couple of examples, many of my decisions and actions would lose the ability to contribute much to the meaning of my life.

Of course, one's life is not the only thing at stake when deciding and acting in one's present finite situation. In fact, even the proponents of the risk argument mentioned above acknowledge that there are many non-existential hazards that one might consider before choosing a course of action. When playing the game of office politics (which is, after all, not the *Game of Thrones*), my dignity and a pay increase might be on the line, but it is unlikely that my life is in jeopardy. And yet, many people still feel quite passionate about workplace drama and seem to find a great deal of significance in 'climbing the ladder.' Why would our ability to find such things meaningful be any different if life had no end? The response of Nussbaum (1994: 229) and Scheffler (2013: 204) seems to be that the possibility of death provides our lives with a more profound background risk that underlies all of the more superficial risks associated with specific activities. If the sense of courage and sacrifice that we currently think is required to 'do the right thing' in an office setting is derived from the more profound sense of courage and sacrifice associated with putting one's life on the line, then it is questionable whether the activities of office politics could offer the same kind of value to an immortal.[11]

Perhaps Scheffler and company are right that the meaning of certain risks would evaporate or become unrecognizable, but Niko Kolodny argues that other risks would only intensify in a life that cannot end. In this category we might find the risk of a life-sentence in prison, the risk of losing the affections of someone you love, or the risk of being jettisoned into space. To be sure, all of these things would be pretty miserable in an ordinary finite life, but without the sweet relief of death the misery might be unimaginable. Kolodny (2013: 167) states, 'Far from immortality removing risk, danger and so forth ... immortality would make risk and danger ... crushing.' Given such intensification, avoiding these crushing scenarios would have to weigh heavily on all of our decisions and actions. I believe that Kierkegaard provides one more example of a risk that could provide life with a great deal of significance, especially when there is no danger of dying.

Just as there would be intensified pressure, given immortality, to avoid being sentenced to life in prison or jettisoned into space, Kierkegaard (or at least Climacus) thinks there would be intensified pressure to cultivate a character that one can tolerate being around forever. One may never be a finished and perfect person, but Wrathall's characterization of *Postscript*'s immortality thought experiment suggests that one ought to project a sense of self that one can embrace and work on indefinitely. If one cannot die, then the prospect of failing to project such a sense of self, whether that means ultimately reaching the dead end of boredom, or worse, becoming the kind of person that one finds despicable, would have to be fairly terrifying. Being an unredeemable asshole in a finite life sounds pretty bad, but 'having to live with oneself for eternity' (Kolodny 2013: 167) sounds infinitely more unpleasant. The risk of being stuck with oneself in this way is both something that (at least some) people can relate to even as mortal beings,[12] and serious enough that it would be hard for immortality curmudgeons of Scheffler's stripe to dismiss it as insignificant in comparison with the risk of death.[13]

Conclusion

In addition to his more explicit discussions of immortality, Kierkegaard's writings obviously provide a variety of other resources to those interested in debating the merits of living forever. But why are these resources suddenly attracting more attention than they have before? I can think of a few reasons for this development, beginning with a growing interest in Kierkegaard generally and a corresponding diversification in the application of his ideas. It also helps that continental philosophers like Thomson and Wrathall are increasingly welcome in what have traditionally been purely analytic debates. And from the analytic side, it was Fischer's attention, of course, that was the catalyst for Kierkegaard's further involvement in this particular debate.[14] While this expanding involvement is both interesting and laudable, Kierkegaard's potential for contribution has not always been properly understood. It seems that certain interpretive errors and perhaps an oversimplification of his complex oeuvre are to blame for these misunderstandings. Once the details are cleared up, a more consistent picture of his views begins to emerge. Even if Kierkegaard, who does not take on the question of the desirability of immortality in exactly the same sense as Williams et al., comes down on neither side of the debate unequivocally, I think it is fair to suggest that he leans more in the direction of immortality enthusiasts like Fischer. What is particularly compelling is the number of ways Kierkegaard's ideas support the notion that living forever could indeed be meaningful and attractive. From the image of crop rotation to various claims about perpetual progress and the cultivation of responsible selfhood, Kierkegaard and his pseudonyms appear to be friends of immortality.

Related topics

'The ethical life of aesthetes,' Ulrika Carlsson; 'Conscience, self-deception, and the question of authenticity in Kierkegaard,' Claudia Welz.

Notes

1 For a helpful discussion of more recent contributions to the latter genre, see Fischer and Curl (2009).
2 These are the things that make one's life worth living, as opposed to what one only desires on the condition that one happens to be alive.
3 Even when using the metaphor of 'rebirth,' believers in spiritual renewal would have to acknowledge that the 'new' person has some essential connection with what came before. There is no narrative of redemption without some acknowledgement of pre-existing sinfulness. The Christian tradition even has the notion of *felix culpa*, which suggests that the joyful later development is predicated on the less than ideal preceding state.
4 If this sounds problematically hedonistic, Fischer (2013: 351) later says that 'it might have been better to put my point as follows: such activities ... might well reliably (and repeatedly) generate experiences that are sufficiently compelling to render an immortal life attractive on balance.'
5 Examples of the 'common' and 'notable' readings of Kierkegaard's works that I mention in this paragraph include Alasdair MacIntyre's (2007: 40–1) suggestion that *Either/Or* presents the necessarily arbitrary choice between the aesthetic and ethical ways of life, and Marilyn Gaye Piety's (2001: 63–6) rejection of MacIntyre's view and corresponding affirmation of a progression to higher stages based on perceived weaknesses in the lower. For another prominent example of the latter idea, see William McDonald (2016).
6 Although his sense of 'the ethical' might be a bit different, Johannes Climacus (another pseudonym) expresses what seems to be a very similar view: 'Only in the ethical is there immortality and eternal life; understood otherwise ... [the affairs of the world go] on and on, but the observer dies, and his observing was perhaps a very important – pastime' (CUP 1, 154/SKS 7, 143).
7 Besides any hope it provides for a personal afterlife (which certainly does veer into the realm of the miraculous), the religious sphere in Kierkegaard's work also has the virtue of resolving the apparent shortcomings of both the aesthetic (its transience) and the ethical (its subjugation of the individual). In the religious, and specifically Christian, way of life one is able to be a part of a community founded on historical events – that is, the life of Jesus – by maintaining a personal relationship with him (cf. Kemp 2015: 228). On Kierkegaard's occasional discussion of an explicitly religious conception of the afterlife, see Marks (2011).
8 Cf. Immanuel Kant (1997: 5:128), who goes further than Kierkegaard in arguing that humans are 'justified in hoping for ... endless duration,' but holds a very similar position on the possibility of 'endless progress' given 'a continuing propensity to transgression or at least impurity.'
9 This argument is related to their larger case that anything that can happen will happen given infinite time. I think discussing this issue would move us too far from the central concern about what Kierkegaard might contribute on the topic of the desirability of immortality, but Mark Wrathall (2015: 433–4) provides a helpful rebuttal, on unrelated grounds, of this dubious claim.
10 Just before considering this topic, Climacus first ponders the related issue of 'what it means to die' (CUP 1, 165/SKS 7, 153). On this thought experiment, see Paul Muench's (2011) thorough treatment.
11 Curmudgeons like Scheffler (2013: 99) have also pointed out that the meaning-giving sense of urgency provided by ordinary finite life's most literal deadline would also go missing in immortality. Unfortunately, while there have been a number of compelling responses to this urgency argument (see e.g., Greene 2016), there is not enough space in the present paper to consider what Kierkegaard might say about it.
12 Although there is probably a religious element to his discussion, wanting to get rid of oneself and in some sense being unable to do so (which has important implications for suicide) is indicative of an especially intensive form of despair experienced by some people according to Anti-Climacus (see e.g., SUD, 20–1, 48–9/SKS 11, 135–7, 163–4; cf. Mjaaland 2011: 85).
13 Also see Buben (2016: 395–7), where I consider other, notably Heideggerian, ways of responding to certain versions of the risk argument.
14 In recent years, Fischer has contributed to this bridge building in other ways. For example, Wrathall's work on Kierkegaard and immortality was both funded by Fischer's 'Immortality Project' grant from the Templeton Foundation, and published in the resulting special issue of the *Journal of Ethics*.

References

Buben, A. (2016) 'Heidegger and the supposed meaninglessness of personal immortality,' *Journal of the American Philosophical Association*, 2, no. 3: 384–99.

Buben, A. (2015) 'Resources for overcoming the boredom of immortality in Fischer and Kierkegaard,' in M. Cholbi (ed), *Immortality and the Philosophy of Death*, Lanham, MD: Rowman & Littlefield.
Chappell, T. (2007) 'Infinity goes up on trial: Must immortality be meaningless?' *European Journal of Philosophy*, 17, no. 1: 30–44.
Duckles, I. (2011) 'Derrida, Judge William, and death,' in P. Stokes and A. Buben (eds), *Kierkegaard and Death*, Bloomington, IN: Indiana University Press.
Fischer, J. M. (2013) 'Immortality,' in B. Bradley, F. Feldman, and J. Johansson (eds), *The Oxford Handbook of Philosophy of Death*, Oxford: Oxford University Press.
Fischer, J. M. (2009) 'Why immortality is not so bad,' in J. M. Fischer, *Our Stories: Essays on Life, Death, and Free Will*, Oxford: Oxford University Press. Reprinted from *International Journal of Philosophical Studies*, 2 (1994): 257–70.
Fischer, J. M. and Curl, R. (2009) 'Philosophical models of immortality in science fiction,' in J. M. Fischer, *Our Stories: Essays on Life, Death, and Free Will*, Oxford: Oxford University Press. Reprinted from G. Slusser, G. Westfahl, and E. S. Rabkin (eds), *Immortal Engines: Life Extension and Immortality in Science Fiction and Fantasy*, Athens, GA: University of Georgia Press, 1996.
Greene, P. (2016) 'Value in very long lives,' *Journal of Moral Philosophy*, 14. DOI: 10.1163/17455243-46810057
Kant, I. (1997) *Critique of practical reason*, M. Gregor (trans), Cambridge: Cambridge University Press.
Kemp, R. (2015) 'Repetition,' in S. M. Emmanuel, W. McDonald, and J. Stewart (eds), *Kierkegaard Research: Sources, Reception and Resources*, vol. 15 (*Kierkegaard's Concepts*), tome 5, Farnham: Ashgate.
Kolodny, N. (2013) 'That I should die and others live,' in S. Scheffler, *Death and the Afterlife*, Oxford: Oxford University Press.
MacIntyre, A. (2007) *After virtue*, 3rd ed., Notre Dame, IN: University of Notre Dame Press.
Marks, T. M. (2011) 'Kierkegaard's understanding of the afterlife,' in P. Stokes and A. Buben (eds), *Kierkegaard and Death*, Bloomington, IN: Indiana University Press.
May, T. (2009) *Death*, Stocksfield: Acumen.
McDonald, W. (2016) 'Søren Kierkegaard,' *Stanford Encyclopedia of Philosophy*. Retrieved from <https://plato.stanford.edu/entries/kierkegaard/> [accessed July 2, 2017].
Mjaaland, M. T. (2011) 'Suicide and despair,' in P. Stokes and A. Buben (eds), *Kierkegaard and Death*, Bloomington, IN: Indiana University Press.
Moore, A. W. (2006) 'Williams, Nietzsche, and the meaninglessness of immortality,' *Mind*, 115: 311–30.
Muench, P. (2011) 'Thinking death into every moment: The existence-problem of dying in Kierkegaard's *Postscript*,' in P. Stokes and A. Buben (eds), *Kierkegaard and Death*, Bloomington, IN: Indiana University Press.
Nietzsche, F. (2001) *The gay science*, J. Nauckhoff (trans), Cambridge: Cambridge University Press.
Nussbaum, M. (1994) *The therapy of desire*, Princeton, NJ: Princeton University Press.
Piety, M. G. (2001) 'Kierkegaard on rationality,' in J. J. Davenport and A. Rudd (eds), *Kierkegaard After MacIntyre*, Chicago, IL: Open Court. Reprinted from *Faith and Philosophy*, 10, no. 3 (1993): 365–79.
Possen, D. D. (2011) 'Death and ethics in Kierkegaard's *Postscript*,' in P. Stokes and A. Buben (eds), *Kierkegaard and Death*, Bloomington, IN: Indiana University Press.
Scheffler, S. (2013) *Death and the afterlife*, Oxford: Oxford University Press.
Schopenhauer, A. (1958) *The world as will and representation*, vol. 2, E. F. J. Payne (trans), Dover: Falcon's Wing.
Thomson, I. and Bodington, J. (2014) 'Against immortality: Why death is better than the alternative,' in R. Blackford and D. Broderick (eds), *Intelligence Unbound: The Future of Uploaded and Machine Minds*, Chichester: Wiley.
Watkin, J. (1990) 'Kierkegaard's view of death,' *History of European Ideas*, 12, no. 1: 65–78.
Williams, B. (1993) 'The Makropoulos case: Reflections on the tedium of immortality,' in J. M. Fischer (ed), *The Metaphysics of Death*, Stanford, CA: Stanford University Press. Reprinted from *Problems of the Self*, Cambridge: Cambridge University Press, 1973.
Wisnewski, J. J. (2005) 'Is the immortal life worth living?' *International Journal for Philosophy of Religion*, 58: 27–36.
Wrathall, M. A. (2015) 'Trivial tasks that consume a lifetime: Kierkegaard on immortality and becoming subjective,' *Journal of Ethics*, 19: 419–41.

Further reading

Barrett, L. C. (2014) 'Immortality,' in S. M. Emmanuel, W. McDonald, and J. Stewart (eds), *Kierkegaard Research: Sources, Reception and Resources*, vol. 15 (*Kierkegaard's Concepts*), tome 3, Farnham: Ashgate.

This entry, in what is essentially an encyclopaedia of important concepts in Kierkegaard's writings, briefly addresses the various ways that immortality comes up in his work.

Buben, A. (2016) *Meaning and mortality in Kierkegaard and Heidegger: Origins of the existential philosophy of death*, Evanston, IL: Northwestern University Press.

Among other issues related to human mortality, this book considers the varying levels of emphasis placed on some notion of an afterlife throughout the history of philosophy, and especially within Kierkegaard's work.

Marks, T. M. (2010) 'Kierkegaard's "new argument" for immortality,' *The Journal of Religious Ethics*, 38, no. 1: 143–86.

This article places Kierkegaard within the nineteenth-century context of debates on the meaning of Christian immortality and resurrection, and argues that (unlike many of his contemporaries) Kierkegaard actually holds onto a more traditional notion of post-mortem existence.

PART 7

Epistemology

30
CHRISTIAN EPISTEMOLOGY AND THE ANTHROPOLOGY OF SIN: KIERKEGAARD ON NATURAL THEOLOGY AND THE CONCEPT OF 'OFFENSE'

Karen L. Carr

Introduction

How do we come to know God? Within the Christian tradition, there are typically two routes: the first is through the exercise of our own rational powers, which leads to natural theology; the second is through revelation. Many, perhaps most, Christian thinkers see a role for both natural and revealed theology. Thomas Aquinas, for example, believes reason can provide us with partial knowledge about God and the nature of our relationship to him while insisting at the same time that certain truths can only be revealed to us. He writes, 'Christian theology also uses human reasoning, not indeed to prove the faith, for that would take away from the merit of believing, but to make manifest some of the implications of its message. Since grace does not scrap nature but brings it to perfection, so also natural reason should assist faith as the natural loving bent of the will ministers to charity' (Aquinas 1969: 55). Both reason and revelation work together in a happy marriage.

Kierkegaard, however, stands apart from this tradition. While he does seem to think we all have some innate awareness of God,[1] and he describes the religion of immanence (or 'Religiousness A') in great detail, he sees no role for natural theology. The nature of Christianity – in particular, its focus on Jesus Christ, the God-man – is such that it can only be revealed to us and its content constitutes the 'Absolute Paradox,' before which reason stands mute. Further, Christianity teaches that we are all defined by sin and are powerless to escape its grip, for all our attempts to extricate ourselves only push us deeper into its grasp. Sin, in other words, is central to Christian epistemology in Kierkegaard's eyes. And it is because of sin that ultimately Religiousness A founders; Religiousness A sees God and our relationship to him as a secure possession, but the truth is that faith, properly understood, has no such security, and exists in a continual state of tension. Kierkegaard's dynamic model of the self, coupled with the ongoing possibility of offense before Christ, means that faith is something the individual must continually and self-consciously will, not with the understanding, but against the understanding.

This chapter examines how Kierkegaard's understanding of sin and offense (offense being the sinful response to Christianity) shapes his religious epistemology. I will argue that, for

Kierkegaard, the reality of sin means that no natural Christian theology is possible, for the very point of Christianity is to bring reason to its knees and force it to submit, humbly, to the Christian revelation. Reason, for Kierkegaard, is our attempt to be *causa sui*, to be God ourselves, and only when we relinquish this effort are we in a position to be in the right relation to God. This relinquishing, however, is not something we do once and then are finished with, because as beings who exist in time, any commitment we make has to be continually and constantly reaffirmed. Further, our attempts to 'conquer' the paradox through reason remain a perpetual possibility that must be suppressed. Thus, I argue that it is not the case that, once embraced, the paradox ceases to be something that can cause offense to the believer – rather, 'faith is carried in a fragile earthen vessel, in the possibility of offense' (PC, 76/SKS 12, 88).[2]

In what follows I will discuss the concepts of sin and offense in three works by Kierkegaard: *Philosophical Fragments* (written under the pseudonym of Johannes Climacus), *The Sickness unto Death*, and *Practice in Christianity* (both written under the pseudonym of Anti-Climacus).[3] Kierkegaard is well known for his analysis of sin as despair, and this is, of course, an important dimension of his understanding of Christianity. Just as central, however, is the concept of 'offense.' This concept figures prominently in the three pseudonymous works just mentioned and arguably, lurks in the not-too-distant background of several others.[4] In *Fragments*, Christianity is viewed from the outside, and offense is linked to the 'absolute paradox' central to Christianity; *Sickness unto Death* and *Practice in Christianity* view offense from within a Christian context, the former connecting it to despair/sin, the latter to the existential response to the confrontation with Christ. While there are important differences between these three works, in all of them offense is connected to the failed attempt to render Christianity reasonable, socially acceptable, easy (or even facile) – in a word, to render Christianity *in*offensive. In Kierkegaard's eyes, all of these attempts reflect human beings' striving to be master, a striving that will inevitably be unsuccessful, given the nature of the human self as a 'derived, established relation' that relates itself to itself and to God (SUD, 13/SKS 11, 130).

I

The stated goal of *Philosophical Fragments* is to explore whether 'an eternal happiness can be built on historical knowledge' (PF, 1/SKS 4, 213). More generally, *Fragments* can be seen as Kierkegaard's attempt to clarify the nature and implications of a distinctively Christian epistemological model. By contrasting the Christian approach to truth with the Socratic, that of the 'pagan' or 'natural man,' Kierkegaard hopes to clarify Christianity's singular status in the world. The goal here is not to prove the truth of the Christian model – something that was an anathema to Kierkegaard – but to lay out what the Christian model must look like if it is to offer a genuine alternative to paganism (or philosophy, or natural theology, or what Climacus will later call 'Religiousness A'). Once having done so, the text goes on to explore the implications of this model for modern-day followers, particularly vis-à-vis historical inquiry into the origins of Christianity.[5] Specifically, Kierkegaard wants to show that, given the nature of Christianity (and the relationship between the believer and Christ, the object of belief), there is no epistemic advantage to be had by having 'been there' with Christ – that there is, in other words, no distinction between the contemporary and the second-hand follower. The concept of offense plays a vital, though not always obvious, role throughout this discussion.

Kierkegaard introduces his subject as a 'thought-project' undertaken by Climacus that will examine human beings' relationship to truth. According to Climacus, the Socratic (or 'pagan') approach to truth emphasizes that 'all learning and seeking are but recollecting. Thus the ignorant person merely needs to be reminded in order, by himself, to call to mind what he knows.

The truth is not introduced into him but was in him' (PF, 9/SKS 4, 218). In this model, the teacher is merely a 'midwife' who is essentially incidental in the process (and who plays a generic role, a role that could, theoretically [or 'easily'], be fulfilled by someone else). The moment of discovery – where the learner recognizes the truth he was seeking – is also 'accidental,' since with the discovery comes the learner's recognition that he or she had already been in possession of the truth.

An alternative epistemological model, Climacus reasons, must affirm the exact opposite of each of these points. In other words, learning must not be the product of recollection, but of revelation; the teacher must be, not an incidental midwife, but a singular and unique saviour. The realization of the truth must be momentous, not accidental, because it imparts something to the individual he or she did not previously possess. Taken together, this means that the learner must 'be defined as being outside the truth (not coming towards it like a proselyte, but going away from it) or as untruth' (PF, 13/SKS 4, 222); he requires not only the truth but 'the condition for understanding it,' which means that 'the teacher, before beginning to teach, must transform, not reform, the learner' (PF, 14/SKS 4, 223).

The contrast between the Socratic and the Christian models thus initially seems quite straightforward. In the Socratic model, one always already possesses or is 'in' the truth; one simply needs to become aware of what one already is. In the Christian model, one stands apart from the truth and must receive it from somewhere (or someone) else.[6]

Yet the contrast is not quite so simple. In the first place, both models presume that the learner is, at least some of the time, marked by ignorance (albeit a different kind of ignorance in each case). In the Socratic model, no less than the Christian, the learner, prior to the realization of the truth, is ignorant of it. Thus while the Socratic model affirms that, in an absolute or eternal sense, one already has the truth, as long as one is (temporally) unaware of it, one is ignorant. True, the ignorance is dissolved with the realization that one always already possessed the truth (hence the moment of discovery is not a transformation, but a moment of immanent self-awareness); ignorance, while not the final word, is nonetheless present, so long as one is not aware that one already has the truth.

In the second place, even on the Christian model, there is a sense in which the learner knows at least part of the truth of which he is ignorant; Climacus emphasizes that the ignorance is a product of an ongoing act of will on the learner's part, an act of will for which he is both responsible and culpable. We can only make sense of this act of will if, on some level, the individual knows the truth from which he is fleeing. That is, the individual, in order to flee the truth, must antecedently know what the truth is, otherwise he could not be said to be willing the flight. Since the attempt is also portrayed as ongoing, this means that the individual continues on some level to know the truth which it doggedly refuses to acknowledge. This 'knowledge,' admittedly, is of a very problematic kind, since Climacus also argues that the individual is unable to become aware himself that he is in a condition of willing untruth. This state of untruth, he suggests, we can label 'sin.' Because we 'know,' on some level, the truth that we are denying, sin can be seen as a form of self-deception, where one both knows and does not know truth at one and the same time.

How does Climacus justify the claim that the individual's state of ignorance or untruth is something he or she must be actively willing (and therefore, responsible for)? The argument defending this claim is frustratingly brief. In a very compressed manner, Climacus reasons as follows. If we are in a state of untruth, it must (1) be caused by God, (2) be caused by an accident (i.e., it must 'just have happened'), or (3) be caused by ourselves. The first option is rejected because God, having created us human, necessarily created us with 'the condition for understanding the truth' (PF, 15/SKS 4, 223). For Climacus, in other words, it seems that this condition is analytically connected to being a human being. Having created us in this form, it would thus be a 'contradiction' for God to arbitrarily take it away from us.[7] In addition, Climacus points out that if we did not initially possess the condition, then the Saviour would be more appropriately called our creator: 'that teacher who gave him the condition along with the truth would make him a human being for the first time' (PF, 15/SKS 4, 223) – in other words, the transformation would not be a rebirth, but a birth; it would be an act of creation rather than salvation.[8]

Why, though, could not the loss of the condition be due to an accident? Climacus initially disposes of this in a parenthetical: '(for it is a contradiction that something inferior would be able to vanquish something superior)' (PF, 15/SKS 4, 223). He goes on to argue that we cannot lose anything 'essential' to ourselves 'accidentally': 'If he could have lost the condition in such a way that it was not due to himself, and if he could be in this state of loss without its being due to himself, then he would have possessed the condition only accidentally, which is a contradiction, since the condition for the truth is an essential condition' (PF, 15/SKS 4, 223). What are we to make of this assertion? What, in other words, would it mean to lose an 'essential condition' 'accidentally,' and why is this impossible?

Taken on an individual level, the claim that it is impossible is plainly false; it is not at all hard to imagine things that are 'essential' to being human that one can lose by accident. If we regard consciousness, for example, as essential to being human, this can be lost through no fault on the part of an individual, merely through a random bad event. (A car accident could leave one in a permanent vegetative state, for example.) But Climacus, presumably, is thinking not in individual terms, but in terms of the general category of what it means to be human. He could, then, be arguing that human beings (understood generically) cannot 'accidentally' lose one of their defining traits, because if they do they then cease to be what they are and become something else.[9] In other words, his point seems to be that if we lose this essential condition, we cease to be human (or we die) – and we are not able to lose this condition once and for all and still be who and what we are. To put this another way, if the condition can be lost accidentally – that is, if some people can lose it while others do not – it cannot be regarded as a defining trait of what it means to be human. The notion that a whole class loses one of its defining traits accidentally is incoherent, since if the entire class lacks the defining trait, it cannot be a defining trait.

If we accept this argument, then it seems that Climacus has not only rejected option (2), but also option (3) as well – that is, this seems to be an argument that, in light of *any* loss of an essential trait, a thing ceases to be what it is (and thus 'it' cannot be said to lose this trait). What's important to note is the way that Climacus describes option (3): while he claims that, given the impossibility of both (1) and (2), the individual must himself have 'forfeited' the condition, he regards this 'forfeiture' as an ongoing process: 'he himself has forfeited *and is forfeiting* the condition' (PF, 15/SKS 4, 223; emphasis added). In other words, the condition is so essential to us that we can 'lose' it only by continually and actively seeking to destroy it. But how is this possible? It is possible only if, in a very real sense, we are unable really to destroy it, only if the condition remains a continuing presence within us that we are perpetually, but fruitlessly, seeking to eliminate.[10] Thus, even though Climacus unequivocally rejects the possibility that we are, through our own efforts, able to realize (or even recognize) the truth, at the same time, he wants to emphasize that our inability to do so is itself a product of our own efforts. Indeed, it is precisely our attempt to be autonomous that imprisons us; we are struggling against the realization of a truth that we must, in a very real sense, already know.

Several things are important to note about the position being developed here. First, even though Climacus goes on, in 'Chapter 3,' to reject at least two of the traditional arguments for the existence of God and to emphasize the essential unknowability of God to any and all efforts at natural theology (discussed in more detail below), the position he has developed nevertheless presumes some sort of awareness of God or, more precisely, dependence upon God, even if the individual is not consciously aware of it. In fact, lack of awareness or consciousness of this innate dependence is crucial to Kierkegaard's understanding of Christianity, since he regards it as one of the most common manifestations of sin. Second, the characterization of our state of untruth as one of 'willed ignorance' anticipates the much more detailed discussion of willed ignorance that can be found in *The Sickness unto Death*, in which willed ignorance is tied to self-deception and despair. In other words, the untruth that Climacus describes us as willing in *Philosophical Fragments* is the same basic condition that Anti-Climacus identifies as despair or sin. Third, offense enters into the picture in two ways: in the claim, on the one hand, that we can be jolted out of our willed ignorance only by God, and in the claim, on the other hand, that our willed ignorance stems from our refusal to accept the image of the self implied by this – as a contingent, derived being. Indeed, the very recognition that we are dependent upon God in order to realize not only what we are, but the error in which we find ourselves is an affront to our desire to be self-determining and autonomous. This affront is what lies at the heart of offense and is, ultimately, the root of all despair/sin. To understand this, we need to turn to *The Sickness unto Death*.

II

In *The Sickness unto Death*, Anti-Climacus remarks, 'It is specifically the concept of sin, the teaching about sin, that most decisively differentiates Christianity qualitatively from paganism' (SUD, 89/SKS 11, 202). Sin, in other words, is central to Kierkegaard's understanding of Christianity and what distinguishes it from other forms of religiosity. Since sin is defined in part as 'despair before God,' and despair itself is described as the failure to be the right kind of self, we need briefly to review Kierkegaard's model of the self and the various ways that people fail to live up to what God wants them to be.

Part One of *The Sickness unto Death* sketches out Kierkegaard's model of the self, a model in which selfhood is understood as something one does or wills, not a static thing one possesses. A human being, writes Anti-Climacus, 'is a synthesis of the infinite and the finite, of the temporal and the eternal, of freedom and necessity' (SUD, 13/SKS 11, 129). This synthesis is the ground or basis for the self, but is not itself the self. The self comes into existence when the individual wills the proper balance of its component parts. To fail to do so, to exaggerate one half of the component pairs at the expense of the other, is to be in despair. (So, the fatalist is in despair because she fails to recognize the existence of freedom and possibility, while the fantasist ignores the bounds and confines of necessity.)[11] The self must also will to be in a proper relation with 'the power that established it' (SUD, 14/SKS 11, 130); it must, in other words, recognize its absolute dependence on God and submit humbly before him. Failure to do so, even if one is attempting to will to be a self, is to be in despair (called defiant despair by Anti-Climacus). Anti-Climacus writes, 'the self in [this form of] despair is satisfied with paying attention to itself, which is supposed to bestow infinite interest and significance upon his enterprises, but it is precisely this that makes them imaginary constructions' (SUD, 69/SKS 182–3). He continues,

> The self is its own master, absolutely its own master, so-called, and precisely this is the despair.... This absolute ruler is a king without a country, actually ruling over nothing; his position, his sovereignty, is subordinate to the dialectic that rebellion is legitimate at any moment. Ultimately, this is arbitrarily based upon the self itself.
>
> *(SUD, 69/SKS 11, 183)*

The only way out of despair is to exist in the following way: 'in relating itself to itself and in willing to be itself, the self rests transparently in the power that established it' (SUD, 14/SKS 11, 130). Later, Anti-Climacus reminds us that this is also 'the formula for faith' (SUD, 49/SKS 11, 164).

In Part Two, Anti-Climacus makes explicit that sin is a form of despair; specifically, it is '*before God, or with the conception of God, in despair not to will to be oneself or in despair to will to be oneself*' (SUD, 77/SKS 11, 191). Thus, 'sin is the intensification of despair' (SUD, 77/SKS 11, 191) and, as noted above, the opposite of despair/sin is faith. Anti-Climacus further explains that 'at the root of the antithesis [between sin and faith] lies the crucial Christian qualification: before God, a qualification that in turn has Christianity's crucial criterion: *the absurd, the paradox, the possibility of offense*' (SUD, 83/SKS 11, 197). 'Offense,' continues Anti-Climacus, 'is Christianity's weapon against all speculation' (SUD, 83/SKS 11, 197).

What is it about Christianity that offends us? It is too lofty for us to accept rationally, as Anti-Climacus explains:

> Christianity teaches that this individual human being ... exists *before God* ... may speak with God any time he wants to, assured of being heard by him – in short, this person is invited to live on the most intimate terms with God! Furthermore, for this person's sake, also for this person's sake, God comes to the world, allows himself to be born, to suffer, to die, and this suffering God – he almost implores and beseeches this person to accept the help that is offered him! Truly, if there is anything to lose one's mind over, this is it! Everyone lacking the humble courage to dare to believe this is offended.
> *(SUD, 85/SKS 11, 198)*

Offense, Anti-Climacus continues, is 'unhappy admiration. ... The uncharitableness of the natural man cannot allow him the extraordinary that God has intended for him: so he is offended' (SUD, 86/SKS 11, 200).

It is no accident that this drive for mastery over oneself and over God/Christianity is intimately tied to what C. Stephen Evans (1992: 61) has called 'imperialistic reason' and to the overabundance of the wrong kind of reflection. Reason, which for Kierkegaard was embodied in speculative idealism, represents the most common and the most pernicious of all efforts to become master; Kierkegaard's focus on the absolute paradox (in *Philosophical Fragments*), on Christ as the 'sign of contradiction' (*Practice in Christianity*), is intended to emphasize how 'the possibility of offense' before Christianity is its 'weapon against all speculation' (SUD, 83/SKS 11, 197). Only if one relinquishes the demands of one's rational, social self and commits oneself wholeheartedly to Christianity in faith does the proper relationship to both God and self ensue.

While offense is undeniably linked to reason's denunciation of Christianity as absurd, this denunciation represents only the surface of the 'offended consciousness' of the non-Christian. Analysis of Kierkegaard's use of 'offense' makes clear that offense is not ultimately offense at a doctrine, not hostile denunciation of the claims of Christianity as self-contradictory and irrational (although this denunciation is a manifestation of the most intense forms of offense). It is rather offense at a particular way of living, at a certain kind of possibility for existence that requires acknowledgement of one's own sinfulness, a sinfulness of which one is culpable yet not healable through one's efforts. Because not only the healing but the awareness of the need for such healing must come from God, the individual's autonomy and sense of self-worth is affronted. Simply put, our autonomy both creates the prison in which we find ourselves and prevents our escape from this prison.

This notion of offense as an affront to one's notion of self-worth becomes particularly evident when one takes seriously Anti-Climacus's claim that offense and envy are analogous phenomena. According to Anti-Climacus, offense 'is related to envy, but is an envy that turns against the person himself' (SUD, 86/SKS 11, 199). Much could be said about this analogy, but for our present purposes, what is important to note is that just as envy may lead us to disparage something we secretly covet, on some level the offended person finds Christianity compelling, even as she derides it – indeed, the more offended she is, paradoxically, the more compelling (on some level) she finds Christianity. This compulsion, however, is thwarted by the errant will of the individual who, despite being drawn by the kind of life Christianity offers – a life of forgiveness, love of neighbour, and 'contemporaneousness with Christ' – is repelled by the dimension of it that requires suffering and self-abnegation. Nonetheless, the quality of offense underscores once again that Kierkegaard views the self as fundamentally oriented towards and defined by its relationship to the creator. And while Kierkegaard's position on offense, by its very nature, precludes the construction of any system of natural theology, it also serves to illustrate how, in Kierkegaard's view, even our resistance to God is both reflection and confirmation of our status as derived, created beings who, to paraphrase Augustine, will never be content until we rest in God.

III

Practice in Christianity is, in part, about what it means to live 'contemporaneously' with Christ, what it means to truly be a Christian, in the Kierkegaardian sense. It contains a lengthy screed against all attempts to ground faith in historical knowledge about Christ. What I want to focus on, however, is its treatment of offense and its relation to faith. Not only does this reveal much about the nature of faith, it also characterizes the sin of rejecting Christianity. Christ, Anti-Climacus argues, is 'the sign of offense and the object of faith' (PC, 9/SKS 12, 17). 'We can learn nothing from history about [Christ],' he continues, 'inasmuch as there is nothing that can be "known" about him. He does not want to be judged humanly by the results of his life, that is, he is and wants to be the sign of offense and the object of faith; to judge him according to the results of his life is blasphemy' (PC, 23/SKS 12, 38).

Anti-Climacus continues to emphasize, as he did in *The Sickness unto Death*, the absolute disjunction between knowledge and faith. 'Jesus Christ is the object of faith; one must either believe in him or be offended; for to "know" simply means that it is not about him' (PC, 33/SKS 12, 47). Or again: 'So inseparable is the possibility of offense from faith that if the God-man were not the possibility of offense, he could not be the object of faith, either' (PC, 143/SKS 12, 146).

Further, the God-man is not only inaccessible to our reason; he stands in opposition to human reason: 'That an individual human being is God, that is, claims to be God, is indeed the offense [in an eminent sense]. But what is the offense, that which offends? That which conflicts with all (human) reason' (PC, 26/SKS 12, 40). Attempts to prove Christ's divinity by appealing to the miracle stories in the Gospels (for example) miss the mark entirely – the miracle stories do not demonstrate the reasonableness of Christianity, rather the reverse:

> The demonstrations for the divinity of Christ that Scripture sets forth – his miracles, his resurrection from the dead, his ascension – are indeed only for faith, that is, they are not 'demonstrations.' Neither do they want to demonstrate that all this is in complete harmony with reason; on the contrary, they want to demonstrate that it conflicts with reason and consequently is the object of faith.
>
> *(PC, 26/SKS 12 40–1)*

Anti-Climacus makes clear that, despite his focus on the God-man as the object of faith, this is not to be understood primarily as faith in a doctrine, but rather as faith in the *person* of the

God-man: 'Christianity is no doctrine; all talk of offense with regard to it as doctrine is a misunderstanding, is an enervation of the collision of offense, as when one speaks of offense with regard to the *doctrine* of the God-man, the *doctrine* of Atonement. No, offense is related either to Christ or to being a Christian oneself' (PC, 106/SKS 12, 115). While offense can take two forms – one can be offended either that Christ is seen as God (offense at loftiness) or that God takes such a humble, lowly form (offense at lowliness) – Anti-Climacus continually insists that offense is not something that is conquered, once for all, when one responds to the 'invitation' of the God-man. Rather, the possibility of offense is ongoing in the life of a Christian. He writes, 'The possibility of offense accompanies the God-man at every moment in one way or another; a person's shadow does not accompany him more inseparably than the possibility of offense the God-man, for the God-man is the object of faith.... [T]he possibility of offense is precisely the repulsion in which faith can come into existence – if one does not choose to be offended' (PC, 121/SKS 12, 127). Or even more clearly: '*The possibility of offense*, as we have tried to show, *is present at every moment*, confirming *at every moment* the chasmic abyss between the single individual and the God-man over which faith and faith alone reaches' (PC, 139/SKS 12, 142–3; emphasis added).

This idea that offense is necessarily a perpetual possibility for the Christian makes perfect sense, given the model of the self discussed above. Just as a self is something that is perpetually coming into existence, rather than a fixed static thing, so too is faith something that the individual continually affirms over time; Anti-Climacus even suggests that it is the collision between reason and faith that generates the passion necessary for faith.[12] To treat religious faith as a secure possession (where one confronts the disjunction between reason and the God-man, makes a leap of faith, and then is 'finished') is to lapse back into paganism, into Religiousness A. Climacus makes clear in *Concluding Unscientific Postscript* that the tension is ongoing. 'For the believer, offense comes at the beginning, and the possibility of it is the continual fear and trembling in his existence' (CUP 1, 585/SKS 7, 532).

IV

In the preceding pages I have argued that we need to think of sin as a decisive shaper of what we can and can't be said to know about God. But even without the pervasive influence of sin, reason is impotent as a basis for religious knowledge. In the third section of *Fragments*, Climacus offers several arguments designed to show that we cannot reason our way to God. Sin, in other words, complicates an already difficult situation: that 'the infinite, qualitative distinction' between God and the self precludes the possibility of any rational comprehension.

Climacus first points out that 'if... [God] does not exist, then of course it is impossible to demonstrate it. But if he does exist, then it is foolishness to want to demonstrate it, since I, in the very moment the demonstration commences, would presuppose it not as doubtful ... but as decided, because otherwise I would not begin, easily perceiving that the whole thing would be impossible if he does not exist' (PF, 39/SKS 4, 245). Thus the very possibility of any existential proof is challenged. As Climacus goes on to explain, 'it is generally a difficult matter to want to demonstrate that something exists.... I never reason in conclusion to existence, but I reason in conclusion from existence. For example, I do not demonstrate that a stone exists but that something which exists is a stone.' Existence, Climacus concludes, 'can never be demonstrated' (PF, 40/SKS 4, 245).

What about the various arguments for God's existence? Climacus discusses (without explicitly naming them) both the teleological and the ontological argument. The ontological argument is handled in a lengthy footnote about Spinoza. Spinoza, Climacus writes, 'by immersing himself in the concept of God, aims to bring being out of it by means of thought, but, please note, not as an accidental quality but as a qualification of essence' (PF, 41n/SKS 4, 246n). To quote Spinoza, '"in proportion as a thing is by its own nature more perfect, it entails a greater and more necessary existence; and conversely, in proportion as a thing entails by its own nature a more necessary existence, the more perfect it is"' (PF, 41n/SKS 4, 246n). Climacus interprets this to mean that 'the more perfect, the more being; the more being, the more perfect.' The problem, however, is that 'what is lacking here is a distinction between factual being and ideal being.... With regard to factual being, to speak of more or less being is meaningless.' Climacus continues, 'A fly, when it is, has just as much being as the god.... Everything that exists participates without petty jealousy in being and participates just as much' (PF, 41–2n/SKS 4, 246–7n). Spinoza's and others' attempts to massage the concept of God and from it deduce that he exists, and exists necessarily, simply will not work. We cannot move from 'ideality' to 'factuality' in the way the ontological argument dictates.

The teleological argument (or the argument from design) is equally problematic, albeit for different reasons. Climacus begins by raising the question of whether one could prove Napoleon exists by inferring his existence from the things that he accomplished. Climacus writes, 'If one wanted to demonstrate Napoleon's existence from Napoleon's works, would it not be most curious, since his existence certainly explains the works, but the works do not demonstrate *his* existence unless I have already in advance interpreted 'his' in such a way as to have assumed that he exists.' There is 'no absolute relation between him and his works – thus someone else could have done the same works' (PF, 40–1/SKS 4, 246). So, unless I assume from the outset that works are Napoleon's, I can never move from the works to Napoleon, but if I have already assumed from the outset what I am attempting to prove, then the proof 'is superfluous.'

But perhaps God is different, because 'between the god and his works there is an absolute relation' (PF, 41/SKS 4, 246). This is, Climacus notes, 'quite correct,' because 'God's works ... only the god can do.' The problem, however, is that reflection on God's works in the world yields ambiguous results. 'The works from which I want to demonstrate his existence do not immediately or directly exist, not at all. Or are the wisdom in nature and the goodness or wisdom in Governance right in front of our noses?' (PF, 42/SKS 4, 248). What's more, 'even if I began [my investigation into the god's works], I would never finish and also would be obliged continually to live *in suspenso* lest something so terrible happens that my fragment of demonstration would be ruined' (PF, 42/SKS 4, 248). Thus, a posteriori attempts to establish God's existence are just as inadequate as a priori attempts, as all of them covertly presuppose that God exists; this presupposition is 'my contribution,' a *'leap,'* that must 'be taken into account' (PF, 43/SKS 4, 248).

What all of this means is that, even without the insidious influence of sin, reason stands mute before God. But things are worse off for us than that, because reason actually goes on the offensive when it comes to the specifically Christian teaching of the God-man. 'The paradoxical passion of the understanding' constantly is seeking its own limit, trying to 'discover something that thought itself cannot think' (PF, 37/SKS 4, 243). For Climacus (and for Kierkegaard), the Incarnation embodies the 'unknown' against which our understanding is always colliding. This 'unknown' cannot be thought, because it is 'the absolutely different' and the understanding 'cannot absolutely negate itself for that purpose' (PF, 45/SKS 4, 249–50). Christianity teaches that a particular human being 'is also the god. How do I know that? Well, I cannot know it, for in that case I would have to know the god and the difference and I do not know the difference' (PF, 45–6/SKS 4, 250). Climacus writes, 'If a human being is to come truly to know something about the unknown (the god), he must first come to know that it is different from him, absolutely different from him. The understanding cannot come to know this by itself ... If it is going to come to know this, it must come to know this from the god' (PF, 46/SKS 4, 251). In other words, a revelation from God is needed if we are to grasp, in any way, the absolutely different.

Specifically, part of what we need to grasp is that our own sinfulness is what is keeping us in 'untruth,' and 'only the god can teach [the consciousness of sin]' (PF, 47/SKS 4, 252).

Climacus recognizes that reason will resist both the teaching of the God-man and the pervasiveness of human sinfulness. It is possible, he says, for 'the paradox and the understanding [to] meet in the mutual understanding of their difference,' in which case 'the encounter is a happy one' (PF, 49/SKS 4, 253). But this is not the norm; instead, what happens is the individual responds to the revelation with offense, which Anti-Climacus, recall, describes as 'unhappy admiration.' Climacus anticipates Anti-Climacus, once again, when he describes offense as a 'suffering . . . similar to that of unhappy love' (PF, 49/SKS 4, 253).

V

Offense at the paradox can take several different forms, as Anti-Climacus details at the end of *The Sickness unto Death*, as well as in *Practice in Christianity*. But at the bottom of all of them is a fundamental misunderstanding: the understanding sees itself as judging the paradox, when this is really 'an acoustical illusion,' as the paradox is actually judging the understanding. Offense, Climacus writes, 'does not understand itself but is understood by the paradox' (PF, 50/SKS 4, 254). Offense 'is the erroneous accounting, is the conclusion of untruth, with which the paradox thrusts away' and this is 'an indirect testing of the correctness of the paradox' (PF, 51/SKS 4, 254–5). Climacus's meaning here is more than a little unclear, but I take him to be saying, in part, that offense is precisely what one would expect to happen, if Christianity were true. In other words, while Christianity itself is not reasonable, the model of faith articulated by Kierkegaard through his pseudonyms makes sense, given his characterization of the Absolute Paradox and assuming the reality of human sinfulness. What this means is that the Christian neither has nor should she seek rational grounds for her belief – Christianity is deliberately designed, as it were, to frustrate all attempts to conquer it through reason. And the fact that we are creatures who exist in time means that the unhappy admiration of offense always remains something that faith must perpetually overcome. The sinfulness of human beings thus shapes, not only Kierkegaard's view of the self, but also his religious epistemology, ensuring that the tension between reason and faith is an ongoing reality in the life of the Christian.

Related topics

'Images of the closed self in *The Sickness unto Death*,' Anna Louise Strelis Söderquist; 'On faith and reason(s): Kierkegaard's logic of conviction,' K. Brian Söderquist.

Notes

1 As Anti-Climacus puts it, 'God is not some externality in the sense that a policeman is. The point that must be observed is that the self has a conception of God and yet does not will as he wills, and thus is disobedient' (SUD, 80/SKS 11, 194).
2 In other words, as opposed to the supra-rationalism of scholars like C. Stephen Evans, I believe Kierkegaard is better characterized as an anti-rationalist, a person for whom the tension between faith and reason always remains. For more on Kierkegaard's anti-rationalism, see Carr (1996) and Carr and Ivanhoe (2010).
3 Climacus and Anti-Climacus are, arguably, the two most important pseudonyms for understanding Kierkegaard's stance on religious faith: Both *Sickness unto Death* and *Practice in Christianity* were explicitly recommended by Kierkegaard to an anonymous reviewer who expressed puzzlement over Kierkegaard's view of Christianity, as was the companion volume to *Philosophical Fragments, Concluding Unscientific Postscript* (see TM, 50/SKS 14, 185).

4 In *Fear and Trembling*, for example, the word 'offense' does not appear, yet one could argue that Johannes de silentio (the pseudonym under which the work is written) offers a reading of the Abraham-Isaac story that emphasizes its offensiveness to human reason, if properly understood.
5 Kierkegaard's preoccupation with the status of historical inquiry into the New Testament was partly a function of the emergence of the 'higher' criticism of the nineteenth century, in which biblical critics focused their attention on trying to discover the historical Jesus (as opposed to the Christ of faith).
6 For a more detailed discussion of the contrast between the Christian and the Socratic paths, see Carr (2001).
7 Note that even if one argues that God causes us to lose the condition as punishment for something we have done (e.g., by invoking the doctrine of original sin), we are still the ultimate cause of this loss; hence it would fall under option (3).
8 Climacus does not invoke the argument that it would be illogical for a good God to create us with the inability to grasp the truth, and also hold us responsible for this failure, but he could have.
9 One might query, given Kierkegaard's existentialist slant, whether it even makes sense to talk generically about 'human beings as a whole' in Kierkegaard. I believe it does; Kierkegaard is quite comfortable detailing the formal elements of what makes up a self (for example). The particular content of selfhood varies with the individual, but what it generally means to be a self does not. In other words, while one cannot be a self 'in general,' we can still talk generally about the characteristics of genuine selfhood or faith.
10 One is reminded of *The Sickness unto Death*, where some forms of despair seek to do away with the self, but always fail, because the self-consuming is 'impotent' (see SUD, 19/SKS 11, 134).
11 It is also, of course, possible to fail to be a self by not even being aware that one has a self (labelled 'unconscious despair' by Anti-Climacus); this is, in fact, the most common form of despair in the world (see SUD, 45/SKS 11, 169).
12 This is very similar to the argument made by Johannes Climacus in *Concluding Unscientific Postscript* about the objective uncertainty of the object of faith generating more passion (see CUP 1, 204/SKS 7, 187).

References

Aquinas, T. (1969) *Summa theologiae*, vol. 1, T. Gilby (trans), Garden City, NY: Image Books.
Carr, K. L. (2001) 'After paganism: Kierkegaard, Socrates, and the Christian tradition,' in J. J. Davenport and A. Rudd (eds), *Kierkegaard After MacIntyre*, Chicago, IL: Open Court Publishing.
Carr, K. L. (1996) 'The offense of reason and the passion of faith: Kierkegaard and anti-rationalism,' *Faith and Philosophy*, 13, no. 2: 236–51.
Carr, K. L. and Ivanhoe, P. (2010) *The sense of anti-rationalism: The religious thought of Zhuangzi and Kierkegaard*, New York: Seven Bridges Press.
Evans, C. S. (1992) *Passionate reason*, Bloomington, IN: Indiana University Press.

Further reading

Alfsvåg, K. (2014) 'In search of the self's grounding power: Kierkegaard's "The Sickness unto Death" as dogmatics for unbelievers,' *International Journal of Systematic Theology*, 16, no. 4: 373–89.
   This article discusses despair and offense in *The Sickness unto Death*, arguing that Kierkegaard is, in part, trying to show how Christianity makes sense (i.e., is internally consistent) even to those who respond to its message with offense.

Deede, K. (2003) 'The infinite qualitative difference: Sin, the self, and revelation in the thought of Søren Kierkegaard,' *International Journal for the Philosophy of Religion*, 53: 25–48.
   Deede provides a detailed discussion of how the concept 'sin' informs and shapes Kierkegaard's understanding of selfhood.

Otte, R. (2014) 'Passionate reason: Kierkegaard and Plantinga on radical conversion,' *Faith and Philosophy*, 31, no. 2: 160–80.
   Otte offers a very different reading of the relationship between faith and reason than the one given above, claiming that Kierkegaard agrees with Alvin Plantinga that religious belief is properly basic (and therefore rational).

31
VARIETIES OF EXISTENTIAL UNCERTAINTY

Rick Anthony Furtak

Introduction

In the *Concluding Unscientific Postscript*, Kierkegaard's pseudonym Johannes Climacus writes about 'the uncertainty of earthly life, in which everything is uncertain' (CUP 1, 86/SKS 7, 85). My aim in this chapter is to examine a number of places in the Kierkegaardian corpus that inform us about the uncertainty of human existence. The varieties of existential uncertainty to which I will attend include the epistemology of religious experience, the problem of other minds, and the limits to knowledge that are entailed by the finite temporal structure of human life. I will focus mainly on three pseudonymous texts, turning from *Fear and Trembling* to the *Concluding Unscientific Postscript* and then to *Stages on Life's Way*.

What Abraham cannot know

Unlike the abstract realm of rationally necessary truth, the realm in which human existence unfolds is one of pervasive uncertainty. About any 'existential proposition' – such as *I heard a voice*, or *the sun will rise tomorrow*, or *I am not dreaming*, or *I can trust this person*, or even *this is another minded being* – we are unable to attain the invincible certainty that attaches only to logical or necessary truth. As Kierkegaard contends, a 'man of conviction' is 'not ignorant of this [uncertainty]; he knows well enough what doubt is able to say' (KJN 4, 78/SKS 20, 79–80).[1] Thus, an Abraham imitator who thinks he *knows* God's intentions would be radically unlike the Abraham who has a passionate conviction that he cannot establish as demonstrably true. So: in the words of Johannes *de silentio*, 'How does the single individual reassure himself that he is legitimate?' (FT, 62/SKS 4, 155). Or, in other terms, that he is justified? He certainly cannot read the mind of God, nor can he rest assured that he has accurately interpreted what God is requiring him to do.

Years after *Fear and Trembling* was published, Kierkegaard returned multiple times to the story of Abraham and Isaac, as if he wanted to expand the 'Tuning Up' section so that it would include more than the four other quasi-Abraham narratives there (each followed by an image of a mother weaning her child). Two notebook entries are particularly of interest, due to the way they address the question of how Abraham might have experienced his divine command. Envisioning the story of Isaac's binding again, Kierkegaard opens up an untold aspect of it, since *how* Abraham heard God's command and *whether* he had any doubts about it are questions left unaddressed in the Genesis account as well (as, largely, in *Fear and Trembling*). No matter how we envisage Abraham's actual experience of God's command, it remains conceivable that he has construed it wrongly. An audible voice, or a sense of God's presence such as Saint Teresa of Avila often felt, or a non-verbal 'inner voice' that transmits specific promptings of the kind that Socrates experienced (see Plato, *Apology* 31c–d, 40a–c; *Phaedrus* 242b–c), would in any case need to be interpreted. Any mode in which God might actually reply to one's appeal for guidance about *what I must do* would also need to be construed and clarified. This imposes a 'dreadful responsibility' on a person, and explains the turmoil that is emblematic of religious experience: individuals 'bear the burden of decoding God's word,' and deciding whether and how to act on it (Sagi 2000: 127–9). Abraham must do more than simply listen and obey. As David Hume (1998: 23) points out, even a voice that speaks from the clouds is not self-validating.

The need for the prophet to take a stand, to make an interpretive decision, accounts for what *silentio* describes as the 'distress and anxiety' without which Abraham is not who he is (FT, 75/SKS 4, 167). In one evident sense, one *cannot* prove, or know, this sort of thing. What we *can* say is that the prophet is open and receptive toward the possibility of being moved, and guided, by a higher power (FT, 21/SKS 4, 117).[2] Yet in Kierkegaard's later notebook passages on this topic, Abraham fails to comprehend what God is trying to tell him: as a result, blood is spilled and confusion ensues. The portrayal of Abraham from a first-person, experiential perspective generates a sense that we as readers are sharing in his spiritual trial: this makes us shudder over what the prophet undergoes and puzzle over how he *could* have felt confident enough to have acted on what he *believed* he had been instructed to do.

In the later of these notebook entries, Kierkegaard recounts of a new variant 'Abraham' that 'he split the wood and he bound Isaac, and he lit the fire,' and then 'he drew the knife' and 'he plunged it into Isaac.' At that moment, God appears in visible form. He asks, 'old man, what have you done? Did you not hear what I said, did you not hear that I cried, Abraham, Abraham, stop!' (KJN 9, 250/SKS 25, 248). And Abraham replies: 'No, o Lord, I did not hear it. Great was my sorrow,' he continues, explaining that the idea of losing Isaac moved him with a sense of imminent loss, so that one feeling that upset him (reasonably enough) was sorrow. The earlier of the two entries (both of which are from the early 1850s) begins similarly, but looks further into what Abraham is experiencing: 'And he split the firewood; and he bound Isaac; and he lit the fire; and he drew the knife – and he thrust it into Isaac!' Then, God shows up beside him, saying:

> What have you done – oh, poor old man! And this was absolutely not at all what had been required. You were of course my friend – I only wanted to test your faith! And indeed I shouted to you at the last instant, indeed, I shouted: Abraham, Abraham, stop!
> *(KJN 8, 379/SKS 24, 374)*

That this 'Abraham' is on the edge of madness becomes more clear when we hear his reply:

> Then Abraham replied in a voice that was partly the faintness of adoration, partly the faintness of madness: 'O lord, I did not hear it. Although now that you say it, it does in fact seem to me that I heard such a voice.... When it is you, my God, who commands, and it is you who commands a father to murder his own child: then at such a moment a person is under some strain. Therefore I did not hear the voice. And if I had heard it, how could I have dared believe it was yours?'

This 'Abraham' *almost* hears God yelling at him to stop: once it is mentioned, he can recall hearing *something*, but it did not register. He is distressed, 'under some strain' [*anstrenget*], to say the least. Like the 'Abraham' of the other notebook passage from the early 1850s, he is passionately agitated; unlike in the other case, his feelings are hard to name. Here is how his explanation continues:

> When you command me to sacrifice my child – and at the critical moment a voice is heard that says, 'Stop,' I am obliged to think it is the tempter's voice that wants to [prevent] me from carrying out your will.... Either I had to assume that the voice that told me to sacrifice Isaac was the tempter's voice, and then I would not have set out, [or] ... since I was convinced that [the first] was your voice, I had to conclude that the other voice was the voice of the tempter.
>
> (FT, 267/SKS 24, 374)[3]

Either he takes to heart the initial command, in light of which the second call, the outcry telling him to stop, must be dismissed as a false temptation which goes against God's will; or else, he doubts the legitimacy of the initial voice, and does not undertake his mission in the first place. No wonder, then, that Abraham was emotionally overstrained as he attempted to execute God's command. He has a conviction, yet he cannot possibly be sure about what he is doing: either way, one might say, 'he will regret it' (Hannay 2001: 194).[4] The two later binding narratives are testimony in favour of the conclusion that Abraham *cannot know* whether he has accurately deciphered God's command, or whether he has taken a mistaken path of action based upon what he heard *or thought he heard*.

Admirably perhaps, Abraham has the 'ability to ... march forward, not knowing where the path will lead,' placing trust in God all the way (Wettstein 2012: 171). Although he cannot foresee how he could possibly retain his son after obeying God's command, he believes and trusts that *somehow* this will be possible, and that ultimately it will not be an absurd loss – as it might appear to be at the moment. Abraham also believes that the son whom he has loved will remain with him, in some way; he has faith that Isaac, and the promise of future generations, will somehow continue to have meaning in the grand narrative of which he is a part. He knows that he was called by name even before the night when God brought him outside to be dazzled by all the stars in the desert sky, asking if he could count them (Genesis 15: 5). And he trusts that 'God is concerned about the smallest things' (FT, 34/SKS 4, 129). The knight of faith *trusts* that all will be well, but not in a naïve way: he knows that 'in the finite world there is much that is not possible' (FT, 44/SKS 4, 138).

As Kierkegaard says, describing his own impulse to write: 'This urge, so copious, so inexhaustible,' which has persisted for years but 'still surges as copiously' as ever, such an urge 'must also of course be a calling from God' (KJN 4, 82/SKS 20, 83).[5] Reassuring himself in this 1847 entry about his own sense of vocation, he almost seems to be inquiring: how *else* could an individualized divine mandate be revealed, if not through one's affective experience? Logical reason can aspire to exact finality, but 'existence is the very opposite' of this (CUP 1, 118/SKS 7, 114). As Climacus points out, we should resist the temptation to regard existential reflection as an unworthy endeavour because it is unscientific compared to systematic thought: 'unscientific,' in a Kierkegaardian context, does not imply 'less difficult.' In an 1846 journal entry, he notes that 'the difficulty with speculating' actually increases to the extent that we are speculating about something that pertains to our existence (KJN 2, 279/SKS 18, 302–3). To 'abstract from existence,' on the other hand, 'is to remove the difficulty' of understanding oneself in the midst of life – yet this is what matters to us as knowing subjects (CUP 1, 351–4/SKS 7, 321–3). When one's epistemic criteria are mainly to find certainty, one's investigations are bound to produce very little knowledge that pertains to existence. Yet this outlook is essentially scepticism, as Kierkegaard explains (see KJN 4, 73/SKS 20, 74), because it leaves us empty-handed regarding issues so practically urgent that we cannot avoid thinking about them as long as we are alive.

On knowledge and difficulty

As Kierkegaard and his pseudonyms never tire of reminding the modern philosophers, it is not as if just any kind of knowledge will help us to understand ourselves in the midst of human existence. If we are wondering about human life and its meaning, and this is a topic about which indubitable knowledge is unavailable, then we will not bring our inquiry any nearer to resolution by deciding to be precise about something else instead. So, rather than allowing our search for knowledge to be motivated by a demand for indisputable certainty, and thus confining ourselves to thinking about pure abstract relations, what if we were to start anew by raising the question: what sort of thing do we have an interest in knowing? This would bring us back to the starting point of the modern epistemological tradition, but with a different sense of how we ought to proceed. Kierkegaard would approve of such a renewal in 'modern philosophy,' which has so far (he claims) been only 'an introduction to making philosophizing possible' (Kierkegaard 1996: 128/SKS 27, 234). As he notes, genuine doubt arises only when a particular someone has an interest in knowing something (see JC, 170–1/SKS 15, 57–8). Thus, the indifference of 'objective knowledge' is a poor substitute for a consciousness that is animated by our 'passionate interest' in understanding existence (CUP 1, 55/SKS 7, 59). And this is something that each existing individual *must* be personally concerned about: after all, 'the difficulty with existence' is what 'the existing person is infinitely interested in' (CUP 1, 302/SKS 7, 275). As living human beings, in other words, we cannot help but care about philosophical questions that are related to the way we live – to 'what it means to exist' (CUP 1, 193/SKS 7, 177) – and that influence how we experience and interpret the world.

What mode of reflection, then, would it be appropriate for us to employ in the search for 'essential knowing' that 'pertains to existence' (CUP 1, 197/SKS 7, 181)? Here, Kierkegaard suggests in the voice of Johannes Climacus, we might want to follow Aristotle's lead. It is obvious, Aristotle claims, that *phronêsis* – wisdom related to human life – is not the same as *epistêmê*, or scientific knowledge (see *Nicomachean Ethics* 1094b, 1142a). Yet that is because scientific knowledge deals only with necessary truths, and – as he states in the *Posterior Analytics* (87b–88b) – much that is true, as well as many aspects of reality, cannot be known scientifically. Since everything is uncertain with respect to the temporal, contingent realm in which we exist, any thinking that pertains to our lives must necessarily take a different form. Philosophers and ordinary mortals alike are drawn to objective reflection not because it is more difficult but because it is *easier* – at least, it avoids one kind of difficulty, substituting the challenges of abstract reasoning for the challenge of trying to understand oneself in the midst of existence. To illustrate this difference, Kierkegaard invites us in a notebook entry to compare the difficulty of scientific research with the difficulty of considering 'the question whether I shall be a scientist' (KJN 2, 266/SKS 18, 288). The former is indisputably challenging, but the latter is difficult in a way that might tempt us to 'make the issue somewhat objective' and thus escape from the 'pain and crisis' that we must face in thinking about it (CUP 1, 129/SKS 7, 121).

When Climacus talks about what it means to die and what death might bring, or when he focuses on the question of whether or not to get married (CUP 1, 165–81/SKS 7, 153–67), he offers us examples of existential questions which involve matters of 'objective uncertainty' and that pertain to every individual human being *as such*. These are 'matters that concern us unceasingly, but about which we are . . . profoundly uncertain' (Possen 2011: 126). It is a 'ridiculous contradiction' to inquire into such matters 'in general,' he says (CUP 1, 174/SKS 7, 161), for they relate to us in our particularity. Death, for instance, is 'the only certainty, and the only thing about which nothing is certain' (TDIO, 91/SKS 5, 460). To bring home the point, he lists many objective truths that he 'knows' about death, ranging from its biological causes to how it has been interpreted by different cultures, and then he adds that even with all this knowledge, he cannot claim that death is 'something I have understood' (CUP 1, 165–6/SKS 7, 153–4). That is, he is not convinced that he has truly succeeded at appreciating how his own life is coloured by the fact of his being finite. To think *this* through as a meaningful truth that concerns him personally, he would need to engage in the type of subjective thinking that is always indefinite and unfinished. As for entering into marriage, that requires nothing less than 'a true conception of life and of oneself' (TDIO, 63/SKS 5, 437), something which is endlessly difficult to attain. This is why there is no need 'to proceed to astronomy or veterinary science' in order to find intellectual challenges: the tasks of subjective thought are sufficiently intricate and complex to occupy us for the rest of life (CUP 1, 181/SKS 7, 167). Not only are we intimately involved in these questions, but the meaning of our existence is at stake in the way that we answer them. Although we continually feel 'an urge to have something finished,' this 'must be renounced' when we are dealing with existential questions that are inherently uncertain (CUP 1, 86/ SKS 7, 85).

The problems that call for subjective thinking share several characteristics. First of all, they have to do with matters that are *not* value-neutral. Secondly, they are subject-involving, in the sense that they concern each of us personally: what someone whom we care about thinks of us, for instance. And finally, they involve at least some degree of objective uncertainty. We do not *know* what death will bring, for example, yet instead of seeking conclusive proofs we might seek to become subjective with regard to this uncertainty, trying to clarify our deepest beliefs about death and immortality in the way that Socrates does (CUP 1, 201–10/SKS 7, 184–92; see Plato, *Phaedo* 91a, 107a–b, 114d. Cf. Howland 2006: 201). Likewise, our epistemic outlook in matters of love is not susceptible of becoming 'absolutely certain' (CUP 1, 455/SKS 7, 413–4) – we cannot *know* whether, or how, we are loved – but even so, we can hardly refrain from having *some* attitude, and holding *some* view, on the topic.

There is no way to prevent second-guessing oneself later on, either: whatever attitude we form, no matter what decision we make, we will be vulnerable to regret (see EO 1, 38–9/SKS 2, 47–9). Our conception of existence and our self-understanding must always be works in progress, containing an element of uncertainty that cannot be eliminated. With respect to the most important issues in human life, we cannot know *for sure* what we are doing; as Kierkegaard notes in an 1843 journal entry, life is lived forward and understood in retrospect, and human existence therefore cannot be known fully while we exist: in his words, 'temporal life' is 'never able to be properly understood' (KJN 2, 179/SKS 18, 194). However, this in itself does not need to be regarded as an embarrassment for philosophy. We might be able to think constructively about issues that are too ambiguous to be known with certainty, as long as we do not render constructive thought about them impossible by confining ourselves to a mode of reason that is inappropriate for the task. What is scandalous is when philosophers are exclusively or too one-sidedly preoccupied with scientific objectivity as the criterion of truth. Because we need to focus more on the subjective aspect of knowledge, philosophers after Kierkegaard must think in terms of attunement and interpretation rather than sheer objectivity. We may still be figuring out how to deal with the 'strenuous difficulties' of human existence (CUP 1, 85/SKS 7, 85), but at least we know that we cannot leave them aside, as if the difficulty of abstract thought were somehow more worthy of attention than the difficulty of concrete reality.[6] In other words, according to Kierkegaard we cannot in good conscience replace the difficulty of existence with the difficulty of mere thinking.

The deceptive allure of certainty

We are sometimes led to imagine that a particular bit of definite knowledge will alleviate our existential uncertainty. One of Kierkegaard's literary narratives in which this temptation is especially evident is the part of *Stages on Life's Way* entitled "'Guilty?'/'Not Guilty?'" Before turning to this text, I would like to comment (for the sake of comparison) on a remarkable passage from *The Captive*, the fifth volume of Proust's long novel. His narrator has the bad habit of watching his girlfriend Albertine while she is napping – and he wonders what is going on in her mind, during her waking life as well as when she is asleep. As he watches her, he recounts what it would require to know her thoughts and secrets. He would need to stop the progress of time, freeze her in a static unchanging state, and then somehow delve into all the layers of her subjectivity: her memories and dreams, her emotions as well as her deceptions. He would need, *per impossibile*, to occupy her mind from the inside, yet *even then* he might not find the resolution he seeks, because her mind is not transparently accessible but harbours mysteries that even she does not understand.[7] So he seizes upon an item of definite knowledge, a yes-or-no question, and becomes obsessed with answering this. He wonders if she has had romantic liaisons with any of her female friends: and this 'did she or didn't she' question becomes a substitute for all that he wishes to know. Strangely enough, he chooses *not* to examine the letters that she has received from these same friends, despite the facts that as she sleeps the letters are available in the pocket of her kimono (where she always keeps them) and that he has no moral qualms about snooping. Again and again he considers reading them, but always he would 'creep back to the bedside' and resume gazing at 'the sleeping Albertine, who would tell me nothing,' all the while seeing 'lying across the arm of the chair that kimono which perhaps would have told me much' (Proust 1929: 88–92).[8] 'Never once,' he says, did the narrator touch the kimono and examine the letters, despite his 'burning curiosity' about what they might reveal. Why is this? I think it's because he realizes that knowing 'did she or didn't she' would not alleviate his uncertainty and provide him with access to Albertine's mind such as he seeks. This bit of definite knowledge does not even help (as he finds, when he learns that the answer to 'did she or didn't she' is that *she did*). His profound wonderings about this other mind are not a matter of having access to something knowable that just happens to be unavailable to *him*. The moral of the story is that our finite condition condemns us even more radically to uncertainty. It might seem that definite knowledge of some fact would help us, but it might not. There is no 'secret note' that *could* explain everything in Kierkegaard's life and work.[9] And that is not by virtue of any peculiar ancestral curses or broken engagements, nor is it because of what one's particular 'thorn in the flesh' might be. The type of difficulty I am pointing out makes human existence incapable of being explained simply because, like the inside of another person's mind, it is opaque to being comprehended.

Quidam, the primary narrator of "'Guilty?'/'Not Guilty?'" is highly susceptible to the allurement of thinking that a specific piece of certain knowledge will alleviate the pervasive uncertainty of his existence. He keeps pondering such questions as whether he has acted rightly, whether he is justified in his sense of having a sacred vocation, and whether he is guilty of something akin to murder by virtue of having broken a person's heart. He is inclined to believe that these questions are answerable, but in fact he never succeeds at getting to the end of them. As Judge William points out, a person 'never finds out in this life' if he is justified in regarding himself as a religious exception (SLW, 183/SKS 6, 170). Quidam claims to be awaiting 'a verdict that will decide whether I was a murderer' (SLW, 198/SKS 6, 185), a verdict in the form of some information that would ostensibly show if the girl's life has turned out well or been ruined – yet this cannot possibly be gained while she is still living, and if she dies then the 'murderer' possibility only weighs more heavily on his soul. Yet he tries to read into her gestures, her silences, her presence and absence, whether she appears more or less pale, searching for information about her state of mind. As for his own, he asks: 'How will my exhausted mind find something on which to rest?' (SLW, 370/SKS 6, 343). Is he perhaps too reflective to be able to love, too depressed to be capable of getting married with a clear conscience? He has 'no factual information that justifies [him] in any conclusion' (SLW, 214/SKS 6, 200). 'I wonder what she is thinking,' he says to himself (SLW, 222/SKS 6, 208), admitting that 'What her state is in a deeper sense, I do not know' (SLW, 250/SKS 6, 233). He does not know whether, or what, she is suffering (SLW, 240/SKS 6, 224). 'And what is the point of all my concerns and plans and efforts? What am I achieving? Nothing' (SLW, 306/SKS 6, 284). Even though all his wondering is in vain, he continues to wonder indefinitely.

The theme of existential uncertainty is especially prominent in a twelve-page section of this book, in which Quidam envisions a 'bookkeeper' who wanders the streets of the Christianshavn neighbourhood. The section is entitled 'A possibility [*En Mulighed*]' and the possibility at issue is that this man may have unwittingly fathered a child after he once visited a brothel (SLW, 276–88/SKS 6, 257–68). He searches the faces of children in the street, fixating on a question with a determinate answer – did he, or didn't he, have a child – as if it would provide the assurance or the resolution he seeks. Furthermore, the man studies physiology and family resemblances, making sketches of how his child's face might look. Here is how he is introduced:

> Some years ago at a specific hour of the day, a tall, slender man could be seen walking with measured steps back and forth on the flagstones in the southern section of Overgaden over Vandet.... His mental disorder manifested itself most clearly ... when he paced the flagstones between Børnehus Bridge and the south end of the street.... The conjecture was that he had been in love with a queen of Spain, [but] this conjecture was an attempt doomed to failure because it did not even pay attention to a very noteworthy piece of evidence concerning him – a decided partiality for children.... It was not merely to have an opportunity [for him] to do good that children occupied him – no, it was the children themselves, and in a most singular way.... As soon as he saw a child, the flat look in his countenance became animated and all sorts of moods [*Stemninger*] were reflected in it. He paused with the child, spoke with him, and during all this regarded the child as attentively as if he were an artist who painted nothing but children's faces.
>
> *(SLW, 278–80/SKS 6, 258–61)*

He had a suspicion that such a child did exist, and this gave him 'a sorrowful certainty that [making] this discovery would confirm for him something sorrowful concerning himself' (SLW, 282/SKS 6, 262). He obsessively looks for this item of definite knowledge, the answer to this yes-or-no question, and is utterly preoccupied with finding it out. 'This possibility pursued him, and he pursued this possibility in his passionate investigation, and this possibility incubated in his silence, and this possibility animated the features of his face ... when he saw a child – and this possibility was that another being owed its life to him' (SLW, 284/SKS 6, 264). He 'wandered ... along the desperate twistings of all possibilities, to find if possible a certainty' and 'wearily tried to change that unknown X into a denominated quantity' (SLW, 286/SKS 6, 266). And he was so greatly tormented that he lost the joy of his youth, came to appear twenty years older than he was, and ultimately 'exchanged understanding for mental derangement' (SLW, 285/SKS 6, 265). Part of his life's tragedy is that he imagines that some knowable information will set his mind at ease, whereas it plainly would not provide him with what he is looking for: namely, the removal of all ambiguity about the meaning of his existence and the resolution of the question whether he has lived well. Frater Taciturnus is right to find in this twelve-page narrative a 'crucial' analogy for Quidam's own experience (SLW, 429/SKS 6, 397).

As Climacus would agree, we might sometimes wish to reach an endpoint where everything is finished and complete, and all knowledge attained, but this longing to reach a conclusive terminus where we *are* finished is a longing to be liberated from the realm of time and change in which we finite beings exist. It is thus a yearning to free ourselves altogether from the human condition. As Kierkegaard writes in his journal: 'One must acknowledge that in the final analysis there is no theory' (KJN 6, 401/SKS 22, 396), none that would provide us with a complete understanding of what we most long to understand. To abandon this longing would itself be to renounce a vital aspect of our humanity: the character who wanders Christianshavn transfixed by the effort to gain some knowledge about the possibility that haunts him is not simply to be denounced.[10] He compares favourably to the untroubled 'cousin' who likes to repeat a cynical saying about how no man knows for sure how many children he has (SLW, 285/SKS 6, 265). Moreover, Quidam himself illustrates far greater spiritual profundity than the Young Man who attends the banquet early in *Stages on Life's Way*, who has hardened himself against the influence of love simply because he 'cannot understand' the power to which he would thereby be surrendering, and wants to keep his wits about him rather than being 'a puppet in the service of something inexplicable' (SLW, 40/SKS 6, 43). Isolating oneself in reason defined thus narrowly must qualify as just one more way to deny our epistemic predicament, rather than finding a way to live *with* uncertainty.

Conclusion

One way in which Kierkegaard offers existential guidance to his reader with regard to 'the uncertainty of earthly life, in which everything is uncertain' (CUP 1, 86/SKS 7, 85) is to portray unsuccessful ways of dealing with the varieties of uncertainty that are entailed by the finite limitations of our epistemic standpoint. There are cases in which what we long to know is, by its very nature, inaccessible to us – such as the mind of another, or what is going to happen in the future. And there are other cases in which the kind of knowledge that we *can* gain does not remove the fundamental uncertainty of our predicament. Yet the aspiration to arrive at definite answers, to have everything resolved and finished, does not just characterize the Cartesian or Hegelian philosophers from whom we can easily distinguish ourselves. This wish to be liberated from the cognitive limits that are a structural feature of the human condition is one that is liable to plague us all – including those of us who are prompted by Kierkegaard's writings to *want* to heed his warning against this very wish. He therefore issues reminders to us in various contexts and in a diversity of voices, continually telling his reader: this pertains to *you*.

Related topics

'The passion of Kierkegaard's existential method,' Lee C. Barrett; 'On faith and reason(s): Kierkegaard's logic of conviction,' K. Brian Söderquist; 'Conscience, self-deception, and the question of authenticity in Kierkegaard,' Claudia Welz; 'Irony and the conversion experience,' Walter Wietzke.

Notes

1 In this journal entry Kierkegaard also states that 'one cannot have a conviction with respect to something mathematical,' because 'no counterproof is thinkable.'
2 Gouwens (1996: 119) writes: 'In Abraham the dialectic of active and passive continues, with even greater emphasis on receptivity. . . . In Abraham the receptivity is even starker; the miracle is that he can receive Isaac back.'
3 If 'the tempter' here is the same one who appears and negotiates with God in the Book of Job, then it is relevant to consider how this trouble-making character is understood in Judaism: see Wettstein (2012: 155–65).
4 Hannay is alluding to an 'ecstatic discourse' in *Either/Or* (see EO 1, 38–9/SKS 2, 47–9).
5 Numerous other Kierkegaardian works return to the idea that 'God may have specific tasks for me,' and 'for every individual as a unique individual,' as C. Stephen Evans (2004: 24–7) has noted.
6 On the difficulty of reality and the difficulty of philosophy, see Diamond (2003); see also Mooney (2017: 175–6).
7 I am grateful to Maria Alexandra Keller for helping me to appreciate this point.
8 Proust's narrator remarks on the 'delicious moment of uncertainty' when 'the uncertainty of awakening revealed by her silence was not at all revealed in her eyes.'
9 The young man in *Repetition* says that he cannot explain 'whether I am beatific in joy or dejected in desolation, whether I have won life or lost it' (R, 221/SKS 4, 88). Maybe this is the kind of thing one never knows for sure.
10 Thanks to Eleanor Helms for encouraging me to mention this, and to Adam Buben and Patrick Stokes for other helpful critical suggestions.

References

Diamond, C. (2003) 'The difficulty of reality and the difficulty of philosophy,' *Partial Answers: Journal of Literature and the History of Ideas*, 1, no. 2: 1–26.
Evans, C. S. (2004) *Kierkegaard's ethic of love*, Oxford: Oxford University Press.
Gouwens, D. J. (1996) *Kierkegaard as religious thinker*, Cambridge: Cambridge University Press.
Hannay, A. (2001) *Kierkegaard: A biography*, Cambridge: Cambridge University Press.
Howland, J. (2006) *Kierkegaard and Socrates: A study in philosophy and faith*, Cambridge: Cambridge University Press.
Hume, D. (1998) *Dialogues concerning natural religion*, R. H. Popkin (trans), 2nd ed., Indianapolis, IN: Hackett Publishing Company.
Kierkegaard, S. (1996) *Papers and journals: A selection*, A. Hannay (trans), New York: Penguin Books.
Mooney, E. F. (2017) 'Difficult faith and living well,' in S. Minister, J. A. Simmons and M. Strawser (eds), *Kierkegaard's God and the Good Life*, Bloomington, IN: Indiana University Press, 173–90.
Possen, D. (2011) 'Death and ethics in Kierkegaard's "Postscript",' in P. Stokes and A. Buben (eds), *Kierkegaard and Death*, Bloomington, IN: Indiana University Press, 122–32.
Proust, M. (1929) *The captive*, C. K. S. Moncrieff (trans), New York: Modern Library.
Sagi, A. (2000) *Kierkegaard, religion, and existence*, Amsterdam: Rodopi.
Wettstein, H. (2012) *The significance of religious experience*, Oxford: Oxford University Press.

Further reading

Carvalhais de Olivera, S. (2013) 'Certainty,' in S. M. Emmanuel, W. McDonald and J. Stewart (eds), *Kierkegaard Research: Sources, Reception and Resources*, vol. 15 (*Kierkegaard's Concepts*), tome 1, Farnham: Ashgate, 175–80.

This chapter on the notion of *Vished* in Kierkegaard's writings elucidates the concept of certitude in relation to the topics of inwardness, earnestness, existence, and faith. It also draws a contrast between certitude and proof.

Levine, M. P. (1983) 'Kierkegaardian dogma: Inwardness and objective uncertainty,' *International Journal for Philosophy of Religion*, 14, no. 3: 183–8.

Especially with reference to subjective inwardness and belief in the Incarnation, this article provides an interpretation of how Kierkegaard's work takes up the question of how a person ought (according to Kierkegaard) to comport himself or herself toward uncertain matters.

Muench, P. (2011) 'Thinking death into every moment: The existence-problem of dying in Kierkegaard's "Postscript",' in P. Stokes and A. Buben (eds), *Kierkegaard and Death*, Bloomington, IN: Indiana University Press, 101–21.

Taking death as a characteristic 'existence-problem,' this chapter addresses the issue of what it means to 'think this uncertainty' [of our mortality] into every moment, for Kierkegaard and his pseudonym Johannes Climacus.

Piety, M. G. (2010) *Ways of knowing: Kierkegaard's pluralist epistemology*, Waco, TX: Baylor University Press.

This book is the most comprehensive account of Kierkegaard's theory (or theories) of knowledge currently available in English. Among the other themes with which it deals is the question of how an epistemic stance of subjective conviction can be appropriate with respect to issues of objective uncertainty.

32
IRONY AND THE CONVERSION EXPERIENCE

Walter Wietzke

Introduction

One of the most remarkable aspects of Kierkegaard's philosophy is the scope with which he explores a certain phenomenon in human experience: the fact that human beings undergo transformations into new types of people, motivated by different interests, beliefs, and values. A range of examples throughout Kierkegaard's writings illustrates this kind of transformation: Judge William's exhortation to the aesthete that he settle down and marry, and Johannes Climacus's musings on how one becomes a Christian are among the most well-known. In these particular cases the personal transformation is significant enough that the individual becomes a new person in at least two senses: as already mentioned, she comes to be defined by a new set of values and beliefs; and as a result, her understanding of who she is and her place in the world changes in ways she cannot anticipate. The standard term for this process is that the individual undergoes a conversion experience. The purpose of the present chapter is to address several specific questions concerning the role human beings play in bringing this experience about.

For one, conversion may be seen as a philosophical *problem* in that it is puzzling how the individual could ever anticipate becoming such a new person when he or she has no understanding of what the 'new-ness' of life will be like. Now, some may believe that this apparent problem is not really worth our concern. For think of a famous case of conversion: the conversion of the apostle Paul. There is a flash of light, followed by blind stupefaction, and then sight is restored with an unexpectedly new insight into one's life and world. Whether or not the story is actually true, it leaves the impression that a conversion experience happens to us without any intentional, conscious contribution of our own. Although we may be able to point to extenuating circumstances retrospectively in order to explain how it happened, the experience itself is essentially beyond our control. In the case of Paul's conversion, God's role as a causal agent seems to be the most important factor. Paul's transformation occurs because God wants to intervene in human affairs.

My purpose is not to contest this version of religious conversions. The reason there is a problem of conversion for *Kierkegaard* is that he maintains that we should seek this experience out. A recurring theme in his authorship is that Christian faith represents the highest good available to human beings, but that this life does not come automatically for us (CUP 1, 15/ SKS 7, 25). Taken together these issues raise a problem for how we are supposed to understand the mechanics of a conversion. As with Paul's experience, some think that God plays a similar causal role for Kierkegaard's understanding of conversions, but in this chapter, I shall argue that his view is far more complicated.[1] First of all, a number of Kierkegaard's writings describe how subjective features of human agency set the individual up for a conversion without assuming God's causal role. For example, the concepts of irony and the leap provide a framework for understanding conversions under the purview of our volitional activity. These concepts do not explicitly invoke divine grace or other forms of external intervention as a necessary condition for conversions. Yet there are also reasons to question this explanation. Close examination of these concepts inevitably raises questions about their ability to account for all the factors of a transformation, even leading some individuals to doubt their capacity to determine the experience themselves. My view is not that this tension means we must postulate both internal and external conditions for such transformations, but simply that it explains the significance of risk and uncertainty in framing the conversion experience.

The nature of the existence spheres

In one of his later works, *The Point of View for My Work as an Author*, Kierkegaard engages in a bit of intellectual autobiography. In this book he surveys roughly a decade's worth of material and settles with the reader that his intention all along had been to show what it means to become a Christian (PV, 55/SKS 16, 36). Another important theme throughout his work is that the vast majority of people living in Christendom are confused about what Christianity means and therefore what it requires of them. The inhabitants of Christendom do not realize how ethically rigorous Christianity is, and in most cases Kierkegaard thinks they would actually prefer not to know. This is unfortunate, since, as Johannes Climacus explains in the *Concluding Unscientific Postscript to 'Philosophical Fragments,'* Christianity aims to provide for each individual human being's deepest existential needs. Christianity promises salvation to those who believe and live by the message that God entered time at a particular moment in history and location in the cosmos. It warps human reason to think that this could be so, but Climacus argues that human nature is uniquely suited for Christianity's paradoxical epistemic and ethical features (CUP 1, 230/SKS 7, 210). We distinguish ourselves by the passion, or pathos, it takes to believe things that can satisfy our greatest needs.

Kierkegaard also recognizes that human existence is problematic: in our default mode human beings are not disposed to act as Christianity demands. For this reason we must view a relation to Christianity as an ongoing project or task. We must work, struggle, and sometimes suffer in this effort, for it is no easy thing to do. But by describing our relation to Christianity in terms of a task, Kierkegaard must think that individuals actually can determine their lives this way. Arguably, his goal of showing what it means to become a Christian is philosophically uninteresting unless he thinks it is theoretically possible for us to achieve it. There must be some meaningful sense in which our efforts can determine this achievement.

The fact that we struggle with this task brings us to another defining feature of Kierkegaard's philosophy. One aspect of Kierkegaard's originality lies in his insight into the various forms the human psyche can take. Many of his works detail how human life is divided between three basic spheres of existence: the aesthetic, the ethical, and the religious. In their most basic sense, the spheres represent competing normative accounts of the world. That is, they describe the different kinds of objects and activities that people find valuable. The primary source for the aesthetic and ethical views lies in the two volumes of *Either/Or*. Although the individual papers collected in the first volume vary in style and content, we can piece together at least one unifying theme to the aesthetic: the organizing principle of an aesthetic life is that it must be interesting to the individual, and so one must do whatever it takes to avoid boredom. By contrast, the author of the second volume, Judge William, argues that certain activities and relationships, such as marriage, necessarily take place within an objective moral order that is defined by a society's cultural and religious institutions. Ultimately the activities within this order are supposed to prove more fulfilling to the individual than a life spent in a never-ending pursuit of the interesting. We also learn from the Judge that central to the ethical is the individual's autonomous conception of herself. An ethical agent can genuinely determine the direction of her life through the decisions she makes.

Finally, there is the religious sphere, the most famous depiction of which is probably found in *Fear and Trembling*. In this book Johannes de silentio explains how religious faith cannot be reduced to an obligation to maintain the social, cultural order. God's command that Abraham sacrifice Isaac is a prime example: divine commands can contradict the prevailing ethical norms and mores of human society. Only faith, it seems, can justify this sacrifice, for only through faith could one believe that God will restore Isaac in order to fulfil Abraham's destiny of fathering a multitude of nations. Religious existence distinguishes itself from aesthetic and ethical existence in that it makes obligation to God fundamental, and this obligation manifests itself in paradoxical ways.

In sum, the particular beliefs and activities that constitute each sphere provide us with substantial normative guidance: they inform us of the things that we should care about and value. In this way, the spheres function as a source of reasons to act. Whenever we reflect on decisions we have to make, we inevitably refer to the values we have in order to formulate reasons that will guide those actions – values give us reasons, and reasons inform actions. Kierkegaard does not spell his view out with this language, but these principles do underlie his account of the spheres.[2] We do express our values through the activities we intentionally commit ourselves to (i.e., our commitments), whether that means getting married or carrying out duties to God.

Furthermore, tied to the value function of the spheres is their psychologically exclusive nature. That is, we can only really appreciate 'what it is like' to value certain beliefs and activities when we reside within the sphere in question. For example, Judge William makes the observation that the qualitative aspects of getting married and having children cannot be conveyed to someone who hasn't experienced them for himself. He says: 'there are things of which one can never have any substantial conception if one has not experienced them, and among these is being a father' (EO 2, 76/SKS 3, 80). This general theme recurs continually throughout Kierkegaard's works.

Fear and Trembling explains how a person outside the religious life will fail to appreciate what it's like to be on the inside. The subjective, phenomenal aspect of Abraham's experience is simply unavailable to someone like de silentio. Of course, in one respect de silentio can describe what Abraham's beliefs and values are – on a certain level that is the reason behind the book – but it's simply an objective description of the difference between ethical and religious existence. And an objective description necessarily fails to impart the subjective quality of what it's like to experience the latter. De silentio himself admits this, explaining to the reader that he cannot understand what it is like to walk in Abraham's shoes, or those of any other Knight of Faith (FT, 37–41/SKS 4, 132–6).

A similar example is found in *The Sickness unto Death*, in which Anti-Climacus argues that an epistemic distinction separating religious existence from other forms of life prevents one from appreciating the full significance of religious doctrine. There in fact exists a qualitative difference between the natural state of human reason and Christian dogma; this is most obvious in the case of sin:

> It is specifically the concept of sin, the teaching about sin, that most decisively differentiates Christianity qualitatively from paganism, and this is also why Christianity very consistently assumes that neither paganism nor the natural man knows what sin is; in fact, it assumes that there has to be a revelation from God to show what sin is.
> (SUD, 89/SKS 11, 202)

Thus, one cannot derive the concept of sin from the natural, unaided use of human reason. Only upon accepting Christian revelation does one appreciate the significance of its doctrine. For the uninitiated it must appear either foolish or offensive.

This understanding of the spheres becomes even more compelling once we consider how Kierkegaard describes the transitions between them. The most explicit discussion of this issue occurs in the two works authored by Climacus. In the first, *Philosophical Fragments*, Climacus explores the difference between two ways of acquiring existential truth – that is, the kind of truth that makes life worth living – the Socratic and the Christian. For the first, the truth is already within us, it is simply obscure, and so at most we only require an effective midwife to help us understand it. In the case of the Christian, however, an individual is fundamentally separated from the truth and may only acquire it through God's assistance. A substantial transformation then occurs: 'When the learner is untruth ... and he now receives the condition and truth ... he becomes a different person ... he becomes a person of a different quality or, as we can also call it, a *new* person' (PF, 18/SKS 4, 227). Climacus states that the transformation must be a qualitative transition between two modes of being. It is a second 'birth' in the sense that a conversion is meant to capture (PF, 19/SKS 4, 227). One's system of values and beliefs fundamentally changes such that she must distinguish her post-conversion self's value system from that of her pre-conversion self. Furthermore, the convert could not have anticipated what her life would be like post-conversion: '[If] the moment [in which the individual receives the truth] is to acquire decisive significance, then the seeker up until that moment must not have possessed the truth, not even in the form of ignorance' (PF, 13/SKS 4, 222). Now, these claims are true only if we acknowledge Christianity as a legitimate way to obtain existential truth. So long as we do, we must view the conversion experience as a radical transformation of the individual's belief and value systems. This explanation confirms the idea that a transition between spheres represents the personal and epistemic break described above.

Although this break does not fully destroy the individual's psychological connection to the person she had been in the past, it seemingly compels her to reassess her former self. As noted, with the acceptance of Christian doctrine comes the realization that one has been so corrupted by sin that one could not have appreciated how separated from the truth one had actually been all along. Ultimately, on the basis of this new perspective the individual will admit she could not have achieved it through her own volitional powers alone. This break therefore sets up the problem posed at the beginning: if conversions truly are radical transformations of an individual's system of values and beliefs, and if an individual requires this system in order to formulate reasons for her decisions, it is a puzzle, at the very least, how a radical transformation could be self-determined. For, to be clear, this transformation means that the individual must transcend her current frame of value reference. Yet how is she expected to choose it, in a genuinely intentional sense, if she cannot access reasons that guide the choice?[3] This is a problem for Kierkegaard insofar as he thinks that becoming a Christian is among the most significant decisions one can make for one's life; so there ought to be some way in which we can meaningfully contribute to our own self-transformation. Nevertheless, the decision must contend with the seeming impossibility of being able to draw on our own internal resources to inform it. Generally speaking, this philosophical issue is not unique to Kierkegaard, though I think that he has a unique way of addressing it.[4] Before taking up his solution let me consider a few possible responses to the argument at this point.

It could be argued that this apparent self-transformation problem is overstated, for the individuals under consideration are actually already committed to the relevant values in their pre-conversion state.[5] If such a commitment exists it then follows that the person one becomes through the conversion is already present in some inchoate sense prior to the experience. Either one is denying a fact about oneself, of which one has some degree of conscious awareness, or it simply has to be elucidated for one how another sphere would better fulfil the values one holds. The latter case requires us to work through an intellectual problem: an individual requires an explanation of how she already values the elements of another sphere. And so long as it is grounded in sound reasoning she presumably must recognize the authority of the explanation on pain of being irrational. Now admittedly, there is textual support for both responses. For the first, self-deception can certainly precede a conversion experience. Conventional wisdom is replete with stories of people who deliberately ignore or attempt to explain away the pull of their conscience, religious or otherwise. *The Sickness unto Death* in fact details a number of the ways in which such self-deception occurs, yet I would argue that there can still be candidates for conversion who do not qualify as self-deceived. Space does not allow me to take up that argument here, unfortunately.[6]

The second objection is that an appeal to an individual's personal values and interests appears to be one of the methods in the Judge's letters. He actually does set out philosophical arguments for why it is in the aesthete's best interest as a human being to choose the ethical life. For instance, the Judge devotes much of his first letter to the idea that so long as the aesthete cares about being in love he should also be able to accept reasons for getting married, as the Judge claims that marriage is the fulfilment of love (EO 2, 60/SKS 3, 66). According to this argument it is irrational for the aesthete to go on ignoring marriage. Specifically, it is his denial of principles he has tacitly committed himself to that marks his irrationality. It is necessary to address this second objection more thoroughly since a proper response will also help us understand how Kierkegaard's work can answer some of the questions surrounding self-transformation.

The leap and conversion experience

The very idea of a transition between two existence-spheres ought to bring to mind one of Kierkegaard's most famous ideas: the 'leap.' There are two items to clarify at the outset. First, the leap does not mean a 'leap of faith': an act of brute willpower in which one arbitrarily summons up a religious belief, regardless of circumstance. This association has been debunked (cf. Ferreira 1997). Kierkegaard did not coin the specific phrase 'leap of faith,' nor does he even use it. Second, although the leap is usually employed to describe transitions to religious existence, the term designates any kind of qualitative transformation, which can include the transition between the aesthetic and the ethical (KJN 3, 373/SKS 19, 375).

Kierkegaard's most sustained analysis of the leap occurs in the *Postscript*. There, Climacus introduces the term for polemical reasons: the *Postscript* must be viewed in part as an argument against the Hegelian philosophy of his day. Climacus argues that in spite of whatever historical factors could explain the prominence of Christianity in culture and society, these factors are irrelevant for whether or not the individual actually lives the way a Christian should. Climacus's way of putting it is that there can be no logical transition between an historical event and an existential truth (CUP 1, 93/SKS 7, 92). An individual's acceptance of Christian doctrine as the foundation for her life does not necessarily happen as a matter of course. The fact that one is raised in a Christian society does not automatically predispose one to do the types of things a

Christian ought; nor does one grow into Christian belief as the result of some normal pattern of human psychological development. Rather, becoming a Christian must be the focus of a deliberate, intentional decision. We have already seen how for Climacus the most significant aspects of Christianity are its radical epistemic and ethical demands, so any genuine decision to become a Christian marks a break with the status quo of human existence.

Therefore, the leap is not a method of deriving new normative content through one's current set of values or beliefs. An individual does not leap by deductively reasoning that another sphere will fulfil her expectations; her present circumstances offer no evidence that could guarantee the result she is seeking. For an individual facing the possibility of transitioning between spheres, then, the leap illustrates the inductive nature of the experience, for which no guarantee of success exists. In this regard the leap reinforces Kierkegaard's specific emphasis on the risk that underlies faith. Faith cannot exist without uncertainty, which is sometimes as formidable as being 'out on 70,000 fathoms of water' (CUP 1, 204/SKS 7, 187). The inability to supply a rational guarantee that one's greatest needs will be fulfilled by another form of life may feel as if there is nothing holding one up, as it were, but it seems incorrect to conclude from this thought that we are *irrational* for committing ourselves to these types of decisions. Rather, Climacus's point is more to emphasize the anxiety and pathos that a lack of complete certainty generates, particularly when the stakes are high – as they should be when one's life and future are at stake.

Existential crises can illuminate when such dramatic decisions are called for. For example, imagine your discovery one day of incriminating evidence that your spouse has been unfaithful. An unexpected crisis such as this compels you to reconsider the major commitments of your life. In other words, you are forced to reconsider the activities and relationships that express your cherished values. One option for you is to renew them, to rebuild your marriage, although you must now contend with the unanticipated challenge of re-establishing trust with your spouse. But the crisis also provides the occasion for you to question the very basis of your marriage. Perhaps it's not the marriage per se that has you anxious, but the entire framework upon which it rests. That is to say, maybe your sudden misfortune has shattered your confidence in finding meaning in your commitment to marriage and other accepted social institutions and conventions – the very things Judge William espoused. Maybe now you are through with these. At this pivotal moment, then, you find yourself in despair: you cannot ignore the decision between continuing with a life that somewhat resembles the status quo, and breaking with that status quo. Moreover, the decision has you anxious because it means you are responsible for your future. In either case it is you who must carve out a path – one that does not derive from life as you thought you knew it. For if your conception of yourself centred upon your role as a faithful husband and family man, what exactly follows after that? Whatever decision you make there is uncertainty and anxiety over the direction it will take you, but you must acknowledge the responsibility of determining it yourself, come what may.

Although in this case the possibility of a leap manifests itself without direct effort on our part, in the final section of this chapter I shall discuss an alternative way of organizing one's life that can cultivate contexts where the leap is equally appropriate. This will show how conversion experiences can fall under the purview of our volitional activity.

Irony and the leap

One form of life that cultivates the conditions for a conversion experience is based on irony, which may explain why Kierkegaard took an explicit interest in the subject. His dissertation, *The Concept of Irony: With Continual Reference to Socrates*, is an analysis of irony in both the character of Socrates and German Romanticism. Five years later in the *Postscript*, however, Kierkegaard criticizes this initial analysis, deeming it incomplete. His reasons for revisiting irony are instructive for understanding its role in a conversion experience.

The most familiar use of irony is probably the ironic speech act, or rhetorical irony: the saying of one thing when you actually mean something else. Here the intention is to communicate an idea indirectly – to say something without actually saying it. Rhetorical irony is also effective at undercutting someone's confidence in having knowledge by exposing her ignorance. This explains the young Kierkegaard's fascination with Socrates, particularly as the early Platonic dialogues depict him. In these texts an ironic comment can be an effective device for disrupting the complacency of those who think they know something when they really do not. But *The Concept of Irony* explores more than the cognitive effect of a disarming remark; it ultimately focuses on the effect of integrating irony into a basic disposition towards life. The *ironist* uses irony not just to undermine the knowledge claims of her peers, but more importantly to distance herself from the cultural customs, practices, and traditions that comprise her social world. This disengagement carries deep existential significance insofar as Kierkegaard refers to these elements as an individual's 'actuality': they structure her identity by representing the various possibilities through which she can express her values (CI, 259–60/SKS 1, 297–8). Hence, the effect of irony's existential use is deeply personal as it separates the ironist from the substance of her own self-understanding. The end result is liberation: she gains independence from the commitments that have personally defined her up to this point.

Yet this view of irony is decidedly negative. For one it is limited to revealing how tenuous a grip the elements of our own self-understanding have on us. Moreover, the consequences of existential irony tend towards the extreme. According to Kierkegaard, unrestrained irony must work its way past our particular commitments to the point where our hold on our values themselves begins to disintegrate. The scope of irony is universal – no person or thing is immune from its critique. This fact betrays the vulnerability of the ironist's own identity, for irony will inevitably probe the ironist's own reasons for espousing existential irony in the first place. Since irony possesses no intrinsic qualities that make it superior to other forms of life (CI, 256/SKS 1, 294), ironic scrutiny will ultimately drain an ironic existence of any authority the ironist may have presumed it had. Thus, irony in its global application implodes, which explains Kierkegaard's conclusion that irony's self-destructive tendencies must be reined in by ethical interests (CI, 326/SKS 1, 355).

By the time Kierkegaard wrote the *Postscript* he had deepened his appreciation for why this conception of irony is unsustainable. Only two years after *The Concept of Irony* Judge William states that: 'Every human being . . . has a natural need to formulate a life-view, a conception of the meaning of life and its purpose' (EO 2, 179/SKS 3, 175). This insight extends well beyond the letters of the Judge. As described above, during the five-year period in between *The Concept of Irony* and the *Postscript* Kierkegaard was busily working out the details of the existence-spheres. It is not necessary to restate those details here; at this point we need only explain how the spheres serve as manifestations of the fundamental human need indicated by the Judge. Human beings cannot function without some value framework for our commitments and identities. It is a condition of human existence that we constitute an identity for ourselves by determining what things are valuable to us, whether that value is aesthetic, ethical, or religious.

Perhaps the most memorable formulation of this idea occurs in the opening passage to *The Sickness unto Death*. Anti-Climacus's definition of the human being as a 'relation' governed by 'spirit' means that the distinguishing feature of one's humanity is the ability to construct oneself into a proper self through the synthesis of particular structural conditions (SUD, 13/SKS 11, 129). First of all, human beings are creatures already defined by concrete, empirical facts that pertain to our biology, psychology, history, and social circumstances. These factors unavoidably shape our character in complex ways beyond our awareness and control, but an individual human being cannot be defined merely as their causal product. We also possess the capacity to transcend them to some degree, for instance by aspiring to make improvements upon character flaws these empirical conditions have wrought. This does not mean we may detach ourselves completely from their influence; we just have some ability to direct the way they shape us. The extent to which we succeed in this effort and achieve a proper synthesis is a separate matter (Anti-Climacus insists that human beings usually fail at this task); for this discussion we need only recognize spirit's structural function in the formation of the human self. Through a human being's interaction with what has already been given to her she actively constructs an identity for herself and thereby takes an evaluative stand (be it aesthetic, ethical, or religious) on that given.

With this advanced account of human agency in mind we can more fully appreciate the incomplete nature of negative irony. Climacus himself emphasizes how negative irony is impractical because it neglects the demands of agency for human existence (CUP 1, 521/SKS 7, 473). To be sure, this is not a new insight – Kierkegaard had already found 'negative' existence problematic – but the *Postscript* modifies the account of ironic agency in order to accommodate this more developed view of human agency.

To begin with, Climacus describes irony as 'the unity of ethical passion ... and culture' (CUP 1, 503/SKS 7, 456), as well as 'joining together the particulars of the finite with the infinite ethical requirement' (CUP 1, 502/SKS 7, 455). In these statements Climacus frames ironic existence according to the aforementioned principles of self-constitution. In this case the ironist is able to recognize how human existence generally consists in an attempt to reconcile absolute ethical imperatives with empirical limitations. The *Postscript*'s discussion is more topical than that of Anti-Climacus or Judge William, but an essential similarity remains: human existence consists in a struggle between its limiting conditions and the imperative to transcend them for the purposes of self-constitution.

The *Postscript* also describes ironic existence as a '*confinium* [a border territory]' between two different existence-spheres (CUP 1, 500/SKS 7, 455). By definition a border region should afford some perspective on all the territory that surrounds it, and since irony is situated between two different spheres it could offer a glimpse of what one of the opposing sides fails to see. In other words, an ironist should be able to appreciate some of the values embodied in both the ethical and the aesthetic, even though she thrives on their continuous disavowal. For example, the ironist can appreciate why people settle into their careers and get married or why they become churchgoers, all the while remaining aloof from these particular commitments. After all, if she were to get 'caught in a relativity,' as Climacus puts it, by adopting one of these identities as her own she obviously would lose her status as an ironist (CUP 1, 502/SKS 7, 455). The unique talent of an ironist, then, consists in the ability to have one's feet in multiple views of life, as it were, so as to imaginatively play with multiple ways of being ironical. Given this fact, she can see how the reasons that justify different identities are compelling for the individuals in question. In fact, it would seem that she must be able to see why they are compelling in order to apply her ironic critique. The more convincing the imaginative construction is, the more effective the ironist's critique.[7]

Yet this process ultimately serves as more than mere play, for it represents a positive development in the understanding of irony. First of all, through the play of irony the ironist builds up different modes of life, finding herself in a position where she can appreciate some of the aspects behind these ways of living. And because a life dedicated to irony offers no substantive guidance for which type of life one ought to live the ironist has no special reasons that could influence her against another view of life. She is free to remain within the confines of irony, but doing so arbitrarily privileges it over the alternatives. Secondly, in the awareness that human existence involves joining disparate elements together, the ironist tacitly acknowledges her capacity to constitute herself as a human agent. In building up various forms of life the ironist simultaneously constructs options for herself that can represent actual existence possibilities. Climacus specifically identifies this attitude as humour, having a sense for the comic. A comic ironist recognizes there is a 'way out' of her position (CUP 1, 520/SKS 7, 472). (By contrast, a tragic ironist despairs over the fact that no overriding reasons can be given to justify another form of life.) The use of humour extends to the ironist who stands within the confines between the ethical and the religious as well. Either way, Climacus's point is not simply that ethical constraints ought to guide irony's use, as Kierkegaard recommended in *The Concept of Irony*, but that irony operates according to a basic assumption about human agency, that the activity of self-constitution structures human existence.[8]

At this point it should be clear how irony sets up a leap. Again, so long as the ironist is talented enough, she will be fluent with at least some of the reasons why people are drawn to their particular lives, which provide her with some sense for what other kinds of life could be like. Yet the ability to project oneself ironically can only do so much, as irony is only designed to bring one to the brink of making a choice. Irony does not compel you in one particular direction. It simply levels the options enough that the ironist finds herself in a situation where she cannot offer reasons *against* the choices facing her. Given that she also possesses an awareness of how others live, the ironist's situation is thus made ripe for a leap.

Conclusion

The ironic conversion experience shows there is no reason to think that divine agency must have engineered our transformation. As hinted at in the introduction, this idea is consistent with the aim of Kierkegaard's more philosophical texts, which is to show that a conversion can be described under the purview of our volitional activity. But as also suggested in the introduction there are certain caveats to this position.

For one, there is a sense of mystery about how worldly events unfold. As noted by Anti-Climacus, we cannot fully account for why our structural conditions have defined us the way they have. One question that picks up on this thought follows from the analysis of the *Postscript*: why does humour define the attitude of some ironists, and thereby provide opportunities for escape, whereas others resign themselves tragically to their situation? Generally speaking, how do we account for the fact that some individuals can lead a humourist's lifestyle when others cannot? For however much we may exhort a tragic ironist to try to see her circumstances differently, that does not mean she can. The *Postscript* does not address this problem, and so some of the reasons why events of life unfold as they do seem to be opaque to us. This fact suggests an aspect of human existence that cannot be exhausted by an agent's attempt to determine her destiny herself. Thus, we cannot state categorically that Kierkegaard's account rules out the possibility of direct divine intervention.

Nevertheless, Kierkegaard's texts leave us with the thought that without definitive evidence of divine intervention (whatever that evidence could be) this issue is a matter of interpretation relative to one's sphere of life. After all, while a religious person believes that God was active in her conversion, her perspective on that event occurs from the vantage point of the religious. My argument is therefore that we need not rule such intervention in.

Ultimately, it is more in keeping with Kierkegaard's methodological aims that God's role remains ambiguous. If divine grace were a systematic factor in conversion it would weaken the demanding nature of the transformation. As we have seen, the themes of passion, risk, and uncertainty help explain how conversions must be more than an intellectual, deductive exercise; for this reason, we should not view a conversion as an accounting of God's responsibilities vis-à-vis ours. That is, we should not approach this transformation by trying to circumscribe our capacity while assuming that God will handle the rest. A calculation of this sort would compromise the character of the transformation insofar as presuming to 'know' that God will intervene on our behalf reduces our uncertainty over the transition. When uncertainty wanes, we have less to risk, which in turn scales down our passion. In the end, given Kierkegaard's emphasis throughout his authorship that people have generally lost their passion for their greatest existential needs we can now understand why he would frame conversion experiences in a way that will maximize their ability to rouse us out of our apathy.

Related topics

'Kierkegaard and the desirability of immortality,' Adam Buben; 'Imagination and belief,' Eleanor Helms; 'On faith and reason(s): Kierkegaard's logic of conviction,' K. Brian Söderquist; 'Logic, language, and knowledge,' Mélissa Fox-Muraton.

Notes

1 Most recently, Andrew Torrance (2017) has argued that properly religious conversions require God's intervention.
2 In Wietzke (2013) I attempt to flesh out this view more fully.
3 See Kemp (2015) for a general analysis of this issue.
4 Though I would argue that the problem reaches back in some form to Plato's *Republic*, a recently debated example appears in Christine Korsgaard's (1996: 183–8, 254–8) discussion of how a Mafioso (i.e., a rational egoist) can be convinced that he has reasons to be moral. See also L. A. Paul (2014) for an analysis of the epistemic difficulties inherent to transformative experiences.
5 In brief, the argument claims there are certain activities that we cannot commit ourselves to without invoking the principles of a later sphere, and that Kierkegaard understood the motivation to ascend to higher spheres through the attempt to resolve this inconsistency. Representatives of this argument include: Davenport (2012); Kosch (2006); and Rudd (2012).
6 See Wietzke (2015) for a discussion of why an agent may not be so self-deceived.
7 Fred Rush (2016: 255–6) argues that the imagination plays a necessary role for understanding how the ironist achieves the transformation between views of life, in that the imagination can hold certain value claims up for her attention until she takes them seriously. Ferreira (1991) has also described the work of the imagination in this way.
8 For this reason I disagree with Andrew Cross's (1997) claim that the 'way out' rests upon one's ethical sensibility. My reading of irony also differs from that of Jonathan Lear's (2011), in that he describes ironic experience as the disruption of the illusion that we are leading the types of lives to which we have aspired. Ironic disruption is therapeutic, though it seems less a matter for the will than as Climacus describes it.

References

Cross, A. (1997) 'Neither either nor or: The perils of reflexive irony,' in A. Hannay and G. Marino (eds), *The Cambridge Companion to Kierkegaard*, Cambridge: Cambridge University Press.
Davenport, J. (2012) *Narrative identity, autonomy, and mortality: From Frankfurt and MacIntyre to Kierkegaard*, London: Routledge.
Ferreira, J. (1997) 'Faith and the Kierkegaardian leap,' in A. Hannay and G. Marino (eds), *The Cambridge Companion to Kierkegaard*, Cambridge: Cambridge University Press.
Ferreira, J. (1991) *Transforming vision: Imagination and will in Kierkegaardian faith*, Oxford: Clarendon Press.
Kemp, R. (2015) 'The self-transformation puzzle: On the possibility of radical self-transformation,' *Res Philosophica*, 92, no. 2: 389–417.

Khawaja, N. (2016) *The religion of existence: Asceticism in philosophy from Kierkegaard to Sartre*, Chicago, IL: University of Chicago Press.
Korsgaard, C. (1996) *Sources of normativity*, Cambridge: Cambridge University Press.
Kosch, M. (2006) *Freedom and reason in Kant, Schelling, and Kierkegaard*, Oxford: Oxford University Press.
Lear, J. (2011) *A case for irony*, Cambridge, MA: Harvard University Press.
Paul, L. A. (2014) *Transformative experience*, Oxford: Oxford University Press.
Rudd, A. (2012) *Self, value, and narrative: A Kierkegaardian approach*, Oxford: Oxford University Press.
Rush, F. (2016) *Irony and idealism: Rereading Schlegel, Hegel, and Kierkegaard*, Oxford: Oxford University Press.
Torrance, A. (2017) 'Can a person prepare to become a Christian? A Kierkegaardian response,' *Religious Studies*, 53: 199–215.
Wietzke, W. (2015) 'Narrativity and normativity,' in J. Lippit and P. Stokes (eds), *Narrative, Identity, and the Kierkegaardian Self*, Edinburgh: Edinburgh University Press.
Wietzke, W. (2013) 'Practical reason and the imagination,' *Res Philosophica*, 90, no. 4: 524–44.

Further reading

Khawaja, N. (2016) *The religion of existence: Asceticism in philosophy from Kierkegaard to Sartre*, Chicago, IL: University of Chicago Press.
   Khawaja provides a cogent analysis of how Kierkegaard shapes the notion of pietistic, religious conversion into the recognizable Existentialist concept of authenticity that was then deployed by Heidegger and Sartre.

Lear, J. (2011) *A case for irony*, Cambridge, MA: Harvard University Press.
   Lear argues that we must cultivate a capacity for having ironic experiences, as these are crucial for human moral development.

Rush, F. (2016) *Irony and idealism: Rereading Schlegel, Hegel, and Kierkegaard*, Oxford: Oxford University Press.
   The chapter on Kierkegaard argues for the centrality of irony in understanding the progression through existence-spheres.

33
LOGIC, LANGUAGE, AND EXISTENTIAL KNOWLEDGE

Mélissa Fox-Muraton

Introduction

Can logic and language provide a foundation for existential knowledge? Can logical reasoning offer a means for providing objective responses to moral and existential questions? Although Søren Kierkegaard is perhaps best known for his claim that existence and logic are diametrically opposed, and has thus been understood by some commentators as a fideist or an irrationalist, we will argue that Kierkegaard does not actually (or at least always) endorse the idea that there must be a strict separation between the spheres of existence and logic, and thus that existential or ethical knowledge is not necessarily opposed to logical reasoning. After examining Kierkegaard's ambiguity with regard to the status of logic and the ways in which logic and existence are opposed in *Either/Or* and the *Concluding Unscientific Postscript*, we will offer a reading of a passage from *Works of Love* which sets forth a realist account of the role of language, and finally examine the ways in which Kierkegaard uses logic and grammatical analysis with regard to problems of moral reasoning and existential choice in 'Does a human being have the right to let himself be put to death for the truth?' Our aim in this article is not to give a full overview of Kierkegaard's understanding of these issues, but more modestly to demonstrate that certain passages in his writings offer the possibility for rethinking the role of existential knowledge in ways which have often been neglected by theological or existentialist interpretations of Kierkegaard's works. We conclude by suggesting that it is possible to offer a Kierkegaardian account as to how logic and language serve as tools for responding to seemingly unanswerable moral and existential questions.

Kierkegaard and the ambiguity of logic

If Kierkegaard's interest in logic may often appear to be secondary, it is clear that this stems from the fact that Kierkegaard himself articulates his task and philosophical orientation in terms that deliberately oppose them to issues of logic. The clearest examples are to be found in the *Concluding Unscientific Postscript*, where Climacus insists on the opposition between logical systems and the problem of existence. As he writes: '*(a) a logical system can be given; (b) but a system of existence [Tilværelsens System] cannot be given,*' (CUP 1, 109/SKS 7, 105) since '[i]n a logical system, nothing may be incorporated that has a relation to existence, that is not indifferent to existence'

(CUP 1, 110/SKS 7, 107). This obligation to exclude existence from the realm of logic stems from the fact that the domain of existence is that of the spheres of subjectivity and of actuality, of the changing and multifarious facets of existence, which cannot be neatly systematized, universalized or objectified. If thus the 'infinite advantage' (CUP 1, 110/SKS 7, 107) that logical thinking has over all other forms of thought is clear, the difficulty is that logic requires abstraction, and thus alienates us from the spheres of life and from the ethical/existential questions which are the most essential to us as living beings. Indeed, Climacus claims that '[a]ll essential knowing pertains to existence, or only the knowing whose relation to existence is essential is essential knowing' (CUP 1, 197/SKS 7, 181). Essential knowing is thus opposed to objective knowledge, which cannot offer responses to the questions that are the most important to us: those questions related to the possibility of leading a meaningful life. And indeed, Climacus writes, for example, that for living/existing human beings, 'the issue is not, after all, a logical issue – indeed, what does logical thinking have in common with the most pathos-filled issue of all (the question of eternal happiness)?' (CUP 1, 362/SKS 7, 329–30).

Since logical thought deals with the spheres of generality, objectivity and necessity, it is necessarily incompatible with existence issues, which 'cannot possibly be understood in general if I am not also such a human being in general. But this I am not' (CUP 1, 167/SKS 7, 154). Kierkegaard's critique of systematic philosophy and ontological logic in the Hegelian vein thus opposes the individual's actual position as an existing subject to what may be perceived as the abstract demands of systematic thinking. For Kierkegaard, refusing to recognize the existential claim of subjectivity as opposed to the objective structure of logical thinking is not only nonsensical, it is also dangerous for the individual, since 'dying to oneself is required' of someone who 'thinks the logical' (CUP 1, 117/SKS 7, 113). Thinking the logical means giving up or losing oneself and one's own life claims in the quest for philosophical abstraction. What is at stake in the rejection of logic is none other than the interest of philosophy itself; whereas Hegel (1841: 9) claimed that philosophy should 'beware of the wish to be edifying,' Kierkegaard's existential approach to philosophy, and his preference for edifying/upbuilding discourses over philosophical treatises, attest to the importance that philosophy should have for actual, living human subjects. In indirect reference to Hegel, *Either/Or* closes with the claim: 'only the truth that builds up is truth for you' (EO 2, 354/SKS 3, 332).

Kierkegaard's critiques of logic have made him vulnerable to a variety of interpretations by commentators who associate his views with strong irrationalism or fideism. One classic example is Georg Lukács (1955: 209), who argues that Kierkegaard promotes 'radical irrationalism' and rejects reason in order to make way for 'the artificially isolated individual.' Lukács (1955: 207) does not fail to note that Kierkegaard often relies on traditional Aristotelian laws of logic in his critiques of Hegelian ontological logic, and especially the principle of mediation, but refuses to recognize that this is anything other than an artifice. Contemporary scholarship has been less polemic in its claims, and generally tends to downplay the emphasis on what might be seen as Kierkegaardian irrationalism, fideism or fundamentalism. While some scholarship has pointed to the necessity of understanding Kierkegaard's notion of existential knowledge in conjunction with Aristotelian practical knowledge and the art of living (see, for example, Taels 2017; Melendo Millán 2016), other approaches have attempted to render Kierkegaard's views on faith compatible with the claims of reason. C. Stephen Evans (2008: 1022–3) has argued, for example, that although Kierkegaard is indeed a fideist of sorts, he does not reject reason and logic altogether, and should therefore be read as a 'responsible fideist,' where 'responsible fideism' is defined as the double claim '(1) that reason is limited and/or defective in certain ways; and (2) that religious faith allows a person to recognize those limits and partially overcome them.' Louis Pojman (1984: 22) attempts to describe Kierkegaard as a philosopher who uses logic in order to demonstrate the rationality of Christianity, through a 'strategy [that] uses reason to undermine the sufficiency of reason, to reach the highest metaphysical and religious truth.' And Eleanor Helms (2013) has argued that Kierkegaard's works should be read as a critique of fideism and a defence of the objectivity of faith.

Despite efforts in contemporary scholarship to offer a more nuanced reading of Kierkegaard, one of their shortcomings is that they generally focus on the rationality of Christian faith. Kierkegaard himself is certainly responsible for this orientation, since he clearly and repeatedly insists on the distinction between reason and faith. However, it is at least curious that scholars such as Pojman (1984: IX, 4, 144) turn to an examination of Kierkegaard's use of logic and epistemology, claiming that he is a 'rationalist' who attempts to demonstrate the 'objective truth' of Christian faith, while at the same time claiming that Kierkegaard is 'not . . . an existentialist' and that 'what we call his "philosophy," his "existentialism," is little more than an attempt at a faithful exposition of the New Testament.' For although the claim can be made that Kierkegaard does indeed attempt to offer a rational justification for Christian faith in his writings – and given the multifarious nature of these, textual evidence can be found for just about any position one wishes to defend – one of Kierkegaard's most consistent claims is that there is indeed a distinct division between the spheres of reason and faith, and that no objective knowledge can serve as a justification for Christian faith, which is the ultimate – if not the only – paradox. Some recent scholarship has attempted to highlight this, notably Karen Carr and Philip Ivanhoe's (2010) reading of Kierkegaard as an anti-rationalist, where anti-rationalism is understood as limited rationality, or more particularly the claim that reason is inadequate, and perhaps antithetical to, a proper understanding of religious truth.

The problem inherent in focussing the debate on rationality with regard to faith in Kierkegaard's writings is that it entails that the existential questions in these are often not taken seriously. Although Kierkegaard indeed defined himself as a Christian thinker, his works, notably the pseudonymous writings (but also the early upbuilding discourses), engage with ethical-existential issues, such as the notions of selfhood and meaningfulness that go beyond, or can be interpreted from outside, a strictly Christian perspective. In this chapter we set aside the question of the rationality of faith and examine the issues of logic and language with regard solely to existential knowledge.[1] Our aim is to give a positive account of the role that logic and reasoning play with regard to moral and existential knowledge. Kierkegaard's initial distinction, as evident in the passages from the *Postscript* quoted above, is not between faith and reason, but rather between logic and existence. Despite this, questions of logic, language and objective knowledge play an important role in Kierkegaard's writings on existence and existence issues. As Paul Holmer (1957: 26) notes, the 'logical and epistemological views which make his writings so effective as argument, which make his issues conceivable, are usually hidden but are not, for this reason, either irrelevant or unimportant.' Kierkegaard's critique of logic should thus not be seen as a blatant rejection of logic in itself, but rather as a protest against forms of 'philosophical rationalism' that attempt to make logic into something more than an instrument for thought (Holmer 1957: 32).

A confusion of the spheres: logic and existence in *Either/Or* and the *Concluding Unscientific Postscript*

While logic is not the focus of Kierkegaard's philosophy, and is given no systematic treatment in his works, there are nevertheless some important discussions of logical issues in many of the texts, notably *The Concept of Anxiety*, *Repetition*, *Either/Or* and the *Concluding Unscientific Postscript*. Questions of logic are also the (indirect) starting point of two of these major texts: *Either/Or* and the *Postscript*. If Kierkegaard sees logic as nothing more than the formal structure of thought and language, it is nevertheless the examination of these formal structures through which philosophizing becomes possible. In his first major published work, *Either/Or*, the title itself is a direct reference to the debate on the Hegelian critique of the law of the excluded middle. While Kant (1900: 98) was the first to introduce the expression '*Entweder-Oder*' into philosophy, and the expression is used in several places in Hegel's *Encyclopädie*, the term *Entweder-Oder* (*aut-aut* in Latin or *enten-eller* in Danish) was largely popularized by Danish Hegelians and anti-Hegelians in theological debates. As Jon Stewart (2003: 184–95) has shown, Kierkegaard's choice of title is not an invention, but rather a catch phrase which would have been immediately identifiable to Danish readers in the 1840s, and which refers back to heavy debates by figures such as Sibbern, Mynster and Martensen, among many others. Rather than an arbitrary reference, Kierkegaard himself directly associates the either/or with logic as an 'indirect polemic against speculative thought' (CUP 1, 252/SKS 7, 229).

To the reader who opens *Either/Or* with this logical reference in mind, the text itself may prove deceiving. Although the text does present a disjunction, it is manifested as a moral question, one of life choices and ways of being, rather than as a logical argument. A closer examination demonstrates, however, that the law of the excluded middle remains the guiding leitmotif of the text. The section of the first part which repeats the title 'Either/Or' offers an illustration of the logical problem through the juxtaposition of mutually exclusive existence alternatives, and suggests that any choice between contrary alternatives is not only meaningless, but also a source of despair and regret: 'Marry, and you will regret it. Do not marry, and you will also regret it. Marry or do not marry, you will regret it either way. . . . Hang yourself, and you will regret it. Do not hang yourself, and you will also regret it. Hang yourself or do not hang yourself, you will regret it either way' (EO 1, 38–9/SKS 2, 47–8). The argument here is that whatever life choice one makes excludes all others, and thus reduces the domain of possibility. Choosing, from the aesthetic perspective, means attributing a predicate, to the exclusion of its contrary. For the aesthete, this is not self-definition, but rather self-privation: definitively depriving oneself of the alternative which was not chosen. The traditional rules of logic apply here as well – and precisely for that reason they are without mercy. The aesthete's claim is that the rules of logic are the abyss into which human choice inevitably plunges. Of course, one is free to marry or not, to laugh or to weep, to trust another or not, to hang oneself or not, but one cannot do both simultaneously, and to believe otherwise 'is a misunderstanding' (EO 1, 39/SKS 2, 48).

Is there no way out of this conundrum? Are our life choices condemned to follow the constraints of logic? In his papers, Kierkegaard did provide a solution which he finally omitted from the published text of *Either/Or*: 'The best thing for you is to go and hang yourself' (EO 1, 529/SKS 19, 214). Is this really the logical solution? If we reinterpret the aesthete's argument, considering the proposition that 'you will regret it either way' not as the conclusion to the argument, but rather as a simple premise, the only logically valid conclusion is suicide. An absurd conclusion? If this conclusion appears absurd, the reason is that it is inherently logically valid. If indeed all life choices are choices which deprive us of possibility and thus push us to despair, the only way out of the cycle would be to put an end to these life choices, and thus an end to life. And yet, such a conclusion is not a response to the problem of existence. 'A' here underscores the fundamental problem of logic: even if logic does describe the structures of thought and meaning, it cannot be fully applied to existence, without denying existence itself. Here we see the premises of the critiques of ontological logic that Kierkegaard will develop throughout his works: logic cannot describe existence, and any attempt to make logic and existence coincide entails existentially untenable conclusions.

While for the aesthete mediation in existence is an impossibility, the ethicist of the second half of *Either/Or* defends a similar position, but for different reasons. Although Judge Wilhelm clarifies that he is 'not a logician' (EO 2, 213/SKS 3, 205), he nevertheless engages the debate on more philosophical terms than does the aesthete. At the same time, it is clear that the ultimate argument given by the ethicist is in many ways less logical than the one provided in non-philosophical terms by the aesthete. In his analysis of the concept of mediation, Judge Wilhelm affirms that what the concept cannot take into account is freedom, and the ethical necessity of the possibility of making an absolute choice. As he notes: 'For thought, the contradiction does not exist; it passes over into the other and thereupon together with the other into a higher unity. For freedom, the contradiction does exist, because it excludes it' (EO 2, 173/SKS 3, 169). Here, Judge Wilhelm largely agrees with the Hegelian account of mediation; with regard to thought and the concept, mediation is effectively necessary and makes becoming possible. However, like the aesthete, the ethicist views this as a problem for the existing being, not so much because of the facticity of any life choice, but rather because it entails problematic consequences. Indeed, if there is no contradiction, if one can always introduce a third term between any two, then there is just no such thing as an absolute choice. The ethicist gives a moral argument against the principles of Hegelian logic: in the end, mediation just cannot be right, because if it were there would be no meaning to life, no individual choice, whereas 'choice itself is crucial for the content of the personality' (EO 2, 163/SKS 3, 160). *Either/Or* thus provides two alternative accounts as to how logic is both valid with regard to existence, and at the same time existentially problematic.

In the *Concluding Unscientific Postscript*, Climacus again takes up these issues. The working title for the *Postscript* was initially *Logical Problems* (JP 5, 295/Pap. VI B 89), and though the text polemicizes against logic (or at least a Hegelian or ontological understanding of logic), it does so through the use of dialectics. Climacus's argumentation aims at bringing to light the question of meaning and, most especially, at pointing out the 'confusion of categories' (CUP 1, 31/SKS 7, 37) inherent in the Hegelian system and modern speculative philosophy. If the title proposes an 'unscientific' treatment of these issues – probably in indirect reference to Hegel's *Science of Logic* – Climacus does not reject ontological logic as a means for attaining objective knowledge, but rather contests the confusion between objective knowledge and existential truth, and the 'mystification' of dogmatic thinking (CUP 1, 111/SKS 7, 107). Although Climacus rejects the methods of direct communication, at least insofar as subjective knowledge is concerned, and offers no direct theses in his writing, the *Postscript* does offer an argument about logic which we could formulate as follows:

(1) Logic is the science through which thought clarifies itself in becoming objective.
(2) As such, logic is necessary in order to ground objective knowledge.
(3) Objective knowledge is possible with regard to all infinite and unchanging beings.
(4) Objective knowledge enables us to define objective truth.
(5) However, the existing being is by definition in movement, becoming, and thus incapable of complete objectification.
(6) *Therefore*, either there can be no knowledge of the existing being, or the type of knowledge, and thus the truth about this being, is qualitatively different from that provided through logic.

The disjunctive conclusion of this argument seems to lead us to a dead end: if no knowledge is possible about existing beings, this fact itself would be something that we could therefore not know, but at the same time if subjective knowledge is qualitatively distinct from objective knowledge, then objective or logical reasoning cannot prove this to us. According to Climacus, however, this apparent dead end only serves to better demonstrate the problems inherent in the philosophical use of concepts. Climacus's critique of logicians, and philosophers more generally, aims to demonstrate that they have confused the categories, and employ terms in such a way that they 'mean something different from what [they] usually do' (CUP 1, 114/SKS 7, 110). Since the categories have become confused, since language contains imprecisions, we can arrive at absurd conclusions. Yet this does not entail that we ought to reject logic and reason, but rather that we must require more precision and clarity in order to arrive at a more correct understanding of existence. As in *Either/Or*, the *Postscript* offers an ambiguous account of logic: if logic fails to enable us to deal with existential questions, it is perhaps less that logic and existence are incompatible, than that our language and logical reasoning have become confused by unclear concepts.

Language: a realist approach in *Works of Love*

In order to get a better grasp on what role logic plays in Kierkegaard's works, it is essential to understand how Kierkegaard conceives of language in the first place. As Stanley Cavell has pointed out, Kierkegaard's method is clearly logical or, perhaps more rightly put, 'grammatical' in the Wittgensteinian sense. Kierkegaard's examinations of logical questions, and more particularly the conceptual confusions which plague idealist philosophy, aim to demonstrate that many issues are problematic not in psychological or empirical terms, but rather in purely conceptual ones. According to Cavell (2002: 168–9), Kierkegaard shows that 'a question which appears to need settling by empirical means or through presenting a formal argument is really a conceptual question, a question of grammar.' However, Kierkegaard's approach to language is not merely negative. Unfortunately, the idea that Kierkegaard gives no real account of language has had a major influence on the ways in which Kierkegaard's writings have been read, especially in the analytic tradition amongst scholars eager to assimilate Kierkegaard with Wittgenstein. Indeed, as James Conant has notably summarized the literature on Kierkegaard and Wittgenstein, most of the accounts (including Conant's) presuppose a certain understanding of Kierkegaard's view of language and the possibilities of logic, which we will hereafter call into question. Conant (1989: 243–4) summarizes this traditional understanding of Kierkegaard as the concern 'to draw a distinction between sense and nonsense ... and to relegate matters of importance (ethics, religion) to a realm beyond the limits of sense; ... to draw a distinction between what can be said ... and what can only be shown ... by drawing limits to what can be said or thought.' The conclusion is that the philosophical endeavour ends in 'self-destruction' and the 'proclamation that silence is the only correct form that an answer to [his] questions could take.' This type of reading draws largely on the idea that Kierkegaard's position is one which is best called irrationalism or fideism, and that Kierkegaard finally rejects the ability of language and logic to answer ethical and existential questions at all.

While it is true that Kierkegaard does sometimes appear to suggest that there are ways in which our objective knowledge is limited, and in which language is unable to express or communicate the existential, it is, however, far from clear that these conclusions really are his own. Indeed, although Kierkegaard offers no explicit 'theory' of language or meaning, some passages in his writings attest to the fact that he did espouse a realist conception of language and offer a solid, if not systematic, account of the way in which higher-order concepts are formed. Notably, in the opening pages of the discourse 'Love builds up,' in *Works of Love*, Kierkegaard offers a surprising analysis of the ways in which language and meaning function. The discourse opens with the affirmation that 'all human speech ... about the spiritual is essentially metaphorical [*overført*, carried over]' (WL, 209/SKS 9, 212). If speech about the spiritual is *carried over*, it is because what we know, or have access to, about the spiritual realm (ourselves as thinking beings, first and foremost) is not immediately given, but can only be derived indirectly through reflexion and language. The world to which language directly refers is that perceived through our 'sensate-psychical' engagement (WL, 209/SKS 9, 212); words describe the world we have access to through empirical evidence. Thus, to speak about what is not immediately given through our senses requires an extension of language practices. Yet, 'metaphorical words are of course not brand-new words but are already given words' (WL, 209/ SKS 9, 212–3). We do not invent a new language or new concepts when speaking about that which is not accessible to immediate perception; rather, we transpose our former language into another domain, give new meanings through the ways in which words are used.

To understand how these new meanings are developed, Kierkegaard suggests that one ought to start with a careful examination of what words '*signif[y] in ordinary speech*' (WL, 210/SKS 9, 213). And Kierkegaard offers a detailed example of how this can be done, through an analysis of the expression 'to build up' (*at opbygge*):

> 'To build up' is formed from 'to build' and the adverb 'up,' which consequently must receive the accent. Everyone who builds up does build, but not everyone who builds does build up. For example, when a man is building a wing on his house we do not say that he is building up a wing but that he is building *on*. Consequently, this 'up' seems to indicate the direction in height, the upward direction. Yet this is not the case either. For example, if a man builds a sixty-foot building twenty feet higher, we still do not say that he *built up* the structure twenty feet higher – we say that he built *on*. Here the meaning of the word already becomes perceptible, for we see that it does not depend on height. However, if a man erects a house, be it ever so small and low, from the ground up, we say that he built up a house. Thus to build up is to erect something *from the ground up*.
>
> (WL, 210–1/SKS 9, 213–4)

If we take this metaphor seriously, Kierkegaard's understanding of language itself is that it is a process of 'building up.' This entails that language is not, for Kierkegaard, a mere arbitrary construction. Like the house, it must have solid foundations. And these foundations reside in what language itself refers to: the empirical world to which linguistic constructions immediately refer. The signs we use to refer to worldly facts may indeed be arbitrary – yet the content to which we refer is not necessarily also arbitrary. Rather, *the foundation through which language acquires its meaning structures* is none other than the empirical world as object of sensate-psychical experience, a starting point upon which the construction of meaning becomes possible as we move up to the more elevated spheres of the psychological/subjective or the spiritual. The view of language and meaning exposed here proves to be an essentially realist view of language: all language (and knowledge) begins with the world we know through experience, yet since language is related immediately to the physical world, and not to the spiritual dimensions of subjective existence, it must be remodelled and reconstructed in order to say something meaningful about non-physical entities.

A second conclusion that can be drawn from this passage is that getting at the meaning of a word is possible through the careful analysis of how it is used in ordinary speech. When we reflect on correct and incorrect grammatical uses of a term, we get a sense of its meaning. Hence, understanding when and where an expression is properly used indicates its meaning. Of course, 'careless and incorrect use of language' (WL, 212/SKS 9, 215) is always possible. Rather than a general critique of the meaningfulness of language itself, however, Kierkegaard suggests that examining how words are used in ordinary language does indeed enable us to see *what they really do mean* – in other words, to what *reality* they refer. As such, linguistic analysis draws us back to the foundations of language, to the conditions of meaningfulness, but also to the facts to which expressions refer.

Kierkegaard thus does indeed seem to be claiming that language refers directly to reality (i.e., to the empirical world as it presents itself to the observer). Of course, this is problematic with regard to non-physical realities. How can we speak about these? Kierkegaard suggests that we cannot simply invent new words and concepts, for if we did, we would not be able to communicate at all. All language involves some possibility of reference to perceptible realities; in order to speak about non-physical states or entities, we therefore have to use the language of the empirical world, but we make sense of it through analogy. Through this change of context new meaning possibilities emerge.

If spiritual meaning is metaphorical, it is not nonsensical; on the contrary, the meaningfulness of any language use about the spiritual relies on the connexion with both the physical world and the ordinary language uses related to that world. It is clear here that Kierkegaard does not suggest that the spiritual cannot be objectively comprehended; he merely affirms that it cannot be objectively comprehended *in the same way* that we might understand the physical reality. We fail to understand the meaning of an expression when we neglect to take into consideration the context in which it is uttered, to what type of reality it is referring, but this does not entail that these realities are in themselves incomprehensible. In light of Kierkegaard's analyses, it seems erroneous to assimilate metaphorical speech with that which cannot be objectively known or said, as Conant and others have. The possibility of carrying over expressions from one sphere of reality to another (from the sensate to the spiritual) does not imply the impossibility of expression itself. Metaphorical language is still *meaningful* language, precisely because it resides upon the foundation of language rooted in sensate reality. Kierkegaard's analysis of language seeks to distinguish meaningful use of expressions from 'incorrect' grammatical use, which leads to 'false' propositions (WL, 212/SKS 9, 215). However, it is through language that we see these distinctions, and are able express different levels of reality; we are able to say and think what goes beyond sensate experience *because* language offers us the possibility of ascribing new and different meanings.

Knowledge and answerable moral/existential questions

If logic and language are important at all, it is because they enable us to ask meaningful questions and provide meaningful answers. However, with regard to Kierkegaard's existential philosophy, this may at times appear problematic. As Patrick Stokes (2013: 378) has pointed out, one of the major difficulties is that many of Kierkegaard's existential discussions 'end up insisting that from within certain world views, some important and perfectly sensible questions are *ethically* unanswerable.' While it is true that Kierkegaard often invites us to act rather than to question moral and existential issues, in other places he does suggest that logical reasoning can be applied to these issues, and even must be if we are to act appropriately. Indeed, early on in his journals, Kierkegaard notes (this passage is often cited, leaving out the essential final clause): 'What I really need is to be clear about *what I am to do*, not what I must know, except in the way knowledge must precede all action' (KJN 1, 19/SKS 17, 24). If, as Kierkegaard claims, the aim of his work is to help others 'to exist more capably' (*for at komme til at existere dygtigere*) (PV, 17/SKS 13, 24), then it would seem that we do indeed need to learn and be able to communicate to others what constitutes a more capable existence, and we do need to be able to reflect rationally on the contents of existence and existential knowledge.

One major example of the way in which Kierkegaard uses logical and grammatical analysis to demonstrate that some apparently unanswerable questions can indeed be answered is in the essay 'Does a human being have the right to let himself be put to death for the truth?' In this essay, H. H. uses logic to show that any attempt to justify exemption from the moral sphere, where universal principles reside, through an appeal to divine authority or religious belief is untenable. The essay focuses on one apparently simple, yet simultaneously morally and existentially complex, question: can an individual ever determine that he legitimately possesses a 'truth' which, though unknown to others, is of such great importance that he can be considered justified in letting himself be put to death for it, despite the fact that there are no objective grounds or proof upon which to found this decision? In other words, can it be considered justifiable to choose to become a martyr for a cause that is not universally accepted or objectively determined? One might suppose that, given Kierkegaard's general theological orientation, his response would be yes. And yet, the text arrives at a very different and categorical conclusion: 'that a *human being does not have the right to let himself be put to death for the truth*' (WA, 84/SKS 11, 88; emphasis added). And this categorical conclusion is proposed as being independent of any particular life-view, of any convictions based on faith or of any psychological dispositions within the individual in question. H. H. here shows that in order to arrive at this conclusion, one is not obliged to ground reasoning on debatable ontological and epistemic issues about the nature of truth or the possibility that an individual may be in possession of the truth. All one really needs, in order to arrive at the 'right' conclusion, is sound logical reasoning – and logical reasoning can also serve to ground solid principles capable of guiding moral behaviour.

How exactly does H. H. use logic and grammatical analysis in this text? Though the presentation is not that of a formal essay or a treatise on logic, the general structure of the essay is clear and points systematically to the fact that in many instances, reasoning on seemingly unanswerable questions such as this is based on missing premises. H. H. thus continually points to the fact that generally with regard to this type of issue, '[o]ne never comes to the real question' (WA, 67/SKS 11, 73). We miss the point of the issue because we tend to focus on ontological or epistemological questions, which are perhaps unanswerable, such as whether it is possible to know the truth, or whether an individual can be certain that he has indeed had a divine revelation. Since we have no means for offering objective responses to these questions, we generally assume that the moral question posed by the individual who believes that he has had a divine revelation and thus that it is his duty to become a martyr is unanswerable. Yet H. H. invites us to look at the issue from another perspective: since we can neither see inside another's mind nor from a God's-eye view, the only method possible is a logical one: to *assume* that the premises are indeed true, and examine their logical consequences with regard to the conclusions that may be drawn.

H. H's essay thus places us in a logical thought experiment: let us assume that a man, through divine revelation, has knowledge of a truth which he should transmit to others, and that he can only do so by being put to death for the truth. Is it then his duty to let himself be put to death? If we reason on the basis of only these initial premises, then the response seems to be yes. However, if we consider the issue further, we see that there are a number of missing premises. H. H. evokes a series of other considerations, among which the major arguments are that in letting oneself be put to death, one makes others guilty of an offense (WA, 72/SKS 11, 76), and that to do so is to presuppose that 'that with regard to the truth I stand so far removed from other people . . . that there is almost no kinship between us' (WA, 77/SKS 11, 81). If this were true, then it must be that there is an infinite difference between the individual and all others, so that the martyr would be able to simultaneously absolve others of their guilt through his death. And yet, as H. H. points out, no human being can, through his death, bring about absolution: only

Christ has this power (WA, 73/SKS 11, 77). Once we have added these premises to our initial argument, it is clear that the initial conclusion was not valid, and that there is only one logically valid conclusion: that a human being never has the right to let himself be put to death, even for the truth. To some moral questions at least, logic and grammar can serve as guides to arriving at valid moral and existential responses.[2]

Are there then unanswerable questions? To some extent, Kierkegaard's answer is yes. We really cannot know objectively whether God exists, what immorality consists in, what happens when we die. Nor whether we ought to marry, to laugh or to cry at the aberrations of the world. However, this does not entail that we have no knowledge pertaining to existence questions, or that the subjective knowledge we do have is of an entirely different sort than objective knowledge about the physical world. And the fact that Kierkegaard distinguishes between existential/subjective knowledge and objective knowledge does not necessarily make him a fideist or an irrationalist. Saying that there are some questions to which it is beyond our scope to find ultimate or even relatively convincing answers, given the limits of our current perspective, can indeed, from a philosophical standpoint, be understood as a form of fideism, but it can also be interpreted as just good science and sound epistemology. Moreover, Kierkegaard does not say that there *are* no answers; indeed, he clearly affirms that 'Existence itself is a system – for God,' albeit unknowable for us now (CUP 1, 118/SKS 7, 114). The obvious and generally recognized conclusion is that Kierkegaard's message is that we need to focus on living and acting, rather than becoming encumbered by abstract questions that estrange us from our lives. While this is certainly true, we wish to make a stronger claim here: as Kierkegaard's continued engagement with questions of logic and language demonstrates, his works are an invitation to make maximum use of all the theoretical tools at our disposal to provide responses to those existential questions that we *can* answer. This means taking Kierkegaard's approach to logic, language and reason seriously, and rethinking some of the general conclusions about what existential philosophy is and ought to be. In so doing, we may find that Kierkegaard's existential philosophy has a lot more to offer than is generally supposed, and that he notably provides tools for examining contemporary moral and existential issues.

Related topics

'Christian epistemology and the anthropology of sin: Kierkegaard on natural theology and the concept of "offense,"' Karen L. Carr; 'Varieties of existential uncertainty,' Rick Anthony Furtak; 'On faith and reason(s): Kierkegaard's logic of conviction,' K. Brian Söderquist; 'Irony and the conversion experience,' Walter Wietzke.

Notes

1 Kierkegaard distinguishes between the existential orientation of his pseudonymous works (up until *The Concept of Anxiety*) as well as the upbuilding discourses, and the specifically religious or Christian orientation of his later writings in the overview of his authorship in the *Postscript*. According to Climacus, the existential writings are purely immanent, whereas the transcendent orientation of the later writings is brought out through the 'paradoxical expression of existence (that is, existing) as sin' (CUP 1, 270–1/SKS 7, 245–6). Our distinction between faith questions and existential questions follows along similar lines: questions of faith refer to particular concepts, such as sin, being before God, and eternal happiness, whereas existential questions more generally do not rely on any form of transcendence or paradox.
2 It may be objected here that we are taking H. H.'s essay too straightforwardly, and that Kierkegaard's writings, and especially the late texts which engage in discussions of martyrdom and the distinctions

between Christendom and Christianity, are significantly less favourable to logic and reason. While it is certainly the case that some of Kierkegaard's Christian writings do offer a different perspective, our intention in this article was not to claim that the whole of Kierkegaard's authorship deals with questions of logic and language with regard to existential knowledge, but much more humbly to suggest that if we do wish to understand how Kierkegaard can be integrated into contemporary debates about epistemology and logic, there are resources available for this. While it goes beyond the scope of this article to demonstrate that the reading we have given here of 'Does a Human Being Have the Right to Let Himself Be Put to Death for the Truth?' is indeed compatible with Kierkegaard's general perspective, we refer the reader to another article (Fox-Muraton 2018), where we make the case that Kierkegaard offers solid arguments throughout his authorship against moral exceptionalism and religious justification for teleologically suspending the ethical.

References

Carr, K. L. and Ivanhoe, P. J. (2010) *The sense of antirationalism: The religious thought of Zhuangzi and Kierkegaard*, New York; London: Seven Bridges Press.
Cavell, S. (2002) 'Kierkegaard's "On authority and revelation",' in S. Cavell (ed), *Must We Mean What We Say?*, Cambridge: Cambridge University Press.
Conant, J. (1989) 'Must we show what we cannot say?' in R. Fleming and M. Payne (eds), *The Senses of Stanley Cavell*, Lewisburg, PA: Bucknell University Press.
Evans, C. S. (2008) 'Kierkegaard and the limits of reason: Can there be a responsible fideism?' *Revista Portuguesa de Filosofia*, 64: 1021–35.
Fox-Muraton, M. (2018) 'There is no teleological suspension of the ethical: Kierkegaard's logic against religious justification and moral exceptionalism,' in H. Schulz, J. Stewart and K. Verstrynge (eds), *Kierkegaard Studies Yearbook 2018*, Berlin: Walter de Gruyter.
Hegel, G. W. F. (1841) *Phänomenologie des Geistes*, Berlin: Verlag von Duncker und Humblot.
Helms, E. (2013) 'The objectivity of faith: Kierkegaard's critique of fideism,' *Res Philosophica*, 90, no. 4: 439–60.
Holmer, P. L. (1957) 'Kierkegaard and logic,' *Kierkegaardiana*, 2: 25–42.
Kant, I. (1900) *Metaphysische Anfangsgründer der Naturwissenschaft*, Leipzig: Verlag von C.E.M. Pfeffer.
Lukács, G. (1955) *Die Zerstörung der Vernunft*, Berlin: Aufbau-Verlag.
Melendo Millán, I. (2016) 'Toward a "positive" defense of existential truth,' *Metafísica y persona: Filosofía, conocimiento y vida*, 8, no. 15: 101–18. DOI: http://dx.doi.org/10.24310/Metyper.2016.v0i15.2705
Pojman, L. P. (1984) *The logic of subjectivity: Kierkegaard's philosophy of religion*, Tuscaloosa, AL: University of Alabama Press.
Stewart, J. (2003) *Kierkegaard's relations to Hegel reconsidered*, Cambridge: Cambridge University Press.
Stokes, P. (2013) 'Death,' in J. Lippit and G. Pattison (eds), *The Oxford Handbook of Kierkegaard*, Oxford: Oxford University Press.
Taels, J. (2017) 'Existential hermeneutics: Kierkegaard and Gadamar on practical knowledge ("Phronesis"),' in A. Grøn, R. Rosfort and K. B. Söderquist (eds), *Kierkegaard's Existential Approach*, Berlin: Walter de Gruyter.

Further reading

Cavell, S. (2002) 'Kierkegaard's "On authority and revelation",' in S. Cavell (ed), *Must We Mean What We Say?*, Cambridge: Cambridge University Press.
    Cavell's analysis of *The Book on Adler* offers a Wittgensteinian reading of the text, showing how Kierkegaard relies on grammatical analysis to demonstrate the conceptual confusion of modern philosophy, and how his works seek to re-activate Christian concepts.

Fox-Muraton, M. (2018) 'There is no teleological suspension of the ethical: Kierkegaard's logic against religious justification and moral exceptionalism,' in H. Schulz, J. Stewart and K. Verstrynge (eds), *Kierkegaard Studies Yearbook 2018*, Berlin: Walter de Gruyter.
    This article examines Kierkegaard's use of logical reasoning and grammatical analysis in order to demonstrate that moral knowledge can be arrived at through reason, and shows that Kierkegaard offers a strong critique of moral exceptionalism.

Holmer, P. L. (1957) 'Kierkegaard and logic,' *Kierkegaardiana*, 2: 25–42.

    Holmer argues that while not a logician in the traditional sense, the logical and epistemological views upon which Kierkegaard's writings are constructed are essential elements in his works. Holmer affirms that Kierkegaard's take on logic could best be described as a surprisingly modern 'via media' position, where logical structure is not directly related to any content, but where logical forms are not pure inventions either.

Pojman, L. P. (1984) *The logic of subjectivity: Kierkegaard's philosophy of religion*, Tuscaloosa, AL: University of Alabama Press.

    Pojman examines how Kierkegaard's use of traditional Aristotelian logic and attempts to contextualize Christian concepts enable him to provide both a negative and a positive account of the objectivity and rationality of Christian faith.

34

THE INCOGNITO OF A THIEF: JOHANNES CLIMACUS AND THE POETICS OF SELF-INCRIMINATION

Martijn Boven

Introduction

Søren Kierkegaard's *Philosophiske Smuler eller En Smule Philosophi* (*Philosophical Crumbs or a Crumb of Philosophy*) was published in 1844 under the pseudonym Johannes Climacus.[1] As the connective 'or' *(eller)* already suggests, the book does not have just one form, but can be interpreted either as multiple *philosophical crumbs* or as a single *crumb of philosophy*.[2] This announces a tension between the outer forms in which the book manifests itself (the *philosophical crumbs*) and the inner existential insight that is expressed in this way (the *crumb of philosophy*). Apparently, the plural manifestation is the only mode in which the singular existential insight can emerge. It cannot be stated directly, but can only unroll itself in contrastive forms that preserve its innerness through tensions and contradictions that still need to be resolved by the reader. In this chapter, I show that these indirect and contrastive forms are animated by a poetics of self-incrimination. By adopting the identity of a thief as an incognito, I argue, the pseudonymous author Johannes Climacus tries to recharge the absolute paradox that he invents/discovers at the heart of Christianity.

Self-incrimination

Climacus' poetics of self-incrimination is already announced in the motto of the book: 'Better well hanged than ill wed' (PF, 3/SKS 4, 214). This echo of the reckless and provocative words of Feste, the jester from Shakespeare's *Twelfth Night*, sets the tone for the entire book.[3] It indicates that Climacus would rather be seen as a criminal (and face the consequences) than join speculative scholarship in its attempts to mediate the offensive nature of Christianity and make it respectable as part of a progressive moment in the development of the Hegelian system. In line with the motto, Climacus deliberately provides the reader with a series of self-incriminating statements.

At crucial moments in *Philosophical Crumbs*, Climacus interrupts his own argument by introducing an imaginary opponent who accuses him of stealing his words from someone else. These accusations do not come from outside, but are an integral part of Climacus' own dialogic discourse. They usually begin with a phrase like 'perhaps someone will say' or 'if someone were to say,' followed by an accusation of theft or plagiarism. This practice of self-incrimination becomes a signature mark for the whole book. By adopting the incognito of a common thief, Climacus puts his own authority in question and dialogizes his own project. At the same time, he bolsters his project by suggesting that he did not steal his ideas from just anybody, but that they originated with 'the god' (*guden*). Moreover, he suggests that theft is the condition for getting access to these ideas, regardless of whether we use them for an attack or for a defense of Christianity. Theft evokes 'sin' and 'guilt,' and the kind of education Climacus advances (as a hypothetical project) can only commence by accepting these incriminations.

Quite a few interpreters (Evans 1992; Fenves 1993; Mulhall 1999; Hale 2002; Conway 2004; Pons 2004; Howland 2006; Muench 2006) have highlighted the role of the imaginary opponent and his accusations of theft and plagiarism. I want to push this point a bit by arguing that it is ultimately Climacus himself who is the source of the accusations that are brought against him. By interrupting his own discourse with dialogical accusations, Climacus invites his readers to join in the ambiguous self-incrimination that he is enacting. In this way, I argue, he deliberately adopts the identity of a thief as an incognito. The aim of this is to re-activate the offensive nature of Christianity, demanding a gesture of self-incrimination as a response, in order to force his readers to take a stance.

If we look at the composition of *Philosophical Crumbs*, it is constructed as a comedy with five acts, preceded by a preface, cut in two by an interlude, and concluded with a moral. This comedy employs several variations on Climacus' incognito of the thief. In chapter 1, Climacus develops a thought-project that, by way of hypothesis, investigates what it means to really 'go further' than Socrates.[4] In the process, he accidentally invents a shadow version of Christianity. Here Climacus adopts the incognito of the thief by presenting himself as a project maker who advances a false claim to an invention that ultimately belongs to no one else than the god. Chapter 2 is composed as a poetical venture, the authorship of which is not clearly assigned but keeps shifting. Climacus, as the disputed writer of this poetical venture, appears in the incognito of a plagiarizer who ends up stealing his words from the god himself. In chapter 3, Climacus takes on the incognito of a capricious fellow who introduces a seemingly ludicrous and completely unreasonable conception that deliberately aims for the collapse of the understanding. In the appendix to this chapter, the incognito of the thief gets a new twist when Climacus admits that he has only been parroting the paradox. In chapter 4 and 5, the poetical venture is taken up again but the accusatory mode of speaking of the imaginary opponent is now mixed with a laudatory mode of speaking. In this way, it simultaneously enacts the dismissive logic of an attack and the jubilant logic of a defense, both of which turn out to be equally problematic. In addition to the five chapters, Climacus inserts an interlude that addresses the difficult issue of coming into existence. This interlude plays with the contrast between the ordinary function of the interlude (shortening time by filling it up with a diversion) and the way it is used here (prolonging time by discussing the most complicated concepts of the whole book).

The maieutic incognito

The first chapter of *Philosophical Crumbs* is announced under the title 'Thought-project.' Climacus argues that the speculative scholarship of his day, despite its attempt at 'going further' than Socrates, ultimately comes down to re-affirming the Socratic conception of recollection. 'All these ideas are that Greek idea of recollection, although this is not always noticed, because they have been arrived at by going further [*gaae videre*]' (PF, 10n/SKS 4, 219). In this way, he identifies speculative scholarship with the Socratic position it supposedly had moved beyond. Climacus presents his thought-project as an experiment in which he will explicate, by way of a hypothesis, what it would mean to really go further than Socrates. It is not easy to summarize this hypothesis, but it goes something like this: if there is a philosophical position that moves beyond Socrates, it must involve a different conception of truth. Socratically speaking, all people have access to the truth through recollection; the condition for reaching this truth is already present within themselves. Going further than Socrates means that this is no longer the case. Instead, the access to the truth is blocked and the condition for reaching it needs to come from somewhere else.

Despite its attempt at going further, Climacus' thought-project overlaps on one important point with the Socratic dialogue: the need for an indirect form of communication. This can be achieved by adopting an incognito (see, for example, Boven 2014; 2018; Muench 2006). In this way, both Climacus and Socrates can ensure that their recipients start to question their own position and turn inwards, rather than simply copying the ideas of an external authority. The term 'maieutic' is derived from Plato's (1921: 34–5/150c) *Theaetetus*, in which Socrates compares himself to a midwife (*maia*). Like a midwife, Socrates can only assist others in giving birth, but remains barren of wisdom (*agonos sophias*) himself (Plato 1921: 34–5/150c). Climacus believes that, humanly speaking, assisting others is the highest goal one can achieve with education. As he states, 'between one human being and another *maieuesthai* [serving as a midwife] is the highest; giving birth [*føde*] indeed belongs to the god' (PF, 11/SKS 4, 220; translation modified).[5] In Climacus' estimation, going further than Socrates means substituting the Socratic conception of recollection (*Erindring*) with a conception of rebirth (*Gjenfødelse*). This constitutes a shift from the Socratic position of a midwife (who assists others to give birth) to the position of a divine creator (who literally gives birth to others). Climacus, as a human being who addresses himself to other human beings, cannot really go further than Socrates and has to stick to a maieutic incognito.

Although Socrates and Climacus use the maieutic incognito for different reasons, its underlying structure is more or less the same. Let us first look at the role of the maieutic incognito in the Socratic dialogues. Given the prominent role Plato's *Meno* plays in *Philosophical Crumbs*, we will take this dialogue as an example. At the start of the dialogue, Socrates adopts the incognito of an ignorant bystander who is willing to accept Meno as his master. Initially Meno is happy to take on this role. He presents himself as an authority on the question 'what is virtue?' and invokes other authority figures like Gorgias in the process. Socrates, on the other hand, presents himself as someone who has no authority to speak about virtue and openly questions authority figures that claim to know all about it (see Plato 1997: 871/71b, 872/71c). By adopting the incognito of an ignorant bystander who only asks a few innocent questions, Socrates forces Meno to admit that he does not know what virtue is and that the issue is in fact perplexing him. In the course of the argument, Socrates complicates the opposition between mastery and slavery on which Meno's initial definition of virtue is based.[6] This comes to a climax in the famous episode in which Socrates questions one of Meno's slaves about geometry. By putting the slave in a position where he – like his master Meno – thinks that he can 'easily make many fine speeches to large audiences,' Socrates ironically identifies the master with his slave (Plato 1997: 883–4/84c).[7] Moreover, he shows that, upon questioning, the slave – unlike his master Meno – is willing to admit that he is at a loss and that his previous claim of authority was utterly mistaken. In other words, in a few simple steps the slave has already surpassed his master in dialectical reasoning. The slave episode is not only an effective mockery of Meno's assumed authority and mastery; it also provides a blueprint for the kind of education that Socrates is propagating.

This kind of education proceeds in two steps. First, by adopting the incognito of the ignorant bystander, Socrates provokes his interlocutor – Meno or his slave – to formulate whatever he thinks he knows about the subject in order to let him run aground on a series of contradictions and difficulties.[8] The aim of this is to make an all too confident interlocutor perplexed, 'numbing him as the numbfish does' and to expose the one-sided nature of his assumptions (Plato 1997: 883/84b; translation modified). In this way, interlocutors become aware that they do not really know what they thought they knew. Instead of relying on assumptions and authorities, they are turned inward and start to long for the truth that is already within them. As a second step, Socrates will remind them of this truth, encourage them to discover it, and let them bring it to light. To determine whether they really gave birth to the truth and not to some kind of phantom, he will subsequently subject their offspring to all possible tests.

From Climacus' perspective, leaving the Socratic viewpoint means that human beings can no longer be defined as having the truth already within them. Instead, they now have to be 'defined as being outside the truth' (PF, 13/SKS 4, 222). As seen from this new perspective, education still proceeds in two steps. The first step still consists of making pupils aware by turning them inwards. However, it can no longer be understood as a progressive movement that brings the pupils closer to the truth within themselves. On the contrary, this first step rather generates a regressive movement that only shows pupils that they are 'not coming toward [*kommende til*]' the truth, but are rather 'going away from [*gaaende fra*]' it (PF, 13/SKS 4, 222). Rather than being reminded of the truth within themselves (the Socratic viewpoint), pupils are turned inward by letting them discover that they are outside of the truth; as such, they are confronted with their own untruth. This state of untruth cannot be communicated directly, but can only be revealed indirectly. Climacus formulates this as follows: 'I can discover my own untruth only by myself, because only when *I* discover it is it discovered, not before, even though the whole world knew it' (PF, 14/SKS 4, 223).

Despite the difference in outcome, the thought-project achieves its effects in a similar way to the Socratic dialogue. In both cases, the first step of education can only be attained by provoking the pupil to turn inward with the help of an indirect form of communication that relies on adopting an incognito. Here 'the teacher is only an occasion, whoever he may be, even if he is a god' (PF, 14/SKS 4, 223). Climacus tries to achieve this effect by presenting himself as a project maker who advances a false claim to an invention that ultimately belongs to no one else but the god. The aim of his ambiguous discourse is to set the first step of education in motion. This prepares the way for the second step, which constitutes a rebirth through which the pupil first receives the condition for discovering the truth. Climacus cannot make this second step happen; it is the prerogative of the god.

An invention without an inventor

At the end of the first chapter, Climacus explicitly hints at his own incognito of a thief. First he claims ownership of his project: 'Look, this is my project [*Projekt*]!' (PF, 21/SKS 4, 229; translation modified). The next moment, however, an imaginary opponent interrupts his discourse, arguing that this project does not in fact belong to Climacus. 'This is the most ludicrous of all projects [*Projekter*], or, rather, you are the most ludicrous of all project makers [*Projektmagere*], for even if someone projects [*projekterer*] something foolish, at least the truth remains that he was the one who projected [*projekteret*] it' (PF, 21/SKS 4, 229; translation modified). At issue is not so much the content of the project, but the assumption that Climacus is the one who projects it. The opponent reproaches Climacus for 'behaving like a scoundrel who charges a fee for showing an area that everyone can see,' someone 'who in the afternoon exhibited a ram for a fee, although in the morning anyone could have seen it free of charge, grazing in the open pasture' (PF, 21/SKS 4, 229; translation modified). In other words, Climacus is accused of taking credit for something that is not at all his own invention.

In his response to these self-incriminating accusations, Climacus complicates matters further by taking two further possibilities into consideration. First he suggests that the invention of his project might be similar to the invention of gunpowder. 'Admittedly, gunpowder was invented centuries ago; so it would be ludicrous of me to pretend that I had invented it. But would it also be ludicrous for me to assume that someone had invented it?' (PF, 21/SKS 4, 229–30). In that case, Climacus would be guilty of stealing intellectual property. However, if we take into account what has been invented (e.g., a certain conception of non-existence that precedes rebirth), it is more likely that nobody invented it. 'Is it not odd that something like this exists, of which everyone who knows about it also knows that he did not invent it, and that this "Go to the next house" does not stop and cannot be stopped, even if one would go to every human being?' (PF, 22/SKS 4, 230; translation modified).

Climacus keeps changing roles. At first he appeared as the inventor of his own project, then as someone who has stolen it from another human inventor, and finally his project turns out to be invented by nobody at all, at least not by a human being. This last option – the invention without a human inventor – fascinates Climacus greatly, 'for it tests the correctness of the hypothesis and demonstrates it' (PF, 22/SKS 4, 230). Here we see that Climacus sees the incognito of a thief as an essential part of his argument. It even provides proof for his hypothetical thought-project. Why is this so? It is not easy to answer this question, as it is part of a complicated play that involves the book as a whole. Nonetheless, a first answer can already be given by reflecting on the second step of education: the rebirth of the pupil.

In Climacus' view, the conception of a rebirth implies a preceding state of non-existence in which the pupil is defined by untruth and has no way of getting access to the truth. 'It would indeed be preposterous to expect that a human being can discover all by himself that he does not exist [*ikke var til*]. But this is the transition inherent to rebirth: from "not existing [*ikke at være til*]" to "existing [*at være til*]"' (PF, 22/SKS 4, 230; translation modified). It is for this reason that rebirth – which, following the hypothetical logic of the thought-project, is implied by going further than Socrates – can only be understood as an invention without a human inventor. It is not possible to discover one's own non-existence and invent a way out of it. However, as we saw, pupils still have to become aware of their own untruth. If someone else does it for them, they do not learn anything new and there will be no transition from untruth to truth. According to Climacus, this transition is tied to what he calls 'the blink of an eye (*Øieblik*),' an ordinary Danish word which simply refers to a very short time-span, an instant. It is within the blink of an eye that the pupil is turned inward and confronted with his or her own untruth. Whether this confrontation results in a rebirth is determined by how the pupil decides to react to this confrontation. The offended pupil is pushed away by the confrontation; the pupil who has faith makes the transition from untruth to truth.

To get a better sense of how this confrontation with untruth takes place, Climacus has to get a sense of the incognito of the god. In contrast to Socrates, who relied on a *maieutic incognito*, the god adopts the *incognito as a true form*. This incognito is necessary to ensure that the first step of education (turning the pupil inward) takes place. In addition, it also provides the condition for the second step (generating a rebirth), regardless of whether this second step takes place or not. The *incognito as a true form* is a bit of a counter-intuitive notion. The second part (as a true form) immediately seems to cancel the first (incognito). This can be clarified with the help of two important notions that are introduced by Climacus: 'the form of a servant' and 'the absolute paradox.' Together they constitute the incognito as a true form. As Climacus makes clear, the god appears in the form of a servant. To the extent that the god really becomes a servant, this appearance is his true form. At the same time, this appearance is also more than that: it is an incognito that confronts the individual with an absolute paradox.

The form of a servant

In chapter 2, the hypothetical thought-project is continued in the form of a 'poetical venture [*digterisk Forsøg*]' (PF, 23/SKS 4, 230) which spreads out over the whole book and is taken up again several times. Echoing the invention without an inventor, this poetical venture will result in a poem without a poet. It is for this reason that the authorship of the poetical venture is not clearly assigned, but keeps shifting. In his attempts to grasp the idea of the incognito as a true form, Climacus identifies himself with two types of poets: the mythological and the religious poet. He speaks in the voice of these poets while simultaneously indicating the limits of what they can say. Moreover, at the end of the chapter, Climacus is exposed as a plagiarizer who ends up stealing his words from the god himself. This reveals a third type of poet: the god. This extended play with the attribution of authorship, which evokes a variety of different voices only to immediately question them, is an integral part of what I have called Climacus' poetics of self-incrimination.

Throughout the chapter, Climacus tries to understand the incognito as a true form that is adopted by the god. He cannot address this incognito right away, but can only get a closer understanding of it with the help of an analogy. 'Suppose there was a king who loved an ordinary girl,' he writes, only to immediately interrupt his own discourse with a possible objection: '– but the reader may already have lost patience with this beginning as it sounds like a mythological adventure [*Eventyr*] that is by no means systematic' (PF, 26/SKS 4, 233; translation modified). Climacus believes, however, that he should be forgiven for the transgression of telling a mythological adventure. He is, after all, 'only a poet [*kun en Digter*] who, mindful of Themistocles' beautiful expression, wants to unroll the tapestry of speech [*Talens Tæppe*] lest the work on it be concealed by being rolled up' (PF, 26/SKS 4, 233; translation modified). This reference to Themistocles indicates that Climacus cannot stick to the systematic vocabulary of the scholarly treatise, but needs to employ the fuller language of mythological poetry to push the boundaries of human language to the limit. Only in this way, can he express the 'kingly concern [*kongelige Sorg*]' that is 'found only in a kingly soul' and which 'many human languages do not name at all' (PF, 28/SKS 4, 235; translation modified).

In Climacus construction of the story about the king, this concern can take on three different forms. First, the king fears that the ordinary girl will not be able to forget the difference in station between her and the king, which might overpower her to such an extent that there is little room left for her to develop her own position. Second, in addition there might be an intellectual difference that separates the ordinary girl from the king, making a mutual understanding between them impossible.[9] Third, even if the king would raise the station of the ordinary girl by dressing her up and letting her forget the differences between them, the misunderstanding between them would not disappear; it would only remain hidden from her. Although Climacus does not unequivocally state how the king can overcome these concerns, it is clear from the text that it is brought about by a descent. The king could, for instance, adopt the incognito of an ordinary man. This would avoid overpowering the ordinary girl and will ensure that she can determine her own relationship to him with frankness and confidence. For Climacus, the concern of the king provides an imperfect analogy for the concern of the divine teacher. In his view, 'human language as a whole is so self-centered that is has no intimation of such a concern' (PF, 28/SKS 4, 235; translation modified). Hence, it falls within the realm of the ineffable and can only be understood by analogy with the story of the king.

'Thus the task [*Opgaven*] is assigned,' Climacus states, 'and we invite the poet [*Digteren*]' (PF, 28/SKS 4, 235). Climacus has already presented himself as a mythological poet earlier. Despite this self-proclaimed role he now feels the need to extend an invitation to a second, religious poet that can address the situation of the god. Climacus does not indicate whether the invitation is accepted by anybody. As a result, the discourse of this religious poet has no clear signature. It is only marked by the invitation preceding it ('we invite the poet') and by a concluding observation ('Thus speaks the poet') (PF, 34/SKS 4, 240). This enables Climacus to approach the realm of the ineffable in a particular way. On the one hand, he advances a position; on the other, he immediately distances himself from it. Let us first look at the position that is taken. The task of the religious poet is 'to find a solution, a point of unity where there is in truth love's understanding, where the god's concern has overcome its pain' (PF, 28/SKS 4, 235). In order to find this point of unity, the god – like the king – has to become the equal of the pupil through a descending movement.

> He will appear, therefore, as the equal of the most insignificant person [*den Ringeste*]. But the most insignificant person is the one who serves [*tjene*] others – consequently, the god will appear in the form of a *servant* [*Tjenerens Skikkelse*]. But this form of a servant [*Tjenerens Skikkelse*] is not something put on like the king's 'cloak of insignificance [*Ringheds-Kappe*],' which just by flapping open would betray the king... – but it is his true form [*sande Skikkelse*].
>
> (PF, 31–2/SKS 4, 238; translation modified)

In Climacus' view, the god adopts the incognito of a servant, but this incognito is not something that he takes on (as in the case of the king); it becomes his true form. Strictly speaking it is no longer an incognito. The god truly becomes the most insignificant person, the servant. Like the maieutic incognito, the incognito as a true form aims to turn the pupil inward (the first step of education). Unlike the maieutic incognito, however, it also aims to generate a rebirth (the second step).

Moving forward, Climacus deliberately creates confusion about the implications of all this. Still speaking in the voice of the religious poet, he suggests that the god does everything in his power to ensure that nobody gets offended. 'He is the god, and yet he walks more circumspectly than if angels were carrying him – not to avoid striking [*stødes*] his foot, but so that nobody will be trampled into the dust because of being offended at [*forarges paa*] him' (PF, 32/SKS 4, 238; translation modified). Moments later, however, he distances himself from this position. 'Thus speaks the poet – for how could it occur to him that the god would reveal himself [*aabenbare sig*] in this way in order to bring about the most terrifying decision?' (PF, 34/SKS 4, 240; translation modified). It is easy to overlook this self-refutation and to take the discourse of the religious poet as the final word on the self-revelation of the god. However, once it is noticed and taken seriously, it becomes increasingly clear that the religious poet leaves out an important part of the story: the offensive nature of the god's incognito as a true form. As will become clear below, it is only by becoming offensive that the god can make the recipient turn inward in order to provoke a decision that might or might not result in a rebirth.

The religious poet has introduced the notion 'form of a servant,' but to fully understand the implications of this a third poet needs to be brought in: the god himself. To this end, Climacus again interrupts his own discourse to make room for an imaginary opponent who accuses him of plagiarism. 'Now if someone were to say, "What you are composing [*digter*] is the crudest plagiarism [*lumpneste Plagiat*] ever to appear, since it is nothing more or less than what any child knows," well then I will have to hear with shame that I am a liar' (PF, 35/SKS 4, 241; translation modified). Climacus does not deny the charge of plagiarism, but he takes issue with the further specification that it is the crudest plagiarism. 'After all, every poet who steals, steals from another poet, and thus we are all equally crude; indeed, my stealing is perhaps less harmful since it is more easily discovered' (PF, 35/SKS 4, 241; translation modified). If this is the kind of plagiarism the imaginary opponent hints at, there is hardly any reason to single Climacus out as the crudest plagiarist. Maybe, Climacus suggests, the opponent tries to say that the poem was not stolen from another poet? Maybe it has a similar status as a proverb that does not belong to any one poet, but seems to be composed by humanity as a whole? In that case, the accusation would not so much concern the plagiarism itself, but the arrogance with which Climacus spoke by pretending to embody the human race as such. This explanation is dismissed as well. In a sense, each human being is equally close to having composed a proverb as all the others. So again there is no reason to single Climacus out as the crudest plagiarist. A final explanation follows:

> You called my conduct the crudest plagiarism, because I did not steal from any single man, did not rob the human race, but robbed the deity or, so to speak, kidnapped him and, although I am only a single human being – indeed, even a crude thief – blasphemously pretended to be the god.
> *(PF, 35–6/SKS 4, 241; translation modified)*

The accusation of plagiarism has entered radical new territory here and is supplemented by the accusation of kidnapping, blasphemy, and megalomania. At this point, Climacus turns the accusation on its head. It is true that Climacus would not be able to write the poem; it is true that he has stolen his words from someone else. It is exactly for these reasons that Climacus has been so ambiguous about his own authorship. He has built up his text in such a way that the reader can only conclude that he is a plagiarist. This conclusion prepares the way for his argument that, ultimately, only the god could have written this poem. After all, it is very well possible that human beings imagine themselves to be like the god or that they imagine the god to be like them. However, it is much harder to conceive that 'the god poetized [*digtede*] himself in the likeness of a human being' (PF, 36/SKS 4, 242). This idea, Climacus suggests, is so absurd that it could not have arisen in a human heart, but must have originated somewhere else. As such, it is an offense to the understanding. This brings us to the second aspect of the incognito as a true form: the absolute paradox.

The absolute paradox

Usually a paradox is understood as an apparent contradiction that despite its counter-intuitive appearance is nonetheless true. Such an apparent contradiction already includes its own resolution. As Climacus suggests, this is not the case with an absolute paradox. The contradiction is real and cannot be resolved, even though it still expresses the truth. Given the absolute nature of the paradox it is hard to say anything about it, without immediately contradicting oneself. As the title of chapter 3 – 'The absolute paradox (a metaphysical caprice [*Grille*])' – already announces, Climacus will address this difficulty by juxtaposing two seemingly incommensurable modes: the absolute and the capricious. Later on, the imaginary opponent highlights this point even more: 'You are such a capricious fellow [*Grillefænger*], I am on to you, there is no way you believe that it would occur to me to be concerned about such a caprice [*Grille*], something so bizarre or so ludicrous that it doubtless has not yet occurred to anyone and, above all, something so unreasonable that I have to exclude everything in my consciousness in order to even find it' (PF, 46/SKS 4, 251; translation modified). As Climacus suggests, the absolute paradox expresses something absolutely unknown that will always remain outside of the reach of the understanding. It cannot be fully conceptualized but can only become manifest as something absurd and ludicrous. Hence the reaction of the imaginary opponent is exactly the kind of reaction that Climacus is aiming for.

Speaking in the voice of the religious poet, Climacus already showed that the god adopts the appearance of a servant. Now we have to find out how this is linked to the absolute paradox. Simply put, the absolute paradox can be summarized as follows: the god has become a human being, while also remaining the god; the eternal has become something historical, while also remaining eternal. One side of this absolute paradox – the divine and eternal – remains unknown. The other side – the human manifestation of the god – can be known immediately. That is why the god's appearance as a servant is both an incognito and a true form. It is an incognito insofar as it is an indirect manifestation of the god who, despite this manifestation, ultimately remains the unknown. It is a true form insofar as it is a direct manifestation of the god's willingness to lower himself in order to create a point of unity that bridges the gap between the human and the divine.

The problem is: how can the individual get an intimation of the absolute paradox if one of its sides cannot be known in any way? It needs a kind of indirect communication that presents the unknown in some way or another without representing it as something that can be known after all. To conceptualize this type of indirect communication, Climacus introduces the noun *Anstød*, which can be translated either as 'collision' or as 'offense.' It introduces the idea of a collision with the unknown. This collision is an offense to the extent that the understanding cannot incorporate the unknown, but runs aground on it. The understanding encounters the unknown as a limit that can only be conceptualized in a negative way, that is, as something ludicrous and absurd. By colliding with the paradox, human beings get so confused by what appears to them as absurd that they no longer understand themselves. In this way, they are turned inward (the first step of education). In response, the understanding either rejects the seemingly absurd by taking offense or accepts it despite its improbable and unreasonable appearance (Climacus calls this faith).

In the appendix to Chapter 3, 'Offense at the paradox (an acoustic illusion),' Climacus analyzes the counter-intuitive causality that animates the Biblical conception of 'a stone of stumbling' or 'a rock of offense.'[10] To get a better grasp on this paradoxical causality, he equates the physical interaction between the stone/rock and the foot to the psychological interaction between the offensive one (who is giving offense) and the offended one (who is taking offense). Just as the rock causes the foot to stumble, so the offense that is given becomes the cause for the offense that is taken. At first sight it might seem that the understanding interprets the absolute paradox, judges it ('this is absurd,' 'this is improbable'), and then takes offense. According to Climacus, however, this is an acoustic illusion. 'While, therefore, the offense, however it expresses itself, sounds [*lyder*] from somewhere else – indeed, from the opposite corner – it is nevertheless the paradox, which echoes [*gjenlyder*] within it, and this indeed is an acoustic illusion' (PF, 50–1/SKS 4, 255; translation modified). In relation to the paradox, the understanding is like the dummy of a ventriloquist. The offense seems to be invented by the understanding, but in fact it originated with the paradox. Its expressions are based on an acoustic illusion. As Climacus argues, the understanding does not articulate its own position, but simply parrots the paradox, 'just as someone caricaturing another does not invent anything, but only makes a distorted copy of someone else' (PF, 51/SKS 4, 254; translation modified). Instead of being a true invention, offense is merely a distorted copy of the unknown that is given by the paradox. In this sense, the understanding merely steals its ideas from the paradox. This already makes clear why Climacus relies on a poetic of self-incrimination. In relation to the paradox everybody is a thief.

Between attack and defense

As we have already seen several times, Climacus adopts the identity of a common thief and dialogizes his discourse by introducing an imaginary opponent who starts accusing him. Throughout the book, this imaginary opponent slowly grows into the role of a real interlocutor who engages with the arguments more fully. The by now familiar charge is repeated. 'But someone may be saying, "Things are truly tiresome with you, for now we have the same story all over again; all the expressions you put into the mouth of the paradox do not belong to you at all"' (PF, 53/SKS 4, 257; translation modified). Again Climacus is caught with stolen goods and accused of thievery, but a new charge is also added. He not only got the words from elsewhere, he also put them into the mouth of the paradox. Climacus admits that some of his expressions are indeed stolen from other authors. At the same time, he insists that these authors were not the true owners of the ideas they expressed, but that these ideas ultimately belong to the paradox. Climacus turns the accusation of the imaginary opponent on its head by suggesting that the second charge – that he has put the words of others into the mouth of the paradox – gives a completely wrong impression of what actually happened. In his view, it is the other way around. Climacus and all the authors he indirectly quotes literally took the words from the mouth of the paradox. Before anyone could articulate these words, the paradox had already expressed them. Anyone else who is saying them is only repeating what the paradox already expressed, regardless of whether these words were meant as an attack ('that is just absurd') or as a defense ('because it is absurd').

In the last two chapters of *Philosophical Crumbs*, the old charge of thievery is reiterated, but in a more subdued voice: 'Once again, knowingly or unknowingly, you have mixed in some words that do not belong to you' (PF, 68/SKS 4, 269; translation modified) and 'you always mix in some little phrase that is not your own' (PF, 105/SKS 4, 301). More importantly, the imaginary opponent's accusatory mode of speaking now repeatedly transforms into its exact opposite. A laudatory mode of speaking that touches upon jealousy: 'I already catch a glimpse of the ramified implications, even if it surprises me that I did not think of it myself and I would give a great deal to be the one who devised it' (PF, 69/SKS 4, 270; translation modified). In a sense, the accusatory and the laudatory mode of speaking are equally problematic since both start from the assumption that it is important to mark who is the owner of the intellectual property that is on display, whereas the whole point is that these ideas cannot belong to anybody since they originate with the god. That is why Climacus has been showing throughout that he was not the one who invented it, but that he only knows it from the paradox.

By employing these two modes of speaking – accusatory and laudatory – at once, Climacus again dialogizes his own discourse. Neither the accusatory mode that fits an attack on Christianity, nor the laudatory mode that matches its defense, is given a decisive impetus. Instead, both these responses are invoked at the same time. In a journal entry, Kierkegaard describes this strategy as follows: 'Joh[annes] Cl[imacus] kept the matter dialectically at a point where no one could see directly whether it was an attack on Xnty or a defense, but that it depended on how things were with the reader, what he got out of the book' (KJN 8, 113/SKS 24, 69). In this way, Climacus assures that nothing resolute can be assigned to him as a separate instance of authority that hovers over the text and guards it, but that the reader becomes responsible for the stance that is taken.

Conclusion

The discourse of *Philosophical Crumbs* is constantly caught up in ambiguities. From the start, Climacus keeps insisting that he is only engaged in a hypothetical thought-project, the aim of which is to discover what it means to go further than Socrates. By presenting the orthodox views of Christianity as a hypothetical thought-project that he just invented, Climacus not only becomes a thief and a plagiarizer, but also remains an outsider who addresses an existential issue in a completely abstract way. At the same time, he highlights this contrast by emphasizing the existential nature of his thought-project and by incriminating himself. I have analyzed this rhetorical strategy as a poetics of self-incrimination. By adopting the identity of a thief, Climacus tries to replicate the incognito as a true form. To the extent that Climacus really turns out to be a thief, this adopted identity is his true form. To the extent that he tries to confront his readers with the paradoxical nature of a non-Socratic conception of truth, it is an incognito. The aim of this incognito is not to hide his own plagiarism, but to draw attention to the fact that going further than Socrates means that the truth needs to be stolen from somewhere else. This is the provocative logic of his thought-project: either we go back to Socrates or we incriminate ourselves and admit that we are thieves.

Related topics

'Johannes Climacus and the dialectical method: from dialectics back to existence,' Claudine Davidshofer; 'Methodology and the Kierkegaardian mind,' Jamie Turnbull; 'Kierkegaard's existential mimesis,' Wojciech Kaftanski.

Notes

1 In the English-speaking world, the book came to be known as *Philosophical Fragments or a Fragment of Philosophy*. However, as Piety (2009: XVI) remarks, '"fragments" is not among a dictionary's favoured options for "Smuler," and it guarantees that the nimble irony of that topsy-turvy title is lost.'
2 This play is continued in the rather elaborate *Postscript* to the *Philosophical Crumbs* that is also attributed to the pseudonym Climacus.
3 Shakespeare (2003: 70) has: 'Many a good hanging prevents a bad marriage.'
4 The notion 'going further' echoes Hegel's speculative vocabulary. It is used in an ironic way and marks a break with the Socratic viewpoint, without presenting this break as a progression in the speculative sense.
5 I have at various points modified the Hong & Hong translation. This does not signify that I take issue with their translation; it simply is a way to get a better sense of the language Kierkegaard used.
6 Early on, Meno defines virtue as the ability 'to rule over [*archein*] people' (Plato 1997: 873/73d). In response, Socrates immediately starts to complicate the issue. See Plato (1997: 876/76b–c, 887/86d).
7 Socrates' phrasing is obviously ironic. The aim is not to present the actual inquiry, but to identify the slave with Meno. See Plato (1997: 879/80b). Note that Meno admits his perplexity, but blames it on Socrates' sorcery rather than on his own lack of knowledge.
8 Mikhail Bakhtin (1984: 110) introduces the notion *anacrisis*, an ancient Greek juridical term, to describe a similar kind of rhetorical technique.
9 There is a thinly disguised reference here to Kierkegaard's engagement with Regine Olsen. In his *Journals and Notebooks* Kierkegaard often explicitly refers to his own incognito (e.g., KJN 4, 256; 5, 259–60, 287; 6, 75, 237; 7, 129, 213, 236; 8, 297). In relation to Regine, these references remain more hidden.
10 The locus classicus for the Biblical conception of offense can be found in Isaiah 8: 14.

References

Bakhtin, M. (1984) *Problems of Dostoevsky's poetics*, C. Emerson (trans), Minneapolis, MN: University of Minnesota Press.
Boven, M. (2018) 'A theater of ideas: Performance and performativity in Kierkegaard's *Repetition*,' in E. Ziolkowski (ed), *Kierkegaard, Literature, and the Arts*, Evanston, IL: Northwestern University Press.
Boven, M. (2014) 'Incognito,' in S. Emmanuel, W. McDonald, and J. Stewart (eds), *Kierkegaard Research: Sources, Reception and Resources*, vol. 15 (*Kierkegaard's Concepts*), tome 3, Farnham: Ashgate.

Conway, D. W. (2004) 'The drama of Kierkegaard's *Philosophical Fragments*,' in H. Schulz, J. Stewart, and K. Verstrynge (eds), *Kierkegaard Studies Yearbook 2004*, Berlin: Walter de Gruyter.

Evans, C. S. (1992) *Passionate reason: Making sense of Kierkegaard's Philosophical fragments*,' Bloomington, IN: Indiana University Press.

Fenves, P. (1993) 'Autopsies of faith: *Philosophical Fragments*,' in P. Fenves, *'Chatter': Language and History in Kierkegaard*, Stanford, CA: Stanford University Press.

Hale, G. A. (2002) 'The other proposition: *Philosophical Fragments* and the grammar of life,' in G. A. Hale, *Kierkegaard and the Ends of Language*, Minneapolis, MN: University of Minnesota Press.

Howland, J. (2006) *Kierkegaard and Socrates: A study in philosophy and faith*, Cambridge: Cambridge University Press.

Muench, P. (2006) 'Kierkegaard's Socratic task,' PhD Dissertation, University of Pittsburgh.

Mulhall, S. (1999) 'God's plagiarist: *The Philosophical Fragments* of Johannes Climacus,' *Philosophical Investigations*, 22, no. 1: 1–34.

Piety, M. G. (2009) 'Introduction,' in S. Kierkegaard, *Repetition* and *Philosophical Crumbs*, M. G. Piety (trans), Oxford: Oxford University Press.

Plato (1997) 'Meno,' in Plato, *Complete Works*, J. M. Cooper (ed), G. M. A. Grube (trans), Indianapolis, IN: Hackett Publishing Company.

Plato (1921) 'Theaetetus,' in Plato, *Theaetetus/Sophist* (Loeb Classical Library 123), H. N. Fowler (trans), Cambridge, MA: Harvard University Press.

Pons, J. (2004) *Stealing a gift: Kierkegaard's pseudonyms and the Bible*, New York: Fordham University Press.

Shakespeare, W. (2003) *Twelfth night or what you will* (The New Cambridge Shakespeare), E. S. Donno (ed), Cambridge: Cambridge University Press.

Further reading

Boven, M. (2014) 'Incognito,' in S. Emmanuel, W. McDonald, and J. Stewart (eds), *Kierkegaard Research: Sources, Reception and Resources*, vol. 15 (*Kierkegaard's Concepts*), tome 3, Farnham: Ashgate.

This entry discusses how the notion of 'incognito' is understood by Kierkegaard's pseudonyms.

Fenves, P. (1993) 'Autopsies of faith: *Philosophical Fragments*,' in P. Fenves (ed), *'Chatter': Language and History in Kierkegaard*, Stanford, CA: Stanford University Press.

In line with his overall focus on the notion of 'chatter,' Fenves' fascinating analysis focuses on language in *Philosophical Crumbs* by highlighting the play of jest and earnestness, the strange practice of naming, and the mock dialogues of the imaginary opponent.

Mulhall, S. (1999) 'God's plagiarist: *The Philosophical Fragments* of Johannes Climacus,' *Philosophical Investigations*, 22, no. 1: 1–34.

In this article, Mulhall interprets Climacus' writing strategy as an attempt to enact the perceived errors of his intended readers in order to make them aware of these errors and to provide an antidote.

Pons, J. (2004) 'Stealing a gift,' in J. Pons (ed), *Stealing a Gift: Kierkegaard's Pseudonyms and the Bible*, New York: Fordham University Press.

This chapter focuses on the use of Biblical quotations in *Philosophical Crumbs* and their status as stolen words. By interpreting the Bible as a gift, Pons intriguingly suggests that stealing these words simply means not accepting them, robbing oneself of what was given.

PART 8
Politics

35

LUKÁCS, KIERKEGAARD, MARX, AND THE POLITICAL

Alison Assiter

Introduction

Despite the fact that they were writing at the same time, Kierkegaard and Marx are usually thought to have little in common. Marx wrote the *Communist Manifesto* in 1847 and Kierkegaard produced *Two Ages* in 1846. Both completed their doctoral dissertations in 1841. But there the similarity is supposed to end. Kierkegaard and Marx are two thinkers who are normally thought to have radically different concerns and opposing theoretical outlooks. Both were intellectually shaped by the work of Hegel or by some follower of Hegel. However, it is commonly held that Kierkegaard rejected Hegel and the Danish Hegelians, while Marx drew heavily on Hegel, and critically developed his theory. Kierkegaard is seen as focussing on individuals working out their own salvations while Marx invites all proletarians of the world to unite.[1] Kierkegaard is said to be concerned, as one commentator has put it, with 'individual inwardness of self choice while Marx focuses on external self-activity in the social practice of material production' (Toews 2004: 420). Marx's works shaped the thinking of Lenin and Lukács, amongst others, whereas Kierkegaard influenced Heidegger and the existentialists. This is the story about the two thinkers that is commonly told. In this chapter, I will challenge the view that Marx and Kierkegaard have little in common. I will do so partly through consideration of a work by Lukács on Kierkegaard. Lukács claims that Kierkegaard has no conception of 'system.' I will challenge this. I will then briefly outline a reading of Marx, drawn mainly from the German Ideology, that shows that, contrary to some readings, and like Kierkegaard, Marx is concerned with human beings and their activity as well as to provide a systematic theory of history.

Lukács and Kierkegaard

One Marxist thinker who did write about Kierkegaard and who saw some similarity between his own Marxism and the work of Kierkegaard is Gyrgy Lukács. The latter was a twentieth-century Hungarian Marxist philosopher whose interpretation of Marx, drawing on the notion of 'class consciousness,' challenged the orthodox Stalinist view. I would like, in this chapter, to consider Lukács' (2010) engagement with Kierkegaard, in his early essay, "The foundering of form against life: Søren Kierkegaard and Regine Olsen", published in the collection *Soul and*

Form. I will then move to outline a response to Lukács and to suggest that there are more parallels between the thought of Kierkegaard and that of Marx than even Lukács suggested.

In his essay, Lukács celebrates what he views as Kierkegaard's understanding of the 'alienation' of humans in his contemporary world. He notes that Kierkegaard deeply understands love and suffering. In this respect he sees Kierkegaard as sharing one of his own abiding concerns. Yet he is critical of Kierkegaard for two central reasons. One of these relates to Kierkegaard's handling of his affair with Regine Olsen. Lukács analyzes Kierkegaard's actions in relation to her as founded upon a 'gesture' that could not possibly work in the way he imagined it would. Lukács claims that, by presenting himself as unworthy of her, Kierkegaard believed he could make Regine understand that he and Regine were incompatible and that she would then be able to move on and find happiness elsewhere. For Lukács, this represents a 'gesture' because the modern social world is so fragmented that there could be no guarantee that she would see his actions in the light he had intended. There could be no certainty that she would not blame herself for the break in their relationship.

For Lukács, and this is his second major criticism of Kierkegaard, this reflects something about Kierkegaard's corpus in general. While Kierkegaard claims, according to Lukács, that there is no 'system' in the world, he nonetheless acts as though there were such a system. Given, to take one example, Kierkegaard's focus on the paradoxical nature of reality, as exemplified through figures such as Abraham, one might have expected him to apply this to his own life as well. Lukács, then, claims that while Kierkegaard properly analyzes the central problem – that of alienation – in the contemporary world, he fails to offer any solution to this problem. He fails, in other words, either to offer a systematic theory of history or to propose any social or historical solution to this problem.

Lukács draws an analogy between Kierkegaard's treatment of Regine and his philosophical outlook. According to Lukács, Kierkegaard refused to consider that historical change might act as a solution to the problem of alienation.[2] Rather than suggesting some major historical event or process that could bring about preferable conditions for all, Kierkegaard, for Lukács, preferred the solution of individual 'faith.' Lukács goes on to make the point that Kierkegaard might have made similar mistakes to the Hegelian (or, one might say the Adlerian) 'speculators' he apparently decries.[3] Lukács writes: 'And so (for Kierkegaard) there is no system anywhere for it is not possible to live a system; the system is always a vast palace while its creator can only withdraw into a modest corner.' He continues, (2010: 48): 'is not the denial of a system itself a system?'

Kierkegaard, according to one commentator on Lukács on Kierkegaard, Price (1999), has analyzed the social world in a similar fashion to Lukács. Yet rather than proposing a 'world historical' solution to the problem of alienation or of the superficiality of conventional Christianity, Kierkegaard argues that only an individual solution is possible. The future, as Price puts it, is uncertain, and therefore, according to Kierkegaard, the only way forward is for people to turn inward to find their 'truth.' For Lukács, however, this view amounts to Kierkegaard 'systematising' hostility towards any system.

Most commentators on Kierkegaard, like Lukács here, have denied that he makes reference to any 'system.' Lukács goes one step further, however, in his claim that Kierkegaard makes a system out of his denial of system.

Kierkegaard: an anti-systematizer?

I'd like, in this section, to consider the claim that Kierkegaard critiques the notion of 'system.' I will note Lukács' extension of this view, namely that Kierkegaard 'systematizes' his hostility towards any notion of system.

Evidence for the claim that Kierkegaard is 'anti-system'

The evidence for Kierkegaard challenging all notions of system can be found in a number of places in his work. One possible place is *Fear and Trembling*. In that text, de silentio claims that 'the philosophers' were attempting to 'sell off' the most significant ideas – those, one might suppose, that concerned matters of faith – in a 'dirt cheap' manner (Kierkegaard 1985: 41/SKS 4, 101). 'Actuality,' de silentio writes, cannot be comprehended in the fashion of the Hegelians – or the Adlerians. 'Actuality' is about real life – about activity and faith – while the discourse of the systematizers is about logical matters or conceptual relations. 'Even if one were able to render the whole content of faith into conceptual form, it would not follow that one had grasped faith, grasped how one came to it or how it came to one' (1985: 43/SKS 4, 103). Or, as Vigilius Haufniensis puts it in *The Concept of Anxiety*, philosophy makes a crucial error when actuality is considered as a part of logic (CA, 9–10/SKS 4, 282–3). Indeed, one might argue, in an extension of this point, that the very form of much of Kierkegaard's writing involves a challenge to the notion of 'system.' Even if one did not accept that all systems involve reference to 'logical' or 'conceptual' relations, Kierkegaard would be critical of all notions of system. For not only does his use of pseudonyms involve an ironic playing with the very idea that it is he that is the author of the works, but he also constantly makes reference to stories – Abraham and Isaac, Adam and Eve, Sarah and Tobias and many more – instead of writing about more abstract theoretical matters. For these and other reasons, he has been labelled the 'father' of existentialism and as focussing on an individual's relationship to a transcendent God. These latter foci are thought to preclude a concern with abstract and 'systematising' theory.

Another text that appears to support the view that Kierkegaard is anti-system is *Continuing Unscientific Postscript to Philosophical Fragments*. Climacus, the pseudonymous author of this text, appears to critique anything that seems to be analogous to a science. He appears, as he does elsewhere, to satirize the 'systematizers.' Climacus seems to suggest that the most significant, the most profound truths can never be presented in such a fashion. Climacus notes that the very possibility of inward truths poses a problem for systematizers, since for them, the system is supposed to encompass everything. The very existence of such truths suggests a 'gap' in the system. Climacus writes: 'The systematic idea is the subject-object, is the unity of thinking and being; existence, on the other hand, is precisely the separation ... existence has spaced and does space subject from object, thought from being' (CUP 1, 123/SKS 7, 120).

However, it is at least possible to suggest that the commonplace view that Kierkegaard is 'anti-system' is open to contestation. I would like, in the next section, to challenge the claim that Kierkegaard is wholly 'anti-system.' The claim that Kierkegaard is hostile to 'system' is a very familiar way of reading him, but it is worth noting that it is a reading that is being challenged by a number of recent authors including Žižek, Michael Burns, Maria Binetti, Steven Shakespeare, and myself.[4]

Challenge to the view that Kierkegaard is 'anti-system'

The first point to note is that the aforementioned critiques of the idea of system perhaps presuppose that all 'systematising thinking' must be internally coherent. It suggests that 'systems' will be free from paradox, free from gaps and perhaps will also fail to provide room for doubt. In *Philosophical Fragments*, by contrast to this, Climacus represents doubt as inherent in thought. There is no possibility of gaining the kind of knowledge Descartes, for example, sought. However, this point, rather than indicating that Kierkegaard is anti-system, might instead suggest that he believes that any system must be open to the view that its claims could be wrong, that it might contain gaps, and that its authors need not claim to be certain that its claims represent truths that could not possibly be shown to be wrong. Although it is undoubtedly the case, therefore, that Kierkegaard doubts that it is possible to gain the kind of knowledge about reality and specifically about the social world that some have thought possible, it does not follow that Kierkegaard is entirely critical of any reference to 'system.'

One recent philosopher, as noted, who takes a different view of Kierkegaard's conception of system is Slavoj Žižek. According to Žižek (2009), referring to Kierkegaard, 'God is the name for the Absolute Other against which we can measure the thorough contingency of reality – as such it cannot be conceived as any kind of Substance, as the supreme thing' (Žižek 2009: 79). Michael Burns (2012: 107) reads Žižek as implying not that there is no system in Kierkegaard's work but rather that the system as a whole must contain contingency. Maria Binetti, as well, writes that 'the history of philosophy has kept Kierkegaard and Hegel apart. I believe that this has been sadly detrimental to both of them, as their longstanding opposition has swept through the speculative greatness of Kierkegaard's thought and the existential power of Hegel's' (Binetti 2007: 183). For Žižek, Binetti, and Burns, as well as for some other recent readers of Kierkegaard, then, the latter offers a metaphysic, drawing on the German Idealist tradition, of contingency. Instead of breaking with the German Idealist tradition, he rather builds upon it and draws from it.

For Žižek, then, the recognition that practical ethical choice precedes every theory itself represents Kierkegaard's theoretical position and it indicates his continuity with the German Idealist tradition. One might be forgiven for thinking that this is mere word play. The very same characteristics that led earlier commentators on Kierkegaard to indicate Kierkegaard's break with the German Idealist tradition are re-cast by Žižek as an engagement with it. However, Žižek has a particular reason for his argument. His reason stems from the work of Kant. Kant had suggested, in his 'First Antinomy' in the *Critique of Pure Reason,* that the conception 'the world as a whole' is both phenomenal and noumenal. It is noumenal in so far it is a concept that lies beyond the possibility of categorical representation. It cannot be known in the way in which phenomena in the spatial and temporal world can be known. Yet it is phenomenal in the sense that it represents, for beings like us, the limits of our world. The mind, for Kant, is necessarily led to speculate up to its own limits and in this sense the 'world as a whole' depicts the limits of our world, our phenomenal world. The transcendental self, then, that experiences these paradoxes, represents, for Žižek, the 'ultimate parallax' (Žižek 2009: 22). By parallax he means an 'insurmountable gap between two closely linked perspectives between which no neutral common ground is possible' (Žižek 2009: 4).

Žižek suggests that Kant is the originator of this notion but that it is Kierkegaard, following Fichte and Schelling, who fully develops it. For Žižek, both Kierkegaard's self and reality-as-a-whole are in some sense contingent and paradoxical in an analogous fashion to the transcendental self of Kant outlined above. For Žižek, this indicates a fact about the relation between a contingent subject – any such subject – and reality. God, in Žižek's interpretation of Kierkegaard, becomes a power, a 'becoming' as opposed to a thing. There is no clear possibility of mediation between the 'ethical' and the 'religious.' As Burns reads Žižek, infinite resignation is the recognition of the lack of any consistent move from the ethical to the religious and the anxiety produced by this recognition (Burns 2012: 108). Burns further suggests that this 'inwardness,' rather than indicating a break from the socio-political, is in fact a precondition of doing anything at all (Burns 2012: 108). If this reading of Kierkegaard has even a modicum of plausibility it already brings him closer to Marx, as the latter is commonly read.

Žižek suggests that Kierkegaard's 'system' is comprised of processes rather than substances or things. This, then, for me, comprises Kierkegaard's 'system.' There are, indeed, other commentators on Kierkegaard – for example, Pattison and Carlisle – who have seen him as a thinker who emphasizes processes. Pattison refers to actuality, for Kierkegaard, as 'containing potentiality or possibility within itself' (Pattison 2003: 40). The world is permeated by temporality or becoming. However, for them, like many commentators on Kierkegaard, he is not a philosopher or a 'systematiser' at all. The reason they draw this conclusion, however, may be because they see philosophy in a particular light – perhaps philosophy, for them, excludes reference to a world that contains movement and process but that also contains wonder, the sublime and paradox. Perhaps they are also influenced in their view by Kierkegaard's own critical and satirical references to 'the philosopher' or 'the system.' It is likely though, as Stewart has claimed, that Kierkegaard's satirical comments concern the Danish Hegelians who exerted such a strong influence over Kierkegaard's contemporaries, rather than Hegel in particular or than 'all philosophers' in general (Stewart 2011: 237–53).

Evidence for Kierkegaard's process system emerges in many places. One piece of evidence is his positive reference to Heraclitus[5], who offers an ontology of process, of movement. De silentio, in the epilogue to *Fear and Trembling*, also mentions Heraclitus' follower, Cratylus, who 'goes further' than Heraclitus. Cratylus wrote, in relation to Heraclitus' claim that one cannot step into the same river twice, that one cannot even do it once (Kierkegaard 1985: 152/SKS 4, 210). Cratylus went too far and rendered both movement and stasis impossible and translated both into an Eleatic doctrine that denies movement altogether. In a journal note, Kierkegaard writes: 'A disciple wanting to improve it said: One cannot even step into the river once. Thereby the nerve is cut; as far as making any sense, the statement becomes the opposite, an Eleatic sentence and denies motion' (JP 3, 511/SKS 18, 152). Also in the *Postscript*, Kierkegaard praises Heraclitus and criticizes the Hegelian notion of movement (CUP 1, 307/SKS 7, 263). Further positive references to Heraclitus occur in *Philosophical Fragments* (PF, 167/SKS 4, 146). There is evidence, then, that Kierkegaard, like Marx, saw the world as in process, as constantly changing.

As Jason Wirth has noted, in his *Introduction* to his translation of Schelling's *Ages of the World*, Kierkegaard's view of time is informed by that of Schelling (Wirth 2000: XXIX). In *The Concept of Anxiety*, Kierkegaard wrote: 'Thus understood, the moment is not properly an atom of time but an atom of eternity. It is the first reflection of eternity in time, its first attempt, as it were, of stopping time' (CA, 88/SKS 4, 358). We cannot capture the moment, for as soon as we attempt to do this, it has gone. In other words, it is impossible for we limited beings, really to capture stasis. We experience the world as in process, as temporal. When we try to catch the moment, it disappears. The above quote from Kierkegaard, then, suggests that 'the moment' is not a category of time because time is always passing. In effect, then, it is an atom of eternity – an atom of a timeless universe.

We might generalize this, as Schelling set out to do, by suggesting that we imagine that reason itself is self-contained, complete. Reason appears to allow us to gain access to the truth. But we cannot even do this with a moment of time. In the *Ages of the World*, Schelling is setting out to capture in language the 'excess' of reason or the ground of reason. The entire world, he writes, seems to be caught in reason, but he poses the question: how did it come to be this way? Schelling suggests, in metaphorical form, that the origin of the intelligible is God becoming time. In turn, this notion relates back to Plato's *Timaeus*, the 'wild unruly matter' or the potency within Being (Schelling 2000: 3–8).

It is perhaps worth speculating that the view that Kierkegaard challenges system may stem partially, then, from an unfamiliarity, within much western philosophical thinking, with the notion of process and also with speculation about the origins of this. In some Islamic thinking, by contrast, both of these ideas may be more familiar. In the thought of Mulla Sadra, for example, God is Pure Act and reality is comprised of energy, or power (Jambert 2007). In this thought, which itself draws, as do both Kierkegaard and Marx, on the ancient Greeks, philosophy is a way of life; it involves more than mere contemplation.

Kierkegaard, then, emphasizes the importance of activity – activity in this metaphysical and deep sense, but also the activity of individual human beings and of groups of people. Many of the characters whose stories he re-writes are people who, in various and different ways, enact their beliefs. Two obvious exemplifications of this are, of course, Christ and Abraham. But there are also characters like Agamemnon, who, while not receiving quite the stamp of approval afforded the former, nonetheless act from principle and for a cause.

Indeed, throughout Kierkegaard's works, there are references to the importance of action – he often uses metaphors of swimming to suggest reasons why it is important not to focus merely on thinking at the expense of action. For example, in a rendering of the good Samaritan parable, Kierkegaard considers someone who sees a person in danger and thinks about how it would be a good idea to help them (WL, 22/SKS 9, 100). But this person doesn't do so in time and then later regrets his decision and returns, but too late. This reaction, Kierkegaard suggests, is inferior to acting immediately. Moreover, it is important to note that it is the act of diving or swimming that Kierkegaard admires, rather than the actor doing the swimming or the diving.

Kierkegaard on living nature

There is one more very specific additional reason, however, that has been given for denying that Kierkegaard makes any reference to system, and specifically for claiming that he broke with the German Idealist tradition. Apart from his many ironic and negative references to Hegelian philosophy, there is also a claim that relates specifically to Schelling. In 1842, Kierkegaard attended the latter's lectures, along with Engels, Burkhart and Bakunin. He was at first transfixed and then disappointed. Many commentators have argued that this is the end of the matter as far as Kierkegaard's relation to Schelling is concerned. However, there is another way of looking at this. Michelle Kosch (2006) has noted that Kierkegaard continued to acquire works by Schelling after he had attended the lectures. Moreover, there are strong resemblances between Schelling's *Freiheitsschrift* and Kierkegaard's *Concept of Anxiety*. Thirdly, there are positive references to Schelling in other texts of Kierkegaard (for a summary of this, see Assiter 2015: 56–8).

In my book *Kierkegaard, Eve and Metaphors of Birth* (Assiter 2015), I point to a common theme in the work of Schelling and Kierkegaard, notably, the suggestion that both offer some sort of process system and specifically that they each see nature, the ground of nature and human nature in terms of a system of powers. I further argue that both can be read as conceptualizing this nature in terms of metaphors of birth. I refer specifically to Schelling's freedom essay where he focuses on evil and on freedom.

I will summarize something of the argument here but if the reader wishes to read more, she will find it in the book. Schelling writes: 'the whole of modern European philosophy since its inception (through Descartes) has this common deficiency that nature does not exist for it and that it lacks a living basis' (Schelling 2006: 355). The *Freiheitsschrift* presents an active process ontology that significantly 'precedes our thinking of it' (Schelling 2006: 421). Ultimately the process is grounded in something that precedes all ground, something that represents an excess in the system of grounding, that Schelling calls a 'non-ground' or an 'ungrund' or in Wirth's words 'an irreducible remainder' (Wirth 2000: XV). God, in this system and specifically in the *Weltalter*, is beyond both Being and Not-Being. Wirth helpfully quotes Lyotard on Wittgenstein, who responded to the latter's claim that we cannot 'say the unsayable.' Lyotard suggests that we must try to do this. For Lyotard, imagining that one cannot speak about the limits of language, as Wittgenstein does, is to suppose a beginning without any presuppositions at all. Instead, the beginning, as noted, for Schelling, is conceived in terms of a potency or a power (Wirth 2000: XII).

Schelling's essay, moreover, claims that freedom must exist in some form 'in' the whole of nature. Haufniensis, in *The Concept of Anxiety*, I have argued elsewhere, (Assiter 2015), presupposes this Schellingian system. Using it, one can make sense of the Adam and Eve story, deployed there, as accounting for the origin of evil. Adam and Eve, given the Schellingian assumptions, existed in a living and active natural world but one in which there was not yet any awareness of right and wrong, good and evil. I have argued, along with others, that Haufniensis, like Schelling in the freedom essay, is partly responding to Kant, the Kant of *Religion within the Limits of Mere Reason*. Summarizing my argument, the claim is that Kant was unable to see how the story of Eve and Adam can explain the origin of freedom and evil because he assumed that Adam and Eve must be either wholly outside history or wholly inside it. Reading the story in terms of a Schellingian process ontology, however, allows for them to be partly inside and partly outside history, and so freedom can 'come into' them. As Kierkegaard puts it 'by the first sin, sinfulness came into Adam' (CA, 33/SKS 4, 305). I suggested that, in Kierkegaard's reading, Adam and Eve existed without knowledge, innocently, in the Garden of Eden, prior to the eating of the forbidden fruit. They were, at that point, neither human nor animal. Since there was nothing, both were anxious. When Eve ate the fruit, freedom and knowledge 'entered into' them via a 'qualitative leap.' The natural world, then, on this view, is made up of living powers, grounded in a force or a power that sets the whole process in motion.

Read in these ways, then, Kierkegaard does have a clear conception of system: his is a system founded on processes or powers, that culminate, as they did in Schelling, in a potency that might perhaps best be characterized as both ground and excess of ground. It is possible to argue, then, that Kierkegaard did offer a conception of system.

There is something else that is important that I would like to mention here. In *Ages of the World*, as well as in the *Freiheitsschrift*, Schelling characterizes intellectuals who describe themselves as devoid of the 'madness of freedom' as in some way physically and morally sick. Schelling writes: 'One could say that there is a kind of person in which there is no madness whatsoever. These would be the uncreative people incapable of procreation, the ones that call themselves sober spirits. These are the so-called intellectuals whose works and deeds are nothing but cold intellectual works and intellectual deeds.... But where there is no madness, there is certainly no proper active, living intellect' (Schelling 2000: XIII). In other words, Schelling is critiquing a conception of system that might be the one held by many commentators on Kierkegaard. This is a conception of system that assumes that reason and madness, indeed reason and action, are diametrically opposed to one another. This may perhaps be a 'scientistic' view of system.

Kierkegaard picks up on Schelling's language. In *Two Ages*, he critiques the 'herd' who mindlessly follow a given outlook on the world. Merold Westphal, in his book *Kierkegaard's Critique of Reason and Society* (Westphal 1991), noting this, has suggested that Kierkegaard offers a critique of the conception of reason expressed in his own epoch.

In this section, I have suggested that Kierkegaard may, contrary to the suggestion of many commentators, have a conception of system. Indeed, I have suggested further that the notion of system he adopts is one that would not be familiar to many philosophers in the western tradition. Furthermore, I have argued that Kierkegaard may have been poking fun not at all systematizers, but rather specifically at those 'systematisers' who adopt a static and ultimately, for we humans, impossible notion of a system. I will now move to sketch a brief picture of Marx's work that demonstrates that he too is concerned with living, active human beings as well as with providing a systematic theory of history. Therefore his outlook shares some characteristics with that of Kierkegaard.[6]

Marx on living nature

Marx, like Kierkegaard, is concerned with natural, living and active beings. Like Kierkegaard, Marx offers a theory of history based on processes of change, processes involving these living and active beings. The focus of his materialist theory of history is human activity. Famously, in the first thesis on Feuerbach of 1845, Marx writes: 'The chief defect of all hitherto existing materialism – that of Feuerbach included – is that the thing [*Gegenstand*], reality, sensuousness, is conceived only in the form of the object [*Objekt*] or of intuition [*Anschauung*], but not as human sensuous activity, practice, not subjectively' (Marx 1968: 28). Then in the eleventh thesis, he famously notes: 'The philosophers have only interpreted the world, in various ways; the point, however is to change it' (Marx 1968: 30). Like Kierkegaard, then, Marx is critical of certain interpretations of Hegelianism, in his case, that of the Young Hegelians, and he writes about them in the *German Ideology* as 'sheep.' He sets out to 'uncloak . . . these sheep, who take themselves and are taken for wolves' (Marx 1965: 29). Their ideas were abstract and irrelevant. In this sense of 'system' then, Marx is critical of the Hegelians in similar manner to de silentio, who pokes fun at the 'systematizers' (Kierkegaard 1985: 41–3). Like Kierkegaard, moreover, Marx is concerned to offer a theory that differs from the pure abstractions of 'the philosophers' and also of any theory that fails to take human activity as central.

Both Kierkegaard and Marx, then, emphasize the importance of action and particularly action carried out freely. The subject matter of Marx's materialist conception of history is material life. What is this? The answer is that it is 'people, their activity and the material conditions under which they live' (Marx 1965: 39). Marx continues: 'We must begin by stating the first premise of all existence and therefore of all history, the premise, namely, that men must be in a position to live in order to "make history." But life involves eating, drinking, a habitation, clothing, and many other things. The first historical act is therefore the production of the means to satisfy these needs' (Marx 1965: 39). Marx is concerned, in other words, with human beings and their conditions of life.

Marx also writes: 'Man is a natural being. He is an active natural being' (Marx and Engels 1975: 167–8). Not only is production an active process but for Marx; additionally, knowledge is active. As Sidney Hook puts it, 'Marx sought to save the idealist's insight that knowledge is active. Otherwise his own historical materialism would result in fatalism. The starting point of perception is not an object on the one hand and a subject opposed to it on the other, but an interacting process within which sensations are just as much the resultant of the active mind (the total organism) as the things acted upon. What is beheld in perception, then, depends just as much upon the perceived as upon the antecedent cause of the perception' (Hook 2002: 88–9).

As human beings live with one another, according to Marx, they develop relations with one another and these relations change with the growth of the productive forces. However, major changes in social relations require a level of consciousness on the part of working-class human beings. Like de silentio, once more, who salutes Descartes for 'doing what he has said' (2002: 41/ SKS 4, 101) as opposed to the Hegelians, who simply speculate for its own sake, Marx emphasizes the importance of human activity that has a point or a purpose.

Both Kierkegaard and Marx, then, are naturalists. They are not reductive mechanistic naturalists, but they rather see a continuity between humans and other natural beings. Each of them accepts an ontology of processes or powers. Both Kierkegaard and Marx claim that nature conditions consciousness. For Marx, famously, 'the production of ideas, of conceptions, is at first directly interwoven with the material activity and the material intercourse of men, the language of real life' (Marx 1965: 40). In the Preface to the *Critique of Political Economy,* he writes:

'legal relations as well as forms of state are to be grasped neither from themselves nor from the so-called general development of the human mind, but rather have their roots in the material conditions of life' (Marx 1968: 181). Neither Kierkegaard nor Marx accepts a reductive form either of materialism or of idealism: rather, for both thinkers, thoughts and actions form part of an active living reality.

I have argued elsewhere that the relation between being and consciousness for Marx can be read as both an identity and a causal relation. The claim that consciousness is identical with being is not a necessary truth, because it holds between items under different descriptions (like the Morning Star and the Evening Star) but specifically the two terms designate different 'time slices' of the same individual (Assiter 1979: 18–20). An individual as a natural being causally shapes that individual as a conscious being, but the two are also the same person. Similarly, for Kierkegaard, the individual and natural being, Eve, who has no consciousness and simply exists in the natural world, is identical with the person who comes to have consciousness after the emergence in her of freedom. But the former, through her actions of eating of the forbidden fruit, caused the latter to come into being.

For both Marx and Kierkegaard, moreover, the self is a natural being partly shaped by a power that lies outside it – for Marx some kind of an ideal and for Kierkegaard a norm stemming from God.

It seems, then, that it is possible to argue that there are commonalities, to a greater degree than is suggested by Lukács, between the thought of the two writers. It might be argued, though, that this might be accepted but it does not answer Lukács' point that Kierkegaard is basically a thinker about the individual in relation to a transcendent God and that he does not accept that there can be any historical solution to the problems of alienation and anxiety. It seems to me, however, that there is some evidence in Kierkegaard's writings that this claim might not be wholly true.

Two ages

In his text, *Two Ages*, written after *Postscript*, Kierkegaard writes about the 'revolutionary' and the 'present' ages. He writes positively about the 'revolutionary age' and contrasts it with the static mindlessness of what he calls the 'present age.' The age of revolution acts passionately in contrast to the present age which is a 'reflective age devoid of passion' (TA, 72/SKS 8, 69). The age of revolution is an age of revelation 'by a manifestation of energy that unquestionably is a definite something and does not deceptively change under the influence of conjectural criticism' (TA, 66/SKS 8, 64).

In some respects Kierkegaard's description of the 'true revolutionary' fits that of the individual suffering before God. Just like the Knight of Faith, 'humanly speaking' the revolutionary may lose everyday taken-for-granted realties; he or she may lose home, family and jobs, but they may also gain a passion for action and for a cause with which they strongly identify. The age of revolution, Kierkegaard writes, can 'prefigure the eternal' while the present age, by contrast, is a 'fossilized formalism' which has lost the 'originality of the ethical' (TA, 65/SKS 8, 63).

Revolution, it must be noted, is not conceived by Kierkegaard quite as Lukács does. Kierkegaard did not view revolution as leading towards a Utopia that would effectively alter the reified and alienated structure of existing society. Indeed, he would probably have doubted that such a future was possible. That in itself might lend support to Price's view that Kierkegaard was a pessimist and that his views were strongly at variance with those of Marx and Lukács on the subject of historical change. Yet Kierkegaard might counter this with the claim that the view that a Utopia is possible for we finite limited beings is itself founded upon a conception of 'actuality' that is Hegelian or Adlerian in the bad sense. It assumes a kind of necessary logical development of the historical process that is inappropriate for the world of real interactions between beings like us. Doubting that Utopia is possible in the full 'communist' sense does not mean that dramatic change is not possible. A revolution, for Kierkegaard, as I have just outlined, shares many features of the relation between an individual and a transcendent God. Yet it is a collective process. If it were really informed by moral ideals akin to those of a truly religious person, then it could, on Kierkegaard's premises, quite properly be regarded as capable of bringing about change for the better.

Conclusion

If this interpretation of the works of both Kierkegaard and Marx is deemed to have any modicum of plausibility, then it casts doubt both upon the view that Kierkegaard was 'anti-system' and on the view that he denied the possibility of change. But it also casts doubt upon the view that Marx was a radically different kind of systematizer from Kierkegaard. How about the other accusation, made by Price, that Kierkegaard both denies the notion of system, and implicitly, accepts it as well? It seems somewhat unfair to describe Kierkegaard's actions in relation to Regine as demonstrating that he believed in a system, at the same time as he theoretically decried the notion of system. It is difficult to judge the actions of any philosopher outside their philosophical thinking, as indicating that their philosophizing is somehow challenged. All of us are finite and limited, and, at times, we act in ways that we might in principle decry. Kierkegaard's brief and somewhat unhappy life has been subjected to more intense scrutiny that have the lives of many philosophers. His texts are often supposed to be either about his relationship to Regine or they are said to contradict his relationship. He is claimed to have acted well in relation to her and to have acted badly. If this is the evidence that is offered for claiming that Kierkegaard contradicts his own philosophical pronouncements, then I suggest it should be taken with a pinch of salt.

In this chapter, I have suggested that the view that Kierkegaard is not a 'systematising' philosopher is open to challenge. But I have also questioned the view that, although Marx and Kierkegaard lived at the same time, this is about all they have in common. Instead I have suggested that both are some kind of naturalist and that both emphasize activity over passivity. Finally, I have questioned the view, held by Lukács, that while Kierkegaard theorized the notion of alienation, he was unsympathetic to any notion of social change or revolution. It may be, then, that Kierkegaard and Marx have more in common than at first meets the eye.

Related topics

'The passion of Kierkegaard's existential method,' Lee Barrett; 'Kierkegaard: the dialectical self and the political,' Shoni Rancher.

Notes

1 For one study of the subject, see Ryan (2014).
2 Marcuse makes a similar point. He writes of Kierkegaard's work that it is the 'last great attempt to restore religion as the ultimate organon for liberating humanity from the destructive impact of an oppressive social order' (Marcuse 1941: 265).

3 Jon Stewart (2007) in his monumental work, has altered understanding of Kierkegaard's relationship to Hegel. He has suggested that Kierkegaard was probably criticizing the Danish Hegelians, and, in particular Adler, rather than Hegel himself. It is important to add, however, that Kierkegaard was also clearly aware of the texts of Hegel himself.
4 See Binetti (2007); Burns (2012); and Assiter (2015).
5 Heraclitus was a pre-Socratic Greek philosopher who believed that change was the fundamental principle of the universe.
6 One of the most significant theorists who emphasizes Marx as a 'systematizer' is Louis Althusser who sees Marx as primarily concerned with offering a 'scientific' theory of history. See Alison Assiter (1990), for a critique of this reading of Marx.

References

Assiter, A. (2015) *Kierkegaard, Eve and metaphors of birth*, London: Rowman & Littlefield.
Assiter, A. (1990) *Althusser and feminism*, London: Pluto Press.
Assiter, A. (1979) 'Philosophical materialism or the materialist conception of history,' *Radical Philosophy*, 23: 12–20.
Binetti, M. J. (2007) 'Kierkegaard's ethical stage in Hegel's logical categories: Actual possibility, reality, necessity, cosmos and history,' *Journal of Natural and Social Philosophy*, 3, nos. 2–3: 357–69.
Burns, M. (2012) 'A fractured dialectic: Kierkegaard and political ontology after Žižek,' in A. Assiter and M. Tonon (eds), *Kierkegaard and the Political*, Cambridge: Cambridge Scholars Press, 103–25.
Hook, S. (2002) *Towards the understanding of Karl Marx: A revolutionary interpretation*, London: Prometheus Books.
Jambert, C. (2007) *The act of being: The philosophy of revelation in Mulla Sadr*, F. Jeff (trans), New York: Zone.
Kierkegaard, S. (1985) *Fear and trembling*, A.. Hannay (trans), New York: Penguin Books.
Kosch, M. (2006) *Freedom and reason in Kant, Schelling and Kierkegaard*, Oxford: Oxford University Press.
Lukács, G. (2010) *The foundering of form against life: Søren Kierkegaard and Regine Olsen in soul and form*, J. Sanders and K. Terezakis (eds), New York: Columbia University Press, 5–44.
Marcuse, H. (1941) *Reason and revolution*, Oxford: Oxford University Press.
Marx, K. (1968) 'Theses on Feuerbach,' in *Marx and Engels Selected Works in One Volume*, London: Lawrence & Wishart, 8–30.
Marx, K. (1965) *The German ideology*, London: Lawrence & Wishart.
Marx, K. and Engels, F. (1975) *The collected works of Marx and Engels*, vol. 42, London: Lawrence & Wishart.
Pattison, G. (2003) *The philosophy of Kierkegaard*, Chesham: Acumen.
Price, Z. (1999) 'On young Lukács on Kierkegaard,' *Philosophy and Social Criticism*, 25, no. 6: 67–82.
Ryan, B. (2014) *Kierkegaard's indirect politics: Interludes with Lukács, Schmitt, Benjamin and Adorno*, Boston, MA: Brill.
Schelling, F. W. J. (2000) *Ages of the world*, J. Wirth (trans), New York: Columbia University Press.
Schelling, F. W. J. (2006) *Philosophical investigations into the essence of human freedom*, J. Love and J. Schmidt (trans), New York: State University of New York Press.
Stewart, J. (2011) 'The notion of actuality in Kierkegaard and Schelling's Influence,' *Ars Brevis: Anuari o de la Càtedra Ramon Llull Blanquerna*, 17: 237–53.
Stewart, J. (2007) *Kierkegaard's relations to Hegel reconsidered*, Cambridge: Cambridge University Press.
Toews, J. E. (2004) 'Antiphilosophical epilogue: Historicising identity in Kierkegaard and Marx, 1841–1846,' in J. E. Toews, *Becoming Historical: Cultural Reformation and Public Memory in Early 19th Century Berlin*, Cambridge: Cambridge University Press, 404–32.
Westphal, M. (1991) *Kierkegaard's critique of reason and society*, University Park, PA: Penn State Press.
Wirth, J. (2000) '"Introduction" to Schelling, F. W. J.,' in J. Wirth (trans), *Ages of the World*, New York: Columbia University Press.
Žižek, S. (2009) *The Parallax View*, Cambridge, MA: Massachusetts Institute of Technology Press.

Further reading

Assiter, A. (2015) *Kierkegaard, Eve and metaphors of birth*, London: Rowman & Littlefield.
  The book offers a speculative naturalist reading of Kierkegaard, viewing nature in terms of metaphors of birth.

Ryan, B. (2014) *Kierkegaard's indirect politics: Interludes with Lucács, Schmitt, Benjamin and Adorno*, Boston, MA: Brill.

    Ryan gives an interdisciplinary reading of Kierkegaard and argues that a radical political gesture can be found in his work.

Toews, J. E. (2004) 'Antiphilosophical epilogue: Historicising identity in Kierkegaard and Marx, 1841–1846,' in J. E. Toews (ed), *Becoming Historical: Cultural Reformation and Public Memory in Early 19th Century Berlin*, Cambridge: Cambridge University Press, 404–32.

    The book is an intellectual history of the period and the final section considers Marx and Kierkegaard. Toews considers common elements in the two thinkers' conceptions of selfhood.

36
KIERKEGAARD: THE DIALECTICAL SELF AND THE POLITICAL

Shoni Rancher

Introduction

At one time it appeared to most scholars that since Kierkegard willed one thing, the highest and absolute good of one's standing alone before God, he had neither an interest in nor a contribution to make to political theory or practice. With the *International Kierkegaard Commentary* on *Two Ages*, however, Robert L. Perkins (1984: XIII) announced the aim of putting to death once and for all this myth of the Kierkegaardian individual as somehow existing in a 'social and political vacuum.' Merold Westphal (1987: 22) furthered this aim in *Kierkegaard's Critique of Reason and Society*, holding that Kierkegaard's critique of reason is a critique of ideology; he argued that Kierkegaard does not reject reason in itself but a form of reason that deifies and legitimates its oppressive order by passing off the contingent and particular as necessary and universal.

Bruce Kirmmse (1990: 458–9, 470, 476) arguably shut the coffin on this Kierkegaard myth with his monumental *Kierkegaard in Golden Age Denmark*, in which he offers the most detailed historical account available of the development of Kierkegaard's authorship, including its culmination in a secular, egalitarian attack on the official church (an attack that squarely situates Kierkegaard in the social-political). Nails were then hammered by Martin Matuštík's (1993) *Postnational Identity: Critical Theory and Existential Philosophy in Habermas, Kierkegaard, and Havel*, Mark Dooley's (2001) *The Politics of Exodus: Søren Kierkegaard's Ethics of Responsibility*, and the essays in volumes edited by George B. Connell and C. Stephen Evans (*Foundations of Kierkegaard's Vision of Community*), Matuštík and Westphal (*Kierkegaard in Post/Modernity*), George Pattison and Steven Shakespeare (*Kierkegaard: the Self in Society*), and John J. Davenport and Anthony Rudd (*Kierkegaard After MacIntyre*).

Today, almost twenty years after *Kierkegaard After MacIntyre,* and over thirty years past Perkins' pronouncement of death to the mythologized Kierkegaard, a eulogy is perhaps all that is left for scholars to write on this score. Today, such introductory remarks warning us against asocial and apolitical readings of Kierkegaard even risk cliché as a sea change seems imminent if not already complete regarding Kierkegaard and politics. For instance, Assiter and Tonon's (2012) collection, *Kierkegaard and the Political*, added six new essays to the work of the two-dozen or so scholars that the editors summarize in their 'Introduction' as having already gone some way in connecting the dots for us.

In the present chapter, I underscore the important role that Kierkegaard's dialectical individualism plays as both a sort of anchor for our thinking about Kierkegaard in this stream of scholarship, and also a compass to mark steady the direction we take in our understanding of his politics. While scholars have offered various names for Kierkegaard's political 'theory' and orientation – for example, the politics of contingency (Kirmmse 1992: 171), the politics of critical theory (Westphal 1987; Morgan 2012), the politics of radical existential praxis (Matuštik 1995), Climacan politics (Perkins 1998), the politics of the emigrant (Dooley 2001) – I will argue that three criteria in dialectical relation persist throughout and provide the axis around which the spokes of such scholarly readings of Kierkegaard's politics must make their revolution. This dialectical relation is, according to Kierkegaard, the self.

Anchor and compass: the dialectical self

The first constituent of the dialectical self is the singularity and uniqueness of the individual. In *Concluding Unscientific Postscript* Climacus expresses this with the thesis that objectivity is untruth and subjectivity truth. Similarly, Kant argued that the ground of moral and human worth was in the freedom of the individual coming to see for itself the authority behind the reasons for its acting. For Kant, here lay the fundamental difference between autonomy and heteronomy, and the absolute value of humanity as an end in itself. While this normative condition of freely choosing for oneself the reasons behind one's actions remains ultimately indemonstrable for both Kant and Kierkegaard, we might call this demand 'existential' the more we move in the direction of the non-verifiable inwardness of the individual, where free choice is decisive for the significance of our actions (Mooney 1992: 86–8). Thus, for example, Dostoevsky argues, in the subtext of the *Grand Inquisitor*, that faith cannot be demonstrated to Christ's persecutors by answering their chiding requests to come down from the cross to prove he is God (cf. PC, 105, 127/SKS 12, 113, 131).

Kierkegaard makes this first demand of the self by distinguishing his existential commitment from Kant's and going further in this direction, arguing that the inner movement that is essential to human freedom and worth, and which escapes what can be objectively demonstrated, likewise eludes the lawful force of rational necessity and universality (Mooney 1992: 86–8). Kierkegaard, in *Fear and Trembling,* most famously and dramatically expresses this with Johannes de silentio's account of faith that requires the teleological suspension of the universal ethical order on the absurd grounds that the individual before God is higher than the universal. But Kierkegaard, under the pseudonym of Johannes Climacus, likewise makes the point sharply, and not incidentally, in terms of the comic by pointing out that if one laughs at a joke simply because others laugh, then one can omit the joke (CUP 1, 325/SKS 7, 295–6). By Kierkegaardian standards, the individual's significance, and value in general, be it aesthetic, ethical, or religious, requires this inner movement of subjective appropriation, of getting the joke oneself or not at all (TA, 74/SKS 8, 71; PV, 106/SKS 16, 85–7).

Still, while the single individual might seem to serve as the necessary *and* sufficient condition for Kierkegaard, equally important is the self's second constituent, the tragically inescapable situatedness of each individual in social-historical practices. Kierkegaard makes this Hegelian point at the outset of his authorship. Beginning at least with 1843's *Either/Or*, aesthete 'A' argues in the essay on tragedy that the comic misunderstanding of the age is its failure to see that 'Every individual, however original he is, is still a child of God, of his age, of his nation, of his family, of his friends, and only in them does he have his truth. If he wants to be absolute in all this, his relativity, then he becomes ludicrous' (EO 1, 145/SKS 2, 144–5). Value requires subjective appropriation, but the individual is not absolute. As I have argued elsewhere (Rancher 2014), the tragic insight of the aesthete's essay is that values are conferred on us first and foremost by our being born into social-historical practices which we never fully outgrow (cf. Battersby 1999: 175). According to 'A,' the socio-historical guides individual thinking, judging and acting to such an extent that the essential tragic collision of *Antigone*, for instance, can be expressed as an unsolvable riddle over whether its *dénouement* is the result of the individual, here, Antigone, or the social-historical practices into which the individual was born (EO 1, 164/SKS 2, 161–2). To relate to the self as severed or untouched by social-historical practices and the values they confer on us not only provides a source for the comic and spells death for tragedy; it also means misunderstanding oneself and others.

Transposing the aesthete's point into the ethical, the Judge in the second half of *Either/Or* repeats the theme, arguing that a 'person who chooses himself ethically, chooses himself concretely as this specific individual … with these capacities, these inclinations, these drives, these passions, influenced by this specific social milieu, as this specific product of a specific environment. But as he becomes aware of all of this, he takes upon himself responsibility for it all' (EO 2, 250–1/SKS 3, 238–9). In short, to be a self also means recognizing one's facticity and its dialectical relation with one's sense of agency, responsibility, and identity (cf. Rudd 2001: 139; Rapic 2014: 63–4). When reading Kierkegaard, it is important to remember this second demand of the self as inescapably situated in social-historical practices, and that the single individual is essentially a dialectical relationship and continual movement between these two terms.

The necessity of this continual movement provides the third criterion of the dialectical self and is, taken together with the first two criteria, key for unpacking Kierkegaard's formulation of the self in subsequent works. In *Johannes Climacus*, for instance, Climacus distinguishes consciousness from mere reflection by arguing that the latter is dichotomous, since it is merely the disinterested possibility of the relation between the immediacy of existing and the mediated ideality of 'the word.' That is, mere reflection on one's possibilities, as mediated by the ideals conferred by one's socio-historical situation, is inadequate for one becoming a dialectical self. Trust a girl, or don't, hang oneself or don't, one will regret it either way! Aesthete 'A' of *Either/Or* expresses this shortcoming with his claim that happiness is thus to be found not 'behind either/or but before it,' that is, in *not* choosing either one possibility or the other (EO 1, 38–9/SKS 2, 47–8). By contrast, Climacus argues that consciousness is *trichotomous* since it presupposes reflection, but in addition is 'something more' in that it requires moving through the either/or by taking a stand in the struggle, collision, and contradiction that it is (JC, 167–71/SKS 4, 146–50). Only when one chooses to affirm or reject a possible ideal and project for oneself *in practice*, does one become conscious of oneself as the distance between existing and thinking. Engaging in practice the ideal of being punctual, for instance, is not something one thereby becomes once and for all. Becoming a self requires the continual movement between thinking and existing that is all the more necessary the higher and more difficult the ideal.

In *Concluding Unscientific Postscript*, Climacus further argues that the mark of the individual's infinite concern for eternal happiness is the dialectical accompanying everything, such that 'a word, a sentence, a book, a man, a society, whatever, as soon as it is supposed to be a boundary, so that the boundary itself is not dialectical, it is superstition and narrow-mindedness. In a human being there is always a desire … to have something really firm and fixed that can exclude the dialectical, but this is cowardliness and fraudulence toward the divine' (CUP 1, 34–5/SKS 7, 41). This is because a human being is neither merely existing nor simply a thinking thing, nor a homogenous unity of the two, but essentially 'the duplexity [*Dobbelthed*] of thought-existence' (CUP 1, 74/SKS 7, 74–5). To remain true to its dialectical nature, then, Climacus prescribes that a person ought to be equal parts comic and tragic, which is to provide the self an interdependent safeguard from the illusion of the comic and the immaturity of pathos (CUP 1, 87–91/SKS 7, 85–90). That is, the double-demand ensures that the individual resists the temptation of resting in the inner or the outer, the individual or the social, but is instead '*continually in a process of becoming, that is, striving*' (CUP 1, 80/SKS 7, 80).

In *Two Ages*, arguably Kierkegaard's most political text, the self as a continually striving dialectical triad continues. Kierkegaard begins his literary review and social-political analysis of the age by expressing his admiration of the author under review for 'remaining true to himself,' which he likens, not incidentally, to Socrates' admiring the constancy of the number three (TA, 8, 97/SKS 8, 11–2, 92–3). In *The Sickness unto Death*, Anti-Climacus also defines the self as a trichotomous relating to oneself as a relation of opposites: 'The self is a relation that relates itself to itself . . . the self is not the relation but is the relation's relating itself to itself. A human being is a synthesis of the infinite and the finite, of the temporal and the eternal, of freedom and necessity. . . . A synthesis is a relation between two. Considered in this way, a human being is still not a self' (SUD, 13/SKS 11, 129–30). In *Practice in Christianity,* pointing to the political and recalling Climacus's warning about coming to restful completion in the inner or the outer, Anti-Climacus holds that every established order requires fear and trembling, which signifies that its constituents are continually in the process of becoming (PC, 88/SKS 12, 96; cf. Mooney 1992: 90).

From Kierkegaard's perspective, and as we can gather from the varied perspectives of his pseudonyms, the basic error and temptation in human life is the one-sidedness that closes the dialectical relationship that is the self, that finishes with the task before life is finished with it. The self is the continual process of taking a stand on the relation between the individual and the social, existing and thinking, the particular and the universal, the finite and the infinite. As Edward Mooney (1992: 80–3) argues, for Kierkegaard, engaging continually these two elements – (1) the immediate self as a product of biology, society, culture, etc., and (2) the inward, reflective self that endorses or rejects the immediate self – is the dialectic that constitutes one's essential humanity (cf. Dooley 1998: 143–5, 150–2; Matuštík 1995: 249, 256–7). Taking a stand and becoming a conscious self is, however, not something done once and for all. One reason for this is, as expressed by the essential tragic conflict, that the socio-historical guides individual thinking, judging and acting to such an extent that the possibility of self-deception arises. In addition, we must continually and critically choose the ideals we strive to live by because existing and thinking are incommensurable. One can never come to possess a value (for example, punctuality) as one owns a car.

When Kierkegaard argues that the single individual is 'the category through which, in a religious sense, the age, history, [and] the human race must go,' this must not be understood non-dialectically as if Kierkegaardian singularity stood for something atomistic or homogeneous (PV, 118/SKS 16, 97–8). For Kierkegaard, the real difficulty and task is to be true to oneself. This requires continual movement between both sides of the dialectic rather than the comfort of one-sidedness or something done once and for all. The self is the fear and trembling of taking a stand within the tension, contradiction, and collision that one continually is.

Political orientations of the dialectical self

Bearing in mind the dialectical nature of one's essential humanity, we arrive at some immediate political implications for Kierkegaard's view. First, and perhaps most frequently noted is that Kierkegaard's view is not that of Hegel's communitarian politics. As Westphal (1987: 32) succinctly puts it in *Kierkegaard's Critique of Reason and Society*, 'Being dialectical [Kierkegaard's] individualism is a social theory of human experience, inherently political in a broad sense. Kierkegaard's task, as he sees it, is to rescue this theory of what it is to be human, and its corresponding practice, from a Hegelian philosophy that is insufficiently faithful to it.' Following Hegel, Kierkegaard's view of the self as a dialectical relation between the I and the We, the individual and the social, is political. However, Kierkegaard begins and ends with the self as the incommensurable relation between existing and thinking, individual and social. By contrast, Hegel starts here but ultimately reduces the individual to the social, namely, to the nation-state, which Hegel sees as the necessary conclusion of reason's movement through history. Kierkegaard rejects this dialectical infidelity and its politics, since he sees it one-sidedly reducing the individual to an abstract process of the whole, to history, the race, the generation, the nation, and so on, such that the individual vanishes along with any genuine ethics, religion, and political community that would require individual responsibility.

In addition, and perhaps of greatest and clearest political import here, Kierkegaard worries about the dangerous deification of an individual or community that follows from such dialectical infidelity. Existence is a system for God, Climacus argues, but not for an existing human being (CUP 1, 118/SKS 7, 114). A system signifies completion in which everything, namely, existing and thinking is unified and finds its properly determined place and function within the system. By contrast, existence for a human being or a collection of them cannot find completion without the individual or collective mistaking itself for God. God serves to delimit what *can* from what *cannot* provide rest from the dialectical striving of one's essential humanity (SUD 14/SKS 11, 129–30). Because God is absolute and man is not, according to Kierkegaard, no *humanly* established order can be absolute instead of precisely what it is, namely, tentative (cf. Kirmmse 1992: 171; Dooley 2001: XVIII).

By failing to maintain this distinction one is led to the temptation of thinking one has arrived at 'something firm that'll hold at bay the dialectical' (CUP 1, 44/SKS 7, 41–2). By Kierkegaard's lights, it is this dialectical infidelity that poses the dangers of the crowd mentality and the deification of the nation-state often linked with totalitarianism (PC, 91/SKS 12, 99; cf. Westphal 1987: 39). In contrast, by properly maintaining its dialectical tension, the Kierkegaardian self resists historical narratives of progressive, communitarian politics that champion the present over the past, and prevents the dangers that an individual's absolute identification with any collective poses (Matuštík 1995: 241; Perkins 1998: 47–8; Dooley 2001: 43–7).

Similarly, Kierkegaard's view of the dialectical self and the political is not that of Plato's aristocracy. Perkins (1998: 44) argues that while Kierkegaard and Plato both find an 'isomorphic' relationship between the individual and society, Kierkegaard prioritizes the particular while Plato prioritizes the whole. In the foundational work of political philosophy, Plato has Socrates seek to know justice in the individual only by first venturing to understand justice in the whole society. This produces the paradox of whether a just society is prior to and necessary for producing just individuals, or the reverse. Plato's theory of recollection provides the solution: knowledge of the whole is prior to the act of cultivating justice in the particular. However, the solution, Perkins (1998: 46) argues, underscores Plato's political elitism, since his ideal society would require a hierarchical caste system supported by the myth of the three metals, and be determined top-down based on the exclusive knowledge and rule of philosopher kings.

By contrast, Kierkegaard reverses the relationship in holding that each individual must arrive by him- or herself at the life, the truth, the way (PV, 105/SKS 16, 86). The religious defined as the single individual before God has priority over the top-down approach to politics (Kirmmse 1990: 410–1). In the preface to 'The Single Individual,' in Kierkegaard's *The Point of View of*

My Work as an Author, he writes: 'the religious is the transfigured rendition of what a politician, provided he actually loves a human being and loves humankind, has thought in his most blissful moment, even if he will find the religious too lofty and too ideal to be practical' (PV, 103/ SKS 16, 83). If it is a genuine political *community*, by Kierkegaard's standards, its constitution first requires the singularity of each individual's relationship to truth as something not commensurable with the demands of universality and objectivity, and so of what can be publicly communicated or cultivated in terms of a top-down political approach.

Consequently, as Kirmmse (1990: 273–4; 1998: 46–7) and others have argued, reversing Plato's terms speaks to Kierkegaard's egalitarianism, or populism, over the political elitism in Plato and against the aristocratic communitarian politics of Danish Hegelians. Whereas Plato's recollection prioritizes knowledge of some fixed, abstract, and systematic whole, as does the looking back of Hegel's world historical process, Kierkegaard prioritizes the particular individual who, like Socrates, turns away from recollection since he wants to exist in truth as an existing thinker (CUP 1, 205/SKS 7, 187–8; PV, 103/SKS 16, 83; cf. Perkins 1998: 45; Dooley 2001: 93–5). The truth and worth of the Kierkegaardian self do not depend on one's membership in and possession of objective and publicly shareable knowledge. Rather, as Climacus writes in *Postscript*, 'to will to be an individual existing human being (which one unquestionably is) in the same sense as everyone else is capable of being – that is ethical victory over life and over every mirage' (CUP 1, 356/SKS 7, 325; cf. CUP 1, 159, 182/SKS 7, 148, 167). Such illusions arise, Anti-Climacus explains further, from mistaking the truths of knowledge with existing in truth, or at least striving to exist in truth. The upshot is that it is a mistake to think there is a shortcut to making a genuine community as there is for making gunpowder, which might have taken its inventor 100 years to do but for those who follow only an hour (PC, 207/SKS 12, 203). As noted in the previous section, to exist in truth signifies the self's continual striving as a dialectical triad. In this every human is equally capable and positioned for life's examination, and no self can do this work for another (PC, 185–6/SKS 12, 185). Thus, while Kierkegaard introduces us to three stages of life rather than a myth of three metals, he also holds that Socrates' access to and responsibility for this labour of wanting to exist in truth and ethical victory, and so to serve as the basis for a genuine political community, is neither greater nor less than any human's, regardless of one's stage on life's way.

Still, despite thinking that all of this rightly points to Kierkegaard's egalitarianism, I worry that the idea of an inverse isomorphism between Kierkegaard and Plato risks losing the dialectical anchor. If the self is dialectical all the way down, as I believe it is for Kierkegaard, then Plato's or Hegel's attempt to solve the paradox by giving priority to the whole is likely to have as much success as prioritizing the particular. Again, Kierkegaard's categorical imperative for the single individual must not be understood non-dialectically as if Kierkegaardian individuality stood for something atomistic and independent of the social (PV, 118/SKS 16, 97–8). The truth that grounds human equality and genuine community is, for Kierkegaard, the religious truth of one's striving to exist as an individual before God. But, again, it is precisely one's relation to God as the absolute that delimits human existence as a continual striving in the dialectical process of becoming. Climacus writes, 'existing is a prodigious contradiction from which the subjective thinker is not to abstract, for then it is easy, but in which he is to remain' (CUP 1, 350/SKS 7, 319). The individual before God signifies that a person continually tarries with the dialectical tension between itself and the social rather than escapes it.

Any solution, then, including a religious, egalitarian one, 'that removes the paradox also fantastically transmogrifies the existing person into a fantastical something that belongs to neither time nor eternity, but such a something,' Climacus warns, 'is not a human being' (CUP 1, 182

/SKS 7, 167). It is necessary to understand the dialectical self in terms of moving between the individual and the social without needing to fix a temporal priority and unilateral direction to one term over the other (Matuštík 1995: 257; cf. Tilley 2014: 104). It is important that, in emphasizing the egalitarian character of Kierkegaard's individual, we are not prioritizing the individual over and against the social in such a way that returns us to the pre-social self of classical liberalism and its own brand of self-deification.

That is, in addition to rejecting the previously considered political positions, the Kierkegaardian self, and the dialectically qualified egalitarianism that flows from it, also requires rejecting the non-dialectical, socially contracted self of classical bourgeoisie liberalism (cf. Westphal 1987: 29–32; Matuštík 1995: 241; Assiter and Tonon 2012: 2). This self is non-dialectical since it is conceived as first and foremost standing outside of society in a state of nature, naked and independent of society's moral, legal, and cultural entrapments, and freely pursuing its self-interest and natural right to life, liberty, and private property (Kirmmse 1992: 161–4). Liberalism's socially contracted individual is, then, apolitical in the sense that the individual's relationship to the social has nothing to do with the individual's essential identity (cf. Assiter 2009: 64–85, 101–7; PC, 19/SKS 12, 29). Rather, the political state is merely a means for expediting the ends of the individual's and others' natural self-interests (cf. Westphal 1987: 31–3; Kirmmse 1992: 161–4; Matuštík 1995: 241). According to Kirmmse (1990: 414), Kierkegaard's single individual endorses this liberal view of the community as *merely* a 'pragmatic association.'

However, I argue that this stands in stark contrast to the second demand of Kierkegaard's dialectical self, namely, the socio-historically situated practices and values in which the individual is to find her truth and take responsibility for it, which points instead to a classical or Rousseauian democratic position. As we have seen, one's essential humanity for Kierkegaard is fundamentally about the relationship between the individual and the social. But we need not place Kierkegaard in either political camp and for no better reason than that doing so would cancel the dialectical tension of the self by reducing it to either the individual or the social. Because liberalism and Rousseauian democracy each does this in their respective ways they enact and promote infidelity to the dialectical self. The democratic self, like the self of Hegel's communitarian holism, risks the ultimate erasure of the individual in the social. But the self of liberalism goes too far towards fundamental independence from the social (Matuštík 1995: 241).

Thus, when Kierkegaard comes to critique the liberal movements of his present age in *Two Ages*, he does so from a standard with two conditions for a community to be optimal and normative: 1) that each individual relates essentially and passionately to an idea, and 2) *together* individuals essentially relate to the same idea (TA, 62/SKS 8, 59–60; my emphasis). These two conditions for a genuine community maintain the dialectical tension between the individual and the social. The emphasis that both scholars and Kierkegaard himself have placed on the first demand for subjective appropriation often risks eclipsing everything else, even though there are criticisms made within Kierkegaard's later works against hidden inwardness (PC, 214–7/SKS 12, 209–12). We cannot forget, then, that here Kierkegaard also posits a second condition for genuine community, namely, that the ideas to which individuals relate are those that both can be shared and, thereby, can also form optimal and normative bonds with others (cf. Westphal 1987: 30). In other words, that an individual must get the joke on his or her own does not mean that individuals cannot or must not laugh together. On Kierkegaard's view, the difficult task is to satisfy both conditions (not simply the first or merely the second), which enables the passionate age of revolution *to act both alone and with many* (Kirmmse 1990: 268).

To help clarify what is at stake here in more concrete terms, consider Kirmmse's (1990: 270) view that in *Two Ages* Kierkegaard's critique of Copenhagen's liberal wave of the preceding years does not apply to 'liberalism's individualism and the principles of constitutional and popular government.' This is apparent since Kierkegaard praises the revolutions beginning in the late 1700s for having acted decisively to establish these same ideals. If the revolutionary age established these ideals both alone and with many by passionately engaging the double-demands of the dialectical self, the present age merely received these ideals as one receives the knowledge of gunpowder or an historical period (PC, 207–8/SKS 12, 203–4). Kierkegaard thus attacks not liberalism, Kirmmse (1990: 271) argues, but the way in which his fellow citizens related to its ideals; they were merely collectively related to the same ideal, without meeting that first demand of individual passion that marks any ethical, religious, or political community as *bona fide*. Consequently, by the time the ideals of the revolutionary age reach Copenhagen, Kierkegaard sees them as having undergone a fossilized formalism (TA, 65/SKS 8, 62–3).

Moreover, Kirmmse (1990: 410) adds that in 1850's *Practice in Christianity* Kierkegaard is able to sustain and extend his 1846 critique of the empty practices of the present age to Copenhagen's own revolution, which began in 1848. While the revolution ultimately overthrew the authoritarian monarchy and replaced it with a constitutional one, Kierkegaard saw that in one fell swoop it also formalized that both government and church were now the official property of a dispassionate and popular majority (Kirmmse 1990: 75–6, 399). The people were then fully led to the misunderstanding, again betraying their lack of passionate fidelity to the dialectical self, that they could possess religion as they did the water pipes and roads (cf. Westphal 1987: 36; Kirmmse 1990: 399).

Last but not least, just as Kierkegaard finds a dangerous self-deification following the one-sidedness of Hegel's communitarian holism, he locates a similar danger in liberalism's demand that the people be everything. Kirmmse notes that Kierkegaard saw the 1848 revolution in terms of a coming of age in which the people rightly freed themselves from political authority that had claimed a divine and inherited right to rule. The problem, according to Kierkegaard, is that the people then proclaimed freedom from all authority, which betrayed the dangerous self-deification that confuses 'the *vox populi* and the *vox dei*' (PV, 123/SKS 16, 102; cf. Kirmmse 1990: 418). On this score, Kirmmse (1990: 416) again reads Kierkegaard as locating the danger not in liberalism *per se*, but in the popular majority's failure to take 'seriously its own modest pretensions and its secularism,' and thus in its 'disastrous confounding of politics and Christianity' (Kirmmse 1992: 171).

The events following the 1848 revolution made the institutionalized confusion of the outer and the inner, the political and the religious, evident to Kierkegaard. According to Kirmmse (1990: 408–10), noticing this confusion ultimately led to Anti-Climacus's demand in *Practice in Christianity* for the established religion's confession of failure to practice what it preached and, when this confession did not come, to Kierkegaard's open attack on the established order in the early 1850s (PC, 7, 226/SKS 12, 15, 220). Consequently, while Kirmmse (1990: 399–401) holds that Kierkegaard is no liberal, his boycott makes clear that he shares liberalism's basic tenet that, regarding non-material, ethical, and religious matters, the individual is higher than the established order. To be sure, laughter imposed officially by popular sovereignty would likewise express a misunderstanding.

However, in light of Kierkegaard's view of the self, it is also important to qualify all of this by underscoring that it is not liberalism's ideals and goals *per se*, but its failure to begin continually within the dialectical tension of the self, that Kierkegaard criticizes in his fellow citizens' collective move toward established religion, mathematical equality and popular, representative democracy (TA, 84–5/SKS 8, 80–2; PC, 215–6/SKS 12, 210–1). In other words, it is true that the liberals of his day, according to Kierkegaard, failed to break with their fossilized formalism and take a passionate stand in order to act both alone and with many, but from the outset this failure results from liberalism's granting independence to the individual over the social-historical in a way that Kierkegaard finds inadequate. The task of every human is that of continually striving to exist in truth by continually taking a stand in the dialectical (Kirmmse 1992: 161–4; cf. 1990: 245–6). But by cancelling the dialectical, Kierkegaard argues, the '[intensity of] passion of the absolute disjunction that leads the individual resolutely to make up his mind is transformed into the extensity of prudence and reflection' (TA, 97/SKS 8, 91–2). This is why the present age, in contrast with the age of revolution, can act neither alone nor with many. The dialectical tension between the individual and the social that constitutes one's essential humanity is the condition for the possibility of choosing continually either/or, that is, the condition for the possibility of freedom, without which genuine community cannot exist.

Consequently, if Kierkegaard's age and its politics lacked the revolutionary age's passion on which the 'coiled springs of life-relationships' depend for their normative health and optimal resiliency, we can say that this is because the age lacked individual inwardness (TA, 78/SKS 8, 74). As Kierkegaard himself explains, however, this lack has a deeper source in the cancellation of the dialectical tension of the self from which passionate action can and must make its stand. The passion of inwardness is not the escape from the self's dialectical collision, which Anti-Climacus makes clear in criticizing such forms of inwardness (PC, 214–7/SKS 12, 209–12). Rather, the passion that grounds revolutionary action and genuine community presupposes dialectical tension (cf. Matuštík 1995: 249–52; Dooley 1998: 147–8). From the outset, it seems that liberalism, and any other political orientation from which this tension is missing, cannot but help to diminish the capacity for acting decisively *both alone and with many* (TA, 62, 72–3/SKS 8, 59–60, 69–70; PC, 223/SKS 12, 217–8; cf. Nicoletti 1992: 191).

Kierkegaard highlights this dialectical infidelity in arguing that the age of revolution upholds the principle of contradiction, whereas the present age nullifies it and thereby evades real choice and action (TA, 66, 97/SKS 8, 63–4, 91–2). Since the age of revolution, like Socrates and the number three, remains true to itself, it 'can become either good or evil,' Kierkegaard writes; 'whichever way is chosen, the *impetus* of passion is such that the trace of action marking its progress or its taking a wrong direction must be perceptible' (TA, 66/SKS 8, 63). Again, the age of revolution maintains the contradiction and with it the passion *to act* both alone and with many (TA, 62/SKS 8, 59–60). By contrast, the present age of reflection cancels the contradiction and with it the passion, which in the silence of action truly speaks. Because of this, Kierkegaard explains, it becomes enough for the present age to know and talk about everything but to do nothing; and because this is enough, it is possible for the individual to be 'everything . . . in contradiction to oneself.' That is, this self-conception contradicts itself since it is not the triad of the self that continually takes a passionate stand on the dialectical relation that it is, and thus, Kierkegaard argues, it is 'nothing at all' (TA, 97/SKS 8, 91–2).

Conclusion

From the anchor and compass of Kierkegaard's dialectical individualism, and from our limited consideration here of the political orientations that might arguably find their bearing and path from it, it seems clear that Kierkegaard's politics is radically anti-authoritarian since he rejects any form of deification as defined by infidelity to the dialectical self (Perkins 1998: 48). From the preceding it is evident that this is not simply because he endorses the liberal separation of church and state. Rather, it is so for the same reason that he rejects any self-conception that removes the dialectical tension between the individual and the social (PC, 89/SKS 12, 97). Kierkegaard does not arrive at religious egalitarianism by beginning from the non-dialectical, pre-social self of liberalism, any more than he begins with the non-dialectical one-sidedness of a communitarian or democratic politics in which the self is to find rest in its identifying with the whole or the majority (PC, 16/SKS 12, 27–8; cf. Quinn 2001: 333–6).

The crucial difference is that for the non-dialectical political views considered here, authoritarian deification always remains a possibility, even a tendency. By contrast, deification seems impossible for the Kierkegaardian self, its egalitarianism, and the genuine community it envisions, precisely because from beginning to end it remains true to the continual striving of the dialectical self. This can also be expressed by stating that the individual stands alone before God. But, once more, the individual's standing here is not something finished, or fixed outside the socio-historical, and so non-dialectical. As I argued earlier, it is precisely infidelity to God that leads to dialectical infidelity to oneself (cf. PC, 88/SKS 12, 96; SUD, 14/SKS 11, 129–30). The restful rewards of faith, human equality and genuine community do not cancel the dialectical relation. The rest promised to all requires that each one engage the dialectal relation between the individual and the established order through the imitation of Jesus Christ, the divinity who was born, lived and died as a lowly servant, and who loved the poor, marginalized, and wretched of the earth (PC, 56–7, 120/SKS 12, 69–73, 126–7; PV, 111/SKS 16, 90–1; cf. Nicoletti 1992: 185).

Related topics

'Johannes Climacus and the dialectical method: from dialectics back to existence,' Claudine Davidshofer; 'Varieties of existential uncertainty,' Rick Anthony Furtak; 'Becoming a subject: Kierkegaard's theological art of existence,' Peder Jothen; 'Kierkegaard, Hegel, and Augustine on love,' Thomas J. Millay.

References

Assiter, A. (2009) *Kierkegaard, metaphysics and political theory: Unfinished selves*, New York: Continuum.
Assiter, A. and Tonon, M. (2012) 'Introduction,' in A. Assiter and M. Tonon (eds), *Kierkegaard and the Political*, Newcastle: Cambridge Scholars Publishing.
Battersby, C. (1999) 'Review of "feminist interpretations of Søren Kierkegaard",' in *Hypatia*, 14, no. 3: 172–6.
Dooley, M. (2001) *The politics of exodus: Søren Kierkegaard's ethics of responsibility*, New York: Fordham University Press.
Dooley, M. (1998) 'Risking responsibility: A politics of the émigré,' in G. Pattison and S. Shakespeare (eds), *Kierkegaard: The Self in Society*, London: Palgrave Macmillan.
Kirmmse, B. H. (1992) 'Call me Ishmael – call everybody Ishmael: Kierkegaard on the coming-of-age crisis of modern times,' in G. B. Connell and C. S. Evans (eds), *Foundations of Kierkegaard's Vision of Community: Religion, Ethics, and Politics in Kierkegaard*, Atlantic Highlands, NJ: Humanities Press International.
Kirmmse, B. H. (1990) *Kierkegaard in golden age Denmark*, Bloomington, IN: Indiana University Press.
Matuštík, M. J. (1993) *Postnational Identity: Critical Theory and Existential Philosophy in Habermas, Kierkegaard, and Havel*, New York: Guilford Press.
Matuštík, M. J. (1995) 'Kierkegaard's radical existential praxis, or: Why the individual defies liberal, communitarian, and postmodern categories,' in M. J. Matuštík and M. Westphal (eds), *Kierkegaard in Post/Modernity*, Bloomington, IN: Indiana University Press.
Mooney, E. (1992) 'Getting Isaac back: Ordeals and reconciliations in "Fear and Trembling",' in G. B. Connell and C. S. Evans (eds), *Foundations of Kierkegaard's Vision of Community: Religion, Ethics, and Politics in Kierkegaard*, Atlantic Highlands, NJ: Humanities Press International.
Morgan, M. (2012) *Kierkegaard and critical theory*, Lanham, MD: Lexington Books.
Nicoletti, M. (1992) 'Politics and religion in Kierkegaard's thought: Secularization and the martyr,' in G. B. Connell and C. S. Evans (eds), *Foundations of Kierkegaard's Vision of Community: Religion, Ethics, and Politics in Kierkegaard*, Atlantic Highlands, NJ: Humanities Press International.

Perkins, R. L. (1998) 'Climacan politics: Polis and person in Kierkegaard's "Postscript",' in G. Pattison and S. Shakespeare (eds), *Kierkegaard: The Self in Society*, New York: St. Martin's Press.
Perkins, R. L. (1984) 'Introduction,' in R. L. Perkins (ed), *International Kierkegaard Commentary*, vol. 14 (*Two Ages*), Macon, GA: Mercer University Press.
Quinn, P. L. (2001) 'Unity and disunity, harmony and discord: A response to Lillegard and Davenport,' in J. J. Davenport and A. Rudd (eds), *After MacIntyre: Essays on Freedom, Narrative, and Virtue*, Chicago, IL: Open Court Publishing.
Rancher, S. (2014) '"Antigone": The tragic art of "Either/Or",' in J. Stewart (ed), *Kierkegaard Research: Sources, Reception and Resources*, vol. 16 (*Kierkegaard's Literary Figures and Motifs*), Farnham: Ashgate.
Rapic, S. (2014) 'Choosing oneself as a process of emancipation: Kierkegaard and Habermas,' in A. Avanessian and S. Wennerscheid (eds), *Kierkegaard and Political Theory: Religion, Aesthetics, Politics and the Intervention of the Single Individual*, Copenhagen: Museum Tusculanum Press.
Rudd, A. (2001) 'Reason in ethics: MacIntyre and Kierkegaard,' in J. J. Davenport and A. Rudd (eds), *After MacIntyre: Essays on Freedom, Narrative, and Virtue*, Chicago, IL: Open Court Publishing.
Tilley, M. (2014) 'Radical individualism or non-teleological community: Kierkegaard's precarious understanding of self and other' in A. Avanessian and S. Wennerscheid (eds), *Kierkegaard and Political Theory: Religion, Aesthetics, Politics and the Intervention of the Single Individual*, Copenhagen: Museum Tusculanum Press.
Westphal, M. (1987) *Kierkegaard's critique of reason and society*, Macon, GA: Mercer University Press.

Further reading

Marsh, J. (1984) 'Marx and Kierkegaard on alienation,' in R. L. Perkins (ed), *International Kierkegaard Commentary*, vol. 14 (*Two Ages*), Macon, GA: Mercer University Press.
  This chapter underscores the dialectical parallels and differences between Marx's and Kierkegaard's respective views on and solutions for the alienation found in modern, capitalist societies.
Matuštík, M. J. (1993) *Postnational identity: Critical theory and existential philosophy in Habermas, Kierkegaard, and Havel*, New York: Guilford Press.
  This book offers an historical account of Kierkegaard's influence on critical theorists such as Adorno, Marcuse, and Habermas, and provides a more exhaustive development of Matuštík's argument in 'Kierkegaard in post/modernity' for why Kierkegaard's dialectical individualism defies liberal, communitarian, and post-modern politics.
Morgan, M. (2012) *Kierkegaard and critical theory*, Lanham, MD: Lexington Books.
  This book focuses on Kierkegaard and critical theory as most recently developed by what Morgan calls the 'Fordham School' of critical theorists, which includes the work of Merold Westphal, Martin Matuštík, and James Marsh.

37
KIERKEGAARD, HEGEL, AND AUGUSTINE ON LOVE

Thomas J. Millay

Introduction

Kierkegaard's doctrine of love is an Augustinian one. This does not mean that Kierkegaard cited Augustine in developing his doctrine of love; nor need it be the case that Kierkegaard intentionally crafted his thoughts on love within an Augustinian framework. Rather, working in a vein similar to Lee Barrett's (2013: 3) definitive book on Augustine and Kierkegaard, I will argue that Kierkegaard and Augustine share certain patterns of thought and that it is mutually illuminating to compare the two. As I will explain here, love for Kierkegaard is always directed toward upbuilding, and this is an Augustinian way of defining the character of love.

Although Kierkegaard's doctrine of love is an Augustinian one, it is forged within an ongoing debate with G.W.F. Hegel. In fact, one could say that Kierkegaard picks up the Hegelian themes of *Moralität* and *Sittlichkeit* and undoes them from within by pushing them in an Augustinian direction. Looking at the interaction between *Upbuilding Discourses in Various Spirits* and *Works of Love* will display Kierkegaard's Augustinian critique of Hegel's social ethics in action.

There are multiple avenues of appropriating Augustine within modern thought, and it can be helpful for clarity's sake to distinguish between them. On this account, I will argue that Kierkegaard should not be confused with a contemporary trend known as Augustinian liberalism. This trend of appropriating Augustine is made up of a group of theologians and social theorists from Reinhold Niebuhr to Jeffrey Stout to Eric Gregory, who all in diverse ways attempt to develop the positive contribution Augustine's thought can make to the project of modern liberal political order. Here I will limit extensive engagement to only one of these figures. Comparing Kierkegaard's doctrine of love to that found in Eric Gregory's *Politics and the Order of Love*, I will show how Kierkegaard challenges contemporary political appropriations of Augustine through his insistence that suffering can be used by love for upbuilding. It is difficult to find a place for the spiritual usefulness of suffering within Augustinian liberalism (even if it can make quite a large space for the lamentable necessity of suffering within the current economic order; see Mathewes 2001); the following reading of Kierkegaard's doctrine of love shows how such contemporary appropriations are departures from Augustine that fail to acknowledge the possibilities that are lost in leaving Augustine, particularly the possibilities lost in relinquishing the spiritual utility of suffering. By picking up this thread of suffering as a potential spiritual good,

I aim to show that Kierkegaard confronts us with an alternative Augustinianism that can make its own contribution to political theory through opening possibilities which modern liberalism shuts down.[1]

One such possibility is Kierkegaard's attack upon Christendom. In this attack, Kierkegaard tells his comfortable, bourgeois society that each individual has a responsibility to embrace suffering. If she is to be a true Christian, the individual must break from the security of Christendom, which attempts to provide the good life in the here and the hereafter. One breaks from Christendom by, for example, ceasing to attend church; for it is an institution that only serves to reinforce the societal delusion that 'one can have it all.' In my conclusion, I will argue that Kierkegaard's attack upon his society should be read as a work of love. As I will show, labelling an encouraged embrace of suffering as a work of love is a description impossible within the confines of Augustinian liberalism. Thus, in comparison to this recent trend, Kierkegaard offers a different possibility for a modern appropriation of Augustine, one that will be explored in what follows.

A final note before turning directly to the texts of Augustine and Kierkegaard: both these thinkers make important contributions to political theory, but not in the sense of advocating a particular mode of political governance. Rather, it is in the asking and attempted answering of the question of how a Christian should act if she is to be faithful to her Christian identity that both of these thinkers make their contribution to political theory. For such a question inevitably informs Christian political participation, if only for those who are thoughtful about how their Christian identity interacts with their civic identity.

Love as a work of upbuilding in Augustine and Kierkegaard

The key definition of love in Kierkegaard's *Works of Love* reads as follows: '*To love God is to love oneself truly; to help another person to love God is to love another person; to be helped by another person to love God is to be loved*' (WL, 107/SKS 9, 111). To love the neighbour is to draw forth her love for God. True love for the neighbour is, in this sense, always upbuilding; that is, it builds the neighbour up out of her everyday, temporal concerns into existence *coram Deo* (before God).

What this means in a practical sense is a matter of some debate. Some, like Theodor Adorno (1939: 413–29), hold that Kierkegaard's exclusive concern for the eternal good of the neighbour leads to an abstract and otherworldly ethic. Others, such as M. Jamie Ferreira, argue that this is a misconstrual of what Kierkegaard is saying. *Works of Love* simply presumes that one is giving material gifts; it then focuses on interrogating one's inner attitude in the giving of those gifts, the result being an ethic that is concrete and this-worldly (Ferreira 1999: 65–79).

Both of these interpretations miss the mark because they fail to see the fundamentally Augustinian character of Kierkegaard's doctrine of love. Material gifts can be given or withheld depending on whether such a gift would be upbuilding to the neighbour's God-relationship. One should give with the following question in mind: can this gift be used by my neighbour to increase her attachment to God?

Implicit within that question is Augustine's dynamic of use and enjoyment (*uti/frui*). In *De doctrina christiana*, he defines that dynamic as follows: 'Enjoyment, after all, consists in clinging to something lovingly for its own sake, while use consists in referring what has come your way to what love aims at obtaining' (Augustine 1996: 107).[2] The human task is thus to order one's love correctly: to love God as the absolute – the one true end-in-itself – and all other things as means for cultivating love for God. This renders the value of all things other than God relative to whether they help one to love God or not.

Later in *De doctrina*, Augustine takes this general principle and applies it to love of the neighbour. First, Augustine speaks to one's own role in this dynamic: one is to love the neighbour not as an end-in-herself, but only as a conduit for increasing one's love of God (Augustine 1996: 114). Second, in loving the neighbour one should try to inspire in her the same approach toward use and enjoyment to which one has oneself subscribed. Augustine summarizes this second conception of love as follows:

> all who love their neighbors in the right way ought so to deal with them that they too love God with all their heart, all their soul, all their mind. By loving them, you see, in this way as themselves, they are relating all their love of themselves and of the others to that love of God, which allows no channel to be led off from itself that will diminish its own flow.
>
> (Augustine 1996: 115)

This is love of the neighbour conceived as the upbuilding of the neighbour in her God-relationship. Whatever one does for the neighbour should be for the neighbour's upbuilding. The goodness of any material gift given to the neighbour is always relative to whether or not it meets such a goal.

Another way to phrase this Augustinian dynamic is to say that the spiritual always has priority. Any temporal, physical, material reality will always be subject to judgment and interrogation. It will be queried to see if it contributes to spiritual development and judged accordingly. Thus, that which is of material benefit to a particular individual is not always right for that person. It all depends on whether that benefit is upbuilding. The singular ethical question in Kierkegaard and Augustine is the same: will this action lead my neighbour to grow closer to God?

When it comes to love, Kierkegaard's mind thinks in Augustinian patterns. Love is building the neighbour up in her love of God, leading her to desire God more and grow in her attachment to the eternal. This is a formal principle that can incorporate any number of concrete actions as appropriate (WL, 215/SKS 9, 218: 'everything can be upbuilding (*Alt kan være opbyggeligt*)'). From providing comfort to allowing suffering to continue, or even prodding the neighbour to take on more suffering in imitation of Christ – all of these are possible loving responses to the neighbour. With the above formal principle in mind, one must simply use one's judgment as to what will be most conducive to the neighbour's upbuilding. Such is also the case in Augustine, but it is not the case in Hegel or those who follow him, as I will now demonstrate.

Kierkegaard's doctrine of love and Hegelian social ethics

While I have emphasized only one text so far, Kierkegaard's doctrine of love should not be gleaned solely from *Works of Love*. In fact, *Works of Love* should be read in tandem with *Upbuilding Discourses in Various Spirits*, as Kierkegaard himself prescribed (JP 5, 363–4/SKS 20, 86). The interplay between these two texts is critical to understanding Kierkegaard on the topic of love.

According to the discourse 'You Shall Love *the Neighbour*,' there are always two moments involved in any act of love for the neighbour. First, one isolates oneself as a single individual before God. Then, one goes out of one's isolation to meet and to love the neighbour that one has been commanded to love in that prior moment of isolation where one is *coram deo*.[3] With the whole of *Works of Love* in mind, such directions are surprising. There is not much material in this text on isolating oneself. Kierkegaard does offer an explanation for such a lack: 'In this little book, we are continually dealing with the works of love; therefore we are considering love in its outward direction' (WL, 282/SKS 9, 280). Everywhere in *Works of Love*, the first moment of isolation before God is presumed, while at the same time focusing on the second moment of going out of one's isolation to one's neighbour. This is why it is essential to read *Works of Love* in tandem with *Upbuilding Discourses in Various Spirits*, for isolation before God is what this previous text is all about.

Upbuilding Discourses in Various Spirits begins with the occasion of confession, in which one actively places oneself as a single individual before God. Confession requires '[t]hat the person making the confession is beyond comparison, that he has withdrawn from every relation in order to concentrate on his relation to himself as a single individual and by doing this to become eternally responsible for every relation he is in ordinarily' (UDVS, 152/SKS 8, 248). During confession, the individual suspends all social relations and all social constitution of the self (wherein the self would gain its identity only through its social role), focusing only on the self's relation to itself.[4]

Once isolated with oneself and therefore before God, one will be able to will the Good for the sake of the Good, without any thought for positive or negative consequences for one's own self. This is purity of heart, and it prepares the newly minted single individual to perform works of love, for these are what the God one meets in isolation bids one to do.

Once purity of heart before God is achieved, one can act directly for the neighbour's good. Acting directly for the neighbour's good is what is laid out in *Works of Love*, where, through outward actions, one helps the neighbour find herself as a distinct individual before God.[5] This is not the end of the story, however. As *Works of Love* makes clear, such outward action for the neighbour's good then increases one's own attachment to God.[6] In a strange way, then, *Works of Love* is always moving back toward the focus of *Upbuilding Discourses in Various Spirits*, which is always moving forward toward *Works of Love*. This is the dialectical movement in Kierkegaard's doctrine of love, which constantly loops from the individual to the neighbour back to the individual: one's own love for God is increased as one acts to build up the neighbour in her love of God. Each stage of the dialectical movement enriches the next.

In setting up such a dialectical movement, Kierkegaard is engaging a Hegelian pattern of thought and undoing it from within.[7] The foundational text for understanding Hegel's ethical teaching is his *Philosophy of Right*. This text also has a dialectical movement, which unfolds over time. The ethical subject first understands himself as a single individual,[8] committed to universal duties to which he owes absolute allegiance, without regard for consequences; this is what Hegel calls *Moralität*, and the debts to Kant should be clear (Hegel 1991: §§105–41). Yet the ethical subject in Hegel must press beyond this first Kantian moment, in which one realizes the reality of moral obligation, to something less abstract. Kantian *Moralität* abstracts the ethical subject from the social ties that bind him and which constitute the only stage on which he can act morally.[9] Hence, Hegel proposes his theory of *Sittlichkeit*, or social ethics, which takes these obligations into account. The ethical individual moves from realizing himself as a creature of universal obligations (e.g., to tell the truth) to realizing himself as a creature of specific obligations to those around him (e.g., to tell the truth in a variety of particular circumstances and social roles, each with their own distinctive shape of truth-telling, from father to husband to civil servant); he moves from inward noumenal identification of himself as an ethical subject to outward identification as a contributing moral member of *this* society (Hegel 1991: §§146–57).

There are several parallels and differences that can be noted when comparing Kierkegaard's *Upbuilding Discourses in Various Spirits/Works of Love* to Hegel's *Philosophy of Right*, but one parallel and one difference stand out as most important.

First, the parallel: there is dialectical movement in each of these thinkers, such that one does not get a proper handle on their respective ethical theories if one isolates only one moment of this dialectic. This has generally been understood fairly well when it comes to Hegel – less so with Kierkegaard.

Now, the difference: in Hegel, the ultimate sphere for moral action is always society (Hegel 1991: §257). The ethical subject is the person who contributes to the flourishing of his society. In Kierkegaard, society is at best a preliminary consideration. The ultimate sphere is always eternity (WL, 6, 252–3/SKS 9, 14–5, 252–3). Ethics in Kierkegaard is all about increasing attachment to this sphere, whether our own attachment or that of others. In Kierkegaard, it is possible that at times the good of society must take a back seat to the flourishing of individual souls before God, a flourishing that can happen even amidst the devastation or dissolution of human society.

When it comes to love, then, Kierkegaard uses a pattern of thinking similar to Hegel's, yet he ends up with a much different result. Kierkegaard takes the Hegelian interplay of *Moralität* and *Sittlichkeit* and makes it subservient to spiritual goods. All temporal societal goods are made relative to the eternal good of each individual before God, such that even if a societal good contributes mightily to the temporal flourishing of a given people group, it is to be dropped immediately if it is seen to be harmful to human souls. This is because all temporal goods or ills are only to be made use of for the purposes of increasing our enjoyment of God. In sum, Kierkegaard takes a modern pattern of thought – Hegelian dialectics – and pushes it in an Augustinian direction, undoing its basic premises in the process.

Kierkegaard and Augustine against Hegel and Augustinian liberalism

The recovery of an ancient, Augustinian conception of love within a situation of regnant Hegelianism is a significant achievement,[10] and the potential uses of Kierkegaard's doctrine of love are many. Here, I will focus on one of the potential ramifications of this recovery: the critique of contemporary Augustinian liberalism. Whereas Kierkegaard appropriates Hegelian patterns of thought and pushes them in an Augustinian direction, I will argue that Augustinian liberals appropriate Augustinian patterns of thought and push them in a Hegelian direction.

Eric Gregory is one of the most sophisticated representatives of Augustinian liberalism, a group that includes philosophers and theological ethicists such as Reinhold Niebuhr, Jean Bethke Elshtain, Oliver O'Donovan, Jeffrey Stout, and Charles Mathewes. Gregory's *Politics and the Order of Love* is particularly notable for the purposes of this chapter precisely because its focus is on love. His book is an attempt to utilize Augustine's thought in order to inspire the sort of love for liberal democratic ideals that results in civic virtue (Gregory 2008: 1–10, 262–3, 383). In so doing, Gregory shifts the focus of Augustinian liberalism from sin to love.[11]

This is a doctrine of love that, from the start, must fit within the governing presuppositions of liberal political order. Although he does not precisely define what the liberal political order is, I take Gregory's meaning to be consonant with what John Locke proposes in *A Letter Concerning Toleration*, namely that the first duty of government is to protect and promote the material well-being of its citizens, with the further proviso that whatever spiritual interests a government may have, those may not contravene government's first duty (2010: 6–7).[12] This is an understanding of political governance that Hegel fully upholds, as *Sittlichkeit* only extends the commitment to individual material flourishing into society as a whole, in addition to providing spiritual benefits that complete without contravening material benefits (Hegel 1991: §§41–53, 160–71). In this respect, Hegel fits comfortably within the lineage of political liberalism (Jakubowski and Bydgoszcz 2014: 237–41). In short, liberal political order is defined by its aim of promoting the material welfare of citizens and, concomitantly, the elimination of the material suffering of those citizens: this is the rather uncontroversial definition of liberalism that Gregory endorses. Gregory does not ask whether Augustine might be critical of the project of liberalism in general; rather, he asks how the use of Augustine might be beneficial to the modern liberal political project (2008: 2). To his credit, Gregory explicitly admits that his goal is not faithfulness to the historical Augustine (2008: 7). I do not object to the creation of a modern political ethic that is inspired by an ancient figure, even if it is not entirely faithful to that ancient figure. Rather, what Kierkegaard's more historically faithful Augustinianism demonstrates is that Gregory has not considered the power of certain objections the historical Augustine would make to the ideals of liberal democracy. These objections still bear considering, and Kierkegaard presses us to do exactly that.

In essence, Gregory (2008: 371) argues that Augustine grants us a 'Christian humanism' that inspires us 'to revisit the moral and religious sources of liberal commitments.' The ethical subject is henceforth motivated to enthusiastically embrace principles such as tolerance, non-violent conflict resolution, and just distribution of material goods. That is to say, the liberal citizen inspired by Augustine will not just formally subscribe to these principles as an abstract condition for living a private life, but actively embrace them; furthermore, she will often be critical of her society for not meeting these ideals (Gregory 2008: 383).

This is fine as far as it goes, and it certainly is an interesting variant upon previous Augustinian liberalisms (such as that of Reinhold Niebuhr), which is just what Gregory intends it to be. The problem is that amongst the ideals of liberalism – and perhaps implicitly present in all of them – is the elimination of material human suffering as an unqualified and unquestionable good (Gregory 2008: 71, 349). This view of material suffering and its elimination would be anathema to Augustine and to Kierkegaard.

Why? Who could be so callous as not to wish human suffering a long overdue goodbye? These outraged questions reveal precisely how pervasive the ideals of liberalism are amongst Western readers.[13] Augustine and Kierkegaard believe that whatever is useful for upbuilding should be what is sought out or allowed to happen, both for oneself and for one's neighbour. Sometimes, this does involve the elimination of suffering, especially in cases where human dignity is at stake.[14] At other times, an increase in suffering is recommended;[15] Kierkegaard's attack upon Christendom, in which he asks his readers to ostracize themselves from the comfortable society of which they are a part, is a clear case in point (more on this below). In this understanding of love, one cannot decide in advance whether one should do everything one can to eliminate the neighbour's suffering or if one should encourage one's neighbour to embrace yet more suffering than she now experiences. Such a view is certainly disturbing in the possibilities it enables; for example, should one withhold food from a hungry neighbour if one has good reason to think the withholding of one's gift will draw the neighbour closer to God? As Stephen Minister has put it, 'ambiguity' is at the heart of Kierkegaard's conception of love; there is an undecidability built in to the structure of material gifts (Minister 2017: 153). Rather than explaining away the disturbing possibilities Kierkegaard and Augustine enable, those readers who choose to follow these thinkers in formulating their own ethical beliefs should admit, as Minister does, that there is an ineradicable element of 'ethical risk' involved in taking this standpoint.

For Augustine and Kierkegaard, there is something truly more important than the elimination of material pain, and that is the good of the soul. If there is a case in which suffering would clearly lead to the good of the soul, then that is what they will recommend. Love, on their understanding, would require it.

In Gregory's quasi-Augustinian schema of love-infused liberal values, it is not clear that suffering could play any positive role in the Christian life. Insofar as that is a problem for the reader, she will also have a problem with Gregory. *Politics and the Order of Love* may not be an attempt to remain faithful to the historical Augustine, and one may grant Gregory's point that this need not be a goal for contemporary Christian ethicists. But in occluding these dynamics that are part of the historical Augustine, Gregory's constructive project fails to consider the potential good of suffering for the Christian. Just as in a non-Augustinian, standard liberal account of politics such as Locke and Hegel's, suffering is only an aberration awaiting its final demolition. The wisdom of ascetic Christianity[16] – Augustine and Kierkegaard included – is left behind, on account of an a priori acceptance of liberal ideals. To the extent that Christians want to make sense of suffering as potentially contributive to spiritual good, Gregory's project is left wanting. The potential spiritual usefulness of material suffering is a reality for which he simply cannot account.

Like Locke and Hegel after him, Gregory is committed to the material flourishing of human society as a first principle of political governance. In opposition, Kierkegaard and Augustine allow that material human flourishing can coincide with spiritual degradation. Concomitantly, the solution to such spiritual degradation may involve the dismantling of a flourishing human society. To show what this might mean, I turn to Kierkegaard's infamous 'attack upon Christendom.'

Conclusion: the attack upon Christendom as a work of love

Kierkegaard did not want his society to flourish. He wanted it to dissolve, at least insofar as it was constituted in his age. This was an age in which material human flourishing and Christianity were equated; as Julia Watkin writes: 'To be an evangelical Lutheran was part of being a Dane; the temporal and spiritual formed one realm of God in which the godly citizen was expected to enjoy earthly prosperity as well as spiritual well-being' (2001: 4).[17] The solvent Kierkegaard applied to this combination of worldly and eternal benefit was the New Testament, which teaches that the true Christian inevitably receives unmitigated hatred from the world (TM, 22–3/SKS 14, 143). With this teaching in mind, one must choose: either the comfortable, secure life of a flourishing modern society, or Christianity. Thus the society Kierkegaard faced, which tried to draw these two incompatible identities together, cannot stand; already it is not the Christian society it claims to be. The belief that one can have it all, that one can be happy in this life and the next, is a delusion.

With this incompatibility in mind, Kierkegaard takes direct aim at the crowning achievement of modern society, the comfortable life (Millay 2013: 144–51), as an anti-Christian ideal. This comfortable life bears close resemblance to an ideal realization of Hegelian *Sittlichkeit*: each person in society is perfectly in her place, is performing her unique contribution for the good of all, and is accorded recognition and respect by the other participating members. This is a life of secure temporal happiness (TM, 20/SKS 14, 143).

The comfortable life modern society affords at least some of its members is a significant achievement. It is also precisely what Christianity calls one to renounce. One should note here, in connection with the theme of ethical risk mentioned above, that Kierkegaard's attack literature is primarily directed to those comfortable members of Danish society who do in fact have something to renounce. If one is disturbed that Kierkegaard's doctrine of love cannot rule out acts generally considered horrific, such as deliberately withholding bread from the hungry, perhaps this disturbance can be somewhat mollified by observing how Kierkegaard himself applied the Augustinian principle of upbuilding love: he attacked not the poor but the comfortable, the latter being a group he considered especially characteristic of his time. Commenting on Christ's statement that '[t]he way is narrow' (Matthew 7: 14), Kierkegaard writes: 'That was a severe *nota bene*; the comfortable – precisely that in which our age excels – cannot be brought into any relation at all to an eternal happiness ... the eternal is obtained only in the difficult way' – that is, the way of suffering (TM, 110/SKS 13, 152–3).

This way of suffering is in fact what God's providence wants to arrange for people, as Kierkegaard makes clear in the eighth issue of *The Moment*:

> We human beings are by nature inclined to view life as follows: we regard suffering as an evil that we strive in every way to avoid. And if we succeed, we then one day on our deathbed think we have good reason to be able to thank God that we were spared suffering. We human beings think that the point is merely to be able to slip happily and well through this world; and Christianity thinks that all terrors actually come from the other world, that the terrors of this world are childish compared with the terrors of eternity, and that the point is therefore not to slip happily and well through this life, but rightly to relate oneself to eternity through suffering.
>
> [T]he God of love is in heaven fondly loving also you. Yes, loving; that is why he would like you finally to will what he for the sake of eternity wills for you: that you might resolve to will to suffer, that is, that you might resolve to will to love him, because you can love him only in suffering, or if you love him as he wills to be loved you will come to suffer. Remember, one lives only once; if it is neglected, if you do not come to suffer, if you avoid it – it is eternally irreparable.
>
> (TM, 293–4/SKS 13, 352)

In the sharp rhetoric of the attack, Kierkegaard calls upon his neighbours to will to suffer so that they might imitate Christ and thereby earn the blessing of eternal comfort. This is a harsh and unpleasant call, by all means – but that does not mean it fails to be an act of love.

Even though the attack upon Christendom is written not to take away the neighbour's suffering, but instead to prod the neighbour toward an increased embrace of suffering, it is still a work of love according to Kierkegaard's definition. The attack literature is an attempt to take an illusion away from the neighbour and, in so doing, enable her to grow closer to God. Precisely in this way, the attack upon Christendom is a pre-eminent example of Christian love-in-action; it is Kierkegaard's attempt to step forth into society and direct people toward greater attachment to God (TM, 91–2/SKS 13, 129–30). The attack is a building up of the neighbour out of her comfortable society into a direct confrontation with the rigorous call of God; it is therefore, quite simply, a work of love.

Sometimes love for the neighbour can take the form of recommending he give up a life of meaningful contribution to society; for example, Kierkegaard explicitly calls upon his fellow Danes to stop attending church, thus interrupting the this-worldly/otherworldly continuum so central to Danish Christendom (TM, 71–8/SKS 13, 109–24). Such a recommendation of renunciation holds even if one's society is progressing toward a more just distribution of material goods and would benefit from one's participation in that project. That is to say: if refusing to attend church excepts one from this grand progressive project, leads to social ostracization, brings suffering upon one, and brings no material benefit to any other person – well, so be it. Recommending such a course of action can only be a work of love if one has a conception of love as upbuilding – that is, if love for the neighbour is doing for the neighbour whatever will draw her closer to God. As I have argued, both Kierkegaard and Augustine hold to precisely such an account of love.

This account departs from a modern liberal preoccupation with material flourishing, a preoccupation shared by Hegel and by Augustinian liberals, where works of love are those actions intended to help the neighbour live a better temporal life (which includes but is not limited to material flourishing). Hegel and Eric Gregory aim to reform modern liberal societies, to make them more just and tolerant; there is of course nothing intrinsically wrong with this, not even in Kierkegaard and Augustine's conception. The problem arises when something more than reform is seen to be necessary for the good of human souls residing in a given society. Kierkegaard and Augustine can affirm that a society should be dissolved, even if such dissolution causes suffering, if such a society is causing harm to human souls. Hegel and Augustinian liberals can only articulate a logic of reform that aims toward the elimination of human suffering in a progressive realization of human flourishing.

In sum: the ancient, ascetic conception of love in Kierkegaard and Augustine is able to make sense of lives lived in renunciation as lives of love in a way that liberalism is not. This conception is able to see suffering as a good, if it is being used by an individual to draw closer to God. And it is able to see suffering as a good both for oneself as a single individual (*Upbuilding Discourses in Various Spirits*), and – more controversially – for one's neighbour in her God-relationship (*Works of Love*). And sometimes it is a pre-eminent act of love to attack the very society that has made the neighbour's life so pleasant. On this, Kierkegaard and Augustine agree, and they continue to call into question the validity of any doctrine of love that cannot admit such a proposition.

Related topics

'Love for humans: morality as the heart of Kierkegaard's religious philosophy,' Sharon Krishek; 'Did Napoleon teleologically suspend the ethical? A dilemma for some 'Hegelian' readings of *Fear and Trembling*,' Ryan S. Kemp.

Notes

1 This chapter therefore occupies similar territory to Alison Assiter's *Kierkegaard, Metaphysics and Political Theory: Unfinished Selves*, though it takes a different approach (Assiter 2009).
2 Cf. WL, 40/SKS 9, 47: 'The despair is due to relating oneself with infinite passion to a particular something, for one can relate oneself with infinite passion – unless one is in despair – only to the eternal.'
3 Kierkegaard uses the image of the closet, taken from Matthew 6:6: 'There is indeed a big dispute going on in the world about what should be called the highest. But whatever it is called now, whatever variations there are, it is unbelievable how much prolixity is involved in taking hold of it. Christianity, however, immediately teaches a person the shortest way to find the highest: Shut your door and pray to God – because God is surely the highest. If someone goes out into the world to try to find the beloved or the friend, he can go a long way – and go in vain, can wander the world around – and in vain. But Christianity is never responsible for having a person go even a single step in vain, because when you open the door that you shut in order to pray to God and go out the very first person you meet is the neighbor, whom you *shall* love' (WL, 51/SKS 9, 58).
4 See, for example, Kierkegaard's description of the apostle: 'An apostle ... leaves out everything else, forgets everything else, does not see it, does not hear it, does not sense it, but has his sights on God alone ... No, for this humble martyr people simply are not present' (UDVS, 336/SKS 8, 426).
5 See WL, 271/SKS 9, 270: 'The small-minded person has never had the courage for this God-pleasing venture of humility and pride: *before God* to be oneself – the emphasis is on "before God," since this is the source and origin of all distinctiveness. The one who has ventured this has distinctiveness; he has come to know what God has already given him, and in the same sense he believes completely in everyone's distinctiveness. To have distinctiveness is to believe in the distinctiveness of everyone else, because distinctiveness is not mine but is God's gift by which he gives being to me, and he indeed gives to all, gives being to all.'

6 See WL, 384/SKS 9, 376: 'The direction is inward; essentially you have to do only with yourself before God.' It is important to see this statement in its context, located in the conclusion to a text that has been focused on outward works.
7 I argue this at greater length in Millay (2018: 23–41).
8 Hegel's understanding of political participation is exclusively masculine. See Hegel (1991: XXIX).
9 See Hegel (1991: §135): 'However essential it may be to emphasize the pure and unconditional self-determination of the will as the root of duty – for knowledge [*Erkenntnis*] of the will first gained a firm foundation and point of departure in the philosophy of Kant, through the thought of its infinite autonomy (see §133) – to cling on to a merely moral point of view without making the transition to the concept of ethics reduced this gain to an *empty formalism*, and moral science to an empty rhetoric of *duty for duty's sake*. From this point of view, no immanent theory of duties is possible. One may indeed bring in material *from outside* and thereby arrive at *particular* duties, but it is impossible to make the transition to the determination of particular duties from the above determination of duty as *absence of contradiction*, as *formal correspondence with itself*, which is no different from the specification of *abstract determinacy*; and even if such a particular content for action is taken into consideration, there is no criterion within that principle for deciding whether or not this content is a duty. On the contrary, it is possible to justify any wrong or immoral mode of action by this means.'
10 On the specific Danish Hegelianism Kierkegaard is combatting in *Works of Love*, see Millay (2018: 27–30).
11 Previous exponents of Augustinian liberalism tend to focus on how due recognition of human sin should cause us to chasten our expectations of what the political order can do. See especially the work of Reinhold Niebuhr (e.g., 1986: 123–41).
12 'Liberalism' is a contested term, but the debates (such as on how active or intrusive the government should be in achieving its aim of material benefit) do not challenge the fundamental principle above summarized (see Ryan 2012: 21–44). Locke is often taken to be a 'founding father' of liberalism (Ryan 2012: 233), and even accounts that challenge how this liberalism is to be defined do not dispute this moniker (Baltes 2016). I have attempted to provide as broad and inclusive a definition of liberalism as possible, *via* a figure who is indisputably important to its intellectual heritage.
13 I do think that, beyond Gregory, the entire group of Augustinian liberals listed above hold to the liberal ideal of the elimination of human suffering, even if – as 'realists' – they doubt the possibility of realizing this ideal. To prove this claim, however, would require a paper of its own; this generalization therefore remains provisional.
14 See Kierkegaard on the elimination of slavery (UDVS, 242–3/SKS 8, 341–2).
15 See FSE, 80/SKS 13, 101: 'Harder sufferings! Who is so cruel as to dare say something like that? My friend, it is Christianity, the doctrine that is sold under the name of the gentle comfort, whereas it is eternity's comfort, yes, truly, and for all eternity – but it certainly must deal rather severely.'
16 By 'ascetic,' I mean to refer to manifestations of Christianity that emphasize suffering and discipline as essential components of a true life of faith. This is in accord with the general definition provided in Guibert (1936: 936–8).
17 Here I use the terms temporal and worldly interchangeably, and equate them with concern for material goods, in line with Kierkegaard's usage. I do not mean to claim that there is a univocal sense for these terms in Kierkegaard's writings, as there is not (especially not for 'temporal'; see McDonald 2015: 163–8). I only mean that these terms come to be associated (amongst other things) with the egocentric, selfish pursuit of material benefit. See Watkin (2001: 77).

References

Adorno, T. W. (1939) 'On Kierkegaard's doctrine of love,' *Zeitschrift für Socialforschung/Studies in Philosophy and Social Science*, 8, no. 3: 413–29.
Assiter, A. (2009) *Kierkegaard, metaphysics and political theory: Unfinished selves*, London: Continuum.
Augustine (1996) *Teaching Christianity*, E. Hill (trans), Hyde Park, NY: New City Press.
Baltes, J. (2016) *The empire of habit: John Locke, discipline, and the origins of liberalism*, Rochester, NY: University of Rochester Press.
Barrett, L. C. (2013) *Eros and self-emptying: The intersections of Kierkegaard and Augustine*, Grand Rapids, MI: Eerdmans Publishing Company.

Ferreira, M. J. (1999) 'Other-worldliness in Kierkegaard's *Works of Love*,' *Philosophical Investigations*, 22, no. 1: 65–79.
Gregory, E. (2008) *Politics and the order of love: An Augustinian ethic of democratic citizenship*, Chicago, IL: University of Chicago Press.
Guibert, J. (1936) 'La notion d'ascèse, d'ascétisme,' in M. Viller, S. J. (ed), *Dictionnaire de spiritualité*, Paris: Gabriel Beauchesne et ses fils.
Hegel, G. W. F. (1991) *Elements of the philosophy of right*, A. W. Wood (ed), and H. B. Nisbet (trans), Cambridge: Cambridge University Press.
Jakubowski, M. and Bydgoszcz, T. (2014) 'Hegel's non-liberal liberalism,' *Hegel Jahrbuch 2014*: 237–41.
Mathewes, C. (2001) *Evil and the Augustinian tradition*, Cambridge: Cambridge University Press.
McDonald, W. (2015) 'Time/temporality/eternity,' in S. Emmanuel, W. McDonald and J. Stewart (eds), *Kierkegaard Research: Sources, Reception and Resources*, vol. 15 (*Kierkegaard's Concepts*), tome 6, Farnham: Ashgate.
Minister, S. (2017) 'An ethics for adults? Kierkegaard and the ambiguity of exaltation,' in S. Minister, J. A. Simmons and M. Strawser (eds), *Kierkegaard's God and the Good Life*, Bloomington, IN: Indiana University Press.
Locke, J. (2010) *Locke on toleration*, Richard Vernon (ed), Cambridge: Cambridge University Press.
Millay, T. J. (2018) 'Concrete and otherworldly: Reading Kierkegaard's "Works of Love" alongside Hegel's "Philosophy of Right",' *Modern Theology*, 34, no. 1: 23–41.
Millay, T. J. (2013) 'The late Kierkegaard on human nature,' in R. Králik et al. (eds), *Acta Kierkegaardiana*, vol. 6 (*Kierkegaard and Human Nature*), Toronto: Kierkegaard Circle.
Niebuhr, R. (1986) 'Augustine's political realism,' in R. Neibuhr (ed), *The Essential Reinhold Niebuhr: Selected Essays and Addresses*, New Haven, CT: Yale University Press.
Ryan, A. (2012) *The making of modern liberalism*, Princeton, NJ: Princeton University Press.
Watkin, J. (2001) *Historical dictionary of Kierkegaard's philosophy*, Oxford: Scarecrow Press.

Further reading

Barrett, L. C. (1999) 'The neighbor's material and social well-being in Kierkegaard's *Works of Love*: Does it matter?' in R. L. Perkins (ed), *International Kierkegaard Commentary*, vol. 16 (*Works of Love*), Macon, GA: Mercer University Press.
   A subtle treatment of a difficult issue in Kierkegaard studies, wherein Theodor Adorno's scathing critique of *Works of Love* is given a more sympathetic read than is usual amongst Kierkegaard scholars.
Doody, J., Paffenroth, K., and Russell, H. T. (eds) (2017) *Augustine and Kierkegaard*, Lanham, MD: Lexington Books.
   This is an insightful collection of essays on Augustine and Kierkegaard that address a wide array of issues.
Ferreira, M. J. (2001) *Love's grateful striving: A commentary on Kierkegaard's Works of Love*, Oxford: Oxford University Press.
   This book offers a textually attentive commentary on *Works of Love*. The result is a significantly different reading than the ascetic interpretation of Kierkegaard on display in this chapter. For Ferreira, material gifts to the neighbour (if needed) are always presumed to be the first order of business for a Kierkegaardian work of love.
Kirmmse, B. H. (1990) *Kierkegaard in golden age Denmark*, Bloomington, IN: Indiana University Press.
   This book provides the most detailed portrait available in English of the society Kierkegaard attacked.

38

THE COVETOUS CANARY: KIERKEGAARD ON THE PROBLEM OF SOCIAL COMPARISON AND THE CULTIVATION OF SOCIAL COURAGE

Paul Carron

Introduction

For much of the twentieth century, interpretations of Kierkegaard stressed his emphasis on the individual. It's not difficult to understand why. After all, he addresses his reader, 'that single individual,' proclaiming 'the crowd is untruth!' Guilt and sin are individual categories: 'every individual becomes guilty only through himself' (CA, 53/SKS 4, 358), and 'the category of sin is the category of individuality' (SUD, 119/SKS 11, 230). Statements like these lead some readers to conclude that Kierkegaard's anthropology consists in an 'extreme "ethical individualism"' (Gottlieb 1979: 351). Fortunately, the tide began to turn in 1984 with the publication of the *International Kierkegaard Commentary* volume on *Two Ages: A Literary Review*. Many Kierkegaard scholars now emphasize Kierkegaard's social analysis and contribution to political thought (see, for example, Tilley 2014; Avanessian and Wennerscheid 2014). However, none locate Kierkegaard's social thought within contemporary social psychology. This chapter fills that lacuna by analysing Kierkegaard's understanding of how the crowd shapes personal identity and how social comparison is a roadblock on the path to authentic selfhood.

I proceed as follows. First, I offer a brief overview of social comparison theory (SCT), an important discovery of twentieth-century social psychology. SCT is evidenced in stories, anecdotes, and numerous laboratory experiments and studies, and suggests that an agent's self-conception is largely determined by social and cultural forces. SCT provides both a theoretical framework and empirical support for Kierkegaard's understanding of the crowd's influence on an agent's self-conception and emotions. Second, I examine several Kierkegaardian texts to show his understanding of the way the crowd influences an agent's self-conception and how the crowd is always a stumbling block on the self's road to authenticity. Finally, I argue that these same texts provide a solution to the crowd's threat to authenticity: developing social courage through emotion regulation strategies. Social psychology is utilized to develop and strengthen these implicit social emotion regulation strategies, especially social attentional deployment.

Social comparison theory

Kathi Hudson, a member of the pro-choice Washington Area Clinic Defense Task Force, was a spy on the anti-abortion group Operation Rescue (OR), and she even testified against several OR members in court. After spending two years as a spy, a man she testified against (and who was subsequently sentenced to jail time) led her in a prayer to become a born-again Christian. She ceased working with the abortion Defense Task Force and reported that because of her conversion, her views on abortion were evolving (Risen 1993; cited in Forsyth 2000: 81).

During the 1930s, the psychologist T. M. Newcomb followed a group of female college students who attended Bennington College. The faculty was liberal and socially active, while the students came from overwhelmingly conservative, affluent families. 62% of students supported the Republican presidential candidate as freshmen; the number plunged to 15% by their senior year. Newcomb concluded (and many social psychologists agree) that 'many Bennington women shifted their attitudes in response to this peer-group pressure' (Forsyth 2000: 84).

Hudson and Bennington College are examples of the influence of social groups on an individual's beliefs and behaviour. Other studies show how the influence of other agents impacts how an individual construes or sees stimuli. A classic study by Solomon Asch asked students to rank a list of professions in terms of their prestige. Prior to ranking the professions, students were told that a sample of their peers had placed 'politician' either at the top of the rankings list or at the bottom of the list. Predictably, the subjects' rankings conformed to their peers' rankings; more surprising was their explanations for why they ranked 'politician' high or low. Subjects who ranked 'politician' high said they understood 'politician' to mean a statesman like Lincoln. Subjects who ranked 'politician' low said they understood 'politician' as corrupt or inept (Ross and Nisbett 2011: 70). Peers changed the subject's construal or perception of 'politician.' While it is impossible to know how individuals would have ranked 'politician' without peer influence, what is clear is that knowing how a peer ranked 'politician' changed the perceptual features of the subject's focus. Knowing that a peer had ranked 'politician' high, the subject's attentional focus keyed in on aspects of a political career that are noble or admirable. Conversely, when told that a peer ranked 'politician' low on the scale of desirable careers, the subject focused on aspects of a political career that are dishonourable or undesirable. The subjects brought to bear a different conception of 'politician' based on how their peers had ranked the careers.

Numerous studies on bystander intervention demonstrate the influence other agents have over an individual's construal. People are less likely to help someone if other people are present, because it seems that *social groups inhibit bystander intervention*. By 1981, one meta-analysis detailed over four-dozen controlled experiments demonstrating this effect (Latané and Nida 1981). In another classic study by Latané and Darley (1968), male undergraduates were sent into a room to fill out a questionnaire. They were either alone, with two other subjects, or with two confederates of the experiment instructed to remain passive and continue working when the planned emergency occurred – smoke came in through the vent and slowly filled the room. If the subjects were by themselves, 75 per cent left the room to report the incident. If they were with two non-responsive confederates, only 10 per cent reported the smoke (Ross and Nisbett 2011: 42). Even more remarkable is what the subjects paid attention to: 'Solitary students in the "smoke study" tended to glance around the room frequently as they worked on their questionnaires, generally noticing the smoke within five seconds. Those in groups typically kept their eyes on their work and did not notice the smoke until it was quite thick – about twenty seconds after the first puff came through the vent' (Ross and Nisbett 2011: 43). Furthermore, while subjects who reported the smoke *recognised* it as a fire emergency, subjects who did not report the smoke did not think that it was due to fire. Rather, they uniformly interpreted the smoke as a 'nondangerous event' (Latané and Darley 1970: 52). The subjects not only construed the situation differently – as an emergency or not – but also allowed others present to affect their attentional focus. These stories and studies show how the presence of other agents changes an individual's construal of a perceptual event by modifying their beliefs to match those of their group, by interpreting data differently (politician as statesman versus politician as corrupt), or by focusing on different aspects of the situation (looking at one's paper instead of paying attention to one's surroundings). These are just a few examples that support SCT.

SCT maintains that 'individuals are driven by a desire for self-evaluation, a motivation to establish that one's opinions are correct and to know precisely what one is capable of doing' (Buunk and Gibbons 2007: 4; see Festinger 1954). Uncertainty about one's opinions, abilities, and emotions can prompt comparison with others (Buunk et al. 1990: 1238). People engage in social comparison in part because other human beings are one of our greatest sources of information about the world (Ross and Nisbett 2011: ch. 3). Furthermore, people 'use comparison to determine whether they are "correct" or "normal"' and to determine their relative standing, especially with regards to things like intelligence, ability, and wealth (Richins 1995: 596).

Social comparison is often a beneficial psychological mechanism. African American soldiers often felt better during their military service during WWII because compared to African American civilians they viewed in Southern towns, they 'had a position of comparative wealth and dignity' (Stouffer et al. 1949: 563; cited in Forsyth 2000: 87). We are often encouraged when we compare ourselves to members of our social group who are coping effectively with their problems – for example, someone diagnosed with cancer looks up to cancer survivors – a process referred to as upward social comparison (Forsyth 2000: 92). However, social comparison also often has negative effects on the individual. This is perhaps most evident in well-documented instances of the previously mentioned bystander effect. In one recent example, a two-year old girl named Wang Yue was run over by two separate vehicles on a narrow road in China. Closed-circuit cameras documented at least 18 passers-by ignoring her over seven minutes. A female garbage scavenger helped get her to the hospital, where she was found brain dead and eventually passed away (Osnos 2011). Cases like this suggest that peer influence changes the individual's attentional focus (we tend to pay attention to whatever the group is attending to) and dampens and diffuses responsible action ('no one else is helping, so I probably don't need to either,' etc.).

Often, we must decide to align our views or behaviours with one of two competing influences, as in the Newcomb study cited above. Consider Milgram's infamous obedience experiments, where the participants were members of the community who were told that this was a study about the effects of punishment on learning. One influence is the learner, who is presented as another volunteer from the community (although he was a confederate of the study, a fact of which the subject was unaware); the second influence is presented as a Yale scientist. The subjects played the role of teacher, asking the learner to recall word pairs. If the learner made a mistake, he received a shock. The electro-shock 'punishment' increased in 15-volt increments up to 450 volts. At several points the learner (who at the beginning noted a minor heart condition) voiced concerns, made agonizing cries of pain and distress, and pleaded for the experiment to stop. If the subject expressed concern or asked to quit, the experimenter gently prodded the subject, telling him to 'please continue' and that 'the experiment requires that you go on' (Milgram 1974: 51). Which influence should the subject follow? *The subjects succumbed to social pressure* (pressure from an authority figure), as two-thirds of subjects went all the way to 450 fictitious volts. (The study was later conducted with women with the same results. See Doris (2002: 39–51) for an overview of the study's many versions.) In response, the philosopher Robert Adams suggests that we should add something like 'moral autonomy' to the traditional list of virtues. He defines moral autonomy as 'a deep groundedness in certain moral ways of viewing people and situations, with a developed ability to interpret situations accordingly and confidently' (Adams 2006: 155). Malcolm Gladwell (2016) describes a similar virtue: 'It takes courage to be good, social courage, to be honest with yourself, to do things the right way.'

It is striking how Kierkegaard anticipates findings like social comparison theory and the bystander effect. But even more striking is his understanding of the need to develop courage to become an authentic self, and the concrete strategies he alludes to that one can employ to develop social courage. After examining Kierkegaard's understanding of the crowd and its negative effects on authentic selfhood, one concrete emotion regulation strategy is explored and developed.

The crowd is untruth!

The role of the crowd in influencing both the concerns and emotions of an agent pervades Kierkegaard's writings, especially the signed authorship. He proclaims, '"the crowd" is untruth!' in 'For the Dedication to "That Single Individual"' (PV, 106/SKS 16, 86), and the problem of social comparison is most clearly seen in Kierkegaard's upbuilding and Christian discourses. This section will focus on those discourses and *Two Ages: A Literary Review*. These texts demonstrate that the Kierkegaardian self is always relational: an agent's self-conception is based either on its relation to the crowd, or on its relation to the Eternal (see Crites 1992). Furthermore, these texts reinforce Kierkegaard's perceptual understanding of emotions. Emotions for Kierkegaard are perceptual construals that stem from and are based on deeper cares or concerns (see Carron 2018). I will focus here on the social construction of the self and the relationship between one's self-perception, concerns, and emotions.

Chapters three and four of *Christian Discourses* – 'The Care of Lowliness' and 'The Care of Abundance' – demonstrate the role the crowd plays in the individual's self-conception. 'Lowliness' and 'abundance' are comparative terms: this is revealed by Kierkegaard's positive invocation of the bird from Matthew, chapter six. Kierkegaard first considers the case of lowliness, which the bird does not have, 'because the bird is what it is, is itself, is satisfied with being itself, is contented with itself. It hardly knows distinctly or realizes clearly what it is, even less that it should know something about the others. But it is contented with itself and with what it is, whatever that happens to be' (CD, 37/SKS 10, 49). The bird only possesses immediate knowledge of itself; it does not have any awareness of its own mental states or the mental states of its conspecifics and therefore has no understanding of how it compares to other birds. In fact, it never questions its relational status to other birds: 'Whether it is a bird just like all other birds, whether it is "just as good a bird" as the others of the same species, indeed, even whether it is just like its mate – of all such things it does not think at all, so impatient it is in its joy of being' (CD, 38/SKS 10, 49). The bird exists in a state of *immediacy* – it does not relate to itself or to others, it simply *is* – and therefore avoids worrying about being less than others.

Due to the bird's lack of awareness, it does not reveal much about the care of lowliness; for that, we must look to human beings. Kierkegaard states, 'In what does the lowliness consist? In the relation to "the others." But on what is its care based? On existing only for the others, on not knowing anything but the relation to the others' (CD, 41/SKS 10, 52). The bird lives in immediacy; humans, however, can both divide themselves up and examine their own thoughts and motivations and understand – at least to some degree – the thoughts and intentions of others. In contemporary psychological terms, humans are capable of both meta-cognition and mindreading (see Bermúdez 2017). Furthermore, humans are intensely social animals. However, Kierkegaard is adamant that when we compare ourselves to other people, only despair will follow: 'What, then, is he (the pagan)? He is the lowly one, nothing else at all – that is, he is what "the others" make of him and what he makes of himself by being only before others. His care is: *being nothing* – indeed, not being at all. Thus, he is a long way from being like the bird, which is what it is. Therefore, in turn, his concern is: *to become something* in the world' (CD, 44/SKS 10, 55). An agent's self-conception – 'what he makes of himself' – stems from his understanding of what the others, the crowd, make of him. If we compare ourselves to others, we will always feel lowly, because there will always be someone better than us: better looking, better off financially, better scholars, better everything. Social comparison creates and fuels the desire for power, money, reputation, or for what Johannes Climacus calls 'world-historical significance.' Here we begin to see why Kierkegaard thinks that comparison is detrimental to authentic selfhood. Comparing ourselves to others that the world deems better than us – upward social comparison – leads to *despair*. 'In this way the despairing lowly one, the pagan, sinks under comparison's enormous weight, which he himself lays upon himself' (CD, 45/SKS 10, 56). The care of lowliness springs from social comparison, and comparison in turn leads to despair over becoming something significant in the world.

Similar results stem from the care of loftiness. The difference is that whereas the care of lowliness comes from upward social comparison – comparison to others that the crowd deems better than an agent – the care of loftiness comes from downward social comparison and the fear that one might become like the 'lowly' ones. Again, the bird is without this care, because 'for the bird there is no one lowlier' (CD, 50/SKS 10, 60). The bird in its immediacy is unaware of the social status of itself or other birds, but the human is not so lucky. 'In loftiness itself there is no danger, and beneath it there is no abyss. Only when beneath it there is a loftiness that is lowlier than it and so on and on – in short, when there is someone beneath it, then there is something beneath it, and then there is also the abyss beneath it' (CD, 50/SKS 10, 60). The care of loftiness only arises when an agent has another person as a point of comparison. Being lofty – having social capital or reputation – means that one is always comparing oneself to those with less prestige, and the greatest fear of the lofty person is that they would be stripped of all their honour and be reduced to nothing in terms of reputation. This continual downward social comparison causes the lofty one to have the care (*bekymring* – concern that gives rise to negative emotions) of loftiness. But the care of loftiness can also take the opposite form: 'A craving to become more and more – for nothing, since the whole thing is indeed nothing; a craving to rise higher and higher in loftiness – that is, to sink lower and lower in the care of the abyss – for what else is the care of worldly loftiness than the care of the abyss' (CD, 57/SKS 10, 67). The lofty person fears losing their loftiness, and therefore craves more honour, more prestige. Loftiness is an insatiable desire, fuelled in part by the fear of losing one's loftiness. And worst of all, just like the care of lowliness, the care of loftiness *dehumanizes*: 'When you speak with him, you do not speak with a human being; in his hankering after loftiness, he has himself become what was coveted: a title regarded as a human being' (CD, 58/SKS 10, 67). The quest for recognition from the crowd results in an inauthentic existence – a loss of the self – as an agent ceases to be a self and instead becomes a replaceable cog in the machine of bourgeois society only recognizable by other inauthentic mob members. When they fall from their lofty position – and they will, because everyone does – the lofty one will be replaced by another honour-seeking pagan, and no one will miss them as they sink into the abyss of the despair of loftiness, the despair over willing to be an inauthentic self.

Both the care of lowliness and the care of loftiness result from an agent letting her self-conception be defined by the crowd. Kierkegaard compares letting oneself be defined by the crowd to an 'optical illusion' (CD, 39/SKS 10, 50). The analogy is apt. Optical illusions confuse us epistemically, causing us to either see an object that isn't there or see the object in a distorted way. Consider a mirage or a stick partially submerged in water. The road *appears* wet; the stick *appears* broken. Furthermore, these distorted perceptions are very difficult to correct through a change in beliefs or by sheer willpower. In fact, one cannot change the appearance of the mirage or the broken stick *unless one looks away*. When the individual focuses on the crowd, then just like in the case of an optical illusion, the crowd causes an agent to have a false or distorted perception, in this case a false *self*-perception. An agent sees herself as lowly or as lofty, but these characteristics only make sense in comparison with the crowd. Looked at in isolation, these characteristics do not exist. Furthermore, an agent concerned with maintaining status experiences a range of emotions: 'Now he ascends loftily, now he descends; he shouts with joy, he sighs, he pants, he groans' (CD, 57/SKS 10, 66). These emotions reveal an agent's self-conception and fundamental concern – loftiness. And if she focuses on the crowd, she will be concerned about her status in relation to the crowd, defining herself in relation to the crowd, and experiencing emotions stemming from those concerns.

The analysis of what happens when an individual succumbs to the temptation of comparison in the *Christian Discourses* is usefully supplemented by Part Two of *Upbuilding Discourses in Various Spirits*, 'To be contented with being a human being.' Again, invoking Matthew 6, Kierkegaard tells the story of a content lily who is befriended by a 'naughty bird.' The bird travelled from far off places, and began telling the lily about far off lands, with exotic birds and beautiful lilies. The bird humiliated the lily by telling the lily that 'in comparison with that kind of glory the lily looked like nothing – indeed, it was so insignificant that it was a question whether the lily actually had a right to be called a lily' (UDVS, 167/SKS 8, 267). The lily had never thought about itself in relation to other lilies before, but the naughty bird generated social comparison. As a result, 'The lily became worried. The more it listened to the bird, the more worried it became; no longer did it sleep calmly at night and wake up joyful in the morning.... Now in self-concern it began to be preoccupied with itself and the condition of its life – all the day long' (UDVS, 167–8/SKS 8, 267). Once the lily began comparing itself to other lilies, it began to care about things it hadn't cared about before – namely, being in a more exotic place and becoming a more beautiful lily – and it developed negative emotions as a result. What happened to the lily? It talked the bird into plucking it out of the ground and transporting it to a more exotic place. On the way, the lily withered and died.

A second story makes a similar point. A wood-dove lived in wonder and let 'each day have its own troubles' until it met two tame doves from the nearby farmer's house. The tame doves told the wood-dove that because of the farmer's storehouse their 'future is secure' (UDVS, 174/SKS 8, 274). The wood-dove became uncertain and insecure about its own life: the wood-dove thought 'it must be very pleasant to *know* that one's living was secured for a long time, whereas it was miserable to live continually in uncertainty so that one never dares to say that one *knows* one is provided for' (UDVS, 175/SKS 8, 274). The wood-dove had no actual needs; it found enough to eat each day. But now the wood-dove 'had acquired an *idea* of need in the future. It had lost its peace of mind – it had acquired *worry about making a living*' (UDVS, 175/SKS 8, 274). The wood-dove's desire for security gets it caught and killed.

Kierkegaard's point in these tales is clear: social comparison and the envy that it causes are detrimental to the development of authentic selfhood. Furthermore, social comparison gives rise to concerns and emotions that the individual otherwise wouldn't have. These emotions are acquired because – like in the Asch study ranking politicians – an agent now brings a different conceptual schema to her self-interpretation and focuses on different aspects of the situation than before. An agent now has a conceptual schema of *security*, looks at herself through that lens, and focuses on the aspects of self and situation that do not meet the new standards of security. Because an agent is now *concerned* with security and focuses on how she compares to secure people, an agent experiences the emotion of worry and covetousness, longing to have the security that others (apparently) possess. An agent now sees herself as insecure and is concerned with and focused on becoming secure. This concern increases worry, resulting in a feedback loop that further intensifies the new attentional focus, leading her to engage in new activities (like building up a storehouse). Soon her basic concerns or beliefs have fundamentally changed – she now believes that she *needs* security and material prosperity to be happy, which she didn't believe before social comparison began. Social comparison changes the self's fundamental concerns, emotions, and actions by contributing to a false, crowd-constructed self-conception.

Social attentional deployment and social courage

When an agent's self-conception arises through comparison with the crowd, a host of negative emotions arise, and an agent will ultimately end up in (conscious or unconscious) despair. How does one avoid inauthenticity and despair? The Christian must change her attentional focus and cultivate social courage. The first sounds simple, but is difficult. Focusing on the crowd creates an optical illusion and a false perception of the self. To avoid this false self-conception, the Christian must stop comparing herself to the crowd, and instead focus on God. 'The lowly Christian, who before God is himself, *exists* as a Christian *before his prototype*' (CD, 42/SKS 10, 53). The Christian believes that Jesus is the prototype to emulate, and therefore all that matters is one's comparison to the prototype. 'He is a lowly human being in the crowd of human beings, and what he is in this way depends on the relationship, but in being himself he is not dependent on the crowd; before God he is himself. From "the others" a person of course actually finds out only what the others are' (CD, 40/SKS 10, 51). Focusing on the crowd results in an agent constructing herself, modelling herself after the crowd. But the Christian stops paying attention to the crowd and focuses on imitating Christ, the prototype. This does not change the Christian's social position in the world: Kierkegaard is clear that in one sense, the lowly Christian is *actually* lowly. She has no social standing or capital to speak of. Her external condition is no different from the lowly pagan's. What is different, however, is how she *sees* herself and the world. She sees herself differently because she does not depend on the crowd, but rather 'stands alone before God.' 'As a Christian, he knows about shutting the door when he is to speak with God – not so that no one will find out that he is speaking with God but so that no one will disturb him. When he speaks with God, he discards all earthly, all sham pomp and glory, but also all the untruth of illusion' (CD, 51/SKS 10, 60–1). Shutting the door to speak to God shuts out the crowd. The person speaking to God behind closed doors has no one else to focus on, no one else to compare to, and therefore can forget the perceptual schema – the optical illusion – of loftiness. Without such a schema, one stops focusing on aspects of the self that would reinforce a comparative self-conception. Changing one's attentional focus is crucial to authentic selfhood, which is not defined in relation to 'the others.'

The Christian who stands alone before God has a different self-conception and focuses on different aspects of the self; he will also have different beliefs. 'He believes that there is a God in heaven who is not a respecter of persons; he believes that the person who ruled over all of humanity, if we will imagine such a one, is not the least bit more important to God than the lowliest – yes, than the sparrow that falls to the ground' (CD, 51/SKS 10, 61). Before God, the Christian knows that God loves all creation, the sparrow as much as the Emperor. And if the Christian really believes in this radical equality before God, then the cares of lowliness and loftiness cannot arise, because before God everyone is on the same level. Without another person to compare oneself to, the Christian realizes that she is both truly lowly (because before God, all creation pales in comparison), yet truly lofty (because Jesus is the human prototype and the Christian has kinship with God). The Christian's self-conception before God is as a creature who is loved – but is loved just the same as all other creatures.

The Christian who stands before God brings a different perceptual schema which gives rise to a different self-conception. Instead of a socially constructed sense of self, the Christian's sense of self is based on her relationship to an idea, the Eternal, the Prototype. This ideally constructed self-conception arises due to an agent's attentional focus: 'He believes (instead of paying attention to all the talk about the many who cannot live without him) that it is he who, in order to live, is in need at all times, indeed, every minute, of this God, without whose will certainly no sparrow comes into existence or exists either' (CD, 51/SKS 10, 61). Merold Westphal (2007: 28) notes that becoming a Christian 'is a matter of attention and arises from what the Christian "bears in mind" and remembers.' But what an agent 'bears in mind' about herself will be largely determined by the object of social comparison. If God is the point of comparison, then an agent will have an accurate yet hopeful construal of itself. If the crowd is the point of comparison, then an agent will have an inaccurate self-conception – seeing oneself as lowlier or loftier than one is – and this false conception will result in negative emotions. Authentic selfhood is only found by focusing on the right object: 'He is a lowly human being in the crowd of human beings, and what he is in this way depends on the relationship, but in being himself he is not dependent on the crowd: before God he is himself' (CD, 40/SKS 10, 51). When an agent focuses on the crowd, she only sees her relational status, her lowliness or loftiness.

Focusing on God allows one to no longer be defined by the crowd. And this change in focus changes both beliefs and emotions. 'But the lowly Christian does not fall into the snare of this optical illusion. He sees with the eyes of faith: with the speed of faith that seeks God, he is at the beginning, is himself before God, is contented with being himself' (CD, 40/SKS 10, 50). If an agent pays 'attention to all the talk about the many who cannot live without' her, then an agent will come to believe that she is lofty and important and will worry about maintaining her social status. But focusing on the Eternal makes one realize one's dependence. This change in attentional focus frees one from the snare of the social 'optical illusion' and gives rise to concern-based emotions such as faith and contentment. A major part of what it means to 'see with the eyes of faith' is to focus on God and how God sees the self instead of focusing on the crowd. Thus, social attentional deployment – focusing one's attention on the proper object of social comparison – is essential for the development of authentic selfhood.

Kierkegaard recognizes that changing one's attentional focus from the crowd to the Eternal is incredibly difficult, especially for the 'lofty' one. 'But then has it not been more difficult for the eminent person to become a Christian (we are, after all, speaking about the eminent Christian) than for the lowly person? To this question Holy Scripture answers yes' (CD, 54/SKS 10, 63). The prototype was lowly, a poor Jewish carpenter with no place to lay his head. So, the route from worldly lowliness to standing alone before God is more direct than the path from loftiness. But in either case, authenticity (seeing the self the way God does and being content with that self-conception) requires developing social courage, because the individual is constantly surrounded by the piercing voice of the crowd. Kierkegaard makes the need for courage clearest in texts such as *An Occasional Discourse*, and 'That Single Individual.' The latter contrasts the contemporary view concerning how truth is found with the Christian view: 'There is a view of life that holds that truth is where the crowd is, that truth itself needs to have the crowd on its side' (PV, 106/SKS 16, 86). This is the view of the present age. The Christian view – like the age of revolution – claims, '"Only one reaches the goal," not by way of comparison, since in a comparison "the others" are of course included' (PV, 106/SKS 16, 86). Furthermore, it's easy to be 'courageous' in a crowd, since acting as a member of 'a crowd either makes for impenitence and irresponsibility altogether, or for the single individual it at least weakens responsibility by reducing the responsibility to a fraction' (PV, 107/SKS 16, 87–8). Just like in instances of bystander non-intervention, the individual does not act responsibly as a member of the crowd. She is cowardly and impenitent. After all, what does she have to be remorseful of? No one acted, no one helped, therefore no one is responsible for not helping. *An Occasional Discourse* proclaims, 'the solitary voice of the conscience ... is so easily outvoted – by the majority' (UDVS, 129/SKS 8, 228). If the individual did at any moment think that she should act, that thought is quickly silenced by the inaction of the herd.

The present age – unlike the age of revolution – is the age of social comparison: '"Just like the others." This phrase expresses the two characteristic marks of being man in general: (1) sociality, the animal-creature which is linked to the herd: just like the others, (2) envy, which, however, animals do not have' (JP 3, 340/SKS 26, 257). Members of the present age do not act, they *reflect*, and when they do act, they act in whatever way the herd acts. They want what others have, and the herd only cares about externalities, that is, external goods such as honour and money (Tilley 2014: 949). Thus, the result of our sociality – at least in the present age – is envy, which generates *apparent* equality. Envy *levels*: 'Envy in the process of *establishing* itself takes the form of *leveling*, and whereas a passionate age *accelerates, raises up and overthrows, elevates and debases*, a reflective apathetic age does the opposite, it *stifles and impedes, it levels*' (TA, 84/SKS 8, 80). In the present age the crowd is the standard and cowardly conformity driven by envy is the natural activity.

One will never become an authentic self as a member of the crowd because one's identity will always be defined in relation to the others. Authentic selfhood requires *courage*: 'Courage is one person holding out alone, as a single individual, against the opposition of the numerical ... courage increases in proportion to the number, and the longer the opposition is endured the more inward the courage becomes' (JP 3, 341/SKS 26, 258). The individual with courage will not let herself be defined by the crowd; rather, she will be passionately committed to an 'idea,' that is, a goal or life ideal that does not follow the whims of the crowd (Roberts 1998: 178). In other words, the individual will display a 'manifestation of energy that unquestionably is a definite something and does not deceptively change under the influence of conjectural criticism concerning what the age really wants' (TA, 66/SKS 8, 64). And as the individual continually follows her passion and defies the crowd, she will grow in inwardness. As Robert C. Roberts (1998: 178) notes, inwardness (*inderlighed*) often implies a contrast 'with "externalities" such as social position, reputation, the "results" of one's actions, and publicly observable natural phenomena.' An authentic individual has passion, character, and inwardness: she is enthusiastically committed to an ethical project – becoming an authentic self – and she does not gauge her success in the same way as the crowd. In fact, the individual who courageously opposes the crowd has a very different measure of success:

> ridicule will even be of advantage to you also by convincing you even more that you are on the right path. Therefore, the opinion of the crowd does have its significance; a person must not haughtily remain ignorant of it – no, he should become aware of it. Then if he just takes care to do the opposite, he usually will hit it right; or if he originally does the opposite and then is so lucky as to have the opinion of the crowd manifest itself as contrary, then he can be fairly sure that the right position has been taken.
> *(UDVS, 136/SKS 8, 235)*

The person who is enthusiastically committed to realizing her ideals and refuses to succumb to the whims of the crowd will suffer ridicule, but this ridicule is a sign of success. Courageously opposing the crowd while focusing on the Eternal and remaining committed to one's ideals deepens inwardness, and as the individual develops inwardness the envious desire for externalities dissipates.

Conclusion

Several connections between Kierkegaard's social psychology and SCT emerge from this analysis. First, Kierkegaard agrees that engaging in social comparison changes what the agent focuses on and how the agent construes the object. The wood-dove was not thinking about future security or building a storehouse until other birds made it aware of those things. The lily never thought it looked inferior to other lilies until the naughty bird came along. Social comparison changed what the wood-dove focused on, and how the lily saw itself. The lily now wished to become 'a gorgeous lily, or even the most gorgeous' (UDVS, 168/SKS 8, 267). Envy and worry soon followed. This illuminates a second connection to SCT. Upward social comparison (like the care of lowliness) produces 'negative affect and lower self-evaluations by reminding one that one is inferior' (Buunk et al. 1990: 1239). Kierkegaard agrees that comparison with other people – especially people one see as better than one's self – adversely alters one's self-conception and generates negative emotions. The poor lily now feels 'inferior' and envious. Finally, social comparison encourages inaction and irresponsibility. The bystander effect shows that a crowd is *less* likely to help in an emergency than a lone individual. Kierkegaard was all too aware of this phenomenon: the present age is the age of anticipation, indecision, and conformity. The crowd *reflects*; only the individual *acts*. And this is why the crowd is untruth. Not because Kierkegaard is an individualist, but because he seeks to release the individual from the bonds of comparison and give her the courage to become an authentic self. Achieving authenticity takes courage, the courage to stop focusing on the crowd and look instead to the Eternal as the only object of comparison.

Related topics

'Becoming a subject: Kierkegaard's theological art of existence,' Peder Jothen; 'Beyond worry? On learning humility from the lilies and the birds,' John Lippit; 'Agency, identity, and alienation in *The Sickness unto Death*,' Justin F. White.

References

Adams, R. M. (2006) *A theory of virtue: Excellence in being for the good*, Oxford: Oxford University Press.
Avanessian, A. and Wennerscheid, S. (eds) (2014) *Kierkegaard and political theory: Religion, aesthetics, politics and the intervention of the single individual*, Copenhagen: Museum Tusculanum Press.
Bermúdez, J. L. (2017) 'Can nonlinguistic animals think about thinking?' in K. Andrews and J. Beck (eds), *The Routledge Handbook of Philosophy of Animal Minds*, London: Routledge.
Buunk, A. P. and Gibbons, F. X. (2007) 'Social comparison: The end of a theory and the emergence of a field,' *Organizational Behavior and Human Decision Processes*, 102: 3–21.
Buunk, B. P. et al. (1990) 'The affective consequences of social comparison: Either direction has its ups and downs,' *Journal of Personality and Social Psychology*, 59, no. 6: 1238–49.
Carron, P. (2018) 'Turn your gaze upward! Emotions, concerns, and regulatory strategies in Kierkegaard's "Christian Discourses",' *International Journal for Philosophy of Religion*, 84, no. 3: 323–43.
Crites, S. (1992) '"The Sickness unto Death": A social interpretation,' in G. B. Connell and C. S. Evans (eds), *Foundations of Kierkegaard's Vision of Community: Religion, Ethics, and Politics in Kierkegaard*, Atlantic Highlands, NJ: Humanities Press International.
Doris, J. (2002) *Lack of character: Personality and moral behavior*, Cambridge: Cambridge University Press.
Festinger, L. (1954) *A theory of social comparison processes*, Indianapolis, IN: Bobbs-Merrill.

Forsyth, D. R. (2000) 'Social comparison and influence in groups,' in J. Suls and L. Wheeler (eds), *Handbook of Social Comparison: Theory and Research*, New York: Plenum.

Gladwell, M. (2016) *This American Life*, Podcast audio, June 24. Retrieved from <http://www.thisamericanlife.org/radio-archives/episode/590/transcript>

Gottlieb, R. S. (1979) 'Kierkegaard's ethical individualism,' *The Monist*, 62, no. 3: 351–67.

Latané, B. and Darley, J. M. (1970) *The unresponsive bystander: Why doesn't he help?* New York: Appleton-Century Crofts.

Latané, B. and Darley, J. M. (1968) 'Group inhibition of bystander intervention in emergencies,' *Journal of Personality and Social Psychology*, 10, no. 3: 215–21.

Latané, B. and Nida, S. (1981) 'Ten years of research on group size and helping,' *Psychological Bulletin*, 89, no. 2: 308–24.

Milgram, S. (1974) *Obedience to authority: An experimental view*, New York: Harper & Row.

Osnos, E. (2011) 'China's bystander effect,' *The New Yorker*, October 18. Retrieved from <https://www.newyorker.com/news/evan-osnos/chinas-bystander-effect>

Richins, M. L. (1995) 'Social comparison, advertising, and consumer discontent,' *American Behavioral Scientist American Behavioral Scientist*, 38, no. 4: 593–07.

Risen, J. (1993) 'A shadow of doubt: Kathi Hudson gave up her job to spy on Operation Rescue: But then she was "born again," sending shock waves through the abortion-rights movement,' *Los Angeles Times*, March 17. Retrieved from <http://articles.latimes.com/1993-03-17/news/vw-11996_1_operation-rescue>

Roberts, R. C. (1998) 'Existence, emotion, and virtue: Classical themes in Kierkegaard,' in A. Hannay and G. D. Marino (eds), *The Cambridge Companion to Kierkegaard*, Cambridge: Cambridge University Press.

Ross, L. and Nisbett, R. E. (2011) *The person and the situation: Perspectives of social psychology*, London: Pinter & Martin.

Stouffer, S. A. et al. (1949) *The American soldier: Adjustment during army life*, vol. 1, Princeton, NJ: Princeton University Press.

Tilley, J. M. (2014) 'Kierkegaard's social theory,' *The Heythrop Journal*, 55, no. 5: 944–59.

Westphal, M. (2007) 'Paganism in Christendom: On Kierkegaard's critique of religion,' in R. L. Perkins (ed), *International Kierkegaard Commentary*, vol. 17 (*Christian Discourses and the Crisis and a Crisis in the Life of an Actress*), Macon, GA: Mercer University Press.

Further reading

Furtak, R. A. (2005) *Wisdom in love: Kierkegaard and the ancient quest for emotional integrity*, Notre Dame, IN: University of Notre Dame Press.

This book compares Kierkegaard's view of emotions with the Stoic view and argues that both Kierkegaard and the Stoics understand that emotions are 'perceptions of significance,' perceptions informed or coloured by beliefs and concerns. However, Furtak contends that while the Stoics view emotions as always negative, Kierkegaard thinks that emotions – especially faith and love – are essential for a fulfilling life.

Krishek, S. and Furtak, R. A. (2012) 'A cure for worry? Kierkegaardian faith and the insecurity of human existence,' *International Journal for Philosophy of Religion*, 72, no. 3: 157–75.

This article argues that Kierkegaard offers a way of dealing with our existential insecurity and overcoming the negative emotion of worry by developing the positive emotion-virtue of Christian faith. Specific suggestions for cultivating faith are gleaned from Kierkegaard's edifying discourses.

Lillegard, N. (2002) 'Passion and reason: Aristotelian strategies in Kierkegaard's ethics,' *Journal of Religious Ethics*, 30, no. 2: 251–73.

This article argues that Aristotle and Kierkegaard affirm the integration of passion/emotion and reason. Furthermore, Lillegard argues that Kierkegaardian passions focus an agent's attention and make certain features of situations salient to an agent.

INDEX

Note: Italicized page numbers indicate a figure on the corresponding page. Page numbers in bold indicate a table on the corresponding page.

Abraham 105–6, 376–9, 388
absent-minded *(distraite)* 273
absolute paradox 141, 365, 370, 416–17
abstractness of human existence 194
acosmic thought 145
acquisition of knowledge 68
active psychology 46
active receptivity 93
actualization 123, 126
Adler, Adolf P. 41, 255
adoxalism 243–6, 243–8
aesthetes *see* ethical life of aesthetes
aesthetics: conversion experience 387–8; of existence 181–2; 'hypernatural' aesthetic world of repetition 181; intellectual thinking 242; of Kant 157; of Kierkegaard 7–8
affective state of self-reflection 158
agential problem 278
Ages of the World (Schelling) 429
agony of the soul 282
alienation 306–8, 311–13
Alznauer, Mark 103–4
ambiguity 25, 294
Améry, Jean 116–17
anatomy studies 319
Andersen, Hans Christian 1, 21
animality 158
Anna Karenina (Tolstoy) 169
anonymous consciousness 269–71, 273
anthropology and selfhood: authentic despair 323–5; historical introduction 10–11, 319–20; human nature as synthesis **321**, 321–7, *322*; inauthentic despair and self-deception 322–3; methodology 320–1; overcoming despair 325–6; summary of 327–8; theological and philosophical 326–7
anti-abortion groups 458
Anti-Climacus (pseudonym of Kierkegaard): anthropology 10–11; despair and 309, 333–8; dialectical self 438; epistemology 11; ethical-religious existence and 162; existential import of 332; faith and Christianity 371–2; fundamental change 331–2; human being, defined 392–3; human existence and 113, 204; imagination and 173–4; paradox of Christianity 245, 247, 252; psychical-physical synthesis 342, 343–4; self-hood and 345; sin and 172, 369–71; true subjectivity 206–9
anti-Hegelians 400
antipathetic sympathy 43
anti-systematizer 424–8
anxiety 42, 43, 114–16, 314
apprehension/concern 234
Aquinas, Thomas 343, 365
Arendt, Hannah 117
arguments against arguments 228–9
argumentum spiritus sancti (proof of the holy spirit) 228, 233
Aristotle 29, 343, 379
Armed Neutrality (Kierkegaard) 197
art *see* 'cognitivist' picture of the arts; theological art of existence
aspirational agency 309, 314
atonement: Christ's receptivity to humans 219–21; humans receptivity to Christ 221–4; *imitatio Christi* 215–18; introduction to 215–16; love and 336; reimagining of 218–19; summary 224
At the Mind's Limits (Améry) 117

Index

Augustine of Hippo 447–52
Augustinian liberalism 447, 450–3
Austin, J.L. 55
authentic despair 323–5
authenticity: conscience and 281–3; defined 286–9; faking it 289–90; introduction to 281; self-deception 143, 283–6, 290
authoritative authorship 41
autonomous self-determination 157

Bacon, Francis 184–5
Barrett, Lee C. 218
Beabout, Gregory 93, 149
becoming 30, 308, 461
Being 30, 428
Being and Time (Heidegger) 111, 113, 118, 281
being a self 124–7, 311
being-between 43, 272
being-in-the-world 48, 113, 118, 247, 314
Berthod-Bond, Daniel 111
Bible (Christian) 205
Binswanger, Ludwig 40, 48–9
Bodington, James 354
Bommarito, Nicolas 96
Book on Adler, The (Kierkegaard) 286
boredom and identity 351–2
'brave officer' paradox 346
Bretschneider, Karl 18
bullet biting 241–2
bystander intervention 458

Caesar 104
Camp. Elisabeth 169
Carr, Karen 399
Cavell, Stanley 402
certainty, allure of 381–3
Christ *see* Jesus Christ
Christendom attack, as work of love 452–4
Christian anthropology 326–7
Christian/Christianity: adoxalism 243–8; analysis of love 23; critique of 3; denunciation of 370; despair and 320–1; dialectics and 34–6; divine revelation in 320; *Efterfølgelse* and 192; epistemology of Kierkegaard 11–12; ethics 326; existence of 30; genuineness of 114–15; God, arguments against existence 25–6; human existence and 34; ideal picture of a Christian 196–7; life-view and 21–2; logic and language 398–9; Lutheranism 254; nature and 55–6, 261–3; paganism and dialectics 31–4; paradoxical account of existence 199–200; paradox of 239–52; Protestantism 140, 208, 255; religious epistemology 365–74; situated in reflection 18; skills model of faith 246–8; suffering in 453; violent nature of atonement in 9; virtues of 116, 117; wisdom of ascetic Christianity 452; *see also* conversion experience; Jesus Christ

Christian consciousness 260–1
Christian Discourses (Kierkegaard) 71, 261, 460–2
Christocentrism 17
Church of Denmark 254
civil rights protests 119
classical bourgeoisie liberalism 441
Clausen, H.N. 19
Climacus, Johannes (pseudonym of Kierkegaard): consciousness 271–4, 277; conversion experience 390, 398; dialectal self 440–1; dialectical method 28–30; emotional tension over philosophical void 229; ethical reflection 68–71, 355; ethics of home and hope 113; existential uncertainty 376; paganism and 31–4, 256; paradox of Christianity 239–40, 242–5, 248–52; passion 172; poetics of self-incrimination 409–19; religious experience 235; sin and offense 366–9; will to believe 232–3; world-historical significance 461
closed self 331–8
'cognitivist' picture of the arts: biblical account 170; emotion 173; human nature and 172–4; imagination 173–4; indirect communication 169; introduction to 166; Kierkegaard's comments about 167–9; as mirror of the self 169–71; in painting 170–1; passion 172–3; pedagogical superiority of art 174; philosophical objections 166–7; science and philosophy 171–2
Coleridge, Samuel Taylor 150–1
coming-into-being 42, 48, 216
coming-into-existence 41–2, 45, 372, 410
communicating life-views 20–2
communitarian politics 438
competitive ego 96
Conant, James 55, 402
Concept of Anxiety, The (Kierkegaard): anti-systematizer 427; anxiety as fate 314; continuity and faith in 300–1; dishonesty, as self-deception 284–5; experimenting psychology 49; imagination 293; living nature 428–9; nature and supernature 178; non-Christian ethics 326; self-consciousness 270; tragic sublime 160
Concept of Irony, The (Kierkegaard) 2, 22, 39, 391–4
Concluding Unscientific Postscript to 'Philosophical Fragments' (Kierkegaard): absolute paradox 141; authenticity 112; communicating life views 20; consciousness and 271; conversion experience 387, 396–7; dialectical self 437–8; the ethical 355; existential uncertainty 376; faith and 229; indirect communication 54; introduction to 2; knowledge and disengagement 68–71; logic and language 399–402; self-deception 285
Conflict of the Faculties (Kant) 159
Connell, George B. 435
conscience and authenticity 281–3
conscious despair 323–5

consciousness *(bevidsthed)*: anonymous consciousness 269–71, 273; Christian consciousness 260–1; ego and anonymity 269–71; egological consciousness 273; God-consciousness 193; interest and 43–4; introduction to 269; I-thoughts 273–4, 276; nature of 9–10, 43; of past actions 346; progression 335; self-consciousness 5, 41, 43, 45, 270, 324, 346; self-thinking 277–8; structure of 271–3; subjective reflection 274–7; teleological structure of 296; unity of 302
Constantius, Constantin (pseudonym of Kierkegaard) 159
continuity and faith 300–1
conversion experience: introduction to 386–7; irony and 391–4; leap and 390–4
conviction, logic of *see* logic of conviction
Corsair, The 2
Critique of Political Economy (Marx) 430–1
Critique of Pure Reason (Kant) 44, 157–9, 426
crowd as untruth 460–3
Crown Imperials 96
Cruysberghs, Paul 275

Dancy, Jonathan 78–87
Danish Golden Age 1–3
Danish Hegelians 400, 423, 427, 440
Danish intellectual society 28
Daseinsanalyse (Binswanger) 48–9
Davenport, John 314, 343–4, 347, 435
decisive heterogeneity 34
De doctrina christiana (Augustine of Hippo) 447–8
defiant/demonic despair 324–5, 327
Deleuze, Gilles: faith as performance 181–2; introduction to 177–8; nature and supernature 178–81
Denial of Saint Peter, The (Caravaggio) 170–1, 174
denunciation of Christianity 370
De Omnibus Dubitandum Est (Kierkegaard) 272, 274
de silentio, Johannes (pseudonym of Kierkegaard) 115, 141, 152
desires and possibility of alienation 306–8
despair: authentic despair 323–5; Christianity and 320–1; conscious despair 323–5; defiant/demonic despair 324–5, 327; divine ladder of 334–7; externalities and 308–9; finitude/infinitude 309–10; human ladder of 333–4; human nature as synthesis for **321**, 321–7, *322*; inauthentic despair and self-deception 322–3; necessity/possibility 310–11; non-conscious despair 322–3; overcoming 325–6; phenomenological description of 320; of possibility 322; selfhood and 308–11, 314, 320, 337; sin, as form of 370
desperate longing 229–30
determinate content in Christ's words 59
Dewey, Bradley Rau 192–3

dialectal self: anchor and compass 436–8; introduction to 435–6; political orientations of 438–43; summary 443–4
dialectical method: Christianity and 34–6; general pattern of 28–30; introduction to 28; paganism 31–4
'Dialectic of Ethical and Ethical-Religious Communication, The' (Kierkegaard) 68, 73, 75
dichotomies of reflection 271–2
difficulty of existential uncertainty 379–81
direct cognitive relation between human/God 57–8
disambiguation 243–6
Discourses at the Communion on Fridays (Kierkegaard) 206
disengagement and ethical reflection 68–72
dishonesty, as self-deception 284–5
divine assistance 209, 326
divine ladder of despair 334–7
divine love 205, 212, 217–18, 336
divine revelation 18, 209, 263, 320, 326, 405
divinity 56–61, 231, 246, 371, 444
Dooley, Mark 435
double-mindedness 287, 322, 323, 325–6
double-reflection 72–4
Duckles, Ian 355
Dupré, Louis 235, 236

Efterfølgelse, defined 191–2
egalitarianism 440–1, 444
ego and consciousness 269–71
egological consciousness 273
Either/Or (Kierkegaard): aesthetic existence 275; belief and illusion 299–300; conversion experience 387, 398; critique of 295–8; dialectical self 436–7; ethical life of aesthetes 136–44; introduction to 2, 7, 24; logic and language 399–402; nihilism and 159; sublime and 159–61
Elements of the Philosophy of Right (Hegel) 101
Elrod, John 314
Emmanuel, Steven 53–4
emotional-spiritual expression 130
emotion of passion 173
empirical psychology 319
empirico-transcendental doublet 5, 48
epistemological particularism 79–82
epistemology of Kierkegaard 11–12
Essay Concerning Human Understanding (Locke) 345
essential unknowability of God 368–9
ethical life of aesthetes: faith and 140–1; introduction to 135–6; letters to 'A' 136–8; meaning 141–4; religious approaches to life 138–40
ethical problem 278
ethical reflection as evasion: existential ethics 72–4; introduction to 67–8; knowledge and

Index

disengagement 68–72; subjective selfhood 355; summary of 74–6
ethico-religious thinking 111, 242
ethics: Christian *vs.* non-Christian 326; existential ethics 72–4, 75; of Kierkegaard 5–7, 159, 257; nature and 259–61; science *vs.* 319–20; social ethics 448–50; theological ethicists 450
ethics of home and hope: authenticity of 112–15; consequence for 116–17; Heidegger's impact on 111–12; introduction to 110–11; Kierkegaard *vs.* Heidegger 117–19
Ethics Without Principles (Dancy) 82
ethnography 319
ethos 19, 118, 138, 140
eudaimonia 323
Europe '51 (Rossellini) 184
evangelical Lutheran 452
Evans, C. Stephen 53, 101–2, 240, 370, 398
Evans, Stephen C. 435
exemplarism 84–6
existence *see* human existence; theological art of existence
existence-communication *(Existents-Meddelelse)* 247
existential anthropology 39–44
existential crises 391
existential ethics 72–4, 75
existential method: communicating life-views 20–2; context of 18–19; freedom pedagogy 24–6; introduction to 17; pathos dimensions 22–4, 25; plurality of life-view 19–20
existential mimesis: comparison 199–200; contemporary debate over 194–5; genuine human existence and 197–200; ideal picture of a Christian 196–7; identifying philosophical meanings 191–2; indirect and intention-driven 198–9; introduction to 191; Kierkegaard's library on 193–4; Kierkegaard's writings on 192–3; plurality of 195; role of the lily and the bird in 195–6; scholarly approach to 192–5; summary of 200–1
existential psychotherapy 47–9
existential questions and knowledge 404–6
existential uncertainty: Abraham and 376–9; certainty, allure of 381–3; introduction to 376; knowledge and difficulty 379–81
existing subjective individual 40
experimenting psychology: eighteenth century Danish psychology 45–7; existential anthropology 39–44; existential psychotherapy and fundamental ontology 47–9; introduction to 39
externalities and despair 308–9

facticity 306–9, 312–15, 321–2, 325, 327, 401, 437
failure to love 127–9
faith: Christianity and 371–2; continuity and 300–1; divine revelation and 320; ethical life of aesthetes 140–1; formula for 370; God and 140–1; hope and 118; imagination and 296; interpreted as openness 337–8; isolation of 106; Jesus Christ as object of 371; knowledge and 35, 371; as openness 337–8; paradox of Christianity 248–50; as performance 181–2; skills model of 246–8
Faith and Knowledge (Hegel) 45
fake it till you make it motto 289–90
false door *(Blinddør)* 333
Fatherland, The 3
Fear and Trembling (Kierkegaard) 60, 100–7, 123, 128–30, 221–3, 228, 388, 436
feeling *(Gefühl)* 45
Ferreira, M. Jamie 192, 193
Fichte, Johann Gottlieb 45
fideism 398, 406
finitude and despair 309–10
First Love concept 298–300
Fischer, John Martin 353
For Self-Examination (Kierkegaard) 24, 71, 170, 277
forward movement *(Fremskridt)* of self 337
Foucault, Michel 5, 48
Frankfurt, Harry 306
free-acting nature of man 319
freedom 24–6, 321–3
Freiheitsschrift (Schelling) 428
French revolution 80
fundamental change 331–2
fundamentalism 398
fundamental ontology 47–9
Furtak, Rick 173

Garff, Joakim 54, 135, 302
Genghis Kahn 103, 104
German Idealists 41, 425, 428
German '*Wissenschaft*' 68
Gladwell, Malcolm 460
Glenn, John D., Jr. 344, 347
God: arguments against existence 25–6; being present in 146; conception of 335; despair and selfhood 320, 337; direct cognitive relation between human and 57–8; essential unknowability of 368–9; existence as system for 439; faith and 140–1; indirect communication and 57–8, 61–2; natural science 256–61; nature and 254–5, 261–3; omnipotence of 148–9; praying to 147–9; relation to 347–8; sin and offense 365–74; as spirit 234; transcendent God 58, 151–2; unconditional obedience to 93; unknowability of 368–9
God-consciousness 193
God-relationship 287
God's will (religiosity) 123, 149
Golden Age Denmark 5
'Gospel of Suffering, The' discourse 95, 199
Gouwens, David 296

471

Grand Inquisitor (Dostoevsky) 436
Gregory, Eric 446, 450–1, 454
Grice, Paul 55
Grundtvig, N.F.S. 1, 3
Guignon, Charles 116
Gyllembourg, Thomasine 2, 20–1, 283

Halliwell, Stephen 191
Hannay, Alastair 40, 309
happiness as eudaimonia 323
harmony 19, 126, 146–7, 150, 290
Harries, Karsten 111
Haufniensis, Vigilius (pseudonym of Kierkegaard) 114, 160, 270, 300–2
Hegel, G.F.W.: Augustinian liberalism 453; communitarian politics 438; Danish Hegelians 400, 423, 427, 440; experimenting psychology 45; indirect communication 55–9; introduction to 1, 29–30; Local Norm Interpreters 100–7; paradox of Christianity 249–50; *Sittlichkeit* theory 449–50; world historical individuals 102–4
Hegelian Idealism 208, 210
Hegel's Ethical Thought (Wood) 103
Heiberg, Johann Ludvig 1, 18, 178
Heidegger, Martin 6, 110–19
Heraclitus 427
Høffding, Harald 46–7
holism 82–3, 84, 441, 442
Holy Spirit 228, 233, 235, 287–8, 337
honest earnestness 288–9
Hook, Sidney 430
hope against hope 327
'How Glorious It Is to Be a Human Being' discourse 92
'how *vs.* what' idea 20
human agency 12, 308–10, 312, 314, 322, 387, 393–4
human existence: abstraction from concrete existence 28; abstractness of 194; aesthetics of 181–2; anxiety and 114–16; coming-into-existence 41–2, 45, 372, 410; ethical-religious existence 162; existence-communication 247; existential mimesis 197–200; inauthentic existence 114; non-concreteness of 194; paradox of 30, 34; spirit and 207; as system for God 439; truth and 34–5; *see also* theological art of existence
human ladder of despair 333–4
human love 123–4
human nature 123–4, 172–4, **321**, 321–7, *322*
humans receptivity to Christ 221–4
human willpower 326
Hume, David 377
humility 93, 94–7; *see also* worry and humility
humour, as indirect communication 53–4
Huntington, Patricia 111

'hypernatural' aesthetic world of repetition 181
hypothesis of work 31

I-thoughts 273–4, 276
ice skater narrative 78, 83, 86
ideal identity 324
idealism (Kantian) 295
ideality 193, 271–2
identity: boredom and 351–2; ideal identity 324; particular identity 125; practical identities 311–13
image-making 158
imagination: belief and illusion 299–300; continuity and faith 300–1; critique of 295–8; infinitude and 309; introduction to 293; in Merleau-Ponty's phenomenology 293–5, 297–8; of passion 173–4; summary of 301–2
imago Dei 194
imitatio Christi 191, 192–5, 198, 203, 215–18
immortality: boredom and identity 351–2; introduction to 351; knowledge and 406; meaning beyond rotation 354–5; repetition, importance of 352–4; risk and value 357–8; summary of 358; as thought experiment 356–7
inactive psychology 46
inauthentic despair and self-deception 322–3
inauthentic existence 114
incognito as a true form 413
indirect communication: of artistic method 169; in context 55–9; defined 52–3; God and history 57–8, 61–2; introduction to 52; methodological approaches 53–5; Socrates and 60–1
indirect existential mimesis 198–9
infinitization 207
infinitude and despair 309–10
inner confirmation *(bekræftelse)* 234
inner experience 47
instar omnium (for all capacities) 42
intentional arc 293
intention-driven existential mimesis 198–9
interest *(interesse)* 43–4
invention and poetics of self-incrimination 412–13
inwardness *(inderlighed)* 270
irony 53–4, 391–4
irrationalism 398, 402
Israelites 336
Ivanhoe, Philip 399

James, William 231–2
Jesus Christ: benefits of medicines 257; existential understanding of 8; hope and 117; humanity of 58–9; human receptivity to 221–4; humility discourse 95; ideality of Christ 193, 196–7; *imitatio Christi* 191, 192–5, 198, 203, 215–18; lily and bird discourses 89, 90–4; as object of faith 371; receptivity to humans 219–21;

reimagining of atonement 218–19; self's relation to 336; true subjectivity and Christ 205–6; *see also* Christian/Christianity
Johannes Climacus, or De omnibus dubitandum est (Kierkegaard) 22, 43
John of the Cross 347–8
Joyce, James 183
joy discourse 93–4
Judge for Yourself! (Kierkegaard) 282

Kant, Immanuel: dialectical self 436; existential anthropology 39–40, 44; idealism 295; introduction to 7, 29; living nature 428–9; reflection philosophy 45; sublime transfigurations 157–9; transcendental psychology 44–5
Kaplan, Eric 249
Kierkegaard, Michael Pedersen 1
Kierkegaard, Peter Christian 1, 3
Kierkegaard and the Political (Assiter, Tonon) 435
Kierkegaard and the Quest for Unambiguous Life (Pattison) 135
Kierkegaard in Golden Age Denmark (Kirmmse) 435
Kierkegaard's Critique of Reason and Society (Westphal) 429, 439
King, Martin Luther, Jr. 119
Kirmmse, Bruce 435
Klossowski, Pierre 180
knowledge: acquisition of 68; answerable moral/ existential questions 404–6; disengagement and 68–72; ethical reflection and 68–72; existential questions and 404–6; existential uncertainty 379–81; faith and 35, 371; immortality and 406; morality and 404–6; objective knowledge 22, 112, 379, 398–9, 401–2, 406; Platonic method of acquiring 142; practical knowledge 398; self-knowledge 40, 73–4, 347
'know thyself' (Socrates) 205
Kolodny, Niko 357–8
Korsgaard, Christine 306
Kosch, Michelle 428
Kripke's theory of direct reference 84
Kroman, Kristian 46, 47
Kupfer, Joseph 94, 95

language *see* logic and language
leap and conversion experience 390–4
Lectures on the Philosophy of World History (Hegel) 102
liberalism 441, 447
Lichtenberg, George 169
life-development 41
life-views 19–22, 41
lily and bird discourses 89, 90–4
The Lily in the Field and the Bird of the Air (Kierkegaard) 145–6, 195–6
Lippitt, John 53, 110

literary genre selection 23
living nature 428–31
Local Norm Interpreters (LNI): implications of 104–7; introduction to 100–2; overview of 101–2; summary of 107; world historical individuals 102–4
Locke, John 342–3, 345–6
loftiness 24, 461–4
logic and language: ambiguity of 397–9; confusion of the spheres 399–402; introduction to 397; realist approach 402–4
logic of conviction: arguments against arguments 228–9; desperate longing 229–30; introduction to 227–8; reason and 230–2; received confirmation 233–4; religious experience 235–6; strength or weakness 236; will to believe 232–3
Logic of Sense, The (Deleuze) 181–2
Løgstrup, K.E. 273
love: Christendom attack as work of love 452–4; divine love 205, 212, 217–18, 336; introduction to 446–7; social ethics and 448–50; as work of upbuilding 447–8
love and morality: being a self 124–7; failure to love 127–9; in *Fear and Trembling* 129–30; human love and human nature 123–4; human nature and 123–4
Löwith, Karl 112
Lukács, György 13, 423–5, 431–2
Lund, Ane Sørensdatter 1
Lund, Henrik 1
Lutheranism 254

Martensen, Hans Lassen 18, 54
Marx, Karl (Marxism) 13, 423, 430–1
Matuštík, Martin 435
May, Todd 357
McCarthy, Vincent 137
McFague, Sallie 217
McInerny, Ralph 53
meaning beyond rotation 354–5
meaning in ethical life of aesthetes 141–4
meaning of life contexts 21–2
Meno's Paradox 31, 32
Merleau-Ponty, Maurice 293–5, 297–8
metaphorical language 404
metaphysical caprice 31
metaphysical particularism 82–4
Metaphysics of Morals, The (Kierkegaard) 282
methodology of Kierkegaard: introduction to 4–5; *see also* dialectical method; existential method; indirect communication
Midwifery metaphor (maieutics) 168
Mikulova-Thulstrup, Marie 192
mimesis *see* existential mimesis
mimetic movement and subjectivity 206–12
Minister, Stephen 451

Modernism 208
Møller, Poul 19
Moment, The (Kierkegaard) 3, 453
Mooney, Edward 54
Moore, A. W. 357
morality: autonomy of 459–60; insignificance/indifference 325; knowledge and 404–6; perfection of 209; in religious philosophy 122–3; *see also* love and morality
moral law 69, 103
moral particularism: epistemological particularism 79–82; exemplarism 84–6; introduction to 78–9; metaphysical particularism 82–4; overview of 79–84; summary of 86–7
moral pluralism 70
moral psychology 327
Moral Reasons (Dancy) 79–80, 82
multivocity 25
Murdoch, Iris 149
mysticism 192, 235, 347
mythological poet 414

Napoleon 104, 105, 373
narrative, defined 143
narrative-driven epistemology 82
natural science 256–61
natural theology 259–61
nature: Christianity and 55–6, 261–3; corruptions of 255–9; as delight and danger 254–5; God and 254–5, 261–3; introduction to 254; invasion into ethics and theology 259–61; living nature 428–31; natural science 256–61; obedience in 147–50; as revelation 150–3; Romanticism and 145, 150–3, 255–6, 263; selfhood and 145–6; supernatura and 178–81; as theophany 7
"necessary boredom" thesis 351
necessity and despair 310–11
neo-Kantians 18
Newcomb, T. M. 458
New Testament 194
nihilism 157, 159
non-Christian ethics 326
non-concreteness of human existence 194
non-conscious despair 322–3
Not-Being 428
Nothing 30
Nozick, Robert 142
Nussbaum, Martha 357

obedience in nature 147–50
objective knowledge 22, 112, 379, 398–9, 401–2, 406
objective psychology 24, 47
object of observation 42
obsessiveness *(indkredsene)* 273
Occasional Discourse, An (Kierkegaard) 464–5

offense and sin 365–74
O'Gorman, Francis 89
'Old Orthodox' party 18
Olsen, Regine 2, 3, 54, 423–4
omnipotence of God 148–9
Omsk (Arad) 127–9
On the Concept of Irony with Continual Reference to Socrates (Kierkegaard) 282
ontological problem 278
openness, faith as 337–8
Operation Rescue (OR) 458
Ordbog over det danske Sprog (Society for Danish Language and Literature) 191–2
Ørsted, A. S. 3
oughtness-capability 72
out-of-character actions 307

paganism 31–4, 256, 342, 461, 463
paradox of Christianity 239–52
paradox of human existence 30, 34
particular identity 125
passion *(lidenskab)* 172–3, 210–12, 270, 379, 431
passive imagination 295
pathos dimensions 22–4, 25
Pattison, George 55, 135, 295
Paul (Apostle) 386–7
pedagogical superiority of art 174
Perkins, Robert L. 435, 439
Phaedrus (Plato) 32
Phenomenology of Spirit (Hegel) 102
philosophical anthropology 326–7
Philosophical Fragments (Kierkegaard) 28–31, 205, 271, 366–9, 389
Philosophiske Smuler eller En Smule Philosophi (Philosophical Crumbs or a Crumb of Philosophy) (Kierkegaard) 409–19
philosophy of art 296
philosophy of mind 9–10, 269
philosophy of personality 46
philosophy of religion/theology 8–9
Philosophy of Right (Hegel) 282, 449
physiological anthropology 319
Platner, Ernst 319
Plato 29, 142, 173, 283–4, 439
plurality of life-view 19–20
plurality of mimesis 195
poetic originality and the soul 40
poetics of self-incrimination: Absolute Paradox 416–17; attack and defense 418; defined 409–10; introduction to 409; invention without an inventor 412–13; servant analogy 414–16; summary of 418–19
poetry and sublime grief 161–2
Point of View for My Work as an Author, The (Kierkegaard) 28, 53, 387, 439–40
political-historical field 158

political orientations of dialectal self 438–43
Politics and the Order of Love (Gregory) 446, 452
Politics of Exodus: Søren Kierkegaard's Ethics of Responsibility, The (Dooley) 435
politics of Kierkegaard 12–13
Pons, Jolita 55
positivism 47
possibility and despair 310–11
Posterior Analytics (Aristotle) 379
Postnational Identity: Critical Theory and Existential Philosophy in Habermas, Kierkegaard, and Havel (Matuštík) 435
post-structuralism 4, 17
potential competence 72–3
practical identities and alienation 311–13
practical knowledge 398
Practice in Christianity (Kierkegaard) 204, 371–2, 438, 442
pragmatic anthropology *see* anthropology and selfhood
pragmatic realism 90
praying to God 147–9
principiis obsta 256
principium individuationis 281
principle-based approaches 84
Protestantism 140, 208, 255
Protestant Reformation 254
psychical-physical synthesis 342, 343–4
psychology *see* experimenting psychology
psychopathological-clinical analysis 48
psychotherapy 39, 47–9
pure science of experience 46
purity of heart 288

radical dependence 94
rationalism 56, 399
rational psychology 44
realist approach to language 402–4
reality 271–2
reason and conviction 230–2
received confirmation 233–4
recollection 143, 410
reductionism 310
reflection: as disinterested 43; philosophy of 45; self as 276; self-reflection 158, 160, 285; subjective reflection 274–7
regional domains of 'Being' 112
Reid, Barbara E. 220
Reid, Thomas 346
relation's relating to itself 345–7
relation to god 347–8
religious epistemology 365–74
religious experience 235–6
religious poet 414, 415, 417
repetition, importance of 352–4
Repetition (Kierkegaard) 178

Ricoeur, Paul 194
Roberts, Robert C. 94, 465
Rocca, Ettore 167
Romanticism 145, 150–3, 255–6, 263
Romantics 23, 41–5, 145–7, 150–3, 167
Rossellini, Roberto 184
rotation, meaning beyond 354–5
Røyen, Kirstine Nielsdatter 1
Rudd, Anthony 314, 435
Rudelbach, Andreas 18

Sade, My Neighbor (Klossowski) 180
Sadra, Mulla 427
Sammenligning, defined 199–200
Sartre, Jean-Paul 270, 271
Scheffler, Samuel 357
Schelling, Friedrich Wilhelm Joseph 2, 428–9
Schlegel, Friedrich 2, 39, 41
Schleiermacher, Friedrich 19
Schönbamsfeld, Genia 55
Schopenhauer, Arthur 351
Schweiker, William 194
science and philosophy in art 171–2
Science of Logic (Hegel) 30
science *vs.* ethics 319–20
second-order volitions 324
Second Schleswig War (1865) 1
security schema 462–3
self-awareness 41, 43–4, 206, 269–70, 333–4
self being/selfhood 124–7
self-centred desire 89
self-confidence 97, 141, 284
self-consciousness 5, 41, 43, 45, 270, 324, 346
self-constitution 146, 276, 306, 393–4
self-deception 143, 283–6, 290, 322–3, 337, 367
self-determination 157, 289, 369, 389
self-interpreting activity 48–9
self-judgments 307
self-knowledge 40, 73–4, 347
self-referentiality 25, 270, 320
self-reflection 158, 160, 285, 355
self-relation 11, 42, 219, 281, 323–4
self-responsibility 19–20, 25, 310
self/selfhood: art as mirror 169–71; being a self 124–7, 311; closed self 331–8; despair and 308–11, 314, 320, 337; forward movement of 337; Kierkegaardian view of 341–3; nature/natural beauty 145–6; as reflection 276; subjective selfhood 355; *see also* dialectal self
self-thinking 277–8
servant analogy 414–16
Sibbern, F.C. 39, 46
Sickness unto Death, The (Kierkegaard): Christian anthropology 326–7; closed self 331–8; conversion experience 388–90; desires and possibility of alienation 306–8; despair as

475

universal sickness 284, 287; dialectical self 438; divine ladder of despair 334–7; experimenting psychology 39; faith and 122, 337–8; forms of despair 146; fundamental change 331–2; human ladder of despair 333–4; imagination and 173–4; introduction to 305–6; loving humans 124, 127; phenomenological description of despair 320; practical identities and alienation 311–13; psychical-physical synthesis 342, 343–4; relation's relating to itself 345–7; selfhood and despair 129, 308–11, 324; sin and offense 369–71; structure of consciousness 272–3

'Silhouettes: psychological diversion' (Kierkegaard) 161

sin 42, 287, 365–74

Sittlichkeit theory 449–50

skills model of faith 246–8

smoke study 458–9

social attentional deployment 463–6

social comparison theory (SCT) 457–60

social courage 457–60, 463–6

social ethics 448–50

social isolation 116

Socrates: conception of recollection 410–11; immortality and 380; indirect communication 60–1; introduction to 19, 28–32; 'know thyself' 205; metaphor of midwifery 168; natural science and 258–9; paganism and dialectics 31–7; phenomenon of conscience 335; unexamined life remark 67

Solomon, Robert 55

soul, agony of 282

soul-body composite 342, 344–5

spinal tuberculosis (Pott's Disease), 3

spirit: of comparison 91–2; contradictory factors of 308; God as 234; human existence and 207; self and 324

Stages on Life's Way (Kierkegaard) 39, 285

Stewart, Jon 54, 56, 400

Stoker, Wessel 298

Stokes, Patrick 70, 194–5, 404

Story of Everyday Life, A (Gyllembourg) 2, 167

strenuous difficulties of human existence 380–1

Streufert, Mary J. 218

subjective psychology 47

subjective reflection 274–7, 278

subjective relativism 17

subjective selfhood 355

subjectivity 205–6, 206–12

sublime transfigurations: introduction to 156; Kantian sublime 157–9; Kierkegaardian sublime 159–60; summary of 162–3; tragic sublime 160–1

suffering, in Christianity 453

supernaturalism 56

supernature 178–81

sympathetic antipathy 43

teleological component of imagination 296

teleological suspension of the ethical (TSE) 101, 105

Tetens, J.N. 45

theological anthropology 326–7

theological art of existence: introduction to 203–4; mimetic movement and 206–12; passion and 210–12; true subjectivity and Christ 205–6; youth's ideal 206; youth's imagination 206–8; youth's will 208–10

Third Synthesis 125

Thomson, Iain 354

Thousand Plateaus, A (Kierkegaard) 183–4

Three Discourses on Imagined Occasions (Kierkegaard) 283

time 47, 142

'To Be Contented with Being a Human Being' discourse 90–1

tragic sublime 160–1

transcendental psychology 44–5

transcendent God 58, 151–2

true subjectivity and Christ 205–6

truth: human existence and 34–5; as subjectivity 203; untruth and 389, 413, 460–3

truth-plus-justification 169

Two Ages (Kierkegaard) 20, 80, 275, 429, 431–2, 441–2, 457, 460

unconditional obedience to God 93

understanding *(Verstand)* 45

unity of the cosmos 19

University of Copenhagen 47

unknowability of God 368–9

untruth and truth 389, 413, 460–3

unum noris omnes (if you know one, you know all) 40

upbuilding, love as 447–8

Upbuilding Discourses in Various Spirits (Kierkegaard) 255, 281, 287, 326, 446, 449, 462

uti/frui distinction 204

utility principle 85

Varieties of Religious Experience, The (James) 231–2

Velleman, J. David 308

visible symbols 297

Washington Area Clinic Defense Task Force 458

Watson, Gary 307

Watts, Daniel 240–2

Weil, Simone 149

welcoming openness 93
Westphal, Merold 277, 345, 435
whimsical idea of work 31
Williams, Bernard 351–2
willing *(Willen)* 45
will to believe 232–3
Wirth, Jason 427
wisdom of ascetic Christianity 452
Wittgenstein, Ludwig 55, 402
women as sinners 219–21
Wood, Allen 103–4
Woolf, Virginia 183
Works of Love (Kierkegaard) 24, 93, 122–3, 127, 129, 281, 289, 402–4, 446, 447–9
world-historical significance 461

worry and humility: humility discourse 93, 94–7; introduction to 89–90; lily and bird discourses 89, 90–4
Worrying: A Literary and Cultural History (O'Gorman) 89
Wrathall, Mark 306–7, 356–8

yearning for forgiveness 221
youth's ideal 206
youth's imagination 206–8
youth's will 208–10

Zagzebski, Linda 78–9, 84–7
Zahavi, Dan 269
Žižek, Slavoj 425